GOLF IN THE CAROLINAS

by

Scott Martin

&

Mitch Willard

The Insiders' Guide®
An imprint of Falcon® Publishing, Inc.
A Landmark Communications company
P.O. Box 1718
Helena, MT 59624
(800) 582-2665
www.insiders.com

•

Sales and Marketing: Falcon Publishing, Inc.
P.O. Box 1718
Helena, MT 59624
(800) 582-2665
www.falcon.com

•

FOURTH EDITION
1st printing

•

©2000 by Knight Publishing Company, Inc.

•

Printed in the United States of America

•

Front cover photo: Pinehurst Resort & Country Club. Back cover photos, clockwise from top left: Bill Woodward; Grove Park Inn; Hilton Head Island; J.J. Bissell; South Carolina Parks, Recreation & Tourism; Hilton Head Island. Spine photo: North Carolina Travel & Tourism.

•

Publications from *The Insiders' Guide*® series are available at special discounts for bulk purchases for sales promotions, premiums or fundraisings. Special editions, including personalized covers, can be created in large quantities for special needs. For more information, please contact Falcon Publishing.

ISBN 1-57380-112-7

Foreword

By Ron Green Jr.

This is golf in the Carolinas:

It's standing on the fourth tee at Tidewater at Cherry Grove Beach, S.C., enjoying the thrill of trying to hit a tee shot into a fairway guarded on the left by the dramatic expanse of the Intracoastal Waterway.

It's the feeling of cool mountain air gently rustling the trees as you play the eternally charming Linville Golf Club.

It's Spanish moss hanging from the live oaks and the musky smell of a Lowcountry lagoon on one of Hilton Head's many golf courses.

It's the sound of clarion bells ringing across Pinehurst on a spring morning as your tee time on No. 2—and your walk among the history—approaches.

It's slipping off one of the bustling highways in Charlotte and finding yourself at a course like Birkdale, where you've got an afternoon free with your friends and the chance to make a birdie or two.

It's framing a 5-iron shot against Mt. Mitchell; having a cold one at the Pine Crest Inn after your round; catching the glimpse of a par 5 as you drive down a backroad; playing six courses in four days at Myrtle Beach; finding a 65-degree January afternoon when winter makes a tee time for you.

When it comes to golf, few places have as many treasures as the Carolinas. For more than a century, golf has been a part of the Carolinas and the game has become part of the region's fabric.

It's more than a game. Golf is what people talk about in big cities and small towns. Like sweet tea and barbecue, golf is part of the Carolinas culture.

The Insiders' Guide to Golf in the Carolinas brings it all together, providing a detailed look at the places where golf comes alive. It offers the nuts and bolts about where to play, how to get there and what you 'll find while giving you a feel for the places you may want to visit.

If there is a single, overriding charm to golf in the Carolinas, it's the diversity of courses. You can find whatever you're after without going far. You can play alongside the ocean at places like Wild Dunes and Kiawah Island. You can head to the high country where the air is thin and the greens are fast. Or, you can pick a spot in between, drive between the oak trees and bunkers and have a wonderful day. Golf in the Carolinas is our own special treasure, but it's one we share with the world.

Myrtle Beach has become a world golf destination with more than 100 courses strung along the Grand Strand. What began as a beach getaway for Carolinians has become a thriving resort built on golf.

Pinehurst had its own special place on the world golf map and with one unforgettable summer week in 1999 when the late Payne Stewart won a marvelous U.S. Open, the gentle village further entrenched itself as the American St. Andrews.

In Charlotte and Raleigh, where more international business is being done, the number of upscale daily-fee golf courses has jumped, giving players more quality options than ever.

Golf has always been a special part of life in the Carolinas. The MCI Classic at Harbour Town on Hilton Head Island is one of the PGA's best stops. Played the week after the Masters in mid-April, the MCI has a habit of producing great champions (Davis Love III, Greg Norman, Tom Watson, Arnold Palmer and Johnny Miller, among others) and there are few golf courses that can match the sheer beauty of Harbour Town.

The Greater Greensboro Chrysler Classic has been played for more than 50 years and, to many, announces spring in the Carolinas. The LPGA Tour visits Myrtle Beach each summer and the Senior Tour comes through Charlotte, Winston-Salem and Myrtle Beach, giving the Carolinas an active schedule of professional golf.

Those are special weeks when the game's best players visit the Carolinas. But golf is a year-round game in these states. Except for the mountain courses, which surrender to Mother Nature for a few months, our golf courses stay open year-round.

In the spring, the azaleas bloom and there's the promise of another year. In the summer, the bermuda fairways turn green, the rough thickens and games are sharpened.

There may be no better time than the fall to play golf in the Carolinas when the weather is wonderful and the courses are in their best condition. Even winter has its own charm. It's chilly and the courses turn brown, but there's a special feeling to stealing a January day to play 18 holes. The game is never far away.

Not when you play golf in the Carolinas.

Ron Green Jr. is a veteran sportswriter for The Charlotte Observer. *His beat includes golf in the Carolinas—each year, he draws the short straw and is forced to cover the Masters, the MCI Heritage at Hilton Head and the Greater Greensboro Chrysler Classic. His job also includes reviewing new courses.*

About the Authors

Scott Martin

... was born in Cincinnati but spent his formative years in Montreal and in London, where he attended Harrow School. In 1984, he accepted a Morehead Scholarship to the University of North Carolina at Chapel Hill where he took creative writing classes with Bland Simpson and Max Steele. He graduated from UNC with a BA in comparative literature. Following graduation, Scott spent a year in Denver where, among other achievements, he coached a high school soccer team to an 0-15 record.

From Colorado, Scott moved to Charlotte, where he worked as a copywriter and typesetter. He then set out on his own as a freelance writer specializing in preparing manuals for financial institutions such as Barclays American Mortgage and Bank of America. He also wrote articles for a number of local publications. In 1992, he became editor of *SouthPark Update* magazine. In 1995, he joined Knight Publishing's Subsidiary Publications department. He is also the editor of *Shouting at Amen Corner,* a compilation of the best of former Charlotte Observer sportswriter Ron Green's articles and columns about the Masters.

Scott took up golf seriously in 1993 and has lowered his handicap from "not listed" to five. Scott continuously updates this guide, researching and reviewing golf and golf courses in the Carolinas. It's a tough job...

Scott is married with a two-year-old son, a slothful rat terrier and a crazed retired racing greyhound. He's a country member of Machrihanish Golf Club in southwest Scotland and regularly participates in tournaments held by the National Association of Left Handed Golfers.

Mitch Willard

... is a freelance writer in North Myrtle Beach, South Carolina. He plays golf every possible moment throughout the Carolinas, Virginia, Tennessee, California, Scotland or wherever an assignment or a whim may take him. He's steadily improving his game and fully intends to be good at it someday.

Mitch grew up in Lynchburg, Virginia, where he earned a master's degree in education and taught elementary school, then college, for more than 13 years. During that time he also learned to play golf and wrote numerous sports-related features for a variety of publications. The sportswriting interest was borne in high school when he was sports editor and photographer for the *High Times* newspaper.

A dedicated runner and fitness buff, Mitch enjoyed road racing for 17 years, then finally recognized that his aching feet would improve on the golf course but not on the road. When he moved to North Myrtle Beach more than seven years ago, his love of golf intensified. Too many courses are readily available and affordable to deny the passion. He travels frequently for golf experiences and other business. Whenever an opportunity arises, a golf course always beckons. When not golfing or writing about it, he actually enjoys his real job as a Realtor, and he will talk to anybody about buying and selling property in any state.

His trip to St. Andrews, the home of golf in Scotland, during the initial research for this book, provided additional inspiration, if not reverence, for the game. Walking the links, seeing the home of the Royal and Ancient Golf Club and learning exactly how and where the phenomenon all began in 1400 AD brought an almost-religious experience into his life.

Mitch returned to his familiar courses in the Carolinas and to writing the first edition of this book with renewed fervor and a true sense of belonging to the universal experience called golf.

Acknowledgments

Scott

Many, many people throughout the Carolinas provided assistance with this book. I would especially like to thank Holly Spofford Bell at Pine Needles; Luellen Cobb at Mid Pines; David Rucker at Myers Park Country Club; John Harrington at Falcon Publishing; Stewart Spencer and Linda Sluder at the *Charlotte Observer*; Dave Troupe, John Buckminster, Jeffrey Craig, Dave Tomsky and Dal Raiford at The Grove Park Inn; Ron Whitten at *Golf Digest*; Melanie McGavran; Charles Hipp; David Craig; Chuck Cordell; Larry Williams (Bam!); Irwin Smallwood; Danny Gore; Stephen Boyd at Pinehurst Resort; Ron Green (both); Dr. and Mrs. Walter Morris; Blair Robertson; Sylvain Blouin; Malcolm and Lauren Campbell; Chuck Lotz; Steven Pandos; Alan Knott; Jay Allred; Russell Breeden; plus Hector and Amy Ingram of Wilmington, North Carolina.

I would also like to thank the numerous hard-working and amenable club professionals who graciously allowed me—often at a moment's notice—to play and review their golf courses. If there's a profession whose members are friendlier and more approachable, please let me know.

I must also thank my wife, Karen, and son, Andrew for affording me the time to chase that little white pill through the woods, mountains, and plains of the Carolinas.

Throughout this book, you will find references to *Architects of Golf* (HarperCollins; 1981, 1993), researched and written by Ron Whitten and Geoffrey Cornish. This 648-page volume is a must for any golfer interested in golf course architecture and design. It includes a history of golf course architecture, profiles of notable golf course architects from around the world and a list of their courses plus a comprehensive list of golf courses and their designers. It's a wonderful book that lovingly details the artists who create (and have created) the golf courses so many golfers enjoy every day.

Finally, I would like to dedicate this book to Thomas Martin, my father, and Karen Martin, my wife, and Andrew, my son, as well as to the greenskeepers, golf course architects, entrepreneurs, pros, volunteers, rangers, manufacturers and others who work so hard and successfully to make excellent golf available to so many in North and South Carolina. Cheers!

Mitch

Writing *The Insiders' Guide to Golf in the Carolinas* is a labor of love and a wonderful experience. What golfer would not want the opportunity to talk about and play some of the finest and best-known courses in the world?

First, I must thank my wife, Liz, who encouraged this project, contributed her ideas and traveled with me to enjoy the golfing, shopping, dining, attractions and accommodations—traveling and writing, which colored our daily conversations and our entire year. Without her, this book could not have been written so easily.

This book could not have been written, of course, without the time and kindness of the club professionals, managers and staff at the golf courses. Their courtesies to us and their knowledge and interest in assisting with our endless information gathering are most appreciated.

Suffice it to say, everyone from club professionals to rangers and other staff is proud of their respective course, and rightfully so. Most are glad to talk about their course and enjoy an opportunity to do a little bragging about their home turf. After all, the Carolinas offer some of the best golfing opportunities in the world.

Many thanks also to my good friends Fred Hickey, Rocky Burton and Jim Wilkes (the Glava group), plus John Moore and Tom Hall, all of whom gave me their constant encouragement and shared with me their knowledge and their time to talk and play golf. I am lucky to have such supportive friends, and I always thoroughly appreciate Sharon and Melvin Godfrey for helping me get a good start in the game of golf.

Preface

Welcome to the Carolinas!

Golf is played with a passion here, and we invite you to sample our Southern hospitality on and off the courses.

In North and South Carolina you have your choice of some of the best golf courses in the world. We have studied and played them to create this guide for choosing your own courses and for planning your golf vacation. The courses within each chapter are listed in alphabetical order for quick and easy reference. The chapters are organized to take you geographically from one end of each state to the other. We start with the self-proclaimed "Golf Capital of the World," Myrtle Beach and the Grand Strand of South Carolina, and end up in the majestic Mountains of Western North Carolina. We recommend a variety of courses—something to suit every interest, whether you are a scratch golfer looking for the toughest challenges or a true beginner ready to learn. Even if you don't want to play, we've found some tournaments that you can enjoy watching.

We want this guide to go beyond just providing great golfing information. We know that not everyone is a golf nut, so in each chapter we offer details about other fun things to do. Plus, we've recommended accommodations and restaurants in each area to make planning your golfing getaway easier and to assure that you take full advantage of what each area has to offer.

Many of the accommodations we recommend at the end of each chapter will include golf in a package for you. Most are suitable for a non-golfing family or traveling companions with other interests (but don't worry—we've kept the recommended accommodations close to your courses for quick access).

We suggest restaurants suitable for any of the golfers we know, and we offer a medley of family activities in every location. Golf can be combined easily with other interests, and much is available to every visitor to the Carolinas.

The Insiders' Guide to Golf in the Carolinas is intended to tempt you with enough basic information to help you understand our states' golfing mentality and add to your golfing pleasure. Please keep in mind that the greens fees for golf vary with the seasons, especially throughout much of the coastal area, with the more expensive golf being found during spring and fall. The farther north you play, the more you'll find summer is the high season in golf. Also, rates typically increase a few dollars each year. We encourage you to call in advance for tee times and ask about the cost as well as any special rates or packages that may be available.

Although many Carolina courses accept walk-ons, it's a good idea to request advance tee times if golf is the main purpose of your trip, especially if the choice of course or time of day is important to you.

Accommodations should be booked in advance to ensure availability, and be sure to inquire about golf packages, senior citizen discounts or other specials based on your length of stay. When calling for reservations, be sure to ask for a clarification of the lodging's policy regarding cancellations. Unless otherwise noted, all accommodations accept most major credit cards.

Price-code Keys

Accommodations

The following price code key gives a general idea of the accommodation rates for the average charge for one room for two people at the places we note in each chapter.

$50 to $75	**$**
$76 to $101	**$$**
$102 to $127	**$$$**
$128 to $153	**$$$$**
$154 and more	**$$$$$**

Restaurants

The following key explains the price range for an average meal for two—excluding appetizer, alcoholic drinks, dessert, tax and tip—at our recommended restaurants. As with accommodations, all restaurants accept at least MasterCard and Visa unless otherwise noted.

Less than $20	**$**
$21 to $35	**$$**
$36 to $50	**$$$**
$51 and more	**$$$$**

We wish you par or better on your golfing excursions. And we hope all your non-golfing companions have (almost) as much fun as you golfers do. Let us know about your Insider experiences from following our recommendations in this guide so we can provide the best information possible in our regular updates.

How This Book Was Written

The authors of *The Insiders' Guide to Golf in the Carolinas* visited each of the courses written about in this book. Courses were assessed either by playing a round or by riding to survey the layout. Also, interviews with the golf professionals or other staff were important in gathering information about the seasonal variations of the courses. The positive aspects of the courses were stressed in the belief that there's something commendable about every golf course, no matter how it may appear upon first inspection. It was physically impossible to review every public-access golf course in North and South Carolina (there are nearly 600!), but we hope this book provides an excellent selection. We certainly tried!

As always, we welcome your comments and suggestions and encourage you to drop us a line at The Insiders' Guides, P.O. Box 1718, Helena, MT 59624, or check us out on the Internet at www.insiders.com.

Happy golfing!

Table of Contents

Directory of Maps

Grand Strand/ Myrtle Beach

Known to most in the Carolinas as simply "The Beach," Myrtle Beach and the Grand Strand are quite unlike any place on the planet.

In some ways, that might be a good thing.

First, before we delve into what this crazed strip of land is all about, let's get our geography and nomenclature sorted out. The Grand Strand, using the most liberal definition possible, stretches from Georgetown, South Carolina up to Southport, North Carolina: a long, arcing, 60-mile portion of coastline blessed with wide sandy beaches. Lining these beaches are all manner of oceanfront resorts, T-shirt shops, fireworks stands, putt-putt courses... you get the idea.

The town of Myrtle Beach is the epicenter of the Grand Strand, but because we're locals, we mostly refer to this area as "The Beach."

The Beach, in addition to hosting nearly 5 *million* rounds of golf a year on more than 100 courses, is a Mecca for an interesting mix of people, depending on the time of year.

December and January are relatively tame at The Beach, a quiet period where the only visitors are conference attendees and golfers who don't mind the occasional cold, windy day on the course. Those who live and work at The Beach can recharge their batteries before the first onslaught of the year from golfing snowbirds.

Golfers who live in Michigan, Wisconsin, Canada and Upstate New York (these are the snowbirds) generally spend the winter months either putting in their basements or ice fishing. This changes for one week a year when they take their annual boys-only expedition to The Beach for golf, drinking, "adult" clubs and some hard-core debauchery. Most of these trips take place during the traditional spring break months of February, March and April.

In May, when the tundra of northern climes has thawed and it's possible to play golf in Green Bay, the snowbirds return home to be replaced by lusty, marauding teenagers in post high school graduation mode. Their goals: sunburn, cirrhosis of the liver, and "interaction" with the opposite sex.

Once this orgy ends, families from as far away as North Dakota minivan in for a week of jungle golf, sunburn, carnival rides, and dodgy seafood.

Come mid-august, schools recommence and The Beach once again becomes the playground of golfers, many of whom visit from overseas, lured from Germany, England and Japan by reports of non-stop golf and outrageous après golf "activities."

The guiding force that guides The Beach must be a Grateful Dead fan, or more specifically, they must have heard and taken to heart the song "I Need a Miracle," which includes the line "Too much of everything is just enough." At The Beach, nothing succeeds like excess: If it's not big, neon, gaudy, and cheap, then it's just not worth the price of admission.

The Grand Strand of South Carolina

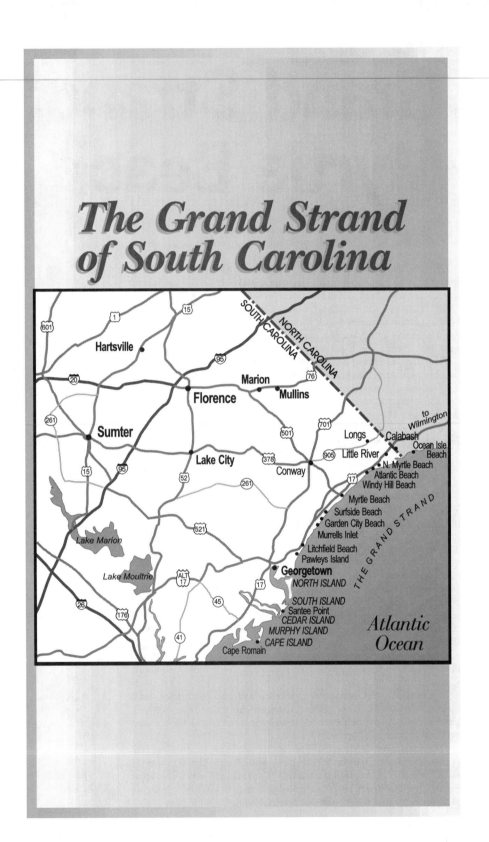

GOLF COURSES ON SOUTH CAROLINA'S GRAND STRAND

Course	Type	Holes	Par	Slope	Yards	Walking	Booking	Cost w/Cart
Angels Trace								
North Course	public	18	72	129	6216	no	anytime	$55
South Course	public	18	72	132	6442	no	anytime	$55
Arcadian Shores Golf Club	resort	18	72	116	6028	no	365 days	$45-90
Arrowhead Country Club								
Lakes/Cypress Course	public	18	72	122	6242	no	365 days	$85
Cypress/Waterway Course	public	18	72	122	6183	no	365 days	$85
Lakes/Waterway Course	public	18	72	122	6179	no	365 days	$85
Azalea Sands Golf Course	public	18	72	116	6287	yes	365 days	$25-54
Bay Tree Golf Plantation								
Gold Course	public	18	72	128	6390	yes	365 days	$40-60
Green Course	public	18	72	126	6492	yes	365 days	$40-60
Silver Course	public	18	72	122	6363	yes	365 days	$40-60
Beachwood Golf Club	public	18	72	117	6344	no	365 days	$24
Belle Terre	public	18	72	127	6672	yes	395 days	$60-75
Blackmoor	public	18	72	118	6217	no	365 days	$35-85
Brick Landing Plantation	semiprivate	18	72	132	6154	no	365 days	$40-70
Brunswick Plantation & Golf Links	semiprivate	18	72	124	6215	no	7 days	$35-60
Buck Creek Plantation								
Cypress/Tupelo Course	public	18	72	126	6306	no	365 days	$30-70
Meadow/Cypress Course	public	18	72	119	6211	no	365 days	$30-70
Tupelo/Meadow Course	public	18	72	119	6115	no	365 days	$30-70
Burning Ridge								
East Course	semiprivate	18	72	124	6216	no	365 days	$30-60

Course	Type	Holes	Par	Rating	Yardage		Season	Price
West Course	semiprivate	18	72	114	6237	no	365 days	$30-60
Caledonia Golf & Fish Club	public	18	70	116	6104	no	365 days	$55-100
CarolinaNational Golf Club								
Egret/Heron Course	semiprivate	18	72	130	6493	no	365 days	$43-80
Heron/Ibis Course	semiprivate	18	72	137	6403	no	365 days	$43-80
Ibis/Egret Course	semiprivate	18	72	138	6452	no	365 days	$43-80
Carolina Shores Golf & Country Club	public	18	72	122	6231	no	3 days	$30-60
Colonial Charters Golf and C. C.	semiprivate	18	72	119	6337	no	365 days	$27-55
Crow Creek	public	18	72	124	6679	no	call	$27-55
Cypress Bay Golf Club	public	18	72	118	6101	yes	365 days	$30-62
Deer Track Golf resort								
Toski Links	semiprivate	18	72	121	6511	yes	365 days	$35-65
South Course	semiprivate	18	71	119	6143	yes	365 days	$35-65
Dunes Golf and Beach Club	private	18	72	130	6565	no	365 days	$100
Eagle Nest Golf Club	public	18	72	116	6417	yes	365 days	$47-62
Eastport Golf Club	public	18	70	111	5400	no	365 days	$30
Glen Dornoch Golf Links	public	18	72	133	6446	no	365 days	$45-110
Heather Glen Golf Links								
1 Red/2 White Course	public	18	72	123	6337	no	365 days	$40-100
2 White/3 Blue Course	public	18	72	126	6510	no	365 days	$40-100
3 Blue/1 Red Course	public	18	72	126	6427	no	365 days	$40-100
Heritage	public	18	71	128	6565	no	365 days	$50-90
Heron Point	semiprivate	18	72	121	6080	yes	365 days	$40
Indian Wells	public	18	72	123	6225	yes	365 days	$50
Indigo Creek Golf Club	semiprivate	18	72	120	6185	no	365 days	$50
International World Tour								
Open/Championship	public	18	72	126	6214	yes	365 days	$100-160
International/Championship	public	18	72	129	6372	yes	365 days	$100-160

Course	Type	Holes	Par	Slope	Yards		Advance	Price
International/Open	public	18	72	129	6633	yes	365 days	$100-160
Island Green Country Club								
Dogwood/Holly Course	semiprivate	18	72	111	5847	yes	365 days	$25-45
Holly/Tall Oaks Course	semiprivate	18	72	111	5864	yes	365 days	$25-45
Tall Oaks/Dogwood Course	semiprivate	18	72	111	5705	yes	365 days	$25-45
Legends								
Heathland Course	public	18	71	117	6190	yes	365 days	$50-90
Moorland Course	public	18	72	121	6143	yes	365 days	$50-90
Parkland Course	public	18	72	127	6460	yes	365 days	$50-90
Litchfield Country Club	resort	18	72	124	6342	yes	365 days	$45-75
Long Bay Club	public	18	72	130	6565	no	365 days	$55-100
Marsh Harbour	public	18	71	121	6000	no	anytime	$50-88
Myrtle Beach National Golf Club								
Kings North Course	public	18	72	109	6033	yes	365 days	$40-100
South Course	public	18	72	118	6089	yes	365 days	$40-100
West Course	public	18	72	113	6113	yes	365 days	$40-100
Myrtle West Golf Club	semiprivate	18	72	118	6191	no	365 days	$30-58
Myrtlewood Golf Club								
Palmetto Course	semiprivate	18	72	118	6495	no	365 days	$30-65
PineHills Course	semiprivate	18	72	119	6112	no	365 days	$30-65
Ocean Harbour Golf Links	resort	18	72	134	6592	no	7 days	$35-80
Ocean Isle Beach Golf Course	public	18	72	122	6146	no	365 days	$25-50
Ocean Ridge Plantation								
Lion's Paw Golf Links	public	18	72	130	6457	no	anytime	$35-80
Panther's Run Golf Links	public	18	72	134	6706	yes	anytime	$35-80
Oyster Bay Golf Links	public	18	70	125	6305	no	365 days	$50-83
Pawleys Plantation Golf & C. C.	public	18	72	127	6522	no	365 days	$50-85

Course	Type	Holes	Par	Slope	Yardage	Walking	Season	Greens Fees
Pearl Golf Links								
East Course	public	18	72	132	6543	no	365 days	$69
West Course	public	18	72	131	6738	no	365 days	$69
Pine Lakes International C. C.	semiprivate	18	71	121	6176	no	365 days	$47-110
Possum Trot Golf Course	public	18	72	113	6388	yes	365 days	$35-60
Prestwick Country Club	semiprivate	18	72	135	6744	yes	365 days	$50-100
Quail Creek Golf Course	semiprivate	18	72	116	6321	yes	365 days	$25-60
River Club	semiprivate	18	72	119	6240	no	365 days	$40-85
River's Edge Golf Club	public	18	72	139	6440	no	365 days	$48-118
River Hills Golf and Country Club	public	18	72	123	6196	no	365 days	$30-60
River Oaks Golf Plantation								
Bear/Fox Course	public	18	72	118	6314	no	365 days	$30-70
Fox/Otter Course	public	18	72	118	6345	no	365 days	$30-70
Otter/Bear Course	public	18	72	119	6425	no	365 days	$30-70
Robbers Roost Golf Club	public	18	72	129	6725	no	365 days	$35-45
St. James Plantation	semiprivate	18	72	132	6428	no	365 days	$40-65
Sea Trail Plantation & Golf resort								
Byrd Course	resort	18	72	126	6263	no	365 days	$40-60
Jones Course	resort	18	72	126	6334	no	365 days	$40-70
Maples Course	resort	18	72	117	6332	no	365 days	$40-60
Surf Golf and Beach Club	semiprivate	18	72	119	6360	no	365 days	$35-88
Tidewater Golf Club and Plantation	public	18	72	118	6000	no	365 days	$70-100
Tiger's Eye	public	18	72	n/r	6628	yes	anytime	$50-80
Tradition Club	public	18	72	n/r	6500	yes	365 days	$43-61
True Blue	public	18	72	128	6840	yes	365 days	$50-130
TPC at Myrtle Beach	public	18	72	136	6600	yes	365 days	$76-175
Waterway Hills								
Lakes Course	public	9	36	115	3001	yes	365 days	$35-60

Course	Type	Holes	Par	Slope	Yards		Open	Fees
Oaks Course	public	9	36	118	3080	yes	365 days	$35-60
Ravine Course	public	9	36	112	2579	yes	365 days	$35-60
Wicked Stick Golf Links	public	18	72	122	6507	no	365 days	$35-70
Wild Wing Plantation								
Avocet Course	public	18	72	119	6614	no	365 days	$54-108
Falcon Course	public	18	72	128	6697	no	365 days	$54-108
Hummingbird Course	public	18	72	123	6310	no	365 days	$45-95
Woodstork Course	public	18	72	111	6598	no	365 days	$45-95
Willbrook Plantation Golf Club	semiprivate	18	72	118	6106	yes	365 days	$52-67
The Witch Golf Links	public	18	71	121	6011	no	365 days	$50-85
Man O' War	public	18	72	126	6311	no	365 days	$40-90
Wizard	public	18	71	126	6402	no	365 days	$50-80

The Beach thrives on tacky gooney golf, loud bars, huge restaurants, musical and theatrical "shows" in massive stucco theaters, aging multi-story hotels, anything NASCAR, anything colored lime or hot pink, anything flashy, anything that's a "deal."

But millions love it, returning year after year to stay at the same motel with the same clapped-out air conditioner, only to get the same stomach ailment from the same all-you-can-gorge buffet. The congestion, particularly in summer, can be catastrophic, and yet people never complain. It's The Beach. What more can you say?

It's a lot easier to understand what makes The Beach so attractive to so many golfers. The Grand Strand boasts 100 courses(!), yet there's meat and substance underpinning this dazzling quantity. While a few of the 100 (and there are more on the way) need some TLC, most are solid layouts, and a select few justifiably rank among the nation's best public-access courses. For all the tackiness elsewhere around town, this is certainly a legitimate golf destination.

Still, there's a sameness to much of the golf at the beach. If you were to abduct and blindfold someone who knows the courses somewhat intimately, take them to a fairway, take off the blindfold then ask them where they were, they might be hard pressed to tell you. The land here is flat as a pancake and there's only so much a golf course architect can achieve given those circumstances. On most Beach courses, the major hazards are drainage ditches, irrigation ponds and quasi-malarial swamp. Ironically, few courses at The Beach actually border the sea.

In all, 12 million visitors descend on The Beach every year; it's crucial to plan and book ahead before you arrive. Many hotels offer golf packages that include lodging and rounds at a handful of courses and employ a director of golf who sets up tee times for guests. Many golfers take advantage of the services of an organization called Myrtle Beach Golf Holiday, (800) 845-4653. It's more than possible to organize a trip yourself but it's often easiest to secure plum tee times at the courses of your choice if you book through a hotel or Myrtle Beach Golf Holiday. Plus it saves time and hassle.

But most importantly, and we can't say this enough, book ahead or suffer the consequences.

Golf course pricing varies tremendously throughout the year. Approximate fees are highest in spring and fall but many courses offer prime time discounts if you book through a hotel or golf package. Many hotels offer similar discounts. Keep in mind that the rates and fees listed in this chapter are provided as a general guideline.

It's possible to binge at The Beach and have a hugely expensive golf vacation. But it's equally easy to come to The Beach and spend remarkably little on a golf holiday while staying at a decent hotel and playing mid-level courses. Perhaps that's part of the attraction of The Beach to so many golfers from around the United States: There's nothing snooty here.

One further geographical note. Myrtle Beach and North Myrtle Beach are two separate entities. People from the latter think they're better that people from the former and vice versa, but that's of little interest to the visitor. Both towns have street grids and thus 17th street could be in either place, plus you need to check whether it's 17th street North or South. Buy a street map when you arrive: Most golf courses are listed.

It's easy to attack and criticize the gaudiness of The Beach and the neon mega-tacky vibe it proudly broadcasts. But something must be a bit more than OK if 12 million people come here before going elsewhere. At its core, The Beach is a playground for all ages and most tastes. If you want refinement, solitude, class, vintage clarets, and Duck à l'orange, visit Pinehurst or Charleston. But if you want raw fun and excitement with an almost infinite variety of courses at your disposal, then you can't go wrong at The Beach. Leave whatever snobbiness and/or aesthetic values you possess at home and you'll have the time of your life on The Grand Strand.

For further information on the area, pick up a copy of the always excellent *Insiders' Guide to Myrtle Beach & the Grand Strand*, available in bookstores nationwide or on the Internet at www.insiders.com.

Angels Trace Golf Links
1215 Angels Club Dr., Sunset Beach, N.C.
• (910) 579-2277, (800) 718-5733

This public, 36-hole complex opened in 1995. It's near The Pearl and a number of other popular courses on the southern edge of North Carolina where scenic courses and tempting seafood restaurants are sprinkled throughout Calabash, Sunset Beach and Ocean Isle Beach. No houses are around the courses, and no noise or distractions will hinder your golf game here.

Both Angels Trace courses offer a pro shop, club rentals, snack shop, driving range and putting green. Walking is not allowed. The greens on both courses are usually fast. Unless your shots to the green can usually hit and stick, it is better to lay up and have your ball roll on to the green.

North Course

Championship Yardage: 6640
Slope: 139   **Par: 72**
Men's Yardage: 6216
Slope: 129   **Par: 72**
Other Yardage: 4524
Slope: 115   **Par: 72**
Ladies' Yardage: 5316
Slope: 111   **Par: 72**

This Clyde Johnston course follows the lay of the land, with natural streams running through it. Gentle mounds and a few man-made ponds add to the character. Nos. 5 and 9 are bulkheaded. No. 5 is the signature: a par 4 dogleg left. The first shot is a placement shot, and the second must carry over water. Traps are inside the fairway; two are in front and one on the side of the green, which is on a hill surrounded by oyster shells.

Water comes into play on at least nine holes. You'll find some good long par 5s that require accurate shot placement. Tees, fairways and rough are bermudagrass, and greens are bentgrass. Fairway width varies. The average golfer will enjoy the North Course.

Approximate fees with cart average $55.

South Course

Championship Yardage: 6876
Slope: 138   **Par: 72**
Men's Yardage: 6442
Slope: 132   **Par: 72**
Other Yardage: 5593
Slope: 122   **Par: 72**
Ladies' Yardage: 4811
Slope: 118   **Par: 72**

Also designed by Clyde Johnston, this course shows similarities to the North Course. Water is a factor on 15 holes. You have a distinct chance of losing your ball on at least 10 of these. No. 4 is a par 3—147 yards from the men's tees. Your tee shot is slightly downhill to a large green with bunkers in front and back. Another good hole is the par 5 14th, 544 yards from the white tees. Besides being long, it requires sensible play to negotiate the double dogleg. Water that bisects the fairway is not visible from the tee. You must play two accurate shots to be able to approach this green for a par. The best approach shot comes from the right side of the fairway to a green that is undulating and well bunkered on all sides.

The challenging finishing hole is a par 5 of 465 yards that doglegs right. You can really let it fly here because the fairway is wide. The best approach to the green is from the left side of the fairway; however, you must be careful not to be too far left. Be aware of water on that side. Conversely, don't be too far right, because trees will block your approach shot. The green is wide and well protected by three small bunkers at its front and one large bunker in the back that runs the entire length of the green.

Approximate fees with cart average $55.

Arcadian Shores Golf Club

701 Hilton Rd., Myrtle Beach
• (843) 449-5217, (800) 248-9228
Championship Yardage: 6446
Slope: 131   **Par: 72**
Men's Yardage: 6028
Slope: 116   **Par: 72**
Other Yardage: 5636
Slope: 113   **Par: 72**
Ladies' Yardage: 5113
Slope: 117   **Par: 72**

Rees Jones designed this course in 1974. The club refurbished the course in 1994. Arcadian Shores includes 64 creatively placed sand bunkers among natural lakes and elevated lush bermudagrass greens. Water comes into play on eight holes. The fairways are wide and beautifully tree-lined. Take an extra club on your approach shots because the greens are all slightly elevated. The fairways are usually soft but well manicured, so you won't get much roll on your drives but you should end up with a decent lie. A challenging hole is the second, a 178-yard par 3. Your shot must travel over water and up a small hill to a fairly large green. The par 4 13th hole is one of the prettiest on the course. If your drive is lucky enough to make it to the top of a knoll, your ball will roll, leaving a relatively easy second shot over water to the green.

The course offers rental clubs, a driving range, practice green, pro shop, bar and restaurant.

Approximate fees range from $45 to $90. Walking is not allowed. Arcadian Shores is affiliated with the oceanfront Hilton Hotel, and the golf course is across the street. The course is bisected by Hilton Road, which connects to U.S. 17 from the oceanfront.

Arrowhead Country Club

1201 Burcale Rd., Myrtle Beach
• (843) 236-3243, (800) 236-3243
Lakes/Cypress Course
Championship Yardage: 6666
Slope: 130   **Par: 72**
Men's Yardage: 6242
Slope: 122   **Par: 72**

Other Yardage: 5713
Slope: 115   Par: 72
Ladies' Yardage: 4812
Slope: 116   Par: 72

Cypress/Waterway Course
Championship Yardage: 6644
Slope: 130   Par: 72
Men's Yardage: 6183
Slope: 122   Par: 72
Other Yardage: 5559
Slope: 115   Par: 72
Ladies' Yardage: 4624
Slope: 116   Par: 72

Lakes/Waterway Course
Championship Yardage: 6612
Slope: 130   Par: 72
Men's Yardage: 6179
Slope: 122   Par: 72
Other Yardage: 5560
Slope: 115   Par: 72
Ladies' Yardage: 4698
Slope: 116   Par: 72

Raymond Floyd and Tom Jackson unveiled this creation in November 1994. The first 18 of 27 holes opened with large bermudagrass greens and bermudagrass fairways unique for their numerous undulations.

The nine-hole Lakes Course measures 3317 yards from the championship tees. The nine-hole Cypress Course measures 3349 yards among hardwoods standing in coastal wetlands. The signature 13th hole is a beautiful 355-yard par 4 that crosses water twice and overlooks the Intracoastal Waterway.

Mounds, pristine woodlands and lakes, which come into play on 17 holes, make the Lakes/Cypress 18 a challenging course. One particularly tough hole is No. 2 on the Cypress, a narrow par 5. Water flanks the left side of the tee shot, which is followed by a lay-up, then another shot across water to a green sitting at its edge.

The nine-hole Waterway Course opened in fall 1995. You guessed it: It also wraps along the snaking Intracoastal and calls upon all your skills to avoid water hazards.

The national trend toward 27-hole courses is growing, and Arrowhead's owners are delighted to have more to offer. They also emphasize their proximity to the airport for visiting golfers in a rush.

Arrowhead Country Club is the first Ray Floyd signature course in South Carolina. Floyd won the *Golf Magazine* Senior Tour Championship played in Myrtle Beach in November 1994, a very good year for him.

Rental clubs, a driving range, putting green,

pro shop, locker room, bar and restaurant are available. The upscale country club atmosphere is classy and comfortable. Walking is not allowed at Arrowhead. Approximate fees include cart and average $85.

Azalea Sands Golf Club
U.S. Hwy. 17 S., North Myrtle Beach
• (843) 272-6191, (800) 253-2312
Championship Yardage: 6902
Slope: 123   Par: 72
Men's Yardage: 6287
Slope: 116   Par: 72
Ladies' Yardage: 5172
Slope: 119   Par: 72

This 18-hole course, designed by Gene Hamm, opened in 1972. Tifdwarf greens are set among lakes, bunkers and trees. One of the toughest holes is the 18th, a 540-yard par 5. Another challenging hole is a 195-yard par 3. The 5th hole requires a shot over a lake to a green well guarded by bunkers.

Amenities include practice greens, bar, snack bar, beverage cart, pro shop and rental clubs. No driving range is provided.

Approximate fees, including cart, range from $25 to $54. Walking is allowed certain times of year, and a pull cart costs $3 to rent.

The course is just minutes from several of the largest golf equipment shops and a couple of miles from Barefoot Landing, a popular destination for lunch or dinner.

Barefoot Resort
S.C. Hwy. 9, North Myrtle Beach
• (843) 272-8349, (800) 854-8619
At the time of printing, Barefoot Resort was still under construction, but much of it was scheduled to open in 2000.

Not to be confused with Barefoot Landing in North Myrtle Beach, Barefoot Resort promises to be one of The Beach's premier facilities. It will feature four courses, designed by Davis Love III, Pete Dye, Tom Fazio, and Greg Norman. That's a pretty strong foursome there! Barefoot is likely to become one of the Beach's most sought-after facilities—make sure you book ahead here.

Bay Tree Golf Plantation
S.C. Hwy. 90, North Myrtle Beach
• (843) 249-1487, (800) 845-6191
You can't miss this golf course on S.C. Highway 9 because of its gigantic golf ball, which doubles as a water tower for the Little River area. Bay Tree has three 18-hole courses, designed by George Fazio, Tom Fazio and Russell

Myrtle Beach courses attract golfers from all over the world.

Photo: Myrtle Beach Chamber of Commerce

Breeden. In 1972, Bay Tree Golf Plantation was the first to build three courses simultaneously. It's a popular club for local memberships among the North Myrtle Beach crowd. All three courses have plentiful water hazards and bermudagrass fairways.

The clubhouse offers a comfortable and scenic bar and restaurant at the 55th hole, a well-stocked pro shop and large men's and ladies' locker rooms. A driving range, practice green and rental clubs are available. Nearby, you'll find condominiums for rent—a great option when you want to be on three great golf courses and a bit away from the beach and its traffic.

Approximate fees range from $25 to $45, and carts are an additional $15. Check for three- and seven-day memberships. Walking is allowed.

Gold Course
Championship Yardage: 6942
Slope: 135   **Par: 72**
Men's Yardage: 6390
Slope: 128   **Par: 72**

Ladies' Yardage: 5264
Slope: 117   **Par: 72**

The No. 1 handicap hole is the par 4 No. 5, which plays 455 yards from the championship tees, 409 yards from the men's tees. Heavy hitters may choose to lay up short of the water— 265 yards out. If you control your drive, you can hit into a narrow landing area approximately 160 yards from the pin. Shots too far right will land in the woods. The green is guarded by a trap on the left that should not come into play, but the green undulates, and pin placement is crucial to making par or birdie here. The 16th tee and fairway flank S.C. 9 in front of the towering golf ball. A birdie is a real possibility here if you carry the water and cut the dogleg. Several fairway bunkers might come into play with errant tee shots. If you do score birdie here, you won't have long to enjoy it; No. 17, a 189-yard par 3, plays longer than it looks. The green is encircled by water and bunkers.

The LPGA championship played on this

course in 1977 was the first nationally televised tournament from the Grand Strand. This course was named to *Golf for Women* magazine's Top Fairways list of the country's 100 most female-friendly golf courses.

Green Course

Championship Yardage:	7044	
Slope: 135		Par: 72
Men's Yardage: 6492		
Slope: 126		Par: 72
Ladies' Yardage: 5362		
Slope: 118		Par: 72

The Green Course has benefited from a recent facelift, with some greens and tees being moved and bunkers being moved or added. It features narrow fairways. You're immediately initiated to the course's muscularity on No. 1, a 563-yard par 5 where you must traverse water to reach a narrow green. Water comes into play on many holes, including the par 4 11th, where a hazard intersects the fairway. Your tee shot must lay up short of the water. The green is guarded by bunkers in front and back.

Silver Course

Championship Yardage:	6871	
Slope: 131		Par: 72
Men's Yardage: 6363		
Slope: 122		Par: 72
Ladies' Yardage: 5417		
Slope: 116		Par: 72

Bay Tree rebuilt and reshaped its Silver Course and reopened it in the fall of 1995. Tees and traps were restructured and senior tees added. The fine George Fazio design and undulations didn't change. The greens were made much larger, and some trees were removed. Target mounds behind some of the greens are helpful for approach shots. Many believe it to be the locals' favorite, and it's often preferred by women.

The Silver course starts with a difficult 388-yard par 4. It's a slight dogleg right on a narrow fairway with woods on both sides. The lone fairway bunker shouldn't pose a problem for long hitters. You should constantly stay right on this hole and have a good approach to the large undulating green.

The back nine includes the tough par 5 12th—518 yards. In order to have a good approach, drives and second shots must be from the center of the fairway left, but beware of a small pond. Reach here safely and you'll have a

nice short iron shot to a triangular green that is well guarded by three sand traps.

Beachwood Golf Club
1520 U.S. Hwy. 17 S., North Myrtle Beach
• (843) 272-6168, (800) 526-4889

Championship Yardage:	6825	
Slope: 120		Par: 72
Men's Yardage:	6344	
Slope: 117		Par: 72
Other Yardage: 5817		
Slope: 115		Par: 72
Ladies' Yardage: 5052		
Slope: 111		Par: 72

The 18-hole course, set between the Intracoastal Waterway and the Atlantic Ocean—as are many Grand Strand courses—was designed by Gene Hamm and built in 1968. Its lush fairways and bermudagrass greens meander through tall pines and lakes and host abundant native wildlife. The signature finishing hole, a par 3, is a healthy 239 yards and calls for a long, accurate shot to reach a green protected by three bunkers.

The multifaceted practice facility offers two large greens, a driving range with multiple target areas, a chipping green and practice bunker.

Approximate fees, including cart rental, range upward from $24. Walking is not allowed.

Belle Terre
4073 U.S. Hwy. 501, Myrtle Beach
• (843) 236-8888, (800) 340-0072
Championship Course

Championship Yardage:	7013	
Slope: 134		Par: 72
Men's Yardage:	6672	
Slope: 127		Par: 72
Other Yardage:	6368	
Slope: 123		Par: 72
Other Yardage:	5880	
Slope: 113		Par: 72
Ladies' Yardage:	5049	
Slope: No rating		Par: 72

Skins Course

Back Yardage:	3201
Slope: 93	
Front Yardage:	2802

There are two 18-hole courses here at Belle Terre, both designed by Rees Jones and opened in 1995. One is the championship course and the other is called the Skins Course and is an

INSIDERS' TIP

If your area has a links-style course, play it one day in a howling gale or light rain to get a sense of what it's like to play in Scotland—where golf began.

executive course with par 4s and par 3s to a par of 58. An interesting feature is the fleet of motorized pull carts for golfers who want to walk.

The name Belle Terre (beautiful earth) came from Jones' description of the property. The Championship Course, with tifdwarf bermudagrass, measures more than 7000 yards. The front nine has water and sand on six holes. The back nine has sand and protected wetlands. The combination of water, sand and wetlands makes this a tight course where course management, club selection and ball placement are paramount. A good short game is another advantage here because most of the greens are well bunkered.

"The soil and natural shape of the land allow for subtle elements of an old-style, classic design, giving the holes clear definition so that a player can stand on the tee and have a clear perspective without using gimmicks. The subtleties make the course different every time you play it," Jones said.

The driving range is lighted and features rolling terrain and tees on each end. The pro shop is fully stocked, and the clubhouse has a nice bar and restaurant with a gourmet chef offering outstanding specialties daily as well as a collection of Jimmy D'Angelo's memorabilia. (D'Angelo is one of the consultants for the course and is well known as the first pro in Myrtle Beach.) Walking is not allowed on the Championship Course. Approximate fees, with cart, are $60 to $75. The staff is extremely friendly here. At the end of your round you are asked to complete a questionnaire—for which you earn a beer.

Blackmoor

S.C. Hwy. 707, Murrells Inlet
• **(843) 650-5555, (800) 650-5555**
Championship Yardage: 6614
Slope: 126   **Par: 72**
Men's Yardage: 6217
Slope: 118   **Par: 72**
Other Yardage: 5774
Slope: 111   **Par: 72**
Ladies' Yardage: 4807
Slope: 115   **Par: 72**

This 18-hole course was built in 1990 and was the first in the Myrtle Beach area designed by 1965 U.S. Open champ Gary Player. Bermudagrass greens and fairways are always perfectly maintained. Several blind shots to the green complexes will remind you to study the course layout. Several interesting holes include No. 3, which is a long par 5 with a narrow fairway; the par 4 No. 8, which features two

routes to the green determined by the degree of risk you want to take; and the par 4 14th, a sharp dogleg to an undulating green guarded by a lake. As with several courses on the southern end of the Grand Strand, Blackmoor was built on the site of a rice plantation along the Waccamaw River. The natural lakes, cypress trees and moss-draped oaks lend tranquility to the course. From the back veranda of the clubhouse, you can oversee the finishing hole, listen to the birds and commune with nature.

The course includes a bar, snack bar, beverage cart, pro shop and rental clubs. Blackmoor offers a practice green and a chipping area as well as a driving range. Approximate fees range from $35 in the summer to $85, including cart, during prime spring and fall golfing seasons. Walking is not allowed, which is odd because Gary Player claims to be such a fitness freak. You'd think that a Gary Player course would allow walking at any time.

Brick Landing Plantation

N.C. Hwy. 2, Ocean Isle Beach, N.C.
• **(910) 754-5612, (800) 438-3006**
Championship Yardage: 6482
Slope: 140   **Par: 72**
Men's Yardage: 6154
Slope: 132   **Par: 72**
Other Yardage: 5792
Slope: 122   **Par: 72**
Ladies' Yardage: 4835
Slope: 114   **Par: 72**

This 18-hole course, designed by H.M. Brazeal along the Altantic Intracoastal Waterway, features ocean views. Hardwood forests and saltwater marshes also characterize this South Brunswick Island layout, easy to reach from either Myrtle Beach or Wilmington.

The first two holes and the last two play along the waterway looking to the Atlantic Ocean. Four holes on the back nine are adjacent to Sauce Pan Creek, which is a saltwater marsh filled with wildlife. The easiest and the shortest hole is No. 2, a par 3 of just 96 yards. This is the first hole you can birdie and the only hole on the course without water. Six bunkers surround the green, and you can forget about the birdie if you land in one of these.

No. 7 is a par 5 of 579 yards, the longest par 5 on the course. Not only is it the longest, but it's also the narrowest. Playing through the pines, you must place your drive in the left center of the fairway to leave the correct angle for your second and third shots. The green slopes left to right with a deep bunker on the right and water on the left. This is a good hole to birdie, but also a hole that can result in a big number. Accuracy is at a premium here. Villas along the fairways and homes along the water or among the hardwoods present no problem to the golfer.

Complete practice facilities include putting greens, practice bunkers, a wide driving range with target greens and instructors. Rental clubs are available. Approximate greens fees including cart range from $40 to $70.

Brunswick Plantation & Golf Links
U.S. Hwy. 17, Calabash, N.C.
• (910) 287-7888, (800) 848-0290
Championship Yardage: 6779
Slope: 131   Par: 72
Men's Yardage: 6215
Slope: 124   Par: 72
Other Yardage: 5791
Slope: 118   Par: 72
Ladies' Yardage: 5210
Slope: 115   Par: 72

Willard Byrd designed this course in 1992. Fairways are bermudagrass, and greens are bentgrass. The greens are undulating and fast, so you may need one club less than usual. Unless your shots are high and come down soft, you will need to lay up and roll on to the green.

The signature hole is the 15th, a par 3 surrounded by oyster shells and water. It's a carry of 197 yards off the back tees over water. Hello! No. 4 is a long dogleg right, with water on one side and sand on the other.

Amenities include practice greens, driving range, pro shop, bar and snack bar, beverage cart and rental clubs. The new clubhouse is upscale, and the restaurant is a spectacular choice for fine dining, including the wine list and daily chef's seafood or other special appetizers, entrées and desserts. You may dine dressed casually straight off the golf course, or you may wish to grab a companion and return later for a leisurely candlelight evening.

Approximate greens fees range from $35 to $60. Walking is not allowed.

Buck Creek Golf Plantation
S.C. Hwy. 9, North Myrtle Beach
• (843) 249-5996, (800) 344-0982
Cypress/Tupelo Course
Championship Yardage: 6865
Slope: 132   Par: 72

Men's Yardage: 6306
Slope: 126   Par: 72
Other Yardage: 5744
Slope: 115   Par: 72
Ladies' Yardage: 4956
Slope: 124   Par: 72
Meadow/Cypress Course
Championship Yardage: 6751
Slope: 126   Par: 72
Men's Yardage: 6211
Slope: 119   Par: 72
Other Yardage: 5688
Slope: 111   Par: 72
Ladies' Yardage: 4972
Slope: 117   Par: 72
Tupelo/Meadow Course
Championship Yardage: 6726
Slope: 128   Par: 72
Men's Yardage: 6115
Slope: 119   Par: 72
Other Yardage: 5574
Slope: 115   Par: 72
Ladies' Yardage: 4684
Slope: 117   Par: 72

This club's three nine-hole courses are played as three 18-hole pairs. All are naturally beautiful and are kept in top condition. A recent ownership change brought improvements to the already popular complex. A hand-held digital caddy is available for measuring to the cup within a yard's accuracy. It's expected to speed play as well as increase shot accuracy. This 137-acre natural wetland sanctuary is home to many varieties of wildlife. All three courses were designed by Tom Jackson, built by John McWhite and opened in 1990. All have bermudagrass greens and plentiful water hazards. The complex was designed to accommodate all levels of play and is exceptionally challenging for the low handicapper. Accuracy and shot placement are imperative.

No. 9 at Tupelo and No. 2 at Cypress are tough holes. The 9th at Tupelo is a big dogleg left, and you easily can miss the green into traps or wetlands. The Cypress' No. 2 is a par 5 where long hitters off the tee must be aware of the water on the right. The second shot is crucial because it must carry water. Aim for the right side of the green; if you shoot left, you might be in another water hazard. If you get to the front of the green without getting wet, you will be in position for a pitch to the green.

INSIDERS' TIP

Limit conversation on the green. Concentration is critical to putting, and players should respect each other's time for mental preparation. You'll also keep the game moving along if you keep the commentary to a minimum.

A putting green, driving range, pro shop, rental clubs, a snack bar and bar are offered. Improvements to the clubhouse were completed in 1997.

Walking is not allowed. Greens fees range from $30 to $70, including cart.

Burning Ridge
U.S. Hwy. 501 West, Myrtle Beach
• (843) 347-0538, (800) TEE-OFFS

Both the East and West courses of Burning Ridge are 18 holes. These adjacent courses were built in 1980 and 1987, respectively; Gene Hamm designed both. They incorporate numerous lakes and huge bunkers, and both feature bermudagrass fairways and greens.

The complex has a practice green, a practice sand trap, driving range, pro shop, bar and restaurant, beverage cart and rental clubs. Walking is not allowed.

Approximate fees range from $30 to $60, including cart.

East Course

Championship Yardage:	6780
Slope: 132	Par: 72
Men's Yardage:	6216
Slope: 124	Par: 72
Other Yardage:	5724
Slope: 114	Par: 72
Ladies' Yardage:	4524
Slope: 115	Par: 72

The par 3 No. 12 measures 210 yards over water from the men's tees. You must choose the correct club, and you must be long and left because your tee shot has to carry over water in front and on the right.

West Course

Championship Yardage:	6714
Slope: 122	Par: 72
Men's Yardage:	6237
Slope: 114	Par: 72
Ladies' Yardage:	4831
Slope: 118	Par: 72

No. 14, a 577-yard par 5, is a slight dogleg left that usually plays into the wind. If you want to play 36 holes in one day, this is an ideal place to be; as the saying at Burning Ridge goes: The first 18 was so good, we decided to stay. Any hooks or slices will definitely find water—it's in view on every hole on this course.

Caledonia Golf & Fish Club
369 Caledonia Dr., Pawleys Island
• (843) 237-3675, (800) 483-6800

Championship Yardage:	6503
Slope: 130	Par: 70
Men's Yardage:	6104
Slope 116	Par: 70
Other Yardage:	5738
Slope: 115	Par: 70
Ladies' Yardage:	4968
Slope: 113	Par: 70

Caledonia opened in early 1994 and continually draws rave reviews from some of the country's most discriminating golfers. Mike Strantz built this 18-hole on the site of a historic colonial rice plantation along the Waccamaw River. The centuries-old live oaks will capture your attention; you'll think you're driving onto a movie set. After your round, the rocking chairs beckon from the back porch of the antebellum-style clubhouse overlooking the 18th green. A precise tee shot is needed for your finish, as the second shot is difficult and the carry on to the green is forced.

Strantz, a former assistant to Tom Fazio, was the architect who made a splash with Caledonia, his first course. Caledonia complements the surrounding natural landscape. Greens are tifdwarf; fairways are 419 bermudagrass. Tees are marked with replicas of the native waterfowl that inhabit the plantation's rice fields: wood duck, mallard, redhead and pintail. Gently sloping fairways with unique landing areas, vast waste bunkers and tough approach shots offer extreme challenges. The hunting and fishing retreat that predates the golf course maintains its old shed where Thursday night socializing remains a time-honored tradition.

A lot of golfers will tell you that Caledonia is their favorite course at The Beach.

The course offers a putting green, a driving net (in lieu of a range), a nice pro shop, a three-hole par 3 course, men's and women's dressing rooms and a comfortable bar and restaurant with good food.

Summer greens fees, including cart, are $55; spring fees are $100. Walking is restricted.

Carolina National Golf Club
1643 Goley Hewett Rd.,Bolivia, N.C.
• (910) 755-5200, (888) 200-6455

Championship Yardage:	7017
Slope: 141	Par: 72
Men's Yardage:	6466
Slope: 137	Par: 72
Other Yardage:	6088
Slope: 127	Par: 72
Other Yardage:	5406
Slope: 117	Par: 72
Ladies' Yardage:	4759
Slope: 108	Par: 72

The Carolina National Golf Club, situated in rolling hills and marshland about a half-hour north of Myrtle Beach, marks the first Carolina design effort of Fred Couples and Gene Bates. The Heron and Egret nines were here first, while the Ibis nine opened in early 2000. The course's live oaks, pines and dogwoods combine with the lakes and wetlands for a certified Audubon wildlife sanctuary, lending credence to the aviary names of the various nines. The fairways are bermudagrass, while the greens are seeded with L-93/Crenshaw bentgrass.

The three nine-hole courses offer five sets of tees, so golfers of all abilities will find a challenge here. The signature hole, the 5th on the Heron Nine, overlooks the scenic Lockwood Folly River. At 203 yards from the tips, the hole will challenge the biggest of hitters to be accurate.

Amenities include a clubhouse and restaurant, large practice chipping and putting green, and a 360-yard driving range. Approximate greens fees range from $43 to $80, cart included. Walking is not allowed at Carolina National.

Carolina Shores Golf & Country Club

99 Carolina Shores Dr., Calabash, N.C.
• (910) 579-2181, (803) 448-2657,
(800) 579-8292

Championship Yardage:	6783	
Slope: 128		**Par: 72**
Men's Yardage:	6231	
Slope: 122		**Par: 72**
Ladies' Yardage:	5385	
Slope: 122		**Par: 72**

This 18-hole course opened in 1974. Tom Jackson designed the course with bermudagrass fairways and tifdwarf greens.

The toughest hole is the 1st—a long par 5 with a lot of sand protected by water in front. Another challenge is No. 11, a sharp dogleg right at 356 yards. If you want to risk the shortcut, you may, but if you miss you will be in the woods and will surely score a high number. If you don't take that risk, you must deal with a fairway bunker. The course is known for its challenge: Note the 96 sand bunkers and 10 lakes. The layout of the front nine definitely brings water into play; sand is more prevalent on the back nine.

Practice greens, a driving range, pro shop, locker room, bar, snack bar, beverage cart and rental clubs are offered.

Approximate greens fees range from $30 to $60, including cart. Walking is not allowed.

INSIDERS' TIP

Many golfers miss putts because they lift their heads too early. A good drill: On the practice green, make a conscious effort to keep your head down and your eye on the spot of the ball until you hear the ball drop in the cup.

Colonial Charters Golf & Country Club

S.C. Hwy. 9, Longs • (843) 249-8809

Championship Yardage:	6769	
Slope: 124		**Par: 72**
Men's Yardage:	6337	
Slope: 119		**Par: 72**
Other Yardage:	6001	
Slope: 115		**Par: 72**
Ladies' Yardage:	5079	
Slope: 120		**Par: 72**

This course's most difficult hole is the 18th. It's been called many names, including one of the 10 toughest "Hell Holes" and the No. 1 hole in Myrtle Beach's "Dream 18." Go ahead and play it and tell us what you think. It always generates comments.

John Simpson designed Colonial Charters in 1988. Swing analysis, lessons, club fitting and club repair are available here. Colonial Charters also has rental clubs, a practice green, driving range, bar, restaurant and locker room, and ladies' play is unrestricted. A special program encourages juniors to play free during the summer.

Approximate fees are seasonal and range from $27 to $55. Walking is not allowed.

Crow Creek

U.S. Hwy. 17, Calabash
• (910) 287-3081, (877) 287-3081

Championship Yardage:	7101	
Slope: 128		**Par: 72**
Men's Yardage:	6679	
Slope: 124		**Par: 72**
Other Yardage:	6099	
Slope: 120		**Par: 72**
Ladies' Yardage:	5097	
Slope: 114		**Par: 72**

Crow Creek, which opened in spring 2000, is Rick Robbins' first effort at The Beach. Robbins is a well-known Carolinas architect who worked with Jack Nicklaus before going out on his own. Much of the course brings the Waccamaw River into play.

Crow Creek is one of the more attractive courses at The Beach—Robbins didn't have to move too much dirt to create the course. The 7th, at 573 yards, should prove to be a difficult hole. Crow Creek should have little problem attracting golfers at The Beach.

Swing analysis, lessons, club fitting and club

repair are available here. Colonial Charters also has rental clubs, a practice green, driving range, bar, restaurant and locker room. A special program encourages juniors to play free during the summer.

Approximate fees are seasonal and range from $27 to $55. Walking is not allowed.

Cypress Bay Golf Club
U.S. Hwy. 17, Little River
• (843) 249-1025, (800) TEE-OFFS

Championship Yardage:	6502
Slope: 122	Par: 72
Men's Yardage:	6101
Slope: 118	Par: 72
Ladies' Yardage:	4920
Slope: 113	Par: 72

This Russell Breeden-designed course opened in 1972. Locals like it a lot for its ample supply of water and sand. The picturesque 8th hole challenges you with 180 yards over water.

No driving range is provided, but Cypress Bay does have putting and chipping greens and practice bunkers as well as rental clubs. After your round, unwind at the friendly bar and restaurant.

Approximate fees range from $30 to $62, including cart. Walking is allowed after 3 PM.

Deer Track Golf Resort
U.S. Hwy. 17 S., Surfside Beach
• (843) 650-2146, (800) 548-9186

Both the Toski Links and the South courses (18 holes each) were designed by Bob Toski and Porter Gibson and built in 1974. Owner-operator Gary Schaal is past president of PGA of America.

The complex offers practice greens, rental clubs, a driving range, pro shop, bar, restaurant and beverage cart. Locker rooms are available for members only.

Approximate fees range from $35 to $65, including cart. Walking is allowed after 1 PM.

Toski Links

Championship Yardage:	7203
Slope: 121	Par: 72
Men's Yardage:	6511
Slope: 121	Par: 72
Ladies' Yardage:	5353
Slope: 119	Par: 72

Bermudagrass fairways and elevated tifdwarf bermuda greens are featured here. No. 8 is a long and narrow hole that plays 458 yards from the back tees—beware of this one! The signature hole on this course is the 17th, a par 3 that requires a tee shot to a green guarded by water and bunkers on three sides. A million-dollar upgrade in 1996 returned the previously

named North, now the Toski Links, to its original outstanding design.

South Course

Championship Yardage:	6916
Slope: 119	Par: 71
Men's Yardage:	6143
Slope: 119	Par: 71
Ladies' Yardage:	5226
Slope: 120	Par: 71

The South Course has bermudagrass greens, more water hazards and more narrow fairways than the Toski Links. It underwent design changes with rebuilt greens in 1994. The signature hole is No. 4, a 204-yard par 3 that requires a tee shot to a peninsula green.

The Dunes Golf and Beach Club
9000 N. Ocean Blvd., Myrtle Beach
• (843) 449-5914

Championship Yardage:	7165
Slope: 138	Par: 72
Men's Yardage:	6565
Slope: 130	Par: 72
Other Yardage:	6175
Slope: 118	Par: 72
Ladies' Yardage:	5390
Slope: 127	Par: 72

Robert Trent Jones Sr. designed this 18-hole course in 1948. It's technically the only private course in Myrtle Beach you can play—if you stay with a member accommodation. Several major hotels maintain memberships with this premier course. When you book your golf vacation, check with hotel golf directors to locate a member property if you want to get on The Dunes, or call the course for a list of "Member" hotels. Also, reciprocal agreements allow members from certain other clubs to play here.

The PGA Seniors used to end their season here, and the Golf Writers Association of America has played its annual championship at the Dunes for close to 50 years. Everyone wants to play this course and with good reason. It's actually one of the few tracks at The Beach that's genuinely close to the beach, with a few holes right up against the sea.

The Dunes features bentgrass greens and many water hazards. Several holes overlook the Atlantic Ocean. The signature hole is the 13th, a par 5 that plays alongside a large lake. *Sports Illustrated* named it one of the best 18 holes in America; it has won numerous other awards as well. In 1995, the championship tee on No. 18 was enlarged and realigned toward the drive-landing area, and another men's tee was added to change the angle of play and stretch the hole to 405 yards.

The clubhouse includes a bar, grill room and

dining room, and the pro shop expanded in 1995. The food is always good, especially the pastry chef's creations.

Members enjoy a pool, tennis courts, memberships for juniors, weekly bridge and frequent dances. Locker rooms are spacious. Driving range and practice green are provided as well as rental clubs.

Approximate greens fees are upwards of $100, including cart. Walking is resticted—a pity.

Eagle Nest Golf Club

U.S. Hwy. 17 N., Little River
• **(843) 249-1449, (800) 543-3113**

Championship Yardage:	**6901**
Slope: 120	**Par: 72**
Men's Yardage:	**6417**
Slope: 116	**Par: 72**
Other Yardage:	**5594**
Slope: No rating	**Par: 72**
Ladies' Yardage:	**5105**
Slope: 115	**Par: 72**

According to legend, it's actually an osprey nest tucked high in the tree on the way to the 8th hole. Don't worry about it too much; you'll keep busy enough looking for your ball. The course provides a wonderful guide to its birds—a great touch for the ornithologically inclined.

This 18-hole course, designed by Gene Hamm and built in 1972, is laid out among woods, water and marsh grass. It boasts three tough finishing holes. The 16th is a 416-yard par 4 with a pond cutting into the fairway from the left. The green is well guarded and undulating. The 17th is a gentle double dogleg of 576 yards. You'll need to lay up short of the pond and pitch to an elevated green, avoiding a trap if you're too short or trees if you're too long. The 18th is the signature hole, a par 3 carrying 164 yards over water to a small elevated green guarded by four traps. Bermudagrass greens are perfectly kept and are a pleasure to play.

Rental clubs, a driving range and a restaurant are available.

Approximate fees range from $30 to $45 with cart an additional $17. The course allows walking at certain times.

Eastport Club

U.S. Hwy. 17 N., Little River
• **(843) 249-3997, (800) 334-9035**

Championship Yardage:	**6047**
Slope: 116	**Par: 70**
Men's Yardage:	**5400**
Slope: 111	**Par: 70**
Ladies' Yardage:	**4560**
Slope: 114	**Par: 70**

Architect Dennis Griffiths designed this track as a finesse course. He did not produce the typical beach layout when he crafted this 18-hole design, built in 1988. It has narrow bermudagrass fairways and large bentgrass greens and is bordered to the east by the Intracoastal Waterway.

Holes 1 through 15 are short, and the course lulls you up to this point. Then, the last three holes are much more difficult. The course is mostly flat, like 95 percent of holes at The Beach. Some tree-lined fairways dogleg. On the 3rd hole, your second shot will vary depending on the placement of your tee shot over the lake.

Rental clubs are available; there's a bar and a restaurant. The new clubhouse is a great addition. Luxury homes are being built along the waterway behind the clubhouse. Eastport has no driving range, but it does have a practice green.

Approximate fees average $30, including cart. Walking is not allowed.

Glen Dornoch Waterway Golf Links

U.S. Hwy. 17 N., Little River
• **(843) 249-2541, (800) 717-8784**

Championship Yardage:	**6850**
Slope: 141	**Par: 72**
Men's Yardage:	**6446**
Slope: 133	**Par: 72**
Other Yardage:	**6035**
Slope: 124	**Par: 72**
Other Yardage:	**5617**
Slope: 116	**Par: 72**
Ladies' Yardage:	**5002**
Slope: 129	**Par: 72**

A tribute to Dornoch, Scotland, where Donald Ross was born, this 260-acre site along the Intracoastal Waterway offers magnolias, pines, oaks, lakes, river, marsh and waterway views among a planned self-contained resort to include a hotel, condominiums and related facilities. The course opened in September 1996. Greens are tifdwarf; fairways are bermudagrass.

At least four holes border the waterway, and dramatic elevation changes (for The Beach), dropping some 35 feet to the waterway, are spectacular. The course has no wide-open fairways. The par 5 5th hole is a mere 590 yards from the tips. You must keep your drive down the left side of the fairway, which is bisected by wetlands that you must carry on your second shot. The second shot should also be on the left side of the fairway in order to give you a good angle as you approach the green, which is guarded by a creek and two bunkers in front. The green is deep, and you must doublecheck your yardage.

Glen Dornoch was created by the owners of

The DuPont World Handicap Tournament is one of Myrtle Beach's biggest events.

Photo: Bill Woodward

Heather Glen and designed by Clyde Johnston. The complex features a driving range, putting green and nice clubhouse. Approximate fees including cart range from $45 to $110. Walking is not allowed, which is a bit of a joke—you'd think that a course that's supposedly a tribute to Donald Ross and Royal Dornoch might pay tribute to one of the key traditions of the game.

Heather Glen Golf Links
U.S. Hwy. 17 N., Little River
• (843) 249-9000, (800) 868-4536

Inspired by Gleneagles and St. Andrews, the Scottish tradition is unmistakable at this 200-acre historic site. Three nine-hole courses with bermudagrass greens are a collective masterpiece designed by Willard Byrd and Clyde Johnston, built in 1987 and named America's top new course of that year by *Golf Digest*. The 50-foot elevation changes, gigantic 100-year-old pine trees, pot bunkers and waste areas are supposed to transport you from South Carolina to Scotland for a few hours. The scrub growth and wooden steps out of the bunkers are designed to be just like courses in Scotland. The mock 18th-century clubhouse, ersatz Scottish pub and pro shop add to your day's pleasure here.

Rental clubs, a driving range, putting area, locker room and beverage cart are available. Approximate fees range from $40 to $100, including cart. Walking is not allowed, which almost completely destroys this facility's attempt to be just like Scotland. (Note to developers who want a "Scottish" golf course: everyone walks in Scotland—whatever the weather.)

1 Red/2 White Course
Championship Yardage:	**6786**
Slope: 130	**Par: 72**
Men's Yardage:	**6337**
Slope: 123	**Par: 72**
Ladies' Yardage:	**5949**
Slope: 117	**Par: 72**

2 White/3 Blue Course
Championship Yardage:	**6791**
Slope: 130	**Par: 72**
Men's Yardage:	**6510**
Slope: 126	**Par: 72**
Ladies' Yardage:	**6200**
Slope: 117	**Par: 72**

3 Blue/1 Red Course
Championship Yardage:	**6791**
Slope: 127	**Par: 72**
Men's Yardage:	**6427**
Slope: 126	**Par: 72**
Ladies' Yardage:	**5959**
Slope: 117	**Par: 72**

The Red Course's par 5 No. 3 has a large fairway bunker on the right. The sloping green also has three smaller pot bunkers behind and left of the green.

No. 8 on the White Course is a beautiful hole. You have a choice of playing it safe or going over the water. The right side of the fairway threatens with mounds and bunkers, and the green has bunkers to the left and around the back.

No. 1 on the Blue Course is a par 4, with a beautiful view of the hole from an elevated tee. The fairway tilts from left to right, and the drive must be slightly left of center. What makes this hole especially tough is a large but hidden green. No. 5 is a short par 3 with huge mounds on the right and pot bunkers placed in the mounds at right, behind and guarding the left side of the green.

The Heritage Club
Kings River Rd., Pawleys Island
• (843) 236-9318, (800) 990-8995

Championship Yardage: 7040	
Slope: 137	Par: 71
Men's Yardage:	6565
Slope: 128	Par: 71
Other Yardage:	6090
Slope: 117	Par: 71
Ladies Yardage:	5325
Slope: 125	Par: 71

The Heritage Club opened in 1986. It was designed and developed by Larry D. Young and was ranked in *Golf Digest's* 1990 Top 50 Public Courses. It is part of a golfing community built on 600 acres of giant magnolias, 300-year-old oaks, freshwater lakes and marshes. An avenue of oaks also leads to the Southern Colonial-style clubhouse of 12,000 square feet that overlooks the Waccamaw River. The Heritage speaks of gracious Southern living and pays tribute to the rice culture of bygone days.

Fairways are bermudagrass; greens are bent. There is always a premium on shot placement. Sculpted bunkers are frequent throughout the course. The par 3 13th requires a carry across water. The 4th hole features an avenue of centuries-old oaks alongside the fairway.

The driving range, putting green, pro shop, dining room and lounge are top-quality.

Approximate fees, with cart, range from $50 to $90. Walking is not allowed.

Heron Point Golf Club
6980 Blue Heron Blvd., Myrtle Beach
• (843) 650-6664

Championship Yardage:	6444
Slope: 129	Par: 72
Men's Yardage:	6080
Slope: 121	Par: 72
Other Yardage:	5335
Slope: 109	Par: 72

Ladies' Yardage:	4734
Slope: 121	Par: 72

Willard Byrd Designed this golf course, which opened in the 1970s with bermudagrass fairways and greens.

Part of an aging condo and retirement community, Heron Point is a relatively tight track with its fairways bordered primarily with pines and OB stakes. There's some water on this mostly flat course, most notably on the par 5 511-yard 18th and the par 3 175-yard 6th. The trickiest holes on the course might be the 367-yard 5th and 355-yard 15th, both of which dogleg 90 degrees.

While there's little interest off the tee here at Heron Point, the mostly small green complexes are well-designed and represent most of the course's challenge. While Heron Point might never stack up against some of the Beach's best, it provides a sensible test for the residents of the community and visitors in search of a low-cost alternative to the more expensive courses.

The course offers rental clubs and a driving range plus a bar and restaurant.

Approximate fees average $40, including cart. Walking is allowed after 3 PM on certain days.

Indian Wells
U.S. Hwy. 17 Bypass., Surfside Beach
• (843) 651-1505

Championship Yardage:	6624
Slope: 125	Par: 72
Men's Yardage:	6225
Slope: 123	Par: 72
Other Yardage:	5811
Slope: 117	Par: 72
Ladies' Yardage:	4872
Slope: 118	Par: 70

Gene Hamm designed this course in the mid-1970s; it has bermudagrass fairways and bentgrass greens and is a member of the Links Group of golf courses.

One of the earlier courses in the Myrtle Beach area, Indian Wells could benefit from a face lift, but still offers decent golf in a rather typical Myrtle Beach setting. The 9th, a 410-yard par 4, used to be on the Myrtle Beach "Dream 18;" it's a tricky hole requiring an accurate drive followed by a mid- to long iron over water and a bunker to one of the smaller greens on the course.

Water comes into play on all but a couple of holes at Indian Wells. On three of the par 5s, trees also come into play—right in the middle of the fairway, something that's rare on a Gene Hamm golf course. While all of us love trees, their place in the middle of a fairway is debatable.

Still, there's a lot of fun to be had on this course. Just avoid the water and play to the middle of the large greens and you should be fine.

The course offers rental clubs and a driving range plus a bar and restaurant.

Approximate fees average $50, including cart. Walking is restricted.

Indigo Creek
U.S. Hwy. 17 S., Surfside Beach
• **(843) 650-0381**

Championship Yardage: 6744	
Slope: 128	**Par:** 72
Men's Yardage:	6185
Slope: 120	**Par:** 72
Other Yardage:	5593
Slope: 113	**Par:** 72
Ladies' Yardage:	4921
Slope: 120	**Par:** 70

This Willard Byrd 18-hole course was built in 1990. It sports bentgrass greens, doglegs, bunkers and water. Note the 90-degree dogleg on No. 12 that crosses the same creek twice. Giant oaks draped with Spanish moss are standard in the Lowcountry, where time seems to stand still.

The course offers rental clubs, a driving range and a bar and restaurant.

Approximate fees average $50, including cart. Walking is not allowed.

Island Green Country Club
455 Sunnehanna Dr., Myrtle Beach
• **(843) 650-2186**
Dogwood/Holly Course

Championship Yardage: 6272	
Slope: 118	**Par:** 72
Men's Yardage:	5847
Slope: 111	**Par:** 72
Ladies' Yardage:	4510
Slope: 115	**Par:** 72

Tall Oaks/Dogwood Course

Championship Yardage: 6123	
Slope: 118	**Par:** 72
Men's Yardage:	5705
Slope: 111	**Par:** 72
Ladies' Yardage:	4996
Slope: 116	**Par:** 72

Holly/Tall Oaks Course

Championship Yardage: 6243	
Slope: 118	**Par:** 72
Men's Yardage:	5864
Slope: 111	**Par:** 72
Ladies' Yardage:	4704
Slope: 115	**Par:** 72

This 27-hole course was built in 1980 by Bill Mooney and has recently undergone major im-

provements under the management of the Links Group. Bentgrass greens are nestled among azaleas and dogwoods. All three 18-hole combinations are similar, with narrow tree-lined fairways and small greens. The Holly Course features an island green on the 9th hole.

These are not exceptionally difficult courses, except for that island green; therefore they can be enjoyed by golfers of all skill levels.

Island Green is not one of the more expensive courses on the Grand Strand, with approximate greens fees ranging from $25 to $45, cart included. Rental clubs and a putting green are available as well as a bar and restaurant. There is no driving range, however. Walking is allowed.

International World Tour
2000 World Tour Blvd., Myrtle Beach
• **(843) 236-2000, (877) 377-7773**
Open/Championship Combination

Championship Yardage: 6525	
Slope: 130	**Par:** 72
Men's Yardage:	6214
Slope: 126	**Par:** 72
Other Yardage:	5826
Slope: 121	**Par:** 72
Ladies' Yardage:	5334
Slope: 120	**Par:** 72

International/Championship Combination

Championship Yardage: 6688	
Slope: 133	**Par:** 72
Men's Yardage:	6372
Slope: 129	**Par:** 72
Other Yardage:	5891
Slope: 124	**Par:** 72
Ladies' Yardage:	5129
Slope: 117	**Par:** 72

International/Open Combination

Championship Yardage: 6688	
Slope: 135	**Par:** 72
Men's Yardage: 6633	
Slope: 129	**Par:** 72
Other Yardage: 5783	
Slope: 123	**Par:** 72
Ladies' Yardage: 5951	
Slope: 115	**Par:** 72

This 27-hole complex opened in late 1999. Its creator, Mel Graham of Charlotte (Rev. Billy Graham's nephew), has produced an interesting concept: a golf course consisting of holes "inspired" by some of the most exciting and famous challenges in the world. Graham essentially tried to re-create some of the world's most notable golf holes for play in a single round. Perhaps you might compare it to a Kiss "tribute band" who dress up like Kiss members and play Kiss songs to Kiss fans.

This controversial course has created quite a stir and has instantly become one of the most sought-after rounds at The Beach. Fairways are 419 bermudagrass; greens are L93 bentgrass.

You could spend upwards of $10,000 traveling to all the courses that inspired IWT, or you could plop down the cash to play IWT. Here are some of the "inspirations" On IWT's three nine-hole layouts:

• The 15th at Seminole.
• The 1st and 17th at St. Andrews.
• The 16th at Pinehurst #2.
• The 12th at Pine Valley.
• The 9th at Royal Melbourne.
• Amen Corner at Augusta National: That's right, the 11th, 12th and 13th all in a row on the Championship Nine.

Many, if not most, of the world's great courses feature some degree of elevation change, which is obviously tough to imitate on the flat land of The Beach. It's difficult to imitate the downhill tee shot on the 11th at Augusta National, but flat land aside, what a fun concept here at IWT.

It must surely irritate members and owners of the clubs whose holes have "inspired" Mel Graham, but for the average Beach golfer, a round here is a treat. The closest they will ever come to playing Pine Valley will be the 6th on the Open Nine, built to resemble the 12th at what most would consider the world's greatest golf course. Who wouldn't want to play a course like this—even if it's just once?

Everything here is designed to be "world class," something that's clearly evident when you see all the international flags adjacent to the sumptuous clubhouse. If you're at The Beach to play the best and most expensive courses, don't miss this one.

The course offers rental clubs, a driving range, putting green plus a bar and restaurant.

Approximate greens fees range from $100 to $160, including cart. Walking is restricted.

The Legends Golf Club
1500 Legends Dr., Myrtle Beach
• (843) 236-9318, (800) 990-8995

The three 18-hole courses at Legends are just off U.S. 501. The Legends Golf Club consists of the Heathland, Moorland and Parkland courses. These courses have been designed in three distinctively different architectural styles.

The Legends Group is owned and operated by Larry Young, one of the major names in the area's golf industry. In addition to The Legends Golf Club, the group's Grand Strand courses

include Marsh Harbour, Oyster Bay and The Heritage Club.

The complex offers rental clubs, a driving range, bar, restaurant, pro shop and beverage cart.

Caddies are mandatory if you wish to walk. Approximate fees range from $50 to $90, including cart. You may book any time.

Heathland at The Legends
Championship Yardage: 6785
Slope: 127   **Par:** 71
Men's Yardage: 6190
Slope: 117   **Par:** 71
Ladies' Yardage: 5060
Slope: 121   **Par:** 71

This 18-hole course—links style with bent greens and bermudagrass fairways—was designed by Tom Doak and built in 1990. The heathland tag is misleading: The goal here was to create a links course.

The first thing that may strike you upon approaching the three-course complex is the magnificent Scottish-style clubhouse, and you'll also notice the distinct absence of trees on the Heathland Course. In lieu of tree boundaries, Doak provided strategic bunkers and deep rough to make this course a challenge. Another significant problem is the wind. Most of the bunkers that guard the greens are deep. No. 8 is the shortest hole on the course. Pin position is crucial here, since the front of the green has a severe contour. No. 14, a par 4, has one of the smallest greens on the course.

Tom Doak is one of the nation's more outspoken architecture critics, but he's also one of the most traveled and erudite, having played and seen almost all the world's great courses at one time or another. His two books, *Anatomy of a Golf Course* and *The Confidential Guide,* are must-reads for anyone interested in golf course architecture.

Doak seems happy with the Heathland course. To build the course, Doak stripped the 175-acre site of its trees, dug two drainage ditches (burns) and created an undulating site using fill dirt. The course boasts just about everything you might find on a true links: open feel, wind, bizarre undulations, open fronts to the greens allowing run up shots when they're called for. The greens and fairways, in order to handle the sheer volume of golf, are large and wide, respectively. It's not impossible to find the fairways but it's important to check pin placement on the greens.

Doak tried to separate Heathland from other courses in Myrtle Beach and most would agree that he succeeded. Of all the courses claiming to be "Scottish" and "Pure Links," this might be the one that comes the closest to the real thing—given the right conditions and conditioning.

Moorland at The Legends

Championship Yardage: 6799
Slope: 128   Par: 72
Men's Yardage: 6143
Slope: 121   Par: 72
Ladies' Yardage: 4905
Slope: 127   Par: 72

The 18-hole Moorland Course, with bent greens, was designed by P.B. Dye and built in 1991. With the Moorland layout, Dye created what is probably one of the most challenging golf courses on the East Coast. It has plenty of natural growth, sand, water and waste areas combined with incredible undulations and many bulkheaded areas reminiscent of PGA West. This is a target golf course. The par 4 2nd hole has a sand trap running almost from tee box to green. No. 17, a par 3, has an island green with a twist: The green is an island in a sea of sand.

Parkland at The Legends

Championship Yardage: 7170
Slope: 131   Par: 72
Men's Yardage: 6460
Slope: 127   Par: 72
Other Yardage: 6230
Slope: 123   Par: 72
Ladies' Yardage: 5570
Slope: 125   Par: 72

These 18 holes were designed by The Legends Group and built in 1992.

The Parkland Course, with bent greens, is distinctly different from Heathland and Moorland because its fairways are tree-lined; it's not unlike the other two in that it has deep bunkers and undulating greens. Water and sand are dominant.

The Parkland has a great finishing hole—a 465-yard par 4. The successful tee shot must be played on the right side of the fairway opposite two large traps. The most challenging hole is the par 5 15th, which has a big fairway. Wetlands carve this fairway into halves running lengthwise. The fairway leading up to the green has seven traps that can cause trouble. No. 11 must be played to the left side. This 515-yard hole is a par 5. To reach the green, the ball must carry over water; if your shot is too long, four sand traps await to catch your ball.

Litchfield Country Club

U.S. Hwy. 17 S., Pawleys Island
• (843) 448-3331, (800) 344-5590
Championship Yardage: 6752
Slope: 130   Par: 72

Men's Yardage: 6342
Slope: 124   Par: 72
Ladies' Yardage: 5917
Slope: 119   Par: 72
Other Yardage: 5264
Slope: 119   Par: 72

One of the area's oldest and most prestigious clubs, Litchfield, was designed by William Byrd and opened in 1966. Greens are tif-dwarf bermuda, and fairways are bermudagrass on this challenging course. Its mature, narrow fairways, lined with moss-draped oaks and large well-protected greens, wind through a former rice plantation to a traditional clubhouse. Although the course is private, a limited number of guests can play.

The traditional layout is tough but fair; never tricked up. Water comes into play on seven of the front nine holes, and water or marsh effects all of the back nine.

Country club cottages are available for vacationers. The course winds through a real estate development, and the scorecard reminds you that you may retrieve your ball from the backyard of a homeowner but must not play from there. The Lowcountry cuisine in the fine dining room is on par with the quality of the golf.

Approximate fees range from $45 during the summer to $75 in the high season, including cart. You may walk the course whenever you like.

The Long Bay Club

S.C. Hwy. 9, Longs
• (843) 399-2222, (800) 344-5590
Championship Yardage   7021
Slope: 137   Par: 72
Men's Yardage   6565
Slope: 130   Par: 72
Other Yardage: 6139
Slope: 126   Par: 72
Ladies' Yardage: 5598
Slope: 127   Par: 72

Jack Nicklaus' signature mounds can't be missed as you approach North Myrtle Beach from S.C. Highway 9. The 18-hole course was built in 1989 and meanders through a lovely residential area and forest. Long Bay has been rated by *Golf Digest* as one of the state's top 10 courses. It has tifdwarf greens and fairways. Numerous waste bunkers dominate the course.

Nos. 7, 8 and 9 are brutal finishes on the front nine. The signature hole is No. 10—a par 4. Your drive must be straight on this hole because a left or right shot will find the sand. You're surrounded by sand from your second shot in. This sand trap is so big that it extends three-fourths the length of the fairway. No. 13 is a 123-yard par 3 with an island green. The abundance of lakes, mounds and bunkers is exciting on this course, which everyone wants to play.

The bar and restaurant are classy and comfortable with a wonderful view of the course. Don't leave home without you-know-what, because the soft drink machines on this course take only credit cards. The pro shop is well stocked. Rental clubs and a driving range are available.

Approximate fees range from $55 to $100 and include cart. Walking is not allowed.

Man O' War
U.S. Hwy. 501, Myrtle Beach
• (843) 236-8000

Championship Yardage:	7027
Slope: 133	**Par: 72**
Men's Yardage:	6311
Slope: 126	**Par: 72**
Other Yardage:	5579
Slope: 118	**Par: 72**
Ladies' Yardage:	5025
Slope: 121	**Par: 72**

This 18-hole public course opened in January 1996. It surrounds a breathtaking 100-acre man-made lake. The rustic red, ranch-style clubhouse is constructed partially over water and is reminiscent of Minnesota's northern fishing lodges. Sixteen holes feature water hazards. Three are considered signature holes. The 9th hole is an island, and two other holes play to island greens. No. 14, a 354-yard par 4, and No. 15, a 126-yard par 3, similar to the famed Sawgrass No. 17, highlight the Dan Maples course. Greens are Crenshaw bentgrass; fairways are bermudagrass.

Amenities include a driving range, putting green, rentals and beverage carts. Approximate fees including cart range from $40 to $90. Walking is not allowed.

Marsh Harbour
Marsh Harbour Rd., Calabash, N.C.
• (843) 249-3449, (800) 552-2660

Championship Yardage:	6680
Slope: 134	**Par: 71**
Men's Yardage:	6000
Slope: 121	**Par: 71**
Ladies' Yardage:	4795
Slope: 115	**Par: 71**

Marsh Harbour sits on the North and South Carolina border just south of Calabash. A good drive with a fade from the 10th tee in North Carolina will cross into South Carolina, then land on the fairway back in North Carolina.

Everyone seems to want to play Marsh Harbour—and its reputation is well deserved. Salt marshes along the Intracoastal Waterway provide exciting scenery and exciting golf play. Larry Young built Dan Maples' design in 1980 and presented a rare combination of elevated ground skirted by low-lying marsh.

The famous hole is the par 5 17th, featuring three distinct targets. Picture trees on the left and large bunkers on the right. You can handle the tee shot; then the second shot must carry across the marsh to a landing area with water on three sides—a toughie. Cross the marsh again to a green beside the marsh. Not too many of us make par on this one.

Approximate fees, including cart, range from $50 to $88. Walking is not allowed.

Myrtle Beach National Golf Club
U.S. Hwy. 501, Myrtle Beach
• (843) 448-2308, (800) 344-5590

This club has three 18-hole courses. All were built in the 1970s and designed by Arnold Palmer and Frank Duane. All feature bentgrass greens and Bermudagrass fairways.

The Myrtle Beach National Golf Club owns another five courses on the Grand Strand, and its reservationist at Tee Time Central can quickly book your entire week for you with one easy phone call.

The course offers rental clubs, a driving range and bar and restaurant.

Approximate fees change at least eight times a year based on the season, not including occasional afternoon and other specials; prices range from $40 to $100. Walking is allowed most of the time—check before you go if you want to hoof it.

INSIDERS' TIP
Proper attire is required on most golf courses. Wear collared golf shirts and Bermuda shorts of standard length for summer dress. Socks are optional on most courses. Jeans, T-shirts, cut-offs, tank tops, short shorts and bathing suits are inappropriate attire.

King's North

Championship Yardage:	6759
Slope: 125	**Par: 72**
Men's Yardage:	6033
Slope: 109	**Par: 72**
Ladies' Yardage:	5047
Slope: 113	**Par: 72**

Built in 1973, this course was one of the beach's initial courses and one of the first anywhere to feature an island green. Arnold Palmer and the Palmer Design Group oversaw substantial changes to this course in 1995, and it reopened in 1996 with its new name, exciting features and increased greens fees. It was previously called The North Course.

What began as a minor update evolved into total design and visual enhancement. The bentgrass greens were reshaped, enlarged and sodded with the new hybrid Crenshaw bent. More than 6,000 trees were removed to open the course. Several fairways feature increased undulation, and bunkers and lakes were dramatically reshaped. The famous par 3 No. 3 includes South Carolina-shaped traps, and it underwent a major enhancement with the addition of bulkheads and a new foot bridge. The par 5 No. 6 is called The Gambler—it was dedicated by singer Kenny Rogers in June 1996 shortly after the course reopened. Play it safe by going right into the fairway, or if you do have a little of the gambler in you, go for the island fairway—your tee shot must carry at least 225 yards from the back tees. The par 4 No. 18 has 41 sandtraps guarding both sides of the fairway, and the green reaches into a lake.

South Course

Championship Yardage:	6416
Slope: 123	Par: 72
Men's Yardage:	6089
Slope: 118	Par: 72
Other Yardage:	5710
Slope: 112	Par: 72
Ladies' Yardage:	4723
Slope: 109	Par: 72

This 18-hole course was built in 1975 and remodeled in 1990. It has flat fairways with some mounding. Compared to its counterparts, this course features the smallest greens and greenside bunkers.

No. 5 is a 355-yard par 4 dogleg, which is unintimidating unless your drive is short, and your second shot could splash into a fairway pond that sits squarely in your line of fire. As you make the turn, No. 9 is a 390-yard par 4 where you must stay right because of the sand down three-fourths of the left side of the fairway. It's tough to make a birdie because of the small green. If you do hit the green, you'll probably be near the hole—it's that small. The 13th, a 166-yard par 3, could be unlucky, as you must shoot over a sea of sand to an island green.

West Course

Championship Yardage:	6866
Slope: 119	Par: 72
Men's Yardage:	6113
Slope: 113	Par: 72

Ladies' Yardage:	5307
Slope: 109	Par: 72

The 18-hole West Course, built in 1974, is the longest course at Myrtle Beach National. Although many tall pines line the fairways and can claim your ball, the course is considered wide open. No. 18 is the only hole on which you'll find a water hazard.

Myrtle West Golf Club

S.C. Hwy. 9, North Myrtle Beach
• (843) 756-0550, (800) 842-8390

Championship Yardage:	6787
Slope: 132	Par: 72
Men's Yardage:	6191
Slope: 118	Par: 72
Other Yardage:	5555
Slope: 108	Par: 72
Ladies' Yardage:	4859
Slope: 113	Par: 72

This course is only a few minutes past the bridge over the Intracoastal Waterway from North Myrtle Beach. Take plenty of balls in case the numerous water hazards claim some, and enjoy the beautiful holes set among Carolina sand and tall pines.

The 18-hole course was built in 1990, designed by Tom Jackson. The entire course is seeded with bermudagrass.

Pick the right tees for your level of ability, the professionals advise. Don't think you have to play macho golf. Where you tee it up defines the difficulty around the greens. No. 17 is one of the most difficult—457 yards, usually playing into the wind.

Amenities include practice putting and chipping greens, a practice sand bunker, driving range, rental clubs, a beverage cart during peak season and a bar and restaurant.

When you visit the well-stocked pro shop, the friendly staff will make you feel like you're at your home course.

A rental cart is included in the greens fee, which ranges from $30 to $58. Walking is not allowed.

Myrtlewood Golf Club

48th Ave. N., Myrtle Beach
• (843) 449-5134, (800) 283-3633

Myrtlewood offers back-to-back challenges, with two 18-hole courses along the Intracoastal Waterway. It's easily accessible on the U.S. Highway 17 Bypass from any part of the Grand Strand.

Amenities include a driving range, practice green, rental clubs, a beverage cart, pro shop, bar and snack bar.

Approximate fees range from $30 to $65,

including cart. Walking is not allowed, which is a shame, because both courses are walkable.

Palmetto Course

Championship Yardage:	6957	
Slope: 121		Par: 72
Men's Yardage:	6495	
Slope: 118		Par: 72
Other Yardage:	6098	
Slope: 115		Par: 72
Ladies' Yardage:	5305	
Slope: 117		Par: 72

Ed Ault designed The Palmetto Course in 1973. It has bentgrass greens and bermudagrass fairways.

Due to its prime location, acceptable design, decent conditioning, sensible pricing, aggressive marketing, and strong playability, the Palmetto Course here at Myrtlewood has long been a Beach favorite.

While the 17th, a 160-yard par 3 fronted by one of the biggest bunkers in creation, is the most photographed hole on the course, the best par 3 might be the 7th, about 175 yards to a shallow and sloping green where par is a great score. The most famous hole on the course is the 410-yard par 4 18th flanked by the Intracoastal Waterway on the left and condos on the right.

Many holes are on the tight side off the tee but most greens are large and undulating. Firing at the pin here is often the best strategy. There are some fine holes on the Palmetto course—while other older courses have faded somewhat, this one remains popular.

PineHills Course

Championship Yardage: 6640		
Slope: 125		Par: 72
Men's Yardage:	6112	
Slope: 119		Par: 72
Other Yardage:	5692	
Slope: 112		Par: 72
Ladies' Yardage:	4906	
Slope: 113		Par: 72

The PineHills opened in 1993—Arthur Hills' first design in Myrtle Beach.

While condos and OB stakes line much of the Palmetto, the PineHills course is further away from civilization and thus much more attractive. Arthur Hills made the most of this pancake flat site, mostly by hauling in what must have been hundreds of truckloads of dirt, creating berms and some interesting undulations, particularly on the back nine. Architecturally, there's more interest, muscularity and strategy on the PineHills course. Thankfully, it's wider off the tee, yet the greens are a little smaller. Very quietly, the PineHills course at

Myrtlewood might be one of the better tests at The Beach.

The most difficult hole might be the par 4 18th, a solid two-shot hole to a semi-peninsula green.

Ocean Harbour Golf Links

Sommersett Dr., Calabash, N.C.
• (910) 579-3588 (in N.C.),
(843) 448-8398 (in S.C.)

Championship yardage:	7004	
Slope: 138		Par: 72
Men's Yardage:	6592	
Slope: 134		Par: 72
Other Yardage:	6148	
Slope: 127		Par: 72
Ladies' Yardage:	5358	
Slope: 126		Par: 72

Built in 1989, Ocean Harbour was Clyde Johnston's first design on the Grand Strand. It crosses the North Carolina-South Carolina border. On the 5th hole, you can drive from North Carolina into South Carolina, then return on the 9th tee.

The 532-yard par 5 7th is the signature hole. The tee is surrounded by a cedar grove. The marsh and waterway views are spectacular. On each shot you will have to clear marshland. As if that's not hard enough, the green's location in the middle of marsh makes it seem as if you are shooting at an island.

All 18 holes are tough; there's a lot of water on this course. Fairways are bermudagrass, and greens are bentgrass. Saltwater marshes and natural elevation shape the course on 500 acres of grass bunkers and gentle rolling fairways. Sand bunkers and multiple ponds contribute to the endless challenges. The panoramic views include rare combinations of the Calabash River, the Atlantic Ocean and the Intracoastal Waterway. The clubhouse is a fine finishing spot with its view of the confluence of the waterway and the river.

Practice greens, a driving range, pro shop, bar, snack bar and rental clubs are available.

Approximate fees range from $35 to $80, including cart. Walking is not allowed.

Ocean Isle Beach Golf Course

Pearl Blvd., Ocean Isle Beach, N.C.
• (910) 579-2610 (in N.C.),
(843) 272-3900 (in S.C.)

Championship's Yardage: 6626		
Slope: 126		Par: 72
Men's Yardage:	6146	
Slope: 122		Par: 72

Wicked Stick is John Daly's first golf course design.

Photo:Bill Woodard

Ladies Yardage: **5075**
Slope: 116   **Par: 72**

Russell Breeden designed this course in 1976. The bermudagrass greens and fairways are carved through rolling terrain, towering pines and live oaks. A tough hole is the 10th, where you have to hit over a ditch to a small green; the ball often will bounce off the back side. The 16th is a dogleg right that plays 451 yards from the championship tees.

Approximate fees range from $25 to $50, including cart. Amenities include practice greens, a driving range, pro shop, rental clubs, a bar and a snack bar. Walking is not allowed.

Ocean Isle is a quiet piece of golfer's paradise: No big city lights, but golf galore. While it's actually in North Carolina, the course aligns itself with the Myrtle Beach golfing scene. The Pearl (see entry below) is the sister course to the Ocean Isle Beach Course, and you can spend many a vacation day trying to master the combination.

Panther's Run and Lion's Paw
U. S. Hwy. 17, Sunset Beach, N.C.
• (910) 287-1717 (in N.C.), (800) 233-1801

Lion's Paw and Panther's Run comprise 36 holes at Ocean Ridge Plantation. The second nine of Panther's Run opened in October 1995.

Willard Byrd designed the first 18 holes, and Tim Nelson Cate designed the newer Panther's Run. All have bermudagrass fairways and bentgrass greens. Walking is not allowed.

Amenities include practice greens, a driving range, pro shop, bar, restaurant, beverage cart and rental clubs.

Approximate fees range from $35 to $80.

Lion's Paw Golf Links
Championship Yardage: **7003**
Slope: 138   **Par: 72**

Men's Yardage:	6457
Slope: 130	Par: 72
Ladies' Yardage:	5364
Slope: 118	Par: 72

The toughest hole on Lion's Paw is No. 3, a 204-yard par 3. Water comes into play on 15 of 18 holes. Fairways are somewhat narrow on the front nine, and the second nine is links style.

Panther's Run Golf Links

Championship Yardage:	7089
Slope: 140	Par: 72
Men's Yardage:	6706
Slope: 134	Par: 72
Other Yardage:	6267
Slope: 128	Par: 72
Other Yardage:	5546
Slope: 118	Par: 72
Ladies' Yardage:	5023
Slope: 116	Par: 72

On Panther's Run, the 4th hole is tough due to the great expanse of water to carry. The course, set along a nature preserve, offers pretty scenery, an interesting variety of elevations and marsh to clear on several holes. Five sets of tees allow every golfer to find a comfort zone. Wide fairways twist and turn around visually appealing lakes, brooks and waterfalls on the new nine. Deer, barn owls and waterfowl frequently are spotted along the course.

Oyster Bay Golf Links
Lakeshore Dr., Sunset Beach, N.C.
• (910) 236-9318 (in N.C.), (800) 697-8372

Championship Yardage:	6685
Slope: 134	Par: 70
Men's Yardage:	6305
Slope: 125	Par: 70
Ladies' Yardage:	4665
Slope: 118	Par: 70

Oyster Bay is another part of the popular Legends Group; it was designed by Dan Maples. Its trademark oyster-shell landscaping and walls have been incorporated into the design. Oyster Bay opened in 1983 and was recognized by *Golf Digest* as the best new resort course in the country that year and was ranked in the top 50 overall courses. It's one of the most beautiful courses here or anywhere.

The 15th and 17th holes are par 3s with island greens. The 17th hole is played from oyster shell-walled tees, and its island green is built on a mountain of shells. The 13th hole has a lake flanking the entire right side, its green guarded by a large cavernous bunker.

Walking is not allowed at Oyster Bay. Amenities include rental clubs, a pro shop, bar, restaurant, beverage cart, driving range and prac-

tice green. Approximate fees range from $50 to $83 including cart.

Pawleys Plantation Golf & Country Club
U.S. Hwy. 17 S., Pawleys Island
• (843) 237-1736, (800) 367-9959

Championship Yardage:	7026
Slope: 132	Par: 72
Men's Yardage:	6522
Slope: 127	Par: 72
Other Yardage:	6127
Slope: 122	Par: 72
Ladies' Yardage:	5572
Slope: 130	Par: 72
Other Yardage:	4979
Slope: 126	Par: 72

A signature course by Jack Nicklaus, Pawleys Plantation is primarily private but play can be arranged though partnering hotels. Call the course or ask the golf director at one of the Sands Properties how to get on this course. You may remember Pawleys Plantation best for the double green and dramatic split fairway. Lake and marsh views and bentgrass greens are spectacular, and similarly spectacular shots must frequently traverse the marsh.

The country club setting includes a clubhouse and lounge where breakfast, lunch and dinner are served. A pool and tennis court for guests are minutes from the beach.

Approximate fees range from $50 to $85, including cart. Walking is not allowed.

The Pearl Golf Links
1300 Pearl Blvd. S.W., Sunset Beach, N.C.
• (910) 579-8132 (in N.C.),
(843) 272-2850 (in S.C.)

The Pearl offers two 18-hole courses, the imaginatively named East and West, both designed by Dan Maples and built on a 900-acre marsh preserve. Both courses opened in 1987 and feature bentgrass greens. The East Course is a traditional layout, and the West Course is "links" style. Both boast spectacular finishing holes: one along the Calabash River, the other on a bluff overlooking the Intracoastal Waterway.

No two holes are alike, and you will definitely use all your clubs. The marsh views and natural wildlife in the undisturbed area are a visual feast. On the West Course, water and/or marsh come into play on every hole; on the East Course, you'll encounter water or marsh on every hole except the 8th and 15th.

A pro shop, driving range, bar, restaurant and rental clubs are available.

Approximate greens fees average $69, including cart. Walking is not allowed.

East Course

Championship Yardage:	6749
Slope: 135	Par: 72
Men's Yardage:	6543
Slope: 132	Par: 72
Other Yardage:	6250
Slope: 127	Par: 72
Ladies' Yardage:	5125
Slope: 129	Par: 72

No. 17 on the East Course is the signature hole. It's a slight dogleg left with three fairway bunkers, oyster beds and marsh down the left side. If you're long on approaching the green, a sand trap flanks the back side, not to mention more marsh.

West Course

Championship Yardage:	7008
Slope: 132	Par: 72
Men's Yardage:	6738
Slope: 131	Par: 72
Other Yardage:	6419
Slope: 129	Par: 72
Ladies' Yardage:	5188
Slope: 127	Par: 72

On the West Course, No. 16 is the signature. It's a 604-yard par 5 that bends twice before you get to the green. Not only do you have to put up with marsh running down the complete right side of the fairway and green, but trouble is compounded by the addition of oyster beds, sand and marsh, also on the right. An abundance of love grass covers this course, especially on the 1st, 2nd, 9th, 11th and 12th holes. Avoid it!

**Pine Lakes International
Country Club**
5603 Woodside Dr., Myrtle Beach
• (843) 449-6459, (800) 446-6817

Championship Yardage:	6609
Slope: 125	Par: 71
Men's Yardage:	6176
Slope: 121	Par: 71

INSIDERS' TIP

Make it or break it: Your tee time is valuable. If you cannot keep it, be sure to call the course in advance to cancel. This is especially important if you've held the time with a credit card and will be charged even if you don't show up.

Ladies' Yardage:	5376
Slope: 122	Par: 71

From the moment you walk into the clubhouse, you begin to soak up the tradition Pine Lakes exudes. It's called the Granddaddy. "When I die, take me to the Granddaddy," a well-known writer instructed.

Pine Lakes International was the first golf course in Myrtle Beach, built in 1927. Robert White, the first president of the PGA and a native of St. Andrews, designed this 18-hole course. It was meant as a playground to complement the million-dollar Ocean Forest Hotel, an elaborate resort for the wealthy. Sunday afternoon croquet matches on its lawn continue another of its age-old traditions. Invitations to members of the neighboring Dunes Club announce the introduction of a "new game."

Among the many significant events Pine Lakes claims, one of the biggest is that *Sports Illustrated* was born here in 1954, when Henry Booth Luce and 66 other Time-Life executives came for a game and left with a brainstorm.

In 1995, it was the first Grand Strand course to spend a million dollars on carts, specifically a lease for buggies with a Rolls Royce motif.

Today Pine Lakes retains the prestige its heritage demands. Scottish flavor and Southern gentility are reflected in every touch, beginning with the tartan-dressed starters, continuing with the mimosa Thomas serves as you approach the 3rd tee, and culminating on cooler days with the signature clam chowder served at the turn. Its special Southern-style Manhattan recipe, heavy with red pepper, is said to add an extra 30 yards to your remaining drives. The cook will sign your score card if any of it is worth writing home about.

The fairways are wide, and while not overly tough, the course can be challenging, depending upon pin placements. Pine Lakes starts with a bang: a 563-yard par 5. The par 3 No. 7 is one of the country's most beautiful holes, according to the editors of *Golf Digest*. Greens here are bermudagrass.

When your game is over, assistants will wash your clubs, shine your shoes and present your crying towel to remind you of this round.

Walking is not allowed—right in keeping with the Scottish motif (yeah, right). Rental clubs and a driving range are available. The bar, restaurant and pro shop are in the 60-room antebellum mansion, and a snack bar overlooks the pool.

Approximate fees start at $47 during summer months and increase to $110 in the high season. A cart is included.

Possum Trot Golf Club

U.S. Hwy. 17, North Myrtle Beach
• (843) 272-5341, (800) 626-8768

Championship Yardage:	6966	
Slope: 127		Par: 72
Men's Yardage:	6388	
Slope: 113		Par: 72
Other Yardage:	5505	
Slope: 108		Par: 72
Ladies' Yardage:	5153	
Slope: 111		Par: 72

One of the older courses on the Grand Strand, this 18-hole layout was built in 1968. It was designed by Russell Breeden. Greens and fairways are bermudagrass. High handicappers welcome the course's openness; yet the 50 bunkers and nine lakes and ponds combine with the length and finesse to challenge any golfer. Watch out for No. 11—430 yards into the prevailing wind from the men's tees. This course's signature hole is the 13th, a 163-yard par 3 with a carry over water.

The extensive practice facility includes a driving range, sand bunkers and separate pitching, chipping and putting greens. Other amenities include a pro shop, bar, beverage cart, snack bar, locker rooms for men and women and rental clubs.

Approximate fees range from $35 to $60, including cart. Walking is allowed after noon.

Prestwick Country Club

1001 Links Rd., Myrtle Beach
• (843) 293-4100

Championship Yardage:	7058	
Slope: 140		Par: 72
Men's Yardage:	6744	
Slope: 135		Par: 72
Other Yardage:	6347	
Slope: 126		Par: 72
Ladies' Yardage:	5210	
Slope: 118		Par: 72

Pete and P.B. Dye designed this course. Many have compared it to Pete Dye's other creations at Sawgrass, Hilton Head and Kiawah Island. The semiprivate club is open to limited public play, so make sure you call if you want to play a round at Prestwick.

The course features much of what you've come to expect from the Dyes: huge mounds, heroic shots, severe penalties for missed greens, deep bunkers, bulkheads, water, waste areas. It's all here.

There's a grand clubhouse, range, putting green, and a pro shop.

Approximate fees range from $50 to $100, including cart. Walking is restricted.

Quail Creek Golf Club

U.S. Hwy. 501, Myrtle Beach
• (843) 347-0549, (800) TEE-OFFS

Championship Yardage:	6812	
Slope: 119		Par: 72
Men's Yardage:	6321	
Slope: 116		Par: 72
Other Yardage:	5955	
Slope: 114		Par: 72
Ladies' Yardage:	5287	
Slope: 112		Par: 72

Gene Hamm designed this bermudagrass 18-hole course in 1968. It has extra-wide fairways lined with trees, well-manicured large greens and easy playing conditions among woods and lakes. No. 11 is a 526-yard par 5 that doglegs left. The somewhat large green is guarded front, left and right by bunkers. Somewhat unique to this area, water comes into play on about six holes only.

The clubhouse, including a bar and restaurant, was recently renovated. A driving range and rental clubs are available.

Approximate greens fees range from $25 to $60, including cart. Walking is allowed.

River Club

U.S. Hwy. 17 S., Pawleys Island
• (910) 237-8755, (800) 344-5590

Championship Yardage:	6677	
Slope: 135		Par: 72
Men's Yardage:	6240	
Slope: 119		Par: 72
Ladies' Yardage:	5084	
Slope: 120		Par: 72

The River Club is an 18-hole Tom Jackson design. Its fairways are wide and open, and the large tifdwarf bermudagrass greens are undulating. More than 100 sand traps and bunkers and plenty of water on 15 holes offer challenges to all skill levels. Its dramatic par 5 finishing hole wraps around a lake and requires a pair of carries for a possibility of eagle. Long hitters may be able to reach the green in two; however, if you miss, you can put at least a bogey on your scorecard.

Amenities include a pro shop, small lockerroom (the room is small, not the lockers, which are standard size, not too large but not too small—you should be able to fit everything you have with you in them, no problem), driving net and a restaurant. There are also adequate facilities for your short game, including practice putting and chipping areas along with a bunker.

Approximate fees range from $40 to $85, including cart. Walking is not allowed.

Rivers Edge Golf Club

2000 Arnold Palmer Dr., Shallotte
• (910) 754-3434, (877) 748-3718

Championship Yardage:	6909	
Slope: 149	Par: 72	
Men's Yardage:	6440	
Slope: 139	Par: 72	
Other Yardage:	6033	
Slope: 126	Par: 72	
Ladies' Yardage:	4692	
Slope: 119	Par: 72	

Rivers Edge opened, without an apostrophe, in 1999. Arnold Palmer designed the course and used 419 Bermuda in the fairways and Crenshaw Bent on the greens.

Taking a pristine site adjacent to the Shallote River, Arnie designed a course that's treacherous yet scenically stunning. It's also a course with tremendous variety; it requires strategic shot-making skills to score successfully. However, play the course from the correct tees and you shouldn't find the marshy layout too much of a problem. Play Rivers Edge from the tips and you'd better bring your best game.

Long hitters will be able to reach the green in two on the the 509-yard par 5 9th but the second shot will be all carry over marsh on this arcing hole. The 9th is just one of many fine risk-reward holes on a course that's bound to attract some attention from visiting and local golfers.

Amenities include a driving range, putting green, and clubhouse. Approximate fees range from $48 to $118, including cart. Walking is not allowed.

River Hills Golf & Country Club

U.S. Hwy. 17 N., Little River
• (843) 399-2100, (800) 264-3810

Championship Yardage: 6829	
Slope: 133	Par: 72
Men's Yardage:	6196
Slope: 123	Par: 72
Other Yardage:	5535
Slope: 113	Par: 72
Ladies' Yardage:	4861
Slope: 120	Par: 72

Tom Jackson designed this 18-hole course in 1988, with bermudagrass greens and fairways. Fairways are somewhat narrow, and water comes into play on 13 holes. The course is laid out in a densely wooded setting and features 40-foot elevation changes—moutainous for The Beach. No. 5 is a challenge: a long par 4 uphill, with bunkers surrounding the hole.

A complete practice facility is available, as are rental clubs, a pro shop, locker rooms for men and women, a beverage cart on busy days and a snack bar.

Walking is not allowed. Approximate fees range from $30 to $60, including cart.

River Oaks Golf Plantation

831 River Oaks Dr., Myrtle Beach
• (843) 236-2222, (800) 762-8813

Bear/Fox Course

Championship Yardage: 6778	
Slope: 126	Par: 72
Men's Yardage:	6314
Slope: 118	Par: 72
Ladies' Yardage:	5133
Slope: 116	Par: 72

Fox /Otter Course

Championship Yardage: 6791	
Slope: 125	Par: 72
Men's Yardage:	6345
Slope: 118	Par: 72
Ladies' Yardage:	5043
Slope: 118	Par: 72

Otter/Bear Course

Championship Yardage: 6877	
Slope: 125	Par: 72
Men's Yardage:	6425
Slope: 119	Par: 72
Ladies' Yardage:	5188
Slope: 118	Par: 72

Three nine-hole courses make up these three 18-hole combinations completed in 1990. Tom Jackson designed the Bear Course, and Gene Hamm designed the Otter and Fox courses. Fairways and greens are bermudagrass. Wildlife, undulating greens, mounded fairways, finger-shaped sand bunkers and large lakes provide scenic beauty along the Intracoastal Waterway.

Water comes into play on the Bear Course, which many believe to be the most difficult of the trio. The 2nd hole on the Bear is, well, a bear, with water and sand prominently coming into play. Some doglegs on the Fox are difficult, although the course plays shorter than the others.

Practice greens, a driving range, pro shop, snack bar, rental clubs and beverage cart are offered.

Approximate fees range from $30 to $70 and include a cart. Tee times may be booked a year in advance. Walking is not allowed.

Robbers Roost Golf Club

U.S. Hwy. 17 N., North Myrtle Beach
• (843) 249-2085, (800) 352-2384

Championship Yardage: 7148	
Slope: 137	Par: 72

Men's Yardage:	6725
Slope: 129	Par: 72
Other Yardage:	6356
Slope: 120	Par: 72
Ladies' Yardage:	5387
Slope: 116	Par: 72

Designed by Russell Breeden, the 18-hole course opened in 1969, with tifdwarf bermudagrass on the tees, fairways and greens.

The prolific Breeden once said that No. 16—a par 5—was the greatest hole he had ever built. The hole is a slight dogleg left with a huge lake between the fairway and the green. If you hit a super tee shot, you have the option to go for it, but you'll need a terrific second shot. Fairway bunkers are on the right, and greenside bunkers are to the left, right and behind. No. 14 is another interesting hole. It's a par 4 measuring 390 yards, but water butts up against the relatively small green, so accuracy is particularly critical. There's no sand on this hole, but the landing area for your drive is extremely narrow.

Water provides a challenge on several holes, and the course's length provides much of the challenge.

The Southern plantation-style porch around the clubhouse is a fine place to unwind after you've finished your round.

A driving range, rental clubs and a bar and restaurant are available.

Approximate fees begin at $35 and go to $45, including cart. Walking is not allowed. You may book tee times a year in advance.

St. James Plantation
U.S. Hwy. 211, Southport, N.C.
• (910) 253-3008, (800) 247-4806

Championship Yardage:	7052
Slope: 142	Par: 72
Men's Yardage:	6428
Slope: 132	Par: 72
Ladies' Yardage:	5048
Slope: 119	Par: 72
Other Yardage:	5845
Slope: 124	Par: 72

P.B. Dye designed this course in 1991 with bentgrass greens and bermudagrass fairways. Views of the waterway are spectacular, and the course also plays along salt marshes. It is a challenge to golfers of all levels with its pot bunkers, bulkheads and shots that must carry water along with multilevel fairways that are trademarks of Dye's architecture. Good course management is a key here. If you hit a bad shot, don't try to be a hero on your next one. Take the penalty and move on. The final three holes play into and over a series of marshes and lakes and offer a fantastic finish to a beautiful layout.

The signature hole is No. 17, a par 4 running along a tidal marsh. It's about 440 yards from the back tees and plays to a peninsula green in the marsh. The lake runs along the left side, and the tidal marsh along the right. A 200-yard carry to the fairway is a challenge. The small green is surrounded by three bunkers.

Facilities include a pro shop, practice greens, a driving range, rental clubs, a restaurant, bar and occasional beverage cart. Approximate fees range from $40 to $65. Walking is not allowed.

There are two additional courses here at St. James, both of which are primarily private, but may accept public play on occasion: The Members Club, (910) 253-9500, designed by Hale Irwin; and the Players Club, (800) 281-6626. Call before you arrive, although most visiting golfers will probably want to play the extremely challenging Gauntlet.

Sea Trail Plantation & Golf Links
301 Clubhouse Rd., Sunset Beach, N.C.
• (910) 287-1100, (800) 546-5748

Sea Trail Plantation is a classy resort community set on 2,000 acres and featuring 54 signature holes of championship golf on bentgrass greens. The three 18-hole courses were designed by Dan Maples, Rees Jones and Willard Byrd, respectively, and named as such. Meeting and conference space plus golf packages make this resort a choice for many golf parties who want their townhouse or villa accommodations right on the course.

Sunset Beach is a great little North Carolina community (right over the state line), with little of the neon hustle and bustle of Myrtle Beach. Views include the golf courses or the river. The beach is about a mile away. Resort amenities include a bar, restaurant, pro shop, fitness room, pool, tennis club and wonderful biking and jogging trails. Walking is not allowed on these golf courses.

Dan Maples Course

Championship Yardage:	6751
Slope: 121	Par: 72
Men's Yardage:	6332
Slope: 117	Par: 72
Other Yardage:	6035
Slope: 112	Par: 72
Ladies' Yardage:	5090
Slope: 108	Par: 72

This course was built in 1986 and promptly nominated by *Golf Digest* as one of the most outstanding resort courses in the country. Maples' Oyster Bay Golf Links is also within

Sea Trail Plantation, and his Marsh Harbour course is nearby. You can stay and play here for a long time if you're looking for some really fine golf.

The par 3 No. 3 is an intimidating hole because of a pond on the right of the green. This hole must be played to the middle or left of the pin regardless of where it's placed. Play the dogleg-left par 4 7th hole in the center of the fairway. The second shot must go over water to a kidney-shape green. An island tee on the 13th is what makes this short par 4 interesting. Bunkers are on the left of the fairway. A good tee shot will leave a mid- to short iron shot to a deceptive green.

Approximate fees range from $40 to $60, including cart.

Rees Jones Course

Championship Yardage:	6761
Slope: 132	Par: 72
Men's Yardage:	6334
Slope: 126	Par: 72
Other Yardage:	5716
Slope: 118	Par: 72
Ladies' Yardage:	4212
Slope: 115	Par: 72

The Rees Jones course opened in spring 1990. Throughout the course, the mounds, swales and pot bunkers present constant challenges and potential migraines. Water comes into play on 11 holes. The par 3 No. 5 has many obstacles. Besides playing over water, it is surrounded by seven sand traps, to the rear, right and left; thus, club selection is crucial. The par 5 No. 8 needs a long tee shot if you hope to reach the green in two; however, you must be careful of the water in front of the green. It's safer to lay up and hit the green in three.

Approximate fees begin at $40 and go to $70 including cart.

Willard Byrd Course

Championship Yardage:	6750
Slope: 128	Par: 72
Men's Yardage:	6263
Slope: 126	Par: 72
Other Yardage:	5590
Slope: 116	Par: 72
Ladies' Yardage:	4717
Slope: 121	Par: 72

The Byrd Course opened in 1990. It's built around lakes ranging from 14 to 20 acres. Shot-making finesse is called for here. The par 3 No. 2 is medium-length, but you must play over water. If possible, try to place your shot so you'll have an uphill putt. The par 4 No. 11 is a narrow dogleg right with four fairway traps. The green is long and narrow and slopes downward

from back to front. Par 5 No. 18 requires a drive down the right-center; otherwise, you're in water. You can reach the green in two with a long iron shot. If the hole is on the front of the green, try to stay below the hole.

Approximate fees are $40 to $60, including cart.

Surf Golf & Beach Club
1701 Springland Dr., North Myrtle Beach
• **(910) 249-1524, (800) 765-SURF**

Championship Yardage:	6842
Slope: 126	Par: 72
Men's Yardage:	6360
Slope: 119	Par: 72
Other Yardage:	5960
Slope: 114	Par: 72
Ladies' Yardage:	5178
Slope: 111	Par: 72

This George Cobb classic was Myrtle Beach's third course when it opened in 1961. The 18-hole layout was rebuilt and enhanced in 1992 then received another facelift in 1996 with conversion to bentgrass greens. The finishing hole is a dramatic par 3 over water. It's 219 yards, usually played against the ocean breeze.

The clubhouse opened in 1990 after a multimillion-dollar expansion and renovation. It's surrounded by an upscale neighborhood just two blocks from the ocean. The bar, the food in the restaurant and the views are excellent.

Other amenities include a pro shop, driving range, large practice green, locker rooms and rental clubs.

Tee times may be booked a year in advance. Approximate fees range from $35 to $88, including cart. Walking is not allowed.

Tidewater Golf Club & Plantation
**4901 Little River Neck Rd.,
North Myrtle Beach**
• **(843) 249-3829, (800) 446-5363**

Championship Yardage:	7150
Slope: 134	Par: 72
Back Yardage:	6530
Slope: 126	Par: 72
Men's Yardage:	6000
Slope: 118	Par: 72
Other Yardage:	5090
Slope: 132	Par: 72
Ladies' Yardage:	4665
Slope: 127	Par: 72

Ken Tomlinson's 18-hole creation was named the top new course of 1990 by both *Golf Digest* and *Golf Magazine*. It continues to draw rave reviews for its bentgrass greens and bermudagrass fairways set on a wooded peninsula between the Atlantic Ocean and the Intra-coastal Waterway. The 3rd, 4th and 12th greens are on the marsh, and the 13th is on Cherry Grove Inlet and the Atlantic. The 16th fairway affords a view straight to the waterway where you might see sailboats and barges passing.

Nothing is artificial here. All of the holes were designed to leave undisturbed the natural surroundings and the lay of the land. An intriguing aspect of Tidewater is the player's variety of choices. For instance, the 360-yard par 4 4th requires a perfect drive close to the marsh; however, if the marsh is too intimidating, you can bail out with a shot to the right but must contend with two fairway sand traps. Then, your second shot must carry over the traps that surround the green.

You might feel intimidated by the extremely large sand trap right off the tees on No. 5, a par 4. The green also is guarded on the left and right by traps. When you arrive at the tee box of the spectacular par 3 No. 12, you will be immediately excited to notice that your tee shot must carry marshland that at high tide is filled with water and at low tide displays the failed shots of previous players. The par 3 17th plays from a tee box with a view of the waterway over water to a green bordered by four sand traps. The signature hole is the 13th, from which you can see all of the Cherry Grove section of North Myrtle Beach.

Rental clubs, a driving range, putting greens, a pro shop, bar and grill and new clubhouse with restaurant are available.

Tee times may be booked a year in advance. Walking is not allowed. Approximate fees range from $70 to $100, including cart.

The Tiger's Eye
Sunset Beach
• (910) 287-1717, (888) 739-6808
Championship Yardage: 7010
Slope: No rating   **Par: 72**
Men's Yardage: 6628
Slope: No rating   **Par: 72**
Other Yardage: 6115
Slope: No rating   **Par: 72**
Ladies' Yardage: 4640
Slope: No rating   **Par: 72**

Tim Cate designed Tiger's Eye, which opened in 2000—yet another fine addition to courses "north of the border." Cate used Tifsport bermudagrass in the fairways and G2 bentgrass on the greens. The course was so new when we went to press that it hadn't yet been rated.

It took five years to get Tiger's Eye off the drawing board and into The Beach's portfolio.

It's part of Ocean Ridge Plantation, where you will also find the popular Panther's Run and Lion's Paw. A 20,000-square-foot clubhouse was under construction at the time of printing. The course features ample water, large traps and undulating greens. The beautiful tree-lined ambiance of the course will set it apart from its competitors. There's even a waterfall on the 18th hole. It also boasts a Pinehurst feel due to the elevation changes. Several holes feature waste bunkers that run directly into the water without any bulkheads.

Approximate fees, including cart, range from $50 to $80. Walking is allowed and Cate designed the course to be walker-friendly.

The Tradition Club
1027 Willbrook Blvd., Pawleys Island
• (843) 626-1658, (800) TEE-OFFS
Championship Yardage: 6717
Slope: No rating   **Par: 72**
Men's Yardage: 6500
Slope: No rating   **Par: 72**
Other Yardage: 5554
Slope: No rating   **Par: 72**
Ladies' Yardage: 4924
Slope: No rating   **Par: 72**
Forward Yardage: 4148
Slope: No rating   **Par: 72**

This stunning 18-hole course was crafted by Florida architect Ron Garl from acres of natural sand waste areas. It opened in 1995. It includes an island par 3 as well as a par 3 strategically placed in the center of a vast waste area. Large rolling greens are set among the sand and towering Carolina pines. Garl created multiple teeing areas to determine the ideal ladies' yardage and to enable every level of golfer to play each hole equitably with the same clubs. This experiment has garnered national attention, as has the Links Group's addition of this masterpiece to their collection along the Grand Strand. The 18th green is guarded by the 8,000-square-foot luxury clubhouse, which houses dressing rooms, men's and women's locker rooms, a dining area, a bar with a fireplace and conversation areas, private members' room and a large pro shop. The clubhouse is decorated with Italian marble, leather upholstery, imported designer pieces and original European artwork.

The elaborate world-class practice area includes a 43,000-square-foot putting green shaped like a clover with four individual locations for practice, a multilevel chipping and pitching area, practice sand bunkers and target greens framed by sand and water to make practice itself an unforgettable experience. Eighteen acres of the practice facility feature multiple greens at varying yardages, and individual coves sit on the left side of the driving range, allowing golfers to practice anything from wedge to full-iron shots.

Tee times may be booked a year in advance. Approximate fees, including cart, range from $43 to $61. Walking is allowed after 3 PM, which is pretty odd for a club that includes the word "tradition" in its name.

The TPC at Myrtle Beach
1199 TPC Boulevard., Murrels Inlet
• (843) 357-3399, (888) 742-8721

Championship Yardage:	**6950**
Slope: 145	**Par: 72**
Men's Yardage:	**6600**
Slope: 136	**Par: 72**
Other Yardage:	**6193**
Slope: 126	**Par: 72**
Ladies' Yardage:	**5118**
Slope: 125	**Par: 72**

The much-awaited and publicized TPC at Myrtle Beach opened in late 1999. Tom Fazio designed it with help from PGA touring professional Lanny Wadkins. The course is a joint venture between the PGA Tour (a non-profit organization) and Myrtle Beach Golf Holiday. There's 419 Bermudagrass in the fairways and L93 bent on the greens. It's one of the few TPC courses in the country that's open to the public 100 percent of the time, and the staff here are keen to let everyone know. *Golf Digest* named it one of the 10 best new upscale public courses in the country in 1999.

Touted as the 100th golf course on The Beach, the TPC at Myrtle Beach (we'll just call it TPC) instantly became one of the best courses in the area when it opened. Fazio and Wadkins hit a home run with this site, building a golf course that's much more Pinehurst that Myrtle Beach—not a bad thing.

In late 2000, the TPC will host the lucrative season-ending Senior Tour Championship and will continue host some sort of professional event every year—it's in the contract.

Tom Fazio, in case you didn't know, has been the world's top architect for most of the 1990s. At this TPC, he shows everyone why.

Unlike many of the TPC courses around the country, the one here at The Beach is less penal, more fun, and less cluttered with housing—there's not a condo or mansion to be seen. The site, unlike most at The Beach, features about 35 feet of elevation change, and this "mountainous" aspect gives the course much of its character. You really might think that

you're in Pinehurst instead of The Beach—we're not kidding.

For the most part, the fairways are wide enough for all but the wildest; greens are mostly large and fairly undulating, although some are smaller than average. Green complex undulations are mostly subtle.

Fazio cleverly designed this course to challenge the best of the professionals while making it playable for the average golfer. A prime example is the par 3 5th, just 158 from the back tees but, for the pros, entirely over water. From the other tees, there's some bail out space to the right of the green from which a good chip and putt will yield a three. Or, you can go for the pin and have to clear the drink: It's your choice, and a golf course that offers choices is always entertaining.

A particularly interesting feature of the course is its variety. The par 4 9th is 472 yards from the tips, while the par 4 12th is just 333. The longest par 5 spans 547 yards, the shortest 502.

There are some excellent gambling holes, particularly on the home stretch. Few will birdie the 445-yard par 4 15th, but good players will have a chance for a 3 on the 390-yard par 4 16th. The 17th, the TPC's signature hole, is a daunting 193 yards from the tips to a peninsula green. The probable "Sunday" pin placement will surely require a precise long iron—almost completely over water to a thin sliver of putting surface. There's room to bail out on the left, but someone who is chasing a tournament title will shoot for the pin—it should be exciting.

The final hole at TPC, a 538-yard par 5, should provide just as much drama. Most pros could reach this hole in two shots, but the second must find another peninsula green. The tee shot is no picnic either, with a stream running down the entire right-hand side of the fairway.

Even though the overall design of the TPC looks somewhat minimalist and traditional, it's going to earn a reputation as a fun golf course—a chance for the normal golfer to play where the pros play. Despite the considerable outlay required to get on here, lots of visiting golfers will want to play a TPC, so book ahead.

The facilities here are first rate, with a massive range, putting green, short game area, etc. The 10,000 square-foot clubhouse feels like a private club; there's a restaurant and bar. You can walk anytime so long as you bring a caddie or rent a motorized handcart. Booking here is almost exclusively through Myrtle Beach Golf

Walking vs. Riding

If you join the United States Golf Association (and you should), you may receive the pamphlet "A Call to Feet," urging more golfers to walk. In the pithy document, the powers-that-be even refer to golf in a cart as "cart-ball." That's pretty stern stuff from the men and women in Far Hills, New Jersey—home of the USGA—for whom golf "is a walking game."

An unscientific survey shows that most public courses in the Carolinas prefer that you use a cart when you play. The courses where walking is restricted far outnumber those where walking is unrestricted. Even on courses where walking is allowed, riders almost always outnumber pedestrians. Many designers and architects, particularly in the last 10 years, have built courses where the only realistic option is to ride—especially true on courses built around a housing or condo development. Most modern courses feature significant distances between green and tee, making walking tedious if not impossible. The modern course that's walkable is a vanishing species. It's all quite sad.

Courses built earlier in the century are walkable and were built to be so. With the arrival of the cart, many of these courses laid ribbons of asphalt or concrete. Many of these same courses started telling customers when they could and could not walk. In addition to the unsightly cart path, the cart's boxy shape invades the beauty of the course. And if the cart is gas-powered, it's also smelly and noisy. (If

Walking the golf course is making a big comeback in the Carolinas.

Photo: Curtis Parker

you haven't guessed by now, we're somewhat the golf purists.)

From our observations and experience, there are numerous myths and problems that surround the cart issue. Many will tell you that cart fees generate income, but that's rarely true when you consider the costs of buying or leasing the cart, insurance, electricity or gas, upkeep, storage and cleaning. Seeing as more people like to ride in carts than walk, the cart generates greens fee income by capitalizing, more or less, on laziness. It's an unfortunate fact that some people simply wouldn't play the game if they couldn't ride. Thus a portion of the greens fee covers part of the cost of keeping carts ready and available; of course, even if you walk, you probably still are paying for a cart.

Many amateurs (and course rangers) will tell you that play is faster in a cart. That may be so when the course is deserted; but that's not always the case when the course is busy. During or after rain, most courses make you keep

A great vacation all about

Contents

Over 3,500 Choices

With more than 3,500 places to choose from, the Myrtle Beach Vacation Center can accommodate everyone from the individual vacationer to large groups...from the oceanfront to golf course locations. The MBVC offers you one-stop access to the very best selection, variety and value on the Grand Strand. The MBVC prides themselves on matching you with the perfect vacation property for your maximum combination of value and fun! Let the MBVC help you find your perfect place at the Beach, today.

Family Vacations

The MBVC is home to the happiest family vacations on the Beach. That's because they specialize in personable properties that really know how make your family's vacation the best the Beach has to offer. With the very best, and safest locations on the Strand, the MBVC custom tailors terrific "fun and value plus" vacations just for you, and your family.

Honeymoons

The MBVC specializes in making certain that your honeymoon is one wonderful memory after another. Their careful attention to all of your honeymoon details assures you of cozy surroundings, scenic vistas, intimate moments and everything else to guarantee the perfect setting for your very special time.

Golf Vacations

With over a half-a-million tee times booked each year, the Myrtle Beach Vacation Center, guarantees you, and your playing partners, the very finest golf vacations Myrtle Beach has to offer. The MBVC offers you custom-tailored golf vacations, with access to the more than 100 Grand Strand courses, at prices designed to assure you the very best value for your vacation investment.

Entertainment Packages

Lights, curtain, action! The MBVC presents "Showtime on the Grand Strand." Enjoy all the dazzling entertainment that Myrtle Beach has to offer: the top talent, the best seats, the best prices are all yours with the MBVC. All the shows you'll ever want to see at one friendly, convenient, quick and easy stop, the Myrtle Beach Vacation Center.

Airline Tickets, Rental Cars and More

The MBVC provides you with the best flights at the best price. They also offer automobiles, vans, motor coaches and any other type of transportation you may require for your personal vacation needs. The MBVC's volume pricing programs further assures you of the greatest variety at the very best price.

MBVC

MYRTLE BEACH VACATION CENTER
Your Personal Vacation Headquarters

Call here: 888.448.3121 or click here: mbvc.com

A great vacation all about

Contents

Over 3,500 Choices

With more than 3,500 places to choose from, the Myrtle Beach Vacation Center can accommodate everyone from the individual vacationer to large groups...from the oceanfront to golf course locations. The MBVC offers you one-stop access to the very best selection, variety and value on the Grand Strand. The MBVC prides themselves on matching you with the perfect vacation property for your maximum combination of value and fun! Let the MBVC help you find your perfect place at the Beach, today.

Family Vacations

The MBVC is home to the happiest family vacations on the Beach. That's because they specialize in personable properties that really know how make your family's vacation the best the Beach has to offer. With the very best, and safest locations on the Strand, the MBVC custom tailors terrific "fun and value plus" vacations just for you, and your family.

Honeymoons

The MBVC specializes in making certain that your honeymoon is one wonderful memory after another. Their careful attention to all of your honeymoon details assures you of cozy surroundings, scenic vistas, intimate moments and everything else to guarantee the perfect setting for your very special time.

Golf Vacations

With over a half-a-million tee times booked each year, the Myrtle Beach Vacation Center, guarantees you, and your playing partners, the very finest golf vacations Myrtle Beach has to offer. The MBVC offers you custom-tailored golf vacations, with access to the more than 100 Grand Strand courses, at prices designed to assure you the very best value for your vacation investment.

Entertainment Packages

Lights, curtain, action! The MBVC presents "Showtime on the Grand Strand." Enjoy all the dazzling entertainment that Myrtle Beach has to offer: the top talent, the best seats, the best prices are all yours with the MBVC. All the shows you'll ever want to see at one friendly, convenient, quick and easy stop, the Myrtle Beach Vacation Center.

Airline Tickets, Rental Cars and More

The MBVC provides you with the best flights at the best price. They also offer automobiles, vans, motor coaches and any other type of transportation you may require for your personal vacation needs. The MBVC's volume pricing programs further assures you of the greatest variety at the very best price.

MYRTLE BEACH
VACATION CENTER

Your Personal Vacation Headquarters

Call here: 888.448.3121 or click here: mbvc.com

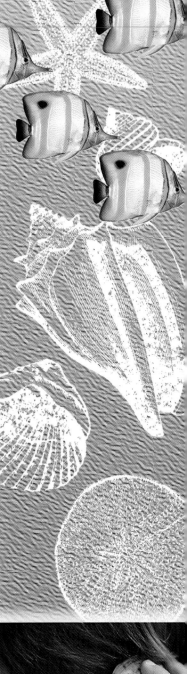

the cart on the path. Thus a twosome will be forced to drive to a point parallel with the ball, walk to where the ball lies, hit the shot, walk back and begin the process again. Under these circumstances, on a walkable course, two golfers walking will play faster than two golfers riding in a cart. Even a walking foursome of decent golfers will rarely delay a foursome that's riding.

And then there's the issue of aesthetics. Great golf course designers craft their layouts to best be viewed from the fairway, not the cart path. From the cart path, you're going to see woods, scrub and the backside of mounds. Walkers see the green complex and the fairway. Walkers see the golf course, not the cart path.

When you play golf, we think you should walk. In Scotland, where the game began, everyone walks. Courses are walkable, and the Scots know how to play in well less than four hours. Most people we know play golf because it's a release from their indoor workplace. The game provides a well-deserved break from the office or factory, from traffic and from the concrete jungles where we work and shop. So why the great need and desire to ride in a cart on a cart path?

The Scots realized, and still realize, the tremendous health benefits of playing golf. Many a recovering heart-disease victim is told to take lessons from a golf pro and take to the links for four hours of gentle walking. If someone with a heart problem can walk a golf course, any physically healthy person can. On walkable courses, we've run into people who think that their poor knees mean that they have to ride in a cart. In most cases, that's garbage. The low-impact exercise accomplished by walking a golf course can only help strengthen leg and back muscles, which in turn sometimes can help alleviate ailing joints.

In the Carolinas, one of the only public-access golf courses with an established and well-run caddie program is Pinehurst Country Club. If you play there (you should at some stage in your life), take a caddie, for a caddie will make the course even more walkable, advise you where to aim and tell you which way a putt will break. A caddie will rake the bunker after you've made a mess, suggest what club might work and tell you exactly how far you are from the pin. This is pure golf, and caddies are part of what make Pinehurst so special. Wouldn't it be great if more public courses could follow Pinehurst's example?

Perhaps one day a course will sell its carts, raze its cart paths, provide golfers with a walking bag or pull cart for free and restore a piece of tradition so sadly lacking in today's game. In this book, we include information about walking courses so those of you who are dedicated to the traditional game can reap the benefits—spiritual and physical—of walking your round of golf.

Holiday. Approximate Greens fees will range from $76 to $175, including cart.

True Blue
900 Blue Stem Dr., Pawleys Island
• (843) 235-0900, (888) 483-6800

Championship Yardage:	7090	
Slope: 139	Par: 72	
Men's Yardage:	6840	
Slope: 128	Par: 72	
Other Yardage:	6488	
Slope: 123	Par: 72	
Ladies' Yardage:	4920	
Slope: 115	Par: 72	

Mike Strantz designed True Blue in 1998. The course is affiliated with the adjacent Caledonia Golf and Fish Club. *Golf Digest* named

it one of the 10 best new upscale public courses in the country when it opened. The same publication named True Blue the 7th best course in South Carolina. *Golf World* named Mike Strantz "America's Hottest Architect" in 1998. Fairways are 419 bermuda and greens are bentgrass.

True Blue might be the most controversial golf course at The Beach, something that becomes clear early in the round on the short 342 yard par 4 second. A good drive to the wide fairway should leave a short iron to a green that's shaped a little bit like a tennis racket. Anything that misses the front half of the putting surface, and it can only be about 10 yards wide, will end up in scrubby sand infested with love grass and shrubs. There's more room to the back of the green, so take an extra club.

Just in case you thought that the 2nd might be just a one-off gimmick, along comes the 3rd, one of the most bizarre yet exciting one-shot holes anywhere. Even though it's listed at 172 from the tips, the hole can play anywhere from 130 to 210 yards depending on pin and tee placement. The shot is all over water to a green that's in two definite sections—the front portion slopes severely front to back and is almost perpendicular to the shallow back section, which can't be much more than 30 feet at its widest point. The green is surrounded by a "beach" of sorts that will likely kick most errant shots into the water. On a windy day with the tees all the way back and the pin in that back section of the green, par is almost completely out of the question. It's a weird and fun hole that can indeed yield a birdie (trust us on that one).

The ride gets a little less exhausting after the third (thankfully), but there are some more wild holes to come—we'll let you discover these for yourself.

Believe it or not, Strantz once worked for Tom Fazio, whose courses tend towards the elegant and traditional. True Blue is much more on the edge than any Fazio course. Whether that's fun depends on how well you are playing. You'll never be bored here although you may well decide to pack it in after nine holes if things are really bad: The par 5 10th is a bear of a hole.

Another exciting par 3 is the 14th, 161 yards from the back tees to a green that's almost 50 yards long and essentially separated into two distinct portions. The tee shot must carry a large waste area.

The best hole on the course might be the par 5 9th, 548 from the back tees, slightly downhill. A well-struck drive will carry a great distance, leaving about 200 yards to a well-bunkered, two-tier punchbowl green.

It's hard to peg True Blue's style, which might be something of a cross between a Scottish Links, Pine Valley, and Studio 54. Even though most visitors will only play it once, it's a course that demands repeat visits.

True Blue stands out at The Beach because it's unique, challenging, different, attractive, relatively condo-free, fascinating, and borderline, uh, borderline. It's out there on the edge and thus, in a roundabout way, provides one of the best imitations of a pure links of any course at The Beach. Anyone who has played links golf in Scotland will tell you that just about every course includes some unfair situations. But who said that golf was meant to be fair?

There's a fine clubhouse at True Blue, an expansive practice facility and a bar. Approximate Greens fees range from $50 to $130 including cart. Walking is an option here.

Waterway Hills Golf Course
U.S. Hwy. 17 N., Myrtle Beach
• (843) 449-6488, (800) 344-5590

One of the most unusual to access, this club includes three nine-hole courses on the west side of the Intracoastal Waterway. You can only get to them by the lift over the waterway. If you're afraid of heights and the rocking ride of a ski lift, you won't know what you're missing. Wilderness surrounds these courses, which are especially popular for that reason. One of the pros says there's an advantage to having nothing but wildlife around.

These courses were built in 1975, designed by Robert Trent Jones Sr., with bermudagrass greens. The terrain is rolling, and water comes into play on many holes—as befits the name.

Amenities include a bar, restaurant, driving range and rental clubs.

Walking is allowed, and pull carts are available. Tee times are accepted a year in advance and may be reserved through the same toll-free number for bookings at Myrtle Beach National Golf Club.

Approximate fees range from $35 to $60, including cart.

Lakes Course

Championship Yardage:	**3190**
Slope: 121	**Par: 36**
Men's Yardage:	**3001**
Slope: 115	**Par: 36**
Ladies' Yardage:	**2490**
Slope: 115	**Par: 36**

Hole No. 9 is a dogleg-left, 390-yard par 4. It has a wide fairway, but traps are left and right of your landing area. If you hit the landing area right, you have a nice iron shot to the undulating green, which is guarded on the right by two small traps.

Oaks Course

Championship Yardage:	**3271**
Slope: 119	**Par: 36**
Men's Yardage:	**3080**
Slope: 118	**Par: 36**
Ladies' Yardage:	**2579**
Slope: 118	**Par: 36**

A general straightforward nine. No. 3 is a par 4 (422 yards), which shoots straight (as you suspect it should), but halfway down the fairway you must contend with lakes on each side. If you go long on your drive either left or right, your ball will get wet.

Litchfield Country Club is as much a feast for golfers' senses as a challenge for their skills.

Photo:Michael Sleary

Ravine Course

Championship Yardage:	2927
Slope: 121	Par: 36
Men's Yardage:	2579
Slope: 112	Par: 36
Ladies' Yardage:	2335
Slope: 112	Par: 36

The 8th hole, a 470-yard par 5, is straight-away. If you try to go for the green in two, a pair of bunkers could be a hindrance, as could a greenside bunker in front. There's yet another bunker behind the green.

Wicked Stick Golf Links

U.S. Hwy. 17 S., Surfside Beach
• (843) 650-2146, (800) 548-9186

Championship Yardage:	7001
Slope: 129	Par: 72
Men's Yardage:	6507
Slope: 122	Par: 72
Other Yardage:	6080
Slope: 117	Par: 72
Ladies' Yardage:	4911
Slope: 123	Par: 72

John Daly's first signature course, Wicked Stick opened in 1995, almost as a celebration of Daly's dramatic win of the British Open at St. Andrews that summer. Daly served as consultant to architect Clyde Johnston on this course, which was developed by Southpark Golf Group Ltd. Partnership, a group led by past president of the PGA of America Gary Schaal.

This 18-hole links-style course with bermudagrass features expansive dune fields, large sand waste areas with gorse-like vegetation, pot bunkers and strategically placed water hazards. A select number of Daly signature tees offer additional length and difficulty, but generous landing areas help the average player. A great course to *"Grip It and Rip It!"*

Amenities include a pro shop, rental clubs, driving range, putting green and beverage cart. Approximate fees range from $35 to $70, including cart. Walking is allowed after noon.

Wild Wing Plantation
U.S. Hwy. 501, Myrtle Beach
• (843) 347-9464, (800) 736-WING

Wild Wing Plantation is a 72-hole golf reserve, and it is a showcase of Pennlinks bentgrass enjoyed by good golfers. Japanese-owned, it shows a distinct Oriental influence in the clubhouse and in its attention to detail and perfection. The plantation is set on 1,050 acres of natural beauty west of Myrtle Beach.

Almost every golfer loves the aesthetics and the variety of Wild Wing's courses; beginners might not excel on these tough layouts, but they will enjoy nature while they improve. Some golfers could spend a four-day golf trip at Wild Wing alone and be more than content with the variety of its four courses.

The bird names are not just incidental; all represented species have been sighted. On the Falcon Course, for example, a falcon sometimes just sits on a mound watching a hole, even when a foursome approaches the green. The operations staff is studying the planting of specific flora to attract the desired fowl to their namesake courses.

The pro shop, bar and restaurant are award winners. A beverage cart, driving range, practice greens and rental clubs are available.

Tee times are accepted up to a year in advance. Approximate fees range from $45 to $95 at the Wood Stork and Hummingbird courses and from $54 to $108 on the Avocet and Falcon courses, including a cart in all cases. Each cart is equipped with a club and ball washer, computerized yardage system and water cooler, can tell the time in several different languages and can book restaurant reservations for you in Tokyo; you may not take a personal cooler. Walking is not allowed.

Falcon Course
Championship Yardage:	7082
Slope: 134	Par: 72
Men's Yardage:	6697
Slope: 128	Par: 72
Other Yardage:	6089
Slope: 117	Par: 72
Ladies' Yardage:	5190
Slope: 118	Par: 72

The Falcon Course, 18 holes built in 1994, was designed by Rees Jones in a "modern traditional" style according to the course literature—whatever that means. With an abundance of mounding, narrow fairways and small bentgrass greens, the Falcon offers diversity in design and play while creating a visually exciting experience. According to the renowned Jones, "The natural appearing features help to contain errant balls and provide a variety of approach shots." Both nines feature large lakes. This course contains Wild Wing's most dominant feature, a 515-yard bunker, that separates the 12th and 13th holes. Now that's a bunker!

Avocet Course
Championship Yardage:	7127
Slope: 128	Par: 72
Men's Yardage:	6614
Slope: 119	Par: 72
Other Yardage:	6028
Slope: 114	Par: 72
Ladies' Yardage:	5298
Slope: 118	Par: 72

The Avocet course opened in 1993 and was recognized by *Golf Digest* as one of the Top 10 Best New Resort Courses for 1994. It was designed as a signature course by Larry Nelson. Bentgrass greens are elevated, and one is a double green. Some fairways are double, and some tees are elevated.

Hummingbird Course
Championship Yardage:	6853
Slope: 131	Par: 72
Men's Yardage:	6310
Slope: 123	Par: 72
Other Yardage:	5796
Slope: 123	Par: 72
Ladies' Yardage:	5168
Slope: 123	Par: 72

The Hummingbird Course—18 holes designed by Willard Byrd—opened in 1992. It's a links-style course with bentgrass greens, native grasses around its perimeter, strategically placed lakes and open fairways. It has an array of pot bunkers and waste areas.

Wood Stork Course
Championship Yardage:	7044
Slope: 126	Par: 72
Men's Yardage:	6598
Slope: 111	Par: 72
Ladies Yardage:	5409
Slope: 121	Par: 72

The Wood Stork Course, its 18 holes also designed by Willard Byrd, opened in 1991. Its parkland setting features significant natural hazards: The first eight holes play through wetlands; the next 10, through a pine forest.

Willbrook Plantation Golf Club
U.S. Hwy. 17 S., Pawleys Island
• (843) 237-4900, (800) 344-5590
Championship Yardage:	6704
Slope: 125	Par: 72

Men's Yardage:	6106	Other Yardage:	5729
Slope: 118	Par: 72	Slope: 118	Par: 71
Ladies' Yardage:	4963	Ladies' Yardage:	4965
Slope: 118	Par: 72	Slope: 121	Par: 71

Dan Maples designed this 18-hole course of bermudagrass on rice plantation wetlands between Litchfield Beach and Pawleys Island.

The par 4 No. 5 is a 383-yard hole. Your drive has to carry water onto the fairway, which has a nice landing area, and the second shot also has to carry water onto a small green that gives the appearance of an island green, surrounded by water on three sides. You won't have to play the true island green until you get to the 127-yard par 3 No. 6.

Public play is limited, with members given preference. A new clubhouse opened in 1995. A driving range and putting green are available as well as rental clubs.

Approximate fees are $35, including cart, with a summer coupon published regularly in Myrtle Beach's *The Sun News*, and $50 in the high season, with a $17 additional cart fee. Walking is allowed, but varies by season.

The Witch

1900 S.C. Hwy. 544, Conway
• (843) 347-2706

Championship Yardage:	6702	
Slope: 133	Par: 71	
Men's Yardage:	6011	
Slope: 121	Par: 71	
Ladies Yardage:	4812	
Slope: 109	Par: 71	

The Witch is an 18-hole course built in 1989 and designed by Dan Maples, with bermudagrass fairways and bentgrass greens. This course, like so many others at The Beach, was built in the middle of a swamp. Wetlands come into play on almost every hole, and 4,000 feet worth of bridges wind through the course. The 15th hole is a par 4 requiring a 200-yard carry over wetlands. The 9th hole features an island fairway surrounded by wetlands; it requires a carry over wetlands on the tee shot and the second shot.

Practice greens, a pro shop, beverage cart, rental clubs, a driving range, bar and restaurant are available.

Approximate fees range from $50 to $85 and include a cart. Walking is not allowed.

The Wizard

U.S. Hwy. 501, Myrtle Beach
• (843) 347-6600

Championship Yardage:	6967	
Slope: 133	Par: 71	
Men's Yardage:	6402	
Slope: 126	Par: 71	

This 18-hole course opened in fall 1996 across the lake from Man O' War. It's another Dan Maples layout. It features the new bentgrass G-2 greens, similar to Crenshaw bent but developed to be more heat tolerant and able to be trimmed to a finer surface. The signature hole is No. 9, an island par 4 of 408 yards. The wind is usually in your face here. Bunkers are on the left, and the island on the right requires an accurate drive. Nos. 14 and 15 are interesting back-to-back island greens.

The bizarre clubhouse is meant to look like a castle. Inside, there's a snack bar, a huge lounge and the knights who say "niiiih." Amenities include a driving range, a putting green and rentals. Walking is not allowed. Fees range from $50 to $80, cart included.

Tournaments

Senior Tour Championship

The Ingersoll-Rand Senior Tour Championship is played in Myrtle Beach every November. It's the year-end tournament for the PGA Senior Tour's cream of the crop and an absolute grand finale for spectators who throng to the Grand Strand during the second week of the month.

This 72-hole tournament features the top 31 money leaders on the PGA Senior Tour and the top 16 Super Senior players (age 60 and older) playing in a simultaneous but separate championship tournament. The largest purse of any PGA Senior event and the largest combined purse of the super senior and senior tournaments are up for grabs.

This championship is played at the TPC Myrtle Beach.

Anyone who loves to watch premium golf will go nuts over this tournament. Set against a sunny backdrop of warm and glorious fall days on this fine course, spectators can watch the year's accumulation of champions vie for the top spots. Despite the tournament pressure and the tough course, players take time out for autographs and conversation and relax by the Atlantic while the world's television cameras tell their stories. If you're lucky, you can watch the tournament then shuttle back to your home or hotel and watch it again on ESPN. (Is that too much, or what?!) If you're really smart, you'll plan at least part of your vacation for early November. You can even play 18 holes a day (except at the Dunes Club, of course) then watch the seniors and super seniors finish their rounds.

Ticket information is available from the PGA by calling (803) 444-4STC.

Accommodations offering ticket packages are listed in Myrtle Beach Golf Holiday's Vacation Planner. To obtain a free copy, call (800) 845-GOLF. Myrtle Beach Golf Holiday is the host organization for the tournament.

DuPont World Amateur
Handicap Championship

Anyone with an established handicap, no matter what it is, can play in this tournament. And anyone can win it!

The DuPont World Amateur Handicap Championship, the world's largest amateur golf tournament, is played the last week in August every year. It will be played for its 17th year in Myrtle Beach in 2000, on more than 50 courses. It's a four-day, 72-hole flighted tournament open to any amateur with a verified USGA handicap (or foreign equivalent).

The DuPont Company of Wilmington, Delaware, is the title sponsor of the tournament, which is owned by Myrtle Beach Golf Holiday.

All types of golfers from all locations compete in the World Am. It began with 680 golfers and has grown to more than 4,200 players. Many participants return year after year to renew golfing friendships and play in a fun tournament. It's a true spectacle when they all bring their guests and gather in the convention center each evening to view scores and swap stories. Just the socializing alone, lubricated by a wide variety of libations, is enough to bring most folks back annually.

Players fly and drive to Myrtle Beach from every state and 20 or more foreign countries. The greatest number of golfers, of course, play in the men's division, although senior men and super seniors are loyal to the tournament, and the number of women increases every year.

Participants have been as old as 86 and as young as 16.

The grand prize is not for the tournament winner, but is a drawing and is often something super-snazzy, such as a Lincoln luxury automobile. All entrants are eligible for the drawings, which include thousands of dollars worth of prizes.

The tournament organizers attempt to weed out carpetbaggers—people who cheat with their handicap. Such low-life are summoned to the tournament office each day issued a red card.

For information, call (800) 845-GOLF.

PING Myrtle Beach Junior Classic

The PING Myrtle Beach Junior Classic will be played for the 12th time in June 2000. It's one of 34 tournaments nationwide conducted by the American Junior Golf Association (AJGA) and is one of the most popular stops on the tour.

Nearly 500 golfers between the ages of 13 and 18 apply annually, and 106 are selected by the AJGA. Another 14 are selected during the first-day qualifying round. Participants typically represent at least 17 states.

Myrtlewood Golf Club hosts the 54-hole tournament.

For information on this event, promoted by Myrtle Beach Golf Holiday, contact tournament chairman George Hilliard at (800) 845-GOLF.

Susan G. Komen
International LPGA

The Susan G. Komen International LPGA was played for the first time in April of 1997 at the new Wachesaw East and is set to return here in 2000 as the City of Hope Classic. For information call (800) 845-GOLF.

Around the Grand Strand...

Fun Things To Do

Entertainment comes in many forms along the Grand Strand. On those days when you're not playing golf or if you and your family come here for golf combined with vacation, you have an almost endless choice of activities. Senior and children's prices are offered on most activities.

You only have to look at the **Atlantic Ocean** for the most obvious entertainment. The entire stretch of beach is public, and free parking is plentiful. If the sedentary life of sunbathing while reading a book isn't for you, you can rent a Jet Ski, take a sailboat ride out into the wild blue yonder or do a little parasailing. Or rent a bike and pedal along the sand with the kids on funny low-slung, three-wheel banana bikes until you've seen it all.

Of course, the ocean also provides fun in the form of fishing, whether from one of the many piers, in the surf or aboard a Gulf Stream charter boat in search of the big ones. Several charters are available in **Murrells Inlet, Little River** or **Calabash**.

Speaking of water, just wait 'til you see the giant water slides on a 10-acre water park at **Myrtle Waves,** off U.S. 17 Bypass at 1001 10th Street N. in Myrtle Beach. This fun is dictated by the heat of the summer season, so call (843) 448-1026 for information on hours and rates. Or visit **Wild Water Waterpark and Family Fun Center,** 910 U.S. Highway 17 S., (843) 238-WILD, a 16-acre park in Myrtle Beach featuring 33 exciting rides, miniature golf, video arcade, food court, picnic facilities and much more. If you tire of the water, the place to race is **Myrtle Beach Grand Prix** with two locations: 3201 S. Kings Highway, Myrtle Beach, (843) 238-2421; and 3900 U.S. 17 S., in the Windy Hill section, North Myrtle Beach, (843) 272-6010.

To combine some nature and education for another big splash of entertainment, take a walk on the wild side and visit **Alligator Adventure** for live shows with exotic wildlife including albino American alligators, giant Galapagos tortoises, dwarf crocodiles of West Africa, enormous pythons, boas and anacondas, all totaling more than 1,000 alligators and reptiles. Call (843) 361-0789 or (800) 631-0789. It adjoins Barefoot Landing, U.S. 17 N., North Myrtle Beach.

When the sun goes down, you don't have to sit around and clean your clubs to get ready for your tee time tomorrow. The fun, entertainment and enjoyment can continue when the moon comes out. The beach is alive with music at one of the many theaters. **Calvin Gilmore's Carolina Opry,** N. Kings Highway at U.S. 17 Bypass, Myrtle Beach, was one of the first to bring country music fans to Myrtle Beach in lieu of Nashville, and his popularity continues. Call (843) 238-8888 or (800) THE-OPRY for reservations.

The newest venue is **House of Blues,** where three stages showcase a variety of musical talent all night every night plus a summer gospel brunch. The fine varieties of spicy Southern food mixed with the outstanding names in music offer something for every taste and every age group. Call (843) 272-3000 or visit the web site at www.hob.com.

Legends in Concert, Third Avenue S., Surfside Beach, features impersonators of Elvis, Marilyn Monroe, Michael Jackson, Whitney Houston and scores of others barely discernible from the original superstars in live, full-stage productions. Call (843) 238-STAR.

Dolly Parton's Dixie Stampede, N. Kings Highway at U.S. 17 Bypass, Myrtle Beach, is an exciting dinner theater with horses and wagons and a friendly north-south rivalry entertaining you while you feast and applaud. Try the melons for desert. New to the show recently were 7-foot-tall, 300-pound racing ostriches, which add a hilarious touch to the fun, and the food is unsurpassed. Call (843) 497-9700 or (800) 433-4401.

Fantasy Harbour, U.S. 501 (behind Waccamaw Pottery), Myrtle Beach, also features live entertainment at **The Gatlin Brothers Theatre** and a variety of other theaters. Call (843) 236-8500 or (800) 681-5209 for information. **Medieval Times** dinner theater, (843) 236-8080, also at Fantasy Harbour, provides a fine feast served by your own wench and a jousting tournament for knightly entertainment from another century.

The group **Alabama** appears several times each year in its namesake theater at Barefoot Landing, U.S. 17 N., Myrtle Beach. Guest performers have included Barbara Mandrel, Waylon Jennings, Merle Haggard, Tammy Wynette and many more of the biggest names in country music. Call (843) 272-1111 or (800) 342-BAMA for information.

The **Palace Theater** offers a varied list of entertainers reaching far beyond country styles. This venue at Broadway At The Beach (see subsequent mention), from 21st Avenue N. to 29th Avenue N., off U.S. 17 Bypass in Myrtle Beach, opened in 1995 with Bill Cosby, Kenny Rogers and The Righteous Brothers (not all together, of course). The Rockettes traveled here from New York City's Radio City Music Hall for a two-month-running Christmas show in 1996 and 1997. From *Cats* to Sawyer Brown, The Beach Boys, Johnny Mathis and Jeff Foxworthy, big-name performers and performances comprise the entertainment du jour. Call (843) 448-0588 or (800) 905-4228 for information.

You may want to add a little culture to your trip. If so, take a trip to **Brookgreen Gardens,** U.S. 17 S., Murrells Inlet, the world's largest outdoor sculpture garden. This beautiful slice of Lowcountry landscape features more than 500 pieces of sculpture. Wildlife and botanical gardens boast more that 2,000 different plants. Children and adults, alike, will enjoy this natural attraction. Call (843) 237-4218 for information.

Shopping is always on the agenda when you are visiting Myrtle Beach, and with the 1995 opening of the **Myrtle Beach Factory Stores,** U.S. 501, west of the Intracoastal Waterway, Myrtle Beach, (843) 236-5100, the variety is even larger. Other familiar places are the **Outlet Park at Waccamaw,** U.S. 501, west of the Intracoastal Waterway, Myrtle Beach, (843) 236-

1400, and **Barefoot Landing,** U.S. 17 N., North Myrtle Beach, (843) 272-8349, still award winners for the bargains and variety plus proximity to theaters and children's entertainment.

Another visitor's delight is **Broadway At The Beach,** from 21st to 29th avenues N., off U.S. 17 Bypass in Myrtle Beach, (843) 444-3200, a unique place to eat, shop and be entertained (see previously mentioned Palace Theatre). You can spend a day or an evening here and never be finished doing it all. The $250 million complex includes more than 100 specialty retail stores and 15 restaurants (including Hard Rock Café, Planet Hollywood, NASCAR Café and All Star Café—described in the Where to Eat section that follows). It also includes miniature golf and the **IMAX** theater, with a six-story-tall screen and surround-sound that brings you feature films bigger than life. **Ripley's Aquarium** opened here in 1997 with thousands of sea creatures in a 1.3 million-gallon tank you may view from the moving sidewalk. Weekly fireworks displays and evening light shows over the lake are scheduled during summer months. Also, eight clubs within **Celebrity Square** have the dance floors, music and cocktails for any style you could choose. Dancin' in the street is literally encouraged here. For one admission ticket, you may mix and match any of the clubs, and street parties on summer weekends are frequent.

The Grand Strand has much to offer vacationers and residents who come here to play golf. It's possibly the miniature golf capital of the world, not to mention the ever popular **Pavilion Amusement Park,** 812 N. Ocean Boulevard, Myrtle Beach, (843) 448-6456, which has been spinning its Ferris wheels for years and luring every kid to rides and amusements that delight the entire family. You might go home tired, but never bored.

Where to Eat

Dining along the Grand Strand is neither for the timid nor the dieter. The Myrtle Beach Area Chamber of Commerce has counted 1,400 places to eat and claims that the area has more restaurants per capita than San Francisco—usually considered the benchmark for abundant and noteworthy dining establishments. Personally, we haven't been able to keep count in Myrtle Beach, but we are diligently trying.

The food is outrageously delicious, no matter what your preference. Of course, fresh seafood is the local specialty, and you will encounter Calabash-style (lightly breaded and fried) cuisine throughout the area. Calabash is actually a little fishing village on the southern edge of North Carolina. Many seafood buffets throughout the area offer all-you-can-eat choices, predominantly Calabash-style. Please don't even think about cholesterol; anything so tasty just has to be good for you.

The other primary local specialty is Lowcountry cooking. The Lowcountry stretches from the southern end of the Grand Strand throughout the Charleston and Hilton Head areas. Wealthy plantation owners settled in the Lowcountry, and their style of cooking depended heavily on locally produced fish, fowl and vegetables. The preparation took its flavorful hints from slaves who brought their ancestral memories of Creoles, sauces and stews from the French.

Plenty of ribs, steaks, burgers and chicken are equally delicious if you don't want seafood.

Also, vegetarian specialties, Italian and Oriental delicacies are equally superior.

Yes, as you might have guessed, we love food, and it's our distinct pleasure to tell you about it. Refer to our Preface for an explanation of the pricing code.

North Strand

The Brentwood Restaurant
$$$ • Luck and Mulberry Sts., Little River • (843) 239-2601

Chef Bill Stublick and his brother Jim of Brentwood, New York, brought their unique culinary talents into the charming restored 1910 home where you'll be seated in one of several small dining rooms, then treated to desserts and after-dinner drinks in the upstairs salon. Fresh-baked bread, crisp house salads, vegetable du jour and a choice of wild rice pilaf or potatoes du jour accompany entrees from the land or sea. Grilled ostrich or twin lobster tails might catch your attention. If not, try the rack of lamb or veal maison. This fine restaurant is out of the mainstream, but convenient to North Myrtle Beach and Calabash-area golf courses. You don't have to dress up to enjoy the dressy meal here. It's open for dinner only.

Chestnut Hill
$$$ • 9922 U.S. Hwy. 17, North Myrtle Beach • (843) 449-3984

Chestnut Hill offers fine dining in a casual atmosphere overlooking a beautiful marsh.

Friendly service by the professional staff adds to the experience, and we think you'll want to come back often. Seafood, steaks, chicken and home-baked breads are the specialties. Be careful not to fill up on the wonderful sweet potato rolls before dinner. We choose the shrimpers platter as an entree again and again. It's cooked three different ways, so you don't have to make up your mind which is best. We finish with a wedge of homemade Key lime pie. Early bird specials are an encouragement to avoid a wait for dinner seating during the summer.

Cucumbers Restaurant
$$ • N.C. Hwy. 179, Calabash
• (843) 575-3003

Cucumbers is a nice little place for a fine quality dinner when you leave Marsh Harbour or any of the Ocean Isle or Calabash area golf courses. It's somewhat hidden within the Shops at Calabash beside the town's tiny post office. Begin with a cucumber salad, which is not a surprising choice. Then try a meatloaf or pork chop entree with some garlic mashed potatoes or other comfort food from a menu that is sophisticated yet packed with simple foods delightfully prepared. It's open for dinner only and is not open Sunday or Monday.

Dick's Last Resort
$$ • U.S. Hwy. 17, Barefoot Landing,
North Myrtle Beach • (843) 272-7794

Yes, Dick's even serves golfers, and the same rough and rude service is dished out to all who want to be loud and crazy in this popular nightspot where the pork chops, catfish or chicken is served in a bucket and eaten with fingers. The food is actually pretty good, too, and if you drink a lot of beer you can especially appreciate (or overlook) the zany atmosphere here.

Hemingway's
$$$ • U.S. Hwy. 17, Barefoot Landing,
North Myrtle Beach • (843) 272-6118

A huge menu offers more than 30 exotic seafood selections plus beef, veal, duck, chicken and pastas. Sidewalk dining is a good place to watch the crowds pass by, but the dining room offers a nice atmosphere, too. A delicious appetizer is salmon crepes au caviar or soft-shell crab Maryland. Our favorite fish dish is mahimahi San Tropez, although many choices are tempting. Maybe try the unusual surf and turf of duck and lobster. Everything here is tasty, accompanied by a fine wine selection, and you'll be anxious to return on every trip. It's open for dinner only.

House of Blues
$$$ • U.S. Hwy. 17, Barefoot Landing,
North Myrtle Beach • (843) 272-3000

It's a unique look straight from New Orleans. You can sample the blues and the food from the backyard pit or the smokehouse. We love the appetizer of Mississippi cat bites with Cajun tartar sauce, but be sure to have a tall, cool beverage handy. For a super salad, try the warm spinach with parmesan fried oysters. An entree of The Big Easy Jambalaya is filled with irresistible chicken, shrimp, ham and andouille sausage in Creole sauce and Cajun rice. All servings are enormous, and many require plenty of beverage to fight the fire lit by the spices. This huge new restaurant with a concert hall and three stages opened with the Blues Brothers and James Brown in early 1997. All night every night, plus summer gospel brunch concerts, it's a smash hit for food, fun and music. Also, the denim clothing or other blues reminders from the retail store are suitable souvenirs of any trip.

Joe's Bar & Grill
$$$ • 810 Conway Ave. at U.S. Hwy. 17,
North Myrtle Beach • (843) 272-4666

The selection of beef, veal, seafood and poultry is good. Begin with an appetizer of scallops en bacon brochette or escargot en brie butter. Then think about the Lowcountry crab cakes, which are the real thing. Desserts are special every day. The atmosphere is golf shirt, but the meal is coat-and-tie. It's in a remodeled rustic home on a saltwater marsh among gnarled live oak trees. Joe's Bar & Grill is open for dinner. Just across the street—and easier to find—is Hamburger Joe's, which is open for lunch of barbecue, sandwiches and beer.

Johnny Rockets
$ • U.S. Hwy. 17, Barefoot Landing,
North Myrtle Beach • (843) 361-0190

The original hamburger or grilled cheese sandwich with American fries and a shake or float from the fountain is served with your choice of jukebox music from the '60s. This is a good, basic, old-fashioned burger, which you can order to go or eat quickly when you're shuttling between Myrtle and North Myrtle for a tee time or if you are browsing through the outlet stores in Barefoot Landing. It's convenient for lunch or dinner.

Marker 350 Restaurant
$$$ • Four Harbour Place,
North Myrtle Beach • (843) 249-3888

A choice on any local's list for dinner, this

restaurant offers great seafood and service plus a view of the marina and the waterway boat traffic approaching the bridge. Daily specials might include blackened tuna or other fish, or you may choose from a wonderful vegetarian pasta and many varieties of pork, chicken or beef. Lobster chunks are a super appetizer, and Key lime pie is a fine finish. It's a bit away from the heaviest tourist population, so you may be lucky here and avoid a wait for summer dinner.

The Old Pro's Table
$$$ • U.S. Hwy. 17, North Myrtle Beach • (843) 272-6060

You'll find the area's only collection of golf antiques here as well as quality steaks or seafood for dinner. This famous haven of golf atmosphere across from Barefoot Landing is convenient and accessible from any golf course. On a good day, you won't have to wait too long. Good entrees include the famous babyback ribs, several varieties of fresh fish, barbecue chicken and shrimp and prime rib or steaks. A new bar menu also offers lighter meals.

The Parson's Table
$$ • U.S. Hwy. 17 N., Little River • (843) 249-3702, (910) 579-8298

The main dining room here was built in 1885 as the Little River Methodist Church. When a new church was built, this became a community meeting place, then was moved to the present location and converted into a restaurant. The antique stained-glass windows, Tiffany lamp and chandeliers plus the flooring and doors have been combined from retained originals and other furnishings collected from various churches and farmhouses and added over the years. Enjoy the architecture and the antiques while you dine, but don't overlook the main reason to visit: the award-winning food.

Beef, seafood, pasta and a variety of duck, veal, pork or chicken dishes are offered. We also like the desserts: apple pie with hot vanilla cinnamon sauce, strawberries Romanoff or banana and pineapple praline. Petite dinners for light appetites and children's specialties also are offered. It's open for dinner only any day except Sunday.

Myrtle Beach

All Star Café
$$$ • Broadway at the Beach, 29th Ave. N., U.S. Hwy. 17, Myrtle Beach • (843) 916-8326

You might prefer the Tiger Woods Club corner, or just choose any sport and find a wall displaying your favorite star's memorabilia. This theme restaurant opened along with Planet Hollywood in early 1997 with the huge fanfare accompanying Bruce Willis, Patrick Swayze, Will Smith, Monica Seles, Andre Agassi and numbers of other noted owners of the two establishments. The food is as interesting as the collections, with sandwiches, salads, entrees and great desserts that any sports fan will enjoy for lunch or dinner or with cocktails anytime. Also, a gift shop is not to be missed.

Bagel Factory
$ • 2012 N. Kings Hwy., Myrtle Beach • (843) 626-4717

The old-fashioned bagels promise no fats, oils or cholesterol. This bakery, deli and café offers a huge variety of breakfast or lunch omelets, sandwiches, burgers, platters and bagels flavored with anything you can imagine and, of course, all the trimmings and stuffings to accompany them. Fresh, quick, casual—it's great food to grab on the run. You can choose a Reuben of corned beef, pastrami or turkey with the standard Russian dressing and sauerkraut on rye. You can also take home eclairs, cannolis or brownies to round off your meal.

Carolina Roadhouse
$$ • 4617 N. Kings Hwy., Myrtle Beach • (843) 497-9911

The Roadhouse is patterned after the supremely popular California Dreaming restaurants in Charleston and Columbia. It smells like the fresh cedar of its high rafters combined with honey-drizzled fresh rolls and fries you can watch being prepared in the show kitchen. For lunch or dinner, try the ribs or one of the giant seafood platters. Slow-roasted prime rib and huge salads with special house dressings are also trademarks. We love the baked potato soup and the fresh fish of the day—try it blackened. It's a fun place for a big crowd to gather. And if you're into shellfish, Carolina Roadhouse has some of the best oyster shooters around.

Collectors Cafe
$$$ • 7726 N. Kings Hwy., Myrtle Beach • (843) 449-9370

A flavor of Europe greets you in the art galleries of Collectors. Also you will notice about 100 selections of wine and 20 different coffee roasts from all over the world. Hand-painted tables, chairs and tiles are scattered among the original art of the owners, all of which is for sale if you can tear your attention from the Mediterranean food long enough to shop. Open for dinner only, the superb menu features grilled Thai shrimp or lobster zucchini pancake for appetizers. Enjoy an original pasta entree or lamb loin and pesto wrapped in phyllo dough. Desserts are decadent but appropriately matched with cappuccino or espresso to finish a special evening. Reservations are suggested.

Croissants Bakery & Cafe
**$ • 504-A 27th Ave. N., Myrtle Beach
• (843) 448-BAKE**

This wonderful bakery has the best muffins in town to grab on the run and also serves a good sit-down breakfast, including quiche or country grits and eggs casserole. For lunch, try a salad in a French-bread bowl, quiche or deli sandwich with a fresh croissant. It's convenient to shopping, the beach and many golf courses.

Giovanni's – A Touch of Italy
**$$$ • 504-H 27th Ave. N., Myrtle Beach
• (843) 626-8995**

Giovanni's menu is based on the regional specialties of Italy's Piedmonte, Vald'Aosta and Liguria. The pasta, shellfish over pasta, beef, veal and seafood specialties are all delicious. From tagliatelle to tortelloni to cappelletti to fuzzoletti to buccatini, it's all here—and you'll feel like you're in Italy (for dinner only). You'll even find Italian coffees and fresh-baked pastries. In a lovely setting, this restaurant's service and menu will never disappoint. Also, the walls are adorned with numbers of photographs of Giovanni with the interesting visiting celebrities who frequent the restaurant.

Hard Rock Café
**$$$ • Broadway at the Beach,
21st Ave. N., U.S. Hwy. 17, Myrtle Beach
• (843) 946-0007**

It's beyond nontraditional with its pyramid shape and Egyptian look. It even surpasses others in the nontraditional chain, which began in London in 1971 and grew to a family of 76 scattered throughout many major U.S. cities and a few other foreign countries. It's a celebration of the All-American burger and rock 'n' roll music. You'll find an array of fascinating memorabilia that is rotated throughout all of the Hard Rock sites. You'll also enjoy the food. The Flying Pig is a nontraditional barbecue sandwich. Salads, sandwiches and entrees are large, and desserts are enough to share. Enjoy the loud music too. That's one of the reasons you'll want to eat here for lunch or dinner or cocktails anytime. Expect a long wait during the summer, but you can go to the front of the line to browse in the gift shop for anything you want to take

home from a visit. A choreographed architectural light, sound and video show outside the pyramid is the only one of its kind and can be enjoyed periodically in the Broadway at the Beach complex or on indoor television screens while you dine.

Key West Grill
**$$ • Broadway at the Beach, Myrtle Beach
• (843) 444-3663**

The Cuban, Spanish and Calusa Indian influences from the Keys are in the tropical atmosphere and unique recipes of this spicy and popular restaurant. Try the garlic crawfish or coconut shrimp to start. We can't resist the Key West conch chowder. Blackened fish specialties of the day or frog legs will transport your taste buds to another place. Pasta is plentiful, and rice with black beans accompanies some entrees. Several lobster combos are tempting. The view of the lake is relaxing while you look around at the sky blue ceiling and unique architecture in this restaurant within the city's newest shopping/dining/entertainment complex. It's open for lunch and dinner.

NASCAR Café
**$$$ • Broadway at the Beach,
21st Ave. N., U.S. Hwy. 17, Myrtle Beach
• (843) 946-RACE**

"Life's a race. The best times win," according to the first official café simulating a racetrack. Surrounding the restaurant/racetrack is the entertainment concourse that simulates the grandstands at a major race track. The exhibits highlight the sights, sounds and personalities of NASCAR teams, drivers and tracks from all 12 of the sanctioning body's racing divisions. It's a tribute to South Carolina's Darlington Raceway and to South Carolinians who have contributed to NASCAR. It's called an interactive eatery because the passive consumption of great food is only part of the experience. NASCAR officials are cultivating new followers for motorsports racing while giving fans access to the entertainment. The all-American fare, plus full alcoholic beverage service, includes delicious chicken, beef or seafood entrees, large salads and all the trimmings for lunch and dinner.

New York Prime
**$$$$ • 405 28th Ave. N., Myrtle Beach
• (843) 448-8081**

It's expensive, and no apologies are made for the charges, just the explanation that the highest possible quality is available for each item on the menu. The prime beef is aged, center-cut Midwestern beef especially meant to compete with the likes of New York's noted steakhouse, Peter Luger's. Lamb chops, fish, veal, chicken, stone crabs and large live lobster also are offered. Roquefort cheese is actually imported from France. Salads and vegetables are large servings. Nothing is ordinary here. You must prepare to relax, eat a lot and enjoy a fine dining experience. The proprietors, Ed Cribb and Jerry Greenbaum, want to know exactly what you think about it, too. Just don't tell them it's too expensive, because they are proud to note that it's worth every dollar. Only dinner is served.

Planet Hollywood
$$$ • Broadway at the Beach, 29th Ave. N., U.S. Hwy. 17, Myrtle Beach
• (843) 448-STAR

Hanging from the ceiling and displayed in every nook and cranny of the new planet-looking sphere are items from the movies of the theme restaurant's owners. A visit here is more than a meal. It's a snippet from a movie and a look into that planet called Hollywood. The food includes salads, sandwiches, burgers, pizzas and pastas, plus fajitas and entrees. A big-hit appetizer is the honeyed, Captain Crunch-coated chicken fingers. A pizza with chicken and artichokes is an unusual and tasty entree. Also a real winner is the ebony and ivory brownie for dessert. Take home a T-shirt or even a jacket to please a collector or brag about your trip. It's open for lunch and dinner.

Rossi's
$$$ • 9600 U.S. Hwy. 17 N., Myrtle Beach
• (843) 449-0481

Italian food is the specialty here, including homemade pasta, but any menu choice is fine; we've never had a bad meal here. Golfers will find their own special corner, and everyone will have fun. A loud crowd usually waits around the bar until seating is available. The cheese and crackers on the bar make the wait worthwhile. Try one of the daily specials for a unique appetizer—or maybe the oysters Rossi, a slight deviation from oysters Rockefeller. Veal, chicken and steak also are good if you tire of our recommended seafood or pasta. If you wish, the wait staff can suggest an appropriate wine to suit your entree choice. Also, the martini is the best in town. Rossi's is open for dinner only.

Sam Snead's Grille
$$ • 9708 N. Kings Hwy., Myrtle Beach
• (843) 497-0580

Sam Snead's serves good food for dinner

only. The sporty atmosphere is pleasing for a casual meal. As good as the food is the memorabilia collected by Snead, one of the greatest golfers of all time. The fourth such restaurant in the country to open, this is a real museum. Snead occasionally greets visitors with his homespun philosophy explaining his self-taught golfing success.

You might tee off with hot cheese and spinach artichoke dip. Then choose a teriyaki chicken salad with honey dijon dressing. Specialties such as oak-fired shrimp Carolina or oak-grilled tuna mignon are good, as are the rattlesnake pasta and burgers or sandwiches. It's a good late-night spot for a beer and a sandwich.

Sea Captain's House
$$$ • 3002 N. Ocean Blvd., Myrtle Beach
• (843) 448-8082

This is one of the oldest local establishments. All the recipes are special Southern secrets. During early breakfast, you and several hundred of your golfing friends can watch the dolphins play while you enjoy specialties of eggs Benedict or traditional eggs, bacon and home fries. A long wait for a dinner table is common (no reservations are taken), but you can add your name to the list and enjoy watching the waves break and the sea gulls flocking to the lights. Lunch and dinner are experiences to remember. The menu choices are predominantly seafood, but you'll find plenty of chicken or salad choices as well. This restaurant serves our favorite she-crab soup. Think about splurging on a special dessert. You'll be hard pressed to find anything comparable.

Shenanigan's
$$ • U.S. Hwy. 17, Myrtle Beach
• (843) 272-1171

Aged steaks, slow-roasted prime rib, fresh seafood and pride in detail characterize this spot, open for dinner only. Any choice is good, but we prefer such specials as the prime teriyaki steak. The accompanying hoppin' johns is a typical choice too. A tempting appetizer is the Savannah spinach and artichoke dip. Kids pay what they weigh, so don't be alarmed by the big scale when you enter the restaurant. You can take home a pint-size souvenir golf bag beer mug to remember your Myrtle Beach round later during the year.

Villa Mare
$$ • 7819 N. Kings Hwy., Myrtle Beach
• (843) 449-8654

Please don't tell all of your friends about this

fabulous Italian restaurant. Don't tell anyone the food is some of the best around, served in large portions and quite inexpensive. This is a secret place among locals, and we don't want it to get so crowded that we can't get our table. Lunch and dinner are real treats in this refreshing little spot. Pasta, soup, salad and bread accompany any entree from seafood to our all-time favorites eggplant parmesan or lasagna. The house red wine goes well with these selections.

Vintage House Cafe
$$ • 1210 N. Kings Hwy., Myrtle Beach
• (843) 626-3918

An eclectic surprise in the midst of old Myrtle Beach, this lovely cafe provides a gourmet menu for lunch and dinner. A favorite luncheon choice is salmon and grits. Dinner entrees include Mediterranean grilled chicken breast over linguine with black olives, tomatoes and feta cheese or grilled New Zealand rack of lamb marinated in olive oil and fresh herbs. Tom and Trina O'Brien specialize in the use of herbs and sauces for their homemade delicacies. Desserts include homemade cheesecakes and similar goodies, with various teas, cappuccino, espresso or wines.

South Strand

Bovine's
$$ • U.S. Hwy. 17 Bus., Murrells Inlet
• (843) 651-2888

Right on the water in the middle of the small fishing village of Murrells Inlet, this restaurant's menu is eclectic and its view a magnet to draw you back often. One tempting daily special is the honey-crust pizza from the wood-fired brick oven. From the wood-fired grill come great steaks or roasted prime rib. A delicious entree is the mesquite-grilled free-range chicken breast stuffed with pancetta, goat cheese and wild mushrooms. Check out the desserts too.

Bovine's, open for dinner only, is popular with locals as well as traveling golfers.

Conch Cafe
$$$ • 1482 N. Waccamaw Dr., Garden City
• (843) 651-6556

Jimmy Buffet would be at home here—maybe he was here when he wrote some of his tunes. Don't come here in a rush. Come for lunch after a summer round of morning golf on the South Strand and plan on languishing with a long, cool salty drink and a sandwich. Salads or sandwiches in any variety are good choices,

and dinner promises seafood entrees concocted from local recipes. Hours are unusual during the off season, so call to check.

Drunken Jack's Restaurant & Lounge
$$$ • U.S. Hwy. 17 Bus., Murrells Inlet
• (843) 651-2044

Plan to arrive long before you expect to be hungry, because the wait in-season, as locals say, might be more than an hour or two. The downstairs lounge provides a view of the inlet fishing fleet at Snug Harbor Marina—and a drink. And if you can wait, the seafood choices upstairs are worth it. Alcoholic drinks are available any day including Sunday, a new feature of the Murrells Inlet restaurants created by popular choice of voters in 1997. We usually choose a fish special (caught today in the Devil's Triangle, the chef says), which can be prepared many ways, or the crab casserole baked in cheese. Word has it Jack might have traded his peg leg for the marinated chicken breast or steak and lobster from the charcoal grill. It's open for dinner only.

Flo's Place Restaurant & Raw Bar
$$ • U.S. Hwy. 17 Bus., Murrells Inlet
• (843) 651-7222

Flo's is one of the few places that offers alligator ribs. Flo's recipes, including the alligator and crawfish specialties, came from her childhood in Louisiana where her father regularly brought home such delicacies. Try the stewpot, with some of everything mixed in. Plan to hold on to your hat unless you want to find it hanging from the rafters, where Flo's collection sports hundreds of them.

Flo's Place is fun and friendly, and it literally hangs over the marsh, creating a definite backwoods bayou feeling. Alcoholic drinks are served here. It's open for lunch and dinner.

Island Cafe & Deli
$$ • U.S. Hwy. 17 S., Pawleys Island
• (843) 237-9527

Locals frequent this cafe once a week for the Wednesday lobster night or the Monday shrimp night. Special price, special drink and seafood cooked to order will keep you coming back too. Reservations are recommended for dinner seven days a week. Everyone driving from one golf course to another on the South Strand stops here for a sandwich for lunch. Our favorite (plus the lobster special) is a big, cool salad with lots of toppings and crusty, hot bread with a glass of wine.

J. Edward's
$$ • 2300 S. Kings Hwy., Myrtle Beach
• (843) 626-9986

The tasty and tender ribs are local award winners in this casual dinner restaurant. If you can't choose which barbecue to eat, try the chef's sampler of ribs, chicken, a pork chop and shrimp. Bread, salad or slaw and baked potato, sweet potato or fries accompany the entree. You won't leave here hungry—nor as clean as when you arrived. Just dig in and enjoy. The people are friendly and the service good.

Where to Stay

More than 100 of the major hotels on the Grand Strand offer golf packages. More than 400 hotels and hundreds of condos offer a total of 55,000 sleeping rooms—we can't possibly describe all of them here. You may call the Myrtle Beach Area Chamber of Commerce at (800) 356-3016 for a complete listing. The following offers a variety of suggestions from basic golfer's accommodations to luxury resorts for a special family vacation. Refer to our Preface for an explanation of the pricing code.

North Strand

T-Time Tours
$$-$$$ • 505 Main St., North Myrtle Beach
• (843) 249-4545, (800) 458-8463

Try this vacation package company for golf, accommodations, entertainment, USAirways booking and Budget car rental. Choose accommodations from one-, two- or three-bedroom fully equipped condominium units with views of the Intracoastal Waterway or the Atlantic Ocean. Golf on any of the area's championship courses, and choose country music or variety shows plus amusement parks, shopping or other attractions.

The Winds Clarion Inn
$-$$ • 310 E. First St., Ocean Isle Beach,
N.C. • (910) 579-6275, (800) 334-3581

It's not part of the North Strand, technically speaking, but this inn apparently prefers it that way. This lovely oceanfront hotel is part of the North Carolina Golf Coast Association, which is seeking to develop its own identity separate from the Myrtle Beach or Wilmington areas—its big-town neighbors to the south and north, respectively. The 73 rooms include oceanfront rooms and one-, two- or three-bedroom suites overlooking subtropical gardens and a 7-mile-long island beach. A heated pool (enclosed in winter), whirlpools, an exercise room, a sauna, bikes, shuffleboard, malletpool, wetbars and refrigerators or kitchens in all suites are additional amenities. The four-bedroom spa houses (which sleep eight golfers) are ideal for golf groups. All five luxurious houses include full kitchens, great rooms and large Jacuzzis. Each bedroom also has a private bath, cable TV, a wet bar with a refrigerator, a private telephone and a balcony.

Golf packages with guaranteed tee times and discounted rates are offered on 20 high-quality Brunswick County courses within a five- to 15-minute drive and a total of some 86 championship courses in the Myrtle Beach area. Golfers are welcomed at a weekly reception during the prime golf seasons—spring and fall. Also, the continental breakfast buffet is more than the usual continental fare: It includes pancakes, waffles or cereal.

If you aren't looking for the big-city lights and other attractions, come here for great golf and great beach access in the family-type Ocean Isle area.

Myrtle Beach

Bar Harbor Motor Inn
$$ • First Ave. N., Myrtle Beach
• (843) 626-3200, (800) 334-2464

This oceanfront property is convenient to the golf courses, and we think you'll enjoy the great views, the outdoor pool or indoor heated pool while traveling on your Southern Escape Golf package. Excellent package prices on any area course are offered year round. Call (800) 554-4546 for information on custom packages. This family-owned accommodation effuses a family-friendly atmosphere. A total of 101 suites, rooms and efficiencies with private balconies are available.

Beach Vacations Inc.
$$ • 357 Lake Arrowhead Rd.,
Myrtle Beach • (843) 449-2400,
(800) 449-4005

One-, two- and three-bedroom accommodations are available in the way of oceanfront condominiums or golf course villas—part and parcel of the golf vacation this company will package for you. Properties feature pools, Jacuzzis, tennis, full kitchens and cable TV. You'll enjoy the quality accommodations, especially if you like to overlook the fairways, and the friendly and helpful staff will assist with your package booking. Their properties are in a number of locations throughout Myrtle and North Myrtle.

The Caravelle
$$ • 70th Ave. N., Myrtle Beach
• (843) 449-3331, (800) 845-0893

One of the first to offer the golf package, this beachfront hotel offers 420 spacious accommodations including rooms, suites, efficiencies or condominiums. The indoor and outdoor pools and whirlpools, a Lazy River, sauna, game room and breakfast buffet will add interesting asides to your golf vacation. Tee times are available on the private Dunes Club as well as almost 100 other championship courses. A "golf widow" package is offered, and you might want to check out the "blizzard escape" winter package too.

The Caribbean Resort & Villas
$$$ • 3000 N. Ocean Blvd., Myrtle Beach
• (843) 448-7181, (800) 845-0883

Oceanfront suites in the tower sleep extra guests in the living room, and oceanfront and oceanview rooms and two- or three-bedroom condominiums with kitchen, living and dining room, and washer and dryer are available. The complex has 278 units. Golf packages are available on any area course including the private Dunes Club. The breakfast included with your golf package will give you the real flavor of a local Myrtle Beach favorite—the Sea Captain's House next door.

Amenities include indoor and outdoor pools, whirlpools and a Lazy River, which is covered during cooler months. Non-golfing family members hang out at the pool or roam a few blocks to the mall.

Coral Beach Resort Hotel
$$$ • 1105 S. Ocean Blvd., Myrtle Beach
• (843) 448-8421, (800)843-2684

Have you ever taken a group to the beach only to encounter an unusually rainy week with nothing to do outdoors? If so, consider staying at the Coral Beach Resort Hotel. Of course, it never rains on the golf course, but sometimes it rains on the kids' pool parties. This quality hotel with 301 units has a bowling alley on the sixth floor, arcade games and a regular entertainment center of its own. It also caters to golf groups, as you'll surmise from the memorabilia adorning its version of the 19th hole plus the indoor putting green and indoor driving range. Golfers who take advantage of the package deal with area courses are invited to complimentary cocktail parties during the season.

The oceanfront suites sleep three golfers or a family of six. Suites and efficiencies include a kitchen with refrigerator, range, microwave, toaster and utensils, and suites feature living and dining areas as well. Suites are oceanfront, and rooms and efficiencies are oceanview, all with private balconies. Amenities include a general store and gift shop, the Atlantis restaurant, a lounge, two snack bars and a pool bar, three indoor whirlpools, two heated outdoor pools, a steamroom and saunas, an exercise room and suntan beds.

Dunes Village
$$ • 5200 N. Ocean Blvd., Myrtle Beach
• (843) 449-5275, (800) 648-3539

The Dunes Village has the feel of a small family resort where everyone knows your name. Catering to golfers and booking packages on any area course including the private Dunes Club, this oceanfront resort offers an attractive year-round pool and tennis courts and is a nice spot for the whole family to enjoy. All 93 rooms are oceanfront with private balconies. The hotel recently completed a renovation project.

The breakfast here is legendary, and many guests return to this same home-at-the-beach year after year.

Fore-Travel
• (800) 800-1103

Focusing on golf packages, Fore-Travel offers room-and-golf deals starting at $79 per person per night. With a handful of accommodations and more than 30 courses to choose from, Fore-Travel can set up golfers of all ages and abilities with appropriate rooms and courses. Carts and taxes are included in all quoted rates. Check them out on the Web at www.fore-travel.com.

Kingston Plantation
$$$$$ • 9800 Lake Dr., Myrtle Beach
• (843) 449-0006

This is one of the classiest resorts around, changing in early 1998 from a Radisson Resort to an Embassy Suites, if you want to splurge on a luxury oceanfront suite and spend some time. Also two- or three-bedroom oceanview condominiums or lakeside villas of one, two or three bedrooms are practical if you're only here for golf. Golf packages get guests on many of the top-rated Grand Strand courses. Be sure to enjoy the oceanfront pool and bar plus the fine dining, especially the weekend dinner buffet. The Swan Sea Conference Center is a convenient site for meetings and reunions. Tennis and racquetball courts, an indoor pool, sauna, whirlpool and health club also are on the property. The Arcadian Shores Golf Course is across the street, and many nightspots are an easy drive from this property.

Myrtle Beach Martinique

$$$ • 7100 N. Ocean Blvd., Myrtle Beach
• (843) 449-4441, (800) 542-0048

One of Myrtle Beach's nicest oceanfront hotels, with 203 units and exceptional attention to quality service, the Martinique splashes its tropical colors and hospitality across just about any size room, efficiency or suite. An indoor pool, oceanfront pool, whirlpool, exercise room, sauna and meeting and convention facilities are available.

The on-site Cafe du Port serves breakfast, lunch and dinner, and the Banana Boat lounge is a popular afternoon and evening spot for socializing. This accommodation is convenient to golf courses, and the staff will book tee times on any area course for guests taking advantage of golf packages.

Ocean Creek

$$$$ • 10600 N. Kings. Hwy.,
Myrtle Beach • (843) 448-8446,
(800) 443-7050

Choose the towers on the oceanfront, or take a short walk back to a villa on the 57-acre resort that welcomes golfers. The variety includes 400 studios plus one-, two- and three-bedroom condominiums.

The Four Seasons restaurant features a buffet breakfast and full-service dining plus banquets or receptions for private groups. A putting green is on site. The knowledgeable and friendly golf department will book packages with any area courses you choose. Seven pools include an indoor pool and whirlpool. A tennis complex and beach club with oceanfront pool also are available. The freshwater creek running through the property provides a unique change of scene for the golfer who doesn't prefer the ocean.

The family that doesn't golf can scoot across U.S. Highway 17 to spend a day at Barefoot Landing and Alligator Adventure, an award-winning entertainment, shopping and dining complex where the new House of Blues also is found.

Ocean Dunes/Sand Dunes Resort

$$$ • 201 74th Ave. N., Myrtle Beach
• (843) 449-7441

This oceanfront resort caters to golfers—it's convenient to any golf course. Packages are booked on any area course plus the exclusive private Dunes Club and Pawleys Plantation. More than 500 rooms, suites, efficiencies, villas and penthouses are available. All have private balcony, refrigerator, in-room movies, cable TV and private safe. Microwaves are available in suites and efficiencies.

The oceanfront Brass Anchor seafood restaurant and lounge offers live entertainment, and the Dolphin pool bar is oceanfront as well. A fitness center, indoor and outdoor pools, a sauna, whirlpools, a beauty salon and massage therapy round out the amenities.

Sands Ocean Club Resort

$$ • 9550 Shore Dr., Myrtle Beach
• (843) 449-6461, (800) 845-2202

Suites or efficiencies in this oceanfront resort hotel are convenient to all major golf courses. Golfers are welcomed at a weekly reception and clinic. Exclusive play on Sands' Pawleys Plantation is a treat for guests here. Each of the 459 units has a private balcony, refrigerator, in-room movies, cable TV and a kitchen with microwave. A poolside cafe, oceanfront restaurant and indoor and outdoor pools are available. A Lazy River, health club, gift shop, convenience store, covered parking and rain insurance round out the amenities.

The area is popular during summer when Sandals lounge and the neighboring Ocean Annie's Beach Bar offer live music, and lots of fun folks dance away the days and nights here. Sands Ocean Club is an easy walk to a few shops. And during November, slip across the footbridge to the Dunes Club for the Energizer Senior Tour Championship. Early reservations are recommended for packages that include tickets to the tournament.

Sea Mist Oceanfront Resort

$$ • 1200 S. Ocean Blvd., Myrtle Beach
• (843) 448-1551, (800) SEA-MIST

Sea Mist is one of the largest oceanfront resorts (with 824 units) that caters to golfers, with customized packages for twosomes or large groups. Perfect for families too, this resort offers supervised and structured summer programs for children.

Accommodations for any size group or family vacation include single rooms, suites, multi-bed apartments and a lacy and romantic honeymoon suite with a red heart-shape Jacuzzi. Eleven pools (two indoor), a Jacuzzi, sauna, steamroom, lounge, cafe and ice cream parlor are on site. Discount theater tickets and limousine service round out the amenities. The Family Kingdom amusement park is nearby, and many other activities are within walking distance.

Sheraton Myrtle Beach Hotel
$$$$$ • 2701 S. Ocean Blvd., Myrtle Beach
• (843) 448-2518, (800) 992-1055

The Sheraton is one of the nice spots to find a room, efficiency or suite. All of the 219 units have refrigerator, coffee maker, in-room movies, cable TV, plus microwave in suites and efficiencies. Golfers and their families will enjoy indoor and outdoor pools, whirlpool, health club, sauna, gift shop and good food and drink in a welcoming setting in Kokomo's beach bar or oceanfront restaurant and lounge. Golf packages booked on any area course include a weekly reception.

Swamp Fox Ocean Resort
$$ • 2311 S. Ocean Blvd., Myrtle Beach
• (843) 448-8373, (800) 228-9894

The Swamp Fox boasts more oceanfront footage than most hotels. A quality and experienced golf department will help you book any package, even on the private Dunes Club, and can include theater tickets if desired. Cocktail receptions for golfers are offered weekly during golf season.

Choose from 377 units, which includes efficiencies or suites in the tower or rooms in the motel. Take a group and enjoy a penthouse with plenty of space, cooking and dining facilities plus an outstanding view. Little ones will enjoy the Lazy River, and everyone will be pleased with indoor and outdoor pools, Jacuzzis, saunas and the adjoining Gabriel's Restaurant.

South Strand

Litchfield Beach and Golf Resort
$$$$$ • U.S. Hwy. 17 S., Pawleys Island
• (843) 237-3000, (800) 845-1897

If you or someone in your party plays tennis or racquetball, wants to find a spa and health club or simply wants to retreat from the busy resort area to the quiet marshes of the South Strand, this is the place for you. Everything you might need is here, with 96 units surrounded by Litchfield Country Club, River Club and Willbrook Plantation Golf Club; plus the resort offers booking on all of the area's other courses. The restaurant is great, entertainment is nearby, and specialty shops are easily accessible. Oceanview, marshview and fairway villas are available. At Litchfield, you could completely miss Myrtle Beach and still have the vacation of a lifetime.

Golf Equipment

You'll find anything you need on the Grand Strand. You won't have any trouble getting to a store, and what you will find is bound to be bigger and better than anything you've seen elsewhere. If you're in the market for new clubs, wait until you get here to shop. In addition to the following suggested equipment shops, professionals at many of the golf courses offer custom fitting. Ask a local golfer if you have any questions.

When golf shopping on the Grand Strand, check out any or all (if you have a week or more to spend just shopping!) of the following golf equipment retailers:

• **Nevada Bob's**, 3100 N. Kings Highway, Myrtle Beach, (843) 448-1779; or 2006 U.S. Highway 17, North Myrtle Beach, (843) 272-4705

• **Golf Dimensions**, 2301 U.S. Highway 17 S., North Myrtle Beach, (843) 272-4630

• **Martin's Golf and Tennis**, 1615 U.S. Highway 17, North Myrtle Beach, (843) 272-6030; 2204 U.S. Highway 17 N., (843) 448-7525, Myrtle Beach; U.S. Highway 501, (843) 236-7878, Myrtle Beach; or 1010 U.S. Highway 17 S., Surfside Beach, (843) 238-1643

• **Scottish Pride Golf**, 1500 U.S. Highway 501, Myrtle Beach, (843) 946-9464

• **Clubmaker's Golf**, 2016 N. Kings Highway, Myrtle Beach, (843) 626-0099

• **Wild Willie's**, U.S. Highway 501, Myrtle Beach, (843) 249-9722 or (800) 249-9722

• **Sam's Discount Golf & Tennis**, 3300-C U.S. Highway 17 S., North Myrtle Beach, (843) 272-6998.

Golf Instruction

Most of these golf schools offer any type of package you'll need to improve your golf game, from short group lessons to day-long individual instruction. Call for specific information or ask at any course you choose to play about private lessons taught by professional staff.

We recommend the following: **Legends Academy**, (800) 552-2660; **The Links Golf School** at The Tradition Club, (800) 833-6337; **Phil Ritson Golf School**, (800) 624-4653 or (843) 237-4993; **The Classic Swing Golf School** at Deer Track Golf Resort, (800) 827-2656 or (843) 650-2545; Riley Golf School, (800) 30-RILEY; and **Myrtle Beach Golf School**, (800) 94-SWING.

South Carolina's

Charleston, Hilton Head and the Lowcountry

Many cities and courses claim to be the home of golf in the United States, but nowhere, save Charleston, can boast the nation's very first track and very first club: Harleston Green and The South Carolina Golf Club—established in 1786. So there. The club and course no longer exist, sadly, but many superb layouts have popped up in the 215 years since, thus rendering the Lowcountry one of the premier golf destinations in the Carolinas.

And with good reason.

The terrain of the Lowcountry—flat, dark, humid, swampy—lends itself to excellent golf, provided the course developers hire a good golf course architect. In the Lowcountry, you'll find some of the finest "pancake land" work by some of the game's finest architects—Dye, Nicklaus, Jones, Fazio. While some of the better clubs in the area are completely private, many of the area's great courses are open to the public, albeit for a hefty chunk of change. Trust us, it's worth the splurge.

Charleston is the epicenter of the Lowcountry, and the city is one of America's most historic and oft-visited destinations. It was also, once upon a time, one of America's wealthiest towns, and the opulence of earlier times is reflected in the pastel ante-bellum architecture downtown. Quite simply, there's a grace, charm, history, and uniqueness to Charleston that makes it one of the world's most wonderful spots, especially for those on a honeymoon or anniversary trip. Oh, Venice may boast more gondolas and romance, but how's the golf there? Eh? Where can you tee it up?

While a visitor would most certainly be excused for thinking that little has changed in Charleston in the past two centuries, the city has actually changed dramatically in the past 20 years. Development in the hinterlands has attracted new residents; an important military base closed; the area's economic foundation broadened. But most importantly, in September 1989, a category four hurricane named Hugo slammed into Charleston, shredding foliage, atomizing boats, destroying buildings, na-

Charleston/Hilton Head/Lowcountry

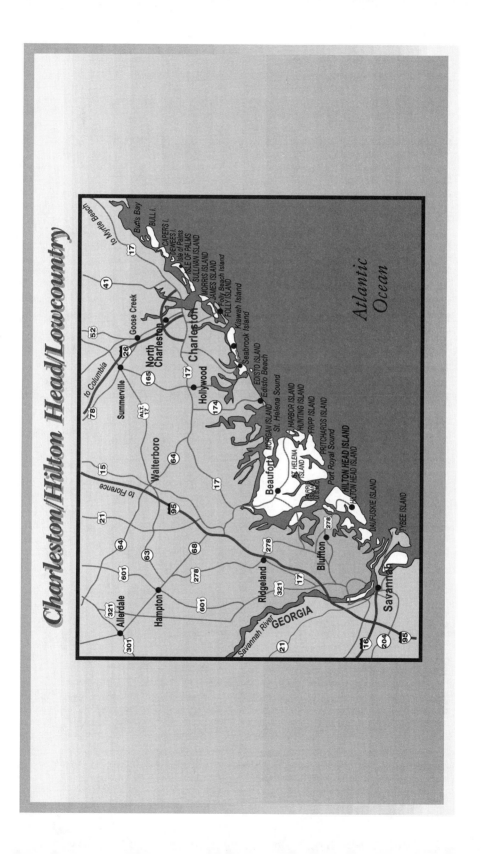

GOLF COURSES IN SOUTH CAROLINA'S CHARLESTON/HILTON HEAD/LOWCOUNTRY AREA

Course	Type	#Holes	Par	Slope	Yards	Walking	Booking	Cost w/Cart
Callawassie Island Club								
Dogwood Course	semiprivate	9	36	n/r	3286	no	call	$52-73
Magnolia Course	semiprivate	9	36	n/r	3275	no	call	$52-73
Palmetto Course	semiprivate	9	36	n/r	3187	no	call	$52-73
Charleston Municipal Golf Course	public	18	72	114	6161	yes	7 days	$25-30
Charleston National C. C.	semiprivate	18	72	125	6661	PM	60 days	$40-60
Coosaw Creek Country Club	semiprivate	18	71	124	6068	yes	7 days	$38-44
C. C. of Beaufort at Pleasant Point	semiprivate	18	72	115	6112	yes	call	$30
Country Club of Hilton Head	semiprivate	18	72	128	6543	no	call	$60-80
Crowfield	semiprivate	18	72	134	6701	yes	call	$30-59
Dunes West Golf Club	semiprivate	18	72	125	6392	no	365 days	$45-75
Golden Bear G. C./Indigo Run	semiprivate	18	72	125	6643	no	30-120 days	$55-73
Hilton Head National Golf Club	public	18	72	125	6260	no	1 year	$45-90
Island West Golf Club	public	18	72	124	6208	no	1 year	$45-75
Kiawah Island								
Cougar Point Course	resort	18	72	130	6523	no	call	$80-125
Ocean Course	resort	18	72	134	6244	no	call	$120
Osprey Point Course	resort	18	72	124	6015	no	call	$110
Turtle Point Course	resort	18	72	132	6497	no	call	$110
Oak Point Golf Club	public	18	72	132	6468	yes	60 day	$55
Ocean Point Golf Links	resort	18	72	124	6060	yes	call	$45-60
Old South Golf Links	public	18	72	125	6354	yes	60 days	$50-85
Oyster Reef Golf Course	semiprivate	18	72	123	6440	no	90 days	$69-79

Course	Type	Holes	Par		Yardage	Walking	Advance Booking	Price
Palmetto Dunes Golf Resort								
Arthur Hills Course	resort	18	72	120	6122	yes	30 days	$40-80
George Fazio Course	resort	18	70	123	6239	yes	30 days	$40-80
Robert Trent Jones Course	resort	18	72	119	6148	yes	30 days	$40-80
Fripp Island Resort								
Ocean Creek Golf Course	resort	18	71	125	6094	yes	call	$45-50
Ocean Point Golf Links	resort	18	72	124	6060	yes	call	$45-60
Eagles Pointe	semiprivate	18	71	n/r	6580	no	call	$50-85
Old Carolina Golf Club	semiprivate	18	71	133	6445	no	call	$50-85
Rose Hill								
East	semiprivate	9	36	n/r	3225	no	2 weeks	$50-65
West	semiprivate	9	36	n/r	3583	no	2 weeks	$50-65
South	semiprivate	9	36	n/r	3239	no	2 weeks	$50-65
Palmetto Hall Plantation								
Arthur Hills Course	semiprivate	18	72	123	6582	yes	60 days	$36-75
Robert Cupp Course	semiprivate	18	72	126	6522	yes	60 days	$36-75
Patriots Point Golf Links	public	18	72	118	6274	yes	call	$35-50
Port Royal Golf Club								
Barony Course	resort	18	72	122	6038	yes	call	$40-80
Planters Row Course	resort	18	72	126	6009	yes	call	$40-80
Robbers Row Course	resort	18	72	129	6188	yes	call	$40-80
Sea Pines								
Harbour Town Golf Links	resort	18	71	126	6119	no	call	$110-180
Ocean Course	resort	18	72	119	6213	no	call	$110-180
Sea Marsh Course	resort	18	72	117	6129	no	call	$110-180
Seabrook Island								
Crooked Oaks Course	resort	18	72	126	6387	yes	call	$60-85

Ocean Winds Course	resort	18	72	130	6395	yes	call	$60-85
Shadowmoss Plantation	semiprivate	18	72	116	6399	weekdays	90 day	$26-35
Shipyard Golf Club								
Brigantine Course	resort	9	36	n/r	2959	after 5 PM	call	$40-90
Clipper Course	resort	9	36	n/r	3132	after 5 PM	call	$40-90
Galleon Course	resort	9	36	n/r	3035	after 5 PM	call	$40-90
Royal Pines Golf & Country Club								
Pines Course	semiprivate	18	72	119	6430	yes	2 days	$22-25
Marsh Course	semiprivate	18	72	101	5659	yes	call	$30-35
The Links at Stono Ferry	resort	18	72	112	6085	no	1 week	$45-50
Wild Dunes								
Harbor Course	resort	18	70	117	5900	no	call	$40-85
Links Course	resort	18	72	121	6131	yes	call	$60-120

palming neighborhoods, gouging golf courses. Locals talk about Charleston pre- and post-Hugo.

While Hugo instigated a period of widespread panic, things are much more laid back these days. In fact, Lowcountry life is mostly extremely relaxed, a general tenor that's reflected in the other municipalities of the Lowcountry: Hilton Head and Beaufort, both of which boast abundant character and excellent golf courses.

Why or how Myrtle Beach has become the more sought-after golf destination in these parts is a bit of a mystery. While the Lowcountry can't offer the same sheer quantity of golf, it certainly wins in the quality category. Plus, trying to compare Charleston to the more visited Grand Strand to the north is like… well… comparing Ella Fitzgerald to Naomi Judd; or a Jaguar to a Ford F-150 (with the off-road package); or James Bond to Walker, Texas Ranger; or a Titleist Tour Balata to a Pinnacle; or Duck à l'orange to a supersized spicy chicken combo… You get the picture.

Still, hats off to Myrtle Beach for its incessant self-promotion: They rock when it comes to plucking hibernating golfers out of the frigid climes of Michigan in February and hurtling them to the northern shores of South Carolina.

This, too, may change.

One day in the not too distant future, golfers from all over the world will to discover that a golf holiday to the Lowcountry is easier on the soul.

You read it here first.

We've divided this chapter up into the main areas covered, with lodgings and restaurants broken down separately for each.

Additional information is available in *The Insiders' Guide to Greater Charleston,* or by calling the Charleston Area Convention and Visitors Bureau, (843) 853-8000; the Edisto Chamber of Commerce, (843) 869-3867; the Greater Beaufort Chamber of Commerce, (843) 524-3163; the Hilton Head Island Chamber of Commerce, (843) 785-3653; or the Greater Summerville Chamber of Commerce, (843) 873-2931.

Charleston Courses

Charleston Municipal Golf Course
2110 Maybank Hwy., Charleston
• (843) 795-6517

Championship Yardage:	6411
Slope: 112	Par: 72
Men's Yardage:	6161
Slope: 114	Par: 72
Ladies' Yardage:	5202
Slope: 114	Par: 72

This 18-hole course, managed by the city, is Charleston's oldest remaining layout—built in 1929. It was designed by John E. Ademes. It's a well-run public course, with bermudagrass greens and fairways.

The scenic 13th, 14th and 15th holes are on the marsh and the Stono River.

Approximate greens fees for visitors are $15 on weekdays and $20 on weekends, and carts are an additional $10. The course hosts as many as 54,000 rounds a year, so call ahead for a tee time.

Practice greens, a driving range, rental clubs, a pro shop, snack bar and bar are available. On busy days, a beverage cart also makes the rounds. Walking is allowed.

Charleston National Country Club
U.S. Hwy. 17 N., Mt. Pleasant
• (843) 884-7799

Championship Yardage:	6928
Slope: 137	Par: 72
Men's Yardage:	6661
Slope: 125	Par: 72
Other Yardage:	6061
Slope: 122	Par: 72
Other Yardage:	5509
Slope: 114	Par: 72
Ladies' Yardage:	5103
Slope: 126	Par: 72

Rees Jones designed the existing 18-hole course in 1990. (The original Jones-designed course was destroyed by Hurricane Hugo in 1989 just days after it opened.) It's home to golf teams of The Citadel and the College of Charleston. Fairways and greens are bermudagrass. Marshland and bridges characterize this course.

One of the pro's favorite holes is the par 4 12th, a dogleg right with a big pond on the right and marsh on the left. It requires a fairly long and accurate tee shot. You have very little rough and are in a hazard if you shoot left or right. Your second shot (hopefully) plays to an elevated and undulating green surrounded by bunkers and backed by the Atlantic Intracoastal Waterway, which usually wafts a gentle breeze over the green. Another challenging hole is No. 6, a par 4—challenging not because of its length but because of its hazards. Your tee shot needs to find a landing area to prevent hitting a second marsh you can't see from the tee. Then your second shot will be over a marsh onto the narrow green.

A practice green, driving range, rental clubs, bar and restaurant are available. Members may access lockerroom facilities, a pool and a tennis center. The pro shop staff is very cordial and ready to answer questions and meet golfers' needs.

Approximate greens fees range from $40 on off-season weekdays to $60 on in-season weekends, including cart. The course is open to the public year-round. Walking is allowed on a limited basis during afternoons only.

Coosaw Creek Country Club
4210 Club Course Dr., North Charleston
• (843) 767-9000

Championship Yardage:	6593
Slope: 129	Par: 71
Men's Yardage:	6068
Slope: 124	Par: 71
Ladies' Yardage:	5064
Slope: 115	Par: 71

Arthur Hills designed this 18-hole course that opened in 1993. Situated on 645 acres of woods and wetlands, Coosaw Creek features bentgrass fairways and bermudagrass greens. A few holes have marsh and a bit of rolling ground somewhat unique to the Lowcountry. This course places a premium on accuracy rather than length, making the approach shots and the short game the keys to scoring well. The best opportunities for scoring are on the front nine, as the course takes charge on the back nine, with more of the water and wetlands coming into play.

Hole No. 11, a 224-yard par 3, requires your tee shot to cross water and wetlands three times. The tee shot on No. 12, a 596-yard par 5, must cross a lake, then avoid a pot bunker in the middle of the fairway. The second shot must be played long and left to avoid pine trees on the right side of the fairway at the entrance to the green. The difficult No. 14 requires a perfect drive,

and even that leaves another 200 yards over a marsh. The signature hole is the par-5 16th, 516 yards from the back tees, requiring a 3-wood off the tee to drive over a big pond. A 40-foot elevation change down, then back up, from tee to green provides a unique situation.

Two practice greens, a driving range and club rental are available. A pro shop, shower facilities and a grill room are on site. A beverage cart makes the rounds on weekends and holidays.

Approximate greens fees range from $38 on weekdays to $44 on weekends year round, including cart. Walking is allowed with some restrictions.

Crowfield Golf & Country Club
300 Hamlet Cir., Goose Creek
• (843) 764-4618

Championship Yardage:	7003
Slope: 134	Par: 72
Men's Yardage:	6701
Slope: 134	Par: 72
Other Yardage:	6471
Slope: 128	Par: 72
Ladies' Yardage:	5682
Slope: 115	Par: 72

Tom Jackson and Bob Spence designed this 18-hole course in 1990 with bermudagrass greens and fairways. It's so popular that it's already hosted the South Carolina PGA Championship three times.

The design takes advantage of the wetlands and forests of an 18th-century plantation. Dense hardwoods surround every hole, and the layout has rolling terrain and plentiful bunkers.

Accuracy is essential on this course. The signature 7th hole is a par 5 measuring 513 yards from the back tees, and mounds are abundant. All greens are elevated, and the course offers extraordinary character and subtleties for the Lowcountry. Every hole has three or more sand traps.

Practice greens, a driving range, pro shop, rental clubs, bar and restaurant are offered. If you need personalized instruction, you can get it at the driving range.

Approximate cost ranges from $30 to $59, including cart. Walking is allowed during the week or after 2 PM on weekends.

INSIDERS' TIP

Plan your shot quickly, and select the club for your next shot while approaching your ball. If you're riding a cart but must walk across the fairway to your ball, take a couple of clubs with you so you'll be sure to have the one you want in hand. Ready golf is the only good etiquette.

The famed lighthouse is the target on the 18th at Harbor Town on Hilton Head Island.

Photo: Hilton Head Island Resort

Dunes West Golf Club
S.C. Hwy. 41, Mt. Pleasant
• (843) 856-9000, (888) 955-1234
Championship Yardage: 6871
Slope: 131 **Par: 72**
Men's Yardage: **6392**
Slope: 125 **Par: 72**
Ladies' Yardage: **5682**
Slope: 118 **Par: 72**

This Arthur Hills design opened in 1991 and has received national attention for its bermudagrass-covered dunes along the Cooper River, set among ancient oaks draped with Spanish moss. It's part of a residential community 10 miles northeast of Charleston. The clubhouse was built on the foundation of an old plantation house.

As with all Lowcountry courses, marshland dominates Dunes West—although the swampy stuff doesn't always come into play. The course is somewhat open. High rough and copious sand

cause trouble around the greens. The signature hole is the 18th, a straightforward par 4 with two different greens. A short green that plays about 420 yards sits in the marsh; the far green plays at 454 yards from the back tees and requires a shot over the marsh to the green for the second shot. Stately oaks line the right side of the fairway, and woods flank the left.

Amenities include practice greens, a driving range, rental clubs, a pro shop, bar, restaurant and beverage cart.

Tee times are accepted a year in advance. Fees range from $45 to $75, including cart. Walking is not allowed.

Kiawah Island
S.C. Hwy. 700, Kiawah
• (843) 768-2121, (800) 654-2924

Kiawah is a barrier island just south of Charleston—as the crow flies. By car, it's about a 45–minute drive that loops inland and reaches the island from the west. Kiawah's developers promote their property two ways: as a retirement community and as a world-class resort. The island works extremely well both ways. Very quietly, it's also becoming a corporate retreat.

Kiawah is pure coastal Lowcountry. Its dense maritime forest and dark marshes are perfect for both golf and relaxation. Its four golf courses are among the best in South Carolina.

Here are just a few of the awards, accolades and prized listings Kiawah and its various courses have received over the past few years.

Top 50 Golf Resorts in the World—*Condé Nast Traveler*

Top 100 Courses You Can Play—*Golf Magazine*

Top 100 Courses for Women—*Golf for Women*

100 Best Modern Courses & 40 Best Public Courses—*Golf & Travel*

50 Best Places to Play for Women—*Golf Digest*

Top 100 Places to Play—*Golf Digest*

Gold Tee Award—*Meetings & Conventions*

#1 Golf Course in South Carolina (The Ocean Course)—*Golf Digest*

#4 Resort Course in America (The Ocean Course)—*Golf Digest*

America's Top 100 Courses—*Golf Digest*

Top 50 Golf Resorts in the World—*Condé Nast Traveler*

Among Top 50 Must Play Courses—*Links Magazine*

Among 100 Best of Golf—*Links*

Best of America's Resort Courses—*The Golfer*

America's 100 Best Golf Shops (The Ocean Course)—*Golf World*

Host 1997 World Cup of Golf (The Ocean Course)

Top 50 Golf Resorts in the World—*Condé Nast Traveler*

#3 Place to Play in South Carolina (The Ocean Course)—*Golf Digest*

#9 Place to Play in South Carolina (Turtle Point)—*Golf Digest*

Ace Award (Top 50 U.S. Resorts for Golf & Meetings) – *Successful Meetings*

Among the "Best for Golf"—America's Greatest Resorts

You get the general idea; it's without question one of the top resorts in the United States. Here's a rundown of the courses at Kiawah.

Cougar Point
Championship Yardage: 6861
Slope: 134   **Par: 72**

Men's Yardage:	6523
Slope: 130	**Par: 71**
Other Yardage:	6090
Slope: 119	**Par: 72**
Other Yardage:	5604
Slope: 112	**Par: 72**
Ladies' Yardage:	4776
Slope: No rating	**Par: 72**

Gary Player's course opened in 1996 on the site of the former Marsh Point. It's completely new and is a wonderful addition to the Kiawah collection. Tifdwarf greens and bermudagrass fairways offer challenge to a scratch golfer and an enjoyable round to players of all levels.

Holes 4, 5 and 6 overlook the tidal marsh, and the stunning views of the Kiawah River are a real treat. The 18th is a strong finishing hole with a three-tiered green and water guarding the left side.

A halfway house greets you at No. 10. Club rentals are available and there's a fully stocked pro shop. Approximate greens fees range from $80 to $125, including cart, and should be booked through the resort where you will be staying. Walking is restricted. Private or group lessons are taught.

The Ocean Course
Tournament Yardage:	7371
Slope: 149	**Par: 72**
Championship Yardage:	6824
Slope: 141	**Par: 72**
Men's Yardage:	6244
Slope: 134	**Par: 72**
Ladies' Yardage:	5327
Slope: 133	**Par: 72**

Pete Dye designed this course in 1990, using tiftdwarf greens and bermudagrass fairways. The course, in classic links fashion, follows the Atlantic coastline on the eastern edge of the island.

Most of the awards we listed earlier in this entry are for the Ocean Course, Pete Dye's controversial track that earned instant fame when it hosted the 1991 Ryder Cup: "The War by the Shore." It's rare for such a young course to host such and important event, but that's just another testament to the quality of this design.

Perhaps the most important accolade the course has received is #1 in South Carolina from *Golf Digest*. That's an amazing honor when you consider all the outstanding golf courses in the Palmetto State. Everyone should play the Ocean Course at least once. It's probably the closest to Scottish links golf of just about any course in the Carolinas and this alone should justify the high greens fees—at least you don't have to pay to fly to Scotland, and the menu in the clubhouse won't include haggis or black pudding.

While most true links courses are "out-and-back," the Ocean Course is laid out in two distinct loops, both beginning at the clubhouse, both wedged between the atlantic and the island's interior marshland.

From the back, back tees, playing up to a whopping 7,371 yards, even the best professionals will find the course overwhelming. At least that was the case in the Ryder Cup and subsequently in 1996 and 1997 World Championships, when the likes of Nick Faldo said that the course would be impossible if the wind really blew.

And the wind is a big part of what makes Kiawah so challenging. With such an exposed site, the wind can really howl out here, and even on a relatively calm day, there's usually a one-club breeze that routinely freshens after lunch.

To add to the challenge, Dye crafted 18 absolutely superb golf holes out of literally nothing. Astonishingly, Dye finished the course in about a year, working furiously between Hurricane Hugo and the Ryder Cup deadline to complete this masterpiece.

Much has been softened since the Cup but the course, with its wildly undulating fairways and greens, deep bunkering and massive dunes, requires nothing less than your A-plus game. If you've played a Scottish links course, like a Western Gailes, a Troon or a Machrihanish, then you'll understand how close the Ocean Course comes to the real thing. And anyone who has played the real thing will understand the severe penalties a links course can exact for missing a fairway—and that there's little that's "fair," especially in the wind. In fact, if there's anything that's slightly easier about Kiawah than a links course, it's the relative paucity of blind shots. At the Ocean Course, most of the challenges are clearly visible—so long as you keep the ball in play.

On your first trip to the Island, do yourself a favor and play from the correct set of tees. And unless your last name is Woods and your first name is Tiger, that's not the tips.

But even if the golf isn't going well, the scenery is superb, with half the course offering full views of the beach and ocean.

The clubhouse offers a restaurant, bar, pro shop, locker rooms and plenty of golf balls. The elevated glass clubhouse overlooks the Atlantic Ocean and offers views of the golf course and practice facility. Make bookings through the resort for an all-inclusive package with every amenity. Approximate greens fees are at least $120, including cart. Fortunately, you can walk here—and you should. The course is flat, and walking will give you something closer to a true links experience.

Osprey Point

Championship Yardage:	6678
Slope: 124	Par: 72
Men's Yardage:	6015
Slope: 124	Par: 72
Ladies' Yardage:	5122
Slope: 120	Par: 72

Tom Fazio used four lakes to challenge you on 15 holes, and moguls will determine the route of your golf ball past marshes and lagoons, sometimes into forests of pines, palmettos, magnolias and oaks. This 18-hole bermudagrass course, opened in 1988, is wider and more forgiving than the other Kiawah courses. A lot of good golfers will tell you they enjoy Osprey Point more than the Ocean Course.

Strong holes include the 453-yard par 4 No. 9 and a pair of par 3s longer than 200 yards. Also, strategic short par 4s tempt the big hitters. A beautiful hole, but possibly intimidating to novices, is the 18th, which is a par 5 with Canvasback Pond stretching along its entire length.

The club has a restaurant, bar, lounge, locker rooms and fully stocked pro shop. The new clubhouse is a Colonial mansion with expansive porches and decks overlooking lagoons and fairways. Five huge chimneys and copper-accented slate roof distinguish the elevated building. Approximate greens fees are more than $110, including cart. Book tee times through the resort for the best prices. No walking is allowed. Inquire about private or group lessons.

Turtle Point

Championship Yardage:	6925
Slope: 132	Par: 72
Men's Yardage:	6497
Slope: 132	Par: 72
Other Yardage:	5986
Slope: 127	Par: 72
Ladies' Yardage:	5285
Slope: 122	Par: 72

Jack Nicklaus designed this 1981 tifdwarf grass course with a spectacular finishing hole. Two other holes along the Atlantic are also beautiful. Lagoons, oak-lined fairways, the ocean and the winds blowing off the Atlantic all contribute to the difficulty here. A keen eye and deft touch are required to master the gentle breaks of this course. Turtle Point makes most every list of top resort courses.

A snack shop is found in the clubhouse. Club

rentals are available in the fully stocked pro shop. Private or group lessons are offered. Approximate greens fees are more than $110, including cart, and can be booked through the resort as part of a fine package including many amenities. Walking is not allowed.

Oak Point Golf Club
4255 Bohicket Rd., Johns Island
• **(843) 768-7030**

Championship Yardage:	6759
Slope: 137	Par: 72
Men's Yardage:	6468
Slope: 132	Par: 72
Other Yardage:	5996
Slope: 126	Par: 72
Ladies' Yardage:	4671
Slope: 121	Par: 72

Clyde Johnston designed this 18-hole course with fairways and greens of bermudagrass. Wildlife is prevalent on this course. Oak Point is now part of the Kiawah Island family of golf courses.

Water comes into play on 16 of the 18 holes. The 3rd hole is an interesting 90-degree dogleg with an island green, measuring 367 yards from the back tees. The 11th is a good par 3 of 193 yards from the back tees with a narrow driving area flanked by water on the right and left; there's water just left of the green as well.

Rental clubs, pro shop, practice green and driving range round out the amenities package.

Cost is $55 year round, including cart. Walking is permitted after 2 PM.

Patriots Point Links
U.S. Hwy. 17 Bus., Mt. Pleasant
• **(843) 881-0042**

Championship Yardage:	6838
Slope: 118	Par: 72
Men's Yardage:	6274
Slope: 118	Par: 72
Ladies' Yardage:	5562
Slope: 115	Par: 72

An 18-hole public course of bermudagrass just across the Cooper River bridges from Charleston into Mt. Pleasant, Patriots Point was designed by Willard Byrd and opened in 1981. The views of the ocean are amazing, as are the panoramas of Shem Creek, James Island, Patriots Point and Sullivan's Island. The wind whistling in from Charleston Harbor is a factor on most shots here, and it adds multiple dimensions to the course.

The signature hole is the par 3 17th, 139 yards from the back tees, with the green stretching into the harbor itself. This is a real test for a par.

Amenities include a pro shop, rental clubs, a large driving range, grill and snack bar. Group or individual instruction is provided.

Patriots Point's rates vary seasonally and range from $35 on weekdays to $50 on weekends, including cart—all a great value. Walking is generally allowed except on weekends before noon.

Seabrook Island
1002 Landfall Way, Seabrook Island
• **(843) 768-1000**

This resort includes a medical center, boat docking and an equestrian center that will rent you a four-legged ride to the trail or the beach. Other resort amenities include clay tennis courts and an excellent beachfront with sailing and fishing arrangements. Babysitters are registered at Seabrook, and you can ask the front desk personnel for assistance with scheduling one.

But we're here to tell you about the golf. Golf packages arranged through the resort are recommended for great family vacations. These courses are only usually available to resort guests or island residents. Amenities include a clubhouse with a large pro shop and private instruction.

Walking is allowed on both courses during afternoons. Approximate greens fees are $60, and high-season rates elevate to $85, including carts.

Crooked Oaks

Championship Yardage:	6832
Slope: 126	Par: 72
Men's Yardage:	6387
Slope: 126	Par: 72
Ladies' Yardage:	5250
Slope: 119	Par: 72
Other Yardage:	6037
Slope: 121	Par: 72

Crooked Oaks is an 18-hole Robert Trent Jones Sr. course that opened in 1981. The bermudagrass course winds through the forest and the blackwater lagoons, and the greens are small. Crooked Oaks is a true Scottish-style layout in that the clubhouse is not at the turn—you play nine out and nine back, and restroom facilities are provided at the 9th hole. As you make the turn, you'll find No. 9, a 170-yard par 3 with a large bunker guarding the front left of the green. The 18th hole, a par 4 of 427 yards, requires that you carry a large body of water before reaching the fairway.

Ocean Winds

Championship Yardage:	6805
Slope: 130	Par: 72
Men's Yardage:	6395
Slope: 130	Par: 72

Other Yardage: 6027
Slope: 125 Par: 72
Ladies' Yardage: 5524
Slope: 127 Par: 72

Ocean Winds, opened in 1973, offers 18 holes designed by Willard Byrd. The bermudagrass greens are large, the layout is flat, and the breeze at this oceanside course is prevalent (hence its name). Only five holes on Ocean Winds do not have water in some form. The 3rd is a 516-yard straightaway par 5, and you must avoid the sand flanking the entire right side of the green. The 6th hole is another par 5, with water bordering the entire left side of the fairway, so play to the right. Also be aware of the bunker on the left side of the green.

Shadowmoss Plantation
20 Dunvegan Dr., Charleston
• **(843) 556-8251, (800) 338-4971**
Championship Yardage: 6701
Slope: 123 Par: 72
Men's Yardage: 6399
Slope: 116 Par: 72
Other Yardage: 6129
Slope: 112 Par: 72
Ladies' Yardage: 5169
Slope: 120 Par: 72

Russell Breeden designed this course with bermudagrass greens and fairways. It opened in 1970 and was extensively renovated in 1986 with the addition of several water hazards.

Beware of the par-5 8th hole, 533 yards from the back tees, with water lining both sides of the fairway and cutting across the path of your second shot. It's a dogleg right with bunkers surrounding the green. The two par 3s on the back are tough as well. Water hazards are primarily off to the side, and they don't come into play if your ball is anywhere near where it should be.

A pro shop, locker room, bar, snack bar, beverage cart, club rental, driving range and practice green make your golfing experience complete. Tennis courts and a swimming pool plus a meeting room are available for a business trip combined with your golf.

Approximate greens fees are $26 during the week, $33 on weekends; during the spring and fall seasons, fees increase to $30 and $35, including cart. Walking is allowed Monday through Friday only.

Wild Dunes
Isle of Palms
• **(843) 886-6000, (800) 845-8880**
Just a 20-minute drive east of Charleston on the northeastern tip of the Isle of Palms lies this dense resort that features two championship 18-hole courses designed by Tom Fazio. It's also a top-rated tennis resort, and the white, sandy beach runs for more than 2 miles. A fitness center, marina and 20 pools (no, that's not a typo) round out the resort amenities. The drive over the causeway to the isle—the new connector to which you will hear locals refer—is a prelude to the treats that await you on this tropical paradise. You can really feel the transition into modern-day resort mode as you drive onto the isle and leave behind any ideas of historical tours or city traffic. Villas and homes for vacation rental have views of the golf course, the ocean, woods or marsh.

The Harbor Course
Championship Yardage: 6446
Slope: 124 Par: 70
Men's Yardage: 5900
Slope: 117 Par: 70
Ladies' Yardage: 4774
Slope: 117 Par: 70

A target golf course, Harbor involves water or marsh on 17 holes and is peppered with heavy bunkering. Fazio claims this 1986 bermudagrass course is one of his favorites. There are 8 holes out and 10 in. Instead of a clubhouse at the finish, a halfway house is located in the middle of everything between the 4th and 5th holes as well as between the 12th and 13th. Bermudagrass greens and fairways are popular. The signature 17th is a 460-yard par 4 that traverses the marsh at Morgan Creek. Marshland and water are intertwined on this winding course.

As the yardage indicates, the course is shorter than some, but it's by no means easier. The numerous hazards mean you have to keep your ball straight.

Practice greens, club rental, a pro shop, bar, deli and pizzeria add to the pleasant atmosphere.

Rates range from $40 during off-season afternoons to $85 during spring and fall, including cart. Walking is restricted.

The Links Course
Championship Yardage: 6722
Slope: 131 Par: 72
Men's Yardage: 6131
Slope: 121 Par: 72
Other Yardage: 5280
Slope: 125 Par: 72
Ladies' Yardage: 4849
Slope: 121 Par: 72

This bermudagrass course opened in 1980 to critical acclaim. In fact, it's probably the course that launched the superstardom of Tom Fazio, now recognized as the country's top golf course architect. Fazio's career would probably have taken off anyway, such is the man's talent, but here's where he got hot.

Based on early photos of the course, the Links Course has changed quite dramatically. Wild Dunes was Hugo ground zero and the hurricane vacuumed away much of the dense maritime forest that surrounded portions of the course when it was built. Then developers lined many of the fairways with condominiums and, in the case of the 17th and 18th fairways, built somewhat obnoxious faux-downtown-Charleston homes that look completely out of place.

Despite the proximity of housing, the course is still one of the best in the Charleston area. The front nine begins with a friendly 501-yard par 5 that usually plays downwind and thus provides an early birdie opportunity. The rest of the front is mostly flat, the highlight being another par 5, the 5th, with its green set behind two prominent dunes.

After a rousing hot dog at the turn, the best and perhaps toughest stretch on the course begins with the 300-yard 10th, a short uphill par 4 with a turtleback fairway. Despite the lack of length here, par is a solid score. The 11th is a moderate length par 4 with a shallow and severely undulating green. The 12th is a superb par 3, about 180 yards downhill from a raised tee to a long green set in a hollow. The more muscular 13th, at well over 400 yards from the tips, requires an accurate drive to the righthand side of the fairway; from there, anything that misses the green may find waste bunkers.

The final three holes head towards the beach, with the final par 5 provides a birdie opportunity for anyone who manages to find the correct side of the most undulating green on the course.

With this and subsequent courses, Fazio established his reputation for building fun golf layouts that offer a wide variety of holes. If you're in the Charleston area, make sure you play this fine course.

There's a driving range and practice green plus a pro shop, locker room, club rental, full restaurant and bar.

Fees range from $60 to $120, including cart. Summer afternoons are the cheapest times to play—maybe hot but often with some ocean breeze. Walking is allowed.

Around Charleston...

Fun Things To Do

It's tremendously useful to stop at the **Charleston Visitor Reception & Transportation Center** at 375 Meeting Street, (843) 853-8000, when you first arrive in the area. You'll easily recognize the renovated train depot. You can park there and tour downtown without the headache of searching for elusive parking spaces. Also, you'll enjoy the video display and the quantity of free maps and brochures describing the spots you'll want to tour. Guided walking tours for the hearty, bus tours for the less adventurous, water tours by reservation or the famous carriage tours are our preference when we want someone to explain what it is we're seeing.

The architecture and the culture of the past two centuries are preserved and displayed in a magnitude in Charleston found in few other areas. Among the churches, house museums and formal gardens are stories of earthquakes, fires, hurricanes and wars. The center is open daily from 8:30 AM to 5:30 PM.

Charles Towne Landing, on S.C. 171 between I-26 and U.S. 17, is an unusual state park. It's an interpretation of the first English settlement in South Carolina, which took root on the plantation site in 1670. It was first established as a site for celebration of the state's tricentennial, then later converted to a state park. The exhibits, 17th-century garden herbs and the animals in natural habitat, will interest the whole family. The park is open year-round. You can enjoy 7 miles of pathways via guided tram tour. For more information, you may call (843) 556-4450.

The **Charleston Museum** at 360 Meeting Street is the oldest museum in America. It showcases the memorabilia of early Charlestonians and defines the social and natural history of the coastal region. The special Discover Me room will occupy your children for hours, as they can touch things as well as learn about toys and clothes from past children's lives. Call (843) 722-2996 for information about hours and prices.

The Battery is a seaside park where you can walk or drive among the cannons, statues and monuments telling of people and events of the American Revolution and the Civil War. Once a significant defense site for the city, it now plays host to laughing children, biking athletes, strolling retirees and blushing brides.

Other activities in the Charleston area worth including in planning a golf trip are the numerous festivals. Whether you love seafood, music, crafts or any combination, you will find a festival that shows it all. One of the best is the popular annual jazz festival, where young and old spend the day in the park sunning and schmoozing and soaking up the brass vibrations. The **Blues and Heritage Festival** usually runs for a week in March and includes a variety of music and venues.

One of the great parts of the Charleston experience still remains the beach activity on the neighboring islands, such as **Isle of Palms**, **Sullivan's Island** and **Johns Island**. Think about biking, walking, fishing, swimming or just relaxing with a book while watching the kids shovel sand over your feet.

If you really like nature, take a ferry to Bull Island and explore the **Cape Romain National Wildlife Refuge**. It's 20 miles north of Charleston and is a pristine wilderness of 64,000 acres home to dolphins, egrets, pelicans and herons including 250 species of birds. Call (843) 928-3411 for information on a day trip to these barrier islands.

Where to Eat

We've found an abundance of great restaurants throughout the Charleston and Mt. Pleasant areas, on both sides of Shem Creek, the port for the area's fishing fleet. Our picks are often in downtown Charleston because it's such a unique town.

We offer our recommendations based on the quality of food, of course, as well as on the service and all-around dining experience, but also for the downtown atmosphere itself. It's only a few miles from wherever you will golf or stay. You can put your vehicle into a parking garage since street parking spaces are hard to find. Then walk around and get a feel for the place—the cobblestone streets, the beautifully restored buildings, the market in the town's center.

Late-night dinners are fashionable, and jazzy dessert cafes or watering holes are open into the wee hours for the crowd that mingles college students with fun-loving golfers and Charleston professionals, not to mention an occasional film star who happens to be on location.

Unless otherwise noted, restaurants are in Charleston proper. Refer to our Preface for an explanation of the pricing code.

82 Queen
$$-$$$ • 82 Queen St., Charleston
• (843) 723-7591

Fine wines accompany elegant lunch, dinner and sometimes Sunday brunch of classic Lowcountry foods served in a historic building created from two townhouses wrapped around a garden courtyard. It's one of the locals' favorite spots for socializing. Cuisine includes veal, beef, fowl, lamb and fresh local seafood.

BJ's Broadstreet Cafe
$ • 17 Broad St., Charleston
• (843) 722-0559

Home of the BJ Burger, this cafe is inside the Music Farm across from the Visitor's Center downtown. BJ's is the place for a quick lunch on weekdays or a late night pizza treat. Check out the burgers or sandwiches from the barn or from the coop, or try chicken wings prepared with a special recipe and a choice of dips. Beers and juices are varied.

Bocci's Italian Restaurant
$-$$ • 158 Church St., Charleston
• (843) 720-2121

Some of the best crusty bread you will ever sample is made at Bocci's. Try to save room for a calzone or the pasta with special sauces, then for pastries galore. You would swear you were in Northern Italy if you didn't step out into the bustling historic downtown of Charleston after a lusty lunch or dinner experience here, all accompanied with suitable wines.

Chef & Clef Restaurant
$-$$$ • 102 N. Market, Charleston
• (843) 722-0732

This is a great place for a late Sunday morning champagne brunch or daily lunch while you listen to fine jazz. Dinner of a special Lowcountry gumbo, beef, pork or seafood is good also, or stop by for a jazzy flambé dessert after a dinner elsewhere and a downtown walk. The different floors for different music styles are interesting and always popular with every age group.

Hyman's Seafood Company
$-$$ • 215 Meeting St., Charleston
• (843) 723-6000

Fresh seafood at Hyman's includes extensive shellfish selections and 15 or more fish choices daily. The non-seafood lover will also find chicken, pasta, beef and deli sandwiches. It's a casual setting in an old warehouse, and Hyman's Half Shell is next door shucking our favorite stuff as fast as anyone can guzzle it with hot spicy sauce. It's a fun atmosphere, where crowds are often spilling out onto the sidewalk for lunch or dinner.

L'Attitude South
$$-$$$ • 130 Mill St., Mt. Pleasant
• (843) 884-5005

"A maverick waterfront kitchen," they call it, this almost-hidden restaurant overlooking Shem Creek. It offers happy hour and dinner daily and a Sunday brunch. Sunset and creek views are spectacular, and the food preparation and service match just fine. A starter to try is the inside-out yellow tomato sandwich with ciabatta bread and basil oil. You've never had this tomato sandwich at home. A typical Southern entree here is shrimp and andouille sausage over creamy grits with veal-stock gravy. Or try the five-spice duck breast with whipped sweet potatoes accompanied by chow-chow with tiny green bean and red onion salad. Cappuccino, espresso or cordials go great with Key lime pie to finish. We always look forward to a meal here.

Louis's Charleston Grill
$$$-$$$$ • 224 King St., Charleston
• (843) 577-4522

Nationally recognized as one of the country's best restaurants, Louis's provides a culinary experience beyond that of any ordinary dining room. You should choose this for one of your most special meals. Louis Osteen uses regional foods splashed with ingenious touches of Lowcountry tradition and prepared with his traditional French training. Choose a basic beef, seafood, chicken or veal dish, but don't expect it to be basic. Take some extra time, and maybe a few extra bucks, and you'll savor the evening you spend with Louis.

One-Eyed Parrot
$-$$ • 1130 Ocean Blvd., Isle of Palms
• (843) 886-4360

Reservations and stress are both unacceptable here. Go for the Caribbean-style seafood, tender steaks, island-style rum punch or piña coladas. Stay for the fun. Lunch starts at the beach level at The Banana Cabana where you can go barefoot and sit in the sun on a beautiful beach. You may enjoy the cheeseburger of paradise or the seafood burrito. For dinner upstairs, begin with

tapas (Spanish for "appetizer") such as fried artichoke hearts or conch fritters. Then try the parrot paella, a medley of shrimp, chicken, sausage with yellow rice, peas, pimentos and tomato rouille. Much food and fun is ready for you here after golf on the two beautiful neighboring Wild Dunes courses. You'll understand why it's called paradise.

Oyster Factory
$-$$ • 85 S. Market St., Charleston
• (843) 722-5877

This is a choice seafood restaurant where you are guaranteed to enjoy oysters raw or cooked any way you like plus complimentary fish chowder and crab dip with a dinner entree. Salads, sandwiches, steaks or prime rib also are good here. Lunch and dinner are served daily. It's often crowded, and you will notice that everyone's having fun along with the great food.

Saffron
$ • 333 E. Bay St., Charleston
• (843) 722-5588

We highly recommend the fresh homemade bread, such as Charleston sourdough, and some healthy and tasty dishes for breakfast, lunch or dinner any day. A great salad is the East-West kiwi salad that includes slivered chicken with hearts of palm, kiwi, mandarin orange and fresh pineapple on greens. Mediterranean specialties of roasted lamb or saffron chicken also are good and spicy. European pastries, croissants,

Who can concentrate on putting with such a dramatic background?

Photo: Hilton Head Island Chamber of Commerce

Danishes, muffins and other daily delights must go home with you on any trip here. For wholesale or retail goodies, check out the Saffron Bread Factory at 1001 Harborview Road on James Island, (843) 762-7636.

Shem Creek Bar & Grill
$$ • 508 Mill St., Mt. Pleasant
• (843) 884-8102

Dine indoors or outside in the gazebo overlooking the tidal waterway, or just order from Sloppy John's, Shem Creek's oyster bar, for fresh shucked oysters and clams on the half shell. For lunch, dinner or weekend brunch, the daily specialties are fresh seasonal offerings such as she-crab soup, seafood gumbo or cioppino (shrimp, oysters, scallops, fish, clams and mussels stewed with tomatoes, onions, bell peppers, garlic and wine over fettuccine). Shem grilled seafood is a specialty with Charleston red rice and fresh vegetables. If you've had your fill of seafood, try the grill thrill of filet mignon, ribeye steak or teriyaki chicken. The food and fun are great, and the view matches.

Southend Brewing Company
$$-$$$ • 161 E. Bay St., Charleston
• (843) 722-0722

The atmosphere is casual and friendly, set in a huge old warehouse where you can see several floors from your table or from the glass elevator. Food is good here, and golfers will feel at home for lunch, happy hour and dinner. Choose a fish special of the day or any variety of seafood, steak or chicken. You can hang around the huge bar area and find a lot of people having fun. Check on weekend evenings for live music. The original Southend is in Charlotte.

Sticky Fingers
$-$$ • 235 Meeting St., Charleston
• (843) 853-7427
U.S. 17 N., Mt. Pleasant
• (843) 856-9840
1200 N. Main St., Summerville
• (843) 875-7969

For ribs and barbecue to eat here, ordered to go, catered or delivered overnight from a mail-order catalog, Sticky Fingers can do it all. Included on the extensive menu are lunch salads and sandwiches or burgers with low-calorie or no-fat choices. We recommend a dinner special

of barbecue pork or half a rotisserie chicken. Side dishes of dirty rice or cinnamon apples round out any meal nicely. The kids menu is sure to please. Be sure to take home a catalog and think about the luxury of receiving these sticky delicacies via FedEx in any city.

TBonz Gill & Grill
$-$$ • 80 N. Market St., Charleston
• (843) 577-2511
166B U.S. 171, Charleston
• (843) 556-2478
Johnnie Dodds Blvd., Mt. Pleasant
• (843) 971-7777

All three locations serve lunch and dinner until late night in a friendly casual atmosphere. Steaks are a specialty, of course, but you may also choose fresh local seafood, Lowcountry dishes or grilled salads. The children's menu is a treat, and desserts from Kaminsky's, also located at the Mt. Pleasant and downtown restaurants, are the finest homemade creations you could ever imagine to go with specialty coffee drinks. Full service bars also are in each location.

The Trawler
$$ • Shem Creek, Mt. Pleasant
• (843) 884-2560

Open daily for lunch, dinner or raw bar, this famous restaurant with a view of the creek specializes in the steam pot crammed with every imaginable seafood or the famous fish stew and crab dip. A shellfish mixed grill or broiled sea scallops are among our favorites, too, or choose delicious beef or chicken anytime in the middle of the huge seafood menu.

INSIDERS' TIP
Good footing is important when hitting from a bunker. Twist your feet into the sand until you're in over the soles of your shoes to prevent slipping as you blast the ball out.

Vickery's
$-$$$ • 15 Beaufain St., Charleston
• (843) 577-5300

Many of the appetizers are large enough for an average eater's entree. Try something made with black beans and dirty rice, and go ahead and pour pepper gravy over your fries so you'll know you've been to the South for a meal. Lots of cayenne and Cuban flavored dishes are tempting. Save room for chocolate diplomattico or bourbon pecan pie for dessert. Micro, domestic, import and draft beers number more than you can name. If beer's not your thing, the wine list is varied, and the award-winning double martinis are famous. The original Vickery's plus two

Fripp Island Resort

Fripp is 19 miles east of Beaufort, and you won't stumble upon this wonderful island by accident. It's midway between Savannah and Charleston, north of Hilton Head Island, but not on the way to anywhere.

It's an ideal resort of 3,000 acres where you can enjoy a family trip, a business meeting or a golf vacation with a group of your peers. Call (843) 838-3535 or (800) 845-4100 for information on complete packages. For daily passes to play golf in the gated community if you wish to vacation elsewhere, call (800) 933-0050.

The 1995 Ocean Creek Golf Course and the origi- nal 1960 Ocean Point Golf Links are the first reasons to notice this resort. (Refer to our course descriptions in this chapter.) The courses are tucked on opposite ends of the island, with challenges and beauty com- mon to the seaside simplicity here. Nearby on Cat Island is South Carolina National Golf Club, which is also booked by the Fripp Company. In its first year,

Ocean Creek was recognized in the top-10 new courses by both *Golf Magazine* and *The Golfer*. It's a classic, minimalist approach to architecture employed by Davis Love III. George Cobb's design on Ocean Point was enhanced during the 1995-96 winter season, and its views of the Atlantic are more dramatic than ever from the elevated tee boxes.

More than 280 lodging choices include intimate one-bedroom villas and rambling beachfront homes, with daily, weekly or monthly rentals. Views may be ocean, marsh or golf course. Transportation on the island may be by rented golf cart during your entire stay if you choose.

Fripp's history began with the pirates. Johannes Fripp, a swashbuckling privateer, was granted the island in the 17th century by King Charles of England as a reward for defending the English settlement of nearby Beaufort. Develop- ment began in the 1960s; and in 1990, the Fripp Company brought its time and

Ocean Point Golf Links on Fripp Island offers panoramic views as well as challenging golf.

Photo: Fripp Island Resort

energy to the island along with $17 million in infrastructure, facility and amenity enhancement.

Beach bums looking for nothing more than a tropical paradise will find their happiness along more than 3 miles of beachfront. It's removed from any big-city noise and feels like the Caribbean. Summer temperatures average 90 degrees, and winter highs average 60. The ocean breezes always ripple over the island.

Families will find sports, nature, planned children's activities and gathering places highlighted by delicious food and leisurely shopping. Interpretive beach walks, kayak excursions and nature hikes may be planned. The Incredible Edibles outings are just one type of family program where participants learn how to catch, cook and eat blue crabs or other island delicacies.

The pool and recreation complex is an open invitation for kids, teens or adults to enjoy a water wonderland with an oval-shaped heated pool, a children's pool with alligator slide, a meandering lagoon pool with secret caves and waterfalls and a bubbling spa for relaxation. Croquet courts, a playground, basketball area, shuffleboard and bocce courts are included in the Beach Club. Ten tennis courts are open year round with two hard surface courts and eight soft fast-dry courts, plus free clinics offered by a USPTA professional to rate adults and suggest drills and instructional options.

Children will also be interested in Camp Fripp, a nature day camp offering exploration of the shore, marshes and forests with lessons in coastal ecology. Kid's Night Out is designed for children ages 3 to 12, and it's a series of theme parties including supper. Teen mixers lure the older kids with bonfires, volleyball and pool parties. Evening programs for families show native birds of prey and reptiles.

Island excursions from the deep water marina offer sunset, shelling, dolphin watching and other cruises tailored to special interests. You can book a private half- or full-day fishing excursion with a local licensed captain who knows where the fish are biting. Kayaks and skiffs can be rented by the hour.

Meeting facilities accommodate small retreats or groups up to 175. The resort can arrange cookouts, cocktail parties and receptions.

Fripp Island is one of the last undiscovered treasures of the South Carolina coast. You'll enjoy the ultimate golf trip here.

others are in Atlanta, so if it's good enough for both of these Southern cities, it's worth a try for lunch, dinner or Sunday brunch of good things like Cuban Benedict or a big ugly biscuit and sausage gravy. You'll see a college crowd mixed with professionals and golfers of all ages.

Where to Stay

Your best trip to Charleston will include someone special and a stay in one of the historic bed and breakfast homes downtown. Man or woman cannot live on golf alone, and a little history tinged with romance adds to any experience. When it's too dark to golf any longer, it's time to enjoy a winter fireplace in your bedroom or a summer sunset from the veranda (you know we spell and pronounce it "verandah" in the Lowcountry) while you turn the clock back several hundred years. We also rec-

ommend a few nice hotels and some basic places for a quick golf trip with no frills.

Please call for information or to book reservations before arriving. You will find many venues filled during the height of summer tourist season and during some festival or convention weekends. Unless otherwise noted, accommodations are in Charleston proper. Refer to our Preface for an explanation of the pricing code.

The Ashley Inn Bed & Breakfast
$$$ • 201 Ashley Ave., Charleston
• (843) 723-1848

This historic inn, c. 1832, is close to the Charleston Visitor Center from which you can easily bike, walk or take a horse-drawn carriage to tour the downtown or drive quickly to any number of golf courses or beaches. The lovely pink house is an architectural treasure. Sausage soufflé, creamy Southern grits casserole with zucchini and cheddar biscuits, and hazelnut peach syrup over crunchy (different!) French toast are breakfasts here you will long remember. Also, the piazza (side porch) setting overlooking the Charleston garden will be a treat during breakfast, afternoon tea or evening sherry. The six guest rooms and suites are furnished with antique four-poster, pencil post or canopied rice beds. All have private bath, air conditioning and cable television.

Charleston Place
$$$$$ • 130 Market St., Charleston
• (843) 722-4900, (800) 611-5545

In the heart of the historic district, this hotel with 440 rooms stands out for its elegance and newness in a city filled with otherwise restored antiquity. Splurge on the club floors where you receive personalized service fit for royalty. Louis's Charleston Grill, one of the most noted restaurants in America, is in this hotel, along with a complete health club, indoor-outdoor pool and world-class boutiques including Polo, Gucci and many other names you will recognize. The location is easily accessible from any golf course, and you will find the downtown attractions a nice diversion.

Hampton Inn-Riverview Hotel
$$-$$$ • 11 Ashley Pointe Dr., Charleston
• (843) 556-5200, (800) HAMPTON

This is a modern high-rise atypical of Charleston architecture but providing the Hampton Inn's standard quality in 177 rooms and continental breakfast along with a view of the Ashley River. Also, it's convenient to the popular California Dreaming Restaurant and not far from downtown for browsing or touring. more importantly, it's near the main routes to all of the golf courses to boot.

Historic Charleston Bed and Breakfast
$$-$$$$ • 60 Broad St., Charleston
• (843) 722-6606

This organization represents more than 60 properties, all of which are private homes with owners who share their area's stories along with extraordinary beds and homemade Southern breakfasts. They include spacious and elegant suites in historic homes aged at least a century or two. The bed and breakfast inns are furnished with antiques and often have piazzas overlooking their own private garden or courtyard or maybe a lake, the Ashley River or the Charleston Harbor. Ask for the size, location and price that suits you.

Holiday Inn
$$-$$$ • U.S. Hwy. 17, Mt. Pleasant
• (843) 884-6000, (800) 290-4004

Going above and beyond the clean and comfortable atmosphere at most Holiday Inns, this is an elegant property with 158 rooms, many overlooking the harbor, just minutes away from Charleston or the golf courses in Mt. Pleasant. A pool, fitness center and sauna are available, and you will appreciate the concierge level's service if you want to be treated accordingly.

Kiawah Island Resort
$$$$ • 12 Kiawah Beach Dr., Charleston
• (843) 768-2121, (800) 654-2924

The resort includes four golf courses, two tennis complexes, three pool complexes, the 150-room Kiawah Island Inn, four restaurants and lounges, shopping arcades and two meeting centers. Also, 350 villas and 22 private homes are for rent. The island is 21 miles from Charleston (though it's close to an hour's drive) and showcases 10 miles of wide beach. You may rent bicycles and catamarans to breeze around the 10,000-acre island.

Kamp Kiawah is a supervised program for children ages 3 to 11, and a teen program includes late-night movies, photo scavenger hunts, basketball and volleyball tournaments, dance contests, billiard tournaments and pizza parties. Families find sand sculpture contests, movies, Jeopardy games, bingo, ice cream socials and aqua aerobics planned. Staff biologists guide interpretive nature excursions. They include off-island tours by boat or tractors, marsh creek canoe excursions, birding walks, night beach walks and bike tours.

This resort choice is superb if you want to play courses by Player, Nicklaus, Dye and Fazio and include a family vacation.

Laurel Hill Plantation
$$-$$$ • 8913 U.S. Hwy. 17 N.,
McClellanville • (843) 887-3708

This country bed and breakfast inn is halfway between Charleston and Myrtle Beach, in a location ideal for reaching golf courses a few miles in either direction. Overlooking the marsh, islands, waterways and the Atlantic Ocean, the plantation house is a restored version of the 1850 historic home that was destroyed in the 1989 hurricane. Four charming guest rooms with private baths are furnished with simple traditional antiques. The hearty country breakfast will be a great start to a day of golf, and the serene fishing pond will be a place to return for recuperation from any stress the course may have inflicted upon you. You could also hide away here for a long vacation and never think of busy city life.

Seabrook Island Resort
$$$$-$$$$$ • 1002 Landfall Way, Seabrook • (843) 768-1000, (800) 845-2475

Ultimate golf, tennis, equestrian and senior citizen packages, along with villa rates, are among the choices you will have here among Seabrook's 160 units. If you're looking for a full family vacation with a multitude of activities along a sun-drenched Southern island, choose this resort 23 miles from Charleston, and you'll never want to leave.

Twenty-Seven State Street Bed & Breakfast
$$-$$$$ • 27 State St., Charleston • (843) 722-4243

This private residence was built in the early 1800s in the French quarter of the original walled city. The two carriage house suites are furnished with antiques and reproductions and include kitchenette and private bath along with a spacious combination bedroom and living room. A veranda brings sea breezes from the harbor two blocks away. Fresh fruit and flowers, a large country breakfast in your suite, newspaper, cable television, phone and bicycles are included amenities. Paul and Joye Craven welcome you to their charming modern accommodation with old-world flavor.

Wild Dunes Resort
$$$$ • Isle of Palms • (843) 886-2260, (800) 845-8880

Boating, tennis, swimming, biking, dining and entertainment add to the golf amenities of this resort. The island is 15 miles from Charleston and totally removed from the traffic and history. If you really want to play golf, and someone else in your party really doesn't, this resort is a perfect compromise, with more than 300 vacation villa rentals near all the recreational choices for a leisurely stay.

Golf Equipment

Discount shopping for your golf equipment and accessories is popular in Charleston. Good choices that also have unusually wide selections for women are **Charleston Golf Center**, 1663

Savannah Highway, Charleston, (843) 763-0800; **Pro Golf Discount**, 966 Houston Northcut, Mt. Pleasant, (843) 881-2255; and **Edwin Watts**, 2037 Sam R. Henberg Boulevard, Charleston, (843) 763-1995.

Golf Instruction

The best golf instruction will be found among the professionals at the top resorts. Call in advance to ask for an appointment. Other instruction is limited to **L.B.'s**, 6656 Dorchester Road, Charleston, (843) 552-1717; and **The Practice Tee**, 3251 U.S. Highway 17 N., Mt. Pleasant, (843) 884-1144.

Beaufort Courses

Country Club of Beaufort at Pleasant Point
8 Barnwell Dr., Beaufort • (843) 522-1605, (800) 869-1617

Championship Yardage:	**6506**
Slope: 118	**Par: 72**
Men's Yardage:	**6112**
Slope: 115	**Par: 72**
Ladies' Yardage:	**4880**
Slope: 120	**Par: 72**

Russell Breeden designed this 18-hole course in 1970. The private sea-island community is set among lakes, saltwater marshes and a deepwater river just a few miles from the historic city of Beaufort. Fairways and greens are bermudagrass. Nature is on display here with occasional young marsh deer bounding along and almost 100 acres of lakes and wide salt marsh adding to the beauty and difficulty of play. Five- to 15-foot elevations sometimes bring a big surprise between tee and green.

The signature hole is the 18th, a slight dogleg left with a lagoon on the right and oaks on the left—a beautiful and difficult par 4 that returns to the clubhouse. The 7th hole requires a carry over water on the right and offers a special challenge to a golfer who needs the roll. Some of the long par 4s are favorites for the long hitters, such as 10, where the drive should go straight and narrow followed by a creative approach shot that must avoid the sand traps and oak trees.

A driving range and a putting, chipping and

INSIDERS' TIP
Take your practice swings while others in your group are hitting, so when your sot comes you are ready to play.

sand practice area are available. You'll also find club rentals, a pro shop, bar and snack bar.

Walking is allowed. Rates begin at $30 for summer afternoon play, including cart.

Ocean Creek Golf Course
90 B Ocean Creek Blvd., Fripp Island
• **(843) 838-1576**

Championship Yardage:	651
Slope: 131	Par: 71
Men's Yardage:	6094
Slope: 125	Par: 71
Ladies' Yardage:	4884
Slope: 119	Par: 71
Other Yardage:	5649
Slope: 121	Par: 71

This fabulous 18-hole course, which opened in October 1995, was the first signature course design of Davis Love III. The rolling dunes and marshlands are on the southern tip of Fripp Island, just past the Ocean Point course. Encompassed within the course are the sites where scenes of the movies *Forrest Gump* and *Jungle Book* both were filmed. You won't recognize either, especially the 5th hole, where Forrest Gump's Vietnam scenes were shot. (The movies preceded the golf course.)

Greens are tifdwarf, and fairways are 419 bermudagrass. Wooden bridges and walkways connect the fairways, and five holes line the marsh. No. 1 is a par 5, a dogleg left of 495 yards where you play up to a small hill. From that point, you are about 175 yards to the pin on an undulating green, guarded on the front by a large trap. No. 3 is a 159-yard par 3 where you must shoot over a small creek, and its green is undulating and guarded by the obligatory traps on the left and right. The water will only come into play if you have a short slice. It's a beautiful hole with palm trees in the back, and all the fairways are bordered by a mixture of palms, pines and old oaks; bunkers are clean white sand.

No. 4 is another great hole. It's 260 yards, and you can expect a crosswind. No. 6 is considered the signature hole, a par 3 surrounded by natural vegetation and salt marsh.

The clubhouse is done in tropical colors of melon and green like a splash of summer sherbet flavored in the Caribbean and flung across the South Carolina landscape. Palm trees and hibiscus wrapped around the course lend it the vacation air.

INSIDERS' TIP

Look for a lost ball a maximum of three minutes per group per hole. The ball can be replaced, but the time you might hold up the entire field cannot.

Fripp Island is private, but tee times are available to resort guests far in advance. Don't be intimidated by the guard because you can visit the welcome center for a daily pass to the golf course.

A driving range, putting green and beverage cart are available. Walking is allowed.

Approximate greens fees with cart range from $45 to $50—a deal for a premier course.

Ocean Point Golf Links
250 Ocean Point Dr., Fripp Island
• **(843) 838-1521**

Championship Yardage:	6590
Slope: 129	Par: 72
Men's Yardage:	6060
Slope: 124	Par: 72
Ladies' Yardage:	4951
Slope: 113	Par: 72

The 18-hole George Cobb course was built in 1964. It was closed during the winter of 1996 for rebuilding and returned for the late 1996 and 1997 seasons in great shape. Mounding was added along with an emphasis on the views of the dunes along the Atlantic Ocean. It's a private course open to resort guests, and attractive golf packages are available for every season. (See our Close-up in this chapter about booking a family vacation on this resort.)

Greens are tifdwarf and fairways are 419 bermudagrass. The 18th, a 486-yard par 5, is the signature hole. It's right on the ocean, bordered by the Fripp Inlet. Typical of an oceanside hole, it's usually windy here. Another classic hole is the 9th, a 365-yard par 4 that also borders the beach; you can expect the ocean breeze to affect the flight of your golf ball. Tight fairways are sandwiched by generous water and woods. Many of the holes have ocean views so beautiful they are a potential distraction to the golfing, but your best judgment is required to succeed on this course.

A practice green, driving range, rental clubs, pro shop, bar, restaurant and beverage cart are available. Private and group lessons are offered by the director of golf, the head professional and first assistant or by the second assistant, at varying price ranges per lesson or for a package of six lessons. Video and playing lessons also are available. Call for information about custom fitting also.

Walking is allowed. Approximate greens

The Rhett House Inn in Beaufort offers fabulous accommodations and food.

Photo: Liz Mitchell

fees, including cart, range from $45 to $60. Ask about a summer afternoon delight—golf related.

On Fripp Island, tennis, boating, beach activities and fine dining are all within easy access, so you won't need to venture off the island unless you are easily bored by one of the world's most gorgeous exclusive golf resort experiences. You'll drive through Beaufort on the way here, and you'll notice additional dining and touring available for anytime before or after your island adventure.

Royal Pines
Golf & Country Club
139 Francis Marion Circle, Lady's Island, Beaufort • (843) 524-3635
Pines Course

Championship Yardage:	**6811**
Slope: 124	**Par: 72**
Men's Yardage:	**6430**
Slope: 119	**Par: 72**
Ladies' Yardage:	**5241**
Slope: 121	**Par: 72**

The 18-hole Pines Course, built in 1969, winds through tall pine trees mixed with moss-draped native trees. It is notable for its par 4 doglegs, and the layout stretches to near 6900 yards from the blue tees. The starting hole is the signature, a 90-degree dogleg left. While the Pines Course is one of the region's challenging layouts, it is not demanding, and players of all levels can enjoy their round. Walking is allowed. Approximate greens fees including

cart are $22 during afternoons and $25 during mornings.
Marsh Course

Championship Yardage:	**5929**
Slope: 104	**Par: 72**
Men's Yardage:	**5659**
Slope: 101	**Par: 72**
Ladies' Yardage:	**5192**
Slope: 107	**Par: 72**

The Marsh Course is noted for its beautiful old live oaks and Spanish moss. Numerous lagoons and ponds dot the course lending charm and some challenge to the idyllic natural setting. It's not a demanding layout, and the average golfer can score well on this fun course, which was built in 1955. No. 18 is a great finishing hole with a well-bunkered elevated green.

Both courses at Royal Pines were designed by Southern Turf Nurseries with bermudagrass fairways. The club requires advance tee times of 48 hours for both courses. Amenities include practice greens, driving range, pro shop, club rental, restaurant for lunch and dinner and a lounge. Walking is allowed. Approximate greens fees including cart are $30 afternoons and $35 mornings.

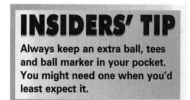

INSIDERS' TIP
Always keep an extra ball, tees and ball marker in your pocket. You might need one when you'd least expect it.

Around Beaufort...

Fun Things to Do

Beaufort is such a small place that you can really walk around and find almost anything you need and any choice of food, especially in the historic area, which includes the entire downtown. It's just minutes from I-95 and a short distance from Hilton Head Island, although you won't know what a pretty and peaceful place this is unless you make a special trip here and spend a few days and nights. It's also on the way to Fripp Island, but you'll surely miss the most charming part of the town and its views if you only pass through.

The city is centuries from any big city noise or clutter. We recommend visiting here on a sunny spring day when you have finished golfing nearby and have nothing else to do except relax on a veranda with a water view. House museums of the **Historic Beaufort Foundation** include the **Verdier house,** c. 1790, at 801 Bay Street, and the **George Parsons Elliott home** of 1844 located at 1004 Bay Street. Call (843) 524-6334 for information about tours on varying days of the week.

The Christmas season is an especially inviting time to enjoy candlelight or holiday events in the homes and area plantations. We also like it here in late September for **Bubba's Beaufort Shrimp Festival,** which includes marine exhibits, shrimp boats, music, family fun and unique cuisine.

Call the **Beaufort Chamber of Commerce** at (843) 524-3163 or visit it at 1006 Bay Street for other information and to book a guided walking tour or join a horse-and-carriage ride, which will afford an excellent view of the historic district. You may also call **Carolina Buggy Tours** at (843) 525-1300 for reservations or group tours in carriages drawn by the beautiful Belgian and Percheron draft horses. The architecture and the history in this lovely town are unmatched. Don't limit your visit to the historic area, as much other fine dining and accommodation options are available too.

The **Beaufort Museum** at 713 Craven Street, (843) 525-7077, provides a series of permanent and changing exhibits on the history and culture of the area. It's in the **Arsenal,** the oldest civic building in the Lowcountry, built in 1795 for the local militia. The **Parris Island Museum** is in the War Memorial Building on Parris Island just south of Beaufort. The displays here tell the story of Parris Island beginning with the French Huguenots in 1562, progressing to the Spanish and English colonists, then to the era when the Federal Navy built a yard and ending with the Marine Corps' establishment of a recruit depot. It's free and open daily. Call (843) 525-2951 for information.

Hunting Island State Park is a large secluded barrier island near historic Beaufort. The historic 19th-century lighthouse offers a stunning view of the coastline and the semitropical flora and fauna. Call (843) 838-2011 for information about park and interpretive center hours, nature programs and camping where 200 sites and 15 cabins are provided for the nature lover.

INSIDERS' TIP

When you're lining up a long putt and one of your partners is tending the pin, have him stand to the uphill side of the hole. That way, you can use his feet at targets as you try to drop the ball down into the cup.

Where to Eat

Refer to our Preface for an explanation of the pricing code.

The Bank Waterfront Grill & Bar
$$ • 926 Bay St., Beaufort
• (843) 522-8831

For fun, food and spirits, visit this historic waterfront landmark, which serves more than 70 menu items including fresh local seafood, steaks, burgers, pasta and huge specialty salads. The appetizer menu, or "beginning balance," presents an extensive list ranging from jalapeño peppers to oysters on the half shell to mozzarella cheese sticks. An unusual sandwich is the salmon BLT. "Junior investors" are welcome, too, for their own size menu items. Chef specialties include Beaufort crab cakes, lobster pasta and frogmore stew. Try the "luscious liquid assets" whether you eat or not. They are items like Kahlua, bananas and cream, any exotic flavor of colada or daiquiri or "lenders" lemonade (vodka, lemonade and Sprite). It's open every day for lunch and dinner, and the waterfront deck and upstairs bar are friendly spots for evening crowds to gather.

Blackstone's Groceries, Deli, Sundries
$ • 915 Bay St., Beaufort • (843) 524-4330

Breakfast or lunch tastes good at this deli in the middle of a grocery store of sorts in downtown Beaufort. Try the smoked salmon plate with goat cheese, capers, onion, lemons and French bread. Deli sandwiches of any meat and cheese are good on crunchy oat bread or croissant. Beer and wine are available. You'll have fun eating here for a quick meal.

Boundary Street Club House
$-$$ • 2317 Boundary St., Beaufort • (843) 522-2115

The mission of the Clubhouse is to help you "escape the distractions of everyday life and relax, unwind and enjoy the company." For lunch start with a Macho Nacho or the Ball Game, which is a combination of many appetizers such as potato skins, buffalo wings and barbecue ribs with a variety of sauces. If you can continue, the house-specialty prime rib is slow-roasted and may be chosen chargrilled with garlic in sizes up to a sportsman cut of a pound. Fajitas, seafood or smothered chicken also are good main courses. Sporting combinations are available for a taste of it all. Extra innings are great desserts, and sharing is common. Lunch and dinner are served daily.

Dockside Restaurant
$ • 11th St. W., Port Royal • (843) 524-7433

On Battery Creek, the views and atmosphere go great with the fresh local seafood and Lowcountry favorites. While waiting for your meal, overlooking the shrimp-boat docks, you might want to try the jalapeño-stuffed shrimp or sunset shrimp, sautéed in garlic butter with green peppers, onion, black olives, artichokes and tomatoes and served over linguine. A steamed seafood pot includes crab legs, shrimp, oysters and a half lobster at an incredible price. A non-seafood lover can appreciate the Southwest chicken or a pound-size charcoal-grilled New York strip sirloin.

Dukes Bar-B-Q
$ • 3166 Boundary St., Beaufort • (843) 524-1128

The buffet at Dukes includes 30 items with country style vegetables, various salads, barbecue pork and fried or barbecue chicken. It's open Thursday, Friday and Saturday for lunch or dinner. This is a place for family dining and for filling big eaters economically with good down-home-style cooking.

Firehouse Books & Espresso Bar
$ • 706 Craven St., Beaufort • (843) 422-2665

All day every day, this is a neat spot to enjoy a bookstore while sampling espresso, cappuccino, latte, juices or tea with sandwiches, baguettes, bagels or cheesecake. For a morning visit, light lunch, afternoon tea or just an any-

The magnificent 18th at Hilton Head features a huge fairway and poses a demanding second shot.

Photo: Hilton Head Island

time visit with a good golf book to read, it's a pleasant stop in the historic district.

The Gullah House Restaurant
$ • 859 Sea Island Pkwy.,
St. Helena Island • (843) 838-2402

Near Beaufort and convenient to Hilton Head golf courses, the Gullah House will teach you a language of the old days on St. Helena Island as well as fill you with delicious home-style meals and a serving of jazz and blues on Friday and Saturday nights. The West African people who originally lived on the island were isolated from the mainland to the point that they developed their own language, some of which is preserved today. For instance you might order Smutta Steak, which is a country-fried steak smothered with sliced potatoes, onions and gravy. Go for the breakfast buffet on Saturday and Sunday or lunch and dinner Tuesday through Sunday. Enjoy the folklore while you're there.

Ollie's Seafood Grille & Bar
$ • Lady's Island Marina, Beaufort
• (843) 525-6333

A good restaurant at the marina, Ollie's features local seafood with steamed shrimp and oysters as well as fresh-cut steaks. You can also enjoy she-crab soup or frogmore stew (a combination of shrimp, sausage, potatoes, corn on the cob, onions, celery and Ollie's own special seasoning), and we recommend the SunShine rice with any entree. Ollie's opens daily for lunch and dinner, and it's popular with the seafaring crowd that arrives by boat and with those who come for the view of the water.

Where to Stay

Refer to our Preface for an explanation of the pricing code.

Cuthbert House
$$$$ • 1203 Bay St., Beaufort
• (843) 521-1315, (800) 327-9275

The 10,500-square-foot house is listed on the National Register of Historic Places. Antiques and reproductions flavor the c. 1790 home, which John A. Cuthbert built for his bride four blocks away, then later moved in two sections to its present location.

Gary and Sharon Groves have lovingly refurbished their historic bed and breakfast inn, and they will welcome you with an afternoon glass of wine and tales of the home's past lives. Parlor suites with adjoining bedrooms are luxurious; two ground-level apartment suites include two bedrooms with a king or queen bed and two twin beds, casual furnishings, full kitchens and private entrances. All six suites have private baths and outstanding views of the Beaufort waterfront. One of the parlors features a marble mantelpiece with carved names and initials left by Civil War Union soldiers.

Gary's special homemade Southern breakfast varies daily from pancakes to eggs, probably some stone-ground grits brought in from Charleston, always with fresh fruit, coffee or tea and juice.

We highly recommend the Cuthbert House for a golf, corporate, romantic or combination getaway trip. All modern conveniences such as telephone, fax, television and e-mail are available during your stay here. Children older than 12 are welcome. No pets and no smoking indoors, please.

Rhett House Inn
$$$$-$$$$$ • 1009 Craven St., Beaufort
• (843) 524-9030

You'll feel at home in the relaxed but elegant atmosphere of this restored antebellum mansion a block from the Intracoastal Waterway and minutes from the historic downtown. Fresh flowers, luscious soft robes (you can buy one to take home) and English or American antiques add to the charm of 10 guest rooms individually decorated and containing queen, king or double beds, television, telephone and private bath. Three rooms also feature fireplaces, and several open onto a veranda, where the only smoking is allowed and where you may wile away an hour or two in the hammock.

Afternoon tea includes linzer tortes or homemade cookies on the veranda. Great coffee, homemade muffins and healthy Southern breakfasts of fruit and pancakes await you in the dining room in the morning, or you may choose a continental breakfast served in your room. You also may request a tray of tea or coffee in the garden or on the piazza (side porch) or a picnic lunch to take out.

The on-site restaurant, Caroline's on Craven, is open for dinner Tuesday through Sunday with reservations. Before or after dinner relax in the parlor and choose a book, cards, backgammon game or compact disk from the library to enjoy in your room.

Children older than 5 are welcome, but pets are not. Small receptions, weddings, meetings and retreats are appropriate here, as are golf outings. Golf, tennis, swimming and massages can be arranged.

Bay Street Inn
$$$-$$$$ • 601 Bay St., Beaufort
• (843) 522-0050

You'll recognize the waterfront antebellum mansion from the movie *The Prince of Tides*. It's on the Intracoastal Waterway in the heart of Beaufort's historic district. Eight rooms with private baths (seven with fireplaces) are filled with antiques and face the water. The library, living room and porches are inviting, and innkeepers Jeffrey and Leslee Peth will make you welcome. Formal gourmet breakfast is served in the dining room; evening fruit, chocolates and sherry top off the day. Bicycles are at your disposal for your tour of the lovely little town.

The Beaufort Inn
$$$$ • 809 Port Republic St., Beaufort
• (843) 521-9000

Built in 1907 by a prominent attorney and converted to a modern inn in 1930, the home has kept the history of local plantations to match the names of its 13 guest rooms while Debbie and Russell Fielden have expanded and restored the entire mansion. It's a block from the Intracoastal Waterway park in the center of the historic district. You will find the inn suitable for a luxury golf or family vacation and for a conference or a group luncheon or dinner meeting. All rooms have private baths, televisions and telephones plus individual thermostats; some have a Jacuzzi or wet bar.

Children older than 8 are welcome; pets are not. A full-service bar and extensive wine list are available. The formal dining room is open to the public as well as to inn guests for dinner and breakfast. Complimentary afternoon tea is served by reservation, and a full Southern gourmet breakfast is included with accommodations. Inquire about golf or other activity packages.

Fripp Island Resort
$$$$ • One Tarpon Blvd., Fripp Island
• (843) 838-3535, (800) 845-4100

Stay in an intimate villa, an oceanfront condo or an oceanfront home and enjoy the exclusive resort that has everything for you and your family for a vacation or business trip. Housing options include 300 villa and house choices. Ask for whatever size and style you like. Camp Fripp provides recreation, activities and natural adventures for children. You only need to take your family, maybe some sunscreen and insect repellent (well, okay, and maybe a few items thrown into a suitcase). You'll have such a good golf vacation that the children can be allowed to decide where to return every year.

Begin your stay with the two championship golf courses, enough to make your vacation perfect. Then add 10 tennis courts, a deepwater marina, year-round restaurants, seaside pools, fitness center and jogging and biking paths, and you've got a full-scale resort. No traffic jams, no noise, no stress, no neon signs, no pollution—shall we say more? Pat Conroy, the author of *The Prince of Tides* and *Beach Music*, lives and writes on this island. Hollywood filmmakers have found perfect settings of several varieties, and so will you.

TwoSuns Inn Bed & Breakfast
$$-$$$ • 1705 Bay St., Beaufort
• (843) 522-1122

This charming inn occupies a restored 1917 Neoclassic Revival-style grand home in a nationally landmarked historic district. The gracious resident owners are Carrol and Ron Kay. Five bayview queen or king guest rooms are complete with modern private baths and a casually elegant ambiance. Handcrafted window and bed ensembles, which Carrol sells, are unique to each room. Amenities include room phones, a parlor cable TV and VCR with video library and a self-serve guest refrigerator with snacks and soft drinks. Croquet and horseshoes are available on the front lawn. Van, carriage, walking, bicycle or boat tours of the historic downtown are convenient from here.

A full breakfast and daily afternoon tea and toddy hour are included. Each breakfast menu offers special entrees, fruit selection, juice and "lovin' from the oven," plus coffee from silver service and a wide tea selection. The inn is suitable for small meetings and special events.

Hilton Head Courses

Callawassie Island Club
176 Callawassie Rd. (S.C. Hwy. 6),
Callawassie Island
• (843) 521-1533

Dogwood/Palmetto Course

Championship Yardage:	6822
Slope: 130	**Par:** 72
Men's Yardage:	6426
Slope: 125	**Par:** 72
Ladies Yardage:	5166
Slope: 123	**Par:** 72
Other Yardage:	6053
Slope: 123	**Par:** 72

Magnolia/Dogwood Course

Championship Yardage:	6956
Slope: 138	**Par:** 72

Men's Yardage:	6514
Slope: 132	Par: 72
Ladies' Yardage:	5237
Slope: 126	Par: 72
Other Yardage:	6124
Slope: 129	Par: 72

Palmetto/Magnolia Course

Championship Yardage:	6956
Slope: 132	Par: 72
Men's Yardage:	6462
Slope 129	Par: 72
Ladies' Yardage:	5201
Slope: 120	Par: 72
Other Yardage:	6035
Slope: 124	Par: 72

The three nine-hole courses at Callawassie Island Club—to be played in tandem pairs to create an 18-hole round—were designed by Tom Fazio and built in 1986. Fazio says it's one of his best; of course, he likes all of his designs, as well he should.

Callawassie Island is an 880-acre sea island that sits among the marshlands between the Colleton and Chechessee rivers. A short drive from Charleston or Hilton Head and just past Beaufort, this island showcases a delightful piece of nature where birds and wildlife disregard your golfing and your round is relaxed and easygoing—but not necessarily easy.

INSIDERS' TIP

If you putt aggressively and roll a putt past the hole, watch your ball as it comes to a stop. Watching it will give you an idea of the line of your putt coming back.

The order of difficulty is Magnolia, Dogwood then Palmetto. The Dogwood is the newest, and its four finishing holes along the river lend dramatics to your game. Greens are tifdwarf, and fairways are bermudagrass. The signature hole at Callawassie is the par 4 No. 9 on the Magnolia Course, where your approach shot must clear a marsh and find an island green. The 4th hole on the Dogwood is tough—a 450-yard par 4 with a wetlands hazard on the right that narrows your driving area. On 15 of Callawassie's 27 holes, you will encounter marshland or ponds.

Practice greens, a driving range, pro shop, rental clubs, locker room, bar and restaurant are available.

Approximate greens fees range from $55 to $80, including cart. Walking is allowed for members only.

By the way, if you've never seen a black river, spend an extra few hours and paddle a kayak or canoe along some barely discovered water where you will find nature like nowhere else. It could be within sight of I-95, and you still can hear not a sound—save an occasional chirp or splash. If you should find Tulifinny Joe's Outpost in Ridgeland (we'll give you the number—(843) 726-5334—to help in the search), where the best kayaks and guides hang out, be sure to ask Leon, Judy or Em to tell you all about this location where the Waterway was born.

Country Club of Hilton Head
70 Skull Creek Dr., Hilton Head
• (843) 681-4653

Championship Yardage:	6919
Slope: 132	Par: 72
Men's Yardage:	6543
Slope: 128	Par: 72
Other Yardage:	6162
Slope: 124	Par: 72
Ladies Yardage:	5373
Slope: 123	Par: 72

Part of Hilton Head Plantation's complex, the 18-hole course was designed by Rees Jones and built in 1985. It features bermudagrass greens and fairways.

The 12th green lies on the Intracoastal Waterway, and others run near it as well as along freshwater ponds and marshlands. Several holes are long par 5s, two of them measuring more than 575 yards each. For instance, No. 18 is 579 yards uphill from the back tees. All in all, you will encounter 13 doglegs as well as water hazards on 14 holes. Elevation changes are constant, including some tees, landing areas and greens. And what about that punch-bowl–shaped green on the 6th?

A practice green, driving range, pro shop, beverage cart and club rental are available.

The greens fees, including cart, range from $60 to $80. Walking is not allowed.

Eagle's Pointe Golf Club
U.S. Hwy. 278, Hilton Head
• (843) 815-3100

Championship Yardage:	6855
Slope: No rating	Par: 71
Men's Yardage:	6580
Slope: No rating	Par: 71
Other Yardage:	6275
Slope: No rating	Par: 71
Ladies' Yardage:	5120
Slope: No rating	Par: 71

Marshes come into play on just about every Lowcountry course.

Photo: Kiawah Island Resort

This Davis Love III 18-hole course opened in 1998. It's a classical design created in the tradition of courses by Donald Ross, A.W. Tillinghast and Alister Mackenzie and reminiscent of Pinehurst No. 2 and Augusta National. It's noted for natural beauty, strategy, variety and superb conditioning throughout the 18 holes. Homesites border one side of seven holes. The course winds through stands of moss-draped live oaks and pines plus freshwater wetlands and lagoons. Spacious corridors and dramatic bunkering plus unique green sites and contoured putting surfaces will create an exciting venue. Generous fairways should allow for few forced carries and open fronts on many of its greens, so it accommodates golfers of all skill levels.

The course includes a driving range and practice putting range. The clubhouse, which opened in the spring of 1998, is a 6,500-square-foot Lowcountry design with pitched roofs, dormers and wide verandas. Inside, it includes locker rooms, a grill room and dining areas for large groups.

Approximate greens fees including cart range from $50 to $85. Walking is restricted.

Golden Bear Golf Course at Indigo Run
72 Colonial Dr., Hilton Head
• (843) 689-2200

Championship Yardage:	**7014**
Slope: 129	**Par: 72**
Men's Yardage:	**6643**
Slope: 125	**Par: 72**

Other Yardage:	6184
Slope: 119	Par: 72
Ladies' Yardage:	4974
Slope: 120	Par: 72

The chief architect for this Nicklaus design was Bruce Borland. Fairways and greens are bermudagrass. Lagoons and freshwater wetlands are sprinkled among oak, cypress and pine forests around the fairways and greens. Mounding and elevation are minimal.

One of the most challenging holes is 446-yard No. 11, a long dogleg left with water to the left of the green. The par 5 15th, a dogleg right of 512 yards, has a substantial landing area for your tee shot. As long as you pass the trees on the right side of the fairway, you should have a somewhat easy shot to the green.

Practice greens, a driving range, pro shop, rental clubs, a bar and grill and a beverage cart all add up to an enjoyable golf excursion.

The Ocean Course at Kiawah hosted the Ryder Cup soon after it was built.

Photo: Kiawah Island Resort

Approximate greens fees range from $55 to $73, including cart. Individuals can book tee times 30 days in advance; if you book through a golf package, that time increases to 120 days. Walking is not allowed.

Hilton Head National Golf Club
1100 U.S. Hwy. 278, Hilton Head
• (843) 842-5900, (888) 955-1234

Championship Yardage:	6779	
Slope: 132		Par: 72
Men's Yardage:	6260	
Slope: 125		Par: 72
Other Yardage:	5589	
Slope: 116		Par: 72
Ladies' Yardage:	4649	
Slope: 109		Par: 72

Gary Player designed this 18-hole course in 1989. Fairways and greens are bermudagrass, and the course is always in superb condition.

There is no residential development here, just marshland. The 9th is a tough hole due to its length, and you're almost always driving into the wind to an elevated green. Marshland lines the entire right side of the hole. The No. 17 signature hole is a par 3 with a fountain guarding the front. Other than the 17th, the narrow fairways and lack of marsh resemble a Northern course more than a typical Carolina layout.

A driving range, practice greens, pro shop, bar, restaurant and rental clubs are available.

Walking is not allowed. Approximate greens fees range from $45 to $90, including cart.

Island West Golf Club
U.S. Hwy. 278, Hilton Head
• (843) 689-6660

Championship Yardage:	6803	
Slope: 129		Par: 72
Men's Yardage:	6208	
Slope: 124		Par: 72
Ladies' Yardage:	4938	
Slope: 116		Par: 72

Fuzzy Zoeller designed this 18-hole course in 1992, and the architect was Clyde Johnston. The 150-acre coastal forest includes live oaks and tall pines around lush wetlands and richly colored bermudagrass greens and fairways.

The course caters to the novice as well as to the veteran and exudes Fuzzy's trademark sense of fun. The forward tees are well-placed for ladies or juniors; on 12 holes they are in front or to the side of the carry—over water or wetlands. Shooting from the back tees... well, you'll have the carry on those 12 holes to have the opportunity to test your skills. Island West's front nine starts with a par 5 that is not overly

difficult and ends with a unique large double green on No. 8 and a beautiful No. 9. The signature hole is the 17th, which also plays to the double green.

Practice greens, a driving range and beverage cart are available. The Southern-style clubhouse has a bar and grill and a pro shop.

Book your tee time up to one year in advance of your game. Approximate greens fees and cart range from $45 to $75. Walking is not allowed.

The Links at Stono Ferry
5365 Forest Oaks Dr., Hollywood
• (843) 763-1817

Championship Yardage:	6606	
Slope: 115		Par: 72
Men's Yardage:	6085	
Slope: 112		Par: 72
Other Yardage:	5710	
Slope: 111		Par: 72
Ladies' Yardage:	4928	
Slope: 119		Par: 72

Ron Garl designed this beautiful resort in 1989 as a Southern experience that can include a polo game after your round of great golf. It lies along the Intracoastal Waterway toward the mainland and has bermudagrass greens and fairways.

The signature hole is the 14th, a par 3 measuring 157 yards. The tee box is built out into the Intracoastal Waterway, and the carry is about 120 yards to the green over marsh and wetlands. Water is prevalent on the back nine and comes into play on five holes.

Practice greens, a driving range, pro shop, rental clubs, a bar and restaurant and a beverage cart are available.

The cost of a round is $30 on weekdays and $35 on weekends. The cart fee is $15. Walking is not allowed.

Old Carolina Golf Club
1 Buck Island Rd., Bluffton
• (843) 785-6363

Championship Yardage:	6805	
Slope: 142		Par: 72
Men's Yardage:	6445	
Slope: 133		Par: 72
Other Yardage:	6065	
Slope: 115		Par: 72
Ladies' Yardage:	4425	
Slope: 121		Par: 71

This new club opened in 1997, with a masterful bermudagrass sculpture by Clyde Johnston. It was built on the site of a thoroughbred horse farm and retains the oak-lined driveway and the original horse barn. It is a sister course to Old South (see write-up below) but showcases a quite different type of terrain with a series of high ground meadows. Johnston calls this a modern links-style course. Dramatic mounding combines with natural wetlands. The fairways are rolling, and hazards are numerous.

The signature holes are No. 9 and 18. Both are par 4s of 430 and 405 yards, respectively. Both carry the same lagoon off the tee to a landing area. No. 9 then has a slight dogleg right, and 18 a slight dogleg left. Rather than a double green, which was originally planned, several big oak trees were saved and now separate the greens. The back tee box is the same for both holes. One hits one way, and one the other, over the same big pond. Then both approach shots are into heavily guarded two-tier greens over another lagoon. Both tee shots could find a big bunker. If you play it right on 9, you need to stay right of the bunker; on 18 you need to stay left of the sand.

Walking is allowed any time of day. Approximate greens fees range from $50 to $85 including cart. A full service pro shop, driving range and beverage cart are available.

Old South Golf Links
50 Buckingham Plantation Dr., Bluffton
• (843) 785-5353

Championship Yardage:	6772	
Slope: 129		**Par: 72**
Men's Yardage:	6354	
Slope: 125		**Par: 72**
Other Yardage:	5779	
Slope: 119		**Par: 72**
Ladies' Yardage:	4776	
Slope: 123		**Par: 71**

This Clyde Johnston course includes 18 holes of bermudagrass greens and fairways, and it's open to the public year-round. It's easy to find on the mainland just before reaching Hilton Head Island.

Johnston's Old South is a tribute to a man working within nature's guidelines. You will experience natural amenities and fabulous views playing this course. Johnston said, "The variety of the setting, from oak forest to open pasture to tidal marsh, provides an opportunity to vary the design elements and strategy of play." This all adds up to marvelous variety. It's a popular and beautiful course featuring seven marsh-front holes and three spectacular island greens among live oaks scattered on rolling terrain. The clubhouse verandas overlook the large putting green and the lagoon, a reminder that you're in the Lowcountry, not in Scotland as the links might persuade you to believe.

The par 4 16th is the signature hole, with two carries over marsh. Lateral water hazards are characteristic. The 7th also requires two shots over water.

The course offers rental clubs, practice greens, a driving range, pro shop, bar, restaurant and beverage cart.

Walking is allowed any time of day. Cost ranges from $50 to $85, including cart.

Oyster Reef Golf Course
155 High Bluff Rd., Hilton Head
• (843) 681-7717

Championship Yardage:	7027	
Slope: 131		**Par: 72**
Men's Yardage:	6440	
Slope: 123		**Par: 72**
Other Yardage:	6071	
Slope: 118		**Par: 72**
Ladies' Yardage:	5288	
Slope: 118		**Par: 72**

Bermudagrass greens and fairways characterize the 18-hole Rees Jones course built in 1982—part of the Hilton Head Plantation complex.

Nine ponds and 66 bunkers contribute to the fairness of the nicely laid out course where every hole is challenging. Doglegs are surrounded by mounds and fairway bunkers. Exact approach shots are required to the large greens with well-defined tiers. The 6th is the signature hole. It overlooks Port Royal Sound, and beautiful oak trees surround the green. It's a par 3 of 192 yards from the tips.

A chipping green, practice green and driving range and club rentals are available. You can also enjoy a pro shop, bar, restaurant and beverage cart. The locker room is for members only. Rates range from $69 to $79, including cart and greens fee. Walking is not allowed.

Palmetto Dunes Golf Course
Palmetto Dunes Resort, 1 Trent Jones Ln., Hilton Head • (843) 785-1138

The three 18-hole courses provide an outstanding golf experience on Hilton Head. The oldest of the trio, the Robert Trent Jones course, involves a winding lagoon affecting 11 holes, and stray shots can easily find their way into one of the many fairway bunkers or lagoons. The Arthur Hills layout, heavily wooded with trademark elevation changes and rolling fairways provided by sand dunes, was overhauled and reopened in the fall of 1995. All greens were rebuilt, some tee areas expanded and the irrigation system reworked.

Unrestricted walking is allowed on all courses any time and any day. According to management, an increasing number of good players are asking to walk, keeping with golf tradition and reaping the fitness benefits. Approximate greens fees, including cart, begin at $40 and go to $80. Specials are available when booking through the resort.

Arthur Hills Course

Championship Yardage:	6651
Slope: 127	Par: 72
Men's Yardage:	6122
Slope: 120	Par: 72
Ladies' Yardage:	4999
Slope: 113	Par: 72

The par 4 12th hole has water running along an entire side from tee to green. The par 5 13th hole, 507 yards from the blue tees, is built for the long driver—your tee shot must carry over water. Your second shot entails a fairway wood, but you must be careful because both fairway and green are guarded by a lake bordering the right side.

George Fazio Course

Championship Yardage:	6534
Slope: 126	Par: 70
Men's Yardage:	6239
Slope: 123	Par: 70
Ladies' Yardage:	5273
Slope: 117	Par: 70

This is a straightforward course with water coming into play on only six holes, which makes it forgiving though not easy. Bunkering is dramatic, and fairways are rolling. The fairways are open on the front nine but are more severe on the back nine. The finishing hole has a large bunker right off the tee that must be carried with your tee shot, and your second shot must also carry a bunker to a short fairway leading up to the green. This course has only two par 5s and three par 3s. The series of long par 4s will test your ability.

Robert Trent Jones Course

Championship Yardage:	6710
Slope: 123	Par: 72
Men's Yardage:	6148
Slope: 119	Par: 72
Ladies' Yardage:	5425
Slope: 117	Par: 72

Fairways on this layout are extensively bunkered, landing areas are generous, and the water hazards are abundant en route to the large well-trapped greens. A winding lagoon system comes into play on 11 of 18 holes here. You go out from the clubhouse to the left of the water, make the turn and return on the right side. The fairways are open, and the greens are large. The majority of the holes on the back nine involve water; exceptions are the 10th, 11th, 16th and 18th. The

signature is the 10th, a par 5 that plays into an ocean breeze and a spectacular ocean view.

The course was named to *Golf for Women* magazine's first list of the top-100 most-women-friendly golf courses nationwide in 1995.

Palmetto Hall Plantation
108 Fort Howell Dr., Hilton Head
• (843) 689-4100

Palmetto Hall features two 18-hole layouts. The Arthur Hills course opened in 1991, the Robert Cupp course in 1993. Unrestricted walking is allowed on the Cupp course, a recent change that management is finding pleases many good golfers who respect the game's traditions. A luxurious 14,000 square-foot Lowcountry-style clubhouse complements the rich sense of history here. The new clubhouse features trophy cases and historic artifacts. Antiques and paintings add an elegant touch. A pro shop, men's and women's locker rooms and lounges are on the main level. The grill room is a typical gentlemen's club with English golf paintings. Upstairs a ballroom is divided into smaller banquet rooms for weddings or corporate parties.

Approximate greens fees, including cart, range from $35 to $74.50.

Arthur Hills Course

Championship Yardage:	6918
Slope: 132	Par: 72
Men's Yardage:	6582
Slope: 123	Par: 72
Other Yardage:	6257
Slope: 117	Par: 72
Ladies' Yardage:	4956
Slope: 119	Par: 72

This first course of the community was spread across the site of a former Civil War garrison. Oaks, pines, willow and lakes wrap the rolling curves of this course. Some greens are edged with bunkers, and water is involved in 12 of the 18 holes, providing a formidable challenge. The par 5, 490-yard 5th hole, for instance, has water up the entire right side of the fairway, so all shots must be placed to the left. Save some strength for the signature par 4, 434-yard 18th hole, which has water running all the way up the left side of the fairway.

Robert Cupp Course

Championship Yardage:	7079
Slope: 141	Par: 72
Men's Yardage:	6522
Slope: 126	Par: 72
Other Yardage:	6042
Slope: 120	Par: 72

Ladies' Yardage:	5220
Slope: 126	Par: 72

As with many courses along the South Carolina coast, this scenic course has a lot of water and sawgrass marshland, although these hazards may not always come into play. Dense forests of oak and pine also wrap around the course. It is somewhat original with straight lines and sharp angles evolving from Cupp's computerized design. The geometric shape includes square greens, angular bunkers and pyramid-shaped mounding. The 6th hole is a par 5, 542 yards from the back tees. It doglegs left. A good second shot will be played to the right because the green is bordered by a pond on the left and rear. The 12th hole is a beautiful 208-yard par 3 with sand guarding the left front and side of the green.

Port Royal Golf Club
10A Graslawn Ave.,
Hilton Head
• (843) 686-8801

The three 18-hole courses at Port Royal offer enough variety to keep you interested for three good rounds any time. All fairways and greens are covered with bermudagrass.

A pro shop, locker rooms, bar and restaurant, rental clubs, practice greens and driving range round out the resort's golf amenities.

Walking is allowed occasionally on all of these courses during the winter, but you should ask before making plans to walk. Fees range from $40 to $80, including cart and greens fees.

Barony Course

Championship Yardage:	6530
Slope: 124	Par: 72
Men's Yardage:	6038
Slope: 122	Par: 72
Ladies' Yardage:	5253
Slope: 115	Par: 72

The Barony Course was built in 1963 and designed by George Cobb. The 12th on the Barony is a good par 4 measuring 428 yards. Water flanks the right and left of the fairway. Most of the greens are small with numerous bunkers, some deep and wide, surrounding the greens. This course brings shot-making ability to the forefront and downplays long drives and iron shots.

Planters Row Course

Championship Yardage:	6520
Slope: 128	Par: 72

Men's Yardage:	6009
Slope: 126	Par: 72
Ladies' Yardage:	5126
Slope: 116	Par: 72

Planters Row was built in 1983 and designed by Willard Byrd. On Planters Row, the hole to fear is the 12th. It's narrow, measures 424 yards and requires a carry over water to the green. The course ends with a 480-yard par 5, with woods to the left and water to the right of the fairway. A good second shot will set up your pitch to the elevated green.

Robbers Row Course

Championship Yardage:	6711
Slope: 134	Par: 72
Men's Yardage:	6188
Slope: 129	Par: 72
Ladies' Yardage:	5299
Slope: 114	Par: 72

The Robbers Row Course was designed by George Cobb and Pete Dye and built in 1967. It was recently redesigned by Pete Dye, who added several water hazards. On Robbers Row take note of the 10th, a long, slight dogleg right that plays par 4 at 454 yards. Most greens are guarded by bunkers, thus requiring precise shot placement.

Rose Hill Country Club
One Clubhouse Dr., Bluffton
• (843) 842-3740

South-East

Championship Yardage:	6464
Slope: 124	Par: 72
Men's Yardage:	6030
Slope: 121	Par: 72
Ladies' Yardage:	5046
Slope: 119	Par: 72
Other Yardage:	5579
Slope: 118	Par: 72

East-West

Championship Yardage:	6808
Slope: 126	Par: 72
Men's Yardage:	6276
Slope: 121	Par: 72
Ladies' Yardage:	5103
Slope: 119	Par: 72
Other Yardage:	5640
Slope: 115	Par: 72

West-South

Championship Yardage:	6822
Slope: 127	Par: 72

INSIDERS' TIP

Because summers are so hot in the Carolinas, greenskeepers let the greens grow out a little to keep the grass from burning. Thus, you'll find that our greens are fastest in spring and fall.

Men's Yardage:	6300		
Slope: 124	Par: 72		
Ladies' Yardage:	5081		
Slope: 118	Par: 72		
Other Yardage:	5681		
Slope: 118	Par: 72		

The 27 holes at Rose Hill designed by Gene Hamm are set along rolling terrain bordered by tall pines, live oaks and magnolias. The course combinations offer many challenges for golfers of all levels. Although it doesn't come into play on every shot, water borders all but five holes. The West is the most-played course. No. 1 on the West is a dogleg over water and is sometimes considered the signature hole. One of the tough holes is No. 2 on the West Course. It's 401 yards with water all along the left side, then cutting into the middle of the fairway so you must clear the water on your second shot. It has bermudagrass fairways and greens. The East Course is more open than the West and South, and it is slightly shorter. The South Course fairways are tree lined, and greens are well bunkered.

No walking is allowed. Club rental, driving range, putting green, beverage cart and restaurant are provided. Approximate greens fees range from $50 to $65 including cart.

Sea Pines Resort
11 Lighthouse Ln., Hilton Head
• (843) 842-8484, (800) 925-4653

These three 18-hole courses are among the most popular on Hilton Head Island and offer preferred tee times and reduced rates to resort guests. Afternoon summer specials may offer you two courses for $130. That's a bargain. Afternoon summer specials at Harbour Town are $110. A more typical price is $170 or more, including cart. Enjoy a half-day school plus 18 holes of golf and cart on the Sea Marsh Course for $165. Eight hours of beginner golf instruction are also available for $200.

Harbour Town Golf Links

Championship Yardage:	6919	
Slope: 136	Par: 71	
Men's Yardage:	6119	
Slope: 126	Par: 71	
Ladies' Yardage:	5019	
Slope: 117	Par: 71	

You've seen this course on TV. It's one of the most popular courses on the PGA Tour and is home to the MCI Heritage Classic, played each year the week after the Masters.

The course is tight off the tee and most of the greens are small and heavily bunkered: it's a shorter, shotmakers course and a great example of early Pete Dye work. The most famous hole on the course is the 450-yard par 4 18th, which plays to a wide fairway with the famous lighthouse in clear view. It sounds like an intimidating hole, but for the pros, it's just a drive and a 6- or 7-iron. Must be nice.

Play this course from the forward tees if you're not a PGA touring professional and be prepared to use your three wood off the tee a lot.

Ocean Course

Championship Yardage:	6614	
Slope: 125	Par: 72	
Men's Yardage:	6213	
Slope: 119	Par: 72	
Ladies' Yardage:	5284	
Slope: 111	Par: 72	

The Ocean Course—the island's first course, and now among its newest—was designed by George Cobb in 1962 and remodeled by PGA veteran Mark McCumber in 1995. Multiple tees accommodate all skill levels, and the restructuring preserved traditional beauty while modernizing the layout. Various hazard placements add to the excitement, and the fabulous ocean vistas, especially on the dramatic beachfront 15th, are tough to beat.

Sea Marsh Course

Championship Yardage:	6515	
Slope: 120	Par: 72	
Men's Yardage:	6129	
Slope: 117	Par: 72	
Ladies' Yardage:	5054	
Slope: 123	Par: 72	

The Sea Marsh Course was designed by George Cobb in 1964 and remodeled in 1990 by Clyde Johnston. The Sea Marsh's varied layout often crosses lagoons or marshes. Fairways are wide, and oaks, pines and palmettos surround them. Medium-size greens are bunkered and slope from back to front, requiring exact approach shots. Distance shots are sometimes required, although the course is not lengthy.

Shipyard Golf Club
45 Shipyard Dr., Hilton Head
• (843) 689-5600

Three nine-hole layouts at Shipyard include the Brigantine, Clipper and Galleon courses. Fairways and greens are bermudagrass. Oaks, pines, magnolias, lagoons and ponds populate these courses and demand driving accuracy and putting delicacy. Water comes into play on 25 of the 27 holes.

Amenities include a practice putting and chipping green and a driving range. A pro shop, locker room, bar and restaurant, beverage cart

A poorly hit shot on a Lowcountry course more often than not finds a watery grave.

Photo: Kiawah Island Resort

and club rental are all on-site. The course also offers memberships.

Summer rates begin at $40 for late afternoon specials and increase to $90 during the spring season, including greens fees and cart. Walking is allowed after 5 PM during the summer, which means it's not really allowed.

Galleon Course

Championship Yardage:	3364
Slope: No rating	Par: 36
Men's Yardage:	3035
Slope: No rating	Par: 36
Ladies' Yardage:	2658
Slope: No rating	Par: 36

The Galleon is a George Cobb design. A nice par 3 is No. 5—179 yards and fronted by two bunkers that may come into play if your shot falls short.

Fairways are defined by trees; they are of medium width and allow enough space to work the ball. The Galleon's second hole is its signature, a dogleg left, par 5, with a bunker to the left that can be carried by a long hitter. Then you have a chance to go for the elevated green, which has water in front and bunkers to left, front, right and rear. The uphill shot cannot be short or it falls back into the water.

Clipper Course

Championship Yardage:	3466
Slope: No rating	Par: 36
Men's Yardage:	3132
Slope: No rating	Par: 36
Ladies' Yardage:	2733
Slope: No rating	Par: 36

The only hole on this George Cobb design that doesn't involve water is the par 4 427-yard 6th.

This was the original back nine for the Galleon when the course began as an 18-hole layout. One of the Clipper's spectacular holes is the 9th, which doglegs left, has bunkers to the right of the fairway and one on the left corner that is difficult to carry. From there in, the hole is well bunkered. The green is somewhat elevated and has bunkers 100 yards out and to the green. Shots that miss the green will be in these bunkers.

Brigantine Course

Championship Yardage:	3352
Slope: No rating	Par: 36
Men's Yardage:	2959
Slope: No rating	Par: 36
Ladies' Yardage:	2457
Slope: No rating	Par: 36

Tree lines also define the fairways here. The 5th hole, a par 3, measures 180 yards from the back tee. A bunker circles the left back portion and around two-thirds of the green. It's a slight downhill shot with water from the tee to the green. A good carry is required.

Watch out for the 6th hole on this Willard Byrd design, a long par 4 with bunkers by the landing area and water on the left. Likewise, beware No. 9, a par 5, 523 yards, with water running down the complete side of the fairway.

Private homes and rental condominiums surround this course but blend with the pines and don't distract from the golfing experience.

Around Hilton Head...

Fun Things To Do

Golf is indisputably the most important of the things you can do on Hilton Head Island. Tennis is especially significant too. Fishing, parasailing, skiing, horseback riding, miniature golf and, of course, dolphin watching and beach walking are also worthy of some vacation time. Shopping includes some unique boutiques and some good outlet malls, enough nice choices for the discriminating. Don't expect the neon resort atmosphere of Myrtle Beach, with a zillion things to do, or a college town with prolific nightlife like Charleston or Wilmington, North Carolina. Go for the sunsets and the sophisticated lifestyle of a privileged few. Just expect a memorable experience, and you've got it.

The **Family Circle Magazine Cup** features top women tennis players annually during late March or early April. Call (843) 785-9602 for information. The **MCI Heritage Classic** features top golfers during the third week of April annually. Check out the **Hilton Head Celebrity Golf Tournament** every Labor Day weekend. For information on both golf events call (843) 671-2448. For general information, contact the **Hilton Head Island Convention & Visitors Bureau,** (843) 785-3673.

Where To Eat

Shrimp, oysters, crab and fish top the menu of local specialties. They're fresh today, and you can count on hushpuppies and red rice to accompany the meal in many seafood restaurants. More than 200 restaurants on the island provide enough variety of international cuisine or basics to please any appetite. You'll also find some really fine wine lists in the classy restaurants. Here's a good start for sampling imported recipes or Lowcountry cooking in the resort atmosphere. Refer to our Preface for an explanation of the pricing code.

Alexander's Restaurant
$$-$$$ • 76 Queens Folly Rd., Hilton Head • (843) 785-4999

This restaurant is conveniently located in the heart of Palmetto Dunes and within walking distance of Shelter Cove, the Hyatt and Hilton Resorts. Enjoy delicious specialties in the cozy dining room, wine bar or enclosed porch overlooking a picturesque lagoon. Appetizers include Oysters Madagascar, which is fresh Cockenoe oysters topped with smoked salmon, caviar and seasoned sour cream, or Seafood St. Jacques, which consists of scallops, shrimp and crabmeat baked in a delicate cheese sauce. Then you may choose a salad such as hearts of palm, mushroom and artichoke hearts á la Greque. Then try an entree such as fresh pecan-crusted mahi mahi served with mixed fruit chutney, black beans and toasted coconut. Or maybe you would prefer wiener schnitzel with scampi, an Austrian classic with a Lowcounty twist: breaded and pan-sautéed veal topped with sautéed shrimp and capers. Alexander's offers more than 100 wines to complement your meal. Go for a very fine dinner.

Aunt Chiladas Easy Street Cafe
$$ • 69 Pope Ave., Hilton Head • (843) 785-7700

Choose Mexican, Italian, seafood, steaks or just about anything else you can think of, and it's probably here in quantities for the whole family for lunch or dinner. Don't go with us if you don't want to be embarrassed during the all-you-can-eat crab-leg feast, which can be quite lengthy, but, oh, so delicious. The owner's Italian mother makes great entrees from the homeland, and steaks are outstanding, even though the restaurant claims a Mexican theme.

Brian's
$$-$$$ • 1301 Main Street Village, Hilton Head • (843) 681-6001

Begin with an appetizer of lump crab and artichoke dip with parmesan cheese, garlic, white wine, cream and toasted pita or beef tenderloin carpaccio. Then for an entrée, choose from fine quality fish, steak, veal, lamb, or other splendid dishes. Also, the chefs are happy to do special items with 24 to 48 hours' notice. Brian's is open for dinner nightly.

Cafe at Wexford
$$ • Village at Wexford, U.S. Hwy. 278, Hilton Head • (843) 686-5969

A great choice for French cuisine, this cafe offers hot appetizers of escargot, traditional French onion soup in a crock with croutons and Swiss cheese or a slice of boneless duck stuffed with spinach, veal and cheese with bing cherry sauce. Paté or smoked Maine salmon are delicious cold appetizers. Entrees include sweetbreads sautéed in cream sauce with mushrooms and julienne strips of ham or crepes stuffed with chicken and mushrooms in a cream sauce with cheese. Daily specials are offered, and dinners are served with bread, salad, potatoes and vegetables.

Crazy Crab
$$ • U.S. Hwy. 278, Hilton Head • (843) 681-5021
$$ • Harbour Town • (843) 363-2722

Crazy Crab's two locations are well known by islanders and golfers alike, and everyone will send you there for lunch or dinner. The crab is the most obvious choice, and steamed seafood pots are usually a favorite. They have almost everything in them and require serious appetites. Dress is casual, and fun is a definite.

Damon's
$-$$ • The Village at Wexford, U.S. Hwy. 278, Hilton Head • (843) 686-6909

Barbecued ribs and prime rib are specialties here. The famous loaf of onion rings is such a tasty huge appetizer that you will miss your dinner if you don't share it with several people. Open for lunch or dinner, Damon's also serves one of our favorite barbecue sandwiches of pulled pork (that means it's not chopped). Homemade rye bread is good, and you will never leave here hungry.

Harbourmaster's Waterfront
$$$-$$$$ • Shelter Cove Harbour, U.S. Hwy. 278, Hilton Head • (843) 785-3030

Fine dining in a dressy and elegant restaurant is a treat here. Linen napkins and proper service are an indulgence for special occasions. The rack of lamb is tender and mouth-watering, and the beef and fish are also good. Dinner is the only meal served, and you should definintely call for reservations.

The Kingfisher
$$ • Shelter Cove Harbour, U.S. Hwy. 278, Hilton Head • (843) 785-4442

At the water's edge, this is one of our favorite Hilton Head restaurants (serving evening meals only), and it offers a view in a bustling center of activity. Happy hour is fun in the harbour lounge or waterside deck, and shrimp, oysters and crab legs are great deals. Entrees are fabulous, including daily selections that can be grilled, blackened, Greek (sautéed with onions, artichoke hearts, black olives, garlic, sherry, lemon and feta cheese), herb encrusted or crab Dijon. Beef and poultry also are broiled or grilled to perfection. Reservations are accepted except for Tuesdays when fireworks displays create huge crowds and parking congestion.

La Pola's
$-$$ • Shelter Cove Harbour, U.S. Hwy. 278, Hilton Head • (843) 842-6400

Upstairs in a cozy indoor restaurant or on the porch, this choice Italian restaurant is the neighbor to The Kingfisher. Frozen drinks, beer and wine are varied. The view is spectacular and the food tantalizing. Artichoke fritters or fried calamari make great appetizers. Italian favorite entrees are good, and the specialties include culinary Olympic winners such as veal and artichoke hearts or chicken Chesapeake. Only dinner is served, and you will need to arrive early on Tuesdays for a parking space to watch the fireworks display over the water. Except for Tuesdays, reservations are accepted.

The Nantucket Seafood House
$$ • 26 New Orleans Rd., Hilton Head • (843) 686-6339

Open for dinner daily, the menu and the dialect are exactly as you would expect in a Nantucket restaurant. Everything includes an "h" whether it's spelled that way or not. You might begin with an "appetizah" of stuffed quahogs, which are "lahge clams baked with homemade stuffing." Then try the "grilled Edgahtown sahdfish" or the Ipswich fried clams flown directly into this kitchen. If you want to stay land-side, you will enjoy the 12-ounce aged "chahgrilled center cut N.Y. strip." Vegetable, potato, house salad and fresh bread accompany any entree.

Old Oyster Factory
$$-$$$ • 101 Marshland Rd., Hilton Head • (843) 681-6040

Seafood of a wide variety is the specialty at the site of the island's original oyster cannery, a landmark experience and location. The atmosphere is casual overlooking the water. Old Oyster Factory is open for happy hour and dinner.

Scott's Fish Market
$$ • Harbourside I, Shelter Cove, Hilton Head • (843) 785-7575

During deck weather you can enjoy the patio on the waterfront for creative fresh seafood,

pasta, beef, pork or chicken. You'll find a full dinner menu, a great kid's menu and Hurricane Harry's Wharf Bar with a bar menu for every size appetite. Hurricane Harry's also features live evening entertainment. Go for happy hour or dinner.

Tony Roma's
$-$$ • 840 William Hilton Pkwy., Hilton Head • (843) 842- 4825

Famous in many states for its ribs and sauces, Tony Roma's won't disappoint the pork or beef lover. Choose from Blue Ridge smokies, Carolina honeys, bountiful beef or red hots. Soups, salads, appetizers, burgers, chicken or sandwiches also are good, but we go for the ribs or maybe a shrimp and rib combo. Side dishes include a good variety, with especially tasty beans and slaw. Go for dinner; Tony Roma's does not serve lunch.

Where to Stay

Resorts are the best choices for Hilton Head visits, as you'll find the top golf courses are easily booked through the resort. Also you will enjoy the luxury and the amenities, not to mention superbly prepared food. The beaches in Hilton Head are usually private, unlike those in much of the Myrtle Beach area; therefore, the premium beach access, as well as the best golf course access, usually comes through the top-quality resorts. Rates are seasonal and vary depending on your choice of location and view of the harbor, marsh, fairway or beach. For Hilton Head Central Reservations call (843) 785-9050 or (800) 845-7018. Refer to our Preface for an explanation of the pricing code.

Accommodations & Golf Hotline
$$-$$$ • 111A Marriott Center, Office Park Rd., Hilton Head • (843) 686-6662, (800) 444-4772

This full-service rental company rents condos, homes and villas of one- to four-bedroom size throughout the island area and specializes in golf packages. Most of the packages include a round of golf for four people once a day for seven days. Cart fee is additional. The condos hold the golf crown award given to the top five percent of the world's condos from Resort Condominium International. Call for a brochure with all the details.

Crowne Plaza Resort
$$$$ • 130 Shipyard Dr., Hilton Head • (843) 842-2400, (800) 334-1881

At Shipyard Plantation Golf Course, this resort includes 340 rooms and suites, miles of beach, a complete fitness center, indoor and outdoor pools, the Van der Meer Racquet Club, two dining rooms, a lounge and a camp for kids. You also have coffee and tea in-room and any luxury you could want.

Disney's Hilton Head Island Resort
$$$-$$$$ • Shelter Cove Harbour,
U.S. Hwy. 278, Hilton Head
• (843) 341-4100, (800) 859-8644

Nestled among live oaks on a 15-acre private island within Shelter Cover Harbour are 123 vacation villas where you may choose a studio or one-, two- or three-bedroom villa. Disney's Beach House is on the Atlantic Ocean with pool, snack bar, arcade, living room and games. Also here is Ben & Stretch's workout room, the Big Strike arcade, the Broad Creek Mercantile and a community hall with games and video library. The resort includes two pools, fishing pier with gazebo, shopping and dining within walking distance. Golf and tennis are available in several nearby areas. Relax here and find your own magic.

Fairfield Inn
$$ • SP9 Marina Side Dr., Hilton Head
• (843) 842-4800, (800) TEE OFF4

Affordable lodging at this Fairfield Inn includes 14 two-room suites, and golf packages are available on any of 20 courses. Rates include cart. Complimentary continental breakfast is included for all guests. Amenities include an outdoor heated pool. Marriott hospitality meets affordable lodging here, and the convenience to golf courses is superior.

Key Realty at Fiddler's Cove Beach & Racquet Club
$$-$$$ • 45 Folly Field Rd., Hilton Head
• (843) 842-5618, (800) 321-1611

This affordable and convenient resort offers free tennis on 10 clay courts and free indoor racquetball. Golf packages for a foursome are a good value here. Some of the villas provide views of the lush fairways of the Port Royal Plantation golf course. Situated on the resort's 23 acres are comfortable two-bedroom villas, each with private balcony, a queen and two twin beds, two baths, living and dining rooms, fully equipped kitchen, color television, wet bar and washer/dryer. Also, you may enjoy two pools with heated spa and sundeck plus a tot lot for the little ones. It's a short walk to a wide stretch of beach and a short drive to shops and restaurants.

Hampton Inn
$$$ • 1 Airport Rd., Hilton Head
• (843) 681-7900, (800) 426-7866

Hampton Inns the world over are dependable if you're looking for a comfortable place that is not an expensive luxury resort. Ask for a king or two double beds. Continental breakfast is quick to grab on the way to an early tee time. An outdoor pool and exercise room are offered. Refrigerators are in suites. Babysitting services may be booked.

Hilton Head Vacation Rentals
$$-$$$ • The Plaza at Shelter Cove,
Hilton Head • (843) 732-7671

More than 125 villas, condos and rental homes are managed by this company. Any size family can be accommodated with small or multi-bedroom homes and every amenity. As part of your rental package, the staff will arrange your tee time on any of the public or semiprivate courses.

Hyatt Regency Hilton Head
$$$$$ • 1 Hyatt Cir., Hilton Head
• (843) 785-1234, (800) 233-1234

The Hyatt has more than 500 rooms and provides a traditional quality accommodation. You can't go wrong here within the Palmetto Dunes complex. The hotel features a health club with massage, whirlpool and sauna, indoor and outdoor Olympic pools and a children's wading pool. Bikes and scooters are available; tennis and racquetball courts are also here. Dining, dancing and live entertainment are part of the experience. Five golf courses will keep you swinging, and others on the island and mainland are minutes away.

Oceanfront Rentals
$$-$$$ • 11 New Orleans Rd., Hilton Head
• (843) 785-8161, (800) 845-6132

This company manages about 175 properties that include your choice of luxurious or budget-type vacation rentals in all areas of Hilton Head. Golf packages can be arranged when you rent a villa or home of any size—from one to eight bedrooms. Some properties are on the ocean; others are on golf courses. Advance tee times are guaranteed on more than 30 area courses; free tennis, group rates and free accompanying non-golfer accommodations are offered.

Palmetto Dunes Resort
$$$$$ • 4 Queens Folly Rd., Hilton Head
• (843) 785-1161, (800) 845-6130

Access to five fabulous golf courses is the

best reason for choosing to stay at Palmetto Dunes. Villas or vacation homes of one to six bedrooms are oceanside, on the harbor or on the fairway. You will enjoy the location and your family will appreciate the boating, 3 miles of beachcombing, pools or tennis on 19 clay, four Supergrasse and two hard courts including eight lighted for night play. The 2,000 ocean-front acres of this sophisticated resort and residential community are adjacent to Shelter Cove Harbour, a Mediterranean-style village with retail stores and restaurants fronting a deepwater marina. Meeting and conference facilities also are superb.

Port Royal Village
$$$ • Port Royal Village, Hilton Head
• (843) 681-9325, (800) 673-9385

Near the 54 holes of Port Royal Golf Club, this collection of vacation villas and townhouse rentals is near the beach as well; it also has a top-rated tennis complex. It has a pool and offers an hour a day at the racquet club. Tennis courts are of all three surfaces. The resort will package golf for you at several nearby courses in addition to the Port Royal Golf Club.

Vacations on Hilton Head
$$-$$$ • The Plaza at Shelter Cove,
Hilton Head
• (843) 686-3500, (800) BEACH ME

A central reservation service claiming to be the largest one on the island, this company will arrange accommodations including a golf package in any price range requested. Discount greens fees and guaranteed tee times can be arranged on any public or semiprivate course, and a variety of accommodations is available with or without other amenities.

Westin Resort & Villas
$$$$$ • Port Royal Plantation, Hilton Head
• (843) 681-4000, (800) 228-3000

More than 400 rooms in a luxurious facility stretching along the beach, spacious meeting rooms, cafe, restaurant and bar, tennis, pools and, of course, championship croquet and golf are all around you. This top-quality resort offers easy Southern charm and some of the best-prepared food you will ever find in a hotel setting.

Golf Equipment

Player's Golf in the Shoppes on the Parkway sells equipment, apparel and accessories; call (843) 785-GOLF. **Nevada Bob's** is another large discount shop on the William Hilton Parkway, with better variety than the one in Myrtle Beach; call (843) 686-GOLF. Also, **Las Vegas Discount Golf**, Buckingham Plantation Drive, (843) 837-3399, is a new superstore that carries golf and tennis equipment.

Golf Instruction

One of the best places to study is where you can also play. **The Golf Academy of Hilton Head Island** helps you learn then helps you receive a discount on greens fees at Port Royal and Shipyard. A full-day program includes four hours of instruction with video analysis, then lunch and 18 holes of golf. The half-day includes a three-hour lesson with video analysis. Special programs are designed for women and juniors, and a mini program will analyze and correct flaws in your swing. Call (843) 785-4540 or (800) 925-0467.

Private instruction is available at many of the other fine resorts, including a variety of quality programs at Sea Pines where you can also study during the morning and play on the Sea Marsh Course during the afternoon. Call (843) 842-1454 for information on a full-day, half-day, beginner or short clinic.

For information on **Marlene Floyd Golf Schools for Women**, call (800) 637-2694. She teaches 12 schools each year at Palmetto Dunes. The two-day sessions allow only 10 or 12 students and specialize in classroom and practice techniques for women only.

South Carolina's
Midlands

Extending from the flatlands of the coastal plain to the rolling and borderline-bucolic farmland west of Columbia, the Midlands of South Carolina represent the heartland of the Palmetto State. Just don't say that to anyone in the Upstate or on the coast.

Columbia, the state's capital, is a city that's tough to love. Primarily a government town buttressed by state politics and a significant army base—Fort Jackson—Columbia boasts all the ambiance of a strip shopping center. In the summer, it's also a city to avoid: The volcanic heat is simply deadly. If it's 90 in Charlotte, just 100 miles to the north, then it's 105 in Columbia. Why? Who knows?

Thankfully, there's a lot of superb golf in the Columbia region. Some of the soil to the east of the city is sandy and presents perfect, almost Pinehurst-like terrain for the golf course architect. Columbia has worked hard to promote its golf packages in an effort to lure touring golfers who usually visit Myrtle Beach and the coast. Still, it's tough to imagine anyone visiting Columbia for a holiday.

And if you should run into a person wearing a baseball hat that says "Go Cocks!" don't panic. They're not employed in the pornography industry, they're supporters of the University of South Carolina Gamecocks, whose stadium in downtown Columbia seats almost 90,000 die-hard Cocks' fans.

South of Columbia is Aiken, a retirement and horse-breeding town dripping with old-South charm. Visit there in July and you'll be dripping as well, but join the legions of golfers who winter here and you'll find some outstanding courses best savored in the cooler spring and fall months. Aiken is just a few miles from Augusta and becomes especially popular during Masters week.

West of Columbia lies the undulating farmland and dense forests of the Greenwood and Abbeville regions. Paper, light industry and agriculture are the mainstays of the local economies.

East of Columbia, in the Pee Dee region, the land flattens. Towns like Sumter, Orangeburg and Bamburg offer sporty courses, many of which attract Canadians and Michiganers looking for good tracks while theirs are used for cross country skiing. Walk into a hotel bar in the Pee Dee in February and the TV will often be showing ice hockey.

While we can't realistically describe South Carolina's Midlands as a "Golf Mecca," good courses can be found—just don't visit them in the summer.

Columbia-area Golf Courses

Charwood—The Country Club of Pineridge
4082 Bachman Rd., West Columbia
• (803) 755-2000

No one seems to know who designed Charwood—The Country Club of Pineridge. Too bad, because we'd like to credit whomever produced these three distinctly pleasing and pleasingly distinct nine-hole courses just west of the state capital. Greens and fairways are all seeded with bermudagrass. The rerouting and revision of some holes is now complete. Note the particularly interesting nuggets of sagac-

South Carolina's Midlands

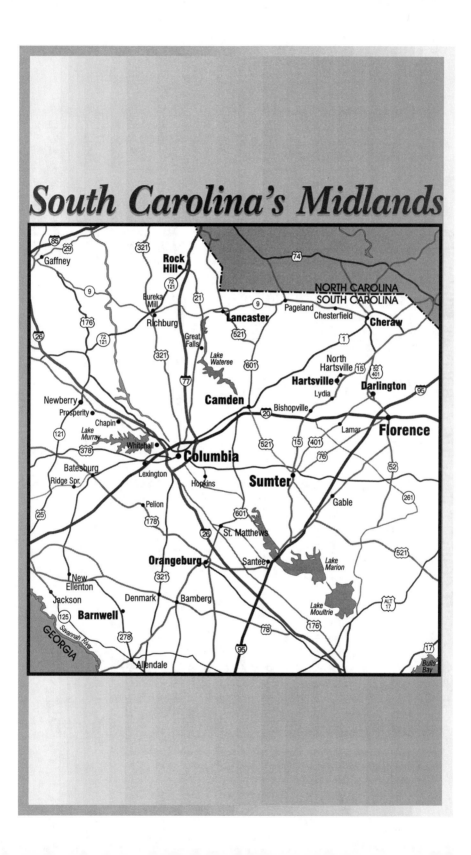

GOLF COURSES IN SOUTH CAROLINA'S MIDLANDS

Course	Type	# Holes	Par	Slope	Yards	Walking	Booking	Cost w/Cart
Allendale County Golf Course	public	9	36	n/r	3789	anytime	anytime	$15
Beech Creek Golf Club	semiprivate	18	72	116	6397	restricted	anytime	$20-27
Bishopville Country Club	semiprivate	18	72	n/r	6448	anytime	anytime	$15-22
Bogeyville Golf Course	semiprivate	18	72	100	5514	anytime	anytime	$14-18
Calhoun Country Club	semiprivate	18	72	n/r	5954	restricted	anytime	$20-25
Cedar Creek Golf Club	semiprivate	18	72	119	6689	restricted	anytime	$30-38
Charwood								
Charwood Course	semiprivate	9	36	n/r	2898	anytime	anytime	$24-29
Ridgewood Course	semiprivate	9	36	n/r	3157	anytime	anytime	$24-29
Pinewood Course	semiprivate	9	36	n/r	3416	anytime	anytime	$24-29
Cheraw State Park	public	18	72	120	6129	anytime	anytime	$30-35
Chester Golf Club	public	18	72	n/r	6273	restricted	5 days	$26-33
Coldstream Golf Club	semiprivate	18	71	118	5733	restricted	10 days	$25-30
Cooper's Creek	semiprivate	18	72	115	6039	anytime	7 days	$30-35
Crystal Lakes Golf Course	public	9	36	110	2935	anytime	anytime	$6-14
Fox Creek	semiprivate	18	72	118	6493	restricted	anytime	$25-29
Golden Hills Golf and Cc C.	semiprivate	18	71	119	6011	anytime	2 days	$35-40
Governor's Run	public	18	72	121	6211	anytime	anytime	$18-23
Green River Country Club	semiprivate	18	72	n/r	6257	restricted	anytime	$20-29
Highland Park Country Club	semiprivate	18	71	n/r	6100	anytime	anytime	$14
Hillcrest	public	18	72	114	6104	anytime	anytime	$23-25
Houndslake Resort	private/resort							
Azalea		9	36	114	3009	restricted	anytime	$35-40
Dogwood		9	36	116	2994	restricted	anytime	

Laurel		9	36	117	3047	restricted	anytime	
Indian River	public	18	71	n/r	6052	restricted	anytime	$32-40
Lake Marion Golf Course	public/resort	18	72	113	6223	no	anytime	$40
Lakewood Links	semiprivate	18	72	116	6027	no	24 hours	$25-30
Lancaster Golf Club	public	18	72	n/r	6140	restricted	3 days	$33-36
LinRick	public	18	73	120	6293	anytime	2 days	$19-21
Mid-Carolina Club	semiprivate	18	72	116	6368	anytime	1 day	$30-33
Midland Valley Country Club	semiprivate	18	72	118	6182	anytime	anytime	$30-35
Northwoods	semiprivate	18	72	118	6485	restricted	7 days	$35-39
Oak Hills Golf and Country Club	public	18	72	117	6449	restricted	anytime	$35-40
Paw Paw Country Club	semiprivate	18	72	117	6649	anytime	anytime	$25-27
Persimmon Hill	public	18	72	117	6449	weekdays	anytime	$30-33
Pineview	semiprivate	18	72	116	6346	restricted	anytime	$26-33
Pocalla Springs	semiprivate	18	71	n/r	5882	anytime	anytime	$20
Sandy Pointe	public	18	72	116	6045	anytime	anytime	$25-29
Santee National	semiprivate	18	72	114	6125	restricted	anytime	$40
Sweetwater Country Club	semiprivate	18	71	n/r	5830	anytime	7 days	$21-28
Timberlake Plantation	semiprivate	18	72	124	6226	anytime	7 days	$33-40
The Traces Golf Club	semiprivate	18	72	117	6449	restricted	anytime	$30-35
White Pines	public	18	72	111	5848	restricted	10 days	$27-35
White Plains Country Club	semiprivate	18	72	n/r	5874	restricted	3 days	$28-33

ity and advice included on the score card for each hole.

Amenities include a practice green, practice range, pro shop, bar, snack bar and rental clubs. You can walk these courses and book a round anytime. Approximate cost for 18 holes, including cart, is $24 weekdays, $29 weekends. The three nines are detailed below.

Charwood Course

Back Yardage:	2898
Slope: No rating	**Par: 36**
Middle Yardage:	2777
Slope: No rating	**Par: 36**
Ladies' Yardage:	2306
Slope: No rating	**Par: 36**

The Charwood Course, also known as the White Course, boasts tight fairways, so accuracy is key off the tee. This nine-hole track is relatively short and poses no major problems until you get to the sloped, slick greens.

Ridgewood Course

Championship Yardage:	3157
Slope: No rating	**Par: 36**
Men's Yardage:	2945
Slope: No rating	**Par: 36**
Ladies' Yardage:	2478
Slope: No rating	**Par: 36**

The Ridgewood Course, or Blue Course, is slightly more open than the Charwood Course. The fairways are flatter and wider. The ball must carry bunkers to reach the built-up greens, which are predominantly flat. If the rough has been allowed to grow up around the greens, getting up and down will not be easy.

Pinewood Course

Back Yardage:	3416
Slope: No rating	**Par: 36**
Middle Yardage:	3074
Slope: No rating	**Par: 36**
Ladies' Yardage:	2580
Slope: No rating	**Par: 37**

The Pinewood Course (a.k.a. Rose Course) is the most interesting and modern of the trio at Charwood. Needless to say, because the course is a typical modern design, there are mounds. This nine offers the most variety and challenge, including big elevation changes and some fun driving holes. The fairways are tight in places, and the holes are relatively longer than on the counterpart courses.

Coldstream Golf Club

Lake Murray Blvd., Irmo • (803) 781-0114

Championship Yardage:	6155
Slope: 122	**Par: 71**
Men's Yardage:	5733
Slope: 118	**Par: 71**
Ladies' Yardage:	5047
Slope: No rating	**Par: 71**

Coldstream, a Michael Mungo design just northwest of Columbia, opened in 1975. Bermudagrass covers the fairways and greens. Some holes are flat, some feature elevation changes. The course is part of a residential development near the shores of Lake Murray.

At Coldstream, we found narrow fairways, plenty of variety, a couple of spectacular holes and, for the most part, small greens. Miss the green here and you might be in trouble: Your ball will roll into deep rough or bounce almost anywhere. Still, the relatively straightforward layout makes for a fun round if you're playing at a relaxed pace. If your approach shots are accurate, you'll score well. Most golfers will enjoy the final hole on the front nine—a 196-yard par 3, which requires a downhill shot through a chute to a green backed by a row of hedges.

Amenities include a practice green, pro shop, bar, snack bar, occasional beverage cart and rental clubs.

Walking is allowed primarily on weekdays. Approximate cost, including cart, is $25 weekdays, $30 weekends.

Cooper's Creek Golf Club

Country Rd., Pelion • (803) 894-3666

Championship Yardage:	6582
Slope: 120	**Par: 72**
Men's Yardage:	6039
Slope: 115	**Par: 72**
Ladies' Yardage:	4565
Slope: 99	**Par: 73**

Cooper's Creek opened in 1973 about 15 miles south of Columbia. Red Chase designed the course. Bermudagrass covers the greens and fairways, and most of the track is set in wooded terrain with some significant elevation changes.

Cooper's Creek offers tremendous variety in a pleasant country atmosphere. Each hole boasts a character all its own. Some fairways are wide, others are narrow. Some holes are flat, others may remind you of a roller-coaster ride. The greens differ in size, shape and undulation. We found that the course is not overly penal, although really awful shots will likely yield really awful numbers. One of the most difficult holes might be the 3rd, a 177-yard par 3 with a nasty bunker right in front of a small and unreceptive green.

Make sure you bring your brain to this course: Cooper's Creek is a thinking-player's track. Concentrate, take what the course gives you, and you'll have lots of fun. Seeing as the course is quite close to Interstate 20 on the way to Augusta, Cooper's Creek would be a fun stop on the way to The Masters in April.

Amenities include a putting green, practice range, chipping green, locker room, snack bar and rental clubs.

If you're fit, the course is walkable, and you can walk anytime. You can book up to seven days in advance. Approximate cost, including cart, is $30 on weekdays, $35 on weekends.

Golden Hills Golf and Country Club
100 Scotland Dr., Lexington
• (803) 957-3355

Championship Yardage:	6461
Slope: 126	Par: 71
Men's Yardage:	6011
Slope: 119	Par: 71
Other Yardage:	5575
Slope: 115	Par: 71
Ladies' Yardage:	4957
Slope: 113	Par: 71

Golden Hills, a Ron Garl design, opened in 1987. Bermudagrass covers the fairways and greens, and most of the holes are set in woodland bordered by a residential development. The course combines undulating and flat terrain, and water hazards come into play on several holes.

Golden Hills used to be an ersatz links course, with tall, ball-eating rough bordering many of the fairways. The members apparently changed all that: What used to be rough is now fairway or light rough. But you'll still find plenty of tight holes, particularly on the back nine. Resist the temptation to swing the driver too much. In many instances, Golden Hills forces you to play target golf—the big stick simply might get you into big trouble.

As you drive up to the clubhouse, you come face to face with the terrifying 10th hole—a 361-yard par 4 requiring a 200- to 215-yard tee shot to a narrow downhill landing area fronted by a large pond. Once you've lobbed an accurate long iron down the fairway, you have to smack the ball about 140 yards over water to a thin green. You should feel very pleased to score par on this wild hole.

The course boasts interesting variety; no two holes are the same. If you're up for a challenge that will test your brain as much as your swing, play Golden Hills. And as one member told us, "The course will give you all you want from the tips."

Amenities include a practice green, pro shop, locker room, restaurant, pro shop, bar and rental clubs. The practice range is open to members only.

You can walk anytime, but it's a tough round on foot. There's a lot of member play here, so make sure you call ahead. Approximate cost, including cart, is $35 weekdays, $40 weekends.

Indian River
200 Congaree Hunt Dr., West Columbia
• (803) 955-0080

Championship Yardage:	6507
Slope: No rating	Par: 71
Men's Yardage:	6052
Slope: No rating	Par: 71
Other Yardage:	5586
Slope: No rating	Par: 71
Ladies' Yardage:	4643
Slope: No rating	Par: 71

Indian River, a Lynn Young-designed course, opened in 1992. Bermudagrass covers the well-maintained greens and fairways. The course is undulating on the front nine and somewhat flatter on the back. The holes are bordered by pine forest, wetlands or both, and water comes into play on several holes.

Indian River boasts a links-style design in a serene and peaceful wooded environment. The mix works well: Indian River is one of the more popular public tracks in the Columbia area. A modern course, you'll find mounds off the tees, wide and rolling fairways, decent variety and some fine views. And for a modern course (typically replete with tricks and trappings), Indian River is fair. We found little trouble off the tee but plenty of challenge around the sizable greens—some of the most undulating in the entire Midlands area. Pat yourself on the back for reaching the green in regulation, but realize that getting down in two once you're on the green will likely produce massive beads of perspiration on your sun-drenched forehead. It's important to look at pin placement and find the best spot for a two-putt. The front nine ends with a stunning par 3—184 yards downhill to a small and, you guessed it, extremely undulating green.

Amenities include a practice green, practice range, pro shop and snack bar.

You can walk the course anytime on the weekdays and after 2 PM on weekends, although

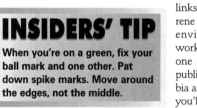

INSIDERS' TIP

When you're on a green, fix your ball mark and one other. Pat down spike marks. Move around the edges, not the middle.

it's not a particularly easy trek. Approximate cost, including cart, is $32 weekdays, $40 weekends.

LinRick Golf Course
356 Campground Rd., Columbia
• (803) 754-6331

Championship Yardage:	6959
Slope: 125	Par: 73
Men's Yardage:	6293
Slope: 120	Par: 73
Other Yardage:	5255
Slope: No rating	Par: 73
Ladies' Yardage:	5086
Slope: No rating	Par: 73

LinRick Golf Course opened in 1971. This Russell Breeden design is operated by the Richland County Recreation Commission. Thus LinRick is essentially Columbia's municipal course. Bermudagrass covers the greens and fairways. Eight lakes bring water into play on several holes.

You might be asking, "Why a funny name like LinRick?" Well, the course is named after Thomas S. Lynton and J.W. Derrick, two gentlemen who played significant roles with the recreation commission. Instead of calling the course the Lynton-Derrick Columbia and Richland County Municipal Golf Course Open to All, they slimmed it down to LinRick.

Nomenclature aside, LinRick is an outstanding municipal course. This Breeden design features lots of water, wooded terrain, doglegs, plenty of challenge, picturesque holes and midsize greens. We have a sneaking suspicion that Russell Breeden must be fairly happy with this layout, particularly the final five holes, which are among the most challenging and picturesque in the Columbia area. The double-dogleg par 5 16th won't yield a lot of birdies; even a low-handicapper should be happy with par. We found wide fairways on the front nine and narrower fairways on the back. The residents of Columbia should be proud; LinRick represents their city well and is well worth a visit—be sure to book ahead.

Amenities include a practice range, putting green, pro shop, snack bar and rental clubs.

You can walk the course anytime. Approximate cost, including cart, is $19 weekdays, $21 weekends (assuming that you share your cart).

Mid-Carolina Club
3593 Kibler Bridge Rd., Columbia
• (803) 364-3193

Championship Yardage:	6595
Slope: 122	Par: 72
Men's Yardage:	6368
Slope: 116	Par: 72
Other Yardage:	5791
Slope: 111	Par: 72
Ladies' Yardage:	5351
Slope: 123	Par: 73

Mid-Carolina is open to the public on weekdays only; on weekends, you must play with a member. Or better still, be a member. Greens and fairways are bermudagrass. The course is development-free and set in wooded terrain.

Mid-Carolina is a good example of a mature, well-maintained Russell Breeden design. Four sets of tees provide challenge for golfers of all levels. Some of the bunkers are larger than those on typical Breeden courses. Water comes into play on nearly half the holes, and it's most noticeable on three of the par 3s.

The course offers some dramatic elevation changes on the back nine. We overheard one regular player saying he has played without his driver for the past 13 years in favor of a fourth wedge. His point is that you won't need to smack the ball a long way to score successfully at Mid-Carolina. The course plays less than 6600 yards from the tips. The premium here is on accuracy off the tee, not distance—particularly true on some of the dogleg holes and some of

Cheraw State Park golf course will remind you of Pinehurst.

MIDLANDS

the tighter holes on the back nine. Even though a portion of the course abuts I-26, Mid-Carolina boasts a relaxed atmosphere.

Amenities include a practice range, putting green, chipping green, pro shop, snack bar and rental clubs.

You can walk the course anytime. The public can book up to a day in advance. Approximate cost, including cart, is $30 on weekdays and $33 on the weekends (if you can get on).

Northwoods Golf Club
201 Powell Rd., Columbia
• (803) 786-9242

Championship Yardage:	6800
Slope: 122	Par: 72
Men's Yardage:	6485
Slope: 118	Par: 71
Other Yardage:	5936
Slope: 113	Par: 72
Ladies' Yardage:	4954
Slope: 116	Par: 72

Northwoods opened in 1990. Bermudagrass covers the fairways and greens. Some holes are set in wooded terrain, others are wide open. The course is hillier on the front nine than on the back, where there is more water.

Northwoods is a modern course designed by P.B. Dye, son of Pete Dye, one of the most famous and highly paid ex-insurance salesmen turned golf course architects in the world. If you've never played a Dye course and you're within striking distance of Columbia, you must play here. Standing on some tees can be a mind-bending experience. Standing in the middle of the fairway can be a mind-bending experience. Standing in the middle of a bunker where the lip is above your head can be a mind-bending experience. Even though it's not a links course, some of the blind shots and deep bunkers will remind you of the Scottish golf experience. You get the picture. There are some massive greens with equally massive undulations, uneven stances in the fairway and some incredible blind shots. Hit a perfect drive down the middle of the fairway on the 14th and you'll have a wedge into the green. The only problem is that you can't see the green—such is the size of the mound in between you, your ball and the pin.

Did we mention bunkers? At Northwoods they come in every shape and size, including a couple that could only have been created through the detonation of a large incendiary device. Have fun at Northwoods but don't be surprised if the course beats you up—physically and mentally. This might be Columbia's wildest yet most interesting course.

The course is walkable for the very fit, and pedestrian play is allowed on weekdays and weekends after 1 PM. Approximate cost, including cart, is $35 weekdays, $39 weekends.

Oak Hills Golf and Country Club
7629 Fairfield Rd., Columbia
• (803) 735-9830, (800) 263-5218

Championship Yardage:	6894
Slope: 122	Par: 72
Men's Yardage:	6449
Slope: 117	Par: 72
Other Yardage:	5666
Slope: 111	Par: 72
Ladies' Yardage:	4829
Slope: 110	Par: 72

Oak Hills Golf and Country Club opened in 1991. Steve Melnyck, a TV commentator, who used to play on the PGA Tour, and D.J. DeVictor teamed up to design this exciting modern track. The course is laid out on terrain that provides a good mix of open and wooded holes. Water frequently comes into play. Bermudagrass covers the fairways and greens.

We found plenty of entertainment and variety at Oak Hills. Greens, fairways, bunkers and water hazards vary in dimension. However, the course provides excellent sight lines, so blind shots are rare. Keep the ball in play off the tee and prepare to play an approach shot possibly from an uphill or downhill stance. Get the ball to the green, and the slope will challenge your abilities with the blade. The management's favorite hole is the par 3 3rd— 175 yards downhill to a receptive green flanked by two bunkers.

Majestic trees frame many of the holes. With four sets of tees, challenges abound for golfers of all abilities. Overall, the course is friendly, playable, pretty and popular.

Amenities include a practice green, practice range, pro shop, locker room, bar, restaurant, beverage cart and rental clubs. The yardage book inside the golf cart is an interesting touch.

Walking is restricted, but you may book anytime. Approximate cost, including cart, is $35 weekdays, $40 weekends.

Persimmon Hill Golf Club
4322 W. Southborough Rd., Saluda
• (803) 275-2561

Championship Yardage:	7063
Slope: 123	Par: 72
Men's Yardage:	6449
Slope: 117	Par: 72
Other Yardage:	5666
Slope: 112	Par: 72

Ladies' Yardage: 4829
Slope: 100 **Par:** 72

Persimmon Hill opened in 1962. The temperature on opening day—Labor Day—was 102, proving beyond any sort of reasonable doubt that Columbia is the hottest city in the world. Russell Breeden designed this popular course. Bermudagrass covers the fairways and greens, and the design wanders through some wonderful and scenic pine forests.

The brochure for Persimmon Hill (an excellent name for a golf course, don't you think?) calls it "The Thrill on the Hill." The course boasts an excellent layout. Russell Breeden might even tell you that it's one of his better tracks. The land provides great variety, and the layout makes commendable use of the natural features. You won't find tremendous trouble off the tee, but you will need to think when playing around the spring-fed water hazards. The greens are large and rolling, and the bunkers are larger than we've seen on other Russell Breeden courses. Perhaps the course favors the long hitter. That's certainly the case on the monster 18th—a 630-yard slightly uphill par 5 (the longest hole in South Carolina). Once you've played Persimmon Hill, you'll understand why it's one of the most understated yet popular courses in the area. It's particularly popular during Masters week.

Amenities include a practice range, putting green, pro shop, snack bar and rental clubs.

Walking is allowed primarily on weekdays. Approximate cost, including cart, is $30 on weekdays and $33 on weekends.

Timberlake Golf Club
1700-A Amicks Ferry Rd., Chapin
• (803) 345-9909
Championship Yardage: 6703
Slope: 132 **Par:** 72
Men's Yardage: 6226
Slope: 124 **Par:** 72
Other Yardage: 5701
Slope: 117 **Par:** 72
Ladies' Yardage: 4829
Slope: 121 **Par:** 72

Timberlake Plantation, a Willard Byrd design, opened in 1987. Bermudagrass blankets the fairways and greens. This well-maintained course winds around the wooded shoreline of Lake Murray, and water hazards come into play on several holes.

Timberlake Plantation is a magnificent modern course without too many of the huge mounds, bunkers and other absurdities often found on contemporary layouts. Byrd created an awesome and varied track that is fairly tight

off the tee box yet lots of fun around the sloped greens. If the rough is grown up any, you'll need to be particularly careful off the tee. Many of the holes are straightforward, but the last four seem more difficult and breathtaking. La crème de la crème is the 18th hole, where Lake Murray guards the right side of the large green. Make par or birdie here and you'll have plenty to be happy about as you down a cold one at the 19th.

Timberlake provides an excellent example of how a modern course can be fun, challenging and visually appealing without being tricked-up. This course is a must-play if you're in the Columbia area.

There's a small marina on Lake Murray adjacent to the new clubhouse, so you can cruise up to the course in your power boat! Call Timberlake to inquire about specific details.

Amenities include a practice green, practice range, pro shop, locker room, snack bar, beverage cart and rental clubs.

Walking is allowed anytime and is manageable if you're fit. Approximate cost, including cart, is $33 weekdays, $40 weekends.

Timberlake Plantation is a little tricky to find. Take I-26 toward Spartanburg. Take Exit 91 to Chapin and take a left into town. About a mile outside Chapin, the road forks; veer right and proceed for about 6 miles. The course is on the right.

Courses Available Through Packages

The Columbia Metropolitan Convention and Visitors Bureau offers a number of package deals that feature some of the better public courses in Columbia as well as some outstanding private courses. Those in the Columbia Golf Promotion include Crickentree, Cooper's Creek, Fort Jackson (on the U.S. Army base), Northwoods, Oak Hills, Timberlake Plantation, Windemere and The Woodlands. Call (800) 264-4884 or (803) 254-0479 for more information.

Aiken-area Golf Courses

In Aiken, you're so close to Augusta, the home of The Masters, that you can almost smell the azaleas at Amen Corner. Sadly, your percentage chance to play at Augusta National is optimistically described as zero or less. Thankfully, golfing options abound in the Aiken area, which is home to some formidable new courses.

Aiken is in the heart of "Thoroughbred Country." This means that when golfers aren't playing golf, they're breeding and riding horses.

The Masters

OK, before you flood the telephone lines, threatening the authors and their editor with a lifetime of putt-putt, we know that The Masters takes place in Augusta, most of Augusta is in Georgia, and this book is called *The Insiders' Guide to Golf in the Carolinas*. But Augusta is such a stone's throw from South Carolina that most golfers in the Carolinas consider The Masters part of their territory; you'll certainly see a lot of people from the Carolinas in the crowd. So we don't feel too bad about a brief blurb about the greatest golf tournament in the world.

Perhaps some would argue that the U.S. Open is more important. Certainly, the British Open (or simply "The Open," as Brits call it) has more of an international reputation. But The Masters is the only major to be played at the same course each year, and that's just part of what makes it so wonderful.

The tournament is run by the members of The Augusta National Golf Club, whose roster includes an interesting mix of well-aged, Southern blue-bloods and corporate titans. They wander around their grounds during the tournament, seeing to it that every detail is just right. The locals call them the "Greencoats"—they don kelly green blazers—not so much a term of derision as one of slightly baffled endearment. The club is secretive, exclusive and authoritarian to point of telling the television companies how much commercial time they can allot to the tournament broadcast and where they can place their cameras.

Thankfully, the members make a lot of great decisions. The field includes the best golfers in the world. The course conditioning is fast and perfect. The turkey sandwiches are $1.50. A hat is just $20. The course bursts with color from a dazzling array of flowering shrubs and trees. And, perhaps most importantly, the imported beer is just $2. Attendees are called "patrons," and they're expected to behave themselves in a manner befitting the tournament; there are no marshals holding up "quiet" signs. Everyone knows when to be still and when to applaud.

The course at Augusta National is much hillier than it looks on television, and the greens are amazingly undulating and speedy. The famous holes of "Amen Corner"—if you've watched The Masters on TV, you've seen them—are everything they are touted to be and then some, but there are plenty of untelevised holes on the front nine that are just as challenging to the pros.

Sadly, it's nearly impossible to get tickets for the tournament days since they are allotted to the same patrons every year. However, the club holds a lottery for the practice days, which is about the next best thing to being there from Thursday through Sunday; call (706) 667-6700 to enter the lottery. Even if the players aren't quite in tournament mood yet, it's still great to be there, absorbing the aura, the sun, the tradition and a couple of adult malt beverages.

Everyone should visit Augusta National at least once in their lives, even if they rate bowling more important than golf.

MIDLANDS

Aiken's downtown area boasts some fine restaurants and is blessed with an old-world, old-South charm. The area has always been a highly rated retirement center, so if the average age of the foursome in front of you is 92 and they're all taking the slow boat to the 19th hole, don't be surprised. Decent people all, they'll probably let you play through. You'll find a variety of courses around here, including young and fantastic Cedar Creek, venerable Midland Valley Country Club and wonderful Houndslake.

The soil is sandy, and pine forests dot the prevailing country scenery. You'll find bermudagrass on the greens and fairways throughout.

Allendale County Golf Course
Barton Rd., Allendale • (803) 584-7117

Men's Yardage:	3789
Slope: No rating	Par: 36
Ladies' Yardage:	2736
Slope: No rating	Par: 36

Allendale County Golf Course, formerly Allendale County Country Club, opened in 1952. The course was designed by Walker Smith, a millionaire with a glass eye who made his fortune in the hat business. Smith, a left-hander with a chronic and incurable slice, designed the course to suit the game of a left-hander with a chronic and incurable slice. So if you're a southpaw and your stock shot is a big, booming, out-of-control fade, you'll love Allendale County Golf Course.

Joe and Audrey Vuknic purchased the course in 1993 after many years running a course in the Hilton Head area. Their renovation project is almost complete. Set in rolling, fairly open terrain bordered by farmland and pine forests, the wide fairways provide comfortable landing areas off the tee. The small to midsize sloping bermudagrass greens, however, will test your ability to read putts. Some greens are protected by bunkers.

The Vuknics operate a small pro shop, bar and snack bar. There's also a practice putting green. Gone are the days when, according to local lore, Mr. Smith would instruct the greenskeeper to pull the flags out of the holes when a group he disliked was on the course. The atmosphere these days is friendly and relaxed. The calendar features five tournaments a year plus a weekly captain's choice scramble in which, as we discovered the hard way, the aristocracy of Allendale County is more than happy to lighten your wallet.

Walking is allowed anytime, and you won't need a tee time. Approximate cost for 18 holes, including cart, is $15. Rental clubs are available.

Bogeyville Golf Course
500 Bogeyville Rd., Bogeyville
• (803) 649-3366

Men's Yardage:	5514	
Slope: 100	**Par: 72**	
Ladies' Yardage:	4622	
Slope: No rating	**Par: 72**	

Bogeyville Golf Course opened at least 35 years ago. The H.D. Wyman-designed course features bermudagrass fairways and greens. Some holes are set in wooded terrain; others are wide open. Water hazards come into play on some holes. The course offers challenging golf in a peaceful country setting. Terrain is undulating, particularly on the back nine.

We found Bogeyville (what a desperate name for a golf course!) somewhat remote, though the many dedicated golfers who were playing in the middle of the week in the heat of the day

apparently found it extremely accessible. You'll certainly encounter plenty of variety on this course, including some remarkable holes, such as a par 5 on the front nine that literally makes a U-turn. The front nine opens with a reachable par 5. Water and bunkers come into play on this mature course bordered by pine trees, water and thicket, although there's decidedly more water and thicket on the back nine. The greens are predominantly flat; make sure, however, that you keep them in front of you because disaster lurks behind some of the greens. It's difficult to sum up Bogeyville's charm any better than the poet who penned the following on the scorecard: "Golf is a fun, relaxing, competitive sport. Enjoy Bogeyville to its fullest potential."

Walking is allowed anytime, and you may book anytime as well. Approximate cost, including cart, is $14 weekdays, $18 weekends.

Bogeyville is definitely off the beaten path or far from the maddening crowd—whichever makes most sense to you. The following directions should help: From Aiken, take U.S. Highway 1 N. past I-20 and look for a signpost for the course on your left. Take an unimproved road for about 3 (bumpy) miles, and the course will miraculously appear on your right.

Cedar Creek Golf Club
2475 Club Dr., Aiken • (803) 648-4206

Championship Yardage:	7206	
Slope: 119	**Par: 72**	
Men's Yardage:	6689	
Slope: 119	**Par: 72**	
Other Yardage:	6277	
Slope: 115	**Par: 72**	
Ladies' Yardage:	5231	
Slope: 115	**Par: 72**	

Cedar Creek, an Arthur Hills design, opened in 1992 as part of a new upscale residential development. The fairways and greens are bermudagrass. Most holes are bordered by trees, and water, wasteland and creeks frequently come into play.

With Cedar Creek, the well-known and respected Arthur Hills has given the golfing world a fine modern course. Challenges come from significant elevation changes, large hilly greens with surrounding bunkers, the occasional mound and some holes where you must hit the fairway or green. You may find yourself flirting with out-of-bounds on a few holes if you're wayward off the tee. For a modern course, the design is not overly tricked-up or difficult. If your last name is Daly and your first name is John, you'll want to play from the tips—a whopping 7206 yards. Thankfully, Arthur Hills also remembered the short hitters in the world: There's a 1000-yard difference between the championship and men's tees. Comparatively speaking, you'll have more fun from the men's tees if you're a mid- to high handicapper.

If you're in the Aiken area, make sure you play this course. You may like it enough to plop down some cash for a house on the 18th! The course hosted the 1995 NCAA Division II National Championship and is a regular stop on the Powerbilt Tour.

Amenities at this top-notch facility include a practice green, practice range, pro shop, locker room, bar, beverage cart and rental clubs.

We do not recommend walking this course, although you can if you like. The approximate cost, including cart, is $30 weekdays, $38 weekends.

Highland Park Country Club
Highland Park Ave., Aiken
• **(803) 649-6029**
Men's Yardage:	6100
Slope: No rating	Par: 71
Ladies' Yardage:	4911
Slope: No rating	Par: 71

Highland Park opened its golf course in 1903. Bermudagrass covers the fairways and greens. The layout winds through some pretty pine forest and is mostly flat.

Venerable Highland Park is just a three-putt from booming downtown Aiken. While wandering around this ancient course, we almost felt the presence of the ghosts of great golfers striding along the fairways, a fleet of doting caddies in their wakes.

Sadly, this excellent layout could use some sprucing up. If someone with a love for old traditional courses would revamp it, perhaps Highland Park could become one of the better tracks around. Still, if you're in the area and want to see a wonderful traditional layout and have some fun, take the time to play Highland Park.

Amenities include a practice green, pro shop, locker room and rental clubs.

You can walk anytime. Approximate cost, including cart, is $14.

Houndslake Country Club
1900 Houndslake Dr., Aiken
• **(803) 648-3333**

Houndslake Country Club is primarily a private club that offers playing privileges if you stay at the Guest House adjacent to the course. The Guest House itself is more than a hotel,

offering more of a resort or corporate getaway-type ambiance. Otherwise, this course is for the members.

Joe Lee designed all three nine-hole courses at Houndslake. The first two opened in 1974; the third nine, in 1979. The courses are set in rolling terrain bordered by homes and pine trees and feature bermudagrass fairways and greens throughout. Lee is well-known in Florida, especially for his courses surrounding Disney World near Orlando. You won't find Mickey or Goofy at Houndslake, but you will find three fine, mature courses that rival any in the Midlands for character and quality of design.

You can't go wrong with any of these courses. Adding to the challenge at Houndslake is a mysterious wind that bounces off the tall pine trees and creates a swirling tempest at times—just like a well-known course in nearby Augusta.

Amenities include a practice green, practice range, pro shop, bar, snack bar and rental clubs.

You can walk these courses and book a round with your reservation at the Guest House. Approximate cost for 18 holes, including cart, is $35 weekdays, $40 weekends.

Azalea Course
Championship Yardage:	3222
Slope: 118	Par: 36
Men's Yardage:	3009
Slope: 114	Par: 36
Ladies' Yardage:	2653
Slope: 121	Par: 36

The Azalea Course is an interesting beginning to the trifecta, offering mostly straightforward holes with wide fairways and large greens. Fairways and greens are guarded by some large bunkers. This nine rewards solid driving and accurate iron play.

Dogwood Course
Championship Yardage:	3253
Slope: 120	Par: 36
Men's Yardage:	2994
Slope: 116	Par: 36
Ladies' Yardage:	2582
Slope: 120	Par: 36

This second nine at Houndslake offers a little more challenge and elevation change. It features one of the most wonderful and picturesque par 5s in the Midlands—the 509-yard 7th. Smack it downhill off the tee toward a small lake, then decide whether you want to go for it or lay up off a downhill lie. Once you're on the large green, two-putting is a serious challenge. Play the course for this hole alone and you'll be quite happy. In places, this nine is a little narrower off the tee, with more out-of-bounds.

Many inland courses in the Carolinas feature plenty of water.

Photo: Curtis Parks

Laurel Course

Championship Yardage:	**3350**
Slope: 122	Par: 36
Men's Yardage:	**3047**
Slope: 117	Par: 36
Ladies' Yardage:	**2642**
Slope: 123	Par: 36

The Laurel Course is the newest, most challenging and least developed of the three courses. If you liked the first two nines, you'll enjoy this course even more. Each hole is unique and fun, offering a variety of shot-making opportunities. The par 5 No. 7, just 435 yards from the white tees, is very reachable for the mid-handicapper.

Midland Valley Country Club

U.S. Hwy. 1, Aiken • (803) 663-7332

Championship Yardage:	**6870**
Slope: 126	Par: 72
Men's Yardage:	**6182**
Slope: 118	Par: 72
Other Yardage:	**5748**
Slope: 111	Par: 72
Ladies' Yardage:	**5545**
Slope: 123	Par: 74

Midland Valley Country Club opened in 1965. The course was designed by Ellis Maples. Jim Ferree, who used to play on the Senior Tour, is the director of golf. Greens and fairways are bermudagrass.

Midland Valley is one of the better courses in the Aiken area. We found an excellent traditional design and a well-maintained, mature track. If you haven't played an Ellis Maples course, definitely try this one. Attention to detail is evident here: The course is meticulous, and yardage markers indicate the distance to the back, middle and front of the green. Towering pine trees and shrubs add to the ambiance, and water comes into play on a few holes.

Maples made excellent use of the sandy undulating terrain to produce a course with great variety and challenge. Maples courses are often defined by midsize sloped greens protected by a bunker or two, one of which might front roughly half the green. Thus, pin placement can play a significant role in what type of approach shot you should play. If the pin is behind the bunker, risk it and go for it, or play it safe and aim for the unprotected part of the green. You'll also find some fun and exciting driving holes where shot placement is often more important than brute strength. Fans of mature, traditional courses will love Midland Valley.

Amenities include a practice green, practice range, pro shop, locker room, bar, snack bar and rental clubs.

Walking is allowed anytime, although the elevation changes will test your stamina. You can book anytime as well. Approximate cost, including cart, is $30 weekdays, $35 weekends.

Paw Paw Country Club

600 George St., Bamberg • (803) 245-4171

Championship Yardage:	**7063**
Slope: 123	Par: 72

Men's Yardage:	6449
Slope: 117	Par: 72
Other Yardage:	5666
Slope: 112	Par: 72
Ladies' Yardage:	4829
Slope: No rating	Par: 72

Paw Paw, a quality Russell Breeden layout, sits peacefully in the heart of Bamberg County about 40 miles southeast of Aiken. Bermudagrass covers the fairways and greens. We found a predominantly flat track, with shallow greens and fairway bunkers providing most of the difficulties. The fairways are lined with old Midland pines. You'll see the occasional mound here, but the challenge off the tee is keeping the ball straight down some relatively narrow fairways. You'll also need to be accurate on your approach shot; if you miss the green here at Paw Paw, only a good chipping game will keep your score from ballooning. There's more water on the back nine than on the front.

Enjoy the difficult finishing hole—a 446-yard par 4 with just enough water to make you nervous. When you're looking for a straightforward yet challenging course should you find yourself in Bamberg, stop by the Paw Paw.

Amenities include a practice range, putting green, pro shop and snack bar.

You can walk this course anytime if you wish, but it's a hike. You can book up to seven days in advance. Approximate cost, including cart, is $25 weekdays, $27 weekends.

Sweetwater Country Club
U.S. Hwy. 64, Barnwell • (803) 259-5004

Championship Yardage:	6248
Slope: No rating	Par: 71
Men's Yardage:	5830
Slope: No rating	Par: 71
Ladies' Yardage:	4680
Slope: No rating	Par: 71

Sweetwater, a Russell Breeden design, opened in 1981 about 35 miles from Aiken. The course sits amid rolling terrain, although many of the fairways are flat. Bermudagrass covers the fairways and greens. Water comes into play on a few holes.

Sweetwater boasts a fine design that's benefited from some improvements. The course is fair and not tricked-up. We found decent variety in a relaxed and pretty setting. The fairways vary in width, the greens in size and shape. A couple of greens are noticeably shallow; others are protected by large bunkers. Chipping areas are mown around the greens. Overall, Sweetwater is a thoroughly playable course. If the round isn't going as well as planned, the

par 5, 471-yard 18th could lift your sagging spirits. It's uphill, but big hitters should reach it in two quite easily.

Amenities include a practice green, practice range, pro shop, handicap computer and snack bar.

Walking is allowed anytime. Approximate cost, including cart, is $21 weekdays, $28 weekends.

Santee-Cooper–area Golf Courses

The Santee-Cooper area (including Orangeburg, Santee, Sumter, Manning and Moncks Corner) is defined by two large bodies of water: Lake Marion and Lake Moultrie. The area is home to some fine golf courses. The recreational atmosphere extends to golf. A number of snowbirds from northern climes come here from February through May as an alternative to Myrtle Beach and Florida. This may explain why Santee-Cooper is surprisingly rich in quality golf courses—and why you'll find plenty of golf-package experts offering excellent winter and spring deals.

We didn't see a bad course around here. The immediate area around Sumter, about an hour east of Columbia, is particularly strong. Why? Perhaps it's the presence of Shawn Weatherly, the 1980 Miss Universe. Perhaps it's the presence of Shaw Air Force Base. Or perhaps it's the water. Who knows.

Overall, you'll find courses from the modern to the traditional and back again. Spend a long weekend in the area playing golf; you won't be disappointed.

Packages are available through the Santee-Cooper Counties Promotion Commission, P.O. Drawer 40, Santee, South Carolina 29142, (803) 854-2131.

Beech Creek Golf Club
1800 Sam Gillespie Blvd., Sumter
• (803) 499-4653

Championship Yardage:	6805
Slope: 120	Par: 72
Men's Yardage:	6397
Slope: 116	Par: 72
Other Yardage:	5956
Slope: 111	Par: 72
Ladies' Yardage:	5247
Slope: 115	Par: 72

Beech Creek opened in 1990. James Goodson designed the course, which today is part of a residential development. The course is well-maintained and somewhat flat. Bermudagrass

419 covers the fairways, and putting surfaces are tifdwarf.

You'll find plenty of variety on this well-designed modern course. Fairways vary from tight to expansive, and greens vary in size and shape. You'll also find mounds, out-of-bounds, water, pot bunkers and other trappings of the contemporary layout that's popular with the top brass. No. 9 is a fun way to end the front nine before heading for the hot dog stand. It's a 530-yard par 5 with water all along the left side of the fairway; just avoid the wet stuff and the two small bunkers front right and back left of the green, and you'll be putting for birdie.

Beech Creek is popular with members of the armed forces stationed at Shaw Air Force Base. The track is one of a host of fine courses in the surprisingly golf-rich Sumter area. For $30 or less per round, including cart, the course is also a fine value.

Amenities at Beech Creek include a practice green, practice range, pro shop, snack bar, yardage book and rental clubs. Walking is restricted on weekends. Approximate cost, including cart, is $20 weekdays, $27 weekends.

Calhoun Country Club

U.S. Hwy. 176, St. Matthews
• (803) 823-2465
Championship Yardage: 6339
Slope: No rating   Par: 72
Men's Yardage: 5954
Slope: No rating   Par: 72
Ladies' Yardage: 4812
Slope: No rating   Par: 72

The front nine at Calhoun Country Club opened in 1959, and the back nine opened a year later. Ashby Gressette designed the course that's a little less than 30 miles southeast of Columbia. Bermudagrass covers the fairways and greens. The layout winds through some fine woodlands, providing a peaceful country setting. The front nine is open and includes some wide fairways. The course narrows on the back nine.

At Calhoun Country Club, we found a fun and relatively straightforward course with plenty of elevation changes. The greens are mostly flat and slightly sloped; some are elevated and bunkered. Water comes into play on some holes, but overall, the course is not overly penal. Low to mid-handicappers should head straight to the tips. On some of the tee shots, you'll be guiding the ball through a chute. The atmosphere at Calhoun is friendly and relaxed. However, if you're looking for an intense round, Calhoun's design is strong and varied enough to provide a solid test. The hardest, yet prettiest, hole on the course is No. 6, a reachable par 5 that's just 463 yards yet still an easy bogey. Perhaps everyone starts thinking about the scenery instead of the hole and starts to whiff.

Amenities at Calhoun include a practice green, practice range, pro shop, men's locker room and snack bar.

The course is walkable weekdays; some restrictions apply on weekends. You can book anytime. Approximate cost, including cart, is $20 on weekdays and $25 on weekdays—an excellent value.

Crystal Lakes Golf Course

Dillon Park, Sumter • (803) 775-1902
Men's Yardage: 5870
Slope: 110   Par: 72
Ladies' Yardage: 5560
Slope: No rating   Par: 72

Crystal Lakes is Sumter's muni. The Eddie Riccoboni-designed track opened in 1990. Bermudagrass covers the fairways and greens.

Just a smooth 3-iron from Shaw Air Force Base, you'll find Crystal Lakes, a small, well-designed nine-hole course that is popular with local golfers. (Yes, we know the true nine-hole course is an anomaly in this book, but this one is a great golfing deal for 18 holes, especially for beginning players.) If your backswing is interrupted by the sonic boom of an F-15 practicing low-altitude bombing runs, it's OK to take a mulligan.

Aeronautics aside, you'll find an aquatic environment on the first four holes. No. 1 is a par 3 over water "infested" by one alligator. Otherwise, Crystal Lakes is a fun, low-pressure, flat, walkable, user-friendly golf course that is challenging enough to entertain the mid- to low handicapper. That player will shoot for birdie on the 475 yard, par 5 No. 4, which should be reachable, especially in summer, when the fairways get as hard as the runways at Shaw.

After your round, if you're not too frazzled

INSIDERS' TIP

Spring is the time to visit the Carolinas if you want to watch the world's best. In addition to the Masters, held in April just across the border in Georgia in April, the PGA Tour makes spring stops in Hilton Head and Greensboro.

by the reptile, bunkers and low-flying, first-strike aircraft, you can relax with a jovial round of darts in the game room adjacent to the pro shop.

Amenities include a practice range, putting green, pro shop, snack bar and rental clubs.

You can (and should) walk this course anytime. Approximate cost for 18 holes, including cart, is $14. You can walk 18 holes for $6 on weekdays.

Hillcrest Golf and Tennis Club
Old St. Matthew Rd., Orangeburg
• **(803) 533-6030**

Championship Yardage:	**6722**
Slope: 119	**Par: 72**
Men's Yardage:	**6104**
Slope: 114	**Par: 72**
Ladies' Yardage:	**5208**
Slope: 107	**Par: 72**

The golf course at Hillcrest Golf and Tennis Club opened in 1972. Russell Breeden designed the primarily flat track. Trees define the fairways, and water comes into play on a few holes but rarely poses a serious threat.

Hillcrest is owned by the City of Orangeburg, about 35 miles south of Columbia. Wouldn't it be nice if every town in North and South Carolina could boast a solid, well-designed muni like Hillcrest? We found a well-kept, well-marked, relatively straightforward course with plenty of variety and fun. Off the tee, the course is basically wide-open, with the occasional raised bunker lurking in the fairway. As you might expect with a Russell Breeden design, the greens are predominantly midsize—undulating but fair—with a couple of bunkers protecting the putting surface. The key to scoring well here is solidly hit, accurate approach shots. The straight, par 4 No. 18 is a fun way to end the round—just a short 373 yards from the tips, and a good chance to end the round with a well-deserved birdie before heading off for an equally well-deserved hot dog all the way (no onions).

Amenities include a practice green, practice range, pro shop, locker room, snack bar and rental clubs.

The course is walkable anytime. You can book anytime too. Approximate cost, including cart, is $23 weekdays, $25 weekends.

Lake Marion Golf Course
S.C. Hwy. 6, Santee
• **(803) 854-2554, (800) 344-6534**

Championship Yardage:	**6615**
Slope: 117	**Par: 72**
Men's Yardage:	**6223**
Slope: 113	**Par: 72**
Ladies' Yardage:	**5254**
Slope: 112	**Par: 72**

Lake Marion Golf Course opened in 1979 and is part of the Santee-Cooper Resort easily accessible from I-95. Eddie Riccoboni designed the course. Bermudagrass covers the greens and fairways. Pine trees border most holes, and water comes into play quite a bit.

At Lake Marion, we enjoyed a wonderful, friendly golf course and staff with an understated charm usually found only at country club and private courses. This definitely is one of the must-play courses in this area and will be well worth the trip (the yardage book gives the distance from Chicago: 919 miles). Majestic pine trees frame equally majestic golf holes that offer both challenge and visual appeal. Design-wise, the brilliance of this traditional layout lies in the strategic placement of bunkers. Just one or two bunkers per hole are enough to guard the midsize to large greens. You'll have to think here and play sound, smart golf. You'll also have a lot of fun driving the ball from some of Lake Marion's elevated tees. Play your cards right on the greens and you'll make some birdies. This is the type of golf course that's fun to play more than once. Be sure to purchase the witty, entertaining and thoroughly useful yardage book. You'll definitely need it on the very first hole, a 502-yard par 5 with a pond immediately in front of the large green. It's early in the round—will you have the guts to go for it?

Amenities at Lake Marion include a practice green, practice range, extensive pro shop, locker room, snack bar, occasional beverage cart and rental clubs.

You need to use a cart to play. Approximate cost, including cart, is $40 weekdays and weekends.

Lakewood Links Golf Club
3600 Green View Pkwy., Sumter
• **(803) 481-5700**

Championship Yardage:	**6857**
Slope: 123	**Par: 72**
Men's Yardage:	**6027**
Slope: 116	**Par: 72**
Ladies' Yardage:	**5072**
Slope: 116	**Par: 72**

Lakewood Links opened in 1989 and is part of a residential development. Common bermudagrass covers the fairways, and 328 bermudagrass is used on the greens. Porter Gibson designed the course. Houses and pine

MIDLANDS

trees border the holes, and water comes into play on 11 of them.

Lakewood Links, as its name implies, is a sort of links-style course with all the trappings of a modern layout built in tandem with a residential development. We found mounds; large, multilevel undulating greens; bunkers around the greens and in the fairways; out-of-bounds terrifyingly near the middle of the fairway; more mounds; and significant distances from tees to greens. The course is especially narrow on the back nine, so if you choose to break out your 300cc titanium-head driver, make sure you bang it down the middle, otherwise you might be in for a long day. The par 4 10th hole is 461 yards from the back tees and 420 yards from the men's, yet the fairway at the 175-yard marker is just 25 yards wide. Therein lies the challenge of this course. You'll be entertained by the par 3s here. The course also features a significant number of doglegs.

Visually, the course is quite appealing. The numerous ponds are so packed with lilies, Monet would have felt like he was at home in Giverny.

Amenities at Lakewood include a practice green, practice range, extensive pro shop, locker room, snack bar, occasional beverage cart and rental clubs.

Use a cart to play here. Approximate cost, including cart, is $25 weekdays, $30 weekends.

Pineview
7305 Myrtle Beach Hwy., Gable
• (803) 495-3550

Championship Yardage:	7084	
Slope: 122	**Par:** 72	
Men's Yardage:	6346	
Slope: 116	**Par:** 72	
Other Yardage:	5951	
Slope: 112	**Par:** 72	
Ladies' Yardage:	5307	
Slope: 119	**Par:** 72	

Pineview, formerly known as Pineland Plantation, opened in 1968 in Gable, about 15 miles east of Sumter. Bermudagrass covers the greens and fairways. The Russell Breeden-designed layout is primarily flat and set in a pine forest.

Recent renovations are finished at Pineview, and many improvements have been made, including a new clubhouse. The course includes all the classic Breeden touches: runway tee boxes, the occasional mound, slightly raised greens, one or two bunkers per green and putting surfaces that are more sloped than undulating. You won't encounter a lot of trouble off the tee, so if you're playing from the tips, go

ahead and take out the big stick. Just make sure you put yourself in a good spot for your second shot. Water comes into play on 11 holes including No. 4 (the No. 1 handicap), where there's a pond right in the middle of the fairway. The 18th is another water hole—a muscular 565 yards from the tips. All you have to do is traverse a stream and a pond and you're on the green—a classic birdie hole with awful possibilities should you stray from the required line.

Amenities at Pineview include a practice green, practice range, pro shop, snack bar and bar.

You can walk anytime on weekdays and after 2 PM on weekends. Approximate cost, including cart, is $26 weekdays, $33 weekends.

Pocalla Springs Country Club
1700 U.S. Hwy. 15 S., Sumter
• (803) 481-8322

Championship Yardage:	6327	
Slope: No rating	**Par:** 71	
Men's Yardage:	5582	
Slope: No rating	**Par:** 71	
Ladies' Yardage:	4682	
Slope: No rating	**Par:** 71	

The course at Pocalla Springs Country Club, an Eddie Riccoboni design, opened in 1955. Bermudagrass covers the fairways and greens. This layout winds along primarily flat ground dotted with live oaks.

Pocalla Springs is a mature course that's popular with local golfers. You might look at the yardage from the back tees, giggle and think this is a silly track designed for "Oh honey, I'm hot today!" old-timers. Think again. According to the locals, Pocalla Springs' tight fairways, large greenside bunkers and hard, smallish greens will flat out "eat your lunch." For golfers used to over-watered bentgrass greens that will hold a sculled 3-iron, the greens here will come as a surprise, particularly when a well-struck 9-iron lands delicately on the green and bounces as if it had hit the cart path.

You'll find five par 3s here. In fact, you'll come face to face with one of them as you drive up to the clubhouse. The 14th is just 127 yards from the back tees, and each of the bunkers that surround and front the green seems larger than the green itself, which is not much larger than a hot tub. Get the ball safely on the green and your birdie putt from the edge might be one of the shortest of your golfing life. Miss the green and you'd better know how to chip or use your sand wedge. You might want to pack away your driver in favor of a fourth wedge!

Amenities include a practice green, practice

range, pro shop, bar, restaurant, beverage cart and rental clubs. Approximate cost, including cart, is $20.

Santee National Golf Club
S.C. Hwy. 6, Santee • (803) 854-3531
Championship Yardage: 6858
Slope: 120   **Par:** 72
Men's Yardage: 6125
Slope: 114   **Par:** 72
Other Yardage: 5415
Slope: 116   **Par:** 72
Ladies' Yardage: 4748
Slope: 116   **Par:** 72

Santee National opened in 1989 and is part of an upscale residential development called Chapel Creek Plantation. Porter Gibson designed the course. Bermudagrass covers the fairways and greens. Most holes are bordered by trees. Water, wasteland and creeks frequently come into play.

At Santee National, we found a modern yet fair course with outstanding variety. The front nine is relatively open; the back nine is more wooded and undulating than the front, which is fairly flat. The variety at Santee National makes it difficult to characterize the fairways and greens as large, medium or small; you'll see it all here. Big hitters off the tee will enjoy the lack of serious trouble spots adjacent to the fairways. Because Santee National is modern, you'll find lots of mounds. No. 2 is a good par 5, a three-shotter for most at 520 yards from the tips. The biggest potential problem here is a pond about 100 yards from the elevated green.

Amenities at Santee National include a practice green, practice range, pro shop, bar, restaurant, beverage cart and rental clubs.

Only members can walk. Approximate greens fees, including cart, are $40 weekdays and weekends.

Pee Dee Country Golf Courses

Pee Dee Country (including Darlington, Florence, Dillon and Marion in the northeast corner of the state) boasts some fine golf courses amid pleasant scenery. You'll find a variety of layouts throughout the area and a cluster of particularly good courses around Florence and Darlington.

Golf packages are available through Pee Dee Golf, (803) 332-2611, or Swamp Fox Golf, (800) 845-3538. These firms may be able to get you on some of the private courses in the area, in-cluding Ellis Maples's Country Club of South Carolina.

Bishopville Country Club
S.C. Hwy. 3, Bishopville • (803) 428-3675
Championship Yardage: 6877
Slope: No rating   **Par:** 72
Men's Yardage: 6448
Slope: No rating   **Par:** 72
Other Yardage: 5675
Slope: No rating   **Par:** 72
Ladies' Yardage: 5620
Slope: No rating   **Par:** 73

Bishopville Country Club opened in 1959. Bermudagrass covers the fairways and greens. Some holes are set in wooded terrain; others are wide open. The course is primarily flat. Water hazards come into play on a few holes. Improvements and renovations were finished in fall 1995. The course offers decent variety, sound design, the potential for a fun round and, with a name like Bishopville, a lot of older men in purple robes swinging incense.

Fairways at Bishopville are primarily wide and lack serious trouble spots, so feel free to take a big rip with the driver. Be careful, however, on the home-lined holes where the fairways narrow and the greens decrease in size. The 16th hole features what surely must be one of the smallest greens in the Carolinas.

Streams, overgrown trenches and water hazards come into play on a few holes but only pose a threat to the really wayward shot. The sloping greens are raised and protected by a variety of bunkers. A couple of the greens are domed. Large tufts of pampas grass are placed at awkward positions around a few of the greens and provide a unique and potentially irritating hazard. Another interesting feature is a double green on the front nine that provides the putting surface for both the 6th and 4th holes.

Amenities at Bishopville include a practice range, putting green, chipping green, pro shop, snack bar and rental clubs.

Walking is allowed anytime. You can book anytime. Approximate cost, including cart, is $15 weekdays, $22 weekends.

Fox Creek Golf Club
S.C. Hwy. 151, Lydia • (803) 332-0613
Championship Yardage: 6903
Slope: 123   **Par:** 72
Men's Yardage: 6493
Slope: 118   **Par:** 72
Other Yardage: 5915
Slope: 112   **Par:** 72

Santee National's course offers outstanding variety.

Photo: John Gibson

Ladies' Yardage:	5271
Slope: 106	Par: 72

Fox Creek opened in 1987, about 10 miles west of Darlington. According to the owners, a committee of architects designed the course. Bermuda 419 covers the fairways, and tifdwarf covers the greens. Most holes are set in rolling, wooded terrain, and water hazards frequently come into play.

Fox Creek boasts wonderful variety. Perhaps the design committee was comprised of 18 individuals, each responsible for laying out a hole. The result is a track featuring just about every design element in the book; believe us, you won't be bored at Fox Creek. The grainy tifdwarf greens add to the difficulties reading the breaks.

The course is completely house-free. You'll find yourself playing all sorts of shots as you navigate this wonderful track. Resist the temp-

tation to hit the driver too much; keeping the ball in the right place at the right time is more important than pure distance.

You won't forget the 18th hole, a magnificent par 5 that doglegs left over water to a large two-tiered green. Overall, it's a playable and fun course with distinct differences from hole to hole. We think you'll find it's well worth the trip.

Amenities include a practice range, putting and chipping greens, a pro shop, snack bar, rental clubs and the occasional beverage cart.

If you're fit, the course is walkable. However, walking is restricted to weekdays. You can book anytime. Approximate cost, including cart, is $25 weekdays, $29 weekends.

Governor's Run
665 Club Dr., Lamar • (803) 326-5513
Championship Yardage: 6900
Slope: 130   Par: 72

Men's Yardage:	6211
Slope: 121	**Par: 72**
Ladies' Yardage:	**4900**
Slope: 110	**Par: 72**

Governor's Run originally opened as Lamar Country Club. A new back nine opened in January 1996. Eddie Riccoboni designed the front nine, which is relatively flat with some mild elevation changes. The back nine features more undulation, contour and water. Common bermudagrass covers the fairways, and bermudagrass 328 covers the greens. The course is set in a peaceful country environment about 15 miles west of Florence.

The front nine is fairly wide open and features a sensible design with a lack of serious trouble. The greens are predominantly medium-size and sloped. Chipping areas surround many of the greens. Bunkers come into play on several holes. Overall, the course is relaxed, fun, straightforward and fair. You'll enjoy driving the ball in this primarily wide-open design, but you'll need to be deadly accurate on the par 3 No. 9, an uphill, 185-yard hole where par is a great score.

Amenities include a practice range, putting green, pro shop and snack bar. A new clubhouse features a bar and grill.

You can walk this course and book a round anytime. Approximate cost, including cart, is $18 weekdays, $23 weekends.

Sandy Point Golf Club

S.C. Hwy. 4, Hartsville • (803) 335-8950

Championship Yardage:	**6840**
Slope: 122	**Par: 72**
Men's Yardage:	**6045**
Slope: 116	**Par: 72**
Ladies' Yardage:	**5203**
Slope: No rating	**Par: 73**

Sandy Point opened its J.B. Ammons-designed course in 1982. Bermudagrass covers the fairways, and bentgrass covers the greens. The course is set in wooded terrain. The back nine features more of a links design than the front— a parkland design.

At Sandy Point, you'll find excellent variety, elevation changes and six holes where water comes into play. Most of the fairways are tight, so you'll need to be straight off the tee. If you play from the tips, you'll also need to be long with the big stick. Bunkers make you think about your approach shot. Once you reach the green, your short game will be challenged by small, undulating greens. Sandy Point is popular with local golfers. Perhaps their least favorite hole (from a scoring perspective) would be

the 8th, a 456-yard par 4 that seems to play a little longer than the card; more of a three-shotter where most golfers are happy with a bogey.

Amenities include a practice green, pro shop, locker room and snack bar.

You can walk anytime. You can book anytime too. Approximate cost, including cart, is $25 weekdays, $29 weekends.

The Traces Golf Club

4322 W. Southborough Rd., Florence
• (803) 662-7775

Championship Yardage:	**7063**
Slope: 123	**Par: 72**
Men's Yardage:	**6449**
Slope: 117	**Par: 72**
Other Yardage:	**5666**
Slope: 112	**Par: 72**
Ladies' Yardage:	**4829**
Slope: No rating	**Par: 72**

James Goodson designed The Traces Golf Club, which opened in 1991. Bermudagrass covers the fairways and greens. Some holes are set in wooded terrain; others are wide open. The course is primarily flat. Water hazards come into play on several holes. The Traces has hosted Nike Tour qualifying play as well as the Powerbilt Tour.

This course provides an excellent example of what a modern, popular golf course should be. Four sets of tees challenge all levels of golfer. The greens are massive and relatively easy to hit. There's potential trouble off the tee on some holes, but you'll be rewarded on most if you keep your ball in play. Mounds are present but don't get in the way. The scenery is pretty, especially on the back nine.

The key to scoring well here is a solid short game, particularly with your putter. You may hit a green and still have a 75-foot downhill slider. We watched one foursome on a par 3 hit decent but not perfect shots, all of which landed on the green. Getting the ball down in two was not as easy. The 12th and 13th holes are unforgettable. On No. 12, if you're playing from the back, you'll need all you have off the tee. The hole measures 471 yards, but the fairway is wide enough to be fair and allow you to hit the driver.

The facility is well-run. If you're in the area, make sure you play this course; it's worth the 80-mile drive from Columbia.

Amenities include a practice range, practice green, chipping green, pro shop, snack bar, beverage cart and rental clubs.

The course is walkable, although the back nine is a trek; walking is restricted on the week-

MIDLANDS

ends. You can book anytime. Approximate cost, including cart, is $30 weekdays, $35 weekends.

Olde English District Golf Courses

Olde English District (including Cheraw, Camden, Chester and Lancaster in the north-central portion of the state) is so named because the area was a significant base for the British Army during the Revolutionary War. It's dotted with a number of fine golf courses. Cheraw State Park's modern course is probably the one you'll want to play the most. Two of the three Springs Industries-owned courses, in Lancaster and Chester, are fine traditional courses worth a visit.

Note: Courses in the Fort Mill area and to the north are reviewed in the N.C.'s Charlotte Region chapter of this book.

Cheraw State Park
S.C. Hwy. 52, Cheraw
• (803) 537-0160, (800) 868-9630

Championship Yardage:	6928
Slope: 130	Par: 72
Men's Yardage:	6129
Slope: 120	Par: 72
Ladies' Yardage:	5408
Slope: No rating	Par: 72

Cheraw State Park boasts a modern course designed by Tom Jackson. And since it's part of the park, you can camp nearby should you be a golfer who prefers a night spent in a tent versus a dry, comfortable and air-conditioned motel room with a big TV and large selection of channels. Fairways are bermudagrass, and the greens are bentgrass, although we're told they may be changed to bermudagrass in the near future. Laid out in a magnificent pine forest (no houses in sight), the course is set on undulating terrain and poses several water hazards, including a significant lake.

In this age of wholesale government downsizing, Cheraw State Park is a rare example of successful government intervention. Based on this effort, we can only hope that the state of South Carolina's budget includes significant earmarks for additional golf courses.

We believe you'd be hard-pressed to find a better course in this area. Its modern design includes the obligatory mounds, big

bunkers and water, plus large, undulating greens that will test your sanity and patience. The course features a number of doglegs. Its variety is evident around the greens; you'll find different contours and extensive bunkering.

The backbreaker is the 13th, a 492-yard par 4 (that's not a misprint). The hole doglegs left down a hill. Assuming you hit your drive 325 yards, you'll be faced with a long and significantly downhill approach shot to a shallow green fronted by water and backed by a cavernous bunker. Hit it hot and you're flying over the green. Hit it fat and you're in the drink. Good luck!

Make a daytrip from Charlotte, Columbia or wherever; it will be worth it. It might be of interest to some golfers that Cheraw is the home of jazz great Dizzy Gillespie.

Amenities include a practice green, chipping green, pro shop, snack bar, practice range, locker room and rental clubs. The clubhouse is particularly impressive.

The course is a hike, but you can walk anytime. Approximate cost, including cart, is $30 weekdays, $35 weekends.

Chester Golf Club
S.C. Hwy. 9, Chester • (803) 581-5733

Championship:	6811
Slope: No rating	Par: 72
Men's Yardage:	6273
Slope: No rating	Par: 72
Other Yardage:	5816
Slope: 112	Par: 72
Ladies' Yardage:	5347
Slope: No rating	Par: 72

Chester Golf Club, designed by Russell Breeden, opened in the early 1970s. The fairways are bermudagrass, and the greens are bentgrass. Holes are mixed between wooded terrain and flat, open stretches. Water hazards come into play on eight holes. The greens are slightly raised, sloped and undulating. As you might expect with a Breeden course, each green is strategically protected by a couple of bunkers.

Chester Golf Club is part of the Springs Industries triumvirate of golf courses. We think the track is one of Breeden's better designs in that it makes tremendous use of the land. Hole after hole is magnificently framed by a backdrop of mature pines and hardwoods.

Dare we recommend

MIDLANDS

that you make the trip from Charlotte or Columbia? Yes, of course we do! We ran into a number of regulars in the pro shop who were justifiably enthusiastic about their course. There's plenty of variety here, without modern trickery. And there are no houses to avoid.

The course closes with the tough 18th, a 421-yard par 4 where you must smack the ball a long way over water with your second shot, even with a good drive. The fairways vary in width, but the course allows and almost encourages you to bring out your big weapon on a few excellent driving holes. Chester is a thoroughly sensible and completely fair course in a wonderful setting.

Walking is allowed (and you should walk) on weekdays and after 1 PM on weekends. Approximate cost, including cart, is $26 weekdays, $33 weekends.

Green River Country Club
Country Club Rd., Chesterfield
• (803) 623-2233

Championship Yardage:	6706
Slope: No rating	Par: 72
Men's Yardage:	6257
Slope: No rating	Par: 72
Ladies' Yardage:	5328
Slope: No rating	Par: 73

The full 18-hole layout opened at Green River Country Club in 1982. The members designed the back nine; R.C. Goodson designed the front, which opened around 1965. The course is set on rolling wooded terrain. Bermudagrass covers the fairways and greens.

The front nine at Green River is spectacularly understated and straightforward. You might look at the course and think, "I'll devour this track." The fairways are wide open. A couple of holes bring water into play. Hit the driver on most holes but be accurate—your second shot will have to avoid bunkers and reach the right part of the green for a birdie attempt. You'll use almost every club in the bag, yet the course comes without all the trappings of the modern layout. Chipping areas flank the greens—a nice touch.

With your score card reading 2-under and a hot dog firmly planted in your stomach, it's time to tackle the back nine—somewhat different from the front, though still fair. For starters, there are many more doglegs. The fairways are more rolling, though still fairly wide. The greens vary in shape and size. The most difficult hole on the course is the 13th, a terrifying and long par 5 that features a pond at the bottom of a large downslope. (If possible, enlist

the guidance of a member who knows how to score par.) Overall, the back nine is more challenging, primarily due to the elevation changes and all the water. Still, the course is a lot of fun; try to visit if you're in the area.

Amenities include a practice green, practice range, pro shop and snack bar.

Walking is allowed mostly on weekdays. You can book anytime. Approximate cost, including cart, is $20 weekdays, $29 weekends.

Lancaster Golf Club
Airport Rd., Lancaster
• (803) 285-5239

Championship Yardage:	6553
Slope: No rating	Par: 72
Men's Yardage:	6140
Slope: No rating	Par: 72
Ladies' Yardage:	5017
Slope: No rating	Par: 73

The front nine at Lancaster Golf Club opened in the 1930s. The course added a back nine more recently. The course is one of three Springs Industries courses. Bermudagrass covers the fairways, and bentgrass covers the greens. *Architects of Golf* lists Donald Ross as the initial designer; Russell Breeden redesigned the track.

The course is well kept and boasts a solid design that wanders through some beautiful woodlands. It's mainly flat, save a few minor elevation changes. The fairways are predominantly wide, and water comes into play on only three holes, including the 7th—an island green. Bunkers abound around the greens, so it's important to consider them if you play aggressively. Lancaster also boasts a golf ball-stealing fox. The No. 1 handicap hole comes at you quickly, on the 3rd hole to be exact—a 408-yard par 4 with a brace of bunkers on the left hand side. It's a magnificent hole, and every golfer should be happy with a par.

Lancaster offers an on-site meeting and banquet facility. Other amenities include a practice range, practice green and snack bar.

Walking is restricted on the weekends. You can book up to three days in advance. Approximate cost, including cart, is $33 weekdays, $36 weekends.

White Pines
614 Mary Ln., Camden • (803) 432-7442

Championship Yardage:	6373
Slope: 115	Par: 72
Men's Yardage:	5848
Slope: 111	Par: 72
Ladies' Yardage:	4806
Slope: 102	Par: 72

White Pines opened in 1969. Bermudagrass covers the greens and fairways. The layout is mostly open and hilly.

To score well at White Pines, you must keep your ball in play. To do so, avoid the numerous ditches and water hazards—they have a yen for dimpled eggs. The greens vary in size, and most are undulating. Some are raised, and all are protected in some fashion by bunkers. Keep your accuracy in tow. Overall, we found a relaxed setting for a fun round of golf. The reachable but heavily bunkered 17th is a par 5 that could yield a birdie and alter the course of your Nassau.

Amenities include a practice range, putting green, pro shop, snack bar, locker room and rental clubs.

Walking is allowed primarily on weekdays. You can book up to 10 days in advance. Approximate cost, including cart, is $27 weekdays, $35 weekends.

White Plains Country Club

White Plains Church Rd., Pageland
• (803) 672-7200

Championship Yardage:	6353
Slope: 117	Par: 72
Men's Yardage:	5874
Slope: No rating	Par: 72
Ladies' Yardage:	4602
Slope: No rating	Par: 72

White Plains, an Eddie Riccoboni design, opened in 1968. Bermudagrass covers the fairways, and bentgrass is used on the greens. The layout is open and undulating, with trees bordering the course and defining the fairways.

At this friendly course, we found a playable and mostly straightforward track. In the heat of summer, White Plains, due to its openness, becomes white hot. The layout is sensible yet challenging, short yet demanding. The fairways are generally wide enough to let you pull out the driver. Greens are fairly large and primarily flat yet gently sloped. You'll end up using most of the clubs in your bag. If you get in trouble, you can blame only yourself (or your clubs, your job or whatever political party you don't like). Overall, this is a fun course that can be as easygoing or intense as you want it to be. The track closes with a birdie opportunity, the 528-yard 18th; just avoid the water that comes into play on your second shot.

Amenities include a practice range, putting green, chipping green, pro shop, snack bar and rental clubs.

Walking is allowed primarily on weekdays. Approximate cost, including cart, is $28 weekdays, $33 weekends.

Around the Midlands . . .

Fun Things To Do

There's plenty to see and do in the Midlands if you've left your clubs or desire to play golf behind. Don't believe it? Read on.

In Columbia, the **Greater Columbia Convention and Visitors Bureau** at 301 Gervais Street should be your first stop. (803) 254-0479 or (800) 264-4884. There's plenty of information and advice as well as historical and audiovisual exhibits. This is also the site of the **South Carolina State Museum**. By appointment only, you can tour the **Governor's Mansion**, 800 Richland Street, free on Tuesdays, Wednesdays and Thursdays; call (803) 737-3000.

On weekdays, you can take a free tour of the **State House**, (803) 734-2323, where the state legislature convenes. The **Columbia Museum of Art**, (803) 799-2810, is at the junction of Senate and Bull streets. There's also the **Movietonews Film Library**, (803) 777-7000, in the **McKissick Museum** at the University of South Carolina.

The Fort Jackson Museum, (803) 782-7668, in Fort Jackson is open from Tuesday through Sunday. And if you've got the kids with you, don't miss one of the finest zoos in the country. **Columbia Riverbanks Zoo**, (803) 779-8730, is about a mile west of Columbia off I-126/U.S. Highway 76 (take the Greystone Riverbanks exit). No one is admitted after 4 PM.

Two **steeplechase races** take place in Camden each year—one in the fall and one in the spring. (Camden is a beautiful small town with quaint shops and restaurants.)

Cheraw is another picturesque town, with a number of historical buildings. **Old St. David's Episcopal Church** on Market Street, (803) 537-3832, for example, dates back to 1770. **Cheraw State Park** on U.S. 1 offers camping, fishing, picnicking, lake swimming, rental boats, a bridle trail (that's horses, not newlyweds) and rental cottages. Call (803) 537-3033 for more information.

More than a few tracks in the Carolinas were designed based on links courses.

Photo: Josh Gibson

If you're in Aiken, and you like horses, visit the **Thoroughbred Hall of Fame**, (803) 649-7770, in Hopeland Gardens (the city park) at the junction of Whiskey Road and Dupree Place. You might also enjoy the **Aiken County Museum**, (803) 642-2015.

For more information about the Aiken area, contact Thoroughbred Country, P.O. Box 850, Aiken, South Carolina 29802, (803) 649-2248.

If you're in the Pee Dee area on Labor Day, spend a day at the **Southern 500** NASCAR race that's held at **Darlington Raceway** on Hartsville Highway, Darlington, (803) 393-5442—the track known as "The Lady in Black." While you're there, check out the **NMPA Stock Car Hall of Fame/Joe Weatherly Museum**, (803) 393-2103, on S.C. Highway 34 next to the raceway. Darlington also hosts a NASCAR race in the spring.

In Florence, there's the **Florence Air and Missile Museum** on U.S. Highway 301 N., (803) 665-5118, the **Florence Museum** at Spruce Street, (803) 662-3351, and the **Francis Marion College Planetarium** on U.S. 301 N., (803) 661-1362.

For more information about the Pee Dee area, contact the Pee Dee Tourism Commission at (803) 669-0950.

In the Santee-Cooper area, **Lake Marion** and **Lake Moultrie** offer some of the best fishing and watersports opportunities in South Carolina, and fish camps dot the region.

In Orangeburg, visit the **Orangeburg Arts Center**, (803) 536-4074, on Riverside Drive and the **Orangeburg National Fish Hatchery**, (803) 534-4828, on U.S. Highway 21 bypass south of Orangeburg.

Sumter offers car racing at the **Sumter Speedway** on Wedgefield Road, (803) 481-3499, the **Sumter County Museum** on N. Washington Street, (803) 775-0908, and the **Sumter Gallery of Art** on N. Main Street, (803) 775-0543.

For further information about the Santee-Cooper area, contact the **Santee-Cooper Counties Promotion Commission** at (803) 854-2131. Call toll-free from outside South Carolina, (800) 227-8510.

Where to Eat

The following are some restaurants that provide a welcome flair and diversion from the chain-run culinary scene, which tends to dominate this area. Refer to our Preface for an explanation of the pricing code.

Columbia Area

Blue Marlin
$$$ • 1200 Lincoln St., Columbia
• (803) 799-3838

Bill Duke's (of Longhorn Steaks; see subsequent entry) latest effort is this retro-ambiance restaurant with dark wood paneling and some of the best Lowcountry cooking you'll find outside the Lowcountry. You'll also find steaks and pasta on the menu. How about shrimp and grits for your out-of-town guests? Or you might try the deviled crab or plump oysters. Finish the meal with homemade cobbler. You won't need a reservation at this dinner spot—and you should dress down, not up. Relax.

The Capitol Cafe
$ • 1210 Main St., Columbia
• (803) 765-0176

Just a smooth wedge from the shadow of the State Capitol building sits The Capitol Cafe, where you'll feel like you've stepped back in time a few years. You get the sense that the comfortable booths have hosted many a heated political conversation or that quite a few "I'll scratch your back if you scratch mine... and pass the mustard" deals have been made here. The menu offers home favorites, ranging from toast to K.C. Sirloin steak (how's that for spanning the gastronomic gamut?). Conversation here centers of the fortunes of the University of South Carolina football team, debauchery, politics and the latest news from The Citadel. Lunch and dinner are served daily.

Hennessy's Restaurant and Lounge
$$$ • Main and Blanding Sts., Columbia
• (803) 799-8280

At Hennessy's, you'll be instantly impressed with the fine ambiance created by white tablecloths and linens. This is a downtown restaurant where you can have a good old-fashioned culinary blowout. And you won't be disappointed. Begin with Oysters Rockefeller or Maryland crab cake. Move on to she-crab soup, then to Steak au Poivre or Shrimp Hennessy. Follow it all with something from the dessert tray. You won't be disappointed. There's also a variety of beer, wine and liquor. Go for it for lunch or dinner. But before you do, make a reservation.

Longhorn Steaks, Restaurant and Saloon
$$ • 902-A Gervais St., Columbia
• (803) 254-5100

This Texas-style eatery is perfect for a casual evening in a fun and laughter-filled environment. Devour a steak or try some uniquely prepared salmon—Longhorn style.

Longhorn is open daily for lunch and dinner.

The Sherlock Holmes
$ • 1440 Main St., Columbia
• (803) 779-3659

Head down a short flight of stairs and you might think you're walking onto the set of *Cheers*—only, this place is slightly smaller and without the highly paid actors. Relax with a cold beer or engage in somewhat raucous conversation. Or hunker down and munch a tasty lunch or dinner from the pub-fare menu. Sherlock's specialty is a juicy pot roast, thinly sliced, served on a French roll with melted Swiss cheese and accompanied by dipping sauce. Or you might try the veggie lasagna. Wash it down with a couple of Killian's Red ales. Good food, I presume, Watson?

Goodfella's Food and Spirits
$$ 105 Amicks Ferry Rd., Chapin
• (803) 345-9827

A sports-themed establishment, Goodfella's is an excellent place to catch a post-round football game on TV, or better still, catch up on your favorite soap opera, which seems to be a pretty popular lunchtime activity. This might be the only sports bar in the world where *All My Children* takes precedence over ESPN. Our advice is not to ask the predominantly large soap addicts if you can change the channel. Instead, you should partake of a dish from a dizzying array of standard American fare for lunch or dinner: wings, fried mushrooms, hamburgers and the like. The chicken cordon bleu sandwich is particularly good, so long as it's smothered with Dijon mustard.

Aiken Area

No. 10 Downing Street
$$$ • 241 Laurens St. S.W., Aiken
• (803) 642-9062

This is not an English restaurant, despite

the fact that the previous owners named this place after the official residence of the Prime Minister of the United Kingdom due to their fondness for Sir Winston Churchill (a fellow alum of one of us). The ambiance of No. 10 is defined by the four cozy dining rooms with fireplaces. The culinary excellence is defined by a menu that changes monthly. No. 10 Downing Street is famous for lunchtime soups and desserts, rack of lamb and shrimp, scallops and feta served over linguine. You'll also find an excellent range of fresh fish entrees for dinner. The restaurant offers a full wine list and mixed drinks too.

Olive Oils Restaurant
$$ • 233 Chesterfield St., Aiken • (803) 649-3726

Italian fare dominates the menu at Olive Oils. You'll find staple basics such as lasagna, spaghetti, fettuccine and the like. But if you're feeling more adventuresome, try something like the Trout Italiano (baked trout served with anchovies, onions, carrots and a special selection of secret seasonings). Or have a go at the stuffed veal chops or the filet mignon. The menu also includes a full range of fresh seafood. Olive Oils is open for dinner only.

INSIDERS' TIP

Before you visit a course, always call to make sure it's open and is not hosting a big corporate outing or tournament.

Santee-Cooper Area

The Chestnut Grill
$$ • 1455 Chestnut St. N.E., Orangeburg • (803) 531-1747

The Chestnut Grill used to be called Mr. Steak and, as that name implied, red meat is one of the more popular menu options. You'll find USDA choice steaks and prime rib plus tasty seafood and a remarkably extensive wine list, a full range of beer and spirits. There's a children's menu as well. Dinner is served daily.

Cole's Family Restaurant and Cafeteria
$$ • 1000 Broad St., Sumter • (803) 773-5664

Cole's is something of a Sumter institution. It's one of those wonderful (and inexpensive) restaurants where you'll find large helpings of home-cooked meals plus a number of super-friendly waitresses who probably served the parents of the current generation of Cole's attendees. Sit down and enjoy a hearty breakfast of bacon and pancakes, or settle in for an evening feast consisting of the prime rib, steak, seafood, chicken, Italian dishes or the tasty pork chops. There's a banquet room and a full selection of basic beer and wine offerings. Breakfast is full-service from 6 to 10 AM. The cafeteria option is open for lunch and dinner Monday to Saturday and for brunch on Sunday.

Georgio's Pizza
$$ • Savannah Plaza, 344 Pinewood Rd., Sumter • (803) 775-7325

Georgio's has been a local pizza and pasta hangout since 1978. Plenty of locals have taken out one of the wonderful and extensive 5-foot-long party subs that can be the centerpiece of any party. Or better still, you should sit down to a wonderful pizza with a thin crust and just about any type of topping imaginable. The menu says that the dough here is made from an "old recipe." That must be what makes it so tasty.

The menu includes a variety of subs and gyros in addition to a number of delicious pasta dishes including lasagna and spaghetti. Try the souvlaki if you're not completely satiated after consuming a large pizza. Or try a salad or one of the other Greek or Italian items on the menu. Georgio's serves lunch and dinner and offers a full beer and wine selection.

House of Pizza
$$ • 910 Calhoun Rd., Orangeburg • (803) 531-4000

Greek-owned and operated, the "Kali Orexi" is a great lunch and dinner place for pizza as well as subs, sandwiches, salads, gyros, souvlaki, shish kebab and baklava. Round out your meal with a draft beer or glass of Italian wine. You'll find another House of Pizza in Orangeburg at 1338 Grove Park Road.

Pee Dee Area

Corona
$$ • 2029 W. Evans St., Florence • (803) 665-6508

Mexican food in Florence? You'd better believe it! After your round of golf, what better way to spend your winnings than on a large Margarita followed by a really massive bowl of chips and salsa and capped off with a creme burrito. Your winnings don't have to be too

MIDLANDS

great to enjoy yourself to the max here. We believe Corona might be the only Mexican restaurant in the Florence area. In addition to Mexican meat-based favorites, the menu also offers a full range of vegetarian dishes. It's open for lunch Monday and Friday and dinner every night of the week.

The Country Barn Restaurant
$ • S.C. Hwy. 151, Darlington
• (803) 395-2257

The Country Barn restaurant presents an array of country cooking in its Country Cooking BUFFET (their caps). It's open 11 AM to 9 PM Thursday through Saturday and 11 AM to 3 PM on Sundays. Also sample the salad bar and dessert bar. Things get really exciting on Friday for the sumptuous seafood buffet. The Country Barn also claims to be a "BBQ Specialist." Bring all the appetite you can muster.

Town House Restaurant
$$-$$$ • 317 S. Irby, Florence
• (803) 669-5083

Adjacent to the public library, the Town House Restaurant is a fine place to enjoy a variety of standard favorites. The menu includes grilled chicken, fried chicken, flounder, shrimp, juicy hamburgers, barbecue, steaks, sandwiches and *deep*-fried onion rings. We can't guarantee that you'll lose weight here, but you'll certainly leave full. Town House is open for lunch and dinner Monday through Saturday.

Olde English District

Lui's Inn Chinese Restaurant
$ • 807 Market St., Cheraw
• (803) 537-4889

You might not think of Cheraw as a place to find an outstanding, albeit small, Chinese restaurant; but Lui's Inn fits the bill. Just a few minutes from the challenging golf course at Cheraw State Park (see the entry in the "Olde English District" section of golf courses), you'll find all your favorite Chinese dishes such as hot and sour soup and General Tso chicken. We suggest you try the surprisingly good shrimp curry. For those of you who love cheap (and tasty) Chinese cuisine for lunch or dinner, you'll be right at home.

The Paddock Restaurant and Pub
$$ • 514 Rutledge St., Camden
• (803) 432-3222

Camden is well known for its steeplechase, so it makes perfect sense that one of its better restaurants is called The Paddock. In addition

to a range of drinking options, The Paddock offers a diverse menu that includes soups, salads, pizza, steaks, seafood (try the linguine in clam sauce) and chicken dishes—even lamb chops. If you can't find anything on the lunch and dinner menu that excites you, you'd better check your pulse.

Where to Stay

There is no shortage of places to stay in the Midlands. Every motel chain you've ever heard of has a large presence, and you'll find some independent players as well. Refer to our Preface for an explanation of the pricing code.

Columbia Area

Adam's Mark Hotel
$$$$ • 1200 Hampton St., Columbia
• (803) 771-7000

This large (301 rooms) full-service hotel is in the heart of downtown Columbia. You'll find a spacious room complete with one king-size or two double beds, color cable TV and a concierge lounge where continental breakfast is served daily. You'll also find a pool and a Jacuzzi. On-site meeting facilities, a gift shop, secretarial services and a health club round out the amenities. Inquire about golf packages.

Claussen's Inn
$$$$ • 2003 Green St., Columbia
• (803) 765-0440

Claussen's is a Columbia landmark. This bed and breakfast inn is in the heart of Five Points near the USC campus and the State Capitol. Rates include continental breakfast and turndown service, with chocolates and complimentary wine, sherry and brandy in the lobby. All 29 rooms have private baths.

Courtyard by Marriott
$$ • 347 Zimalcrest Dr., Columbia
• (803) 731-2300

This no-frills, down-to-earth lodging with 149 rooms is convenient to Columbia's main thoroughfares. Amenities include a whirlpool, an outdoor pool, in-room coffee makers and ironing boards, cable TVs with pay-per-view movies plus a restaurant that's open for lunch and dinner. If you want to do some laundry, your detergent is free.

Embassy Suites
$$$$ • I-126 at Greystone Blvd., Columbia
• (803) 252-8700

The seven-story atrium makes this one of

the most visually arresting hotels in the Columbia area. There's a complimentary cocktail reception in the evening, and breakfast is included in your room rate. In each suite—there are 214 in all—you'll find a coffee maker and color cable TV. The hotel offers golf packages.

Super 8 Motel
$ • 2516 Augusta Rd., West Columbia
• (803) 796-4833

Clean, sensibly priced and convenient to Downtown Columbia and the University of South Carolina, West Columbia's Super 8 Motel boasts 88 rooms, which must make it popular among numerologists and bingo players everywhere. You can choose from rooms with either two double beds or a king-size bed. The room rate includes cable TV with free Showtime and ESPN plus access to the swimming pool. Group rates and senior-citizen discounts are available as well.

Super 8 Motel
$ • 5719 Fairfield Rd., Columbia
• (803) 735-0008

Four miles from Downtown Columbia and 4 miles from Fort Jackson is Columbia's newest Super 8 Motel, built in mid-1996. Most importantly, it's fewer than 2 miles from one of Columbia's better public golf courses: Oak Hill (see this chapter's entry in the "Columbia Area" section). Golf packages are available. The motel offers 43 rooms, including a Jacuzzi suite, whirlpool suite and several king suites. Nonsmoking rooms are available. The reasonable room rate includes continental breakfast plus cable TV (with HBO and ESPN).

Aiken Area

Best Western Aiken
$$ • 3560 Richland Ave., Aiken
• (803) 649-3968

Within easy striking distance of beautiful downtown Aiken, this Best Western offers 60 rooms with microwaves, TVs, refrigerators and coffee makers as well as VCRs and movie rentals. Some rooms even have Jacuzzis. Amenities include a lounge, continental breakfast and meeting facilities. Note that the price increases somewhat the week The Masters is played.

Comfort Suites Aiken
$$ • 3608 Richland Ave. W., Aiken
• (803) 641-1100

Tired after a long day in business meetings? Have a bad day on the course? Consider the small extra investment to get a Jacuzzi suite.

You'll also find an in-room cable TV, and your room rate includes access to the swimming pool and weight room. The 68-room hotel offers full corporate meeting facilities.

Holley Inn
$$ • 235 Richland Ave., Aiken
• (803) 648-4265

When in Aiken, check out the charming Holley Inn—a place so old that the elevator is hand-operated and the floorboards in the hallways are uneven, creating quite a challenge should you, yourself, be uneven after a visit with the bartender. Each of the 30 rooms includes cable TV and private bath. Relax in the courtyard or sip a drink in the bar. The service in the Holley Inn Restaurant will remind you of a bygone era when hotel guests were treated like royalty.

Santee-Cooper Area

Best Western Orangeburg
$$ • 475 John C. Calhoun Dr., Orangeburg
• (803) 534-7630

The Best Western Orangeburg is a modern and convenient motel with 104 rooms. The room rate includes continental breakfast, cable TV with Showtime and access to the swimming pool. A conference room is also available should you want to organize a meeting.

Pee Dee Area

The Inn Downtown
$$ • 121 W. Palmetto St., Florence
• (803) 662-6341

The Inn Downtown is yet another of Florence's many hotels and motels offering good value. This 110-unit property offers spacious rooms and suites, fax service, a restaurant that's open for lunch and dinner, a bar, transportation to the airport, banquet rooms and cable TV with HBO and ESPN. As the name implies, the Inn Downtown is extremely close to downtown Florence.

Swamp Fox Inn
$ • I-95 and U.S. Hwy. 76, Florence
• (803) 665-0803

The Swamp Fox Inn is a self-confessed "mom and pop" hotel where you'll find a clean, comfortable room at an extraordinary price: Approximately $25 scores you one of the 60 rooms. You'll also get free cable TV (with HBO and ESPN) and access to the restaurant, which serves meals from 6 in the morning until 9 at night. There's an on-site pool, and the hotel

MIDLANDS

can help book golf packages at many of the fine local courses.

clude an outdoor pool and a daily continental breakfast.

Olde English District

Days Inn Cheraw
$ • 820 Market St., Cheraw
• (803) 537-5554

The Days Inn Cheraw offers 50 comfortable rooms in the town that's best known in the jazz world as the birthplace of the late, great Dizzy Gillespie. You won't find much about Dizzy here at the Days Inn, but you will be provided with a clean room and all the cable TV (with HBO) you care to watch. Other amenities include an exercise room and a full breakfast buffet. If you're hungry, thirsty and in the mood for a dance in the evening, head for Plum's Restaurant and Lounge.

INSIDERS' TIP

Park your cart or place you bag on the far side of the green so you can move along quickly when finished. Make sure you don't leave any clubs behind at the green.

Holiday Inn of Camden
$$ • U.S. Hwys. 1 and 601, Lugoff
• (803) 438-9441

The 117-room Holiday Inn of Camden is actually just down the road in Lugoff, but it's near enough to Camden to warrant its name. Your room rate includes cable TV, access to an exercise room and a full breakfast buffet. If you're hungry, thirsty and in the mood for a dance in the evening, head for Plum's Restaurant and Lounge.

South Carolina's
Upstate

While the coastal regions of the Sandlapper State attract vacationers from all over the United States, Upstate attracts visitors of another ilk: businessmen seeking sites for new enterprise or contracts from one of the thousands of companies who call the Greenville-Spartanburg area home.

Even though Columbia is the state capital, Upstate is South Carolina's economic and political powerhouse. The drive down I-85 from Gaffney to the border with Georgia demonstrates the area's industrial muscle: Factories, warehouses and related facilities line the interstate to the point that there's barely room for another Wendy's or Motel 6.

The crown jewel of this roaring hinterland is the BMW factory in Greer, about midway between Greenville and Spartanburg. Since it opened in 1994, the facility has pumped out thousands of those spunky Z3 convertibles and is now producing BMW's sport-ute, the X5. To get an idea of the type of moolah involved in all this, consider that BMW invested $600 million in 1999 to expand its Greer plant to accommodate X5 production, creating 1,000 new jobs. Before the Greer BMW plant opened, major suppliers like Bosch and Michelin opened factories and warehouses to support Z3 manufacturing.

So, if you're wondering why Interstate 85 in the Upstate seems to be under construction almost permanently, now you know why: The state is trying to accommodate the traffic created by the region's pullulating business and industry.

The influx of newcomers to the Upstate is creating a bit of culture clash between the hard-core conservative natives and more liberal influxees.

Interestingly, golf course development, like the aforementioned interstate, has not caught up with the new prosperity, and there have been no significant public golf course developments in recent years, something that's likely to change.

But Upstate residents should not be ashamed of their portfolio of public golf courses. North of Greenville-Spartanburg, there are some spectacular courses nestled in the foothills of the Appalachians, while in the "low" country around Greenville and Spartanburg, the topography is perfect for inland courses: gently undulating parkland with an abundance of streams and natural hazards.

It's not a stretch to say that the Upstate could be South Carolina's most underappreciated golf region. Proof of this might be the fact that George Cobb, Russell Breeden, John LaFoy, and Tom Jackson make (or made) their homes in this area. While none of these men are household names, these prolific and successful golf course architects are well known to golfers throughout the Carolinas. And Tom Fazio, perhaps the nation's foremost golf course architect, lives just an hour's drive from the Upstate in Hendersonville, North Carolina. Other fine architects like P.B. Dye and Gary Player produced work near Greenville and Spartanburg.

Pick of the private tracks might be Chanticleer, the Valley and Cliffs Courses at Glassy Mountain and the Pine Valley-like Musgrove Mill.

So, while the Upstate is best known for its industrial and political clout, it's worth a visit if you're interested in lesser-known good golf

South Carolina's Upstate

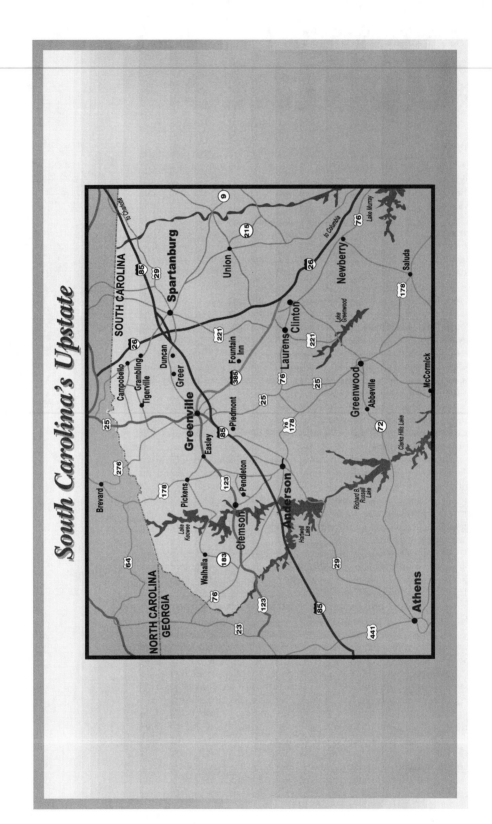

GOLF COURSES IN SOUTH CAROLINA'S UPSTATE REGION

Course	Type	# Holes	Par	Slope	Yards	Walking	Booking	Cost w/Cart
Bonnie Brae Golf Course	semiprivate	18	72	113	6255	anytime	7 days	$28-30
Boscobel Golf Club	semiprivate	18	72	n/r	6184	anytime	2 days	$26-30
Carolina Springs Golf and CC								
Pines/Cedars Course	semiprivate	18	72	122	6248	anytime	5 days	$30-37
Pines/Willows Course	semiprivate	18	72	120	6416	anytime	5 days	$30-37
Cedars/Willows Course	semiprivate	18	72	117	6204	anytime	5 days	$30-37
Cobb's Glen C. C.	semiprivate	18	72	120	6470	restricted	2 days	$40-45
Cotton Creek Golf Club	semiprivate	18	72	113	6170	anytime	anytime	$20-27
Falcon's Lair	semiprivate	18	72	119	6444	anytime	7 days	$22-25
The Gauntlet Golf Club	semiprivate	18	72	130	6233	anytime	5 days	$34-45
Greer Golf and C. C.	public	18	72	116	5730	anytime	anytime	$30-35
Hickory Knob	public	18	72	n/r	5951	anytime	anytime	$25-30
Hunter's Creek								
Maple/Willow Course	semiprivate	18	72	n/r	6407	restricted	7 days	$25-35
Willow/Oak Course	semiprivate	18	72	n/r	6301	restricted	7 days	$25-35
Oak/Maple Course	semiprivate	18	72	n/r	6376	restricted	7 days	$25-35
Lakeview Golf Club	semiprivate	18	72	110	6016	anytime	3 days	$20-25
Links O'Tryon	semiprivate	18	72	122	6230	restricted	2 days	$45-55
Oak Ridge Country Club	semiprivate	18	72	111	5487	anytime	2 days	$28-30
Parkland Golf Club	semiprivate	18	72	120	6140	anytime	anytime	$25-34
Peach Valley Golf Club	public	18	70	92	5925	anytime	anytime	$25-30
Pickens Country Club	semiprivate	18	72	117	5966	anytime	2 days	$30-35
River Chase	semiprivate	18	71	114	6086	anytime	anytime	$23-26
River Falls Plantation	semiprivate	18	72	121	6238	no	anytime	$35-45

Rolling Green Golf Club (27 holes)								
First & Second Nines	semiprivate	18	71	118	5635	anytime	7 days	$25-29
Second & Third Nines	semiprivate	18	72	n/r	5705	anytime	7 days	$25-29
Third & First Nines	semiprivate	18	71	n/r	5610	anytime	7 days	$25-29
Southern Oaks Golf Club	semiprivate	18	72	115	6449	anytime	2-7 days	$30-38
Stoney Pointe	semiprivate	18	72	117	6129	anytime	7 days	$28-35
Summersett	semiprivate	18	72	108	5420	restricted	anytime	$26-35
Table Rock	resort/semiprivate	18	72	114	6038	anytime	anytime	$25-30
Verdae Greens Golf Club	semiprivate/resort	18	72	118	6249	restricted	7 days	$39-49
Village Green Country Club	public	18	72	117	5873	anytime	2 days	$27-32
The Walker Course at Clemson University	public	18	72	129	6560	anytime	anytime	$32-42
Willow Creek Golf Course	public	18	72	n/r	6222	restricted	5 days	$37-45

courses. And if you're visiting on business and will have some spare time in your itinerary, pack those golf clubs.

In this chapter, we include courses in the Greenville-Spartanburg and Greenwood-Abbeville regions.

A note about greens fees: As with all courses in the Carolinas, where golf is a year-round activity, expect seasonal variations and occasional discounts. Rates listed in this chapter can change.

Bonnie Brae Golf Course
1316 Fork Shoals Rd., Greenville
• (864) 277-9838

Championship Yardage:	6579
Slope: 115	Par: 72
Men's Yardage:	6255
Slope: 113	Par: 72
Ladies' Yardage:	5468
Slope: 116	Par: 74

Bonnie Brae Golf Course opened in 1961. According to the well-informed staff, Charles Willimon designed the course, which is set on wooded and mostly undulating terrain. You'll find bermudagrass in the fairways and on the greens.

Charles Willimon may not be the best-known architect in the great golfing state of South Carolina. That doesn't matter. Bonnie Brae is one of those wonderfully basic golf courses that proves you don't need a big-name architect for a fun course. The greens vary in size, shape and slope. No two bunkers look the same. The fairways are wide in some places, narrow in others. It's just difficult to characterize this course, which is what makes it interesting. It's also popular with locals.

Bonnie Brae starts with a bang: a 457-yard par 4. On some holes, the superintendent left chipping areas. Water comes into play on a few holes but won't ruin your day unless you're hitting the ball just terribly. There's nothing earth-shattering or jaw-dropping about Bonnie Brae, but it's certainly worth a look if you're in the mood for a relaxed round on a mature course.

Amenities include a practice green, range, snack bar, rental clubs, the occasional beverage cart, pro shop and help with crossword puzzles (the pro shop staff are wizards!).

The course is walkable anytime. You can book a tee time seven days in advance. Approxi-

INSIDERS' TIP
Unless otherwise instructed, play "real" golf—play the ball where it lies.

mate cost, including cart, is $28 weekdays and $30 on weekends.

Boscobel Golf Club
U.S. Hwy. 76, Pendleton
• (864) 646-3991

Championship Yardage:	6449
Slope: No rating	Par: 72
Men's Yardage:	6184
Slope: No rating	Par: 72
Other Yardage:	5776
Slope: No rating	Par: 72
Ladies' Yardage:	5023
Slope: No rating	Par: 72

Boscobel opened in the 1930s. *Architects of Golf* lists Fred Bolton as the original designer, although Russell Breeden has worked on the course. You'll find bermudagrass fairways and bentgrass greens amid rolling terrain.

Boscobel is a decent and challenging course set among mature trees. According to the experts in the pro shop, the course is "sneaky long" and plays every bit of its 6500 yards from the tips. You need accurate mid-iron play and well-honed short-game skills—most of the greens are small, and there will be plenty of those sneaky short putts we all love. The front nine is hilly; the back is slightly flatter. And water is a factor on three holes.

No. 8 is a difficult hole—just 410 yards from the tips, yet the most challenging on the course—you'll need two great shots and two excellent putts to make par.

Amenities include a practice green, locker room, bar, snack bar and pro shop.

Walk anytime you wish. You won't need a tee time during the week, and you can book for the weekend on Thursday. Boscobel is a good value too. Approximate cost, including cart, is $26 weekdays and $30 on weekends.

Carolina Springs Golf and Country Club
1680 Scuffletown Rd., Fountain Inn
• (864) 862-3551
Pines/Cedars Course

Championship Yardage:	6676
Slope: 125	Par: 72
Men's Yardage:	6248
Slope: 122	Par: 72
Other Yardage:	5833
Slope: 116	Par: 72
Ladies' Yardage:	5084
Slope: 116	Par: 72

Pines/Willows Course
Championship Yardage: 6815
Slope: 123　　　　　　Par: 72
Men's Yardage:　　　　6416
Slope: 120　　　　　　Par: 72
Other Yardage:　　　　5988
Slope: 113　　　　　　Par: 72
Ladies' Yardage:　　　　5084
Slope: 119　　　　　　Par: 72

Cedars/Willows Course
Championship Yardage: 6643
Slope: 121　　　　　　Par: 72
Men's Yardage:　　　　6204
Slope: 117　　　　　　Par: 72
Other Yardage:　　　　5773
Slope: 113　　　　　　Par: 72
Ladies' Yardage:　　　　4996
Slope: 113　　　　　　Par: 72

Carolina Springs opened in 1968. Russell Breeden designed this course with bermudagrass fairways and bentgrass greens on gently rolling terrain. Most of the 27 holes are wooded.

This course is somewhat typical of a Russell Breeden track in that it presents ample difficulty while appearing straightforward. The recent change in ownership portends improvements in the courses and facilities.

There's trouble off the tee in the form of the occasional raised bunker, but the fun begins when you consider your approach shot. Most of the green complexes include one, two or three large bunkers. The beauty of the course is that each hole presents its own set of challenges and decisions without a lot of silly mounds and other contrivances. Water comes into play on a few holes but should only affect the truly awful shot. Play the course from the tips and you'll have your hands full.

On first inspection, there isn't a massive difference between the three 9-hole courses; play them in any combination for a wonderful round. The 5th on the Willows is a great par 3. It's slightly downhill, just 172 yards from the tips and 154 yards from the middle tees. The narrow green, flanked on the left by a bunker, slopes downhill toward water on the right. You can bail out short or long, but only a perfect chip and putt will yield par—right of the green is wet, and a sand save requires a touch as soft as minister's handshake. It's a simple hole that demands precision and rewards finesse over power. Big numbers lurk.

Amenities include a practice green, range, snack bar, rental clubs, a beverage cart and pro shop.

The course is walkable anytime. You can book a tee time five days in advance. Approxi-mate cost, including cart, is $30 weekdays and $37 on weekends.

Cobb's Glen Country Club
2201 Cobbs Way, Anderson
• (864) 226-7688
Championship Yardage: 7002
Slope: 129　　　　　　Par: 72
Men's Yardage:　　　　6470
Slope: 120　　　　　　Par: 72
Other Yardage:　　　　5952
Slope: 115　　　　　　Par: 72
Ladies' Yardage:　　　　5312
Slope: 121　　　　　　Par: 72

Cobb's Glen opened in 1975. The name says it all: George Cobb designed the course with help from John LaFoy on pleasant, rolling terrain. Houses and woods border many of the holes. In the fairways, you'll find bermudagrass; on the greens, bentgrass.

At Cobb's Glen we found a fun, traditional, mature, well-designed and challenging course that's well worth a visit if you're in the Clemson/Anderson area. It's a hefty course from the back tees, so you might want to play it from the middle or front if your last name isn't Daly and your first name isn't John. If the bermudagrass rough is long and the fairways hard, you might be in for a long day. Adding to the challenge off the tee are numerous fairway bunkers. The greens are mostly large and undulating. These, too, are heavily bunkered. Water comes into play on a couple of holes.

With a tasty hot dog in your belly, you might enjoy the 10th, a reachable par 5 just 446 yards from the forward tees and 508 yards from the tips. A good drive over a couple of bunkers (come on—go for it!) leaves a fairway wood or long iron to a heavily bunkered, raised green. A good pitch and a firm putt later, it's off to No. 11, one-under for the back nine.

Amenities include a practice green, range, locker room, bar, snack bar, restaurant, rental clubs, an occasional beverage cart and a pro shop.

The course is walkable, and you can walk late in the day. You can book a tee time 48 hours in advance. Approximate cost, including cart, is $40 weekdays and $45 on week-ends.

Cotton Creek Golf Club
640 Keltner Blvd., Spartanburg
• (864) 583-7084
Championship Yardage: 6653
Slope: 116　　　　　　Par: 72
Men's Yardage:　　　　6170
Slope: 113　　　　　　Par: 72

Ladies' Yardage: 5070
Slope: 118 **Par: 72**

Cotton Creek Golf Club opened in 1968. Russell Breeden designed the course, which is set on slightly rolling terrain. In the fairways and on the greens, you'll find bermudagrass.

Cotton Creek is a typical Breeden design. The routing and overall layout are sound and basic. The occasional raised bunker lurks in the fairway. The green complexes feature two or three bunkers, a pampas grass bush here and there, a mildly undulating putting surface and some small mounds. But you'll also find grass bunkers—a rarity on a Breeden course.

Overall, this track is open, straightforward and fun, providing a venue for an enjoyable round of golf in a country setting. Keep the ball in play, smack it to the middle of the medium-size greens, two-putt, and you'll leave with a smile on your face. Easy game, isn't it?

The toughest hole might be the par 4 No. 6—449 yards with a second shot over water to a difficult green. But you might get a shot back from the course on No. 7, a 485-yard par 5.

Amenities include a practice green, range, chipping green, locker room, bar, snack bar, restaurant, rental clubs, a beverage cart and a pro shop.

The course is walkable anytime, and you can book a tee time whenever you choose. Approximate cost, including cart, is $20 weekdays and $27 on weekends.

Falcon's Lair

1308 Falcon's Dr., Walhalla
• (864) 638-0000
Championship Yardage: 6955
Slope: 124 **Par: 72**
Men's Yardage: 6444
Slope: 119 **Par: 72**
Other Yardage: 5913
Slope: 113 **Par: 72**
Ladies' Yardage: 5238
Slope: 123 **Par: 74**

Falcon's Lair, a Harry Bowers design, opened in 1991 and features bermudagrass fairways and bentgrass greens set on undulating terrain.

After graduating from Michigan State University with degrees in park planning and turfgrass science, Bowers joined Robert Trent Jones as an associate designer. He supervised several new designs and remodeled others. In 1991, Bowers and Curtis Strange built Odyssey Golf Course in Illinois.

Falcon's Lair is a challenging course that demands accuracy off the tee. Several greens are tricky, and trouble spots exist on almost every

hole. There are some extremely pretty holes on the course as well.

The No. 1 handicap hole, the par 4 13th, is just 370 yards from the tips and 327 yards from the forward men's tees! It's a hole that requires absolute precision—big numbers await the wayward drive. Lock away the titanium driver for this hole.

Amenities include a practice green, range, chipping green, locker room, snack bar and rental clubs.

You can walk anytime; book a tee time up to seven days in advance. Approximate cost, including cart, is $22 weekdays and $25 on weekends.

The Gauntlet Golf Club

253 Chinquapin Rd., Tigerville
• (864) 895-6758
Championship Yardage: 6713
Slope: 135 **Par: 72**
Men's Yardage: 6233
Slope: 130 **Par: 72**
Other Yardage: 5543
Slope: 124 **Par: 72**
Ladies' Yardage: 4545
Slope: 119 **Par: 72**

The Gauntlet Golf Club, a P.B. Dye design, opened in 1992. Most of the holes are bordered by woods, and the course is very hilly. Fairways are bermudagrass; greens are bentgrass.

The Gauntlet is one-third of a triumvirate of perilous Carolinas golf courses, including The Gauntlet at St. James Plantation in Southport, North Carolina, and Myrtle West Golf Club outside North Myrtle Beach. One company developed all three tracks.

The "PB" in P.B. Dye must stand for Pin Ball, which is how your ball will behave if you miss the green just slightly or, on occasion, if you actually hit a green. This is a Pete Dye course on steroids. (P.B. Dye is Pete Dye's son.)

The Greenville version of The Gauntlet is set in the foothills of the Smoky Mountains and provides one of the greatest challenges in the Upstate—a challenge that borders on the absurd in places. Earth was moved. Sands were shifted. The sky was shaken. The golfing world has never been the same. No two holes are alike, and all are difficult. Score par on most holes and you should be extremely pleased with yourself. Each hole has a name with a King Arthur and the Round Table motif. If the course beats you up in a particularly nasty fashion, our advice is to restore your sense of humor by renting *Monty Python and the Holy Grail*.

As you might expect with a modern course,

Hickory Knob is one of the best state-sponsored courses in the country.

Photo: Hickory Knob State Resort Park

there are plenty of mounds, bunkers, steep drop-offs, water, blind shots and uneven stances. Some holes defy description. The par 5 16th, a 521-yard monster, looks innocent enough off the tee, but that's because the shot is uphill to a flat landing area. From here, you can lay up to a series of terraced landing areas or fire away at a massive green divided by what appears to be an elephant buried in the shallowest of graves. We tried to putt from one end to the other while keeping the ball on the green and failed miserably. Consider yourself warned. The other hole of anxiety is the par 5 11th—more than 500 yards straight uphill to a difficult green.

The Greenville-Spartanburg area is full of solid layouts, but visit here for the experience of playing a Dye course. Whether or not you'll return depends on your ability to suck up mental anguish. There's nothing that comes close to describing the semi-hallucinogenic thought processes that went into designing the aptly named Gauntlet.

Amenities include a practice green, range, chipping green, snack bar, rental clubs, an occasional beverage cart and a pro shop.

You'll only add injury to insult if you try to walk this course, but you can if you want to. You can book a tee time five days in advance. Approximate cost, including cart, is $34 weekdays and $45 on weekends.

Greer Golf & Country Club

2990 Gap Creek Rd., Greer
• (864) 877-9279

Championship Yardage:	**6321**
Slope: 121	**Par: 72**
Men's Yardage:	**5730**
Slope: 116	**Par: 72**
Ladies' Yardage:	**5083**
Slope: 110	**Par: 72**

Greer Golf & Country Club opened nine holes in 1954. The club added nine more holes in 1965. There's no record of any one designer. Bermudagrass covers the fairways; bentgrass, the greens.

As mentioned in this chapter's introduction, Greer is known around the world as the site of the young and massive BMW automotive factory. However, this friendly South Carolina town is also home to a decent golf course—once again proving you don't need a big-name, hot-shot architect to provide a challenge. The track is popular with locals, many of whom find time in their schedules to exercise their beer drinking muscles in the clubhouse, which is well equipped with a few card tables and a state-of-the-art (in 1954) television.

The course is relatively straightforward until you reach the undulating greens. The fairways are tree-lined. The course has a pleasant country ambiance, well removed from the hustle and bustle of life in the rapidly expanding and booming Greenville-Spartanburg metropolis. Have fun.

Amenities include a practice green, range, locker room, bar, snack bar, restaurant, rental clubs, a beverage cart, TV and pro shop.

The course is walkable for the limber, and you can walk anytime. You'll need a tee time on the weekend, and you can book that starting on Wednesday. Approximate cost, including cart, is $30 weekdays and $35 on weekends.

Hickory Knob State Resort Park Golf Course
S.C. Hwy. 378, McCormick
• (864) 391-2450

Championship Yardage:	6560
Slope: No rating	Par: 72
Men's Yardage:	5951
Slope: No rating	Par: 72
Other Yardage:	4905
Slope: No rating	Par: 72
Ladies' Yardage:	4905
Slope: No rating	Par: 72

Hickory Knob State Resort Park Golf Course opened in 1982. Tom Jackson designed it amid rolling, wooded terrain. Fairways and greens are bermudagrass.

Hickory Knob is part of McCormick State Park. We found it to be an excellent course with plenty of challenge—a good example of sound government and well-spent tax dollars! We found hickory, but we failed to find a knob. You won't encounter the abundance of mounds that typically defines Tom Jackson courses; the attraction lies in the variety. You'll find greens of all sizes and shapes. Some are sloped, while others pitch and roll. Bunkering is extensive, and there's plenty of water, some of which comes from the picturesque lake bordering the course.

You'll barely have time to limber up before the course delivers the No. 1 handicap hole as its second challenge. A stunningly narrow par 5, No. 2 spans 501 yards from the middle tees, and only the bravest drivers will risk taking out the big stick to try to reach the green in two.

You won't have to bang the ball a mile here to score well, but you will need to keep it in play and take what the course gives. You'll also have to carry the ball over water on a few occasions. The setting alone is worth the modest price of admission. Seek this place out.

Amenities include a practice green, range, chipping green, locker room, bar, snack bar and pro shop.

You can walk and book a tee time at Hickory Knob whenever you choose. Approximate cost, including cart, is $25 weekdays and $30 on weekends.

Hunter's Creek Plantation
702 Hunter's Creek Blvd., Greenwood
• (864) 223-9286

Maple/Willow Course

Championship Yardage:	7089
Slope: No rating	Par: 72
Men's Yardage:	6407
Slope: No rating	Par: 72
Other Yardage:	5723
Slope: No rating	Par: 72
Ladies' Yardage:	4977
Slope: No rating	Par: 72

Willow/Oak Course

Championship Yardage:	6927
Slope: No rating	Par: 72
Men's Yardage:	6301
Slope: No rating	Par: 72
Other Yardage:	5704
Slope: No rating	Par: 72
Ladies' Yardage:	4931
Slope: No rating	Par: 72

Oak/Maple Course

Championship Yardage:	6920
Slope: No rating	Par: 72
Men's Yardage:	6376
Slope: No rating	Par: 72
Other Yardage:	5765
Slope: No rating	Par: 72
Ladies' Yardage:	5000
Slope: No rating	Par: 72

The Oak Nine at Hunter's Creek Plantation opened in 1995. Tom Jackson designed the course. Many of the holes are open, while others are bordered by woods. You'll find bermudagrass on both the greens and fairways.

All three nines are now open at Hunter's Creek. Each of the courses is a modern treat complete with mounds, tough greens, big tee shots and a variety of nasty bunkers. All three nines are extremely challenging from the back tees too. If you're a fan of modern and difficult courses, take the challenge at Hunter's Creek.

The first hole on the Oak nine is much more than the average warm-up opener. At 506 yards from the tips, it tempts even the moderately long golfer into going for it. A stiff green with plenty of trouble awaits those who are a bit too bold.

Amenities include a practice green, range, chipping green, bar, snack bar, restaurant, rental clubs, a beverage cart and a pro shop.

The Oak nine is walkable, while you need a cart on the other two. You can book a tee time

Choosing Golf Clubs

There are so many golf clubs on the market these days that choosing the perfect set is a daunting task. Ironically, it's easier than ever to find the right clubs for your game due to one of the most important developments in the past five years: custom club-fitting.

It used to be that most players purchased clubs straight off the rack from the pro shop or discount store. This was fine for the golfer with average height, average weight, average hands and average swing speed. Anyone who differed from normal simply had to make do. Nowadays, most new sets are tailored to match the swing characteristics of the purchaser. The result is greater consistency, and the golfer will be more likely to benefit from sound swing mechanics and fundamentals. It takes less than a half-hour to complete a club-fitting session, and there's usually no cost—as long as you purchase the clubs!

There are so many materials available on the market that it's impossible to list their characteristics in a short space. However, space-age materials are unlikely to produce amazing results in the hands of a duffer; it's still wise to spend money on regular lessons from a good pro before splashing out on a new set.

Putters—The Stroke-savers

A lot of putting is feel, thus it's important to try out a number of putters before settling on one model. Pick the one that feels right and instills a sense of confidence and consistency, particularly when it comes to speed. Even putters can be custom fitted—something that could be valuable if you're very tall or very short. Your arms should hang freely to the handle of the putter (hence shorter people need a shorter putter). A putting lesson from a pro is always a good idea before choosing your weapon. Tiger Woods putts with a $500 putter, while Steve Elkington's costs about $60. Find the one that works best for you and sort out your mechanics before deciding that it's time to find another putter. Most faults emanate from the puttee, not the putter. Consider the typical speed of your home course's greens when selecting the best putter for your needs.

Wedges

Wedges are tremendously important scoring tools. Most pros carry three wedges, which is also a good idea for the average player. A 60-degree lob wedge can be a valuable addition to your arsenal once you learn how to use it. Even wedges come in a vast array of sizes and shapes; ask you pro to recommend a set that suits the course conditions you encounter. A sand wedge that's good out of soft sand may not work too well in hard or coarse sand; a sand wedge with a lot of bounce can be difficult to use on hard fairways. Once again, there's no need to spend a massive amount on wedges, even though the average player might use one on almost every hole.

Irons

Irons are your workhorse clubs. Pros often use finely tuned, forged "blades" with sweet spots the size of dimes; such clubs require precise ball striking and tend to be unforgiving. Hit 400 practice balls a day and you might use blades as well. Some manufacturers produce hybrid, cavity-backed, forged clubs that combine degrees of workability with some forgiveness. Many low-handicap players prefer this type of club for the wonderful feel.

However, far and away the most popular iron on the market is the ultra-forgiving cast club. In the past few years, many cast-iron clubs to hit the market boast greatly improved feel and workability. Cast clubs offer such tremendous performance, in fact, that many pros are now using them. And these can be custom-fitted as well. We think most golfers should use cast irons.

Shaft technology has improved over the past 10 years, and this probably has resulted in better distance for all players. The shaft is the most important component in a club, and it should be properly matched to a golfer's swing speed. While many players, particularly seniors, enjoy graphite and boron shafts, such exotic materials aren't necessary for accuracy or distance. Steel shafts, particularly in irons, tend to produce better distance control. However, most average golfers will benefit tremendously from the extra distance a graphite shaft can produce in a driver or 3-wood.

Drivers—The Big Sticks

Woods aren't woods anymore, and it's rare to find a persimmon driver in anyone's bag. Metal and titanium heads dominate the market, and these materials offer excellent control and compensation. If you can swallow the cost of titanium woods, then it's well worth the extra cash; the huge head promotes confidence and is incredibly forgiving. Better players miss the feel but can still work the ball successfully. Steel-headed drivers are a close second: they were state-of-the-art three years ago and work very well today at half the cost of titanium. Golfers with slow swing speeds will benefit from utility woods, and these should replace long irons. A number of LPGA pros carry 7- and 9-woods instead of 3- and 4-irons.

Choose Wisely . . . and Patiently

It's not difficult to spend more than $3,000 on a complete set of 14 clubs if you choose every exotic material available. However, brand-name equipment is available in pro shops and discount stores at excellent prices; there's nothing that beats the confidence generated by a club produced by a brand manufacturer. If you want to save money, the secondhand section often can be a treasure trove; let the manager of the store know that you're looking for quality used equipment and he or she can be quite helpful—just be patient. If you want new clubs at discount prices, then a number of "hole-in-the-wall" stores can set you up with no-name component clubs, which can be just as effective as the brand-name stuff at half the price.

Well-fit, quality equipment can shave strokes off your game—just like the ads say. But avoid rushing into a club-purchasing decision. Try out demos and ask golfers of similar abilities what works for them. A trustworthy pro or shop manager will point you in the right direction; if you want to keep your expenditure low, tell them. Spending a lot of money for clubs that don't promote confidence is a waste. Dollar-for-dollar, the best money you will spend will be on a custom-fit putter.

UPSTATE

seven days in advance. Approximate cost, including cart, is $25 weekdays and $35 on weekends.

Lakeview Golf Club
315 Piedmont Golf Course Rd., Piedmont
• (864) 277-2680

Championship Yardage:	6455
Slope: 116	Par: 72
Men's Yardage:	6016
Slope: 110	Par: 72
Ladies' Yardage:	5036
Slope: No rating	Par: 73

Lakeview Golf Course opened in 1954. In the fairways, you'll find 419 bermudagrass; the greens are 328 bermudagrass. Although we searched high and low, we could not determine who designed this course.

Lakeview offers a fun and relaxing round in a pleasant country setting. Like its neighbor, Bonnie Brae, the course is set on gently rolling terrain. Some of the holes are wide open, while others are set in woodland. One of the first things you'll notice, depending on the time of year, is that the first fairway is crosscut—a landscaping touch evident from the elevated tee.

The greens are small to medium-size and not overly undulating. The layout is predominantly straightforward—what you see is what you get. There's a distinct lack of water and heavy bunkering. Perhaps the back nine is a little tighter than the front. The course offers enough challenge and variety to keep the novice as well as the low-handicapper happy, which may explain its evident popularity.

Amenities include a practice green, range, chipping green, snack bar, rental clubs and a pro shop.

You can walk the course anytime. You won't need a tee time during the week, but you should call on Wednesday to book for the weekend. Approximate cost, including cart, is $20 weekdays and $25 on weekends.

Links O'Tryon

11250 New Cut Rd., Campobello
• (864) 468-4995

Championship Yardage:	**6728**	
Slope: 130		**Par: 72**
Men's Yardage:	**6230**	
Slope: 122		**Par: 72**
Other Yardage:	**5539**	
Slope: 113		**Par: 72**
Ladies' Yardage:	**5051**	
Slope: 114		**Par: 72**

Links O'Tryon, a Tom Jackson design, opened in 1987. The course is set on gently rolling terrain bordered by woods and houses. Fairways are blanketed with bermudagrass, and greens are bentgrass.

Links O'Tryon is well known in the Upstate as one of the area's most popular courses, and it's often the site of local amateur tournaments. For a number of years, *GolfWeek* magazine voted the course No. 1 in Upstate South Carolina.

The layout offers many Tom Jackson touches even though it's a parkland course, not a links. The course is somewhat forgiving and rewarding. Perhaps this course is less penal than other Tom Jackson designs. The open aspect that defines most of the course and its proximity to the foothills of the Smoky Mountains mean that wind may be a factor in your round here.

Many of the holes are quite memorable, including the uphill, 562-yard, par 5 No. 8, which requires considerable heft off the tee. The hole features a small and undulating green fronted by a large and deep bunker. The 6th hole, a 377-yard par 4, requires an excellent tee shot to avoid the trees on the left of the fairway.

The key to this course's attraction is the

variety. You'll have to place all of your shots to score well here. No two holes are the same. It's a great example of why Tom Jackson is such a well-respected architect. Bunkers come in all shapes and sizes; some are massive. Jackson took a page out of Robert Trent Jones's book with a couple of cloverleaf bunkers that are fun to look at but no fun to be in. Water comes into play on a few holes, but it shouldn't pose too much of a problem unless you're shots are very wayward.

Amenities at this fine golfing facility include a practice green, range, chipping green, locker room, bar, snack bar, restaurant, rental clubs, a beverage cart and a pro shop.

The front nine is more walkable, and you can walk after 2 PM. Book a tee time whenever you choose during the week, but you'll need to call after 1 PM on Thursday to schedule for the weekend. Approximate cost, including cart, is $45 weekdays and $55 on weekends (including Friday).

Oak Ridge Country Club

5451 S. Pine St., Spartanburg
• (864) 582-7579

Championship Yardage:	**6156**	
Slope: 121		**Par: 72**
Men's Yardage:	**5487**	
Slope: 111		**Par: 72**
Ladies' Yardage:	**4491**	
Slope: 112		**Par: 72**

Oak Ridge Country Club opened in 1980. George Cobb designed the course on picturesque rolling terrain. Fairways are 419 bermudagrass, and greens are bentgrass.

The club remodeled the course in 1992. Much of the difficulty on this well-designed track is the result of the hilly terrain. At times, you might feel like you're on a mountain layout. The greens vary in shape but are primarily midsize and sloped, with some subtle undulations. The combination scorecard/yardage book is a useful aid. You'll find bunkering in the fairways and around most of the greens. Keeping the ball in play on this somewhat short course is crucial, so you might want to leave your big stick in the trunk. The course narrows a touch on the back nine, and water comes into play on a few holes. You can't go wrong with a George Cobb design, so visit this course if you can. It's also an excellent value.

Amenities include a practice green, range, chipping green, snack bar, rental clubs, a beverage cart and pro shop.

The course is walkable for the physically fit, and you can walk anytime. You can book a tee time two days in advance. Approximate cost, including cart, is $28 weekdays and $30 on weekends.

Parkland Golf Club
295 E. Deadfall Rd., Greenwood
• (864) 229-5086

Championship Yardage:	6520
Slope: 124	Par: 72
Men's Yardage:	6140
Slope: 120	Par: 72
Other Yardage:	5710
Slope: 114	Par: 72
Ladies' Yardage:	5130
Slope: 115	Par: 72

Parkland Golf Club opened in 1986. John Park designed the course (maybe he named it after himself too) on rolling wooded terrain, with bermudagrass greens and fairways.

The aptly named Parkland is a fine and formidable country course crafted by a little-known architect. Overall, the layout is relatively flat and features a number of tricky holes surrounded by towering pine trees. Some of the holes are tight off the tee. Streams and ponds come into play, particularly on the back nine.

The short, par 4 16th hole and the longer par 4 17th could ruin a good round. Both are flanked by water and could produce some big numbers.

You'll find a great deal of sand around the greens and an occasional bunker in the fairway. The greens undulate and vary in size. There's nothing tricked-up about the course; it exudes an old-style, country club feel. Definitely play here if you can.

Amenities include a chipping green, snack bar and pro shop.

The course is walkable for the fit, and you can walk anytime. You won't need a tee time. Approximate cost, including cart, is $25 weekdays and $34 on weekends.

Peach Valley Golf Club
2363 Chesnee Hwy., Spartanburg
• (864) 583-2244

Championship Yardage:	6225
Slope: 109	Par: 70
Men's Yardage:	5925
Slope: 92	Par: 70
Ladies' Yardage:	No rating
Slope: 97	Par: 76

Peach Valley opened in 1960. The course is set on open and primarily flat terrain. In the fairways, you'll find bermudagrass; on the greens, you'll find both bentgrass and bermudagrass. Who designed this course? We

don't know, and neither did anyone or any text source we consulted.

Peach Valley offers low-cost, worry-free, relaxed golf in a pleasant setting. Greens are raised and small to medium-size, with subtle slopes. The fairways are wide and open, so feel free to take out the boron-shafted big daddy you just purchased from the clubmaker in the pro shop and let the big dog eat.

Even though it's just 350 yards, the 1st hole is a little bit intimidating and could easily wreck your round from the outset. There's a relatively short carry over water followed by an approach to a green with water to the right. Don't slice.

Amenities include a practice green, range, chipping green, snack bar, restaurant, rental clubs and a pro shop.

The course is walkable—you should walk and you can do so anytime. You can book a tee time whenever you choose as well. Approximate cost, including cart, is $25 weekdays and $30 on weekends.

Pickens Country Club
1018 Country Club Rd., Pickens
• (864) 878-6083

Championship Yardage:	6250
Slope: 120	Par: 72
Men's Yardage:	5966
Slope: 117	Par: 72
Ladies' Yardage:	4912
Slope: 115	Par: 72

Pickens Country Club opened in 1954 with nine holes, and the club added a back nine in 1958. Willie B. Lewis designed the course. Woods border some of the holes, and most of the fairways are defined and delineated with evergreens and hardwoods. The course is set in rolling terrain; water comes into play on only a couple of holes. You'll find bermudagrass in the fairways and bentgrass on the greens.

At Pickens Country Club, we found a fine, mature, traditional layout. You won't encounter anything tricked-up or gimmicky here; it's fairly straightforward. The trees are mature and magnificent, there's barely a house in sight anywhere, and many of the holes sweep majestically right and left, giving you the feeling that you're on a country club track—which you are. You might ask yourself why modern courses aren't like this one.

Like a lot of older, more traditional designs, the degree of trouble off the tee depends on the length of the rough. If it's long and shaggy, you'll need to keep your ball in the short grass with a little less stick off the tee. The greens are small, undulating and, according the staff, fast outside the summer months. They're probably harder than they look. Though you won't find an overabundance of them, some strategically placed sand and grass bunkers make you think about your approach shot.

Older courses offer something modern courses often lack: interesting short par 4s. And Pickens Country Club might offer the best crop of short par 4s in the Upstate. The dogleg 8th hole is just 314 yards from the middle tees—a long iron downhill to a narrow landing area leaves a pitching wedge or short iron shot uphill to one of the Pickens' small greens entirely fronted by a large bunker. Sound easy? Anyone caught trying to overpower the hole may be staring at a big number.

The course offers a yardage book that includes swing thoughts and golf tips on each page, including one tip that encourages you not to over-think . . . a good example of yardage-book irony.

Amenities include a practice green, range, chipping green, locker room, bar, snack bar and pro shop.

You can walk anytime. Nonmembers can book a tee time two days in advance. Approximate cost, including cart, is $30 weekdays and $35 on weekends.

River Chase
459 Fairwood Blvd., Union
• (864) 427-3055

Championship Yardage:	**6607**
Slope: 121	**Par: 71**
Men's Yardage:	**6086**
Slope: 114	**Par: 71**
Ladies' Yardage:	**5138**
Slope: 103	**Par: 71**

River Chase, a fine Russell Breeden design that opened in 1976, is set in rolling wooded terrain, with bermudagrass greens and fairways.

You'll find there isn't much room off the tee, which makes the course play longer—as if it weren't long enough already (6607 yards from the tips). The green complexes are challenging and feature numerous bunkers and extreme undulations. The most difficult hole might be the 5th, a 432-yard par 4. It's particularly narrow, and the long-iron second shot will not find a receptive wel-

come on the green. Par is an excellent score here.

The renovation of the course is complete and makes it one of the better challenges in the Upstate.

Amenities include a practice green, range, locker room, snack bar and pro shop.

River Chase is walkable for the fit, and you can walk anytime. You can book a tee time whenever you choose. Approximate cost, including cart, is $23 weekdays and $26 on weekends.

River Falls Plantation
100 Player Blvd., Duncan
• (864) 433-9192

Championship Yardage:	**6697**
Slope: 127	**Par: 72**
Men's Yardage:	**6238**
Slope: 121	**Par: 72**
Other Yardage:	**5702**
Slope: 116	**Par: 72**
Ladies' Yardage:	**4928**
Slope: 125	**Par: 72**

Gary Player designed the golf course at River Falls Plantation, which opened in 1990. Most holes are bordered by woods, and some holes have a mountain feel. In the fairways, you'll find bermudagrass; on the greens, bentgrass.

Player designed an excellent course here. He routed the course exceedingly well, and the result is a track with a number of memorable holes. We found outstanding variety: It's the sort of course where, as the old saying goes, you'll have to use every club in your bag. You'll find yourself forced to plan a strategy with just about every shot. Some holes offer great elevation changes. Fairway widths vary a great deal, and on certain holes you'll want to throttle back with a long iron. On other holes, take out the big stick and fire away. Water frequently comes into play. The green complexes vary in size, shape and protection to the point where it's impossible to generalize. On certain holes, you might think of this course as a sort of kinder, gentler Dye-ish effort.

You'll find two tremendous holes: The par 5 12th is 591 yards downhill to a shallow green fronted by a stream. The par 4 13th is short at 327, but the blind

INSIDERS' TIP

Early in the morning or late in the evening are often the best times to see the subtleties in a golf course, as shadows highlight the contour of greens and fairways. Many courses offer discounts if you tee off in the late afternoon. Plus, in the Carolinas anyway, these can be the most comfortable times to play.

second shot severely downhill to a narrow green is one of the most spectacular in Upstate golf.

Amenities include a range, chipping green, locker room, snack bar, restaurant, rental clubs, a beverage cart and pro shop.

Walking is not allowed, but you can book a tee time whenever you choose. Approximate cost, including cart, is $35 weekdays and $45 on weekends.

Rolling Green Golf Club
386 Hester Store Rd., Easley
• (864) 859-7716
First Nine/Second Nine
Championship Yardage: 6116
Slope: 118   **Par: 71**
Men's Yardage: 5635
Slope: 114   **Par: 71**
Ladies' Yardage: 4546
Slope: 114   **Par: 71**
Second Nine/Third Nine
Championship Yardage: 6159
Slope: No rating   **Par: 72**
Men's Yardage: 5705
Slope: No rating   **Par: 72**
Ladies' Yardage: 4679
Slope: No rating   **Par: 72**
Third Nine/First Nine
Championship Yardage: 6083
Slope: No rating   **Par: 71**
Men's Yardage: 5610
Slope: No rating   **Par: 71**
Ladies' Yardage: 4625
Slope: No rating   **Par: 71**

Rolling Green offers 27 holes. The first nine opened in 1968, the second nine two years later, and the third nine opened in 1991. Willie B. Lewis designed the first nine, while the owners, the Dacus family, designed the second and third nines. The course is set on rolling terrain and is bordered by woods. Water comes into play on a number of holes. You'll find bermudagrass in the fairways and bentgrass on the greens.

As you might expect from a course built in three stages, each section has its own character and feel. The front nine is relatively narrow and pretty yet straightforward. You won't find any significant water. The greens are medium-size, sloped and protected by bunkers. Keep the ball in play and you'll have some fun. On the second nine, the bunkers seem a little deeper and a bit more menacing; the greens are a little larger. The layout retains the traditional feel of the first nine. Water also comes into play. The third nine offers a bit more variety, with fairways defined and delineated by evergreen trees.

More and more women are playing golf, and courses are catering to their needs.

Photo: Robert Lahser

There are some significant elevation changes on the final nine plus a bit more water. Considering that the final nine is just a few years old, it feels remarkably mature. Overall, Rolling Green offers three fun, varied and interesting nine-hole layouts.

Amenities include a practice green, range, chipping green, locker room, bar, snack bar and pro shop.

You can walk anytime. Nonmembers can book a tee time seven days in advance. Approximate cost, including cart, is $25 weekdays and $29 on weekends.

Southern Oaks Golf Club
105 Southern Oaks Dr., Easley
• (864) 859-6698
Championship Yardage: 6701
Slope: 119   **Par: 72**
Men's Yardage: 6449
Slope: 115   **Par: 72**
Other Yardage: 6044
Slope: No rating   **Par: 72**
Ladies' Yardage: 5000
Slope: 110   **Par: 72**

Willie B. Lewis designed Southern Oaks Golf Club, which opened in 1989. The course is set on gently rolling terrain and is predominantly open. Fairways are bermudagrass; greens, bentgrass.

An important fact about Southern Oaks:

Head PGA professional Wayne Myers shot here what might be the world-record golf score for 18 holes—57. Obviously, there were numerous eagles and birdies during this impressive round, but don't think that Southern Oaks is a push-over. This is one of the finest courses in the Greenville-Spartanburg metroplex, and it surely rates as one of Willie B. Lewis' best efforts. We'd also call it somewhat underrated.

The course is modern inasmuch as it was built fewer than 10 years ago, but the design borrows more from the traditional than from today's trickery and treachery. In many ways Southern Oaks reminded us of Tanglewood in Clemmons, North Carolina, without the 100-plus bunkers. Most of the holes are open. Each hole has a distinctive character. There's usually plenty of room off the tee. The greens are mid-size to large, with plenty of slope and/or undu-lation. Bunkers come into play on quite a few holes, and water poses a hazard on several holes as well.

You'll enjoy the tee shot on the par 4 No. 3, where you must clear nearly 200 yards of water to reach a peninsula landing area; the hole mea-sures 465 yards from the back tees. There's also a 625-yard par 5 on the front nine. So make sure you bring your big stick and be ready to smack it on a few holes, although some holes favor placement over distance off the tee. Over-all, Southern Oaks is a course you must play if you're a fan of traditional yet challenging golf courses. Southern Oaks is an excellent value, especially if you walk.

There's something special about Southern Oaks.

Amenities include a practice green, range, chipping green, locker room, snack bar/grill, rental clubs and a pro shop.

The course is walkable, you should walk, and you can anytime (amazing for a modern course!). You can book a tee time for the week-end on the preceeding Thursday, seven days in advance for the weekdays. Approximate cost, including cart, is $30 weekdays and $38 on weekends.

Stoney Pointe
709 Swing About Rd., Greenwood
• (864) 942-0900

Championship Yardage:	**6681**
Slope: 125	**Par: 72**
Men's Yardage:	**6129**
Slope: 117	**Par: 72**
Other Yardage:	**5449**
Slope: 111	**Par: 72**
Ladies' Yardage:	**4962**
Slope: 120	**Par: 72**

Stoney Pointe opened in 1991. Tom Jack-son designed the course to be open in some places and bordered by woods and houses in others. In the fairways, you'll find 419 bermudagrass; the greens are seeded with bentgrass.

Stoney Pointe is a wonderful design and, for our money, it's one of Tom Jackson's best ef-forts. In places, the course has a links feel, with mounds bordering the fairways and undulations within them. Many fairways are tight, with OB and water lurking off the tee. The greens vary in size, and many are sloped and rolling. If the rough is tall, you must avoid it to score well. The yardage book/scorecard is a useful tool.

The difficulties begin on the 1st hole, a mod-erate-length par 4 with a clump of trees flank-ing the left edge of the fairway. It's a shot-makers delight right off the bat.

As with many Jackson courses, bunkers come in all shapes, sizes and depths. If the rough is grown up around the greens, it will hamper your finesse pitches and chips. You'll also find some grass bunkers—just to make the course all the more difficult. Stoney Pointe is a really fun and challenging course that we suggest you play on more than one occasion. It's also a good value.

Amenities include a practice green, range, chipping green, locker room, bar, snack bar, rental clubs and a pro shop.

You can walk anytime and book a tee time seven days in advance. Approximate cost, in-cluding cart, is $28 weekdays and $35 on week-ends.

Summersett
111 Pilot Rd., Greenville
• (864) 834-4781

Championship Yardage:	**6025**
Slope: 114	**Par: 72**
Men's Yardage:	**5420**
Slope: 108	**Par: 72**
Ladies' Yardage:	**4910**
Slope: 119	**Par: 74**

Summersett opened in the late 1930s. *Archi-tects of Golf* lists Tom Jackson as the man who revamped the track in 1979. The course is set on undulating terrain, and you'll play on bermudagrass fairways and bentgrass greens.

Summersett is short from the back tees (6025 yards), but it's also tight off the tee. In rework-ing it, Tom Jackson resisted the temptation to lengthen the course to absurd proportions. In-stead, it appears that the renovation made good use of the original routing, and the course was made more difficult by adding variable pitch

South Carolina boasts two excellent state park courses in Cheraw and Hickory Knob.
Tom Jackson designed both tracks.

Photo: S.C. Parks, Recreation & Tourism

and roll to the greens. There's plenty of variety here, and you'll discover it's most sensible to keep the driver in the bag, especially on the back nine.

With the foothills of the Smoky Mountains surrounding it, the course has a mountainous feel, and the rolling terrain makes for some interesting tee shots. It's definitely worth a visit if you're looking for a good game on a short but well-planned course.

Amenities include a practice green, chipping green, snack bar, rental clubs, a beverage cart and a pro shop.

You may walk the course anytime except weekends before 2 PM. You can book a tee time whenever you choose. Approximate cost, including cart, is $26 weekdays and $35 on weekends.

Table Rock Resort
171 Sliding Rock Rd., Pickens
• (864) 878-2030

Championship Yardage:	**6514**
Slope: 118	**Par: 72**
Men's Yardage:	**6038**
Slope: 114	**Par: 72**
Ladies' Yardage:	**5085**
Slope: 112	**Par: 72**

The golf course at Table Rock Resort was designed by Willie B. Lewis and opened in 1983. Table Rock is a mountain course—most of the holes are bordered by woods, while others are wide open, with a couple of shared fairways. You'll find common bermudagrass in the fairways and bentgrass on the greens.

Table Rock's management recently made several improvements and many locals praised the changes. The basic layout and design is sound, with some fine holes beautifully framed by trees. If everything goes according to plan, the modifications should make the course both more fun and more playable.

Many of the fairways are narrow, particularly on the back nine where the course is more wooded. There are a couple of fun driving holes where you need to bang it through a chute. Locals advise keeping the driver in the bag unless you know you can keep it straight. The greens are primarily small, flat and interestingly shaped, although the recent changeover to bentgrass may alter their character. Most holes are flat, although a few feature significant elevation changes. Water comes into play mainly in the form of pretty mountain streams that need be avoided: Take a photograph, but don't let your ball anywhere near them. A smattering of bunkers lurk here and there. Overall, Table Rock boasts a course with a lot of potential.

If you're fed up with golf, the resort also offers horseback riding, hiking, tennis or fishing in a stocked lake. Table Rock State Park is just a few minutes away.

Amenities include a practice green, range, chipping green, locker room, bar, snack bar, restaurant, rental clubs and the occasional beverage cart.

You can walk anytime, and the course is walkable for the fit. You can also book anytime. Approximate cost, including cart, is $25 weekdays and $30 on weekends.

Verdae Greens Golf Club
650 Verdae Blvd., Greenville
• (864) 676-1500

Championship Yardage:	**6773**
Slope: 126	**Par: 72**
Men's Yardage:	**6249**
Slope: 118	**Par: 72**
Other Yardage:	**5470**
Slope: No rating	**Par: 72**
Ladies' Yardage:	**5012**
Slope: 116	**Par: 72**

Verdae Greens opened in 1990. Willard Byrd designed the course in rolling terrain. Woods border many of the holes. In the fairways, you'll find bermudagrass, while Pencross bentgrass covers the greens.

Verdae Greens (an interesting name) is owned by Embassy Suites Hotels (note the large multistory Embassy Suites adjacent to the course; call (864) 676-9090 for reservations). Thus the course is a magnet for golfers on corporate outings, retreats and getaways.

S&P 500 aside, Verdae Greens is home to one of the most difficult and prettiest golf courses in the Greenville-Spartanburg area, an excellent example of Willard Byrd's magic. The course has hosted the Nike Greater Greenville Open (see our Tournaments section in this chapter). We found excellent variety and some serious challenges. Water comes into play often. The course is not overly long, but it's narrow and exacting in places. You'll need to play some target golf to play well. It's important to be in the right place at the right time. Bunkers taunt you off the tee and around the relatively large but sometimes mercilessly undulating greens.

The par 4 No. 4 is only 352 yards from the middle tees but surely must be one of the most exacting holes anywhere in the Upstate. The tee shot is downhill to a narrow fairway, which slopes precariously towards a stream on the left side of the course. The approach must carry the stream to a narrow green with a tiny pot bunker on the left—short but hair-raising. It seems that almost every hole on the course features woods or a stream. This brand of target golf will really mess with your head the first or second time out.

If you're a mid-handicapper, play from the "Other" tees and you'll have a good time at this must-play course in the Greenville-Spartanburg area. A useful purchase is the witty yardage book: Heed its advice.

Amenities include a practice green, range, chipping green, bar, snack bar, restaurant, rental clubs, a beverage cart and pro shop.

The course is walkable for the fit and dedicated, and you can walk anytime on weekdays. You can book a tee time seven days in advance. Approximate cost, including cart, is $39 weekdays and $49 on weekends.

Village Green Country Club
S.C. Hwy. 176, Gramling
• (864) 472-2411

Championship Yardage:	6372	
Slope: 122		**Par: 72**
Men's Yardage:	5873	
Slope: 117		**Par: 72**
Ladies' Yardage:	5280	
Slope: 123		**Par: 74**

Village Green Golf Course opened in the mid-'60s. *Architects of Golf* lists Russell Breeden as the course designer; give an assist to Dan Breeden. The course is seeded with bermudagrass fairways and bentgrass greens.

Village Green is a fine course—a playable and attractive track that provides good value for your hard-earned golfing dollar. The course features all the typical Breeden elements and includes a number of truly fine golf holes. There's a definite lack of hardship off the tee, but you'll have to plan your approach shot to avoid the bunkers and leave yourself a viable birdie putt. The back nine is slightly hillier. As the shadows lengthen at the end of the day, the subtle undulations in the green become more evident. To score well, keep the ball in the fairway and avoid the deep rough around the greens. True to Breeden form, the course becomes a little tougher as you come home.

Village Green is worth a visit. Oh, and call ahead on the 9th and 18th tees for your Kenburger and adult beverage from Ken's Grill.

Amenities include a practice green, range, chipping green, bar, snack bar/grill (Ken's), rental clubs, a beverage cart and pro shop.

You can walk anytime. No advance tee times are necessary during the week, but book on Thursday for the weekend. Approximate cost, including cart, is $27 weekdays and $32 on weekends.

The Walker Course at Clemson University
110 Madren Center Dr., Clemson
• (864) 656-0236

Championship Yardage:	6911	
Slope: 137		**Par: 72**
Men's Yardage:	6560	
Slope: 129		**Par: 72**
Other Yardage:	5934	
Slope: 121		**Par: 72**
Ladies' Yardage:	4667	
Slope: 103		**Par: 72**

The Walker Course at Clemson University is the official course of the Clemson Tigers. D.J. DeVictor designed the course with bermudagrass fairways and bentgrass greens. The course is set in primarily open and rolling terrain.

Clemson welcomes you not to Death Valley (the university's football stadium) but to the Walker Course, an amenity made possible primarily through the donations of several wealthy, orange-clad alumni. DeVictor designed an impressive and challenging course with plenty of trouble for the wayward. From many of the holes, the campus is clearly visible. The most difficult hole, the par 4 No. 9, is 460 yards from the "Tiger" tees. A creek runs through the middle of the hole, meaning longer hitters might have to lay up. If you do stop short, it's 200 yards over water to an undulating green set in a bowl. You should be extremely happy with par here. If you're a diehard "my blood runneth orange" Clemson fan, then you'll love the 17th hole, a moderately difficult par 3 shaped like a tiger's paw. Only at Clemson...

The course offers tremendous variety. DeVictor made good use of the land to create a number of truly challenging and interesting holes. There isn't a great deal of trouble off the tee except for wayward hitters. The greens are predominantly large and rarely flat. Bunkers and other hazards are placed to make you think quite hard—play the percentage shot and you'll be in great shape. Unless you're a superstar All-American golfer, play the course from the white tees for the most fun. The Walker Course at Clemson is the newest course in the Upstate, it's one of the prettiest, and it's a course you definitely should visit, even if you graduated from the rival universities of Georgia or South Carolina.

You'll enjoy the local color on the right flank of the 7th hole, where the odor of fresh ordure from the university's Department of Agriculture facility creates a uniquely pungent olfactory hazard.

Ironically, the Walker Course is barely

walkable even if you are fit. But you are allowed to walk at anytime. Approximate cost, including cart, is $32 weekdays and $42 on weekends.

Willow Creek Golf Course
205 Sandy Run, Greer
• (864) 476-6492
Championship Yardage: 6698
Slope: No rating   **Par: 72**
Men's Yardage: 6222
Slope: No rating   **Par: 72**
Other Yardage: 5640
Slope: No rating   **Par: 72**
Ladies' Yardage: 4846
Slope: No rating   **Par: 72**

Willow Creek Golf Course, a Tom Jackson design, opened in summer 1995. The course combines open holes with some bordered by woods. Water frequently comes into play. You'll find bermudagrass in the fairways and state-of-the-art Crenshaw bentgrass on the greens.

Willow Creek demonstrates that Tom Jackson is not a cookie-cutter designer. The course is flatter and apparently less penal than some of Jackson's other tracks—the mounds bordering the fairways aren't quite as large. Still, the course has a links feel, and if the wind is blowing, you're in for a challenge. The tee boxes are massive, and clearly were built to withstand the expected heavy play. The greens are also large, and the influence of the bunkering and slope of the green will vary depending on pin placement.

Based on the looks of the clubhouse and the track record of the ownership, there's an initial commitment to make this young course one of the better facilities in the area. This should be achieved once the course has had some time to grow and mature.

Amenities include a practice green, range, chipping green, locker room, snack bar, restaurant, rental clubs and a pro shop. There's no beverage cart, because your cart is the beverage cart: The course supplies you with your own personal cooler.

The course is not especially walkable, but you're allowed to walk on weekdays. You can book a tee time five days in advance. Approximate cost, including cart, is $37 weekdays and $45 on weekends.

Around Upstate South Carolina . . .

Fun Things To Do

While you're driving through the Greenville-Spartanburg area in the reckless pursuit of golfing nirvana, you might begin to feel somewhat awed by the sheer volume of industry. On I-85, construction crews busily prepare new interchanges and add lanes in an effort to support all the traffic produced by the area's pulsing industrial base. People work hard here. When their work is done, they like to play. And many of them play golf on the fine selection of aforementioned courses.

Visitors to the area might wonder what there is to do besides view factories from arterial roads or play golf. Well, you might be surprised at the variety of attractions here—we were. Downtown **Greenville** has undergone a fine renovation, and you'll find all sorts of eclectic opportunities for dining and drinking. The NFL's **Carolina Panthers** spend summer camp at Wofford College in Spartanburg. There's dirt track stock-car racing at the speedway in Gaffney. But perhaps most importantly, minor league icehockey has arrived in Greenville; the **Greenville Grrrowl** began play in the rock 'em-sock 'em East Coast Hockey League in the 1998-99 season.

Here are just a few other activities you might find interesting.

The **Greenville Braves**, Double-A minor league affiliate of Major League Baseball's Atlanta Braves, play at Greenville Municipal Stadium on Mauldin Road, Greenville, (864) 299-3456. The season runs from April through September, and tickets are $5 to $25. Take Exit 46 off I-85 to reach the ballpark.

If you strike out at the stadium, a real hit, especially with the kids, is the **Greenville Zoo**, 150 Cleveland Park

INSIDERS' TIP

Here's a drill to help you can those troublesome three-foot putts. On the practice green, select a hole that lies on a slope, and make a circle of about a dozen balls all the way around it. Work your way around the circle making putts, and start over if you miss one. You'll face putts of every angle, and that tester on 17 should fall a little easier.

UPSTATE

Drive, Greenville, (864) 467-4300. You'll find 14 acres of exotic animal kingdom, featuring lions and other big cats, miniature deer, kangaroos, tortoises and myriad wild beasts roaming about in a natural setting. Go ahead and make your day (and your kids' day too) with a visit to Dirty Harry, the boa constrictor. The zoo is open year round; ticket prices are $4 for adults and $2 for kids 3 to 15 years old.

Another educational attraction is **Roper Mountain Science Center**, 504 Roper Mountain Road, Greenville, (864) 281-1188. All types of fun and scientifically oriented activities await the entire family, including observatory/planetarium shows, hands-on exhibits and nature trails. Go to the intersection of I-385 and Roper Mountain Road. The center is open to the public every second Saturday of each month and on Friday nights for "Starry Night," a special presentation for astronomers. Admission is $3 for adults, $2 for children (5 and younger get in free).

For more information about activities and events in the Greenville area, contact or stop by **The Greater Greenville Convention & Visitors Center**, 206 N. Main Street, Greenville, 233-0461. Or you may also call or write **Discover Upcountry Carolina Association**, P.O. Box 3116, Greenville 29602, (800) 849-4766.

Northeast of Spartanburg, **Cowpens National Battlefield** was the site of one of the more important battles in American history. On a grim January day in 1781, Gen. Daniel Morgan and his militia beat up a group of British soldiers in less than an hour. The National Parks system site includes a visitors center, auto trail, walking trail and picnic area. Cowpens National Battlefield is at 4001 Chesnee Highway near Gaffney, (864) 461-2828. It's run by the United States Department of the Interior.

If you're a member of a YMCA, you can get in shape for longer drives at the **Spartanburg YMCA**, 226 S. Pine Street, Spartanburg, (864) 585-0306. This branch is the largest single-unit YMCA in the Southeast and features two indoor pools, basketball and handball courts, Nautilus equipment and a cardiac-rehab center.

For more information about Spartanburg, call the **Spartanburg Convention and Visitors Bureau** at (864) 594-5050.

Where to Eat

There's no shortage of places to eat in the Greenville-Spartanburg area. As we've indicated repeatedly, Upstaters are a hard-working lot who like to play golf. They also enjoy food, as evidenced by the plentiful locally owned eateries where local folk have feasted for years. You'll find all your favorite chain restaurants (we haven't written many of these up) plus an excellent variety of ethnic- and regional-fare establishments including Chinese, Italian and down-home, country-style favorites.

Abbeville

Yoder's Dutch Kitchen
$$ • S.C. Hwy. 72 E., Abbeville
• (864) 459-5556

It may come as some surprise to you that one of the top 10 Pennsylvania Dutch restaurants in the country is right here in the thriving submetropolis known as Abbeville. Yoder's declares itself a "nice place to bring your family or friends"—except on Sunday, Monday and Tuesday, when the restaurant is closed. There's a smorgasbord-style dinner buffet, so if you're particularly hungry, you can indulge to your stomach's content here. Also try the lunch buffet Wednesday through Saturday. In addition to the tasty Pennsylvania Dutch treats, you can purchase whole pies, apple butter and cinnamon-nut rolls.

Greenville

The Blue Ridge Brewing Company
$$ • 217 N. Main St., Greenville
• (864) 232-4677

Walk in the door, head straight for the bar and ask yon fair bartender for a pint of Colonel Paris Pale Ale, an outstanding hand-crafted beer the likes of which you won't find anywhere else in the Upstate. Then look around to discover that this relatively new establishment has an Old World feel and a trendy, well-to-do younger clientele—although beer lovers of all sizes, shapes and ages seem to enjoy themselves here.

Sample other fine pints, including Dove Field Wheat, Strumhouse Scottish Red Ale and the Rainbow Trout Amber Ale. There's an abundance of food as well—basic appetizers, soups, salads and sandwiches, plus some interesting pub-type entrees including pan-seared trout and a half-rack of brewhouse ribs. There's pizza too. For brewpub lovers, this is heaven.

UPSTATE

Peter David's Fine Dining
$$ • 921 Grove Rd., Greenville
• (864) 242-0404

Peter David's offers an elegant atmosphere—white linen and beautiful decor—at affordable prices. Dinner items include fresh seafood, beef and veal, and there's a value-priced wine selection. Peter David's is a member of the Blue Plate Society.

Greenwood

Little Pigs Barbeque
$ • 414 Montague Ave., Greenwood
• (864) 229-1314

Owner Barbara Sprouse and her staff want you to enjoy what she calmly refers to "the best barbeque in town." This popular establishment serves plates and sandwiches in the traditional way, replete with fries, slaw, hush puppies and all the essentials of the essential barbeque experience. But there's fare here for non-pork eaters too: homemade chicken salad, hamburgers, hot dogs, chef salads, barbeque chicken, roast beef, club sandwiches and fish plates.

Simpsonville

Country Earl's Chompin' & Stompin'
$$ • I-385 at Exit 31, Simpsonville
• (864) 967-8569

You'll get good, hearty down-home cookin' here at Country Earl's, in addition to a full evening of country entertainment. Perhaps you'll hear a rendition of co-author Scott Martin's favorite country song, "All My Ex's Live in Texas." Indulge in fried chicken, beef tips, chicken and gravy and all your favorite fixin's. And enjoy various bands, clogging exhibitions and all types of dancing to work off your meal. Tour-bus groups are welcome to come chomp and stomp.

Spartanburg

Le Baron Restaurant
$$ • 2600 E. Main St., Spartanburg
• (864) 579-3111

Le Baron's tag line invites you to "Discover the difference between eating out and real dining pleasure." This enormous restaurant, with banquet facilities for up to 500 hungry souls, offers a full menu featuring fresh seafood, charbroiled steaks, succulent prime rib and a host of veal dishes. There's live entertainment on Saturday evenings as well. And if you need catering services, call Le Baron's catering service, Sophie's Choice. Who chose that name?

Longhorn Steaks
$$ • 1793 E. Main St., Spartanburg
• (864) 585-9400

On U.S. Highway 29 near Hillcrest Mall, this version of the popular chain offers all that you've come to expect from a Longhorn. Begin your meal with a beer and some sizzling appetizers, then delve into a thick and juicy steak cooked to your specifications. If steak is not your cup of tea, devour a chicken dish or try Longhorn's famous salmon. Round out the meal with a beer or a Texas-size bowl of ice cream.

Papa Sam's Breakfast Nook
$ • 191 E. St. John St., Spartanburg
• (864) 582-6655

Papa Sam's serves breakfast 24 hours a day, seven days a week. The menu includes standard early morning fare such as pancakes, waffles, eggs cooked to order, biscuits, toast, orange juice, grapefruit juice and even some sandwiches. But the item you must order is the famous (on E. St. John Street at least) Trashcan Omelette. This work of art is stuffed full of ham, American and Swiss cheeses, mushrooms, onions, peppers and probably anything else you could possibly want. Adjacent to the breakfast-seating area of the restaurant, a bigger dining room features a full menu of prime rib, steaks, seafood and other more filling items. Papa Sam's also is home to the famous (again, on E. St. John Street) Monster Burger, which is as enormous as its name implies.

Stefano's Authentic Italian Cuisine
$$ • 1560 Union St., Spartanburg
• (864) 591-1941

Stefano's proclaims itself Spartanburg's premier Italian restaurant. It's certainly worth a visit if you love Northern Italian cuisine. This large restaurant specializes in banquets and catering. You'll find your favorite pasta dishes as well as some unique recipes featuring chicken, veal and fresh fish. Wash down your Veal Valdostana with a bottle of Valpolicella, and top it off with tiramisu.

Where to Stay

With all the business activity in the Greenville-Spartanburg area, it's important to book a room before you arrive, particularly for a weekday visit. Try to call four weeks before your arrival.

Abbeville

Westbrook Motel
$$ • S.C. Hwy. 72 W., Abbeville
• (864) 459-5533

The 18 rooms at the Westbrook Motel are reasonably priced. They include air conditioning, wall-to-wall carpeting (a rarity in these parts, we're told) and color TVs with free HBO and ESPN. And if your travels take you to beautiful Abbeville for a week or more, the hotel offers special weekly rates.

Greenville

Hyatt Regency Greenville
$$$$ • 220 N. Main St., Greenville
• (864) 235-1234

Enter the spacious atrium lobby and you'll immediately be at ease in this outstanding downtown hotel. There are 327 guest rooms, many with fine views. There's also a pool, health club and a full-service business center. It's probably the most expensive place to stay in Greenville, but it's also the most pleasant and plush. In-room amenities include cable TV (complete with ESPN) and a coffee maker.

Holiday Inn Express
$$ • McAlister Square Mall,
27 S. Pleasantburg Dr., Greenville
• (864) 232-3339

This 74-room Holiday Inn Express is off I-385 and U.S. Highway 291, two blocks from the Palmetto International Exposition Center and close to McAlister Square Mall. Breakfast is included in your room rate. Amenities include fax and other business services and cable TV in each room.

The Phoenix
$$ • 246 N. Pleasantburg Dr., Greenville
• (864) 233-4651

The 183-room Phoenix is a full-service inn with outdoor dining at the Courtyard Grille, plus romantic dining in the Palms Restaurant. There's dancing and entertainment in The Bar. The Phoenix exudes a much more intimate setting than the typical motel. In-room amenities include cable TV plus full bathroom en-suite.

Pettigru Place
$$$$ • 302 Pettigru St., Greenville
• (864) 242-4529

In the heart of downtown Greenville, Pettigru Place offers five individually decorated guest rooms, each with private bath and televi-

sion. A full gourmet breakfast is included in the room rate.

Greenwood

Holiday Inn Greenwood
$$ • 1014 Montague Ave., Greenwood
• (864) 223-4231

The Holiday Inn Greenwood offers 100 recently remodeled rooms as well as a courtyard with a pool and decks. It's a good value as well, particularly if you make use of the corporate, group and special weekend rates; kids and teens stay free. A free full breakfast and local calls are included in your room rate, and fax and copy services are available. Relax in Simon's Bar and Grill after golf or take in the bountiful Sunday brunch before you venture forth onto the links for your afternoon round. If it's raining on your golfing parade and you and your foursome are stuck inside, the in-room televisions offer cable with ESPN.

Spartanburg

Best Western Spartan Inn & Conference Center
$$ • I-85 Bus. and S.C. Hwy. 9,
Spartanburg • (864) 578-5400

This comfortable and accessible Best Western enjoyed a complete renovation just four years ago and is popular among the business-traveler set. This hotel offers 122 rooms with free cable TV. There's a business center, banquet and meeting rooms, a tennis court and an outdoor pool. Corporate rates are available. After your busy day of golf and/or business, retire to Bigoli's Restaurant and Lounge.

Courtyard by Marriott
$$ • 110 Mobile Dr., Spartanburg
• (864) 585-2400

Designed by business travelers for business travelers, as the chain's saying goes, Spartanburg's version of the well-known and liked Courtyard concept is perfect for the person who is coming to the Upstate to close a deal. But it's also an excellent place for the golfer. The restaurant offers a great breakfast buffet and serves a solid sandwich and dinner menu. Choose a guest room or indulge in a suite at this 108-room lodging. Courtyard has a reputation for good value.

Holiday Inn North
$$$ • I-85 and S.C. Hwy. 9, Spartanburg
• (864) 578-5400

The Holiday Inn in Spartanburg is a good

UPSTATE

place to stay and eat. There are 122 recently renovated rooms and suites, each with cable TV with HBO, ESPN and CNN. There's a business center for the corporate traveler as well as meeting rooms. The hotel offers corporate rates. If you're in town for business, unwind on the

tennis court, by the pool or in Bleachers! Sports Bar and Grill.

Residence Inn by Marriott
$$$ • 9011 Fairforest Rd., Spartanburg • (864) 576-3333

The Residence Inn chain tends to cater to long-term guests: Weekly and monthly rates are available. Residence Inn Spartanburg offers 88 one- or two-bedroom suites, each with a fully equipped kitchen, a living room with a fireplace and cable TV with HBO. A complimentary breakfast and access to a swimming pool are included in the room rate.

INSIDERS' TIP

Join the USGA or your local golf association.

Outer Banks

The Outer Banks of North Carolina conjure images of big sand dunes, fishing villages, hammocks, hang-gliding, windsurfing and glorious, relaxing family vacations. The area is also a secret golf paradise. Popular and upscale as well as mid-range courses here offer excellent golfing experiences, and the surrounding beach communities offer everything else for a complete vacation.

The Outer Banks north of Oregon Inlet include Corolla, Duck, Southern Shores, Kitty Hawk, Kill Devil Hills and Nags Head; Roanoke Island to the west includes Manteo and Wanchese; and to the south are Hatteras and Ocracoke islands. All of the golf courses are easily accessible from Manteo, Duck, Southern Shores, Kill Devil Hills, Kitty Hawk or Nags Head. Then head south to Hatteras or Ocracoke for some easy days of pure relaxation, maybe with a fishing pole or just a good book.

From Virginia north, the Outer Banks are perhaps the best know and most popular parts of North Carolina. Perhaps that's because much of the Outer Banks are more accessible to Virginians than many in central North Carolina.

The best guidebook to this area, in our humble opinion, is *The Insiders' Guide to North Carolina's Outer Banks,* available at bookstores or through www.insiders.com.

Currituck Club
N.C. Hwy. 12, Corolla
• (252) 453-9400,
(888) 453-9400

Championship Yardage: 6885	
Slope: 136	**Par: 72**
Men's Yardage:	**6404**
Slope: 128	**Par: 72**
Other Yardage:	**5814**
Slope: 121	**Par: 72**
Ladies' Yardage:	**4766**
Slope: 120	**Par: 72**

Carolinas Golf Group created the Currituck Club, Corolla's only golf-resort community, as part of a 600-acre development. It promises the upscale ambiance appropriate for the Outer Banks gentry and like visitors. The land was used by a shooting club in 1857. That clubhouse, rebuilt in 1879 and listed on the National Register of Historic Places, is preserved on one end of the development.

The 18-hole Rees Jones course opened in July 1996. The dense vegetation and several spectacular dunes provide an opportunity for a true links-style layout. Abundant wetlands, maritime forests and two lakes all come into play. The number-one handicap hole is the 12th, a par 4 dogleg right that measures 454 yards from the tips. It's narrow at the turn with three bunkers on the inside of the dogleg. If you drive it about 250, it's a 3-wood to a narrow approach, which bottles to about 30 yards wide in front of the green. Then it drops severely on the left with a collection area on that side of the hole and a big hill wrapping around the right of the green. The two-tier green is high in the back, so if you can hit it there you can play down to the lower level.

The 7th is a beautiful signature hole on Currituck Sound. It's a 532-yard par 5. Water runs along the left side, plus there's a thinned line of maple and oak trees. You can hit a 300-yard drive to a big oak tree where the fairway narrows; then you can go for the green and avoid the three bunkers in a row on the right. The green is raised on the

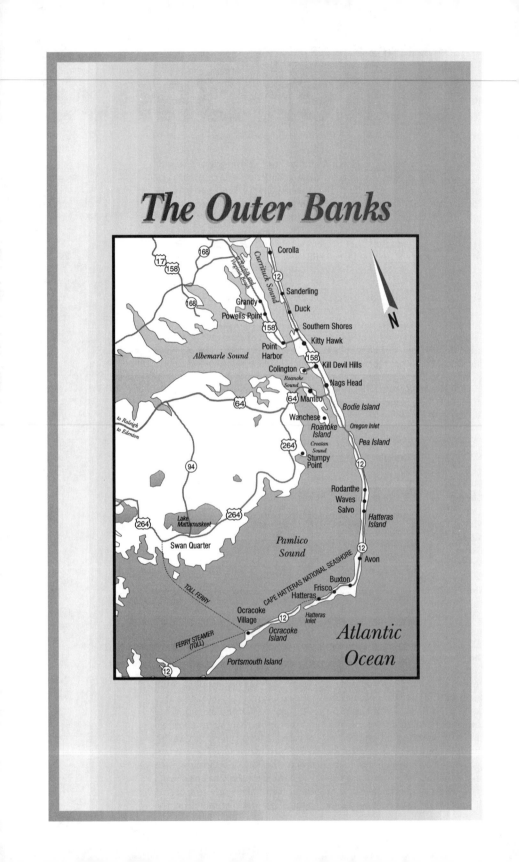

GOLF COURSES ON NORTH CAROLINA'S OUTER BANKS

Course	Type	# Holes	Par	Slope	Yards	Walking	Booking	Cost w/Cart
Currituck Club	semiprivate	18	72	128	6404	no	365 days	$45-90
Duck Woods Country Club	semiprivate	18	72	123	6161	no	1 week	$45
Goose Creek Golf & C. C.	semiprivate	18	72	109	5943	no	2 days	$35-40
Nags Head Golf Links	semiprivate	18	71	126	5717	no	365 days	$45-75
The Pointe Golf Club	semiprivate	18	71	113	5911	yes	call	$37-52
Sea Scape Golf Resort	semiprivate	18	72	123	6052	no	90 days	$40-60

How to Get Here

Only three vehicle access routes will bring you to the Outer Banks from the mainland.

The Wright Memorial Bridge, four lanes wide across two spans, is the main access to the Outer Banks from the north. The Monitor-Merrimac Memorial Bridge-Tunnel (I-664), connecting Chesapeake and Newport News in Hampton Roads, Virginia, is a time-saver. If you're coming from the Washington, D.C., area or points north, take I-95 S. to I-295 north of Richmond, and follow signs to I-64 E. toward Norfolk and Virginia Beach. Follow I-64 E. until you get to Hampton. Go south on I-664 toward Newport News and through the tunnel; then take I-64 toward Norfolk/Virginia Beach; go south on U.S. Highway 17 at Deep Creek, Virginia, to South Mills, North Carolina. Pick up N.C. Highway 343 S. to U.S. Highway 158 E., which will take you directly to the Outer Banks.

An alternative from Hampton is to follow I-64 E. to Exit 290B (Battlefield Boulevard S.). Proceed past Chesapeake General Hospital (on the right) and exit right onto Va. Highway 168 S. Remain on Va. 168 into North Carolina; it eventually merges with U.S. 158 E. at Barco. Then follow U.S. 158 E. to the Outer Banks.

From points west and south, take I-95 to Rocky Mount, North Carolina, and pick up U.S. Highway 64 E. This route will take you to Manns Harbor, across the William B. Umstead Bridge to the north end of Roanoke Island and into Manteo. Follow U.S. 64 E. through Manteo and across the Manteo-Nags Head Causeway to access the beaches. At Whalebone Junction, take N.C. 12 south to reach Oregon Inlet, Hatteras Island and Ocracoke Island, or U.S. 158 to Nags Head, Kill Devil Hills, Kitty Hawk, Southern Shores, Duck and Corolla.

If arriving from the south you may choose the ferry from Cedar Island to Ocracoke — an experience in itself, although not when you're in any rush to reach the golf courses on the northern end. The North Carolina Department of Transportation Ferry Division operates seven routes within its system. The ferry service runs its fleet of more than 20 vessels year-round. Some trips (Hatteras-Ocracoke) take as little as 45 minutes. Others (Ocracoke-Cedar Island) last as long as 2½ hours. Call (800) BY FERRY for information about reservations, varying costs and schedules. The trip from Cedar Island to Ocracoke Island costs $10 per car, and the ferry from Ocracoke to Hatteras Island is free. Along N.C. Highway 12 from the southernmost tip of Hatteras Island through Pea Island National Wildlife Refuge to Oregon Inlet, you will enjoy a scenic drive.

The Herbert C. Bonner bridge spans Oregon Inlet and links the South Nags Head beaches and Pea Island National Wildlife Refuge on Hatteras Island.

Photo: Dare County Tourist Bureau

right, sloping flat toward the sound across the fairway. One huge bunker guards the left side of the green.

A driving range with multiple tees and several target greens will provide a good warm up, and the practice green is expansive.

Approximate greens fees with cart range from $45 to $90 depending on the season. Walking is restricted.

Duck Woods Country Club
50 Dogwood Tr., Kitty Hawk
• (252) 261-2609

Championship Yardage:	**6589**	
Slope: 128	**Par: 72**	
Men's Yardage:	**6161**	
Slope: 123	**Par: 72**	
Ladies' Yardage:	**5411/5764**	
Slope: 129/120	**Par: 72**	

This country club is the oldest course on the Outer Banks. It boasts a pristine setting among tall pines and other foliage. The club aims to accommodate its 900 members, many of whom are non-locals, but accepts public play year-round as time permits.

Housing surrounds parts of the course but does not inhibit play. You shouldn't be afraid to cut loose with a long shot; you won't find a window close enough to break.

Ellis Maples designed the course. Fairways are narrow, and water comes into play on 14 holes. The bentgrass greens were reconstructed in 1996 and 1997.

INSIDERS' TIP

Playing at coastal courses, the wind can make a difference of several clubs on one hole. The par 3 you reached with a 7-iron yesterday may require a 4-iron today. Keep the breeze in mind when you're making your club selection.

Warm up before playing Duck Woods because the course begins with a bang: a 481-yard par 5. Stay warm for the entire round because it ends with a 506-yard par 5. Shot placement is key on this course. For example, on the par 5 14th, you must lay up in front of the water bisecting the fairway. Duck Woods is a friendly but unforgiving course; again, every shot must be placed carefully.

The driving range, putting green, target greens and a practice bunker are open to the public the day of play only.

Club rentals are available. The pro shop is stocked primarily with balls and tees but includes limited equipment and apparel as well. A clubhouse, locker rooms for men and women, a bar and restaurant are available to members.

Walking is allowed for members only. Booking is accepted a week in advance. The greens fee, including cart, varies according to season and time of day. Approximate cost is $45.

Goose Creek Golf and Country Club
U.S. Hwy. 158, Grandy
• (252) 453-4008, (800) 443-4008

Championship Yardage:	**6191**	
Slope: 114	**Par: 72**	
Men's Yardage:	**5943**	
Slope: 109	**Par: 72**	
Ladies' Yardage:	**5558**	
Slope: 116	**Par: 72**	

Technically speaking this course is not on the Outer Banks, but it's just minutes away across the Currituck Bridge on the mainland. Besides, we think Goose Creek has the right idea. The club's philosophy summed up on its scorecard: "Golf is a fun, relaxing, competitive sport. Enjoy Goose Creek to its fullest potential."

Goose Creek is one of the most player-friendly courses anywhere. The main objective is for golfers to have a good time and come back again. This is not a course where you will lose countless balls and go home frustrated. This is a course for the whole family. In fact, family golf outings are encouraged, and children are welcome during a recommended time frame conducive to young golfers who are learning the game.

The clubhouse is a former hunting lodge. The owners have converted the small bedrooms into private locker rooms for players. The homey atmosphere is derived from the owners' receptive attitudes as well as the ambiance of the pine-paneled lounge and snack bar, which retain the feel of the lodge living room and kitchen.

Steve and Bill Jernigan built the course in the early '90s using a Jerry Turner and Associates design. The Jernigans believe in their golfing concepts and are interested in the development of packages to bring golfers to the Outer Banks for the fun aspects of the game in a comfortable Southern-style atmosphere.

Bermudagrass greens and fairways grace the flat Goose Creek course, which is not a typical beach layout. The tree-lined fairways are relatively tight on the front nine and more undulating and open on the back. Greens are relatively small.

The 13th is considered the signature hole. During fall and winter, the wind in your face presents the difficulty; during summer, the wind is at your back, thus the hole plays quite differently. A few water hazards exist and could come into play on five holes.

After playing Goose Creek, you should feel confident and upbeat about your game. It's a course for high-handicappers as well as seasoned golfers.

A driving range and practice green are available.

Only members can walk. Approximate greens fees range from $35 to $40 for prime morning tee times. The course offers a three-day golf pass for approximately $99.

Nags Head Golf Links
Village at Nags Head, 5615 S. Seachase Dr., off U.S. Hwy. 158, Milepost 15, Nags Head • (252) 441-8073, (800) 851-9404

Championship Yardage:	6126	
Slope: 130	Par: 71	
Men's Yardage:	5717	
Slope: 126	Par: 71	
Other Yardage:	5354	
Slope: 123	Par: 71	
Ladies' Yardage:	4415	
Slope: 117	Par: 71	

This course offers enticing beauty along the Roanoke Sound. Views of the water are spectacular on almost every hole. Architect Bob Moore remembered not to mess with Mother Nature too much when he designed this course, and he left intact almost all of the wonderful natural landscape.

With the wind whipping around the course, its proximity to the ocean and its design, this course could easily be mistaken for a Scottish links. If your ball travels out of the fairway, plan to spend time searching the dense undergrowth. The distance is fully realized because of the strength and influence of the constant winds. This is especially true on the 583-yard par-5 18th. It runs dangerously close to the Roanoke Sound and, therefore, truly tests your skills as a golfer. This course is difficult, and a less experienced golfer may want to play from the mid-front ("Other") tees. You also may want to leave your woods in the bag, because your drive can easily get caught in the wind and blown off-line.

In addition to the wind, water and wetlands present challenges, coming into play on all but four holes. Nags Head Golf Links requires both muscle and mind. Houses on the course may present a fear of breaking glass if you don't have control of your tee shots. One thing you can't control is the wind.

Of the five par 3s, none is a "gimme." The cruelest par 3 is the 221-yard 15th. With one quick gust of wind, your ball could either be in sand on the right or in the pond in front of the green. This course changes almost minute by minute. You can be standing on the tee box with wind hitting you in your face, take a quick glance at the flag and notice the wind blowing the exact opposite direction on the green.

Nags Head Golf Links has a pro shop, bar, restaurant, driving range, putting green and rental clubs. The Links Grille overlooks the 9th green and Roanoke Sound.

Walking is restricted. Approximate greens fees, including cart, range from $45 to $75. A three-round pass is available and may be used also on The Currituck Club. Kids play free after 5 PM on Fridays and Saturdays.

This is a golfing experience that every golfer should appreciate, regardless of ability. A round here will make your visit to the Outer Banks unforgettable. It's also the place to remember that golf is just a game. But golf on this beautiful course, regardless of your score, is a game worth playing.

Pointe Golf Club
U.S. Hwy. 158 E., Powells Point • (252) 491-8388

Championship Yardage:	6320	
Slope: 120	Par: 71	
Men's Yardage:	5911	
Slope: 113	Par: 71	
Other Yardage:	5428	
Slope: 108	Par: 71	
Ladies' Yardage:	4862	
Slope: 110	Par: 71	

Pointe Golf Club opened in 1995. It's a Russell Breeden design and was the first course in the country seeded with A1 bentgrass. This new disease-resistant, dense grass has been researched extensively at Penn State University, and Keith Hall, Pointe owner and president of United Turf, is a perfectionist when it comes to lush grass. The site of the course formerly was a turf farm, thus a special bit of attention was given these perfect greens. Hall and his friendly staff are devoted to providing the finest course conditions, including lush tifdwarf fairways.

No development surrounds this course, save the few scattered farmhouses that add to the character of this rural Carolina-mainland community.

Retirees are moving to the Carolinas from all over the United States; one of the big reasons is golf.

Photo:Bill Kiser

Although built in an area known for links-style golf courses, the Pointe is more of a traditional layout. The scenery is quite beautiful, as the Pointe overlooks the Currituck Sound. Strategically placed water hazards come into play on 15 holes, and generally windy conditions ensure that the course will never play the same way twice.

The signature hole is No. 6, a 457-yard par 4 with a carry over wetlands, a blind shot to the fairway, water, bunkers and slopes to the right.

The 18th hole plays an exciting 619 yards from the back tees. Your drive has to hit the fairway. Three perfect shots will make your birdie for the day.

A driving range, practice bunker, full-size putting green, clubhouse, pro shop and restaurant are available. The clubhouse is quite classy, and you'll appreciate the course's beauty.

Walking is allowed after noon from October through May for greens fee pass-holders. Approximate greens fees are $52 in summer and $37 after October. Packages are available through area rental companies.

Sea Scape Golf Club

300 Eckner St., off U.S. Hwy. 158 E.,
Milepost 2½, Kitty Hawk • (252) 261-2158

Championship Yardage:	**6408**
Slope: 127	**Par: 72**
Men's Yardage:	**6052**
Slope: 123	**Par: 72**
Ladies' Yardage:	**5536**
Slope: 114	**Par: 73**

This course is cut into the maritime forests of Kitty Hawk and the signature dunes of the Outer Banks. It was designed by Art Wall, with bentgrass greens and fairways. The fairways are somewhat wide. During the winter of 1997, the course was redesigned and remodeled by

Paragon Construction and Nicklaus Design Company. Waste areas, new tees and Scottish-style bunkering were added, making it a true links course.

Sea Scape is the second-oldest course on the Outer Banks, and it has aged beautifully since opening in 1965. At Sea Scape, as at virtually all seaside courses, but particularly those on the Outer Banks, you not only play the course but also the wind. The course derives its character from the natural surroundings, with ocean views from 15 holes. If the wind is unforgiving and your shot lands in the rough, you will be looking for your Titleist in sand and sea oats as well as scrub.

The most challenging hole is No. 11. It's long and always plays against the prevailing wind. The par 3 141-yard 9th is aesthetically appealing from its elevated tee. Club selection is imperative here depending on the direction of the wind. Your shot easily could bounce off the road if you have a good tail wind.

With its five par 3s and five par 5s, Sea Scape is a true test of your golfing ability as well as your patience. Housing along Sea Scape is sometimes close to the course and surrounded by woods.

Sea Scape has a teaching center, club fitting, rental clubs, a driving range, bar, restaurant and a fully stocked pro shop.

Walking is not allowed. Approximate greens fees range from $40 to $60, including cart. Advance tee times are available whenever you call, which means you should call well in advance of your arrival if you plan to be here during the busy summer season.

Around the Outer Banks . . .

Tourism is king on these once barren, now booming barrier islands. As a result, the type, price range and selection of accommodations, restaurants and activities span the gamut. Regardless of your personal preferences and tastes, we think you'll find something here to satisfy you and yours.

Explore the options, especially in the off-season when locals' spirits rise and temperatures and lodging rates fall into a comfortable range. We suggest you pick up a copy of *The Insiders' Guide to North Carolina's Outer Banks* to help in your search for a wonderful stay. These books are available in bookstores nationwide or through direct order, (800) 582-2665. Or, check out the Insiders' Guide homepage on the Internet at www.insiders.com.

Fun Things To Do

On the Outer Banks, you're sure to enjoy the beaches and the huge sand dunes, which are unlike any others anywhere else in the world. Looking for something unique? Try recreational clamming at **Hatteras Village Aqua Farm,** off N.C. Highway 12, just north of Hatteras Village, (252) 986-2249. Rent a rake and bucket for $3 and sift the tidal flats of private clam beds to find your own dinner (22 cents per clam up to 100 in aggregate) at the only rake-your-own clam farm on the East Coast.

If you tire of harvesting mollusks, we suggest you follow Tony Bennett's advice: "When in Rome, do as the Romans do. . . ." On the Outer Banks, you must do some fishing, even on a golf trip; it's the greatest lure for most vacationers here, and many locals do it for a living, so there must be something to it, right? In fact, these barrier islands are renowned for offering some of the best fishing opportunities in the world. Call **Oregon Inlet Fishing Center,** N.C. 12 at the northern terminus of the Bonner Bridge, (252) 441-6301, or **Pirate's Cove Marina,** Nags Head-Manteo Causeway, (252) 473-3906, to get on a head boat or arrange a charter. Or stop by one of the many bait and tackle shops to get the gear you'll need for shore or pier fishing.

If angling isn't your activity, enjoy any one of the many quaint villages where biking or strolling is better than driving. Appreciate the native arts and crafts in the galleries, shops and boutiques prevalent all along the Outer Banks. You will find some enticing buys to remind you of your vacation here.

The **Wright Brothers Memorial,** U.S. Highway 158, Milepost 8, Kill Devil Hills, (252) 441-7430, will teach you all about the world's first flight in a heavier-than-air plane. Plan on spending a couple of hours at this educational and interesting site. National Park Service interpreters lead you through the historic events that started humankind's love affair with air travel, and the monument near the location of those first flights is a worthwhile stop. An entrance fee of $2 per person or $4 per car is charged.

OUTER BANKS

Dowdy's Amusement Park, U.S. Highway 158 (S. Croatan Highway), Milepost 11½, Nags Head, (252) 441-5122, is open from late spring through Labor Day, with a Ferris wheel and rides for the kid in all of us.

Hang-gliding and windsurfing are important sports on the Outer Banks, for good reason: The wind here is as consistently good as anywhere on earth for related recreational activities. Surfers also find consistent seasonal breaks at a number of spots, especially on Hatteras Island. Shops to help get you catching the big one, be it wave or wind, are all over the place.

The *Lost Colony* **historical drama** tells the story of the first attempt at English settlement in the New World. Summer nights are enchanting when you enter the outdoor amphitheater and immerse yourself in the mystery. Call (252) 473-3414 or (800) 488-5012 for information about tickets ($14 for adults, $7 for children younger than 12). The curtain goes up nightly except Saturdays, from early June through late August. **Waterside Theatre,** performance site of the Lost Colony, is off U.S. Highway 64/264 on the north end of historic Roanoke Island.

The **North Carolina Aquarium,** Airport Road, on the north end of Roanoke Island, (252) 473-3494, is open daily. Become acquainted with crabs, sharks, Loggerhead turtles and other marine creatures from the nearby Atlantic. The aquarium is open 9 AM to 6 PM Monday through Saturday and 1 to 5 PM on Sunday. Admission is $3 for adults, $2 for senior citizens and active military, $1 for kids ages 6 through 17 and free for children younger than 6.

The *Elizabeth II* is a representative 16th-century sailing ship, commemorating Sir Walter Raleigh's Roanoke Voyages. The **Elizabeth II State Historic Site,** (252) 473-1144, is a museum about life in the 16th century. It's easy to find on Ice Plant Island. Just follow the signs to Roanoke Island.

The country's oldest-known grapevine grows off Mother Vineyard Road in Manteo. The **Mother Vine** is believed to be 400 years old. A small winery owned by the Etheridge family cultivated the vine on Baum's Point, making the original **Mother Vineyard** wine until

It's never too early to start playing golf.

Photo: The Charlotte Observer

the late 1950s. Mother Vineyard Scuppernong is still produced, and the sweet pink wine is available locally.

The **Elizabethan Gardens,** off U.S. Highway 64/264 on the north end of Roanoke Island, were initiated in 1951 by the state garden club as a memorial to the people of Sir Walter Raleigh's lost colony. Herbs, wild and native flowers and statuary combine with the history and mystery for a fantastic and beautiful adventure. Admission is $3 for adults, $1 for youths ages 12 through 17 and free for children younger than 12. Call (252) 473-3234 for information on seasonal hours. And, if you go, take a camera.

Want to pick up a few bargains? Check out **Soundings Factory Stores,** U.S. Highway 158, Milepost 16½, Nags Head, (252) 441-7395, where you'll find discount prices everyday on major name brands such as Bass, Bugle Boy, Van Heusen, Corning, Pfaltzgraf and more. Browse through several collections of boutiques on the northern beaches from Corolla to Duck: **Scarborough Faire, Wee Winks Square, Osprey Landing,** the **Waterfront Shops, TimBuck II** and **Corolla Light Village,** to name just a handful.

The **Cape Hatteras Lighthouse,** off N.C. Highway 12, Cape Point in Buxton, is probably the most recognizable symbol of the Outer Banks, and, perhaps, North Carolina. Explore the visitors center, with its interesting exhibits and gifts, or climb the 268 steps to the top of this 180-foot, black and white spiral-striped structure. Climbing is permitted from May through Columbus Day. (Please note: It's a strenuous climb.) The National Park Service recently spent $9.2 million to relocate the structure to a site less prone to erosion.

Where To Eat

Seafood in any type of appetizer, sandwich or entree is a standard favorite on the Outer Banks. It's fresh and served up in a wide variety of tempting dishes. An increasing number of eateries stays open for most of the year; however, hours are limited, so don't plan on late night (or all night) dining at too many places. Check for availability of specials everywhere you go too, as daily fresh fish is often more exciting than the standard menu.

Liquor by the drink is not served on Roanoke Island, so enjoy the choices of beer and wine or ask about brown bagging at many establishments if you wish to partake of spirits.

Refer to our Preface for an explanation of the pricing code.

Corolla

Grouper's Grille & Wine Bar
$$$ • TimBuck II, N.C. Hwy. 12, Corolla
• (252) 453-4077

This restaurant—opened in 1996—offers recipes with influences from Thailand, India and Greece, among other locales. The pasta, chicken, steak and local seafood entrees are eclectic and tasty. The vegetarian offerings include wonderful things, such as an appetizer of our favorite Portobello mushrooms with vegetable pesto or a spinach lasagna with seasonal vegetables and a white wine tomato marinara sauce. Or, try the blackened shrimp salad with orange thyme vinaigrette dressing. Everything is fresh and original. Dessert is an experience all

its own. We suggest the chocolate bag with white chocolate mousse and raspberry sauce garnished with fresh fruit. An extensive selection of wine and beer is available to accompany your meal, which is served on white tablecloths bathed in candlelight. Don't dress up if you feel casual. Reservations are recommended. Grouper's serves lunch and dinner.

Duck

Duck News Cafe
$$ • N.C. Hwy. 12, Duck
• (252) 261-1549

Italian entrées, shrimp served three ways and creative local crab and tuna entrees are good choices here. The aged beef tenderloin is delicious, and the perfect evening topper is Key lime pie or the Lady Godiva, a sinful concoction of ice cream drowned in chocolate liqueur. Reservations are recommended for this family restaurant across from the Sanderling Inn. Dinner is served spring through fall.

Blue Point Bar & Grill
$$$ • The Waterfront Shops, Duck
• (252) 261-8090

This is a favorite locals' haunt for imaginative, expertly prepared food, served in an atmosphere that doesn't take itself too seriously. The menu centers on what's fresh, rather than a set selection. Try a tuna entree, prepared in a way you never would have thought up yourself but will wish you could duplicate. Enjoy a steak and potato dinner that's anything but usual. And, if you usually don't have dessert, make an exception here. Reservations well in advance are a good idea, as is a visit to this waterfront bistro for lunch, dinner or Sunday brunch. Watch for the sunset from the porch for a magnificent dinner show.

Elizabeth's Cafe & Winery
$$$ • Scarborough Faire, off N.C. Hwy. 12, Duck • (252) 261-6145

As the name implies, wine is a primary focus here. If you like wine and want to learn a few things, you'll appreciate the choices at this warm and casual establishment, recognized since 1991 by *Wine Spectator* magazine. For shopping, there's a walk-in wine cellar and a retail sales area. The changing menu offers eclectic country French and California dishes. Fresh seafood is prepared with fresh ingredients in cre-

ative and varied ways, and all desserts are homemade and delicious.

Dinner is served year-round, and lunch is served in season. Reservations are needed. Ask about the prix-fixe dinner for $80 per person, which includes six courses and accompanying wines. Elizabeth's has a strict no-smoking policy.

Fishbones Raw Bar & Grill
$$ • Scarborough Ln., Duck • (252) 261-6991

Fishbones is in the Scarborough Lane Shoppes next to Scarborough Faire. It opened in the summer of 1995 and was immediately popular and successful. This restaurant has a good raw bar with cold drinks to accompany the choices. The raw bar is open all day, with more than a dozen selections.

Fishbones also serves the usual burgers and chicken entrees for lunch, or try a big salad or veggie burger.

If you can't get there for lunch or the raw bar, don't fret: Fishbones also serves dinner. A fish special is fresh everyday, and it's great in a barbecue mesquite; or try sautéed pork medallions topped with backfin crab and hollandaise. Evenings during the season, live music adds to the nice atmosphere.

Before you leave, check out the array of T-shirts. You'll want one to remind you of your trip.

Kitty Hawk

Ocean Boulevard
$$$ • Beach Rd. (N.C. Hwy. 12), Milepost 2, Kitty Hawk • (252) 261-2546

This restaurant was created by the same people who operate The Blue Point in Duck. Ocean Boulevard is in the former 1949 Virginia Dare Hardware Store building. The food is fresh and original. A good appetizer is poached oysters with horseradish risotto and fresh dill. The delightful entrees feature pasta, beef,

After a round of golf, how about some cool refreshments at one of our eateries?

Photo: J. Aaron Trotman

shrimp, pork chops or fish, and you're sure to find a wine selection to accompany any dish. Reservations are recommended, and hours vary seasonally. The cigar and martini bar was added in 1997. This is a classy restaurant—popular with good reason.

Kill Devil Hills

Awful Arthur's
$$ • Beach Rd. (N.C. Hwy. 12), Milepost 6, Kill Devil Hills • (252) 441-5955

Awful Arthur's is popular for steamed seafood and beer—lots of each. Locals keep it busy and even have their own specials offered all day Mondays. It's a casual and typical beach place, with some of the biggest fresh oysters shucked by fast and friendly bartenders who also serve a variety of drinks. Landlubber sandwiches and platters are available if you're not a seafood lover.

Bob's Grill
$ • U.S. Hwy. 158, Milepost 9, Kill Devil Hills • (252) 441-0707

This is one of the late night places to eat on Wednesday through Saturday and also one of the best breakfast spots. Omelets, served during any meal, are Greek, Western, Mexican or three-cheese. A fine inexpensive lunch can also be found here, such as grilled veggies over brown rice, a tuna sandwich or spinach salad. For dinner, you will also find a good prime rib or grilled chicken breast with rice or baked potato and veggies.

Goombay's Grille and Raw Bar
$$ • Beach Rd., Milepost 7½, Kill Devil Hills • (252) 441-6001

Come to this fun spot if you're looking for a great time to go with your great food. It's noisy at times, but it's the sound of people having fun, so just join in. The food is built around a Caribbean theme (as is the colorful decor) and centers on fresh seafood and pastas. Our absolute favorite chicken-wing appetizer is served here. Or try the spicy crab balls or sweet coconut shrimp. Daily specials also include some kind of stir-fry. There's a full line of beer, wine and spirits to wash it all down. And, of course, the Key lime pie (our favorite)

is irresistible. For the price, quality of food and fun atmosphere, this place is hard to beat for lunch or dinner.

Chardo's
$$ • U.S. Hwy. 158, Milepost 9, Kill Devil Hills • (252) 441-0276

Go during the winter for the pasta buffet or anytime for the steak and pasta specials. Veal chops also are a specialty. Italian or California wine accompanies the entrees and salads. A coffee bar is available for after-dinner beverages. Desserts are made fresh here, and the cannolis, tiramisu or napoleons make for a great finish to any meal. Chardo's is open all year for lunch, dinner and Sunday brunch.

Nags Head

Kelly's Outer Banks Restaurant & Tavern
$$$ • U.S. 158, Milepost 10½, Nags Head • (252) 441-4116

There are those people who feel their Outer Banks experience isn't complete without a visit to Kelly's. What keeps them coming to this place in droves? Well, it could be the great seafood, or the extra-fun atmosphere, or the bar where you can dance the night away to live bands. Maybe you see all your friends here. Go see for yourself.

The raw bar is a great place to begin the meal. Dinner is the only meal served here, and choices include fresh seafood dishes, chicken, pasta or beef. You might like the sweet potato biscuits so much, you'll be full before the entree.

Stinky Bean's Gourmet Eatery
$ • U.S. Hwy. 158, Milepost 11½, Nags Head • (252) 480-0727

Monty and Colleen Jones opened this shop in 1997 and offer a great wine selection along with the best take-out breakfast on the beach. A breakfast burrito or croissant can be stuffed with fresh peppers and eggs and lots of other tasty embellishments. For lunch, try some of Colleen's fresh baked breads—Italian, French, grain, white rye, sunflower, pumpernickel, Kaiser rolls, bagels, cheese bread, challah or eight grain—with Boar's Head meats and cheeses. A

INSIDERS' TIP

Count your clubs before beginning play and be sure to take the same number home with you. Be especially careful around the greens, an area where players are most likely to leave a club behind.

good choice for a big eater is the Good Reverend Hollywood, "so good it's a religious experience," states the menu, with turkey, roast beef, bacon, muenster cheese, cole slaw and Russian dressing. The apple pudding with lemon sauce is a wonderful dessert. Gift baskets are made to order for a gourmet treat.

Penguin Isle Soundside Grill
$$$ • U.S. Hwy. 158, Milepost 16, Nags Head • (252) 441-2637

Another place with an outstanding wine list—*Wine Spectator* has recognized it for excellence since 1992—Penguin Isle also offers off-season wine dinners and full-time nice ambiance. The views of the Roanoke Sound are as soothing as the sunsets are spectacular. Fresh pasta, seafood or aged beef plus breads and creative pairings are delectable. If you like escargot, try it here Southern-style over black bean cakes with tequila horseradish sauce. Duck Roanoke or shrimp Aristotle are our favorite entree choices. The desserts are also worth a taste. Penguin Isle is open from March through December.

Soundside Pavilion
$$$ • U.S. Hwy. 158, Milepost 16½, Nags Head • (252) 441-0535

All summer long, you will find a full surf-and-turf buffet here, and the view of the Roanoke Sound adds to the attraction. Fruits, salads, rolls, desserts and ice cream are included with such delectable items as fish, chicken, clams, barbecue, pasta, oysters and crab legs. A breakfast buffet is served daily in season, including pancakes, ham, corned beef hash, sausage, bacon, eggs, grits, French toast, fruit and all the coffee you can hold.

The Dunes
$ • U.S. Hwy. 158, Milepost 16½, Nags Head • (252) 441-1600

Breakfast and lunch are popular here—especially the breakfast bar, where you will see a big crowd being efficiently handled daily during the summer and weekends from February through November. If you don't like a buffet, try the crab omelet. Delicious seafood or steaks at moderate prices for dinner also are served with a salad bar, and everyone can find something good. Keep an eye out for the all-you-

can-eat specials (we don't miss the soft-shell crab nights). The Dunes is also known for its friendly service.

Owens' Restaurant
$$-$$$ • Beach Rd., Milepost 16½, Nags Head • (252) 441-7309

This restaurant is an Outer Banks tradition. In 1996, Owens' celebrated 50 years of fine dining and attentive service. It's the area's oldest restaurant continuously owned and operated by the same family. Seafood reigns supreme here, and it is prepared to perfection. Try the crab cakes—they melt in your mouth. Or pick a live Maine lobster from the tank for steaming. And beef tops the list if seafood isn't your choice. Homemade chowders are good beginnings, and homemade desserts are good endings.

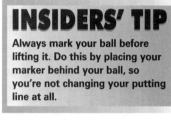

INSIDERS' TIP

Always mark your ball before lifting it. Do this by placing your marker behind your ball, so you're not changing your putting line at all.

The wine list is substantial, or you can enjoy a drink from the upstairs piano bar. One visit to Owens' and we bet it will become a dining tradition for you too. Owens' is open for dinner only from mid-March through New Year's Eve.

Hurricane Mo's Restaurant & Raw Bar
$$ • Pirate's Cove, Manteo-Nags Head Cswy. • (252) 473-2266

A cozy dining room or covered outdoor porch will each offer a view of the marina and all the tasty steamed or raw seafood plus steaks or seafood entrees you desire. A very good choice is the blackened tuna. Early discounts are offered for dinner, and you can sometimes choose daily specials such as the Monday clams for a quarter each. Brown bagging is allowed, and beer or wine are served. Service is good, and it's a friendly, fun place to take a crowd for lunch or dinner. It closes during the winter months.

Roanoke Island

1587
$$$ • Tranquil House Inn, Queen Elizabeth St., Manteo • (252) 473-1587

Named after the year the English colonists attempted to permanently settle Roanoke Island, 1587 is one of the finest restaurants on the Outer Banks. The presentation is superb and meets the chefs' goals of standing apart from the mainstream.

Savor some of the best-prepared delicacies at 1587, creations of Executive Chef Donny King, who offers a constantly changing menu. For an appetizer, we like the grilled Portobello mushroom Rockefeller with a tarragon-accented asiago cheese and vegetable stuffing. A great entree is chargrilled North Atlantic salmon over a wild mushroom soufflé, accompanied by an herbed tomato caper sauce and finished with fried spinach. Vegetarian requests are encouraged, and a familiar children's menu is offered. A fine selection of wine and beer is available, and brown bagging is allowed. Don't be in a rush. This is an experience, not just a meal. Reservations are suggested, and you should call for dinner hours, which change seasonally. Lunch is not served, and the restaurant closes during the winter.

Full Moon Cafe

$$ • The Waterfront, Queen Elizabeth St., Manteo • (252) 473-MOON

A cozy café overlooking Shallowbag Bay from its second-story vantage point, this eclectic eatery opened in late 1995 and is popular with local and visiting patrons. The cuisine here is creative and fun, featuring items not frequently seen on Outer Banks restaurant menus. Hummus spread, baked Brie and crab dip are our favorite appetizers. Lunch includes gourmet sandwiches, vegetarian offerings, seafood, chicken and homemade soups, such as Hungarian mushroom, curried spinach and spicy tomato, that change daily. Each entree is served with chips and Full Moon's own salsa. A separate dinner menu offers enticing seafood dishes, stuffed chicken breasts, roasted eggplant and nightly specials. All the desserts are delightful. Beer and wine are served.

You can eat inside the lovely little dining room, dine outdoors in the courtyard beside the soothing fountain or order any meal to go. Reservations are not accepted. Full Moon is open for lunch and dinner seven days a week in summer. Hours are more limited in the off-season, so call for specific schedules.

Weeping Radish Brewery & Bavarian Restaurant

$$ • U.S. Hwy. 64, Manteo
• (252) 473-1157

The most important thing here is the beer—varieties and flavors you'd never dream of. Enjoy some samples with a hearty Bavarian meal, or go during the afternoon for brewery tours. The Weeping Radish features an outdoor beer garden, separate pub, children's playground and two-story dining room. The traditional fare includes veal, spaetzle, sauerbraten and, of course, cooked red cabbage. It's open all year for lunch and dinner. There's also a pub in Monterey Plaza in Corolla. The restaurant's name comes from the radish that is served with beer in Bavaria. It's cut in a spiral, sprinkled with salt, then put back together. The salt draws out the moisture and gives the radish the appearance of weeping.

Hatteras Island

The Froggy Dog Restaurant
$$ • N.C. Hwy. 12, Avon
• (252) 995-4106

Go to the Froggy Dog for a big breakfast, quick lunch or affordable dinner. Check out entertainment nightly in the Lily Pad Lounge and take home a T-shirt from the upstairs gift shop. And drop in daily for the happy-hour steamed shrimp. The restaurant is open every day year-round, which is important on Hatteras Island: Not many establishments here stay open in winter. The steaks, pasta and chicken are good if you ever tire of seafood. We like the broiled, fried or sautéed seafood entrees.

Ocracoke Island

Howard's Pub and Raw Bar
$ • N.C. Hwy. 12, Ocracoke
• (252) 928-4441

Probably the only place on Ocracoke Island open for a late-night visit in the off-season, everyone congregates here; it's a good destination for casual fun, occasional live music and dancing. The raw bar is good (and the only one around), and simple, tasty burgers, pizza and sandwiches are served day and night. Jalapeño poppers are good appetizers, and prime rib is a good entree. Beer and wine are served, including some 200 types of domestics, imports and microbrews.

The Back Porch
$$$$ • 1324 Country Rd., Ocracoke
• (252) 928-6401

Owners John and Debbie Wells renovated this older building to blend with the natural

INSIDERS' TIP

Carry a copy of the current United States Golf Association rule book (which, of course, you've read and memorized) in your golf bag.

landscape (note the waist-high cacti!). It's a quiet place to enjoy a first-class meal and comfortable conversation. Many folks don't think twice about the two-hour drive from Nags Head—including the free ferry ride—just to eat here.

Where To Stay

Please refer to our Preface for an explanation of the pricing code.

Duck

Advice 5¢
$$$$ • 111 Scarborough Ln., Duck
• (252) 255-1050, (800) 238-4235

This charming bed and breakfast inn opened in 1995 and offers four guest rooms and one suite, all with private baths, rocking chairs and decks. The suite includes cable TV, stereo and Jacuzzi. The atmosphere is warm and inviting, as is the hospitality you'll receive from owners Nancy Caviness and Donna Black. Quiet-time activities, such as games, puzzles and books, are at hand. You may use locking storage for your gear—golf clubs, surf boards or fishing poles. A continental breakfast buffet of fresh-baked breads and fruit salad is served in the morning, and an afternoon tea tempts guests with homemade goodies and hot and cold drinks. The inn is open all year and is a non-smoking accommodation.

Sanderling Inn Resort and Conference Center
$$$$ • 1461 Duck Rd. (N.C. Hwy. 12),
Duck • (252) 261-4111, (800) 701-4111

The Sanderling Inn Resort occupies 12 acres of wilderness along the ocean. It's like an old beach home (a *big* one), with wooden siding and rocking chairs on the porch. The 86 rooms include robes for lounging, continental breakfast, afternoon tea and complimentary wine and cheese. The 28 rooms in the main building have kitchenettes. Another 32 rooms in the Sanderling Inn North are equipped with wet bars and refrigerators, and a newer south wing has 26 rooms with wet bars, refrigerators, microwaves, stereos with compact disc players, 1½ baths, king-size beds and double sleeper sofas. Two guests per room will have privacy and comfort here.

Conference and meeting facilities are offered in another building. The beaches are private; the health club includes an outdoor pool, indoor pool, whirlpool, two exercise rooms, locker rooms, tennis courts and a walking/jogging trail.

Ask about seasonal discounts or special holiday packages. Handicapped-accessible rooms are available at this year-round inn.

Kitty Hawk

Outer Banks Golf Getaways
$$-$$$$ • U.S. Hwy. 158, Milepost 2,
Kitty Hawk
• (252) 255-1074, (800) 916-OBGG

This real estate company packages golf at four Outer Banks courses and offers private homes and condominiums from simple oceanside retreats to spacious homes for large groups. Tee times are confirmed in advance for you, and private or group lessons or club rentals can be scheduled. All packages include accommodations, a breakfast allocation, one round of golf per day, linens, towels and departure cleaning. Non-golfer rates also are available.

We recommend Outer Banks Golf Getaways if you travel with a group of golfers or possibly a large family. The ease of booking your golf and accommodations with one phone call is appealing for simple vacation planning.

3 Seasons Guest House
$$$$ • U.S. Hwy. 158, Milepost 2,
Kitty Hawk
• (252) 261-4791, (800) 847-3373

This is a perfect bed and breakfast inn if you want to play Seascape Golf Course every day. The house overlooks the 9th green and is across the street from the clubhouse and pro shop. The ocean is just a few blocks away too. Bicycles, a common area, a Jacuzzi, complimentary cocktails and a full breakfast cooked to order add just about anything you could want for a great golf vacation. Other courses are only a few minutes away. Susie and Tommy Gardner offer five bedrooms—four of them for double occupancy. This inn is open April through October and is suitable for non-smoking adults.

Beach Haven Motel
$$ • Beach Rd. (N.C. Hwy. 12),
Milepost 4,Kitty Hawk • (252) 261-4785

This is a small hotel with six semi-efficiency units across the street from the beach. Coffee makers, refrigerators, hair dryers and porch chairs are provided. A portable phone is available. Some units are large enough for up to four people. Croquet, canoes, boats, rafts, grills, picnic tables and a putting green provide additional outdoor opportunities. It's open April through October.

OUTER BANKS

Kill Devil Hills

Tanglewood Motel
$$$$ • Beach Rd. (N.C. Hwy. 12),
Milepost 8¼, Kill Devil Hills
• (252) 441-7208

Eleven one- or two-bedroom apartments are available in this oceanfront motel. The one-bedroom units have a sleep sofa and accommodate four adults. One of the large apartments can accommodate up to 10 people. They have complete kitchens, cable television and full baths. A phone is available by request. Amenities include an outdoor pool, sun deck, outdoor bathhouse, boardwalk to the beach, picnic tables and grills. The motel is open April through October.

Cavalier Motel
$$$ • Beach Rd. (N.C. Hwy. 12),
Milepost 8½, Kill Devil Hills
• (252) 441-5584

This oceanfront motel has 40 rooms with double and single beds. Six one-room efficiencies have two double beds and kitchenettes. Two pools and volleyball and shuffleboard courts are within the three one-story wings. Another 13 cottages are available as weekly rentals. Pets are allowed in the cottages. The Cavalier, a well-maintained family property, is open year round.

Colony IV Motel
$$$ • Beach Rd. (N.C. Hwy. 12),
Milepost 9, Kill Devil Hills
• (252) 441-5581,(800) 848-3728

You can practice your putting at the nine-hole miniature golf course, then challenge your partners to a game of horseshoes at the pits here. Cindy and Tom Kingsbury run a nice family oceanfront motel with 87 units. They offer rooms with two doubles or one king-size bed. Fourteen units are efficiencies; one has a Jacuzzi. Some have direct beach access, and others have oceanfront balconies. The Colony is open March through November.

Cherokee Inn Bed and Breakfast
$$$ • Beach Rd. (N.C. Hwy. 12),
Milepost 8, Kill Devil Hills
• (252) 441-6127, (800) 554-2764

This former hunting and fishing lodge across the road from the beach offers six rooms with private baths, remote-control televisions, ceiling fans and comfortable wicker furnishings. Five rooms have queen-size beds, and the other has a double and a twin bed. The atmosphere is homey. Guests may borrow bikes or gather on the porch for conversation. The inn is owned by Kay and Bob Combs, second-generation proprietors. This property has been an inn for 18 years and a bed and breakfast inn for nine. Continental breakfast is included. No smoking is allowed. The inn is open April through October.

Nags Head

Surf Side Motel
$$$$ • Beach Rd. (N.C. Hwy. 12),
Milepost 16, Nags Head
• (252) 441-2105, (800) 552-7873

The friendly folks at this oceanfront hotel will go out of their way to make your Outer Banks experience a good one. The rooms in this five-story structure all have ocean views, and some even have sound views also. All rooms have refrigerators, cable TV, phones and private balconies. Why not book the honeymoon suite—you can make this visit a second or third honeymoon!—with a king-size bed and private Jacuzzi? Complimentary coffee and sweets are provided for early-morning convenience, and an afternoon wine and cheese get-together is the perfect way to end a great day on the golf course. Indoor and outdoor pools, an indoor Jacuzzi and strolls on the beach are other recreation options.

The Nags Head Inn
$$$$ • Beach Rd. (N.C. Hwy. 12),
Milepost 14, Nags Head
• (252) 441-0454, (800) 327-8881

This crisp, white oceanfront hotel with 100 rooms is near the golf courses and the Oregon Inlet Fishing Center as well as Nags Head, Kill Devil Hills and Roanoke Island attractions. Amenities include an indoor/outdoor pool and refrigerators in every room plus a wide, inviting beach expanse. One suite includes a sitting room, wet bar and Jacuzzi.

Oceanfront rooms have private balconies; streetside rooms have sound views. Nonsmoking and handicapped-accessible rooms are available on each floor. The conference room accommodates up to 30 people. The inn is open year-round except for three weeks in December.

Blue Heron Motel
$$$ • Beach Rd. (N.C. Hwy. 12),
Milepost 16, Nags Head • (252) 441-7447

This small family-owned motel is a fine choice for a well-managed beachfront property. Double or king-size beds are available in 19

Developers left much of the land intact when designing premier Outer Banks golfing communities. Wildlife, such as this red winged blackbird, is a common sight.

Photo: Mary Ellen Riddle

rooms, and 11 efficiencies provide full kitchens and sleep up to four people. All rooms have coffee pots, refrigerators, microwaves and televisions. One room is wheelchair-accessible. Private balconies are available on the second- and third-floor rooms. The motel is open year round and offers weekly rates.

First Colony Inn
**$$$$ • U.S. Hwy. 158, Milepost 16, Nags Head
• (252) 441-2343, (800) 368-9390**

This landmark hotel has been moved and refurbished since it opened in 1932. In 1988, the Lawrence family rescued the beachfront hotel from demolition, sawed it into pieces and moved it to its present site, where it underwent a three-year renovation. This Old Nags Head-style inn is listed on the National Register of Historic Places. The 26 rooms are now both traditional and modern, enduring reminders of the old days at the beach.

Deluxe continental breakfast and afternoon tea are included in your stay. Classical or jazz background music in the reception area are reminders of earlier days, as are the English antique furniture and toiletries. A television, heated towel bars, tile baths, a telephone, refrigerator and individual climate control are standard in each room. Some rooms offer wet

bars, trundle beds, Jacuzzis, VCRs and private balconies. The oceanfront gazebo across the street is a pleasant spot to while away some time after you leave the pool. The inn is open year-round.

Roanoke Island

Scarborough Inn
**$$ • U.S. Hwy. 64, Manteo
• (252) 473-3979**

This is one of our favorite places to stay, especially when traveling without very young children or large groups of golfers. Furnished with authentic antiques, the inn has a charming and friendly atmosphere, carefully created and preserved by the family and managed by Fields and Rebecca Scarborough. Each room, piece of furniture and collectible holds a story the family can relate. Although on the main street of this delightful village, the inn is tucked away and private, more so than the larger beach accommodations. Continental breakfast—muffins and a pot of coffee—is provided in your room. Borrow a bicycle and explore historic Roanoke Island or walk across the street for some food or drink. If Scarborough Inn is full, the family also operates Scarborough House in another nearby, lovely part of town. The inn is open year-round.

White Doe Inn
$$$$ • Sir Walter Raleigh St., Manteo
• (252) 473-9851, (800) 473-6091

When you're looking for luxurious accommodations with the personal attention found at a bed and breakfast, look no further than the White Doe Inn. Bob and Bebe Woody, owners of this Queen Anne-style house, restored the property and added modern conveniences and niceties such as fireplaces (in every room), antique furniture, tile bathrooms (two with a Jacuzzi), stained-glass windows, lovely linens and finishing touches (Godiva chocolates on your pillow).

The inn is in a quiet neighborhood in Manteo—a perfect starting point for exploring all that Roanoke Island has to offer (see our "Fun Things To Do" section).

The inn serves a full breakfast each morning and offers tea and coffee with sweets in the afternoon. Guests may take the inn's bicycles out for a spin on the 6-mile Manteo Bike Path or just sit in the front porch swing and watch the goings-on of this charming little town. The inn is open all year, and you should inquire about off-season rates.

Hatteras Island

Lighthouse View Motel
$$-$$$ • N.C. Hwy. 12, Buxton
• (252) 995-5680

The Hooper family has operated this establishment on the big curve in Buxton for more than 36 years. The 73 oceanfront and oceanside units include your choice of efficiencies, duplexes, motel-style rooms, villas or cottages. Amenities include an outdoor pool and a hot tub. Windsurfers, surfers and fishing vacationers all enjoy this motel, which is close to the landmark Cape Hatteras Lighthouse, renowned windsurfing mecca Canadian Hole and myriad restaurants and shops.

Cape Hatteras Motel
$$$$ • N.C. Hwy. 12, Buxton
• (252) 995-5611, (800) 995-0711

Owners Carol and Dave Dawson offer basic rooms as well as efficiencies that sleep six, with double beds as well as kings and queens. Part of the motel has been here for more than 30 years. Nearby Canadian Hole is a notable venue for windsurfers. The motel is also popular among anglers, beachcombers and surfers. Guests enjoy an outdoor swimming pool and spa. The motel is open all year.

Ocracoke Island

Berkeley Center
$$$, no credit cards • N.C. Hwy. 12,
Ocracoke Village • (252) 928-5911

This nine-room bed and breakfast inn is renowned for its hand-carved paneling of redwood, pine, cypress and cedar. Seven rooms have private baths, and the other two rooms share a bath. The manor house was built in 1860 and remodeled in 1950; the ranch house dates from the mid-'50s. This inn is tucked away from everything, and the spacious rooms are furnished without telephones or televisions for the times you really want to escape. A television is available in the guest lounge if you suffer from withdrawal without one. The living and dining rooms, with their country estate-type atmospheres, are gathering spots for guests. Continental breakfast includes coffee and fresh breads and fruits served in the breakfast room of the manor house. The inn is open April through October.

Golf Equipment

Teed Off Discount Golf and Tennis, Three Winks Shoppes, U.S. Highway 158, Milepost 1, Kitty Hawk, (252) 261-GOLF, offers major pro-line equipment, club repair service and custom clubs as well as supplies and apparel. Another option is **Smash Hit Tennis & Golf**, Scarborough Faire, Duck Road (N.C. Highway 12), Duck, (252) 261-1138, which stocks a limited supply of golf clothing, equipment and accessories. These two places might have just what you're looking for. If not, you'll probably find what you need at the pro shops, especially those at Nags Head Golf Links and Sea Scape.

New Bern, Edenton & Eastern N.C.

Much of Eastern North Carolina is rural, the scattered towns deriving their character from their industries—agriculture, fishing, clothing manufacturing, boat building, cabinet making and, in the case of Camp Lejeune, producing U.S. Marines. Few visit the area on golf vacations, but there are quality courses nonetheless. The locale is quiet, and most courses are just enough off the beaten path to be appreciated by golfers who like to include a relaxing round with their vacations.

Bath is North Carolina's first town, founded in 1705, and the notorious pirate Blackbeard reportedly was one of its early residents. Today you can enjoy the historic district with the state's oldest church and three restored historic house museums from the 18th and 19th centuries.

The river town of New Bern is the second-oldest city in North Carolina, named by its Swiss settlers in 1710 after the Swiss capital, Bern. The black bear emblem emblazoned throughout the town also came from Bern. New Bern is at the confluence of the Neuse and Trent rivers, which join to make the widest river in the country and influence most of the area's recreational pursuits. New Bern's downtown has been carefully restored to display a panoply of architecture along with antiques shops, restaurants, specialty shops and art galleries. One of the city's many claims to fame: New Bern is where Pepsi-Cola originated.

Don't plan on wild nightlife or fast-paced activities here: go to Myrtle Beach for those. Just come to New Bern for some peace and quiet, and to appreciate its history—along with watersports and golf.

Historic Edenton lies on Edenton Bay at the head of the Albemarle Sound, and it's home to a prestigious collection of 18th-century buildings. A guided tour of the historic district includes St. Paul's Church, Cupola House, Chowan County Courthouse National Historic Landmark, James Iredell House State Historic Site, Barker House and other outstanding examples of period architecture. Little has changed in this small town while centuries have crawled past; only the new golf courses, downtown shopping boutiques and modern conveniences will remind you of the date.

In fall of 1999, portions of eastern North Carolina suffered tremendous and devastating floods. The area is slowly recovering and many golf courses sustained damage. Thus it's particularly important to call ahead before playing the courses listed in this chapter. Check to see that all 18 holes (and greens) are open. And be patient: The people of this area went through hell and, literally, high water, and are working hard to put their lives back together.

For more information on Eastern North Carolina, pick up a copy of *The Insiders' Guide to North Carolina's Central Coast and New Bern* or *The*

New Bern, Edenton, and Eastern North Carolina

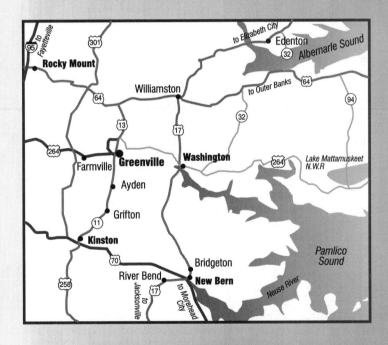

GOLF COURSES IN EASTERN NORTH CAROLINA

Course	Type	# Holes	Par	Slope	Yards	Walking	Booking	Cost w/ Cart
Ayden Golf & Country Club	semiprivate	18	72	117	6282	yes	3 days	$12-25
Carolina Pines Golf & C. C.	semiprivate	18	72	111	5845	yes	30 days	$27-30
Chowan Golf & Country Club	semiprivate	18	72	118	5921	yes	1 day	$35
Cypress Landing	semiprivate	18	72	130	6421	no	14 days	$40-45
Emerald Golf Club	semiprivate	18	72	124	6451	no	2 days	$40-45
Farmville Country Club	semiprivate	18	71	111	5702	yes	1 day	$30-35
Harbour Point Golf Links	public	18	72	113	5998	yes	2 days	$25-35
Indian Trails Country Club	public	18	71	120	6172	yes	7 days	$19-24
Ironwood Golf & C.C.	semiprivate	18	72	119	6625	yes	call	$40-45
Quaker Golf & C.C.	semiprivate	18	72	117	6334	yes	4 days	$17-30
River Bend Golf & C. C.	semiprivate	18	71	109	5043	yes	5 days	$22-25
Rock Creek Country Club	semiprivate	18	72	126	6233	yes	no	$25-30
The Sound	semiprivate	18	72	119	5836	no	9 months	$30-35

(both available online at www.insiders.com).

NEW BERN, EDENTON & EASTERN N.C.

Ayden Golf & Country Club
Golf Club Rd., Ayden • (252) 746-7859
Championship Yardage: 6784

Slope: 117	**Par: 72**
Men's Yardage:	6282
Slope: 117	**Par: 72**
Ladies' Yardage:	5057
Slope: 106	**Par: 72**

This is a straightforward, compact course—not extremely demanding. Water comes into play on only four holes. The 18-hole layout, designed by Clay Stroud, opened in 1952. Bermudagrass covers the greens and fairways.

The front nine has narrow fairways, so accuracy counts from the beginning. No. 7 is a 515-yard par 5 with an extremely narrow fairway for your tee shot. It opens a bit, but the green is small.

The 18th is a long hole (618 yards) that doglegs slightly right. Bunkers surround the front of the green.

Amenities include practice greens, a driving range, pro shop, locker room, bar, grill and club rentals.

Walking is allowed. Year-round greens fees are $12 to walk and $20 to ride during the week and $17 and $25, respectively, on weekends. Tee times may be reserved three days in advance.

Carolina Pines Golf & Country Club
390 Carolina Pines Blvd., New Bern
• (252) 444-1000
Championship Yardage: 6270

Slope: 115	**Par: 72**
Men's Yardage:	5845
Slope: 111	**Par: 72**
Ladies' Yardage:	4784
Slope: 108	**Par: 72**

Bermudagrass during summer and winter rye during colder months grace this 18-hole course designed by Frank Marmarose, Ron Broissoit, Jim Stallings and Joe Hughes. It's not exceptionally long and, therefore, is often preferred by some of us who need all the help we can get to score well. This course wanders among residential areas and over lagoons near the Neuse River.

The signature 15th hole is a medium-length par 5, reachable in two shots with a good drive. Trouble spots are left and right and behind the green, so the hole requires a decision and some straight shooting.

Carolina Pines has a pro shop, club rentals,

a driving range and target greens. Also available are tennis courts, a pool and a clubhouse with lounge and patio.

Daily year-round greens fees, including cart, are $30 before noon and $27 after. Walking is restricted.

Chowan Golf & Country Club
1101 W. Soundshore Dr., Edenton
• (252) 482-3606
Championship Yardage: 6392

Slope: 122	**Par: 72**
Men's Yardage:	5921
Slope: 118	**Par: 72**
Ladies' Yardage:	5062
Slope: 112	**Par: 72**

Although this 18-hole course has more than 300 members, public play is welcome. Fairways are bermudagrass; nine greens are bermudagrass and nine are bentgrass.

No. 3 is a par 4 that runs along S. Sound Drive, and a stream bisects the fairway 35 yards from the green. If you clear the stream, you still must contend with four bunkers in front of the green. Pine trees are widely spaced along the fairway.

The 4th hole is an unusual par 4. You have to play it like two par 3s because of the water that juts out in the path of your tee shot and flanks the fairway on the left and out-of-bounds on the right; water also extends into the landing area. Then you must hit to an elevated green.

The 5th, originally a par 5, has been changed to a par 4. It's a sharp dogleg right off the tee with out-of-bounds to the right and water to the left. The green slants away from you and is not particularly receptive.

Amenities include a practice green, driving range, pro shop, beer and beverage sales, club repair and regripping. Lessons are available.

The cost is $35 for greens fee and cart. Walking is generally allowed but is restricted during the weekend morning hours.

Chowan Golf & Country Club is a few miles outside historic Edenton.

Cypress Landing
600 Clubhouse Dr., Chocowinity
• (252) 946-7788
Championship Yardage: 6849

Slope: 134	**Par: 72**
Men's Yardage:	6421
Slope: 130	**Par: 72**
Other Yardage:	5976
Slope: 125	**Par: 72**
Ladies Yardage:	4989
Slope: 123	**Par: 72**

This course opened in July 1996. Weyerhaeuser Real Estate Company has developed a community with homes overlooking either water or the tree-lined course. Cypress Landing is an 18-hole semiprivate club on the Pamlico River. Ault, Clark & Associates designed this course with bentgrass greens and bermudagrass fairways. Each hole offers four sets of tees, so golfers of all abilities can enjoy a game here.

This beautiful course is laid out on rolling woodland and many holes offer fine views of the Pamlico River.

You'll find a driving range, putting green, rental clubs, a pro shop and a beverage cart on weekends.

Walking is not allowed. Approximate greens fees with a cart range from $40 to $45.

The Emerald Golf Club
5000 Clubhouse Dr., New Bern
• **(252) 633-4440**

Championship Yardage:	6924	
Slope: 129	Par: 72	
Men's Yardage:	6451	
Slope: 124	Par: 72	
Other Yardage:	6123	
Slope: 120	Par: 72	
Other Yardage:	5441	
Slope: 111	Par: 72	
Ladies' Yardage:	4813	
Slope: 114	Par: 72	

Rees Jones designed this course in 1988 to attract golfers of all skill levels. It's placed among tall pines within a 700-acre residential community developed by Weyerhaeuser Real Estate Company. Greens are beautiful bentgrass, and fairways are bermudagrass. Additional tees recently were added and others adjusted to accommodate golfers' varying abilities. We appreciate the handicap specification on the score card, which leads us to the appropriate tees to make the course most challenging. Jerry Briele, PGA professional, and Jim Lanier, golf course superintendent, have done a fine job of upgrading this course.

Don't be intimidated by the plentiful and prominent water here. Of the four par 3s on this course, three must carry the drink. The 5th hole (par 5) measures 521 yards. The fairway snakes beside the highway up to the green. Water borders the right, and trees line the en-

tire left side. A bunker comes into play on any short approaches to the green.

The signature hole is the 18th, a delight for its characteristic rolling mounds on the left side and water lining the fairway on the right.

The first round of the PGA qualifying school was conducted here in 1992 and 1993. Emerald also is home to the Curtis Strange Shrine Classic.

A pro shop, driving range and lessons are available. Memberships entitle visitors to use tennis, swimming and club facilities as well as play golf.

Approximate cost Monday through Thursday is $40, including cart; Friday through Sunday and holidays, it's $45. Carts must stay on the path. Only members are allowed to walk the course.

Farmville Country Club
308 Bynum Dr., Farmville
• **(252) 753-3660**

Championship Yardage:	6206	
Slope: 115	Par: 71	
Men's Yardage:	5702	
Slope: 111	Par: 71	
Ladies Yardage:	4759	
Slope: 109	Par: 71	

Farmville's front nine was built during the 1930s, and the club added the back nine in the 1970s. The 18-hole course has bermudagrass greens and fairways. Small greens and tight fairways characterize the front nine; wider fairways and larger greens may surprise you on the back. Farmville is kept in top condition with good-quality greens and beautiful fairways.

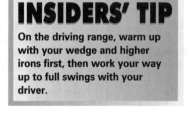

INSIDERS' TIP

On the driving range, warm up with your wedge and higher irons first, then work your way up to full swings with your driver.

This course demands accuracy. Every hole varies according to the natural landscape. A ditch runs through most of the front side, except on the par 3s. A creek crosses the 11th and 18th holes, and ponds add additional hazards on the back side. Except for the par 3s, you must continually contend with a ditch, creek or pond. Bring extra golf balls unless you can consistently keep one in the air.

A practice green, chipping area, pro shop, locker rooms, a bar and grill are available. The short driving range is for warm-up purposes only. A cart path is provided for nine holes and planned for the additional nine.

Approximate cost for greens fee and cart is $30 weekdays and $35 on weekends. Walking is permitted Monday through Thursday and after 2 PM on Friday, Saturday, Sunday and holidays.

Harbour Pointe Golf Links
750 Broad Creek Rd., Bridgeton
• (252) 638-5338

Championship Yardage:	**6554**
Slope: 117	**Par: 72**
Men's Yardage:	**5998**
Slope: 113	**Par: 72**
Ladies' Yardage:	**5778**
Slope: 110	**Par: 72**

Harbour Pointe is one of two 18-hole courses at the Fairfield Harbour resort community that are available to residents and time-share owners. Occasional overflow from Harbour Pointe is booked at Shoreline, Fairfield Harbour's private club.

Greens at Harbour Pointe are bentgrass, and fairways are bermudagrass. The course was designed by Tom Johnson and D.J. DeVictor. Sand and water combine to test players of every skill level.

The most challenging hole is No. 4. This par 4 measures 395 yards, a dogleg right with water from tee to green down the right side to penalize those who try to cut the corner to tight.

The driving range is two-tiered. A pro shop, club rentals, a snack bar, lounge, tennis courts and a swimming pool round out the amenities.

Walking is allowed after 1 PM. Approximate greens fees and cart range from $25 to $35.

Indian Trails Country Club
Country Club Dr., Grifton
• (252) 524-5485, (800) 830-4822

Championship Yardage:	**6634**
Slope: 124	**Par: 71**
Men's Yardage:	**6172**
Slope: 120	**Par: 71**
Ladies' Yardage:	**4796**
Slope: 115	**Par: 71**

Part of this 18-hole course has been open since the early 1960s, and the rest has developed progressively. Many travelers are surprised to find a course like Indian Trails in such a small town. The public is welcome here, and member programs are under way to encourage junior and women's golf as well as executive networking. It's easily accessible via I-95 to N.C. Highway 11 and is one of the only area courses

completely open to public play. Fairways and greens are bermudagrass.

The course is entirely surrounded by forest. It's hilly, with frequent left or right doglegs and wandering finger lakes that come into play on seven holes. The 1st tee is on the shoreline of what geologists believe was the ocean several million years ago, and the elevation varies significantly. The 9th hole is notable: It's 440 yards from the back tees has a pond on the right and trees on both sides. The green is elevated and slopes from left to right—into trouble.

INSIDERS' TIP

Allow faster players to play through. You'll have more fun by observing proper etiquette and you won't feel rushed by someone waiting for you.

A putting green, driving range, pro shop, club rentals, a snack bar and beer sales are offered. A beverage cart is available occasionally on weekends. And a paved cart path complements the course.

Approximate cost is $19, including cart, for weekdays; weekend fees increase to $15 plus $9 for a cart. Walking is allowed during the week and after 3 PM on weekends.

Ironwood Golf & Country Club
200 Golf Club Wynd (U.S. 43), Greenville
• (252) 752-6659, (800) 343-IRON

Championship Yardage:	**7069**
Slope: 124	**Par: 72**
Men's Yardage:	**6625**
Slope: 119	**Par: 72**
Other Yardage:	**5965**
Slope: 113	**Par: 72**
Ladies' Yardage:	**5359**
Slope: 116	**Par: 72**

Ironwood is the first Lee Trevino design east of the Mississippi. The 18-hole course is private, with limited daily fee play. Members are given preference. The course is surrounded by a development with wooded lots and cluster home lots. The signature hole is the 18th, a slight dogleg left with water all the way down the left side to about 50 yards from the green. Three bunkers are about 100 yards out on the right side, and three more bunkers surround the green. This pretty hole is almost tucked into the woods. The 6th is also a tough hole because it's dead into the prevailing wind. It's a 418-yard par 4—wide open but hard to play. Water could come into play with bad shots on seven holes.

The club includes a 1,500 square-foot clubhouse, conference room, fitness room, grill room, dining room, bar, golf shop, men's and ladies' lounges, a pool and clay tennis courts. It's a prestigious community with a course designed to match.

Approximate greens fees including cart are $40 on weekdays and $45 on weekends. Walking is restricted.

Quaker Neck Golf and Country Club
299 Country Club Rd., Trenton
• **(252) 224-5736, (800) 657-5156 (in N.C.)**

Men's Yardage:	6334
Slope: 117	**Par: 72**
Other Yardage:	6010
Slope: 109	**Par: 72**
Ladies' Yardage:	4978
Slope: 108	**Par: 72**

This semi-private course opened in 1967 and has bermudagrass greens and fairways. Russell Burney designed this course. This enjoyable layout has only about 25 traps. Small lakes or ponds flank three holes, and a meandering creek comes into play on nine more. The signature hole is the 16th, a par 3 across water to a green along the Trenton River. Another notable hole is the 15th, a 425-yard par 4 dogleg left with a tee shot across water. The 15th green also flanks the river and is guarded by traps.

The full practice facility includes a range, putting and chipping greens and practice sand traps. Locker rooms are available for members only. A snack bar is open, and a beverage cart makes the rounds on weekends.

Approximate greens fees including cart are $30 on weekends and $25 on weekdays, with a $17 special available in winter, after noon in spring and after 2 PM during summer. Walking is allowed.

The club is a full-service recreation facility tucked into the Sandhills of Jones County. A picnic area, playground, horseshoe pits, a boat ramp and swimming pool provide other family activities besides golf.

River Bend Golf & Country Club
94 Shoreline Dr., River Bend
• **(252) 638-2819**

Championship Yardage:	6404
Slope: 117	**Par: 71**
Men's Yardage:	5043
Slope: 109	**Par: 71**
Ladies' Yardage:	5012
Slope: 105	**Par: 71**

Greens and fairways are bermudagrass, and fairways are wide open on this Gene Hamm design. This 18-hole course (built in 1963) is open to the public and playable by the average golfer.

The signature hole is the 13th, a par 3 across water that plays 184 yards from the back tees. The green slopes away from left to right, with bunkers on the left and right front. Five holes on the back nine have water. The front side is tighter and weaves through a residential neighborhood. It's a fun layout, often referred to as player-friendly.

River Bend offers a driving range, practice green, club rentals, a snack bar, bar, pro shop, tennis courts and an Olympic-size pool.

Approximate cart and greens fees range from $22 to $25. Walking is allowed, and the management is very helpful in booking advance tee times for out-of-towners; just call with your request.

Rock Creek Country Club
308 Country Club Blvd., Jacksonville
• **(910) 324-5151**

Championship Yardage:	7108
Slope: 116	**Par: 72**
Men's Yardage:	6233
Slope: 126	**Par: 72**
Ladies' Yardage:	5389
Slope: 112	**Par: 72**

This 18-hole course, designed by Jerry Turner and built in 1971, is well kept and playable. It's also well off the regular route (from U.S. Highway 17, take N.C. Highway 1308, then N.C. Highway 1390), so it won't be as busy as many others in this area during high season. Fairways were sprigged in 1996 with bermudagrass 419, and greens are bentgrass. Staffer Mitzi Johnson says the course is "deceptively tough, but obligingly forgiving." Whatever that means.

The signature hole is the 15th—a par 4. Your tee shot must fly between water and a ditch.

Rental clubs and a restaurant are available here. Walking is restricted. Greens fees, including cart, begin at $25 and increase to $30 on weekends.

The Sound Golf Links
101 Clubhouse Dr., Hertford
• **(252) 426-5555, (800) 535-0704**

Championship Yardage:	6504
Slope: 124	**Par: 72**
Men's Yardage:	5836
Slope: 119	**Par: 72**
Ladies' Yardage:	4665
Slope: 113	**Par: 72**

The Sound is an 18-hole course in Albemarle Plantation, a 500-acre world-class golfing and boating community outside Hertford. It's

The 18th hole at Ironwood Golf & Country Club stretches out in emerald majesty as viewed from the clubhouse.

Photo: Chip Henderson

tucked away at the tip of Albemarle Sound. You have to be familiar with the really good golf courses in the Carolinas to know about this Dan Maples original. Owner and designer Maples stamped his signature here. As with all Maples-designed courses, you get a break on the par 4s and 5s, but the par 3s are extremely difficult. It's a target golf course with a few similarities to a links course.

Fairways are wide, but there's plenty of marsh to carry off the tee. It's critical to hit where you aim. It's a fair course overall, but it's tough from the back tees. The pro's advice: "Don't bite off more than you can chew."

On the 7th and 13th holes, the landing areas are extremely small. Both are par 4s.

This course is surrounded by undisturbed wetlands and tall pines. Enjoy the ride over the wetlands from the 16th green to the 17th tee. In fact, you'll probably enjoy all of the cart rides over the bridges. The three finishing holes stretch along the water and provide breathtaking views.

The classy, 12,000-square-foot clubhouse overlooks the sound and has a pro shop and restaurant. A driving range and putting green also are available. Amenities for members include a swim and fitness center and a separate recreation center, and the marina is the largest in the area.

Approximate greens fees, including cart, range from $30 to $35. Walking is restricted.

Around New Bern, Edenton and Eastern North Carolina...

Fun Things To Do

Antiques shopping, historical tours and, of course, watersports are major interests for many golfers during their extra time in eastern North Carolina.

New Bern invites you to wear walking shoes or hop on the trolley and enjoy art galleries, gardens in bloom and especially the restored homes, churches and stores reflecting internationally flavored 18th-century architectural influences. The three distinct historic districts include the downtown and the Ghent and Riverside neighborhoods. More than 200 homes here are listed on the National Register of Historic Places, and the 2,000 crape myrtles surrounding them are an attraction themselves.

In New Bern, browse through the **Firemen's Museum,** 410 Hancock Street, (252) 636-4087, or the **Civil War Museum,** 301 Metcalf Street, (252) 633-2818. The early fire-fighting equipment includes steam pumpers and a variety of photographs and Civil War relics, plus the mounted head of the fire horse who died in his tracks. The Civil War Museum showcases an important private collection of weapons, uniforms and battlefield artifacts. There's also a gift shop here.

Be sure to leave an afternoon to amble through the **Tryon Palace Historic Site and Gardens,** Pollock and George streets; call (252) 638-1560 for information about tour options and hours. It's open daily year-round and is the setting for summer re-enactments of historical events. The Georgian brick mansion was reconstructed from the remains of one originally built on the site in 1770 by William Tryon, the British colonial governor. Delegates gathered in this palace for the first state legislature meeting in 1777. As part of the palace tour, visit the **New Bern Academy Museum,** the oldest public school in North Carolina, founded in 1764. Exhibits here feature education and architecture as well as the history of New Bern, which was a Union city within the Confederate states.

We suggest you plan a golfing vacation here each April so you can also attend the **Home and Garden Show.** This event is a must for garden lovers—the quiet, self-guided stroll through some of the town's most beautiful homes is enchanting, and you can get great decorating ideas for your own home.

An important stop if your children accompany you is **Kidsville,** a playground at 1225 Pine Tree Drive. This isn't just your regular playground. It's a planned interactive site with an extensive grouping of creative equipment including a slide and a maze in a fort-like setting.

Spend some quiet time in this small town. You won't hear the sounds of a big city. Talk to the people here—folks aren't shy about sharing their life stories with new friends who are here to enjoy local golf courses.

You also might enjoy the **Croatan National Forest,** where deer, bears, alligators and Venus' flytraps are preserved. You can access the forest at 141 E. Fisher Avenue, just a few miles south of New Bern. Pick up a map at the forest headquarters here before venturing into an undeveloped area unprepared. Call (252) 638-5628 for more information. Swimming, boating, fishing, hunting, hiking and picnicking are popular activities during most of the year. Overnight camping is ideal. However, the park is sometimes closed in winter, so be sure to call ahead. Saltwater fishing in the park is popular, as are flounder gigging, crabbing and oystering along the river shoreline. Fishing tournaments and sailing competitions are other major events for enthusiasts, spectators and even photographers.

Visit Eastern North Carolina during any festival, and you'll absorb some real flavor of the region and its people as well as be entertained and fed like royalty. Call (800) 437-5767 for general tourist information and a listing of events that span the calendar.

Call (252) 482-2637 for information about Edenton or (800) 775-0111 for the **Tourism Development Authority.** And when you arrive here go straight to the **Visitors Center,** 108 N. Broad Street, for a genuinely warm welcome by the knowledgeable and courteous staff. Watch the introductory film, then take a guided tour of the more than 50 historic buildings along the tree-lined downtown streets. If you enjoy celebrations, visit Edenton during the September shrimp festival, the October peanut festival or the Christmas candlelight tour of private homes.

The 1730 **Newbold-White House,** North Carolina's oldest surviving home, is on N.C. Highway 1336 near Hertford, one of the state's oldest towns. Its medieval English architecture has been modified by Colonial touches. Call (252) 426-7567 for tour information.

Nearby in Bath, the state's first town, you can tour three restored house museums. Go to the **Historic Bath Visitor Center** on Carteret Street (N.C. 92), (252) 923-3971, for information on tours of the **Palmer-Marsh House,** the **Van DerVeer House** and the **Bonner House.** Here you can also get directions to **St. Thomas Episcopal,** the state's oldest church. Call (252) 923-3971 for more information.

The prestigious **Albemarle Craftsman's Fair** at Knobbs Creek Recreation Center on Ward Street in Elizabeth City, one of the oldest demonstrating shows in the country, has been celebrated in October for 39 years. This event showcases myriad crafts of exquisite design and workmanship. Call the **Elizabeth City Area Chamber of Commerce,** (252) 335-4365, for information on events and nearby attractions. Also, make time for a walking tour through the historic district.

Lake Mattamuskeet National Wildlife Refuge, on N.C. 94 a mile north of U.S. 264 and east of Washington, encompasses 50,000 acres of marsh, lake, timber and cropland. The shallow lake provides a winter refuge for various waterfowl, including more than 45,000 tundra swans and 150,000 birds. Also, thousands of snow and Canadian geese and 22 species of ducks arrive for the season. Fishing, including herring dipping and blue crabbing, and boating are popular here. For information about the refuge, call (252) 926-4021.

Pettigrew State Park, just off U.S. Highway 64 outside Creswell (follow signs once you've entered town), features 5 miles of trails through virgin forests and displays Native American dugout canoes along the trail. A fishing pier and boat launch along the west side of the 16,600-acre lake make great starting points, as do the hiking trail and the biking trail. Fishing, camping and nature programs are available. Call (252) 797-4475 for information.

Somerset Place in Pettigrew State Park, (252) 797-4560, presents hands-on educational programs about the plantation system and daily life during the antebellum period. The main house, a restored early Greek Revival-style coastal plantation home, is furnished with period pieces. Its outbuildings include a smokehouse, dairy, kitchen and the original Colony House where the family lived while the mansion was being built in the 1830s. This state historic site is open for tours year-round, and admission is free, but groups planning to visit should call in advance for reservations.

The **Great Dismal Swamp Canal** is the oldest continually operating man-made canal in the country. You can view the National Civil Engineering Landmark from the visitors center here; call (252) 771-8333. The **Dismal Swamp Wetlands Boardwalk** in northern Currituck County measures a half-mile long and leads to 639 acres in the Dismal Swamp. An observation tower provides panoramic views of the area. Admission is free, but you must ask permission to go on the boardwalk or tower, both of which are owned by Elizabeth City State University. For information call (252) 335-3375.

Hope Plantation, near Windsor, is the Federal plantation home of Gov. David Stone. You can tour the entire complex for a glimpse of a statesman's life on a self-sustaining plantation in the early 1800s. Call (252) 794-3140 for information.

The historic district of the small town of **Washington** (a.k.a. "Little Washington") is the site of 30 noteworthy structures dating from the late 1700s. This town is replete with restaurants and accommodations. Self-guided walking tours near the Pamlico River make for a full afternoon's activity.

INSIDERS' TIP

Pay attention while others in your group putt. Watching the others will help you read the speed and line of your putt.

Call the **Washington-Beaufort County Chamber of Commerce,** (252) 946-9168, or drop by the chamber offices, 102 W. Stewart Parkway, for information.

Where to Eat

Fresh seafood abounds in eastern North Carolina restaurants and is prepared in a variety of ways: fried, blackened, grilled, baked, broiled or steamed. Country cooking with homegrown vegetables and homemade meat loaf, pork chops or fried chicken is also prevalent, and you won't go home hungry. Barbecue is a North Carolina specialty—usually pork but sometimes beef, seafood or chicken—and you can expect French fries and cold slaw to round out the meal. We believe in eating well when we're on golf trips; actually, we promote eating well all of the time. We'll recommend a few favorite spots offering variety, and you'll find others featuring local specialties and international cuisine. Unless otherwise indicated, the following restaurants accept most major credit cards. Refer to our Preface for an explanation of the price code.

New Bern

Annabelle's Restaurant & Pub
$-$$ • Twin Rivers Mall, Clarendon Blvd. (U.S. Hwy. 17), New Bern
• (252) 633-6401

Here you'll find a variety of food served in a casual atmosphere. The lunch and dinner menus are the same and include something for almost any taste. Chicken, ribs, beef and seafood entrees are featured. Mexican dishes also are available. It's a great place to enjoy a quick soup, salad and a beer before an afternoon tee time. Desserts are plentiful too—we recommend the hot fudge cake to finish any meal.

The Berne Restaurant
$ • 2900 Neuse Blvd., New Bern
• (252) 638-5296

Menu selections include fried or broiled shellfish, trout, flounder and oysters (in season). We think the always-full parking lot at this easy-to-find eatery (it's at a major intersection) is a sign of the good food served within. The Berne offers down-home country and seafood meals. Pork barbecue, a regional specialty, is featured; if that doesn't appeal to you, choose steak or seafood. Don't miss the breakfast buffet served each Saturday and Sunday. A traditional country breakfast is featured every day.

The Chelsea – A Restaurant & Publick House
$$-$$$ • Broad and Middle Sts., New Bern
• (252) 637-5469

Shellfish, steaks or sandwiches are good choices for lunch or dinner at The Chelsea. Regional cuisine sports a contemporary flair here. Watch for the daily specials listed on the chalkboard and enjoy the healthy house salad, vegetable, potato or rice and fresh bread that accompany every entree. The large bar is popular with locals and offers domestic and imported beers and mixed drinks. Live entertainers perform many nights.

Caleb Bradham, founder of Brad's Drink (the original Pepsi-Cola), once used this building as his drugstore. The colorful wall mural tells the story.

The Harvey Mansion
$$-$$$ • 221 Tryon Palace Dr., New Bern
• (252) 638-3205

This restaurant and lounge with a water view are housed in a beautifully restored building constructed by John Harvey in the 1790s. Before it became a restaurant in 1979, the building went through various incarnations—home, mercantile establishment, boarding house, military academy and community college. Chef Beat Züttel and his wife Carolyn now own and operate the mansion and live there with their children.

Gourmet dinners, served here nightly, include fresh seasonal offerings of grilled, poached or sauteed seafood. The menu changes frequently and reflects the chef's heritage and influences from his native Bern, Switzerland. Homemade desserts are delicious. Downstairs, the cellar lounge boasts a copper bar, an informal menu and an inviting atmosphere in which to relax before or after dinner.

This acclaimed establishment, with linens and candlelight, encourages guests to enjoy a dressy and leisurely evening.

Henderson House Restaurant
$$$ • 216 Pollock St., New Bern
• (252) 637-4784

This award-winning restaurant in a restored historic home is perfect for candlelight dining on a special occasion. Original art adorns the walls—a nice complement to your meal. And exquisite menu selections—creatively prepared veal, duck, lamb and pheasant—match the decor. The shrimp almondine is one of our favorites. The international wine list is extensive. Henderson House is open Wednesday through Sunday evenings.

Kress Café '50s Rock & Roll Diner

$ • Kress Bldg., 309 Middle St., New Bern
• (252) 633-9300

In the Kress Building—formerly home of the S.H. Kress & Co. Diner—this diner's menu has a large selection of breakfast specials including eggs Benedict and French toast. Lunch and dinner items include a variety of delicious salads, sandwiches and burgers. Beer, wine and cocktails are available. It's open daily.

Latitude 35

$$ • 1 Bicentennial Pk., New Bern
• (252) 638-3585

This restaurant in the Sheraton Hotel and Marina showcases fine dining, but you need not avoid it when you're wearing golf attire. Come as you are and enjoy the views of the Neuse River and the marina. Locals enjoy the breakfast buffet, which includes eggs, grits, breakfast meat, waffles, muffins, fabulous biscuits, fresh fruit and cereal. Try a tasty salad or sandwich for lunch and seafood specialties in the evening. You won't be disappointed with the shellfish or other seafood, served broiled, baked, fried, grilled or blackened. If sea fare is not to your taste, order pasta, chicken or beef. A full salad bar is included with each entree.

Moore's Barbecue

$ • U.S. Hwy. 17 S., New Bern
• (252) 638-3937

No trip to North Carolina is complete without barbecue, and this is a good place to sample some. Pork, seafood or chicken and all the trimmings make for a fine Carolina-style lunch or dinner feast to eat in or carry out. Call for hours, which vary on weekends. If you're planning a big party, consider Moore's to cater a pig pickin'. You've not eaten real Southern food until you've tried this.

Pollock Street Delicatessen and Restaurant

$-$$ • 208 Pollock St., New Bern
• (252) 637-2480

If you are visiting and homesick for food from a New York deli, Pollock Street serves breakfast, lunch or dinner to please any Yankee palate—and Carolinians love it too. Salads, bagels, quiche, pasta, sandwiches and other entrees are delicious and followed by great desserts. Call for hours, which vary daily.

Sandpiper Restaurant

$ • 2403 Neuse Blvd., New Bern
• (252) 633-0888

As soon as you sit down at Sandpiper, your hot hush puppies and butter will arrive. This gets your meal off to a good start, but don't fill up yet. You have many fried seafood platters from which to choose: fish, shrimp, oysters, deviled crab, scallops. We recommend the trout fillets or fried shrimp. Get a baked potato or fries and a hearty serving of cole slaw. Oyster stew, clam chowder, shrimp and oyster cocktails are specialties. The same menu is available for lunch and dinner.

Scalzo's

$$ • 415 Broad St., New Bern
• (252) 633-9898

Scalzo's huge variety of pastas with a choice of 18 sauces plus fresh lamb, seafood, beef, veal or chicken selections should please any palate. One of the best and most unusual sauces is the black olive and caper creation. Others include mixed seafood, red or white clam sauce or a standard marinara. Not a typical Carolina eatery, this place is more typical of an Italian restaurant. Choose a complementary wine and an Italian dessert and spend a memorable evening here. Dinner is served Monday through Saturday.

Yana's Ye Olde Drugstore Restaurant of New Bern

$ • 242 Middle St., New Bern
• (252) 636-5440

Styled after a 1950s luncheonette, this restaurant offers a typical breakfast and lunch bill of fare. From the massive pancakes to chocolate nut sundaes, there is something to please every taste. It's closed on Tuesday.

Washington

No. 1 Chinese Restaurant

$-$$ • 1308 John Small Ave., Washington
• (252) 975-7445

Whether you prefer Cantonese, Szechwan or Hunan cuisine, you're in luck here, because this restaurant features in all three. We recommend the General Tso chicken, but be sure to ask for extra beverage to accompany this hot and spicy dish. This small restaurant in this equally small town offers one of the most extensive Chinese menus we have ever seen. Many items can be ordered as a combination plate, such as chicken with garlic sauce, roast pork egg foo young or pepper steak. Combination plates include pork fried rice and egg roll. Other special dishes include spare rib tips, fried shrimp, chicken wings or half a fried chicken. We also recommend Cantonese special No. 110 (a.k.a. subgum won ton), a combination of won ton, lobster, chicken and pork with vegetables and white rice.

No. 1 Chinese Restaurant serves lunch and dinner daily.

PJ's Creekside Restaurant
$-$$ • 1052 E. Main St., Washington
• (252) 946-9483

Whether outside in the gazebo or in one of the dining rooms (Patty's Porch, The Solarium or Grandpappy's Bedroom), you can enjoy good food from an entertaining menu at this restaurant near the Pamlico River. Featured menu items include the Annette Spinachello (spinach salad with tomatoes, eggs and bacon bits) and the Hugh Heffer (roast beef with cheddar cheese, onions and barbecue sauce on a honey wheat roll). Sweets for My Sweet desserts change daily.

Patty Lovely's vision of 35 years became a reality here. It's A Small World children's menu includes sandwiches dubbed by entrants in a sandwich-naming contest: That's A Bunch of Bologna, Nutter Butter Jelly Jubilee, Mexican Puppy. For the adults, sandwich choices include several varieties of Fowl Play, Ham It Up, Beef Encounters and Chicken of the Sea. For dinner, try an Italian chicken or prime rib entree.

Edenton

The Dram Tree Restaurant
$$$ • 112 Water St., Edenton
• (252) 482-2711

Next door to the lovely bed and breakfast inn of the same name, this restaurant features beef, veal, lamb, poultry, pasta and seafood entrees. A tasty beginning is the Dram Tree coconut shrimp or the seafood crepes. One of our favorite entrees is chicken colliers, a fricasseed breast of chicken over fettuccine topped by a sherry Dijon sauce with almonds. The vegetable ravioli combines our favorite eggplant and spinach with tomato and a roasted red pepper marinara sauce. Desserts are made fresh every day. The restaurant and inn take their shared name from the dram tree where the English captains of outgoing vessels during the 17th and 18th centuries partook of a dram of rum as a token of a safe voyage.

Lane's Family BBQ and Seafood
$ • E. Church St. Ext., Edenton
• (252) 482-4008

Authentic North Carolina barbecue with all the proper trimmings is served here. In case you don't know, the main accompaniments to a chicken or pork barbecue (sliced or chopped)

sandwich or plate are slaw and French fries or onion rings. Take home a pound or two of barbecue for another meal. You can also choose clam strips or a basic delicious hamburger. Daily specials include such offerings as chicken pot pie on Mondays or ham and collards on Wednesday. Don't miss the banana pudding or lemon meringue pie for dessert.

Where to Stay

The few major hotels in this part of the state are dependable, and the modest local motels are fine for a short stay. But, to sample the real flavor of eastern North Carolina, we suggest a bed and breakfast inn in a Victorian or Greek Revival-style restored home. The fine selection of accommodations throughout these historic towns presents a tough choice. If you're here for golf only, you'll want to consider an accommodation that offers a package and helps you book a tee time at your chosen course. Refer to our Preface for an explanation of the price code.

New Bern

The Aerie
$$$ • 509 Pollock St., New Bern
• (252) 636-5553, (800) 849-5553

This is a good place to talk to the locals at the on-site Tea Room, serving tea and coffee, scones and jam Wednesday through Saturday afternoons. A block from Tryon Palace, this 1880s Victorian home includes seven rooms with twin, queen- or king-size beds. Each room has a private bath and cable television. Complimentary wine, beer, soft drinks and light refreshments are provided, and a full gourmet breakfast is served daily.

Comfort Suites & Marina
$$ • 218 E. Front St., New Bern
• (252) 636-0022, (800) 638-7322

Golf packages are a specialty at this motel, within walking distance of New Bern's downtown and historic area. Many of the 100 suites have waterfront balconies overlooking the beautiful Neuse River—a perfect setting to reflect on your golf round. All suites have refrigerators, microwaves and coffee makers. Golfers can enjoy a complimentary continental breakfast prior to their daily round.

Fairfield Harbour
$$$ • 750 Broad Creek Rd., New Bern
• (252) 638-8011

Timeshare units are available for twosomes

or several foursomes, including small condominiums (for two) and two- to three-story houses. In addition to golf privileges at two on-site courses, amenities include tennis, pools, an exercise room, game room and miniature golf to practice your putting. Although the 237 units are timeshares, they're available for rent to the public.

Hampton Inn
$-$$ • 200 Hotel Dr., New Bern
• (252) 637-2111, (800) 448-8288

This hotel off U.S. Highway 17 at the U.S. Highway 70 bypass has 101 clean and comfortable rooms (maintaining this chain's national standards for quality). Guests have convenient access to golf courses and attractions. A continental breakfast is served daily; heartier breakfasts can be had at any of a number of nearby restaurants. Golf and historic district tour packages are available.

Harmony House Inn
$$-$$$ • 215 Pollock St., New Bern
• (252) 636-3810, (800) 636-3113

Enjoy the interesting architecture, the antiques and the hospitality, including a delicious breakfast and afternoon social hour, at this bed and breakfast inn in the downtown historic district. Golf courses and historic tours are nearby. The house was built in 1809. Around 1900, it was cut in half and the west side shifted to allow for an addition and a staircase; new porches also were added. Harmony House Inn has nine guest rooms and one suite, each furnished with antiques or reproductions and including private baths and decorative fireplaces. A full breakfast is served daily in the dining room, and beverages are offered in the evening.

The Magnolia House
$$$ • 315 George St., New Bern
• (252) 633-9488

You'll think you're in Charleston, South Carolina, when you see this pink-painted bed and breakfast inn, just a short distance from Tryon Palace. Don and Kim Trudo's home sits within walking distance of the town center and waterfront. The three guest rooms are cozy, and all have private baths. Family heirlooms, locally gathered antiques and local art adorn each room. Fresh-baked breads and muffins, sea-

sonal fruits and fresh-ground coffee await guests each morning. Guests are invited to lounge and enjoy refreshments daily at 4 PM.

New Bern House Inn
$$ • 709 Broad St., New Bern
• (252) 636-2250, (800) 842-7688

You can enjoy the porch swing and forget about your day if you didn't have a good golf round. The seven guest rooms in this bed and breakfast inn are air-conditioned; all have private baths and either twin, king or queen beds. You can't miss this Colonial-style home, just a block from the Tryon Palace complex. In case you didn't get enough exercise on the golf course, this inn provides a bicycle built for two to spin around historic New Bern. When you call for reservations, ask about the monthly mystery weekends. They are great fun for guests as well as the innkeeper.

The Sheraton Grand
$$-$$$ • New Bern Hotel and Marina, 1 Bicentennial Pk., New Bern
• (252) 638-3585, (800) 326-3745

Comfortable rooms overlook the Trent River and on-site marina. Packages include golf at your favorite course. A covered walkway leads guests to rooms, suites and minisuites (reminiscent of grand Southern hotels) with waterfront and city views. The hotel and inn have two restaurants for dinner and two lounges for relaxing. This is a one-stop choice if you don't want to venture any farther than the golf course and the hotel.

INSIDERS' TIP
After you hit, get your clubs and be ready to proceed to your ball once everyone else in your group has played.

Vacation Resorts International
$$$ • Broad Creek Rd., New Bern
• (252) 633-1151

Condominiums at Fairfield Harbour (see entry above) overlook one of the golf courses, and rental packages for one- to three-bedroom units include golf, a pool, marina and other amenities. Units will accommodate six to 18 people. A three-day minimum stay is required year-round.

Washington

Acadian House Bed & Breakfast
$ • 129 Van Norden St., Washington
• (252) 975-3967

Leonard and Johanna Huber renovated this

1902 house and furnished it with antiques and local crafts, some of which are for sale. Each of the four lovely guest rooms has a private bath. Acadian House is a block from the Pamlico River and a pleasant walk to the historic sites. It's also near good golf courses. True to their New Orleans roots, the innkeepers serve southern Louisiana specialties as well as traditional North Carolina eggs and meats for breakfast.

Pamlico House Bed & Breakfast
$-$$ • 400 E. Main St., Washington
• (252) 946-7184, (800) 948-8507

In the center of the historic district, this large turn-of-the-century home exudes the warmth and friendliness found so often in small Southern towns. The Colonial-style house, once the rectory of St. Peter's Episcopal Church, is appointed with period antiques and modern creature comforts such as air conditioning and color TV. Four spacious guest rooms include private baths and king, queen or twin beds. Guests awaken to a delicious breakfast each morning.

Putting surfaces on courses in the Carolinas vary from bermudagrass to bentgrass, tifdwarf or poa annua.

Photo:Bob Leverone

Edenton

Captain's Quarters Inn
$$$$ • 202 W. Queen St., Edenton
• (252) 482-8945

Phyllis Pepper offers golf-and-snooze or sail-and-snooze two-night packages. Hors d'oeuvres are served the first night, followed the next morning by an in-room continental breakfast and then a three-course gourmet breakfast served in the dining room. After breakfast, go sailing or golfing for a few hours, then hurry back to Captain's Quarters for a two-hour guided tour of Edenton's historic district. Next, enjoy afternoon refreshments back at the inn. A four-course gourmet dinner rounds out the evening. A continental breakfast followed by a breakfast buffet is served the second morning. Sailing or golf at Chowan Country Club or The Sound at Albemarle Plantation (see previous entries), the aforementioned meals and refreshments all are included in the package.

Captain's Quarters Inn features eight spacious and comfortable rooms with private baths.

Governor Eden Inn
$$-$$$ • 304 N. Broad St., Edenton
• (252) 482-2072

Governor Eden Inn is just 1½ blocks from the visitors center in the historic district and seven blocks from the downtown shopping district. It's near Chowan Country Club, and The Sound at Albemarle Plantation is about 20 miles away. (See entries above for each.) The turn-of-the-century Victorian inn includes four rooms with private baths. The wraparound porch and the upstairs balcony are inviting places to relax. As an added enticement, owner and operator Ruth Shackelford serves a hearty breakfast each morning.

The Granville Queen Themed Inn
$$-$$$ • 108 S. Granville St., Edenton
• (252) 482-5296

Nine guest rooms with private baths are individually designed to carry out unique themes ranging from Egyptian to Italian, and furnishings, art and accessories are actually imported from Italy, China, Holland, Thailand and England. This inn in the heart of historic Edenton is a good place for a leisurely visit in an elegant setting. It is nonsmoking and not suitable for children or pets. Along with lodging the visit includes a five-course gourmet breakfast based around grilled chicken breast or filet mignon and accompanied by eggs folded with fresh basil and diced tomatoes. Weekend evening wine tastings also are available. Don't be in a rush for a morning tee time when staying here. Spend the morning lounging over breakfast and then touring the historic district.

Lords Proprietors' Inn
$$$$$ • 300 N. Broad St., Edenton
• (252) 482-3641, (800) 348-8933

Three restored homes offering a total of 20 rooms spread over an acre of ground make up this inn in the historic district. Each room includes private bath, cable television, VCR and use of porches, parlors and the library. Gourmet dinner and a hearty breakfast are included with the price Tuesday through Saturday nights, and rates are adjusted (lowered) to exclude dinner Sunday and Monday nights. Special historic preservation weekends during February and March include a reception Friday night before an elegant dinner. On Saturday afternoon private historic homes are opened for touring. Then enjoy another wonderful dinner and entertainment.

Trestle House Inn Bed & Breakfast
$$ • Soundside Rd. (N.C. Hwy. 1114), Edenton • (252) 482-2282

This secluded inn is a wonderful hideaway just about 4 miles outside historic Edenton. The owners will even pick you up from the Edenton Municipal Airport if you want to arrive on your private or corporate jet. This is an ideal setting for business meetings, with outstanding golf courses nearby. The inn was built in 1972 as a private estate. It features massive exposed redwood beams milled from abandoned railroad trestle timbers, which came from trees estimated at 450 years old. Guest rooms are spacious, and each includes a private tiled bath, remote color TV with cable and HBO, ceiling fan and air conditioning. The delicious complimentary breakfast is accompanied by a view of the pasture and the private lake. Also, the exercise room, billiard table, shuffleboard and sun deck are suggested for a few relaxing hours.

Golf Equipment

Wild Bill's Golf Shop, 3817A U.S. Highway 17 S., (252) 633-9820 is the only golf equipment shop in New Bern. Custom clubs are available as well as same-day service for regripping. For additional golf-equipment options, we have noted in the respective course entries those pro shops in the area that are especially well-stocked.

North Carolina's Central Coast

North Carolina's Central Coast—also known as the Crystal Coast—is halfway between Myrtle Beach (South Carolina) and Norfolk (Virginia) or, if you prefer, directly below North Carolina's Outer Banks. This 65-mile stretch of beaches comprising North Carolina's southern barrier islands is similar to little else on the east coast of the United States. The area comprises Atlantic Beach, Beaufort, Down East, Emerald Isle, Morehead City, Pine Knoll Shores, Salter Path and Indian Beach.

Bogue Banks is a 26-mile island stretching from Atlantic Beach (to the east) to Emerald Isle (to the west) and bordered by the Atlantic Ocean (to the south) and Bogue Sound and the Atlantic Intracoastal Waterway (to the north).

North Carolina's Central Coast is known for its historic fishing villages and boat-building communities. Seafood festivals provide a background for some enjoyable family-oriented visits.

All other factors being equal, it's unlikely that you would come here for a golf holiday. But if you find yourself here for some other reason, the area boasts some decent tracks. For the lowdown on the wealth of activities, attractions, services and more to be found along North Carolina's Central Coast, pick up a copy our favorite guide to the area, *The Insiders' Guide to North Carolina's Central Coast & New Bern* (also available online at www.insiders.com).

Bogue Banks Country Club
152 Oakleaf Dr., Milepost 5,
Pine Knoll Shores,
Atlantic Beach
• (252) 726-1034

Championship Yardage: 6008	
Slope: 116	**Par: 72**
Men's Yardage:	**5757**
Slope: 113	**Par: 72**
Ladies' Yardage:	**5075**
Slope: 116	**Par: 73**

This 18-hole, Morris Bracket-designed course is the only one on Bogue Sound in Atlantic Beach. It features narrow bermudagrass fairways and bermudagrass greens.

Although relatively short, this course is deceptively difficult; it runs between the sound and the ocean, and the back nine includes three holes flanked by the sound; one green and one tee overlook the sound. It's a picturesque layout.

The most challenging holes here are the 5th and 16th. The former has a slight dogleg with trees and bushes on the right, water to the left. On the 16th, another slight dogleg leads to the narrow landing area. Water runs along the sides of many holes, patiently waiting for an errant ball.

The course has a pro shop, snack bar and tennis courts.

Approximate greens fees in summer are $35 if you walk or $45 if you ride.

Brandywine Bay
U.S. Hwy. 70, Morehead City
• (252) 247-2541

Championship Yardage: 6609	
Slope: 119	**Par: 71**
Men's Yardage:	**6150**
Slope: 115	**Par: 71**
Other Yardage:	**5389**
Slope: 113	**Par: 71**
Ladies' Yardage:	**5191**
Slope: 113	**Par: 71**

This 18-hole layout was designed by Bruce Devlin and revised by Ellis and Dan Maples. Its rolling fairways and bentgrass greens are set among tall oaks and private resi-

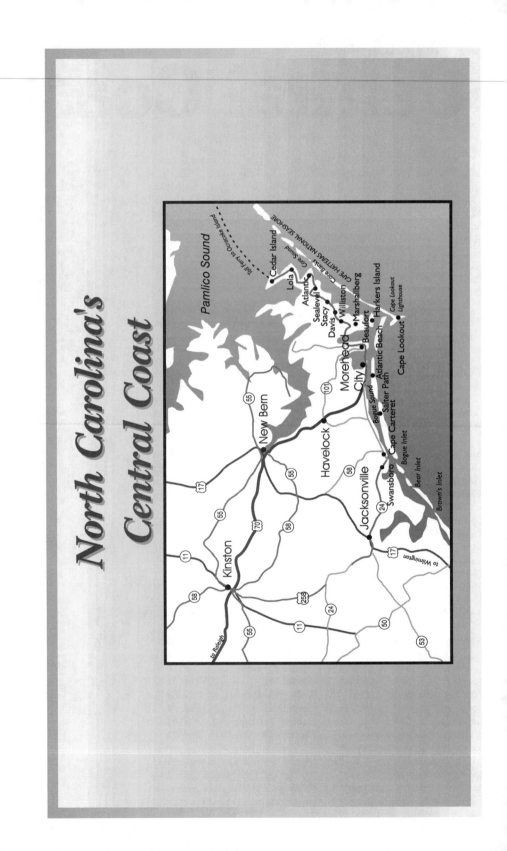

North Carolina's Central Coast

GOLF COURSES ON NORTH CAROLINA'S CENTRAL COAST

Course	Type	Holes	Par	Slope	Yards	Walking	Booking	Cost w/Cart
Bogue Banks Country Club	semiprivate	18	72	113	5757	yes	7 days	$33-45
Brandywine Bay	semiprivate	18	71	115	6150	yes	call	$20-35
Morehead City Country Club	semiprivate	18	72	110	6116	yes	3 days	$35
Silver Creek Golf Club	public	18	73	113	6030	yes	call	$35-40
Star Hill Golf and Country Club								
Lakes Course	semiprivate	9	35	56	2897	yes	365 days	call
Pines Course	semiprivate	9	36	53	2998	yes	365 days	call
Sands Course	semiprivate	9	36	56	2889	yes	365 days	call

dences. The front nine opened in 1980, and the back nine opened in 1983. It's a demanding course where water or woods come into play on every hole. Accurate tee shots and exacting approach shots are needed here.

The 2nd hole is noteworthy, with a winding lake guarding the fairway and green. Your tee shot must carry the lake; your second shot must be of equal accuracy. The 4th hole is a double dogleg right that requires an accurate tee shot followed by a lay-up to a small landing area guarded by water on the left and woods on the right. The green is somewhat elevated and flanked by water on the left. The par 3s are short but not necessarily easy.

Amenities include a pro shop, putting green and snack bar. A pool and two tennis courts are available to members and their guests.

Approximate greens fees are $20 for walking or $35 with cart. Walking is restricted to certain times.

Morehead City Country Club
Country Club Rd., Morehead City
• (252) 726-4917

Championship Yardage:	**6345**
Slope: 113	**Par: 72**
Men's Yardage:	**6116**
Slope: 110	**Par: 72**
Ladies' Yardage:	**4991**
Slope: 105	**Par: 72**

This 18-hole layout, built in 1952 by C.C. McCuisto, is somewhat walkable and easily walkable. The county's oldest course roams along the Newport River. The club is private, but public play is accepted as time permits, usually during the week. Bermudagrass greens and fairways are well maintained.

Some holes are tight, and some are more open. The 1st hole is a good one, albeit a tough start. It's a position hole, a dogleg of 409 yards from the back tees. Several ditches run parallel to the fairways, but otherwise there's not much water to worry about.

The 18th is the signature hole, the only one where marsh comes into play. It's a par 5 of 509 yards from the back tees. The tee shot requires you to hit out of a chute to a fairly wide landing area. Then you have the option of trying to hit over the marsh or laying up short and leaving another 175 yards or more to the green. It's a beautiful hole, with the Newport River running behind the green.

The course offers rental clubs, a driving range, bar and restaurant.

Approximate greens fees are $40, including cart.

Silver Creek Golf Club
N.C. Hwy. 58, Swansboro
• (252) 393-8058

Championship Yardage:	**7005**
Slope: 122	**Par: 73**
Men's Yardage:	**6030**
Slope: 113	**Par: 73**
Ladies' Yardage:	**5526**
Slope: 110	**Par: 71**

Gene Hamm designed this course with bermudagrass fairways and bentgrass greens. It's open, flat and easy to walk. Stands of small pines dot the course but don't create much of a problem. Ponds come into play on 12 holes, but most are not extremely difficult. The toughest hole is No. 8, a par 3 measuring about 185 yards from the back tees with a pond around the front and the right side.

You will encounter at least seven doglegs. The 11th hole doglegs right over two ponds; it's a par 5 that requires a lay-up followed by a long iron over the water. On the second it's also hard to position your drive over the lake, which runs down the hole from right to left. The farther left you go, the longer the carry. Then, a trap on the right in the landing area makes it even tougher. No. 14 is a straightaway par 4 of 460 yards that usually plays tough with the wind in your face.

The 16th is another interesting hole—par 3, 145 yards—with terracing on the front and back of the green. And the 18th is a par 4 of 445 yards with a pond on the right of the green.

The clubhouse is inviting, and amenities include a locker room, driving range, putting greens, a pro shop, tennis courts, a swimming pool and a grill.

Approximate greens fees, including cart, are $35 to $40. Walking is allowed after 2 PM every day.

Star Hill Golf & Country Club
Club House Dr., Cape Carteret
• (252) 393-8111

The 27 holes of Star Hill offer more than 9000 yards of great golf. The three nine-hole courses are played as three 18-hole pairs, each set between the Intracoastal Waterway and the Croatan National Forest. All three are flat with narrow tree-lined fairways and bermudagrass greens. Russell Burney designed the courses.

Despite the proximity of the Waterway, only about five holes have water.

A fully stocked golf shop, a driving range, rental clubs, a clubhouse, grill, tennis courts and a pool add to this facility's desirability. Corporate outings are welcome, and a banquet facility is available.

Approximate greens fees, including cart, range from $35 to $45. Walking costs from $25 to $35 and is sometimes restricted. Call for details when you book your round.

Lakes Course

Championship Yardage: 3254	
Slope: 58	Par: 35
Men's Yardage:	2897
Slope: 56	Par: 35
Other Yardage:	2662
Slope: 52	Par: 35
Ladies' Yardage:	2507
Slope: 52	Par: 36

No. 1 on the Lakes is considered the signature hole of this complex, and the Lakes is the most challenging course of the three because of, that's right, the big lake. From the back tees, No. 1 requires a 200-yard carry. You must cross the lake to the landing area, then play over a creek that runs in front of the green.

Pines Course

Championship Yardage: 3194	
Slope: 55	Par: 36
Men's Yardage:	2998
Slope: 53	Par: 36
Other Yardage:	2497
Slope: 49	Par: 36
Ladies' Yardage:	2390
Slope: 52	Par: 36

On the Pines, you'll need a good tee shot on the par 5 No. 2. But don't leave your power stroke at the tee; you'll need to follow up with two more big shots. This course actually has more water on it than the Lakes Course.

Sands Course

Championship Yardage: 3107	
Slope: 60	Par: 36
Men's Yardage:	2889
Slope: 56	Par: 36
Other Yardage:	2672
Slope: 52	Par: 36
Ladies' Yardage:	2279
Slope: 56	Par: 36

No. 1 on the Sands requires a good tee shot, or you will need a long iron shot into a slight dogleg left surrounded by trees.

Around the Central Coast . . .

Fun Things To Do

In addition to golf, the best things to do here include fishing, swimming and sunning. It's a real getaway from busy resort areas, and you won't find a more beautiful spot for a quiet family vacation and easygoing fun. Eat plenty of seafood and spend sunny days beachcombing and ocean swimming.

Shop at the **Golfin' Dolphin,** N.C. Highway 58, Cape Carteret, (252) 393-8131, for golf equipment or apparel. Your big or little children can keep busy with arcade games, miniature golf and bumper boats at this family entertainment complex, while the golfers browse, buy and then break in their new accessories on the 50-tee driving range.

Children of all ages will enjoy amusements such as an arcade, miniature golf, bumper boats and other rides at **Jungleland,** Salter Path Road (N.C. 58, Milepost 4.5), Atlantic Beach, (252) 247-2148; **Pirate Island Park,** Salter Path Road (N.C. 58, Milepost 10.5), Salter Path, (252) 247-3024; or **Playland,** 204 Islander Drive, Milepost 20.5, Emerald Isle, (252) 354-6616. The boardwalks in Emerald Isle and Atlantic Beach also are must-stops on any beach trip.

If you crave some educational activity to give your trip a culturally redeeming quality, visit **Fort Macon State Park,** E. Fort Macon Road (N.C. 58, Milepost 0), Atlantic Beach, (252) 726-3775. On occasional weekends, you can witness militia musket firings and living history in the Civil War fortress at Fort Macon; call for specific dates and times.

Check your map to differentiate between Beaufort, North Carolina, and Beaufort, South Carolina. Both cities are delightfully historic yet distinctly different, beginning with their pronunciations—in North Carolina, it's "Bow-fort;" in South Carolina, "Byu-ford." **Beaufort Historic Site** (N.C.), 100 block of Turner Street, (252) 728-5225 or (800) 575-7483, under the auspices of the **Beaufort Historical Association,** is the focus of, among other things, guided tours of a 21-block historic district that features homes, buildings and gardens dating from 1732. Seasonal celebrations revolve around the architecture and heritage included therein. Also in Beaufort, visit the **North Carolina Maritime Museum,** 315 Front Street, (252) 728-7317, which celebrates the state's coastal heritage, maritime and natural history and natural resources. The museum maintains an impressive collection of watercraft models, including sailing skiffs and full-rigged ships.

In Pine Knoll Shores, enjoy the **North Carolina Aquarium at Pine Knoll Shores,** Salter Path Road (N.C. 58, Milepost 7), (252) 247-4004. Tucked away in the maritime forest of the **Theodore Roosevelt Natural Area,** the aquarium bustles with fun and educational activities between spring and fall, including films, talks and workshops on coastal topics, on-board collecting cruises, canoe trips, snorkeling instruction, saltwater fishing and excursions to remote barrier islands. For a special treat, take a narrated sightseeing cruise on a paddle-wheeler.

Enjoy outdoor drama presentations at the **Crystal Coast Amphitheater,** N.C. 58, Pelletier (near Cape Carteret). The long-running professional production *Worthy Is the Lamb*, a passion play depicting the life and times of Jesus Christ, draws audiences from miles away to its mid-June through September performances. Call (252) 393-8956 or (800) 662-5960 for ticket and schedule information.

For a taste of regional culture, stop by the **Carteret County Museum of History,** 100 Wallace Dr., Morehead City, (252) 247-7533. Examine changing exhibits of American Indian artifacts as well as memorabilia of the county's settlers, some dating to 1722.

Small specialty shops dot the villages and tempt shoppers with antiques, art and local crafts. The fresh fare at the prevalent seafood markets will entice you to cook your own deep-sea delights, although world-class local restaurants will be happy to prepare their delectable bounty for you.

Festivals are based on such important leisure activities as kite flying, melon eating, fishing (of course) and the ever-shining convention of bald folks in Morehead City.

One of the year's greatest events—featuring entertainment as well as unsurpassed cuisine—is the **North Carolina Seafood Festival,** held the first weekend in October on the Morehead City waterfront. It's a three-day celebration of the area's heritage and all that makes life delightful along the Central Coast. Call (252) 726-6273 for more information. Other events revolve around boats, art, antiques, music and even sandcastle building, and the welcome mat is always rolled out for visitors or newcomers.

Call (800) SUNNY NC or pick up a copy of *The Insiders' Guide to North Carolina's Central Coast & New Bern* for complete Central Coast information.

Where to Eat

Fresh seafood abounds all along the Central Coast, and most of our favorite shellfish or saltwater fish entrees are served in the casual atmosphere befitting a golf trip along the coast. If you prefer fine dining with international flair, it's also available here. Read on for some real finds that we can personally recommend for your dining pleasure. We also keep an eye out for the steak and potatoes meals, which a couple of our golfing buddies *must* have, so that's no problem here either. You'll also enjoy some outstanding homemade breakfasts in several of the country inns. Don't diet while visiting here; too many tempting delicacies call out to you.

(Note: Refer to our Preface for an explanation of the pricing code.)

Beaufort

Beaufort Grocery Co.
$$-$$$ • 117 Queen St., Beaufort • (252) 728-3899

The restored town grocery store is now famous for its fine cuisine including salads, soups and sandwiches for lunch. Be adventurous and try the gougeres, which are herb pastries stuffed with wonderful salad mixes such as crab, shrimp, chicken or eggs. For dinner, try fresh seafood, choice steaks, chicken, duck or lamb—all served with creative sauces. Definitely begin

INSIDERS' TIP

Learn how to fix a pitch mark on the green in the correct fashion. And as the signs constantly remind you, "repair your ball mark and one other."

with a Carolina crab-cake appetizer and end with a luscious dessert. Sunday brunch is great, and the small bar is well stocked and invites conversations among locals and visiting golfers who all blend into the relaxed setting.

Clawson's 1905 Restaurant
$$ • 429 Front St., Beaufort
• (252) 728-2133
Old and new wares represent the atmosphere of the early days along the waterfront in Beaufort. Go early and expect a crowd during the summer. Wonderful appetizers include battered and lightly fried vegetables. Entrees feature fried, grilled or sauteed seafood, chicken, pasta or steaks; and wine, beer and mixed drinks are available. For a great lunch, we recommend the hearty baked potato stuffed with seafood, vegetables or meat.

Finz Grill & Eatery
$ • 330 Front St., Beaufort
• (252) 728-7459
Finz offers seating on its great porch overhanging the creek as well as in the restaurant or the bar. Gumbo or black bean items enhance the varied choices of seafood such as flounder, Spanish mackerel or king mackerel. You could be eating next to the person who caught your meal, because local fishermen provide the fresh seafood. Entrees from the sea can be ordered grilled, blackened or fried. Other dinner entrees include steaks and pasta. The lunch menu offers all sorts of sandwiches, subs, burgers and soups (we recommend the black bean). Finz is a friendly place to relax, with good food, nice people and all beverage permits for beer, wine or mixed drinks.

Net House Steam Restaurant & Oyster Bar
$$-$$$ • 133 Turner St., Beaufort
• (252) 728-2002
Conch or clam chowder and every steamed mollusk plus other dinner choices and delectable desserts (did we mention the Key lime pie?) are enough to bring any golf group to this

family-owned and operated establishment for lunch or dinner. The atmosphere is distinctly maritime—the restaurant is bedecked in weathered pine and nautical antiques.

Morehead City

Calypso Cafe
$$$ • 506 Arendell St., Morehead City
• (252) 240-3380
Creative cocktails and a tropical atmosphere welcome you into this world of fine food. We like to begin a meal with the black bean torta or the stuffed jalapeños. Then, move on to the entrees, which spotlight local seafood with island accents of fruit and spices. Shrimp curry with tropical salsa and grilled fish with ginger salsa are two of our favorites. Pork, pasta, seafood fajitas and blackened or grilled seafood will also delight your taste buds. Don't leave without trying the Paradise Pie, which is a brownie and ice cream covered with strawberry puree. (You may be limited to one of these per customer!) Enjoy your meal at a table, the bar or

Solid sand play is essential—particularly on the beach courses of the Carolinas.

Photo: Ortega Gaines

Back to School

You have made the commitment to improve your game by taking lessons on how to hit the ball like the pros—or as much like the pros as you can. So what is the next step? You should decide whether to seek help from your local club pro with whom you feel comfortable, or go to a school. If you go to your club pro, fine. You know the pro; you feel at ease and like the idea of the give and take the two of you have. So if everything is right, set a schedule of once or twice a week and settle in—and be sure to be on time for each lesson.

But suppose you want totally new ideas and techniques to improve your game. And what if you want intense instruction for two, three, maybe four days in a row. In that case, attend a golf school. But take note: The multi-day schools are not for everyone. However, if you really wish to improve your game, then the multi-day school is a good route to take. That's because results will be more immediately apparent following concentrated instruction at a multi-day school. Ostensibly, you leave all distractions behind, and golf is the only thing on your mind for a few days. (Characteristically, folks are more likely to retain what they've learned when continuously immersed in the golf setting, even if only for a few days.) The instructor can teach at a pace that matches your needs. And you probably will not feel like everything is being crammed in, as it sometimes is in a one-hour lesson.

OK, so you have committed to taking a few days off work and going to a golf school. What next? Get brochures, look at videos and, if possible, talk to folks who have attended these schools. Of course you should find out about the student-teacher ratio. One-on-one is an ideal situation, but it's not always viable. Three- or 4-to-1 is a fine ratio at any school. Remember, in a group situation, you can learn from others being instructed.

The amount of instruction time each day is also important. Ninety minutes of instruction time and the rest of the time playing is not that much different from going to your local pro and then playing on your home course. And the reputation

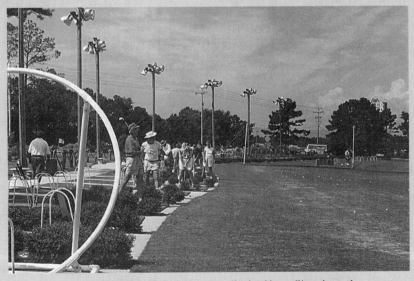

A big consideration when choosing a golf school is pupil/teacher ratio.

Photo: Charles Mitchell

of the teachers at your chosen school is very important. Above all, enlist a PGA professional. Look for success stories of students who have attended your chosen school. Also, find a situation where you are hitting at real fairways and greens, not just on a driving range.

Of course you want to be comfortable at day's end, so the overnight accommodations are also important. If you can get away from daily encumbrances and sources of stress, you'll better retain what you've learned in your lesson if you settle in for the night in satisfactory accommodations; otherwise, you may be more concerned with strange surroundings than applying the proper technique to your backswing. When you get back home, you should feel like you have been on vacation.

Cost is another consideration. The multi-day school is pretty cost-effective— usually cheaper than paying for five or six hourly lessons. If you go to a golf school that offers accommodations, then you can expect to pay more. But do a little logical thinking. If you go to a three-day school that includes accommodations and instruction for $400, and your room is $125 a day, your three-day lessons are costing you $25 a day total. Ask yourself if this is really worth it.

Going to a golf school is a big step toward improving your game. The seemingly costly short-term investment is worth it in the long run because of the progress you stand to make.

on the patio. We like the casual atmosphere as well as the food.

Capt. Bill's Waterfront Restaurant
$$-$$$$ • 701 Evans St., Morehead City • (252) 726-2166

Lunch and dinner on the waterfront have been a tradition here since 1941. Now owned by John and Diane Poag, Capt. Bill's continues its legacy as a place for good food in Morehead City. A daily lunch special, such as baked chicken, two vegetables and hush puppies, can cost less than $4. Specials change daily, but they're always good. Try the all-you-can-eat fish on Monday or all-you-can-eat fish and popcorn shrimp on Friday. Wednesdays and Saturdays feature conch stew. Desserts are made from family recipes and created from scratch; one of the best is the Down East lemon pie. By boat or by car, just get here quickly and sample any of the 13 flavors of fudge made at the restaurant. And, after your meal, you can visit the Ship's Wheel Gift Shop.

Nikola's
$$-$$$$ • Fourth and Bridges Sts., Morehead City • (252) 726-6060

Nikola's serves creative and delicious Italian fare in this Victorian house. Try the rack of lamb or any pasta or seafood entree for a delightful treat. The spinach soup is unsurpassed. Reservations are recommended for weekends.

Raps Grill and Bar
$$ • 715 Arendell St., Morehead City • (252) 240-1213

Locals and visiting golfers enjoy Raps' bar, with its popcorn and wide-screen television. Enjoy lunch or dinner here in a casual atmosphere. The original Raps Burger with anything or everything on it is a good bet, or try the ribs and salads. Steamed clams and crabs are our favorites; they're fresh and make a great companion to a beer after your golf round.

Bogue Banks

Bistro By The Sea
$$ • 401 Money Island Dr., Milepost 1.25, Atlantic Beach • (252) 247-2777

You don't have to *eat* here—the bar serves mixed drinks, beer and wine. Just the same, we recommend that you dine at this small, casual restaurant—a local favorite—beside Sportsman's Pier. Seafood entrees vary nightly according to season, freshness and availability, and include such tasty choices as cappellini with pesto, vegetables and scallops and eggplant Parmesan (a personal favorite). You won't be disappointed by the Caesar salad with chargrilled tuna or the leafy spinach salad with shrimp. If seafood is not your choice, we recommend the chargrilled steaks or the liver in orange liqueur (c'mon, your mom would be proud!). And if you're watching your cholesterol, try the stir-fried chicken with rice and wontons.

The Watermark
$$ • Milepost 3, Atlantic Beach
• (252) 240-2811

Look carefully for this restaurant in the Atlantic Station Shopping Center; it has a new name and a new owner. It's a fine choice for Black Angus beef lovers. Open for dinner only from 5:30 PM Wednesday through Sunday, the restaurant specializes in steak and prime rib and also serves good fresh fish in a variety of ways.

Bushwackers Restaurant
$$ • 100 Bogue Inlet Dr., Emerald Isle
• (252) 354-6300

Bushwackers is a great spot for broiled or steamed seafood and appetizers such as 'gator and shark bites. Entrees include prime rib and Black Angus steaks. Try the Rock 'n' Roll Cheesecake for a luscious dessert. Mixed drinks, beer and wine are served, and the lively atmosphere in the lounge will put a smile on your face. Enjoy the fun wait staff, the wonderful oceanfront view and the great decorations too.

Frank and Clara's Restaurant & Lounge
$$-$$$ • Milepost 11, Indian Beach
• (252) 247-2788

Locals love the crab cakes or anything made with fresh crab. Try any of the seafood offerings as well as the steaks. Relax in the upstairs lounge if there's a wait for a table at dinner, or return to the lounge for a nightcap. Locals and visitors alike feel at home here.

Mazzella's Italian Restaurant
$$ • N.C. Hwy. 58, Cape Carteret
• (252) 393-8787

You can't go wrong with this authentic, family-owned Italian restaurant where the pasta is fresh, the sauces are homemade, and the seafood and pizzas are scrumptious. To add to the positives, it's affordable and convenient to accommodations and golf courses to boot!

Rucker Johns—A Restaurant & More
$$ • 140 Fairview Dr., Milepost 19.5, Emerald Isle • (252) 354-2413

If you find a beach house to rent in Emerald Isle, you'll probably love the area so much that you won't want to venture any farther away than a golf course or this restaurant for all the excitement you could hope for in a vacation. If you're searching for fried calamari, you've found a home here; and that's just one of the special appetizers. Steaks and ribs are great, and we never tire of the crab cakes, shrimp entrees or seafood and pasta choices. The lounge doubles as a popular nightspot.

Tradewinds
$$-$$$ • Royal Pavilion, Milepost 5.5, Pine Knoll Shores • (252) 726-5188

Sunday brunch is the best time to eat here. Sample the large selection of bread, entrees, fruit and desserts. Pasta, chicken, seafood and aged prime beef specialties are menu highlights, along with good soups and salads. We recommend the Jack Daniels rib-eye—and maybe a drink of the same to go with it. Live entertainment is featured often.

Choose a golf ball to suit your game; your pro can help.

Photo: John D. Simmons

Where to Stay

Since the Central Coast is becoming more of a year-round resort, it would be impossible to mention all of the area's accommodations. So we've listed some of our favorites in each price range (see our Preface for the price-code key). You can also get good information about lodging from the Carteret County Tourism Development Bureau, P.O. Box 1406, Morehead City, North Carolina 29557, (800) SUNNY NC. The bureau staffs visitors centers at 3409 Arendell Street (U.S. Highway 70) in Morehead City and on N.C. Highway 58, just south of its intersection with N.C. Highway 24, near Cape Carteret.

Stay in Beaufort if you're looking for history and variety. You'll certainly find copious amenities and wonderful atmosphere at many accommodations, most of which are near golf courses. Some inexpensive local motels provide standard options, both in Beaufort and at the beach. Or, if you're looking for ocean access and fishing options coupled with convenient proximity to golf courses, stay at one of the islands' super beachfront resorts.

Beaufort

Beaufort Inn
$$$ • 101 Ann St., Beaufort
• (252) 728-2600, (800) 726-0321

Head into this historic town and you'll find the Beaufort Inn on Gallant's Channel. Enjoy the rocking chairs on the porch as well as a friendly welcome and the famous breakfast. The 41 guest rooms, all with private porches, feature early American decor created by local artists and craftspeople.

Captain's Quarters Bed & Biscuit
$$$-$$$$ • 315 Ann St., Beaufort
• (252) 728-7711, (800) 659-7111

A complete English-style breakfast, featuring Ms. Ruby's famous "Riz" biscuits, and the traditional toast to the sunset, with complimentary light wines and fresh fruit juices served on the veranda or by the parlor fireplace, are among the reasons to enjoy the Captain's Quarters. The family atmosphere in this three-bedroom Victorian home will make you feel... well, like part of the family.

It's in the heart of the historic district, a block from the waterfront shops and restaurants. Rated "excellent" by the American Bed & Breakfast Association, the "home of hospitality with quiet elegance" is furnished with family heirlooms and antiques. Yet Ruby and Capt. Dick Collins are as modern as it gets, offering guests use of their computer, modem and fax.

The Cedars Inn at Beaufort
$$$-$$$$ • 305 Front St., Beaufort
• (252) 728-7036, (800) 732-7036

The inn is created from two period homes (c. 1768 and 1851). The Grady family offers 16 standard rooms and suites, all of which are en suite (private baths); some also have sitting rooms or fireplaces. Second-floor porches include rocking chairs where you can sit back, relax and contemplate your next day's golf round. The hospitality is warm, and breakfast (included in your room rate) is a treat. The Cedars Inn is easy to find at the corner of Front and Orange streets.

Delamar Inn Bed & Breakfast
$$$ • 217 Turner St., Beaufort
• (252) 728-4300

The Delamar Inn (c. 1866) offers Scottish charm and homemade bread for breakfast plus afternoon cookies and refreshments. Mable or Tom Steepy will be glad to help you with tee times or arrangements for other activities, such as chartering a boat or exploring Beaufort by bike. Delamar is open all year. The three guest rooms have private baths and antique furnishings.

Inlet Inn Bed & Breakfast
$$$-$$$$ • 601 Front St., Beaufort
• (252) 728-3600

Harborfront rooms with sitting areas, bars, refrigerators and ice makers, homemade continental breakfast, and afternoon wine are among the amenities at the Inlet Inn, which opened in 1985 on the same block as the 19th-century inn of the same name. Enjoy a little respite in the courtyard garden or the rooftop lounge, with impressive views of the Atlantic Ocean, Morehead City Harbor, Cape Lookout Light, Fort Macon, the wild ponies on Carrot Island and the Beaufort waterfront. The inn is also near the North Carolina Maritime Museum (see the previous "Fun Things To Do" section) and many fine restaurants and shops.

Langdon House
$$$, no credit cards • 135 Craven St., Beaufort • (252) 728-5499

Fishing poles, beach baskets, arranged dinner reservations and a full breakfast with Jimm's famous pecan waffles are a few of the treats here. All four rooms are comfortable and include private baths. Langdon House is open year round.

Pecan Tree Inn
$$$-$$$$ • 116 Queen St., Beaufort
• (252) 728-6733

Combine your honeymoon with your golf trip and you can enjoy the Jacuzzi in the bridal suite plus Susan's homemade muffins and special ground coffee in this charming historic home. The other six rooms effuse individual character, and each includes a private bath. The half-block walk to the waterfront is a treat. The Johnsons will help arrange tee times or other activities, including box-lunch excursions or bicycle rides through the historic district. In the morning, you can enjoy a continental breakfast on the wraparound porch or in the formal dining room.

Morehead City

Best Western Buccaneer Inn
$$ • 2806 Arendell St. (U.S. Hwy. 70), Morehead City
• (252) 726-3115, (800) 682-4982

Golf packages are arranged here for two nights or a week, with tee times booked on any area course. A full hot breakfast, comfortable accommodations, greens fees and cart are included in your price. The Buccaneer Inn is near shopping destinations and historical tours for fun in your spare time. You may choose king or double beds among the 91 rooms, all with TV. Pool, restaurant, lounge and meeting facilities also are available.

Bogue Banks

Atlantis Lodge
$$$ • Salter Path Rd., Milepost 5, Pine Knoll Shores
• (252) 726-5168, (800) 682-7057

Atlantis Lodge is one of the oldest hotels on Bogue Banks. It's situated among large live oaks on the ocean side of Salter Path Road. All of the 42 units are efficiencies with kitchens and separate dining, living and sleeping areas. Each unit also has either a patio or deck that faces the ocean. Lounge around the pool and get psyched up for tomorrow's tee time. During fall and spring, the hotel offers package deals.

Harborlight Guest House
$$$-$$$$ • 332 Live Oak Dr., Cape Carteret
• (252) 393-6868, (800) 624-VIEW

Stay in one of the seven suites at this bed and breakfast inn. Once used as a restaurant by the ferry service, this three-story establishment is known for its beautiful views of more than 500 feet of shoreline and its choice setting close to Emerald Isle beaches. Enjoy your breakfast privately in your upstairs suite or have it served in the dining room or on the waterfront terrace. The guest house is open year-round and is ideal for a 20-person conference.

Holiday Inn On the Ocean
$$ • Salter Path Rd., Atlantic Beach
• (252) 726-2544, (800) 733-7588

On the oceanfront, with deep-sea fishing, sailing, pier fishing and golf courses nearby, this hotel is a convenient choice for outdoor enthusiasts as well as for golfers. Amenities include a pool, restaurant and lounge. Hotel staff can customize golf packages and golf widow packages, including greens fees, a cart, daily full breakfast, golf towel and tees plus an oceanview or poolside room. The best deal is a two-night stay with two days of golf from early November until March.

Iron Steamer Resort
$$-$$$ • Salter Path Rd., Milepost 6¾, Pine Knoll Shores
• (252) 247-4221, (800) 332-4221

Families and anglers are welcome at Iron Steamer, open from Easter until Thanksgiving. The resort is named for a Civil War-era blockade runner, the remains of which are visible from the on-site pier. Oceanfront rooms offer access to the beach, a pool and the pier. Request an in-room refrigerator or private balcony if you'd like.

Oceanana Resort Motel
$$-$$$ • E. Fort Macon Rd., Milepost 1½, Atlantic Beach • (252) 726-4111

This is a basic motel, with comfortable standard rooms, oceanfront rooms and suites. Amenities include a pool, children's play area (this place is great for families), fishing pier, picnic tables and grills and more. It's open from spring through fall only. Inquire about golf privileges.

INSIDERS' TIP
In hot weather, drink plenty of fluids (especially if you're walking). Beer will only dehydrate you. Drink water before you feel thirsty, and mix a sports drink in every once in a while to replace some of the salt you lose through sweat.

Parkerton Inn
$$ • N.C. Hwy. 58 N., Cape Carteret
• (252) 393-9000, (800) 393-9909

You'll have convenient access to the golf courses and the Crystal Coast Amphitheater at this somewhat new accommodation (less than 2 years old). Room options include efficiencies with kitchenettes. A complimentary continental breakfast is served daily. Be sure to inquire about golf packages.

Royal Pavilion
$$-$$$$ • Salter Path Rd., Milepost 5½,
PineKnoll Shores
• (252) 726-5188, (800) 533-3700

This is a familiar property to longtime visitors of Bogue Banks. Newly named after the John Yancey Motor Hotel was renovated, the Royal Pavilion offers oceanfront rooms and a conference center. The neighboring Tradewinds Restaurant will cater meals in the conference rooms—a perfect arrangement if a business meeting is part of your stay. The Pavilion's amenities include efficiency kitchens, an outdoor pool, private beach and arranged tee times.

Sheraton Atlantic Beach Resort
$$$-$$$$ • Salter Path Rd., Milepost 4½,
Atlantic Beach
• (252) 240-1155, (800) 624-8875

This full-service beach resort has a bar, restaurant, nightclub and pool, and a fishing pier is nearby. All rooms offer private balconies, refrigerators, microwaves and coffee makers, and suites include Jacuzzis.

Showboat Motel
$-$$ • Atlantic Beach Cswy.,
Atlantic Beach
• (252) 726-6163, (800) 540-BOAT

Golfers who care to bring their fishing poles might want to stay here, since you can fish from the motel's wharf. You can cook your catch on a grill in one of the picnic areas that the motel maintains. If fishing isn't your thing, but you'd like an up-close and personal look at these creatures of the deep, take advantage of Wreckreational Divers, a complete on-site dive shop for golfers who want to go on a Sea Hunt. All rooms have refrigerators. The year-round property offers corporate and other special rates, so be sure to inquire.

Windjammer Inn
$$$-$$$$ • Salter Path Rd., Milepost 4½,
Pine Knoll Shores
• (252) 247-7123, (800) 233-6466

All of the Windjammer's rooms are spacious and oceanfront, with private balconies, cable TV and refrigerators. Getting to your room via the glass-enclosed elevator offers a beautiful ocean view. No need to go out early for your cup of coffee—the Windjammer offers complimentary java each morning. There's a two-night minimum stay on summer weekends and a three-night minimum on holiday weekends; but, hey, it's a fun place to hang around for a while.

CENTRAL COAST

Wilmington and the Cape Fear Coast

Wilmington is one of North Carolina's oldest and most vibrant cities. Its location, tucked up the Cape Fear River yet within easy striking distance of any number of wonderful coastal destinations, annually attracts thousands of new residents and swarms of summertime visitors, plus a horde of academically dedicated students who attend the University of North Carolina at Wilmington.

There's something a little bit sexy about Wilmington: the film industry. While nobody would confuse Market Street for Rodeo Drive, film and TV producers routinely use Wilmington's studios and streets for shows like *Matlock* and movies like David Lynch's eerie *Blue Velvet*. Wilmington basically provides a low-cost alternative to shooting in Hollywood and putting up with all that traffic, smog, and general haughtiness. Wilmington's residents seem relaxed and less impressed with themselves than can be the case in other similar cities. Nobody in Wilmington says, "I'll have my people call your people."

Wilmington's stature and history as a major port rivals that of Savannah (Georgia) and Charleston (South Carolina). While the latter cities may be larger and more publicized, Wilmington, especially downtown, boasts just as much character and charm. Massive homes built by 18th and 19th century commodity and transportation magnates peer down majestically at tourists and locals. Developers have turned former cotton and sugar warehouses into upmarket restaurants, all-day all-night coffee shops and heaving bars.

While Wilmington's suburban hinterland of fast-food outlets and cheap motels is no different from any other in the United States, its downtown and adjoining neighborhoods, draped in oak and magnolia trees, make it a delightful city that's remarkably unspoiled by tourism.

The biggest threat to Wilmington over the last few years of the 20th century arrived in the form of four sizeable hurricanes. Each of these monster storms rocked up the Cape Fear River, downing trees, flooding roads, eroding beaches and giving that old guy at The Weather Channel an excuse to say "Wilmington, North Carolina may be completely destroyed" a gazillion times. In his oh-so-droll way, John Hope helped put Wilmington on the map.

Thankfully, most of the coastal communities remained intact and relatively unharmed by the hurricanes. Places like Wrightsville Beach, Figure Eight Island, Topsail Beach, Kure Beach, Carolina Beach, and Oak Island are tremendously important for the local economy. Visitors from up and down the East Coast visit these wonderful seasonal retreats.

They also play golf.

Wilmington's seaside terrain and semi-sandy soil make for outstanding coastal golf. While Wilmington will never be confused with Myrtle Beach (just a one-hour drive to the south), the southern coast of North Carolina attracts more than its fair share of golfing tourists.

Wilmington and The Cape Fear Coast

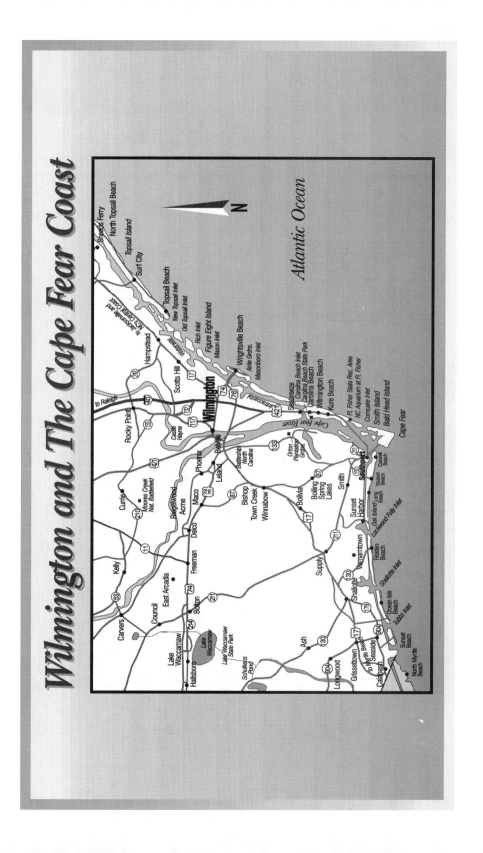

GOLF COURSES IN NORTH CAROLINA'S WILMINGTON AREA

Course	Type	# Holes	Par	Slope	Yards	Walking	Booking	Cost w/Cart
Bald Head Island Country Club	semiprivate	18	72	136	6239	yes	7 days	$71
Beau Rivage Plantation	semiprivate	18	72	129	6166	no	30 days	$30-50
Belvedere Plantation Golf & C. C.	semiprivate	18	71	126	6021	no	6 months	$18-43
Brierwood Golf Club	semiprivate	18	72	121	6170	yes	7 days	$38
Cape Golf & Racquet	semiprivate	18	72	125	6129	no	365 days	$30-45
Duck Haven Country Club	public	18	72	122	6053	yes	none	$20
Echo Farms Golf & Country Club	semiprivate	18	72	126	6073	no	24 days	$25-30
Fox Squirrel Country Club	semiprivate	18	72	123	6208	yes	7 days	$25-32
North Shore Country Club	semiprivate	18	72	123	6358	yes	14 days	$40-55
Oak Island Golf and Country Club	semiprivate	18	72	124	6135	yes	2 days	$40
Old Fort Golf Course	public	18	72	103	5773	yes	none	$22
Olde Point Golf and Country Club	semiprivate	18	72	123	6253	no	14 days	$35-50
Porters Neck Plantation and C. C.	semiprivate	18	72	136	6818	no	60 days	$60-70
Topsail Greens Golf & Country Club	semiprivate	18	71	118	6010	yes	7 days	$25-30
Wilmington Municipal Golf Course	public	18	71	116	6267	yes	7 days	$15-20

We included courses in parts of the Brunswick Islands, stretching south from the Southport area, in our Grand Strand chapter. These tracks, though found in North Carolina, align themselves with the Myrtle Beach area.

For more information about this area, contact the Cape Fear Coast Convention & Visitors Bureau, (910) 341-4030 or (800) 222-4757, or pick up a copy of *The Insiders' Guide to Wilmington & the Cape Fear Coast.*

Bald Head Island Country Club
Bald Head Is., Southport
• **(910) 457-7310**

Championship Yardage:	6855
Slope: 143	**Par:** 72
Men's Yardage:	6239
Slope: 136	**Par:** 72
Other Yardage:	5536
Slope: 124	**Par:** 72
Ladies' Yardage:	4810
Slope: 132	**Par:** 72

This George Cobb course opened in 1975. It has bermudagrass greens and fairways and is routed through dense coastal forest. The club recently regrassed the greens and improved its facilities.

The golf course at Bald Head Island is *special,* and any golfer who visits the Wilmington area should make the time to take the ferry over to this secluded island to play this course.

If Bald Head were more accessible and more publicized, it would easily rate as one of North Carolina's finest courses. But thankfully, Bald Head is neither publicized or highly rated by magazines—and therein lies part of its charm.

While a lot of coastal golf courses advertise themselves as "pure links" or "a Scottish links experience," most of these claims are rubbish. And while very few true links courses resemble Bald Head, Bald Head might come the closest to being the real thing of all but a very few of the hundreds of courses on the Carolina coast.

Wind is always a factor at Bald Head, whether it's the prevailing south-westerly or the colder, stormier nor'easter. If your ball flies above the tops of the dense coastal forest, it can be blown all over the place, thus Bald Head invites shotmaking. In particular, it favors low, piercing, controlled shots that can run up to a green.

Because of the wind and the fact that most

people are on vacation when they visit Bald Head, George Cobb didn't "overdesign" the course. Another more modern architect could have gone overboard with this site, shaping it into a monster: Bald Head's understated architectural elegance is part of the course's appeal and character.

Still, there are plenty of superb golf holes. The par 3 second, 190 yards from the tips, is one of our favorite one-shot holes. After walking off the first green, you dash through a gap in the woods and there it is: simple, gracious, majestic and completely away from everything.

The final three holes on the back nine typically play into the wind and if you can follow par (5-3-4), you're a player. Many fine golfers are ecstatic to leave the ninth with a bogey: the drive, which must split two wetland areas, is sheer terror.

The par 5 11th, dare we say it, must be somewhat modeled after Augusta National's 15th. It's 510 yards from the tips, usually downwind, leaving a second shot of about 225 yards; a small pond guards the ever-so-shallow green. See what we mean?

The par 3 sixteenth tees off from what might be the highest point on Bald Head Island (with the exception of the lighthouse). When the prevailing wind blows, it's 180 yards over water right into the teeth; many will pull out their drivers to reach this green in regulation—and come up short.

Bald Head's greens are large, its bunkers relatively few and far between and its fairways mostly generous, but the course is never a pushover. Condos and civilization impede the view on only the last two holes, but for 16 holes, at least, Bald Head is pure golf and pure fun and, of all the courses we've seen, comes closest the ideals of Scottish seaside golf.

Amenities include a driving range, practice green, pro shop, locker room, bar, rental clubs, a beverage cart and snack bar. Two croquet greenswards, four tennis courts and a swimming pool are available. The club dining room and restaurants are popular and comfortable.

Greens fees average $71, including cart. It's best to stay here if you want to play here. Temporary club memberships, including use of all club facilities, are provided with packages. Walking is allowed most times of the day, and it's a great walking course.

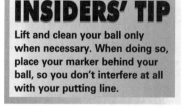

INSIDERS' TIP
Lift and clean your ball only when necessary. When doing so, place your marker behind your ball, so you don't interfere at all with your putting line.

A few words about Bald Head Island: It can only be reached by private boat or passenger ferry, a 30-minute ride from Indigo Plantation in Southport, 2.5 miles across the water. No vehicles larger than electric golf carts are allowed here. From atop Old Baldy, built in 1817, you get a view of the 10,000-acre island's dunes, marshes, creeks and beaches—home to abundant wildlife and a few human residents. The island lies at the mouth of the Cape Fear River where it meets the Atlantic Ocean.

At the yacht harbor, you can spend several hours on the restaurant deck at Eb & Flo's, the island's gathering place for the general public. You'll fit right in if you drink your Heineken from the can and play cards while eating fresh seafood from a paper plate with your fingers.

Beau Rivage Plantation
6230 Carolina Beach Rd., Carolina Beach • (910) 392-9022, (800) 628-7080

Championship Yardage:	6709
Slope: 136	**Par: 72**
Men's Yardage:	6166
Slope: 129	**Par: 72**
Other Yardage:	5610
Slope: 126	**Par: 72**
Ladies' Yardage:	4612
Slope: 114	**Par: 72**

This 18-hole championship course was designed by Eddie Lewis and built in 1988 with bentgrass greens and bermudagrass fairways. It's considered a difficult course and somewhat resembles a desert around many holes. Except for the tricky sand traps, the course's topography includes gently rolling hills dotted with Carolina pines and live oaks draped in Spanish moss. It has unusually high elevations (it's the highest point in the city of Wilmington) and a unique character created by these rises. Water comes into play on eight holes, but the course is playable—not penal. The natural forest between the 3rd, 4th and 5th holes is a conservation area filled with wildlife, including alligators. If your ball goes in there for some odd reason, wish it well and leave it alone.

The 2nd hole is a 515-yard par 5 dogleg right with trees flanking the right side. You may want to lay up for your third shot because the green has an obligatory bunker guarding the front side.

The 18th hole is a par 5 of special interest. It snakes to the right, then cuts back to the left. This course is on rolling hills and holds a number of blind shots among its narrow fairways.

Amenities include chipping and putting greens, a driving range, club rentals and a clubhouse with a bar, grill, restaurant, pro shop and locker rooms. A pool, tennis courts and gourmet dining are available for lodge guests at this family-vacation destination, just a few miles outside Wilmington.

Approximate cost, including cart, ranges from $30 to $50. Walking is not allowed.

Belvedere Plantation Golf & Country Club
2368 Country Club Dr., Hampstead • (910) 270-2703

Championship Yardage:	6401
Slope: 132	**Par: 71**
Men's Yardage:	6021
Slope: 126	**Par: 71**
Ladies' Yardage:	4992
Slope: 117	**Par: 72**

This course was designed by Russell Burney in the early 1970s and refurbished in 1991. It's 15 miles north of Wilmington and just north of Old Pointe Golf and Country Club (see the subsequent entry in this chapter) on U.S. 17 N.—convenient if you want to play 36 holes in a day. The wide fairways are 419 bermudagrass, and the elevated greens are bentgrass. The course is set among 1,000 homesites, none of which are too close to the course, and the condos can be rented for an extended golf vacation.

The course is popular for its scenery, including the wildlife in the surrounding forest. Osprey, gray heron and Canada geese can be spotted among the tall pines, and the waterway view from No. 5 is peaceful.

Both No. 3 and No. 8 are considered signature holes. No. 3 is a par 3 requiring a carry over a lake. It's 180 yards from the back tees to an elevated green that slopes toward the lake. No. 8 is a par 5 that also requires a drive over a lake, which extends down the entire right side of the fairway. A creek crosses the fairway in front of the small, elevated green. If you're a long hitter, you can go for the green in two. Water comes into play on eight holes, and groomed waste areas are abundant.

Only members may walk. Approximate cost, including cart, ranges from $18 to $43. A practice green and driving range are available. Tennis courts, a marina and a restaurant are also on site.

Brierwood Golf Club
10 Brierwood Rd., Shallotte • (910) 754-4660

Championship Yardage:	6607
Slope: 129	**Par: 72**

You'll always find a warm welcome on golf courses in the Carolinas.

Photo: Bob Leverone

Men's Yardage:	6170
Slope: 121	Par: 72
Ladies' Yardage:	4812
Slope: 114	Par: 72

Dr. Ben Ward designed the first (now the back) nine holes, which opened in 1976. The second (front) nine opened in 1979. Brierwood was the first course built in the South Brunswick Islands.

The course is set on flat terrain with houses bordering most holes. You'll find bermudagrass on the greens and in the fairways.

With water on 14 holes, Brierwood offers a challenging but fair test. Even from the back tees, the course is not a backbreaker; however, your wayward drives may find one of the ponds or end up out of bounds and in someone's back yard. Even with all the water, you won't find many long carries. The emphasis is on accuracy, particularly off the tee. The few bunkers you'll find are around the greens, which are midsize and somewhat flat.

Overall, your shots off the tee need to be sensible and straight. If your approach shot misses the green, you still have a good chance at getting up and down. But, if you reach the green in regulation, a good putt will yield a birdie—you can't ask for more than that!

Amenities include a putting green, bar, snack bar, pro shop, rental clubs and a beverage cart. Tennis courts are adjacent to the course, and the local fishing is excellent.

Walking is for members and their guests only. Approximate cost, including cart, is $38.

The Cape Golf & Racquet Club
535 The Cape Blvd., Wilmington
• (910) 799-3110

Championship Yardage:	6790
Slope: 133	Par: 72
Men's Yardage:	6129
Slope: 125	Par: 72
Other Yardage:	5629
Slope: 120	Par: 72
Ladies' Yardage:	4948
Slope: 118	Par: 72

This 18-hole layout by Gene Hamm encompasses an area on the peninsula between Cape Fear River and the Atlantic coast. Ponds, a marsh and 24 lakes lend character and challenge to this course.

The 3rd hole is a 197-yard par 3. If your tee shot is short, you face a narrow landing area due to water on the left and right of the hole. Woodland and bunkers back the green. The 13th hole is another notable par 3 (221 yards). You must cross two bodies of water from the championship (blue) tees—a deceptive shot with the wind in your face. Also of interest, the 15th and 17th holes have double greens. Water comes into play on 16 holes.

A driving range, practice putting and chipping greens, a pro shop, restaurant and lounge are on site. A pool and tennis courts, adjacent to the clubhouse, are available to members and guests.

Approximate cost, including cart, ranges from $30 on weekdays to $45 on weekends. Walking is not allowed.

Duck Haven Country Club
1202 Wood Rd., Wilmington
• **(910) 791-7983**
Championship Yardage: 6506
Slope: 125   **Par: 72**
Men's Yardage: **6053**
Slope: 122   **Par: 72**
Ladies' Yardage: **5361**
Slope: 121   **Par: 72**

Raiford Trask designed this 18-hole course with bermudagrass fairways and greens. Pine trees line the wide fairways. The layout features just 18 sand traps—fewer than on the average course.

While nobody would flatter Duck Haven by placing it among Wilmington's elite courses, the course caters to those who enjoy a simple, inexpensive round on a straightforward yet attractive golf course with no condos or other impediments.

Most of the holes are tantalizingly straightforward with all the hazards—mostly drainage ditches—in clear view. Those in search of la crème de la crème should head elsewhere, but those in search of a low-cost game will find Duck Haven to their liking. Perhaps one day, the owners will hand this excellent site over to a first-rate golf course architect. But why bother?

There's a practice green but no driving range. The course amenities include a pro shop (of sorts), locker room, snack bar, rental clubs and a beverage cart (on weekends).

The year-round cost is $20, including cart. Walking is allowed.

Echo Farms Golf & Country Club
4114 Echo Farms Blvd., Wilmington
• **(910) 791-9318**
Championship Yardage: 6708
Slope: 131   **Par: 72**
Men's Yardage: **6073**
Slope: 126   **Par: 72**
Ladies' Yardage: **5142**
Slope: 121   **Par: 72**

Gene Hamm designed Echo Farms in 1974 on a former dairy farm. The owners made a number of improvements in 1995, upgrading the bentgrass greens. Most of the bermudagrass fairways are tree-lined. Ian Scott-Taylor made further improvements in 1998.

The 8th hole is a par 5 on which your second shot must account for a dogleg left (you have to lay up); your third shot must carry over a pond to an elevated green. The 16th is a long, straightaway par 5 with three fairway bunkers in the driving area. Play your drive to the right of the bunkers to avoid trouble. Wide fairways and plenty of water characterize the course.

This course is well maintained, and the staff is proud of its quality. Echo Farms is set in a residential community, and a large nature preserve within its boundaries is home to abundant and diverse wildlife.

Amenities include a driving range, practice greens, a pro shop, locker room, club rentals, a bar and restaurant. Lessons and clinics are taught here.

Greens fees range from $25 to $30, including cart. Walking is allowed only with a member.

Fox Squirrel Country Club
591 S. Shore Dr., Boiling Spring Lakes
• **(910) 845-2625**
Championship Yardage: 6762
Slope: 125   **Par: 72**
Men's Yardage: **6208**
Slope: 123   **Par: 72**
Other Yardage: **5485**
Slope: 116   **Par: 72**
Ladies' Yardage: **5349**
Slope: 117   **Par: 72**

Bermudagrass greens and fairways blanket this course, which was designed by Eddie Riccoboni. Water comes into play on almost every hole on the front nine. The fairways tighten on the back nine along corridors of tall longleaf pines.

The 2nd hole is an interesting par 3—173 yards from the men's tees, and your tee shot must carry a lake.

The 9th hole is a difficult dogleg left with barrier trees that flank the left side and a ditch that runs about 80 yards in front of the green. The hole measures 426 yards from the men's tees, and the prevailing wind is often in your face.

You won't find a single straightaway hole on the back nine, and the numerous doglegs make for interesting shots. Several of the doglegs on the back nine are fun; almost every one provides a chance for birdie or par. The 18th is a good way to finish—a par 5, dogleg left with large centered mounds in the fairway and natural white sand outlining the hole.

Wildlife is prevalent at Fox Squirrel, including (you guessed it!) North American melanistic fox squirrels as well as deer, alligators and birds in the wildlife preserve and bird sanctuary. The retirement-community atmosphere is quieter than many resort-type courses, and the staff is friendly. The course's beauty makes it a locals' favorite.

Eagles Grille and Pub is in the newly remodeled clubhouse, with an outside deck overlooking the "big lake." This full-service facility is suitable for tournaments, outings, banquets or corporate functions.

Greens fees range from $25 to $32, including cart. Walking is allowed anytime, so take advantage of it.

North Shore Country Club
off N.C. Hwy. 210, Sneads Ferry
• (910) 327-2410, (800) 828-5035

Championship Yardage:	6866	
Slope: 134	Par: 72	
Men's Yardage:	6358	
Slope: 123	Par: 72	
Other Yardage:	5636	
Slope 119	Par: 72	
Ladies' Yardage:	5039	
Slope: 122	Par: 72	

Bob Moore designed this 18-hole course, which opened in 1988. It's a few minutes from Topsail Island Beach. The relatively wide bermudagrass fairways are adorned with extensive mounding, tall pines and lakes. Greens are seeded with bentgrass.

Water and wind remind you that you're near the ocean and require a different game plan every round. Water comes into play on more than half the holes. The course is scenic, with frequent views of the Intracoastal Waterway. It is always well maintained.

The finishing holes on both sides are challenging and require long carries over water off the tee.

The 18th hole emphasizes length—it plays 460 yards from the back tees, with a slight dogleg left and usually into the prevailing wind. You tee off over water and then must clear another pond to a large, slightly elevated green with two bunkers guarding the front. Drive down the right side and forget about those traps, but realize this adds length to the hole.

Amenities include a pro shop, driving range, practice green, rental clubs and a bar and grill.

Greens fees range from $40 to $55, including cart. Walking is allowed after 3 PM.

INSIDERS' TIP
Record your score at the next tee box or while driving to the next tee, not on or near the green.

Oak Island Golf & Country Club
928 Caswell Beach Rd., Caswell Beach
• (910) 278-5275

Championship Yardage:	6608	
Slope: 128	Par: 72	
Men's Yardage:	6135	
Slope: 124	Par: 72	
Ladies' Yardage:	5437	
Slope: 121	Par: 72	

This George Cobb course, completed in 1964, is one of Brunswick County's oldest. It was improved in 1995 and is inviting to golfers of all levels who enjoy its bermudagrass fairways and greens.

You'll definitely need all your clubs to play Oak Island. The sea breezes are the challenge here. The wind may help you on one hole, then hurt you on the next. Water, sand, open fairways and the differences in individual hole layouts lend character to this course. You won't find adjacent fairways here. If you shoot wide of the fairway, you're in the trees.

One of the more notable holes is the par 3 7th, which plays 191 yards from the back tees. You must carry over water to an elevated green, heavily trapped on both sides.

Both finishing holes are interesting. The 9th is a slight dogleg right with a trap in the corner. It measures 426 yards from the back tees usually into a head wind; it can be 475 yards on some days. The 18th is a 553-yard par 5. It's a straightaway shot, but you must hit into the same head wind. You must clear water on the third shot, which, depending on the wind, may require as much as a 3-wood.

Amenities include a pro shop, rental clubs, a bar, restaurant and lounge, locker rooms, a driving range, putting green and a pool.

The approximate cost is $40, including cart. Walking is allowed on weekdays after 1 PM. Tee times are accepted up to two days in advance.

Old Fort Golf Course
3189 River Rd. S.E., Winnabow
• (910) 371-9940

Championship Yardage:	6311	
Slope: 108	Par: 72	
Men's Yardage:	5773	
Slope: 103	Par: 72	
Ladies' Yardage:	4580	
Slope: 99	Par: 72	

This 18-hole course, designed by Raiford

Are You Green-friendly?

Picture this: You go to your pro shop, golf store or golf outlet to buy a new pair of shoes. You find the right size and color, take them to the counter, and as you are about to pay for them, you read a small label on the box: "THESE SHOES ARE NOT GREEN FRIENDLY."

OK, that scenario might be a little farfetched. However, at more than 1,300 golf courses nationwide, you are not allowed to play unless you have green-friendly shoes. More and more courses are requiring golfers to shed their old steel spikes and have green-friendly spikes inserted in their shoes. The principal reason, of course, is that they don't tear up the greens like traditional metal spikes do. In fact, that's how these spikes came to be.

In 1992, two golfers in Boise, Idaho, looked for an alternative to metal spikes, which were outlawed during winter play because they tore up the frozen greens of their home course. The spikes they designed are the basis for the Softspike that's available today in golf shops across the country.

There is strong sentiment to maintain the traditional metal spikes, and these feelings die hard. Besides the fact that they sound so cool walking across the parking lot to the clubhouse, they provide the necessary traction to stabilize you during your swing. But at the end of the day, after countless foursomes have trampled back and forth, the greens take the brunt of the treading and are torn up. That's where Softspikes come in. Thus, this spikeless revolution should be good news to all of us who have had that four-foot putt roll off line because of a spike mark.

With the help of the PGA's Senior Tour, Softspikes is offering $20,000 to any player who wins a tournament while wearing their golf shoes. As a result, these alternative spikes are beginning to lose their "newfangled" stigma. Still, the pros are playing for hundreds of thousands of bucks, so the question remains: Would they even take the risk of less traction during the swing for a (relatively) measly $20,000?

You will soon have to choose the soft spike you like best.

Photo: Charles Mitchell

If you are still not ready to try the green-friendly spikes and want to stick with the traditional steel spikes, then you're in luck—some manufacturers are now making a 6-mm steel spike with a plastic flange that fits tight with the sole of the shoe. Thus you get a spike that is more green friendly—but it's still steel. Psychologically speaking, you may get just as much traction with the 6-mm spike as with the standard 8-mm variety.

Most of the green-friendly spikes are made of polyurethane. They have a varied array of swirls, bumps or knobs that provide some degree of traction. Whether they give the traction you need is for you to determine, and we suggest you experiment with the different types. Again, there are many to choose from, but all of the following have a polyurethane shaft that screws into the sole. Here are a few options:

- Softspikes—swirl pattern; somewhat hard to clean
- Softspikes Extra Traction—12 nubs of about 2mm
- Softspikes XP— eight nubs around the sole's perimeter and raised in the center
- Turf-Mates—made by Foot-Joy, swirl pattern
- Turf-Mates Plus—essentially the same as Turf-Mates but with optional 1-mm steel spike
- Greenspikes—self-threading spike (said to keep it from coming loose) with no nubs or swirls, but rather circular grooves around the perimeter
- Tred-lite II—four knobs close to the center and a threaded metal shaft that screws into the sole of the shoe like traditional metal spikes
- Tred-lite Combi-lite—threaded metal shaft and a steel post like traditional metal spikes, but it is only 3mm long

Besides these golf shoes with screw-in, green-friendly spikes, other shoe manufacturers have come on board with their own versions. Etonic has a golf shoe with a sole that looks very much like a runner's training shoe. Rockport has The Groove, with six removable slides containing from three to five spikes per slide. These slides can be removed to replace the worn spike. Foot-Joy has the Dri-Joys Spikeless, with a series of small, soft rubber cleats joined by 10 larger, harder rubber spikes.

We suggest you try the green-friendly spikes for yourself. The only difference we found is that they are harder to clean than metal spikes. So the next time you replace your spikes, try out a set and see what you think. You still might not make that 4-foot putt for birdie; but, your partner will not have your spike marks as an excuse for knocking his 4-footer off line either.

Trask Sr., opened in 1990. Bermudagrass covers the greens and fairways. This wide-open layout has few trees and few traps. Fairways are wide, and greens are large. Water is a factor on about half of the holes, more so on the back nine.

The owner's favorite hole, the par 3, 196-yard 8th, is a toughie because of its length and small green with surrounding sand trap. The 17th is an interesting par 4—433 yards from the back tees—as it requires both tee and second shots that carry water.

Wind is also a factor on this course near the Intracoastal Waterway.

Practice greens, a driving range and rental clubs are available.

Approximate cost is $22, including cart. Walking is allowed at the same price.

Olde Pointe Golf and Country Club
1300 Country Club Dr., Hampstead
• (910) 270-2403

Championship Yardage:	6913
Slope: 136	Par: 72
Men's Yardage:	6253
Slope: 123	Par: 72
Other Yardage:	6008
Slope: 120	Par: 72
Ladies' Yardage:	5133
Slope: 118	Par: 72

Jerry Turner designed this 18-hole course in 1974. Fairways are 419 hybrid bermudagrass, a big improvement from the previous coastal bermudagrass. The spacious greens are bentgrass. The rolling and scenic terrain ambles amid woods, lakes and streams.

The 12th, 13th and 14th holes are all considered signatures because of their scenic beauty on the lake.

The tricky 11th hole is (in)famous. It's a narrow par 5 of 589 yards with a gradual dogleg right and a downward slope into the woods. It's hard to score par on this hole—the wind from the ocean almost always comes into play.

A large putting green, driving range, chipping area, practice sand bunker, pro shop, snack bar and club rentals are available. Construction of a large member clubhouse is complete. The pro shop offers a good selection of gear, including women's clothing and accessories.

Lighted tennis courts and an Olympic-size pool are available to members. A boat ramp on the Intracoastal Waterway invites golfers to arrive by boat and is adjacent to a recreation area where tournaments can conclude with social functions.

Greens fees, including cart, are approximately $35 on weekdays and $50 on weekends. Walking is allowed by members only.

Porters Neck Plantation and Country Club
1202 Porters Neck Rd., Wilmington
• (910) 686-1177, (800) 423-5695

Championship Yardage:	7209
Slope: 140	Par: 72
Men's Yardage:	6818
Slope: 136	Par: 72
Other: Yardage:	6287
Slope: 130	Par: 72
Ladies' Yardage:	5268
Slope: 124	Par: 72

Porters Neck Plantation along the Intracoastal Waterway originated in 1732 when John Porter purchased 930 acres of King George II's original land grant from then-owner Maurice Moore. It remained a working plantation until a few years ago. Today, it's a private country club community, but the golf course is available for limited public play. The course, homesites and amenities were carefully placed among the rolling hills and dogwood and pine forests, and a traditional ambiance has been preserved. Beautiful custom homes are mingled with patio homes and provide a distinctive air, yet they don't interfere with the golf course's playability.

The 18-hole bentgrass, Tom Fazio-designed course was built in 1991. The trecherous par 4

14th features water up the entire left side of the hole; the second shot must be well placed on the green. If the pin's up front, aim short of the hole. With the flag to the rear, well... you'll probably want to look ahead to the 15th.

No. 8 favors the straight hitter. It's a par 5 measuring 506 yards. You do have a chance to reach the green in two with well-played shots. The bunkers right of the green should be avoided at all costs. Also, a fairway bunker on the left could be deadly.

The 20,000-square-foot clubhouse offers a grill room, locker facilities and pro shop complete with quality items and rental clubs. Practice facilities are nearby. The staff is friendly and helpful, and we heartily recommend the spectacular course. Ladies' events are offered frequently, and the course stays busy. It's minutes from Wrightsville Beach and convenient to downtown Wilmington. In 1999, the course hosted the North Carolina Amateur.

Monday through Thursday, approximate greens fees are $65 per person, including cart. Weekend rates are higher and subject to change. No walking is allowed.

Topsail Greens Golf & Country Club
U.S. Hwy. 17 N., Hampstead
• (910) 270-2883

Championship Yardage:	6324
Slope: 121	Par: 71
Men's Yardage:	6010
Slope: 118	Par: 71
Ladies' Yardage:	5033
Slope: 113	Par: 71

Topsail Greens—more than 20 years old—was designed by Russell Breeden. This 18-hole course is tight and, typical for an oceanside layout, windy. Fairways and greens are bermudagrass. It's considered a shot-making course that favors brain over brawn. Water comes into play on seven holes, and several greens are elevated.

The island green on the par 3 No. 8, the signature hole, plays 159 yards from the men's tees. This scenic beauty of a hole is a true test of accuracy.

The 11th has a water hazard about 220 yards from the tee, which still leaves some 180 yards over the large lake to the green. It's a solid par 4.

The staff here is friendly, and the course is kept in fine condition. A new large practice green, driving range, pro shop, bar and restaurant, beverage cart and club rentals are available.

Approximate greens fees range from $25 to $30, including cart. Walking is allowed after 3 PM.

Wilmington Municipal Golf Course

311 S. Wallace Ave., Wilmington

• (910) 791-0558

Championship Yardage:	6564
Slope: 118	Par: 71
Men's Yardage:	6267
Slope: 116	Par: 71
Ladies' Yardage:	4978
Slope: 114	Par: 72

This 18-hole Donald Ross design, which opened in 1926, has fewer water hazards and more flat terrain than most area courses. Fairways and greens are bermudagrass. Generally, fairways are relatively wide, and water hazards are not extreme. The city completed a successful renovation of the course in 1998.

One of our favorite holes is the 4th, a par 3 of 184 yards that plays from an elevated tee to an elevated green. A big valley in between leads to a big hill afterward if you shoot too long. To the right and left are woods. To the far right is a pond.

The clubhouse has showers and lockers for men. Practice greens, a pro shop, rental clubs and beer sales round out the amenities.

Greens fees are inexpensive: $7 to $8 for residents and $11 to $12 for nonresidents. The cart fee is an additional $8.

Walking is allowed, and you may set a tee time seven days in advance. This is one of the busiest 18-hole courses in the Carolinas, hosting 80,000 golfers annually. It's popular for its playability and low cost, and the friendly staff is a big plus.

Around Wilmington and the Cape Fear Coast...

Fun Things To Do

The city of Wilmington is surrounded by attractions, and every day dishes up something new to do. The **Riverwalk** is a fine place for strolling along the Cape Fear River, and it's here you can appreciate the historic area's shopping and dining as well as the waterfront's leisure and commercial activities. We recommend walking, boat or horse-and-carriage tours for seeing the sights. Sunset, moonlight or dinner dance cruises offer a scenic view of the town from the *Henrietta II*, a stern-wheel paddleboat that's docked by the Wilmington Hilton on N. Water Street. It has an observation deck and a complete bar, and its dining salon is heated and air-conditioned. Call (910) 343-1611 or (800) 676-0162 for information about cruises April through December. A knowledgeable guide with a straw hat and cane leads **adventure walking tours** from the foot of Market Street on the site of the old ferry landing. Call (910) 763-1785 for information about group tours (including multilingual service). The horse-drawn carriage or trolley tour, narrated by a costumed driver, departs from Water and Market streets. Call **Springbrook Farms,** (910) 251-8889, to arrange private tours.

Our favorite time to spend a weekend in Wilmington is during the **North Carolina Azalea Festival** in mid-April. Call (910) 763-0905 for information about the annual event, which includes a parade, a street fair and many activities in addition to fascinating home and garden tours. You don't even have to like gardens or historic walking tours to appreciate the multicolored spectacle in bloom throughout the city. Everyone else visits during this weekend too, so you'll need advance reservations for accommodations and many restaurants.

The **Battleship *North Carolina*,** across the river from downtown, is easily accessible at the junction of U.S. highways 17 and 74. Dedicated to veterans of World War II, it was the first modern U.S. battleship. It carried a crew of 2,339 who made history in the combat zones of the Pacific from 1941 to 1945. It's open for tours every day and is a summer evening host to a spectacular sound and light show. The complex includes a gift shop, seasonal snack bar and riverside picnic area. Call (910) 251-5797 for schedules, which vary with the seasons.

Enjoy live entertainment at **Thalian Hall,** home of the country's oldest community theater and current host to national touring companies as well as numerous local theater companies. Built between 1855 and 1858 as a theater and city hall, it continues to serve both purposes. It's at the corner of Chestnut and N. Third streets in downtown Wilmington. For more information, call (910) 343-3664 or (800) 523-2820.

Art enthusiasts can view the permanent collections of 19th- and 20th-century North Carolina artists in the **St. John's Museum of Art,** (910) 763-0281, 114 Orange Street, in downtown Wilmington. The three restored, architecturally distinctive buildings date from 1804 and are united by a sculpture garden. Some 80 contemporary North Carolina artists and craftspeople are represented in the sales gallery.

Wilmington Railroad Museum, on the corner of Water and Red Cross streets in downtown Wilmington, includes exhibits from the important rail era of the city's history. The railway system was once the largest in the world and an important contributor to Wilmington's economic development in the mid-1800s. For more information, call (910) 763-2634.

The **Cape Fear Museum,** (910) 341-7413, 814 Market Street, displays an interesting nautical exhibit and provides information about the social, cultural and natural history of the region. Changing exhibits and weekend programs offer diverse entertainment. The **Michael Jordan Discovery Gallery** offers a hands-on exploration of southeastern North Carolina where you can feed a Venus' flytrap or crawl through a beaver lodge. (And yes, it is named for the basketball player, who grew up here before going on to six NBA championships with the Chicago Bulls after a stellar career at the University of North Carolina.)

The **Bellamy Mansion,** Fifth Avenue and Market Street, is another downtown museum. This restored structure was built on the eve of the Civil War. Tours and changing exhibits on history and the design arts are offered. The antebellum home was originally the city home of a prominent planter, and all 22 rooms on four floors are open to the public. Call (910) 251-3700 for information.

Shopping is a good way to spend a few hours in Wilmington. The **Cotton Exchange,** 321 N. Front Street, recalls the days when cotton was king and one of the world's largest export companies was located here. Eight restored buildings connected by brick walkways, open-air courtyards and gigantic heart-pine beams house 33 specialty shops and restaurants. **Chandler's Wharf,** nearby at Water and Ann streets, houses a variety of specialty shops as well as two fine restaurants with outdoor dining.

Poplar Grove Plantation is on U.S. Highway 17 outside Wilmington. It showcases an 1850 Greek Revival house on a 628-acre plantation. Costumed guides and scheduled events depict the history of the period. Call (910) 686-9518 for information about prices and schedules.

Take the family to **Treasure Island Family Fun Park** in Sneads Ferry for go-cart racing, bumper boats, kiddie rides and miniature golf. It's a few minutes north of Topsail Island. Call (910) 327-2700 for information. The **Jubilee Amusement Park** has go-carts, water slides, a Ferris wheel and other fun things you'd expect to find at an amusement park. It's on U.S. Highway 421, just over the bridge into Carolina Beach; call (910) 458-9017.

The **North Carolina Aquarium** at Fort Fisher on Kure Beach, (910) 458-8257 or (910) 458-7468, offers films, live animal exhibits and field trips. Other features include an alligator pond, touch tank, life-size whale sculpture, shark, stingray exhibits and other marine life of the Cape Fear Coast.

The **Fort Fisher Civil War Museum** on Kure Beach, (910) 458-5538, is an earthen fort that kept the Cape Fear River and the port of Wilmington open to blockade runners, which delivered supplies to Confederate armies. It's at the site of two major battles.

The **Southport Maritime Museum,** 116 N. Howe Street, (910) 457-0003, houses a collection of nautical memorabilia of the lower Cape Fear area.

Fishing, swimming, sunning, sand-castle building, snorkeling, boating and sailing are always popular, and the Cape Fear River and the Atlantic Ocean welcome visitors year-round. For serious beach or fishing time, visit any of the coastal villages. Surf fishing or pier fishing will yield bluefish, spot, flounder, trout, striped bass or pompano. For inshore charter services including custom charters and custom rods, plus remote surf fishing trips or inshore light tackle trips, contact Capt. Rick Bennett in Wilmington at (910) 799-6120. His specialties include Spanish mackerel, trout, drum and bluefish. A specialist in Gulf Stream fishing—tuna, wahoo, dolphin and billfish—is **Capt. Fred Holland.** Call him in Carolina Beach at (910) 458-5482 or (800) 284-5482. **Capt. Chuck Harrill** of Carolina Beach also specializes in Gulf Stream and inshore fishing; call (910) 458-4362 or (800) 288-FISH.

For more information, contact the **Cape Fear Convention and Visitors Bureau,** (910) 341-4030 or (800) 222-4757, or pick up a copy of *The Insiders' Guide to Wilmington & the Cape Fear Coast.*

Where to Eat

Food in these parts is a Southern experience that attracts visitors from far and wide, and locals use mealtimes as gathering times, especially during sunny spring or fall days. Food plays a big part in outdoor socializing along Wilmington's downtown riverfront. And visitors and locals alike gather in eateries throughout the villages dotting the Cape Fear Coast to

Wilmington-area courses usually play close to the water.

Photo:N.C. Travel & Tourism

enjoy glorious views from indoors or outdoor decks overlooking the Cape Fear River or the Atlantic Ocean. Seafood is abundant and fresh, and other offerings reflect regional as well as international flair.

Restaurants accept most major credit cards. We recommend that you call for hours of operation, as varying schedules are common during different seasons. Refer to our Preface for an explanation of the price code.

Wilmington

Bocci
$$ • Mercer and Wrightsville Aves., Wilmington • (910) 763-0067

This bistro offers an assortment of specialty pizzas, pastas and main dishes of healthy and unique Mediterranean cuisine. Robust servings of assorted veal, chicken and beef also are served in well-prepared, creative dishes. Black and white photographs of boccie players adorn the walls, along with murals and interesting decor. Valet parking is required because there's really no place for you to put your car—it's not meant to be pretentious. The spirited (read: loud), fun atmosphere attests to the friendliness here. Try Bocci for dinner any evening.

Caffe Phoenix
$$$ • 9 S. Front St., Wilmington • (910) 343-1395

Don't complain about a short wait in line to dine here—it's worth it. Italian by nature, the restaurant's seasonal specials are always tasty. This downtown luncheon or dinner spot provides terrific atmosphere as well as delicious food. The decor is attractive, the staff attentive; from appetizer to dessert, it's a treat.

Charlotte's
$ • 130 N. Front St., Wilmington • (910) 343-9883

Charlotte's is Wilmington's first Internet cafe. Surf the World Wide Web for a nominal fee while enjoying breakfast or lunch of bagels, sandwiches, salads, soups or frozen yogurt. Daily specials include reasonably priced offerings such as shepherd's pie, hoppin' John or a rice, bean and cheese burrito. It's possibly the newest trend for a downtown historic district eatery.

Franko's Caffe & Trattoria
$$$-$$$$ • 10 Market St., Wilmington • (910) 763-8100

Authentic Italian dishes are prepared with fresh seafood and complemented by Italian wines. Prime rib and lobster are touted here, along with daily specials of risotto or pasta. Breads and desserts also are homemade and oh-so-tempting. We sample Italian cuisine in every city we visit and critique wine selections too, and this trattoria certainly measures up with the best. Reservations are a good idea. You can walk here from any part of downtown.

Front Street Brewery
$-$$ • 9 N. Front St., Wilmington • (910) 251-1935

This addition to downtown Wilmington should be around for a long time to come, as it's popular with any age golfer or non-golfer for lunch, dinner or just a good brew. It's a block from the Cape Fear River in the Foy-Roe building, an 1883 dry goods store and, later, a prominent menswear store. Tin ceilings and heart-pine floors are original, and the new woodwork has been specially crafted.

Try a raspberry wheat ale in the spring or a spiced ale or oatmeal stout in the cooler months. Hand-crafted brews are the current rage and can satisfy a taste for variety in any size up to 24-ounce jumbos. The pub food complements the beer and can be selected from a before- or after-5 PM menu. For an appetizer, try the Southwestern stromboli—spicy sausage and jalapeño jack cheese baked into a loaf of sourdough bread. Then try the artichoke ravioli pomodoro entree—flavored with fresh tomatoes, basil, garlic and olive oil.

The Pilot House
$$$ • 2 Ann St., Wilmington • (910) 343-0200

The historic Craig House is home to a riverfront restaurant that serves good seafood and pasta, including regional recipes such as seafood au gratin and flounder stuffed with crab meat—all prefaced by the seafood bisque. It also offers frequently changing specials. Try a huge burger or sandwich for lunch, and choose from the notable wine list to accompany your dinner selection. Lunch and dinner are served daily except Sunday. The atmosphere is casual for lunch and a bit dressier for dinner.

Roy's Riverboat Landing Seafood & Steaks
$$-$$$ • at the foot of Market St., Wilmington • (910) 763-7227

In historic downtown, this restaurant is on one of the city's oldest building sites. The Eilers Building was constructed in 1857 as a dry-goods warehouse. In the 1890s, the third story was used as one of the original U.S. Weather Bureau's

Observation Stations. Now you can choose from four dining rooms on two separate floors or a private balcony with a beautiful view of the riverfront and the Battleship *North Carolina*. Drop in for lunch, dinner or drinks.

The signature dishes of the seafood specialist are Jefferson seafood turnover served with caviar; lobster imperial; grouper royale or Carolina clam chowder. Seasonal offerings may include quail, venison, lamb, veal or vegetarian dishes; and beef lovers will be happy with the New York strip or filet mignon. The beef marinade with herbs and spices is another specialty. Pastries and breads are baked to perfection, and desserts include such delights as Miss Margaret's renowned four-layer coconut cream cheese pie.

Trails End Steak House
$$$ • Trails End Rd., Wilmington • (910) 791-2034

Beef and history are served in equal portions. The view of the Intracoastal Waterway adds to the interest of the old restaurant, which has many stories to tell. Call for reservations and directions when you're ready for authentic broiled steak or prime rib, salad and appetizers. The hospitality bar includes salads and hors d'oeuvres with all entrees. The genuine hardwood charcoal-cooked entrees are always a treat, and beer, wine and cocktails are plentiful.

Water Street
$-$$ • 5 S. Water St., Wilmington • (910) 343-0042

This sidewalk cafe provides a nice view of the Cape Fear River. Good soups, salads, burgers and various entrees are available for lunch or dinner. Jalapeño poppers make tasty appetizers. Water Street seafood chowder is an unusually tasty combination of shrimp, scallops, clams, fish and fresh vegetables, which can be served in sourdough boule (sort of a bowl made of bread) and makes a fine meal. Pita-pocket sandwiches can be filled with a choice of salad, such as herbed chicken, tabouli or hummus. Jambalaya and Greek-style scampi add flair to the entree selections.

The Beaches

J. Council's
$$ • 205 Charlotte Ave., Carolina Beach • (910) 458-9411

Fresh herbs and spices are added to fresh seafood and fine cuts of meats for a variety of entrees. Begin with a tasty appetizer such as country pâté or grouper nuggets. Proceed to a spinach or fruit salad. Then choose a fish, chicken, veal or beef entree such as pan-grilled scallops with tomatoes and artichokes—you won't be disappointed. Chef Pete Herring welcomes you for dinner Tuesday through Sunday evenings.

The Cottage Restaurant
$$ • 1 N. Lake Park Blvd., Carolina Beach • (910) 458-4383

Lunch and dinner are served here—indoors or outdoors, Monday through Saturday. Sample a slice of beach history in this 1916 cottage while you enjoy the Bloomin' Onion appetizer followed by the crab cakes or other seafood, steak, chicken or a pasta entree.

The Marina's Edge
$$$ • 300 N. Lake Park Blvd., Carolina Beach • (910) 458-6001

Come casual or dressed to the nines to enjoy the fine cuisine—fresh steak, chicken or locally caught seafood—prefaced by something from the raw bar. The Marina's Edge is open for dinner daily and for lunch on the weekend. This restaurant is near myriad beach attractions. Check out the tropical saltwater aquarium and waterfall as well as the big-screen TV in the lounge.

Sweetwater Café
$$ • 106 Carl Winner Ave., Carolina Beach • (910) 458-0500

This comfortable, casual place serves up a good view of the activity happening around the marina. It serves fresh seafood as the dominant dish, but you'll also find tasty chicken and beef entrees. Consider the fish of the day blackened, or try any shellfish.

Big Daddy's Seafood Restaurant
$$$ • 202 K Ave., Kure Beach • (910) 458-8622

A trip to the beach isn't complete without a seafood platter, and Big Daddy's is a great place to enjoy one. Or try lobster tails or Alaskan snow crab. Have your seafood broiled, fried, grilled, steamed... however you like. Steaks and chicken also are available in this casual setting. If you're really hungry, get the all-you-can-eat buffet. This huge restaurant has been dishing out tasty food for many years, and we keep coming back.

The Bridge Tender
$$$ • 1414 Airlie Rd., Wrightsville Beach • (910) 256-3419

The view from this restaurant is of the Wrightsville Beach drawbridge over the Intracoastal Waterway. The decor is enhanced by lamp light and high, raftered ceilings. The food includes frequent specials of grilled seafood or Angus beef. The nationally recognized wine list is excellent. Our favorite entrees include any of the Cajun-spiced seafood. Locals frequent this restaurant, and the atmosphere is welcoming to visitors, many of whom especially enjoy the lounge.

Gardenias
**$$$ • 7105 Wrightsville Ave.,
Wrightsville Beach • (910) 256-2421**

Fresh pasta, fresh-baked bread, local seafood, Angus beef, vegetarian dishes and delectable desserts are well matched by fine wines at Gardenias. It's west of the Waterway and presents a dinner experience to suit any budget or taste. If you like wine and enjoy learning, the wine dinner specials are for you. Winemakers and chefs create complementary blends for each course and add commentary. Reservations are accepted but are only necessary for the wine dinners.

Mollie's
**$ • 107 N. Shore Dr., Surf City
• (910) 328-0505**

Mollie's is casual and quick. It's right across the street from the ocean and easy to find as you drive into town. The home fries and biscuits are homemade, and the country ham or omelettes will start your day right. For lunch, a good sandwich for seafood lovers is the crab melt. If you're here for dinner, the Captain's Choice platter contains about all the seafood a big eater can handle plus pasta, chicken or steak . . . at a great price. Desserts are always fresh-made. It's open every day except Tuesday.

One Eyed Parrot
**$$ • Roland Ave. at Shore Dr., Surf City
• (910) 328-3326**

This casual, shoreside restaurant is an enjoyable stop for lunch, dinner or drinks and a snack. Try the indescribable pepper-seared scallops appetizer. Specialty sandwiches for lunch feature oysters, fish, shrimp, steak or chicken. For dinner, try the smoked and grilled baby back ribs made from a secret recipe. Or enjoy fried or broiled seafood entrees, grilled chicken breast or rib-eye steak with all the trimmings. Surf

City is part of Topsail Island and is renowned for its relaxing atmosphere, which you're bound to notice.

Where to Stay

We understand... you'll probably want to stay near your favorite golf course. So we recommend a few special accommodations that are nearby; most offer golf packages. Refer to our Preface for an explanation of the price code.

Wilmington

219 South 5th
**$$$ • 219 S. Fifth St., Wilmington
• (910) 763-5539, (800) 219-SOFI**

This bed and breakfast inn is a gracious Greek Revival structure built in 1871, restored and decorated for modern comfort. Three rooms and a suite include king- or queen-size beds and fireplaces. All accommodations have private baths and access to common areas. A full breakfast is served, and golf packages are arranged at nearby courses. Private walking tours of the historic district also may be arranged. This inn bills itself as "uniquely unpretentious."

Beau Rivage Plantation
**$$$-$$$$ • 6230 Carolina Beach Rd.,
Wilmington
• (910) 392-9021, (800) 628-7080**

Luxurious suites furnished with antique reproductions, balconies overlooking the golf practice facility, a pool and restaurant welcome you into the true plantation life while you enjoy a golf vacation. Modern facilities are combined with old-fashioned elegance and Southern hospitality in a country club atmosphere. Golf packages are available, but family or business visits are good reasons to stay here as well.

Catherine's Inn
**$-$$ • 410 S. Front St., Wilmington
• (910) 476-0723**

A full breakfast and use of all of the inn's amenities are included in your stay at this classic Southern home, which has been restored to its 1883 splendor. The home was built by the Forshee family, and its five guest rooms are comfortable and inviting, each with private bath. The spacious lawn overlooks a sunken garden

---

INSIDERS' TIP

Always check in 20 to 30 minutes before your tee time, so you'll have time to change your shoes and hit a few practice shots or putts. You are expected to tee off at your scheduled time, not arrive at that time, then warm up and load your cart.

and the Cape Fear River. Morning coffee is delivered to your room. Extras include complimentary afternoon refreshments, turndown service and bedtime liqueur.

The Curran House
$-$$ • 312 S. Third St., Wilmington • (910) 763-6603, (800) 763-6603

Vicki and Greg Stringer offer three uniquely furnished guest bedrooms with private baths, king- or queen-size beds, central air-conditioning and ceiling fans. This was the McKay-Green House built in 1837 in Wilmington's downtown. The exterior architecture is an unusual combination of Queen Anne and Victorian Italianate. Cable television and VCRs are available by request at no extra charge. A delicious full breakfast is included. The historic district's walking tours, shopping or dining are nearby, as are all area golf courses.

Front Street Inn
$$-$$$ • 215 S. Front St., Wilmington • (910) 762-6442

Stefany and Jay Rhodes have decorated Front Street Inn with American art that they gathered at galleries, fairs, auctions and attics, and each of eight suites is spacious and inviting. Fireplaces, Jacuzzis, full kitchens and wet bars, and king or queen beds can keep you comfy for brief or lengthy stays. This historic downtown building is in a convenient location with off-street parking. Continental breakfast—muffins, breads and fruit—is fresh and emphasizes natural ingredients. The Sol y Solbra bar and breakfast room is the setting for your morning meal as well as healthful beverages, beer, champagne and wine. Room service also is available. Each suite has a TV and phone.

The Inn on Orange
$$ • 410 Orange St., Wilmington • (910) 815-0035, (800) 381-4666

The Inn on Orange, a beautifully restored 1875 Italianate Victorian home, is completely furnished with antiques and reproductions collected by the Vargas family during its travels with the military. There are four bedrooms, all with private baths and fireplaces and two with sitting rooms. A full gourmet breakfast is served every morning in the elegant dining room or outside around the small backyard swimming pool. Also included in your stay are morning coffee service, afternoon refreshments, evening cordials and chocolates. The Inn is just four blocks from the Cape Fear River and an easy walk to dozens of restaurants, nightclubs and upscale shops.

Wilmington Hilton
$$$ • 301 N. Water St., Wilmington • (910) 763-5900, (800) HILTONS

Overlooking the Cape Fear River, the restored downtown district and the Battleship *North Carolina,* this 178-room hotel is in an ideal spot for shopping and dining. It's also just a short drive to area golf courses. Almost every amenity you could want is available, including a pool, restaurant, lounge, fitness center, conference space and courtesy van. You also can choose the concierge level for extra amenities, such as beverages and continental breakfast.

The Wine House
$$ • 311 Cottage Ln., Wilmington • (910) 763-0511

The tiniest-ever bed and breakfast inn is this two-room cottage replicating an 1860s wine house. It's tastefully furnished with antiques, completely comfortable and located downtown, providing easy access to just about anything you'd need. The entire house is a private retreat tucked away behind a historic home and church. The variable breakfast menu includes traditional eggs and accompanying meats and bread.

The Beaches

Bald Head Island Resort
$$$$ • Bald Head Is. • (910) 457-5002, (800) 234-1666

The management group here handles cottage, condo and villa rentals. This might be the farthest away from the real world you'll ever get, and it's no more than a 30-minute ferry ride. Golf carts and bikes are the only modes of transportation here faster than your feet, so imagine the noise and pollution levels dropping accordingly. Not the least expensive of resorts, this exclusive residential and vacation island boasts a luxurious golf course and upscale atmosphere. Golf packages include the round-trip ferry ride, cart and greens fees. Weekday fees are more affordable than weekend rates.

The Beacon House Inn Bed & Breakfast
$$$ • 715 Carolina Beach Ave. N., Carolina Beach • (910) 458-6244

The ocean view is just one reason to choose this 1950s beach house. Another is the country breakfast with homemade breads. Named after lighthouses and decorated in a nautical motif, each of the nine air-conditioned rooms offers a private or semiprivate bath. There's also a three-bedroom cottage that sleeps eight. Special rates are available for private functions, and a private murder-mystery weekend can be arranged for a group of six or more. Midweek and off-season packages are available. Hosts Peggy and Jerry Emerson and Mary and Larry Huhn, both retired military couples, share their knowledge of the area's dining and attractions as well as a warm welcome. You may contact them via e-mail: lhuhn@ix.netcom.com.

Blockade Runner Beach Resort and Conference Center
$$$-$$$$ • 275 Waynick Blvd., Wrightsville Beach
• (910) 256-2251, (800) 541-1161

Golf, sailing and children's packages are offered at this fine oceanfront resort with 150 rooms that overlooks the windsurfing and sailing center. The standard package includes waterfront accommodations and greens fees. The deluxe golf package includes room, greens fees, a cart fee and breakfast and dinner at the hotel's gourmet Ocean Terrace Restaurant. Additional holes may be played regularly at no extra charge, except cart fee, on many Wilmington-area courses. A bar, restaurant, health center, pool, beach and comedy club provide diversions when you're not on the golf course—especially convenient if you're traveling with a family. The Sandcampers children's program is an attractive option for golfing couples traveling with the kids. The views at this resort are spectacular, and public beach access is great.

The Cottage
$$$ • 275 Waynick Blvd., Wrightsville Beach
• (910) 256-2251, (800) 805-2252

This remodeled 1935 boarding house is adjacent to the Blockade Runner Beach Resort (see previous entry) at Wrightsville Beach. The 13 spacious rooms can be reserved individually or collectively—a good choice for large families or groups. Shared amenities include a pool, health spa, Jacuzzi, lounges, live entertainment, oceanfront dining and children's programs. An on-site golf director can arrange your tee times. The Cottage is reminiscent of years past when beach cottages were the sole accommodations.

Lois Jane's Riverview Inn
$$ • 106 W. Bay St., Southport
• (910) 457-6701, (800) 457-1152

A full breakfast, afternoon hors d'oeuvres and evening sweets are included with your stay in this beautifully restored 19th-century home overlooking the Cape Fear River. A room with a private bath is available by request. This is a comfortable and charming four-room bed and breakfast inn in the wonderful little village of Southport where you can stroll along the River Walk to antique shops, restaurants or the Maritime Museum (see the previous "Fun Thing To Do" section). Golf courses, especially Bald Head Island's, are easily accessible from here.

Seven Seas Inn
$ • 130 Fort Fisher Blvd., Kure Beach
• (910) 458-8122

Twenty efficiencies, 12 rooms—connected, if you like—or two-room suites are offered here, along with cable television, refrigerators and coffee pots in the rooms. The whole family can enjoy the oceanfront and kiddie pools as well as a playground, picnic area with grills, ice cream parlor, game room and nearby amusement park, water slide and miniature golf. Laundry facilities also are available. Golf or fishing packages are offered.

The Surf
$$-$$$ • 711 S. Lumina Ave., WrightsvilleBeach • (910) 256-2275

Luxury oceanfront suites are convenient to golf courses as well as charter, surf or pier fishing and boating. Each of the 45 suites offers a combined living room/kitchen, cable television, queen-size sleeper sofa and a separate bedroom with queen-size bed. Meeting rooms and catering also may be arranged if you're here on business. The pool, sun deck and gazebo are oceanfront, and the Oceanic Pier and Restaurant are nearby.

Golf Equipment

Tee Smith Custom Golf Clubs, 1047 S. Kerr Avenue, Wilmington, (910) 395-4008, is one place you can visit for new clubs. Regripping service and various brands are available. Nearby **Pro Golf Discount**, 914 S. Kerr Avenue, (910) 392-9405, offers a large selection of major-brand equipment and accessories and provides professional club fitting, repair and regripping services on site. **The Golf Bag**, U.S. 17 S., Hampstead, (910) 270-2980, has a good selection of items, with emphasis on ladies' equipment and accessories. It's easy to find north of Porter's Neck Plantation and Country Club near Olde Pointe Golf and Country Club (see this chapter's previous entry).

North Carolina's
Pinehurst/ Sandhills

Pinehurst is the crown jewel of golf in the Carolinas. It's also the cradle of American tournament play and one of the foremost golf destinations in the world. For these three reasons alone, every golfer should make time to spend at least a weekend here and challenge one of the over 30 wonderful courses that welcome and thrive on public play.

First, a word about the word "Pinehurst," because the situation surrounding that name has become a bit confusing and contentious over the past few years.

If you look at a map of North Carolina, not far to the west of Fayeteville, there's a dot with the word "Pinehurst" next to it: that's the "Village of Pinehurst," the quaint collection of shops and magnificent homes laid out almost 100 years ago by Frederick Law Olmstead. The epicenter of the Village is Pinehurst, the famous resort. A golfer who says "I'm going to Pinehurst" may not go anywhere near Pinehurst the resort, or Pinehurst the village. He'll probably visit a golf course that's technically in Southern Pines or Aberdeen or one of the other towns in what's also called "The Sandhills" or "southern Moore County." Confusing isn't it?

Pinehurst the resort attempted to end the confusion recently by trademarking the name "Pinehurst," preventing companies like "Pinehurst Embalming and Massage" from using the golden name. The resort argued that a "Pinehurst Hamburger Shack" or a "Pinehurst Exterminators" would detract from their franchise. While they might have a point, it's extremely rare and difficult to trademark a geographical name, particularly one with the resonance and import of Pinehurst. Most locals, particularly those in the Village of Pinehurst, decried the decision and pressured the resort to hand back the name. In January, both sides agreed not to Brinks any more cash to the lawyers and called a truce. Pinehurst the village could be Pinehurst, and companies in the area could use the name, so long as they aren't in the golf or resort business. All's well that ends well: The good people at Pinehurst Proctology can keep their name.

Despite all the flak that Pinehurst the resort received from locals, it must be noted that Club Corp., the company that owns Pinehurst Resort and Country Club, has worked extremely hard in the past decade to improve this national treasure. Although official numbers aren't available, it's clear that Club Corp. must have spent close to $100 million renovating buildings, constructing new courses, sprucing up the existing layouts and generally restoring Pinehurst to what it should be. Lost in much of the punch-up over the name is the commitment of all those who work for Pinehurst Resort and Country Club to maintain their property to world-class standards. Kudos to them for getting it right.

For the purposes of this book, we use "Pinehurst" to describe the entire area. In the entry for the resort, we say just "Pinehurst" so that we don't have to wear out the 'r' key on the keyboard. We hope this ends the confusion.

The Sandhills

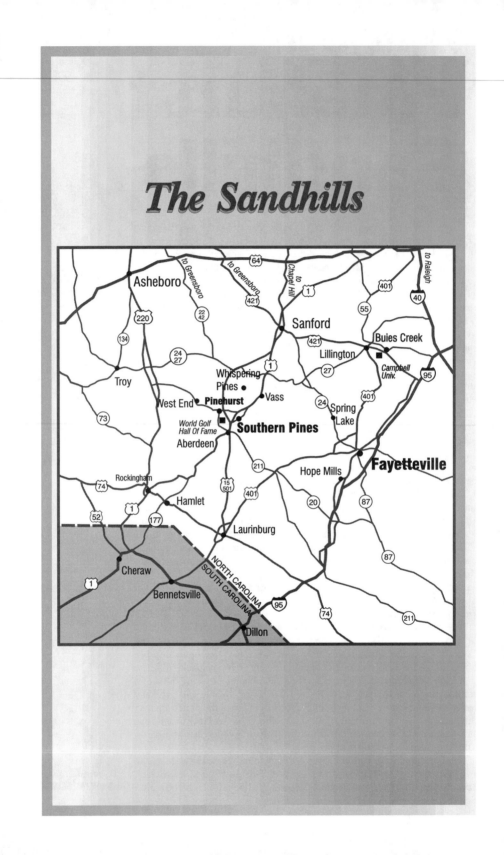

GOLF COURSES IN NORTH CAROLINA'S PINEHURST/SANDHILLS AREA

Course	Type	# Holes	Par	Slope	Yards	Walking	Booking	Cost w/ Cart
Beacon Ridge	semiprivate	18	72	123	6143	restricted	anytime	$40-60
CC of Whispering Pines								
West Course	semiprivate	18	71	125	6007	restricted	anytime	$46-66
East Course	semiprivate	18	72	124	6406	restricted	anytime	$46-66
Cypress Lakes	public	18	72	118	6585	anytime	anytime	$25-30
Deercraft	semiprivate	18	72	120	6185	restricted	anytime	$37-65
Foxfire								
East Course	semiprivate/resort	18	72	123	6286	restricted	anytime	$51-77
West Course	semiprivate/resort	18	72	123	6333	restricted	anytime	$51-77
Hyland Hills	public	18	72	113	6111	restricted	anytime	$41-60
Keith Hills	public	18	72	124	6129	anytime	anytime	$35-40
King's Grant	semiprivate	18	72	118	6222	anytime	3 days	$35-40
Knollwood Fairways (9 holes)	semiprivate	18	72	121	5218	anytime	anytime	$24
Legacy	public	18	72	124	6505	no	anytime	$60-95
Little River Farm	public	18	71	n/a	6505	restricted	anytime	$40-70
Longleaf Country Club	semiprivate	18	71	110	6073	restricted	anytime	$45-70
Midland Country Club (9 holes)	semiprivate	18	70	n/r	5714	restricted	anytime	$25
Mid Pines Golf resort	resort	18	72	122	6121	anytime	anytime	$60-110
Pine Needles	resort	18	71	126	6318	anytime	anytime	$85-110
Pinehurst								
#1	resort	18	70	114	5873	caddies	anytime	$59-94
#2	resort	18	72	127	6354	caddies	anytime	$225
#3	resort	18	70	117	5593	caddies	anytime	$59-94
#4	resort	18	72	117	6396	caddies	anytime	$59-94

#5	resort	18	72	123	6357	caddies	anytime	$59-94
#6	resort	18	72	132	6603	restricted	anytime	$59-94
#7	resort	18	72	114	6692	restricted	anytime	$104-200
#8	resort	18	72	135	7092	caddies	anytime	$130-200
The Pit	public	18	71	128	6138	anytime	anytime	$55-90
Seven Lakes	semiprivate	18	72	122	6151	restricted	anytime	$55-70
Talamore at Pinehurst	public	18	71	134	6393	llamas	anytime	$50-94
Tobacco Road	public	18	71	142	6304	restricted	anytime	$60
Whispering Woods	semiprivate	18	70	n/a	6334	no	anytime	$35-45
Woodlake Country Club	semiprivate	18	72	129	6584	restricted	3 days	$55-85

So, let's get back to what Pinehurst is all about: great and wonderful golf in one of the game's great settings.

Golfers find more courses and spicier nightlife in Myrtle Beach, and the coastal gems of North and South Carolina offer an abundance of charm and character. The Eastern Seaboard of the United States, in fact, boasts some sensational pockets of resort golf. But nothing compares to Pinehurst for tradition, history, relaxation, ambiance and the quality of golf. Pinehurst is a haven for those among us who love and respect pure golf and who want to retreat from the pressures and hassles of city life.

It's not easy to get to Pinehurst. The area is at least 1½ hours by car from North Carolina's urban areas, and the journey is mostly along country roads. Pinehurst's airport can only handle commuter planes and the smallest of jets. And yet despite the relative inconvenience of getting there, golfers from all over the world flock to Pinehurst—which says a great deal about the quality of its resorts and courses.

The epicenter of the Pinehurst area is the Pinehurst Resort and Country Club, 100-plus years old and the area's most important landmark. Its eight courses are all superb, and the famed Pinehurst #2 is usually rated as one of the 10 best in the world. In 1999, it hosted one of the best U.S. Opens ever, with the late Payne Stewart holing a number of difficult and dramatic putts—including a gut-wrenching 12-footer on the 18th green—to snatch the tournament from Phil Mickelson. The event was such a smashing success that the United States Golf Association has already announced that the country's Open Championship will be returning to Pinehurst in 2005—a quick repeat performance indeed.

Perhaps the most important celebrity in Pinehurst is Donald Ross, universally acknowledged as one of the greatest and most influential golf course architects in the history of the game. After leaving Scotland in the early 1900s, Ross settled in Pinehurst where he lived until his death in 1948. His legacy lives on strongly in the Sandhills, where locals and visitors revere his courses and personality.

Ross loved the Pinehurst area because he adored the rolling topography and the sandy soil, both of which reminded him of Royal Dornoch, his home course in northern Scotland. The Sandhills provide perfect land for golf courses, easily workable while providing excellent drainage and pristine scenery. Tom Fazio, Gene Hamm, Robert Trent Jones, Ellis Maples, Dan Maples, Tom Jackson, Ed Seay and Jack Nicklaus are a few of the well-known architects whose work is enjoyed in and around the area.

Pinehurst is also the home of tournament golf in the United States. Every course boasts a history of competition ranging from the North Carolina Dentist's Four-Ball to the Ryder Cup and U.S. Open. The list of champions reads like a Who's Who of golf and includes the likes of Watson, Irwin, Nicklaus, Palmer, Stewart, and Hogan.

The 1999 U.S. Open wasn't the first tournament awarded to the area by the United States Golf Association. Pine Needles hosted the 1996 U.S. Women's Open and will hold the tournament again in 2001.

In 2000, Legacy, another fine course in the Pinehurst area, will host the U.S. Women's Public Links. But the grandaddy of all the tournaments in Pinehurst must be the North and South Amateur, played each spring on Pinehurst #2. There are categories for men, women, men's seniors, juniors, and women's seniors. After the national championships, the North and South is probably the most important amateur tournament in the country.

Something else that makes the Pinehurst area so special is that just about every course is accessible to the public in one way or another. Out of the approximately 35 courses within 30 minutes of the traffic circle at the junction of U.S. highways 211 and 15/501, all but three or four are open to the public golfer. Some are more public than others—in other words, some courses are resort-oriented and your chances of getting a choice tee time at a famous track are better if you're staying in a room that's just a few feet from the first tee. But there's always a way to get on a chosen course should you be willing to ask around.

The key to getting on the course you desire is getting to know the professional staff at a local club or, better still, at the resort where you're based. In the Pinehurst area, everyone knows each other. The pro at resort #1 knows the pro at resort #3, who can get a tee time at #3 because he knows the guy in the starting tower who, in turn, plays golf with the guy who used to caddie on tour for the friend of the pro at course #4, where the greenskeeper is friendly with the bartender at bar A, which also happens to be Wayne Gretzky's favorite watering hole when he's down with family, friends and Mark Messier for a week of 36 holes a day. Ask around and you'll be amazed at what you can organize.

A lot of young and aspiring professional golfers come to Pinehurst to work, teach and hone their games for what they hope will be a life of professional golf on the big boys' tour. There are plenty of professionals and directors of golf whose knowledge and skills are excellent. What better place to be a professional than in Pinehurst, the capital of the golfing world?

The first major "in-season" period begins at the end of February and extends through late May and early June. You'll find plenty of fine sunny days with perfect temperatures interspersed with a few days of rain and gloom. The summer months are primarily quiet on most of the courses. The intensity of the summer heat and humidity makes golf a chore, and the frequent late-day thunderstorms render it dangerous and wet. In deep summer the fairways are excellent, but the greens will be slow as the greenskeepers fight to save them from death by heat by raising the blades on the greens mowers. Fall brings a second season: You'll find the greens back to championship speed and the courses filling up. The fall season ends around Thanksgiving. Winter is somewhat dead, but the courses are usually playable and the rates can be at their lowest. There can be plenty of wonderful and comfortable days in the winter season, and most area courses offer outstanding rates.

Even though the price of golf in Pinehurst has increased significantly in the past few years, there's still a course for nearly every budget. Inexpensive but comfortable lodging options abound, and if you're eating on a budget, Ronald McDonald has a secure presence here. You can spend a fortune in Pinehurst and feast on quail and rare clarets, but you don't need to take out a second mortgage to have an excellent time. Still, it's fun to have a couple of blowouts, and there are plenty of opportunities in Pinehurst to pullulate your visa balance.

Whatever the size of your wallet or golfing desires, the key is to plan and book ahead. Many, many courses host large outings and leagues, and there's nothing more depressing than showing up at a course only to find that you've arrived (without a tee time) smack-dab in the middle of the annual tournament of the Mid-Atlantic Chapter of the Association of Undertakers and Mortuary Professionals. After an hour wait as the pro struggles to get your foursome on the course, the pace of play will be, well, funereal. Just remember, the desk clerk at your hotel or the pro at your resort can be incredibly resourceful if you're polite.

A pleasing trend in Pinehurst is the return of walking on many courses that previously made golfers cruise around in a cart. Pinehurst Resort offers caddies to its guests. Sadly, many architects designed the newer courses with carts only in mind, while the older courses are much more walkable. Our advice is to leave the carts at the cart shed and walk. It's how real golfers play real golf. And, as you should know by now, Pinehurst is all about real golf.

We come to Pinehurst to relax and enjoy the greatest of games. A trip to Pinehurst is a pilgrimage of sorts, a quest for golfing purity among the quiet and stately pines. In Pinehurst, golf is all that matters, which is why our hearts beat a little faster when, as we drive along those country roads, we see the soil turn from clay to sandy loam and we pass the signs that say "Welcome to Pinehurst, Golf Capital of the World." If a trip here fails to get you excited about the game, then you should sell your clubs and take up Scrabble.

Beacon Ridge Golf and Country Club
Seven Lakes W., West End
• (910) 673-2950

Championship Yardage:	6414
Slope: 125	Par: 72
Men's Yardage:	6143
Slope: 123	Par: 72
Other Yardage:	5354
Slope: 114	Par: 72
Ladies' Yardage:	4730
Slope: 115	Par: 72

Beacon Ridge Golf and Country Club, a Gene Hamm design on rolling, wooded terrain, opened in 1988. This well-maintained course has bermudagrass fairways and bentgrass greens.

About 10 minutes outside the main Pinehurst area, Beacon Ridge offers some fine golf in a relaxed environment. It's part of a housing development, but houses don't interfere with play too much, if at all.

You'll find that the back nine is less undulating than the front and, therefore, a little less difficult by comparison. But overall, the course is challenging without being impossible—a happy medium that will satisfy golfers of all levels.

Perhaps what sets Beacon Ridge apart from a number of other area courses is the variety. Just about every hole boasts its own character. There isn't too much water to contend with, but when it comes into play, it will definitely affect your plan of attack. There are plenty of bunkers lurking to distract you as well—most of which are large and flat, with no lip. The greens are mostly large and sloped. You'll find decent room off the tee, but if you miss the fairway, you'll end up in deep rough and pine trees and might not find your ball. Keep it in play and your score should be sensible.

The most picturesque hole might be the par 4 13th, short at just 344 from the tips, and downhill off the tee with a bunker on the right hand side of the fairway. There's water and a large tree to the left of the green, which is also flanked by two large bunkers. A solid short hole requiring more precision than pure muscle.

Amenities include a practice green, range, chipping green, locker room, bar, restaurant, rental clubs and a pro shop.

The course is walkable for the extremely fit, but you'll be better off with a cart. Approximate cost, including cart, is $60 high season, $40 low.

Country Club of Whispering Pines
2 Clubhouse Blvd., Whispering Pines
• (910) 949-2311

The Country Club of Whispering Pines opened the East Course in 1959 and the West Course in 1970—both Ellis Maples designs. The East Course is set on rolling terrain; the West Course is relatively flat. In the fairways, you'll find bermudagrass; on the greens, bentgrass.

The housing around the course is mostly owned by retirees who purchased the club from the developers a few years ago. There's a big membership push going on and the club is close to becoming private. The club offers a limited number of on-site condos for rent. The clientele here is mostly retirees.

Amenities include a practice green, range, chipping green, locker room, restaurant, rental clubs and a pro shop.

Both courses are walkable, but you must take a cart if you're not a member. Approximate cost, including cart, is $66 high, $55 medium and $46 low.

West Course
Championship Yardage:	6340
Slope: 128	**Par:** 71
Men's Yardage:	6007
Slope: 125	**Par:** 71
Other Yardage:	5525
Slope: 118	**Par:** 71
Ladies' Yardage:	5135
Slope: 121	**Par:** 71

Let's start with the West Course—newer, shorter and tighter than its sister track. There's plenty of water to negotiate on the back nine,

and thus this course rewards accuracy and sound judgment over big hitting. There's a great variety of interesting holes and relatively few homes—the course is mature enough that tall pines tend to obscure the back porch of Ted and Millie Morris' place.

The key from the tee is to keep the ball in play on the tight fairways; the key to scoring from there is to avoid the many and mostly large bunkers that protect the large greens. If you miss the green and the rough is deep, then getting up and down requires a bit of good fortune.

Even though it's rated as the easiest hole on the course, the par 3 14th could yield a big number. The large green is set at 45 degrees to the tee and is flanked by two bunkers. There's water short left and long right, but at just 160 yards from the tips, it shouldn't cause too much difficulty for the better player and could even yield a birdie.

With its emphasis on accuracy over brute length, the West course is set up perfectly for the membership.

East Course
Championship Yardage:	7110
Slope: 125	**Par:** 72
Men's Yardage:	6406
Slope: 124	**Par:** 72
Other Yardage:	5943
Slope: 117	**Par:** 72
Ladies' Yardage:	5542
Slope: 123	**Par:** 72

Speaking of accuracy versus distance, perhaps the opposite could be said of the East Course, a track that's more than 7100 yards from the back tees. Of course, you don't have to play from the tips. The course will play somewhat friendlier from other tees. The fairways are mostly wide, and there seem to be quite a few of the epic and sweeping doglegs that made Ellis Maples famous. The track is really extremely fair and somewhat challenging, and most holes offer difficulties without gimmicks.

On the back nine, you'll find a couple of holes where water comes into play—it helps to be somewhat straight off the tee. You'll have plenty of chances to risk aiming for a certain segment of the fairway—the reward for a well-placed shot will be an easier approach. The greens are large, sloped and protected primarily by large bunkers. There are quite a few fairway bunkers. This fun and challenging course will test even the scratch golfer (from the back tees).

The most interesting hole might be the par 5 11th, a whopping 583 yards from the tips with water threatening off the tee and then the entire left-hand side. Even though the tee shot

The green on the 18th at Pine Needles—site of the 1996 U.S. Women's Open.

Photo: Pine Needles

is downhill, Maples designed it to be a true three-shotter where par is gladly accepted.

Cypress Lakes Golf Club
Cypress Lake Dr., Hope Mills
• (910) 483-0359

Championship Yardage:	7217
Slope: 126	**Par: 72**
Men's Yardage:	6585
Slope: 118	**Par: 72**
Ladies' Yardage:	5060
Slope: 116	**Par: 74**

Officials told us that Cypress Lakes opened in 1968, although we think (and we'll tell you why later) that it's much older. L.B. Floyd designed the course on rolling, wooded terrain, with bermudagrass fairways and bentgrass greens.

There are probably better golf courses in the greater Fayetteville metropolitan area, but this one stands out because it was previously owned by L.B. Floyd, father of golfing greats Raymond and Marlene Floyd. If you've ever read Ray Floyd's *From Sixty Yards In*, you know about young Raymond splashing about in the bunkers on his father's course. This is where the younger Floyd learned how to get the ball up and down so impressively . . . and so lucratively. Considering Raymond is 50-something, we think the course must have opened before 1968. The scorecard amusingly describes Cypress Lakes as an "Open, Championship Course."

The course itself has been under new ownership for quite some time, and a renovation is complete. The layout is somewhat straightforward, and the obvious hazards or difficulties that need to be negotiated are easily visible from wherever you lie. Still, it's a fun track that's well worth a visit if you're into finding out where the Floyds originally played golf.

The front nine ends with a tricky par 3, a whopping 245 from the tips, mostly over water to a small green. Par this one and the hot dog at the turn will taste like filet mignon.

Amenities include a practice green, range, chipping green, locker room, bar, restaurant, rental clubs and a pro shop.

You can walk your round and book a tee time anytime. Approximate cost, including cart, is $25 on weekdays and $30 on weekends.

Deercroft Golf and Country Club
U.S. Hwy. 15/501, Pinehurst
• (910) 369-3107

Championship Yardage:	**6745**
Slope: 125	**Par: 72**
Men's Yardage:	**6185**
Slope: 120	**Par: 72**
Ladies' Yardage:	**5443**
Slope: 113	**Par: 72**

The golf course at Deercroft Golf and Country Club opened in 1984. Gardner Gildy designed the track, which is set in wooded and undulating terrain.

Deercroft is roughly 15 minutes south of Aberdeen on U.S. Hwy. 15/501. As you approach the pro shop, a large sign tells you that *Golf Week Magazine* hailed Deercroft as "One of America's Best Golf Courses."

Deercroft is a course cut out of some fine and mature pine forest, thus you'll always feel like you're far from civilization and all of its accompanying hassles and distractions. The preponderance of trees means you must keep the ball straight off the tee. Take whatever club you need to keep it out of the woods and away from the out-of-bounds markers that can often be quite close to the fairway. Adding to the fun are a number of deep and nasty fairway bunkers that may keep your ball from skidding into the woods but may also create an extra shot or two. There isn't a huge amount of water here at Deercroft. Among local cognoscenti, Deercroft is feared as a difficult and demanding golf course.

Most of the greens are large and sloped and often surrounded by a series of flat bunkers with little or no significant face. A good player will probably not find it too difficult to get up and down. The real challenge here at Deercroft comes from keeping it long and straight off the tee, especially on some of the more muscular par 4s: There are six two-shotters of more than 400 yards from the tips, including the 18th, which is a 470-yard par 4.

Deercroft is walkable for the fit, and you can walk when the course isn't too crowded. You can book a tee time at your convenience. Approximate cost, including cart, is $65 during the high season and $37 during the low season.

Foxfire Resort and Country Club
Hoffman Rd., Pinehurst • (910) 295-5555

First, a note about the resort and accommodations: Plenty of people live all year at Foxfire, but many visit for a conference or just for golf. There are plenty of condominiums for rent, each with various bedroom/bathroom configurations. Call (800) 736-9347 for a brochure with all the details. Foxfire also specializes in conferences, tournaments and outings.

Once you've completed all your business, spend some quality time on the golf course. The resort's new management, as part of its extensive renovation plan, built a completely new and spacious clubhouse. Everyone here is friendly, and if you're looking for a relaxed setting for whatever sort of golf outing suits your fancy, you can't go wrong at Foxfire. With an advance call to the pro shop, the public can get a tee time on either course. Despite all the recent improvements (and accompanying rate hikes), Foxfire still represents one of the better values in Pinehurst.

Now, on to the golf courses. Gene Hamm designed both of them. The East Course opened in 1968 and the West Course in 1973. Both are set in rolling terrain, with pine forest bordering the bermudagrass fairways. Greens are covered with bentgrass.

Amenities include a practice green, range, chipping green, locker room, bar, restaurant, rental clubs and a pro shop.

Both courses are walkable for the fit, and the management now encourages walking at most times. Approximate cost, including cart, is $77 high, $65 medium and $51 low.

East Course

Championship Yardage:	**6834**
Slope: 129	**Par: 72**
Men's Yardage:	**6286**
Slope: 127	**Par: 72**
Other Yardage:	**5864**
Slope: 119	**Par: 72**
Ladies' Yardage:	**5256**
Slope: 122	**Par: 72**

Let's start with the East Course. You'll begin with the No. 1 handicap hole, a medium-length par 5. There's plenty of length from the back tees and plenty of width on most of the fairways. If you spray it a little off the tee, you may find either deep rough or a nasty bunker, heavily infiltrated with love grass. You'll find some of those same bunkers around many of the greens. The greens are primarily large and sloped. You can push or pull the ball a little, be pin high and still have a long putt for birdie. Water could prove irritating if you miss a shot badly. You might enjoy the back nine a little more than the front: It's completely undeveloped, and you really feel like you're away from it all. Some of the finest holes are on the back nine and require your best form and behavior. Most intimidating is the par 3 12th, 212 from the tips to a green where anything left means bogey and anything right means triple.

West Course

Championship Yardage: 6742
Slope: 128   Par: 72
Men's Yardage: 6333
Slope: 123   Par: 72
Ladies' Yardage: 5273
Slope: 115   Par: 72

The West Course is fun, well designed and perhaps a little easier in places than its counterpart, although it's plenty difficult in other spots. Water comes into play on a few holes but shouldn't pose much of a problem unless you're particularly wayward. The greens are large and mostly flat, as are the bunkers. The challenges are evident; there's nothing tricked-up or artificial. If we had to choose between the two courses, we'd probably pick the East, but you'll be just as satisfied with the West, which has a bit more eccentricity, quirkiness, and undulation. Foxfire is fortunate to have two good golf courses at its disposal.

The most memorable hole might be the 9th, a 519-yard par 5 with a difficult tee shot downhill; club selection is critical as it's important to clear the trees and thus leave a clear second shot to the green.

Hyland Hills Golf Club

4100 U.S. Hwy. 1 N., Southern Pines
• (919) 692-3752
Championship Yardage: 6726
Slope: 120   Par: 72
Men's Yardage: 6111
Slope: 113   Par: 72
Ladies' Yardage: 4677
Slope: 109   Par: 72

Hyland Hills Golf Club opened in 1973. Tom Jackson designed the course on rolling, wooded terrain bordered by houses and pine forest. Fairways are bermudagrass; greens, bentgrass.

Just north of Southern Pines, Hyland Hills offers a fine and fun golf course in a pleasant, primarily open setting. It's one of Tom Jackson's earlier efforts and offers plenty of well-designed holes. You won't find too much trouble off the tee, although wayward shots might find the deep rough in the summer, some nasty bunkers or the occasional small mound. Around the large and interestingly shaped greens are bunkers, more mounds and some greens with considerable slope and undulation. The greens pose the most difficulty, so bring your best putting game.

Hyland Hills offers a little more undulation than its local counterparts, a facet that is particularly noticeable on the downhill 5th, a precipitous 409 yards to a large green. The bold will try to cut the corner.

Overall, Hyland Hills provides outstanding variety. It's a good example of what made Tom Jackson such a sought-after designer. Mid- to low handicappers should play the course from the back tees for the full effect and the most challenge. The course is an excellent value and justifiably popular.

Amenities include a practice green, range, chipping green, locker room, bar, restaurant, rental clubs and a pro shop.

The course is walkable for the extremely fit, but walking is restricted. Approximate cost, including cart, ranges from $60 down to $41.

Keith Hills Country Club

Keith Hills Rd., Buies Creek
• (910) 893-1371
Championship Yardage: 6660
Slope: 129   Par: 72
Men's Yardage: 6129
Slope: 124   Par: 72
Ladies' Yardage: 5535
Slope: 120   Par: 72

Keith Hills opened in 1977. Ellis Maples designed the course, and Dan Maples, his son, assisted. The course is set in primarily rolling, wooded terrain bordered by houses, with bermudagrass fairways and bentgrass greens.

Keith Hills is a well-regarded course that's owned and operated by Campbell University, so if you see a camel wandering across the first fairway, you'll understand why (and if you don't understand—the university's mascot is a camel). The course is so popular that it's often difficult to get a tee time during peak seasons.

This beautiful course has the reputation for being kept in excellent condition. The fairways are wide, but the rough can get thick. The greens are large and sloped. A couple of elevated tees make for some dramatic tee shots. There's a reason why a course that's a little off the beaten track is so busy—it's not necessarily the hot dogs in the snack bar.

In October 1995, Keith Hills opened the largest practice facility in North Carolina, designed by Dan Maples. There's also an indoor teaching center. If you're in the Buies Creek or Sandhills area, check out Keith Hills.

Amenities include a practice green, range, chipping green, locker room, snack bar, rental clubs and a pro shop.

The course is walkable, and you can walk anytime, although in the busy seasons you will be charged a cart fee whether you ride or not. Make sure you call ahead for that tee time. Approximate cost, including cart, is $35 weekdays and $40 on the weekend.

King's Grant Golf and Country Club
198 Shawcroft Rd., Fayetteville
• (910) 630-1114

Championship Yardage:	6634
Slope: 125	Par: 72
Men's Yardage:	6222
Slope: 118	Par: 72
Other Yardage:	5814
Slope: 113	Par: 72
Ladies' Yardage:	5060
Slope: 115	Par: 72

Jim Holmes designed King's Grant Golf and Country Club, which opened in 1990. The course is set in rolling, wooded terrain bordered by houses. In the fairways, you'll find bermudagrass; on the greens, bentgrass.

Fayetteville is best known throughout the world as home to one of the largest army bases in the United States: Fort Bragg. This is where you'll find paratroopers and green berets. You'll also find King's Grant, a housing-development course that's quite a challenge, particularly from the back tees. Many of the holes are extremely close to the houses, but if you ignore the back tees and the out-of-bounds markers, you'll find some fine, well-designed holes offering lots of challenge and interest.

The final hole is a 510-yard par 5 with water running along the entire right hand side of the fairway and coming into play on the left-hand side off the tee. The big hitters could reach the green in two, but they'll have to be dead accurate. It's a solid closing hole that could yield anything from a three to a snowman.

Amenities include a practice green, range, chipping green, locker room, snack bar and a pro shop.

You can walk anytime. Book a tee time three days in advance. Approximate cost, including cart, is $35 on weekdays and $40 on weekends.

Knollwood Fairways Golf Club
1470 Midland Rd., Southern Pines
• (910) 692-3572

Championship Yardage:	5398
Slope: 123	Par: 70
Men's Yardage:	5218
Slope: 121	Par: 70
Ladies' Yardage:	4730
Slope: 120	Par: 70

C.A. Pitts designed Knollwood Fairways. The course is set on flat terrain bordered by pine trees and condos. In the fairways, you'll find bermudagrass, while bentgrass blankets the greens.

Knollwood Fairways is a fun, short and entertaining layout that's great for a practice round

or for the beginning or seasoned golfer who doesn't want to play a huge course. You start off with a short par 3 over water followed by a longer par 3 over land. Then you begin a series of short, tight par 4s. A local pro told us that he and his friends play the course with one rule: You *must* use your driver on every par 4. You might not have that same degree of control with your big stick, so take a little less club with you. The course boasts a couple of full-length holes in the middle of the course. The massive driving range is popular with locals. Knollwood Fairways is a great place for an after-work practice round.

You can walk anytime, and you should walk here. You can book a tee time anytime you choose. Approximate cost, including cart, is $24 for 18 holes.

Legacy Golf Links
U.S. Hwy. 15/501 S., Aberdeen
• (910) 944-8825

Championship Yardage:	7008
Slope: 133	Par: 72
Men's Yardage:	6505
Slope: 124	Par: 72
Other Yardage:	594
Slope: 122	Par: 72
Ladies' Yardage:	5080
Slope: 128	Par: 72

Legacy Golf Links opened in 1992. Jack Nicklaus II, son of the Golden Bear, designed the course on rolling, wooded terrain, with bermudagrass fairways and bentgrass greens.

Jack Nicklaus II is perhaps best known as his father's son, but don't underestimate the design skill of the "second edition." Don't underestimate his golfing skill either: The younger bear won the North and South Amateur Championship in 1985.

After graduating from the University of North Carolina, Jack II tried various pro circuits but soon decided to concentrate on working with his father's golf architecture business. His other efforts include Ibis Golf and Country Club in Florida and Hanbury Manor in England.

At Legacy, Jack II created a course that's extremely well respected among locals, who will not hesitate to recommend that their out-of-town friends visit this course. Legacy is a totally public course with an upper-market atmosphere. At the bag drop, an attendant takes care of placing your bag on the cart, and there's a shoeshine waiting for you after the round.

The course is a good one—one of the better tests in the area, particularly from the back tees. Jack II and his design team built challenging, fun and playable holes. Water comes into play frequently and could lead to a big score if you're not careful. Off the tee, stick to the middle of the fairway; however, balls struck to the left and right sometimes come back to the middle due to favorable mounding. It's not death to miss the fairway here, but you may find a bad lie or your view of the green obstructed by a pine tree. The course is not heavily bunkered. The greens are large and mostly sloped. Some of the par 3s are flanked by large slopes that could prove very nasty.

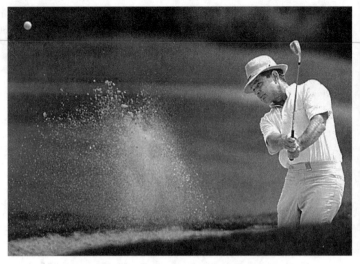

Just about every course in the Carolinas features tough bunkering, so be prepared to play from the sand.

Photo: Dick Van Halsema

The closing hole is a massive 459-yard par 4 with an uphill blind tee shot. However, a well-struck wood should get plenty of roll once it gets over the crest of the hill. The second shot has to be one of the most difficult in the area, probably a long iron or fairway wood downhill over water to one of the largest greens on the course. A huge four.

Golf Digest praised the layout and the course's value —a true rarity. If you like sensible and playable modern tracks, you'll enjoy Legacy. Play it and you'll understand why locals give it well-deserved kudos. Make sure you book well ahead in the peak season as the course is immensely popular.

Amenities include a practice green, range, chipping green, locker room, bar, restaurant, rental clubs, a beverage cart, shoeshine and a pro shop.

Carts are required. Approximate cost, including cart, is $95 high, $75 medium and $60 low.

Little River Farm
500 Little River Farm Rd., Carthage
• (910) 949-4600

Championship Yardage:	**6931**
Slope: 132	**Par: 71**
Men's Yardage:	**6505**
Slope: 125	**Par: 71**
Ladies' Yardage:	**4705**
Slope: 118	**Par: 71**

Little River Farm opened in 1996. Dan Maples designed the course. It's set in wooded terrain just north of Pinehurst on the road to Carthage. You'll find bermudagrass in the fairways and bentgrass on the greens.

Little River Farm is Dan Maples' third course in the Pinehurst area, and the three couldn't be much more different. You'll find full descriptions of The Pit and Longleaf (his other Pinehurst courses) in this chapter. The big factor at Little River is the soil; unlike the Pinehurst courses, the soil here at Little River Farm is Piedmont clay, thus there's more of a traditional park land feel to the track. There are more hardwood trees here than pines.

Little River Farm features some significant elevation changes, much more compared to other courses. The fairways vary in width, so be careful to leave some room for error on the tighter holes. In general, there's more room on the front nine, but the back nine gets tighter and a little more difficult. Difficulty off the tee comes in the form of ball-swallowing wetlands—make sure you know where they are.

Greens are not as large as some found on new courses, and they are more sloped than severely undulating. The greens are not tricked up in any way, and the head pro here thinks these are Dan Maples' best greens. Unlike many courses, the shorter par 4s feature greens that are banked away from the fairway. The courses are not overly bunkered, but traps are strategically placed around each green. We'd certainly take a look at Little River Farm, an interesting addition to the Pinehurst portfolio.

Little River Farm is walkable for the fit, and

you can walk anytime. Approximate cost, including cart, is $70 during the high season and $40 during the low season.

Longleaf Country Club
1010 Midland Rd., Southern Pines
• **(910) 692-2114**

Championship Yardage:	**6600**		
Slope: 117		**Par:** 71	
Men's Yardage:	6073		
Slope: 110		**Par:** 71	
Ladies' Yardage:	4719		
Slope: 108		**Par:** 71	

Dan Maples designed the golf course at Longleaf Country Club, which opened in 1988. The back nine is set in rolling, wooded terrain bordered with houses; the front is generally open. Fairways are bermudagrass, and greens are bentgrass.

As you drive down Midland Road for the first time, likely awed by the sheer number of golf courses concentrated on one road, you may pass Longleaf thinking it's a horse farm. Actually, the front nine is built on a former horse-training facility and Dan Maples kept many of the old fences and hedges intact. The 100-, 150- and 200-yard markers are furlong markers. In case you're wondering why Dan Maples was chosen as the designer, he's part of the partnership that's developing this course.

The front and back nines at Longleaf are very different. It's sort of like Kyle Petty's hair: short front, long back. The front is wide open. The back is wooded and somewhat tight in places due to the intrusion of homes. There's a bit of water on the back nine, and one hole includes a tree right in the middle of the fairway—a Dan Maples eccentricity. There's plenty of room off the tee, and you should have lots of fun driving the ball. The greens are predominantly large, subtly undulating and well guarded in places. The fairways feature some mounds and the occasional bunker. Overall, this fun course is suitable for all golfers.

There's a lot more interest to the back nine, but the par 5 5th on the front has to be one of the prettiest holes on the entire course. It's a solid 525 yards, and big hitters could reach it in two, seeing as the second shot is predominantly downhill. It's rated the most difficult hole on the course, but the 14th is more likely to incur a big number.

Amenities include a practice green, range, chipping green, locker room, bar, restaurant, rental clubs and a pro shop.

The front nine is very walkable, and the back nine is walkable for the fit; you can walk anytime but still must pay a cart fee. Approxi-

mate cost, including cart, is $70 high, $60 medium and $45 low.

Midland Country Club
2205 Midland Rd., Southern Pines
• **(910) 295-3241**

Championship Yardage:	**6186**		
Slope: 119		**Par:** 70	
Men's Yardage:	5714		
Slope: No rating		**Par:** 70	
Ladies' Yardage:	5066		
Slope: 113		**Par:** 70	

Tom Jackson designed this nine-hole course on flat terrain bordered by houses. In the fairways, you'll find bermudagrass; on the greens, you'll find bentgrass.

Midland is owned by the same crew that's in charge of Knollwood, and you'll find the same ambiance and similar characteristics: fun, walkable, decently challenging, tight in places and an excellent value. While this is not one of Jackson's extravaganzas, the course is wonderfully playable and well worth the approximately $25 per round. Before and/or after your round, challenge the Dunes Restaurant, just a lob wedge from the pro shop.

Amenities include a practice green, restaurant and rental clubs.

The course is extremely walkable, so walk if you can. Approximate cost, including cart, is $25 for 18 holes.

Mid Pines Golf Resort
1010 Midland Rd., Southern Pines
• **(910) 692-2114**

Championship Yardage:	**6515**		
Slope: 127		**Par:** 72	
Men's Yardage:	6121		
Slope: 122		**Par:** 72	
Ladies' Yardage:	5592		
Slope: 128		**Par:** 72	

The golf course at Mid Pines Golf Resort, a Donald Ross design, opened in 1921. The course is set in rolling, wooded terrain, with bermudagrass fairways and bentgrass greens.

First, a word or two about the resort: Mid Pines is well known in the Carolinas as a great place for corporate meetings and conferences. Adjacent to the course are numerous houses available for rent; these wonderful old homes are a pleasant change from the typical hotel setting.

Should you want more of a hotel atmosphere, Mid Pines offers one of the most attractive and well-run facilities in the area. The rooms are traditionally appointed, many with antiques. We can't think of a more wonderful setting for a conference or weekend getaway.

There's also some great food and drink. Other amenities include a lounge, outdoor deck, bikes, indoor game room, volleyball, baby-sitting services, outdoor swimming pool, tennis courts, a children's play area and shuffleboard. You can also organize or be part of a golf clinic.

Until recently, word was that the course was not in the best condition. That's all changed since Peggy Kirk Bell and some investors purchased Mid Pines in 1994. Bell also owns Pine Needles, and you can read more about her in the Pine Needles review below. The same superintendent who keeps Pine Needles in such great shape has been at work at Mid Pines. The result of this union: A great Donald Ross layout is enjoying a well-deserved renaissance.

Mid Pines offers classic Ross resort golf on a course with some intriguing quirks and difficulties that combine to make it less forgiving than its sister, Pine Needles. Still, you'll find all the characteristics that made Ross so great: plenty of room off the tee, wonderful landscaping and tough greens rippled with subtle undulations. It's exciting that such an excellent design is back on the map. And although you're more likely to get a good tee time if you stay at the resort, the course is open to public play.

The opener will test only the wayward, yet the second has to be one of the most demanding par 3s in the Pinehurst area and could easily ruin a round very early on. It's 160 yards from the middle tees over a ravine to an L-shaped and very undulating green. The first shot is difficult enough, as club selection will play such a pivotal role, but it's second shot that will prove the most demanding. Don't be too disappointed with a four.

Mid Pines ends with a wonderful par 4 of 411 yards, downhill to a narrow fairway. Miss the flag above the hole with your approach shot and par is virtually out of the question. The 18th at Mid Pines is regarded as one of the best finishing holes in the region.

If you're a fan of Donald Ross layouts and you enjoy a more traditional course, you'll really enjoy Mid Pines. And make sure you visit the locker room—one of the oldest, most traditional and untouched in the area, it's like stepping back into the 1920s.

Amenities include a practice green, range, chipping green, locker room, bar, restaurant, rental clubs, a beverage cart and a pro shop.

You may walk the course at any time. Approximate cost, including cart, is $110 high, $78 medium and $60 low.

Pine Needles Resort
1000 Midland Rd., Southern Pines
• (910) 692-7111

Championship Yardage:	**6708**
Slope: 131	**Par: 71**
Men's Yardage:	**6318**
Slope: 126	**Par: 71**
Other Yardage:	**6003**
Slope: 124	**Par: 71**
Ladies' Yardage:	**5039**
Slope: 118	**Par: 71**

The golf course at Pine Needles Resort opened in 1927. Donald Ross designed the course on rolling, wooded terrain, with bermudagrass fairways and bentgrass greens. The course has hosted numerous significant tournaments and in 1996 was the site of the U.S. Women's Open, which it will host again in 2001.

Speaking of the resort, you're best off staying here if you want to play Pine Needles during the spring and fall seasons. The course has opened its doors to the public during the summer and winter but public-access tee-times are rare in the busy seasons. Like its relative, Mid Pines, Pine Needles is an excellent corporate retreat or weekend getaway. The resort has villas and apartments for rent, and you'll find the accommodations welcoming and well appointed. Instruction is big here at Pine Needles: One of the finest teaching facilities in the Southeast is just seconds from the accommodations and is staffed by some fine instructors, including one of the most famous in the country: Peggy Kirk Bell. The course is also home to touring professional Pat McGowan, who is married to the former Bonnie Bell, a relative of Peggy Kirk Bell. A family atmosphere predominates; you'll feel right at home at Pine Needles. The place exudes golf, relaxation and Southern hospitality.

Pine Needles is one of the southeast's great golf courses. Pinehurst #2 receives more accolades and some of the more modern tracks in the area are more treacherous, but Pine Needles stands head and shoulders above the crowd for a number of reasons.

INSIDERS' TIP

Plan now for a trip to the 2005 U.S. Open at Pinehurst #2. This should be a very special event, and if you enjoy golf tournaments, you'll love this one: the greatest golfers on the greatest Donald Ross course.

PINEHURST/ SANDHILLS

Pine Needles' owner, Peggy Kirk Bell, was instrumental in bringing the U.S. Women's Open to her course.

Photo: Pine Needles

First, it's a mostly untouched Donald Ross classic on a perfect piece of land. Anyone who loves Donald Ross courses should visit Pine Needles to view for themselves the architectural features normally associated with Ross: the sensible width of the fairways; the inverted saucer greens; the open approaches to the green complexes; reachable par 5s; superb par 3s; solid two-shot holes; subtle, tricky putting surfaces; grass-faced traps; and almost impossible up-and-downs from behind the greens.

Second, the routing is near perfect. The par 5s may be short, but they both require long, uphill shots. The longer par 4s are mostly downhill, while approach shots on the shorter par 4s are only easy if the drive has been precise. The best spot in the fairway is often perilously close to a massive fairway bunker.

Third, Pine Needles is a fine example of a fair, strategic golf course without the need for gimmicks. It's not long by modern standards, yet it will not necessarily yield to the big hitter who will likely be outfoxed by the straight-hitting thinker who can find the best spots in the fairways and around the greens from which

to score. That's one reason why Annika Sorenstam won the U.S. Women's Open here in 1996 while Laura Davies struggled at times, even bogeying the short par 5 10th on one occasion during the tournament.

Fourth—ambiance. Great golf courses have a great and stately air. There's something special about Pine Needles.

Fifth—history and tradition. The short par 3 third is a devilish hole that's completely untouched since Ross' day. Look around the reserved yet elegant clubhouse and you'll see photos of all the great golfers who have played here. When you play at Pine Needles, you're walking in the footsteps of the greats.

Sixth, you *can* walk in the footsteps of the greats—anytime you choose. Carts are not required.

Seventh—Peggy Kirk Bell, one of the most important and influential figures in the game. She's the keeper of this great course and it shows.

Every hole at Pine Needles is solid, yet more than a couple stand out. The aforementioned par 3rd, just a short iron or wedge to a narrow green, is the most photographed hole on the course, but the most difficult par 3 comes just two holes later and registers a severe 210 from the tips. The green is well bunkered and has to be one of the most difficult on the course, especially if you're above the hole; par is a great score. Another well-documented hole is the par 5 10th, with its drive over water, the shortcut to the green protected to the left by a nasty bunker. Even for mere mortals, it's a birdie hole. Another fine yet under-appreciated par 3 is the 16th, about 170 from the middle tees, ever so slightly uphill to a long and narrow green flanked by some of the deepest bunkers on the course.

The 16th is one of four tough closing holes culminating in the par 4 18th, another solid medium-length par 4 all downhill.

Today's PGA Tour player with his titanium driver and hot ball would probably bring Pine Needles to its knees, but so what? Pine Needles boasts more than enough charm, challenge, tradition and outstanding golf to make up for whatever length it might lack. Anyone who visits the Pinehurst area should make the time to play this old and wonderful golf course. Play it once, and you'll want to play here each and every time you visit.

Amenities include a practice green, range, chipping green, locker room, bar, restaurant, rental clubs and a pro shop.

You can now walk anytime at Pine Needles. Approximate cost, including cart, is $110 high and $85 low.

Pinehurst Resort
Carolina Vista Dr., Pinehurst
• (800) ITS GOLF, (800) 487-4653

Here it is—the golf resort of golf resorts. If there's a resort that's more golf-oriented than Pinehurst, please show us. If there's a resort where golf is more celebrated and important, please take us there. If there's a resort with more high-quality courses, we'd love to see it. If there's a course with more history and prestige than Pinehurst, prove it.

People come to the Pinehurst Resort and Country Club from the all over the globe, and they're not coming for the logoed golf towels in the golf shop or the beer and hot wings in the Ryder Cup Lounge. Yes, there's lawn bowls and other activities available through the resort, but people come here for golf. That's what Pinehurst is all about.

The actual resort dates back to 1895 when Boston soda fountain magnate James Walker Tufts bought about 5,500 acres of timberland in the middle of North Carolina. Tufts hired Frederick Olmstead to design and plan the resort and accompanying village. Olmstead designed New York City's Central Park as well as the grounds of the Biltmore Estate in Asheville, North Carolina (see our North Carolina's Mountains chapter).

The first golf course opened in 1897. Tufts hired Donald Ross as the professional and greenskeeper in 1900, and it was from Pinehurst that Ross built a reputation as the finest golf course architect ever.

The hotel that now dominates the scenery opened in 1901. It's called The Carolina. The resort flourished and even stayed open throughout the Great Depression, when staff were compensated in coupons redeemable for merchandise in the Pinehurst Village General Store.

In 1943, the Holly Inn, the first hotel in Pinehurst, began year-round operations. In 1970, the Tufts family sold the resort to the Diamondhead Corporation, which in turn sold it in 1984 to present owners, Club Corp. For a better picture of the history of the course, take a stroll down the hallway on the first floor of the hotel where the staff has intelligently laid out the story behind the Pinehurst resort. There's more history in the clubhouse, where the stories and pictures are more golf-oriented.

As soon as Donald Ross began sculpting great golf courses here, great golfers followed— coming here for tournaments and other events or just for pleasure. You'll see their names in the clubhouse. Palmer, Nicklaus, Snead, Hogan, Pavin, Love, Bobby Jones, Miller, Watson and Faldo are just a few of the greatest of the greats who have come for the challenge, usually on course #2—in Ross's opinion the greatest test of championship golf he designed. Others must think so too: Pick virtually any golf publication, and Pinehurst #2 is consistently ranked in the top 10 of all golf courses throughout the country. The course proved its worth magnificently at the 1999 U.S. Open, and will again hold the tournament in 2005.

Pinehurst #2 has also hosted what has to be the most prestigious amateur tournament outside the U.S. Amateur: the North and South Championship. Some of the greatest names in the sport have won this tournament on their way to stardom as professionals. Once a professional tournament, it was Ben Hogan's first win. Other tournaments hosted by Pinehurst include the PGA Tour Championship, the PGA Championship, the Ryder Cup, the U.S. Senior Open, the PGA Junior Championship and the U.S. Amateur.

As part of Pinehurst's centennial celebration, the resort opened a new Tom Fazio-designed course, Pinehurst #8, in late 1995. In early 2000, the resort opened the Fazio redesign of #4.

Golf amenities at Pinehurst include a range (called Maniac Hill), chipping and putting greens galore, a full golf school with some wonderful packages, restaurants, a bar called the 91st hole, locker rooms, shoe-shine service, rental clubs and pro shops. On course #1 through course #5, you can book ahead for a caddie. The cost will range from $25 to $50, depending on tip and the number of bags carried.

Unless you're a member of Pinehurst Country Club, you typically need to stay at the Pinehurst Hotel to play here. At least, that's the official word. Some local hotels and some other resorts in the area offer limited access to Pinehurst courses, but you didn't hear that from us, OK? But why not get the full experience and stay at the hotel anyway: It's the centerpiece of Pinehurst hospitality, and it's well worth the price of admission, which fluctuates seasonally. The hotel offers several packages, many of which are good values, especially in the evergreen season (winter).

Pinehurst's Carolina hotel has 220 rooms in all. The Manor Inn, which is closer to the village, offers 49 rooms. And golf course condominiums are available as well. The resort recently purchased the Holly Inn and completed a multi-million dollar refurbishment.

The hotel provides ample meeting and exhibition space. In addition to the golf courses, which we promise to get to soon, there are 24 tennis courts, a lake for sailing and other watersports, swimming pools, a croquet court and a bowls lawn. A shuttle service can whisk you around the resort. And, of course, the hotel offers a full range of dining and drinking options, all serviced by staff dressed in britches. We think you'll love the hotel, and we're certain you'll love the golf courses. It's expensive but a great value if you believe in the tradition and excellence of a truly world-class resort. Go ahead! Get out the credit card, close your eyes, think of Donald Ross and have a great time. You won't regret it.

A note about rates. Pinehurst's courses are reserved entirely for resort guests, and most resort guests are here as part of golf packages. The average rate for a three-day stay in the high season runs about $700 per person (double occupancy), and surcharges of about $70 apply for golf on #2, #7 and #8. Caddies—and you

really should indulge in this—cost $37.50 per person excluding gratuity.

Pinehurst #1

Championship Yardage: 6102
Slope: 117   **Par: 70**
Men's Yardage: 5873
Slope: 114   **Par: 70**
Ladies' Yardage: 5307
Slope: 117   **Par: 73**

Pinehurst #1 opened with nine holes in 1899; a second nine opened in 1901. Dr. D. Leroy Culver, an amateur architect, designed the first nine. Donald Ross revised the first nine, added a second nine and made major changes to the course in 1913, 1937, 1940 and 1946. This rolling, wooded track has bermudagrass fairways and bentgrass greens.

As the number implies, #1 was the first course built at the Pinehurst resort and probably the first course that Donald Ross designed—unless you count the work he completed at Oakley Country Club near Boston. For Donald Ross fans, #1 is a shrine of sorts and a great example of his work. Although the course is not long by modern standards, it's still a fine test of golf: rolling fairways and tough, small greens. A couple of holes offer decent length off the tee. The fairways reveal examples of devilish Ross bunkers with steep grass faces—a true hazard for any golfer. Around the greens you'll see more grass-faced bunkers, and if you have a bad day with your short game, your score is likely to become larger than you'd care to admit. If you're a low handicapper, this course will provide a good tune-up for some of the other challenges that await you. If you're a mid- or high handicapper, you'll find this course pleasantly manageable if you keep the ball straight and putt well. The course plays a lot longer that it seems.

You can walk and carry your own bag on this walkable course. Approximate cost, including cart, is $94 high, $72 medium and $59 low.

Pinehurst #2

Championship Yardage: 7053
Slope: 131   **Par: 72**
Men's Yardage: 6354
Slope: 127   **Par: 72**
Ladies' Yardage: 5863
Slope: 135   **Par: 74**

Pinehurst #2 opened with nine holes in 1901; an additional nine opened in 1906. Donald Ross designed the course and made major changes in 1922, 1933, 1934, 1935 and 1946, although he constantly made minor improvements. Changes were made after Ross's death in 1948, but descendants of the Tufts family

The 11th hole at Pine Needles is one of the best driving holes in the Pinehurst area.

Photo: Pine Needles

and others have brought the course back to its original form and shape. Rees Jones recently supervised the refurbishment of the greens in time for the 1999 U.S. Open.

So much has been said and written about #2, particularly for the U.S. Open, that it's somewhat unfair to summarize the course and the experience in just a few paragraphs. It's easily the finest golf course in the Carolinas as well as one of the best public-access courses in the world. And it's the main reason why serious golfers come to Pinehurst. It's hosted several major and professional tournaments and is home to arguably the top amateur tournament in the country (behind the U.S. Amateur)—the North and South. For many professional golfers, this is the finest course anywhere.

In summer and fall 1996, the course completed a number of grassing changes to get ready for the U.S. Open. Management re-seeded the greens with a strain of bentgrass called G2, and the areas around the greens are now a finer strain of bermudagrass.

So what makes #2 No. 1? At first, you might wonder. There are courses with better scenery and better views. There are courses with bigger clubhouses. And there are courses that will make your jaw drop more, that are more difficult. Yet for any perceived shortcomings, Pinehurst #2 routinely remains at the top of the list of

the greatest golf courses. Even with a somewhat moderate slope rating, few of the world's best beat up #2 during the U.S. Open—Payne Stewart won the tournament by shooting one-under par for four rounds. So, what's the big deal?

Two big deals. First, this is the course that Donald Ross built and nurtured to what he thought was perfection. He eventually built a house next to the 3rd green near the confluence of the 3rd, 4th, 5th and 6th holes. He deemed Pinehurst #2 the greatest test of championship golf that he designed—that the person who won a championship here would be a golfer who had come as near as possible to all-around excellence.

The terms "championship course" and "you'll have to use every club in your bag" have become well-worn clichés, but they apply at #2 perhaps more than anywhere in the Carolinas. Donald Ross built more than 400 courses in his lifetime—and this was his best.

Second, and perhaps more importantly, #2 is a golf purist's dream. Pinehurst #2 is a stunning example of what makes a great golf course: a designer who understands that a course is defined by the variety and fairness of the strategic test.

Each hole here has its own set of difficulties and problems. Lose your concentration and your score will mushroom. In fact, it's a course where even the low to mid-handicapper will find that the score has somehow reached levels that mirror the national debt. From the back tees, we were humbled to the point of tears by the end of the round. Thankfully, on a second non-golfing visit, we spent two hours in the company of legendary starter and ranger Americus "Max" Lamberti, former curator of the PGA Hall of Fame. Mr. Lamberti pointed out that many great golfers have been similarly humbled by the course. They may drive the ball well (you must) and hit their fair share of greens (you must), but it's the golfer with the creative and wizard-like short game who will ultimately prevail. Notice how it was Phil Mickelson against Payne Stewart down the stretch at the U.S. Open. Stewart won because he routinely got up and down on the back nine from a variety of tortuous spots.

The fairways are generous at #2, but it helps to be in the right place—and where you want to be often is where Ross placed a bunker or love grass. From there, your approach shot, often with a long iron, needs to hit the right portion of the green for a birdie putt. The route to the correct portion of the green is guarded by deep grass-faced bunkers or rough-infested hollows or a swale. And more often than not, the green plays smaller and the less-than-perfect iron shot will roll off the edge. This is where the fun begins—and where the wizard of the short game will prevail.

To get up and down requires such a masterful touch that if you do so with relative ease you'll feel ready to give a short game clinic or write a book.

At #2, if you play to the top of your game, you'll be rewarded; but if you're off, you'll be in for a long, frustrating round. What could be closer to the true spirit and challenge of the game?

Low handicappers will love the constant challenge and should play from the back tees. Mid-handicappers should play from the middle tees and hold on to their hats. High handicappers: Try to play within yourself, take in the experience, ignore the score and try not to impede the progress of the group behind you. Pinehurst #2 is a course you should play before you pass away. Despite the fee, you'll want to come back time and time again, constantly drawn by the addiction and timelessness of the greatest of all Donald Ross courses.

You must take a cart unless you take a caddie. Go ahead and take a caddie to experience the full effect and to keep you loose and limber.

You can book a tee time with your reservation at the hotel. Approximate cost, including cart, is $225.

Pinehurst #3

Championship Yardage:	5593
Slope: 117	**Par:** 70
Ladies' Yardage:	5307
Slope: 117	**Par:** 71

Pinehurst #3 opened in 1907. An additional nine opened in 1910. Donald Ross designed the course and made major changes in 1936 and 1946. The course is set on rolling, wooded terrain, with bermudagrass fairways and bentgrass greens.

Pinehurst #3 is similar to #1: short yet still quite challenging. And, like #1, it should not be discounted as too short to be interesting, and it plays a lot longer than its yardage. It's a course where you must be straight off the tee and sharp with your short game to score well. The greens are small and crowned; there's plenty of trouble lurking off the tee in the form of deep grass-faced bunkers and irritating swales and hollows. Pinehurst #3 will be best appreciated by those whose strength is accuracy, not distance. Many of the holes on #3 have been praised by avid Donald Ross fan Ben Crenshaw, who spent some time here studying the greens.

You can walk on this walkable course or take a cart. Approximate cost, including cart, is $94 high, $72 medium and $59 low.

Pinehurst #4

Championship Yardage:	6919
Slope: 126	**Par:** 72
Men's Yardage:	6396
Slope: 117	**Par:** 72
Ladies' Yardage:	5696
Slope: 119	**Par:** 73

Pinehurst #4 opened nine holes in 1912 and nine more in 1919. Donald Ross designed the course, and Robert Trent Jones revised the layout in 1973, lengthening it and adding water. Rees Jones revised the layout once more in 1982. In 1999, Tom Fazio completely redesigned the course, re-routing several holes.

At the time of writing, Tom Fazio had just completed his work. Early word is that Fazio's reworking of #4 has been a success, giving it a degree of consistency lacking in the original layout(s).

Pinehurst #5

Championship Yardage:	6929
Slope: 130	**Par:** 72
Men's Yardage:	6357
Slope: 123	**Par:** 72
Ladies' Yardage:	5720
Slope: 131	**Par:** 73

Pinehurst #5, an Ellis Maples design, opened in 1961 on rolling, wooded terrain. Fairways are bermudagrass; greens, bentgrass.

This one of the lesser-known courses in the Pinehurst crown and perhaps its most underrated. Maples lived in the Pinehurst area and supervised construction on Donald Ross's final design at Raleigh Country Club. Maples was a fine golfer who once shot 62. But he was also a teacher of the game and understood the needs and desires of the average player. Maples became one of the most sought-after architects in the Southeast. It's fitting that Pinehurst tapped Maples to design a course, and he provided the resort with one of his finest efforts.

This course plays long from the back tees. But it's still fair and fun—though more so for the average player from the forward tees. Ironically, although Maples is sometimes considered the master of the long, sweeping and majestic dogleg, you won't find much of that here. Instead, you'll play some wonderful straightaway holes that demand accuracy. There's plenty of variety, from long and short par 4s to par 5s where the long-hitter will feel somewhat inclined to gamble. Pinehurst #5 is a tremendously playable course as well as being just plain fun to play.

This walkable course allows walking. Approximate cost, including cart, is $94 high, $72 medium and $59 low.

Pinehurst #6

Championship Yardage:	7157
Slope: 139	Par: 72
Men's Yardage:	6603
Slope: 132	Par: 72
Ladies' Yardage:	5430
Slope: 125	Par: 72

Pinehurst #6 opened in 1979. George Fazio and nephew Tom Fazio tag-teamed the design here. The course is set in rolling, wooded terrain, with bermudagrass fairways and bentgrass greens.

Although it has been ranked as one of North Carolina's better golf courses, Pinehurst #6, like #5, is underrated. This course is "off-campus," and you'll have to drive or take the shuttle bus to get there. It's away from the main bulk of the Pinehurst courses and its topography is more undulating. Fazio did not want to compete with the Ross designs, thus you'll find #6 quite different from its counterparts. The site is more dramatic, and there are some significant elevation changes.

When #6 opened, many felt Fazio had created the most difficult Pinehurst course. You have to keep the ball in play here; if you miss the fairways, you might end up in thick vegetation or water or on steep fall-offs, and you may have to negotiate some mounds and swales. It doesn't look difficult, but as we all know, looks can be deceiving. Better golfers will have all they can handle from the back tees.

Tom Fazio returned to the course in 1991 to soften some of the green contours, but it's still possible to shoot some big numbers here. For a kinder, gentler ride, shoot from the forward tees; it's still an exciting track from there.

The course is walkable for the fit, but walking is restricted. Approximate cost, including cart, is $94 high, $72 medium and $59 low.

Pinehurst #7

Championship Yardage:	7152
Slope: 117	Par: 72
Men's Yardage:	6692
Slope: 114	Par: 72
Ladies' Yardage:	4996
Slope: 117	Par: 72

Pinehurst #7 opened in 1986. Rees Jones designed this lengthy course on rolling, wooded terrain with homes bordering some of the holes. In the fairways, you'll find bermudagrass; on the greens, bentgrass.

Pinehurst #7, like #6, is another "off-campus" golf course. It's been consistently rated as one of the top 10 golf courses in North Carolina and as one of the best resort courses in the country. Locals, however, feel that it's a little overrated and are happy to leave it to the legions of resort golfers who flock there.

Rees Jones is one of the most in-demand golf course architects in the nation, and he's created a significant course here. Some golfers are not excited about Jones's work, and a few locals feel there are too many uphill or blind shots. Still, it's impossible to describe the course without being positive. There's simply too much variety, interest and natural beauty to ignore.

Pinehurst #7 blends elements of links golf with elements of Pine Valley (as if most of us will ever play at Pine Valley!). There are lots of downhill tee shots, mounds and severely tiered, undulating greens to make life extra-interesting. There's also quite a bit of water, as well as bunkers of all shapes and sizes.

If you're a traditionalist, perhaps you'll enjoy some of the older Pinehurst courses. But if you're a fan of Rees Jones and modern architecture, you'll absolutely love #7. We found Pinehurst #7 to be a spectacular course, deserving of its high ranking. It's worth a visit if you're in the Pinehurst area. It will certainly provide a serious challenge.

You must take a cart, although efforts are being made to introduce walking on the course. Approximate cost, including cart, is $200 high, $117 medium and $104 low.

Pinehurst #8

Championship Yardage:	7092
Slope: 135	Par: 72
Men's Yardage:	6692
Slope: 125	Par: 72
Ladies' Yardage:	4996
Slope: 112	Par: 72

Pinehurst #8 opened in late 1995. Tom Fazio designed the course on typical Sandhills terrain: slightly undulating land replete with sandy waste areas and pine forest. In the fairways, you'll find bermudagrass; on the greens, a new strain of bentgrass called G2, which is supposed to let the greens remain firm and fast in hot weather and is now used on Pinehurst #2 and other Pinehurst courses.

The owners of Pinehurst Resort and Country Club hired Tom Fazio to design and build the course that would celebrate the 100-year anniversary of their great golfing destination—quite an honor and challenge for Fazio, who stepped up to the plate and hit a home run with #8. There are so many excellent golf courses in the Pinehurst area that it's difficult for one track to stand out among all the others, but #8 succeeds in making the statement, "I want to be one of the top resort courses in the world even though I'm just a youngster." Apart from Pinehurst #6, which is really the work of his uncle, #8 represents a rarity: a public-access Fazio course in the Carolinas, even if the price is way up there. And in case you didn't know, Tom Fazio is regarded as probably the top golf course architect in America today.

Pinehurst gave Fazio a pretty good piece of land with which to create #8. It's certainly spacious, and, thankfully, there are no houses or condos bordering the fairways. If you enjoy the feeling of being away from everything, you'll really like #8.

But you've paid the significant fee for the golf, right? During your first tussle with this golf course, several things will strike you. From the tee, the best place to aim is not easily discerned: There's a bunker here and there, a clump of trees close to the fairway or a waste area or a swale. You want to bang it down the middle with your driver, but sometimes it's not always clear exactly where you'll find the hallowed ground of the center cut of the fairway. Also striking are the excellent variety of the challenges and the holes. No two holes are the same, and each hole boasts a unique set of challenges achieved without being artificial and without water hazards. There are short par 3s and extremely long par 3s. There's a brutally long par 5 and a reachable one. And there's no easy way to summarize and characterize the par 4s.

The fairways here are wide, and bunkers often lurk near the best position for your approach shot. But perhaps the greatest challenge exists in and around the green complexes, which seem like a tribute to Donald Ross, only harder and larger. Many of the greens are simply enormous, but many play much smaller, what with some severe slopes near the edges—edges that can send your ball into a swale or a bunker with a 5-foot grass face. It's all rather intimidating at times, thus you'll need to bring your very best short game to shoot anywhere near your handicap. With five sets of tees, #8 helps the higher-handicap golfer—at least from the tee box.

Memorable holes. The 1st: a downhill short par 4 of just 361 yards from the tips. The landing area narrows a bit from 150 yards in, with woods and a bunker on the left-hand side that could cause difficulty. Approach shots must be hit to a large green that slopes away from the fairway. The 6th: a monster par 5, 604 yards uphill from the tips; third shot is a wedge or shot iron to a green that features complete death if you go over it.

Over the years, you'll find that #8 will certainly be rated as one of the best golf courses in the Southeast, and *North Carolina Magazine* rated it as the best new course in the state. It's quirky and fun and quite a test. If you're wealthy enough to play it over and over again, you'll find that #8 will provide a different challenge each time out. It's not #2, but it's certainly a wonderful golf course and a fitting tribute and addition to the cradle of American golf.

INSIDERS' TIP

Remember that Pinehurst was originally designed as a winter resort. The temperatures can be mild, the days sunny and the rates for hotels and courses at their lowest in winter. If you're looking for a way to enjoy the Pinehurst area at a reduced price, it's worth taking a risk with the weather and going in the off-season. Most courses overseed the fairways and, thus, they remain in excellent shape throughout the winter.

This course is walkable for the fit, and you can walk anytime. See if you can take a caddie with you. Approximate cost, including cart, is $200 during the high season.

Ranking the best of the best. So far, we've resisted the temptation to rank courses in this book. But here's how we'd rank the Pinehurst octet: 2, 8, 4, 6, 5, 1, 3, 7.

The Pit Golf Links

N.C. Hwy. 5, Pinehurst • (910) 944-1600

Championship Yardage:	**6600**
Slope: 139	**Par: 71**
Men's Yardage:	**6138**
Slope: 128	**Par: 71**
Other Yardage:	**5690**
Slope: 120	**Par: 71**
Ladies' Yardage:	**4759**
Slope: 121	**Par: 72**

Dan Maples designed The Pit Golf Links, which opened in 1984. The course is set in pine barrens, with bermudagrass fairways and bentgrass greens.

Ask locals, even good golfers, what they think about The Pit and there's a sudden moment of silence followed by a slightly glazed look punctuated with "It's like going to the dentist," "It's quite a track" or "It's awesome." You'll either love or hate The Pit.

Oddly, The Pit has its devotees among the mid- to high handicappers. We say "oddly" because The Pit, in addition to being one of the most daring golf courses in the area, is the most penal. If you miss the fairway, that's it. Lost ball. Hole over. As soon as a foursome of duffers arrives and pays the greens fee, you can see Titleist's stock shoot up. You're going to lose a lot of balls if you're not hitting it straight, so be prepared.

You know something's wrong at a golf course when the back tees are called the screw tees. You know something is wrong, or different, when you drive up to the course through the rear end of Southern Pines past industrial plants. Word is The Pit was an excavation site for sand eventually used to build roads in the Great North State. It's a wild site.

The result is a true test of target golf. Maples shows you the landing area (in most cases) and says "hit this or else." It's a truly punishing course in an area known for its less-than-penal tracks. The Pit isn't a beautiful layout by any stretch of the imagination. In fact, it might be the least attractive course in the Pinehurst area. But it makes for exciting golf.

There are some truly unbelievable holes where par seems almost impossible. Take the par 5 15th, for example—the No. 1 handicap hole. From the back tees, at 550 yards, it demands that you bang it straight down the middle. Your approach shot to the small green must tumble through two massive mounds. The next hole, a 100-yard par 3 from the middle tees, features a green on which there is no such thing as a flat pin placement.

But by far the goofiest hole is the par 5 8th. It's just 480 yards from the back, and it plays from an elevated tee. Keep it dead straight or you'll lose your ball—a recurring theme. A solid 3-wood might leave you just 200 yards from the green. However, the green is only 20 yards deep, and a tree to its left makes the hole completely inaccessible if the pin is on the lefthand side. It must be the most puzzling golf hole anywhere. Despite holes like this, the course begs a repeat visit; there is simply nothing like it.

Amenities include a practice green, range, chipping green, locker room, bar and a pro shop.

The course is not very walkable, but you can walk at certain times. Approximate cost, including cart, is $90 high, $80 medium and $55 low.

Seven Lakes Country Club

Seven Lakes Dr., West End
• (910) 673-1092

Championship Yardage:	**6927**
Slope: 133	**Par: 72**
Men's Yardage:	**6151**
Slope: 122	**Par: 72**
Ladies' Yardage:	**5186**
Slope: 128	**Par: 73**

Seven Lakes opened in the early 1970s. Peter Vail Tufts designed the course on rolling, wooded terrain flanked with houses. In the fairways, you'll find bermudagrass; on the greens, bentgrass.

You won't find seven lakes, but you will find a sound course designed by Donald Ross's godson. When the Tufts family decided to sell the Pinehurst resort, Peter Vail established Seven Lakes as a housing development built around a golf course. It should come as no surprise that someone so close to Donald Ross produced such a fine golf course. We didn't see a rip-off of a Ross design. Rather, we saw a well-conceived, challenging, yet playable course with a good reputation among local golfers.

Water comes into play here and there. The fairways are relatively wide, but it will help to play your shot carefully. A few bunkers lurk in the fairways, ready to create trouble. Some greens require daring shots over water from uneven lies. Overall, this fun and thoroughly worthwhile course probably would have made Tufts' godfather proud.

Amenities include a practice green, range, chipping green, locker room, bar, restaurant, rental clubs and a pro shop.

The course is walkable for the fit, but walking is restricted; call for details. Approximate cost, including cart, is $70 high, $65 medium and $55 low.

Talamore at Pinehurst
1595 Midland Rd., Southern Pines
• **(910) 692-5884**

Championship Yardage:	7020
Slope: 142	**Par: 71**
Men's Yardage:	6393
Slope: 134	**Par: 71**
Other Yardage:	6058
Slope: 126	**Par: 71**
Ladies' Yardage:	4995
Slope: 125	**Par: 72**

Talamore at Pinehurst, a Rees Jones design, opened in 1991. The course is set in rolling, wooded terrain. Fairways are bermudagrass, and greens are bentgrass.

Yes, this is where you'll find the llama caddies. Perhaps (?) this is a publicity stunt, but so what? It's a fun addition to a course, and it means that some people are out there walking. And golf needs more walking. The llamas go out about 30 times each year, and it will set you back an additional $100 per person for the luxury of having one of these beasts carry your bag for you. The service is only available from late fall through early spring. Llamas are social creatures, so you must bring them out in pairs or not at all. Book well ahead for llama service, and make sure that you are quite fit: Talamore is not a particularly walkable course, and you'll have to negotiate about 6 miles of undulating terrain.

Let's meet the llama caddies. Dollie Llama (no relation) is the first-known llama caddie in the world; her hobbies include tree pruning and mud wrestling. Jack began caddying in August 1993 and is the quiet and somewhat reserved type. Sir Hogan (again, no relation) is fond of apples and carrots and takes the game fairly seriously. Freddie loves kids and prefers a bad day on the golf course to a good day at the office. Reg the Wonder Llama is still in the opening credits of *Monty Python and the Holy Grail* and is unable to caddie at this time.

We've discussed the llamas, now what about the golf course? It's been highly rated and touted and is a fine example of Rees Jones's work. Rees apparently wanted to make this a thinker's course rather than a muscle layout. Well, he made the course a par 71 that plays more than 7000 yards from the back tees. Of course, you won't have to play the track from there, but you will find plenty of length, even from the front; the course seems to play a bit longer than stated on the card.

The course is picturesque. The bunkers and mounds are attractively shaped and visually appealing—unless your ball happens to be in the bunker or on top of the mound. The greens are undulating and can be particularly difficult if fast. Plenty of trouble lurks, and you'll find that Talamore offers a serious challenge, whatever your ability.

On a course that's remarkably devoid of any truly memorable holes, perhaps the par 3 13th comes to mind, but mostly because it's quite steeply downhill.

Amenities include a practice green, range, chipping green, locker room, bar, restaurant, rental clubs, a beverage cart and a pro shop.

The course is not walkable without a llama, so you'll want to take a cart if you're not taking a llama. You can book a tee time anytime. Approximate cost, including cart, is $95 high, $65 medium and $50 low.

Tobacco Road
442 Tobacco Rd., Sanford
• **(877) 284-3762, (919) 775-1940**

Championship Yardage:	6554
Slope: 150	**Par: 71**
Men's Yardage:	6304
Slope: 142	**Par: 71**
Other Yardage:	5886
Slope: 132	**Par: 71**
Ladies' Yardage:	5094
Slope: 124	**Par: 72**

Tobacco Road, designed by Mike Strantz, opened in 1999. The course is routed through sandy waste areas. Fairways are bermudagrass, and greens are bentgrass.

Like Strantz's True Blue at Myrtle Beach, Tobacco Road is a controversial course that people seem to love or hate. While water isn't a defining feature at Tobacco Road, there's just as much trouble—in the form of desolate looking waste bunkers and love grass infested traps. Thus Tobacco Road is, in many ways, a target golf course where poor shots receive significant punishment. The course also boasts a number of blind shots that are less difficult than they look. Remember: a blind shot is only a blind shot once. Right?

The fairways are mostly fairly wide and

Pinehurst #2 will host its second U.S. Open Championship in 2005.

Photo: Pinehurst Resort & Country Club

somewhat undulating. The greens are large; some undulate considerably, others not so much. Overall, Tobacco Road is one of those courses that everyone should play at least once. If you hate it, head for something more traditional. If you like it, you'll want to come back over and over again.

The course offers a clubhouse and full practice facilities plus a pro shop. Approximate cost, including cart, is $60. Walking is an option most of the time.

Whispering Woods Golf Club
26 Sandpiper Dr., Whispering Pines
• (910) 949-4653

Championship Yardage:	6334	
Slope: 122	Par: 70	
Men's Yardage:	6006	
Slope: No rating	Par: 70	
Ladies' Yardage:	4924	
Slope: No rating	Par: 70	

Whispering Woods opened in 1974. Ellis Maples designed the course on rolling, wooded terrain bordered with houses. In the fairways, you'll find bermudagrass; on the greens, bentgrass.

This fine and relatively mature design is going through something of a renaissance. Whispering Woods has sometimes been confused with the Country Club of Whispering Pines, just a few doors down the way. The new own-

ers of Whispering Woods have pumped a lot of cash into the course, and the result is consistent conditioning and improved play.

Don't let the lack of length fool you. There's plenty of heft from the back tees, particularly if the course is wet. Whispering Woods is more difficult than it looks—and it looks plenty difficult in places. It's probably one of the area's most underestimated courses, and its final hole is one of the most interesting in the area. It's a severe dogleg to the left where the second shot is a short iron over water to a smallish green. Hit the tee shot too far to the left and you must negotiate a steep bank. If you're looking to play a good course in the Pinehurst area at a very affordable price, Whispering Woods is an excellent venue.

Amenities include a practice green, locker room, snack bar, rental clubs and a pro shop.

You must take a cart but may book a tee time anytime. Approximate cost, including cart, is $45 high, $40 medium and $35 low.

Woodlake Country Club
150 Woodlake Blvd., Vass
• (910) 245-4693

Championship Yardage:	7012	
Slope: 134	Par: 72	
Men's Yardage:	6584	
Slope: 129	Par: 72	
Other Yardage:	6144	
Slope: 120	Par: 72	

Ladies' Yardage:	5080
Slope: 128	Par: 72

The golf course at Woodlake Country Club opened in 1969. We bet you didn't know the course was originally called Lake Surf Country Club. Dan and Ellis Maples tag-teamed the design on mostly flat terrain next to a lake. Fairways are bermudagrass; greens, bentgrass.

Woodlake is an outstanding course well worth the short drive from Pinehurst. Its reputation among Pinehurst golfers is excellent. The first few holes border a lake called Woodlake, and you'll have to be accurate. The lake is not a large man-made pond but a seriously massive lake that can generate significant wind. Thus the first few holes can be very difficult, and the wind will play havoc with club selection.

After this potentially brutal introduction to Woodlake, the course leaves the lake and heads for the woods, where the wind is not quite as much a factor. In the woods you'll find plenty of sweeping doglegs the likes of which gained Maples notoriety. There's decent room off the tee, but your ball might find a tree or two if you're not careful. The greens are well-bunkered and large. These "inland" holes offer great variety and challenge, but you'll be glad to know that the course returns to its lakeside location for the final three holes.

The 18th, a wonderful par 5, begs you to go for glory with a second shot over water to a small, well-protected green. Are you gutsy enough? This course is certainly worth the price of admission.

One notable item here is an aquatic driving range. You actually hit balls into the water, and a large subsurface net shags them.

Amenities include a practice green, range, chipping green, locker room, bar, restaurant, rental clubs and a pro shop.

The course is walkable for the fit, although walking is restricted. Approximate cost, including cart, is $85 high, $70 medium and $55 low.

Around Pinehurst and Southern Pines . . .

Fun Things To Do

So you're in Pinehurst and you're not playing golf. What's wrong? It must be raining to the point where even the Japanese golfers are off the courses. Or perhaps it's snowing. Or dark. That's it: It's dark and raining, and even the Japanese are looking for other entertainment.

The **Village of Pinehurst,** built by the original owner of Pinehurst and laid out by Frederick Law Olmstead, is quaint and picturesque with its New England feel. Even the owner of the local bookstore has a New England accent, but she's become Southern enough to greet you with a smile as you walk in.

The village offers some excellent shopping and dining. If you're looking for a unique golf-oriented gift, take a few minutes to visit **Burchfield's Gallery,** (800) 358-4066. Take away a chess set made of golf figurines, a map of Pinehurst #2 in a solid frame, a personalized golf ball, framed golf cartoons, a hole-in-one memento, Pebble Beach bookends—even a ball-drying rack. Perhaps what you'll find most amusing are some of the framed sayings, including "I once gave up golf; it was the most terrifying weekend of my life." If you're looking for a great gift for the golfer who has just about everything, then you'll love Burchfield's.

For those of you who are more culturally inclined, check out the **Performing Arts Center,** 250 N.W. Broad Street, Southern Pines, (910) 692-3611; call for information about upcoming events.

One of the most interesting and least publicized attractions in Pinehurst is the **Tufts Archives** in the **Given Memorial Library,** which is right in the heart of Pinehurst Village. The Tufts Archives are wonderfully arranged, and the result is a presentation that provides the visitor with a comprehensive history of the development of Pinehurst. Call (910) 295-6022 for more information. If it's too wet to play golf, then the Tufts Archives provide an interesting diversion, and it's 5-minute walk from the main Pinehurst Hotel.

Those of you who enjoy gardening and gardens should head towards the **Sir Walter Raleigh Historical Garden,** which is part of **Sandhills Community College,** on Airport Road in Southern Pines. You can reach the garden at (910) 695-3882. The lush wonderland is designed to resemble the type of garden you might have seen when Sir Walter was alive.

For comprehensive information about Pinehurst, contact the **Pinehurst Area Convention and Visitors Bureau,** P.O. Box 2270, Southern Pines, NC 28388, (800) 346-5362.

Where to Eat

You'll find plenty of great places to eat in the Pinehurst vicinity. And you'll discover that most of the better hotels still believe in the importance of matching the quality of the accommodations with the restaurant—something of a rarity these days. Anyway, there's a better variety of cuisine than you might expect in Pinehurst and close surrounds (Southern Pines and Aberdeen), and we've included but a few of the many fine establishments. We also give you a couple of good choices in the Fayetteville area.

It's worth noting that many of the options we give you for accommodations in the next section of this chapter also sport excellent restaurants on their premises. Round out your dining choices by perusing these selections. Refer to our Preface for an explanation of the pricing code.

Beefeater's
$$ • 672 W. Broad St., Southern Pines
• (910) 692-5550

As the name implies, Beefeater's is an outstanding place for beef, from filet mignon to prime rib. There's more, however, in the form of seafood, chicken and lamb chops, the latter being somewhat of a rarity in these parts; serve it up with mint jelly and a big baked potato and you're in fine fettle. The ambiance is low ceilinged and white tableclothed but not stuffy—and more casual than you might think. Get dressed up if you want, but feel free to visit the lounge after a round and still dressed in shorts.

According to our waitress, Beefeater's is popular with those who hail from climes north of the Mason-Dixon Line. Evidently, the bartender is just a little rude to those folks, but no one seems to mind too much: He's not particularly conservative when it comes to pouring mixed drinks.

The restaurant is busy on most nights, particularly so on the weekends and during the peak season. It's the type of restaurant where golfers in the area for a week come over and over again.

The Coves
$-$$ • Market Square, Pinehurst
• (910) 295-3400

Just opposite the Holly Inn and right in the thick of the village of Pinehurst is The Coves, an eatery and drinkery with two distinct characters.

Upstairs, you'll find a restaurant where the atmosphere is on the casual side of formal. Downstairs, you'll find a subterranean bar that looks like it could become a touch raucous in the later hours of the evening.

The restaurant is open for lunch and dinner.

For lunch, go downstairs and ask the bartender to pull you a pint of Bass ale, then order a hamburger—one of the best around. For dinner, impress your better half with the varied menu and the better-than-average selection of wine. Then head downstairs for a game of Putt-Putt, another Bass ale, a shag on the dance floor and a game of darts.

The Coves is a locally owned gem that's, dare we say it, not quite as stuffy as some of the other eateries in and around the village. Perhaps that's why it's so popular.

Henning's Restaurant
$$ • U.S. Hwy. 1, Southern Pines
• (910) 692-8585

A local favorite pops up in a somewhat unlikely place: the Southern Pines Holiday Inn. We're told that "All Dishes are Personally Supervised by Mrs. Henning," but that may just be an advertising slogan. Still, the menu is strong and varied, with such excellent fare as veal scaloppini alla Drew, broiled baby flounder with crabmeat, North Carolina rainbow trout, steak and oysters and the always popular fresh fruit au Kirch. On Sundays, march over to the extremely famous Sunday buffet. Even if you're not staying at the Holiday Inn, Henning's is worth a visit if you are hungry for a big meal at a moderate price.

The Lobster House
$$$ • 448 Person St., Fayetteville
• (910) 485-8866

The Lobster House is so well known it's almost a landmark. As the name implies, the Lobster House is the place to go for live Maine lobster—if you're into that sort of thing. If lobster is not your game, sample other fresh seafood entrees. If beef is your taste, try the prime rib or charcoal steaks. It's closed on Mondays and is only open for dinner.

The Pine Crest Inn Restaurant
$$$ • Dogwood Rd., Pinehurst
• (910) 295-6121

The Pine Crest Inn is a place where a lot of people stay, but more still come to the excellent restaurant that serves breakfast and dinner. Breakfast is a hearty affair complete with fresh fruit, eggs cooked to your liking, waffles, pancakes and other such goodies. After a round or two of golf, dinner is a slightly more formal affair served in one of two elegant dining rooms adjacent to the bar. Once again, there's a lot to eat. Start out with some fried button mushrooms in horseradish, then follow them up with entrees like rack of lamb, prime rib or filet mignon. Finish it all off with the greatest of all English desserts: trifle. Afterwards, return to the bar, where there is usually much merriment to be found.

Raffaele's
$$ • 1550 U.S. Hwy. 1, Southern Pines
• (910) 692-1952

Raffaele's is situated at the northern end of the main business district in Southern Pines. The cuisine is Italian, and you'll find a real attention to detail in the preparation of the food.

Raffaele's is a local favorite, so much so that one local told us not to write about it so it won't become too full of tourists. That's probably as good a recommendation as you can find in the Pinehurst area.

Begin your meal with stuffed mushrooms, move on to spaghetti with Italian sausage and complement everything with a beefy bottle of Valpolicella. The menu isn't massively extensive, but we feel confident you'll find something you really enjoy. Raffaele's is open for lunch and dinner.

Roma Gourmet Italian Restaurant
$$ • 3729 Sycamore Dairy Rd., Fayetteville
• (910) 864-1313

At Roma Gourmet you'll find a menu that includes live lobster, steaks, seafood and Roma's brand of Italian cuisine. With advance notice, Giovanni Giannone will prepare anything your stomach desires. In addition to cooking, Giovanni will sing any of your old Italian favorites—although he doesn't necessarily need advance warning for this. For your information, Giovanni came to America from Sicily more than 25 years ago, jumped ship and ended up in Fayetteville.

The Squire's Pub
$$ • 1720 U.S. Hwy. 1 S., Southern Pines
• (910) 695-1161

The Squire's is a fun watering hole and restaurant that's popular with locals and out-of-town golfers alike. The ambiance approaches that of an English pub, and you'll certainly find the same sort of friendliness. When the professional tours are in town, Squire's is a magnet. For in-

stance, when the LPGA cruised through, long-hitting Laura Davies arrived with an entourage of 10 and proceeded to fill up the bar. The manager quantified the final bill as "plenty." If you're angling to see a famous golfer enjoying a drink and meal, this is a place where it might happen.

Squires is a fantastic place to enjoy a drink. Choose from among more than 40 beers, most of them from England, and if you're in the mood for something stronger, how about a martini? (Two of these, and your handicap is five strokes less; three, and you'll be telling everyone that you just took £20 off Laura Davies.)

Thai Orchid
$$ • 1404 Sandhills Blvd., Aberdeen
• (910) 944-9299

And now for something completely different. Thai Orchid is the only restaurant that serves good Thai food in an unpretentious setting. You won't be coming here for the atmosphere necessarily, but if you're a devotee of Thai food and you need a fix while golfing in Pinehurst, you'll want to come here.

Try the Thai grilled steak, Bangkok duck or spicy and sour fish. Start with koong da bog (shrimp roll) and wash the whole meal down with a cool Singha beer from Thailand. You can have your food prepared Thai hot, extra hot, medium or mild. The restaurant also offers excellent lunch specials. You'll leave with change from a $5 bill.

Where to Stay

As we've mentioned, one of the attractions of Pinehurst is the fact that there's something here for everyone's budget. You can spend a lot of money here on places to play, or you can spend a lot less on your hotel room and spend what you save to play on the better golf courses. If you want tradition, service and amenities, you'll find it here (for a price); if all you want is a basic room with Clint Eastwood movies and a shower, you'll find that here as well.

It should be noted that most of the following hotels have excellent restaurants and wonderful dining rooms, some of which we've mentioned above. They are all worth visiting for their restaurants, even if you are not staying there as a guest. Refer to our Preface for an explanation of the pricing code.

Fairfield Inn by Marriott
$$ • 562 Cross Creek Mall, Fayetteville
• (910) 487-1400, (800) 228-2800

Fayetteville's Fairfield Inn by Marriott is by

the All-American Freeway at U.S. Highway 401—one of the city's busiest intersections. The inn offers 135 clean and comfortable rooms at reasonable rates. You'll get free cable TV and local calls plus access to an outdoor pool. Children 17 and younger stay for free.

Foxfire Resort and Country Club
$-$$$ • Hoffman Rd., in Foxfire Village, Pinehurst • (910) 295-5555

We've already told you that Foxfire has two fine Gene Hamm golf courses, but even if that were not so, you should consider staying at Foxfire anyway, particularly if you're looking for great value in a setting that's relaxed and secluded. Foxfire is also well suited for conferences.

At Foxfire, you'll stay in a condominium equipped with fireplace, telephone, TV with ESPN and the Golf Channel, a living room, ample sleeping space and facilities to allow you to do your own cooking. Or wander over to the lodge for breakfast or dinner. There's also a lounge where the bartender will stay as late as you do.

Play at other fine courses in the area can be arranged by the courteous and well-connected staff. You'll really enjoy the hospitality and value at Foxfire.

Hampton Inn
$$ • 1675 U.S. Hwy. 1, Southern Pines • (910) 692-9266, (800) 626-7866

The Hampton Inn is a modern motel-style accommodation that's always popular with golfers and visitors. There are 126 guest rooms, and rates include free continental breakfast. Amenities include a pool, cable TV with HBO, meeting room, guest laundry room and fax service. Local phone calls are free. There are golf packages with access to 18 local golf courses. The Hampton Inn's location could not be better.

The Holiday Inn
$$ • U.S. Hwy. 1 Bypass and Morganton Rd., Southern Pines • (910) 692-8585, (800) 647-STAY

As you enter Southern Pines from the north, you can't help but notice the Holiday Inn—it will be on your right just before you enter the main drag. For years the Holiday Inn has been a local stalwart and a popular place to stay among the golfing public. The hotel offers more than 160 guest rooms and suites. Enjoy the pool, room service, cable TV with HBO and four tennis courts plus a game room and fitness center. Golf packages are available, and most packages

include free breakfast. Meeting and exhibit space is available as well.

On-site Hennings restaurant offers three meals a day and serves a surprising variety of dishes plus a sizeable breakfast buffet. But most importantly, there's TAMS lounge, where, a few years ago, author Scott Martin served notice of his karaoke prowess with a show-stopping rendition of George Strait's "All My Ex's Live in Texas."

The Holly Inn
$$-$$$ • Cherokee Rd., Pinehurst • (910) 295-2300

The Holly Inn was the first hotel in Pinehurst, and it lives on today as one of its finest. There's a wonderful and understated charm to the place that's both relaxing and timeless. You'll feel like you're stepping back in time as soon as you pass through the doors.

That feeling hasn't left, even though Pinehurst Resort and Hotel recently purchased the property and outspent an unlimited budget restoring it to its former glory. Estimates vary, but Pinehurst is rumored to have spent about $10 million on this building. The results are truly magnificent.

The restaurant is also worth mentioning because it's one of the best in Pinehurst. The dining room, with its cupola roof, is like a scene out of *The Great Gatsby*; check out the intricate molding. Feast on duck with a smoked salmon appetizer; wash it down with a robust claret.

The rooms are all quite different, each wonderful and traditionally appointed with antique furniture. The inn offers a number of golf packages, and the golf course access is excellent, especially now that the Pinehurst runs the hotel. Once you've finished your round, relax with a gin and tonic in the garden, under a shade tree or on the veranda. The inn is part of the Historic Hotels of America and the National Trust for Historic Preservation.

Mid Pines Inn and Golf Club
$$-$$$ • 1010 Midland Rd., Southern Pines • (910) 692-2114

If you've read the description of the course at Mid Pines, you know the inn has always been a popular spot for meetings—and for good reason. Pinehurst Hotel notwithstanding, there might not be a more charming and stately building in the area.

All 118 guest rooms are graciously furnished with period antiques. Other amenities are geared toward business meetings and include full conference facilities that are perfect for small to midsize groups. The inn actually dates back to 1921. The cuisine in the restaurant is wonderful, and you'll feel like you're getting away from it all in the traditional atmosphere.

Golf packages are available, and the staff will work to get you a tee time at a course of your choosing other than Mid Pines or its sister course, Pine Needles.

The Pinehurst Hotel at Pinehurst Resort and Country Club
$$$-$$$$ • Carolina Vista Dr., Pinehurst • (910) 295-6811, (800) 487-4653

We've already gone through what makes the golf courses at Pinehurst so special, and golf is what Pinehurst is all about, so read about the courses before you read about the hotel. Driving through the Village of Pinehurst, you will surely stumble across the grand and magnificent Pinehurst Hotel, now renamed The Carolina. It's hosted all the great golfers in addition to some of the most famous people in the universe. And it's been an award-winning accommodation 13 years in a row.

As soon as you enter the hotel, your bags will be handled by a bellhop in plus-fours. Enjoy this new and wonderful experience as you're taken care of in 1920s fashion. The rooms are traditionally appointed but offer all modern conveniences. In addition to the golf courses, the hotel offers children's programs, a swimming pool, a lake, tennis courts, croquet, lawn bowls and historical tours. You'll find a variety of restaurants as well as the Ryder Cup Lounge, where you can have a drink and discuss whether Lanny should have picked Curtis as the wildcard choice (he shouldn't have). It's a place for a blowout, so get out the Osmium credit card . . . you'll enjoy every second of it.

The Pine Crest Inn
$$-$$$ • Dogwood Rd., Pinehurst • (910) 295-6121

Donald Ross purchased the Pine Crest Inn in 1921 and owned it until his death in 1948. Thus, for the golfing purist, the Pine Crest Inn is a special place—almost hallowed territory.

Today's Pine Crest Inn is known as one of the most popular and famous places to stay, eat and drink in Pinehurst. It's also one of the

most fun and, at times, rambunctious—but in a polite way.

The rooms are wonderfully appointed and offer modern amenities—in-room telephones and color TV with the all-important Golf Channel. The atmosphere is like being at home. The inn's excellent restaurant serves traditional cuisine. But perhaps the most famous part of the Pine Crest is Mrs. B's Bar where, since the inn's inception, golfers have come to recount their day of adventure and calamity on the links. The bartender, in addition to dispensing adult beverages, also flows with wit and wisdom about golf. And did we mention the occasional well-directed barb? One employee has said: "We have no featured or specialty drinks as such, but whatever the golfers drink, they usually end up singing."

There's nothing pretentious about the Pine Crest; it's pure fun and pure golf. If there's a hotel with better access to local golf courses, please let us know. In addition to all the Pinehurst Courses (including #2), the folks at the Pine Crest can get you on just about anywhere, often at a special rate.

Pine Needles
$$-$$$ • 1000 Midland Rd., Southern Pines • (910) 692-7111

For a full description of the magnificent course at Pine Needles, see the entry earlier in this chapter. The course is reserved for hotel guests only. The hotel offers 71 sleeping rooms in Swiss-style lodges. Room amenities include full bathrooms and showers, cable TV with ESPN and the Golf Channel and a great view of the enormous practice facility. Guest services include a heated pool, grass tennis courts, sauna, dining rooms, a lounge and learning center. The golf packages include unlimited greens fees on the Pine Needles course. The staff can arrange tee times for you at other courses in the area as well.

Prince Charles Hotel and Conference Center
$$$ • 450 Hay St., Fayetteville • (910) 433-4444

In historic downtown Fayetteville, the Prince Charles Hotel and Conference Center is

> **INSIDERS' TIP**
> Several private courses offer tee times in tandem with golf packages. These courses and their designers include: Pinehurst Plantation (Ed Seay and Arnold Palmer), Pinehurst National (Jack Nicklaus), Pinewild (Gene Hamm) and Southern Pines Elks Club (Donald Ross).

PINEHURST/ SANDHILLS

an elegantly restored 105-room hotel that's one of the finest in the region. Luxurious suites with wet bars are available. You'll find conference space for up to 350 people. Ask about corporate rates as well. Chloe's restaurant features continental cuisine and is a great place to indulge in Sunday brunch. The Prince Charles is also home to Babe's, a nostalgic sports bar that serves an express lunch.

Golf Equipment

A number of Pinehurst area courses have excellent golf shops where you'll find just about everything you'll need to outfit yourself for a round. And it's here that a number of PGA pros have been trained in the art of personal club fitting.

Three prominent golf shops are in Southern Pines near the junction of U.S. highways 1 and 15/501. **Spoon and Mashie**, (910) 944-1982, on U.S. 1, is one the largest and best-equipped golf stores in the Carolinas and carries just about every type of club made. The store can custom fit clubs and offers full repair services as well. **Robert's Golf and Tennis**, (910) 944-2757, offers a full range of gear and clubs in a friendly atmosphere; it's on U.S. 1 in Aberdeen. And at **Carolina Custom Golf**, behind the Chamber of Commerce on U.S. 15/501, Southern Pines, (910) 695-1670, you'll find a massive store as well as a range with mats where you can pay $5 and hit balls all day.

Golf Instruction

As you might expect, Pinehurst is a great place to learn how to play or to improve your technique. Just about every course has excellent practice facilities, many of which have been specially designed by well-known architects. And most courses have PGA professionals who are qualified to help you with your game. A couple of courses boast teaching professionals

who are sought after by the better golfers in the Sandhills and the Carolinas. Probably the two best-known golf schools are at Pinehurst and Pine Needles.

The **Golf Advantage School** at Pinehurst Resort and Country Club, Carolina Vista Drive, Pinehurst, is designed to help golfers of all skill levels improve their games. The school is supervised by former PGA president Don Padgett. The maximum student-teacher ratio is 5-to-1, and you'll get a chance to test your improved game on any of the eight great Pinehurst courses. If you really want to get serious, you can stay for a week's worth of school. Or, if you haven't got the time, stay for the weekend. Either way, the program includes lodging for the entire stay, three meals a day, daily greens fees and carts, unlimited range balls, personal video analysis, personalized club fitting, access to all the amenities and a graduation cocktail party. Quite a gig! Call (800) 795-4653 for the brochure and rates. Junior programs are also available.

At Pine Needles, on Midland Road in Southern Pines, Peggy Kirk Bell and her staff will lead you on a **Golfari**. Either Bell or PGA touring pro Pat McGowan will begin your day with an instructional session before helping you on an individual basis with your swing. After lunch, play golf all afternoon on the great Pine Needles course. The facilities at Pine Needles are excellent, and there aren't many instructors with a better reputation than Peggy Kirk Bell. For more information about instruction at Pine Needles, call (800) 747-7272.

Taking a slightly different approach is the **Woodlake Total Performance Golf School** at Woodlake Country Club, 150 Woodlake Boulevard, in Vass. In addition to a full instructional program and access to a wonderful golf course, your instruction includes fitness and nutrition evaluations. Call (800) 334-1126 for more information.

INSIDERS' TIP

If you're going to play several golf courses and stay at a local hotel, go for the golf packages. This will save you the hassle of making telephone calls to several different courses and will often save you money off the advertised walk-up rates; plus you're more likely to get a preferred tee time. This strategy works best at many areas in the Carolinas, including Pinehurst and Myrtle Beach.

North Carolina's
Triad

While it might be sensible to assume that the Triad is an area defined by three cities, it actually comprises four: Greensboro, Winston-Salem, High Point and Burlington. More accurately, it should be called the "Quad." Actually, if you're a public golfer fortunate to live in the area, the only name change you might consider would be to "Paradise."

The Triad is so rich in outstanding public courses that it must be one of the best "urban" areas in the United States for the daily-fee golfer. In fact, there's no real need to fork over the cashola join a private club, such is the depth and quality of public golf in the Triad. And should you tire of all the wonderful courses here, Pinehurst is but an hour's drive down a four-lane highway. Even though the PGA Tour brings its circus here each April for the Greater Greensboro Chrysler Classic (still known to most by its original name, the Greater Greensboro Open), golf in the Triad is one of the nation's best kept secrets.

Bryan Park near Greensboro, Tanglewood near Winston-Salem, and Oak Hollow in High Point are three mature courses designed by Rees Jones, Robert Trent Jones and Pete Dye respectively. National publications like *Golf Digest* and *Golf Magazine* routinely and justifiably rate this majestic triumvirate among the nation's best daily-fee courses. Other diamonds include Grandover Resort, Oak Valley, Mill Creek, Meadowlands, and Stoney Creek.

Visitors to North Carolina bent on playing golf usually head for the mountains, the coast or Pinehurst. Visitors here for business, if they're not going to Charlotte, head for the Triad. The bi-annual furniture shows in High Point attract buyers and sellers from around the world. Winston-Salem is R.J. Reynolds' manufacturing home, and Greensboro boast Sara Lee and a host of manufacturing facilities. The Triad is busy and industrious.

Still, there's a down-home and small town feel to the Triad that somehow makes it seem a little more liveable and tranquil than a major city. Add all the golf courses to this mix and you can understand why many in the Triad would quite happily re-name it "Paradise."

Note: The Triad is well served by one of the best regional golf periodicals in the United States: *Triad Golf Today*, published by Jay Allred. Check out its Website for regular updates and news at www.triadgolf.com.

Walkers: You are treated well in the Triad, with some of the most walker-friendly policies in the Carolinas. Most courses are walkable; very few prohibit walking altogether while more than a select few let you walk on Saturday and Sunday mornings. That's how golf should be.

Asheboro Country Club
Old Lexington Rd., Asheboro
• (910) 625-6810

Championship Yardage: 6417	
Slope: 132	**Par: 70**
Men's Yardage:	**6169**
Slope: 128	**Par: 70**
Ladies' Yardage:	**4695**
Slope: No rating	**Par: 70**

Asheboro Country Club opened in the early 1950s, designed by its then membership. The course is open in places, wooded in others. Jim Bivins redesigned the greens and much of the course in 1996. Fairways are bermudagrass and greens are A1 bentgrass.

To many North Carolinians, Asheboro is best known as home of the North Carolina Zoo. It's not,

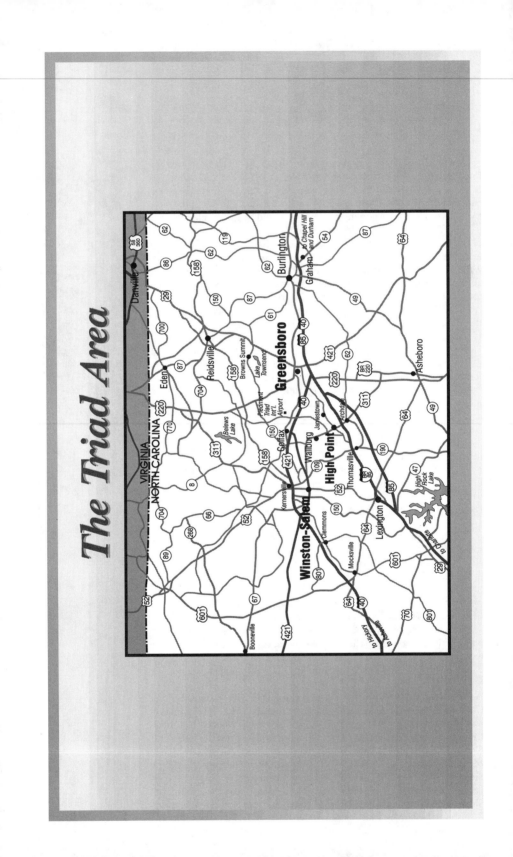

The Triad Area

GOLF COURSES IN NORTH CAROLINA'S TRIAD

Course	Type	# Holes	Par	Slope	Yards	Walking	Booking	Cost w/Cart
Asheboro Country Club	semiprivate	18	70	128	6169	restricted	anytime	$30-34
Bryan Park								
Champions Course	public	18	72	125	6622	restricted	30 days	$35-37
Players Course	public	18	72	120	6499	anytime	30 days	$35-37
Challenge at Hideaway Farms	public	18	72	133	6461	anytime	30 days	$40-48
Cresent Golf Club	public	18	72	125	6331	restricted	7 days	$30-37
Grandover Resort								
East Course	resort	18	72	n/a	7100	restricted	anytime	$50-60
West Course	resort	18	72	125	6499	restricted	anytime	$50-60
Greensboro National	public	18	72	n/a	6922	restricted	anytime	$35-45
Hickory Hill Country Club	semiprivate	18	70	110	5902	restricted	3 days	$24-28
Indian Valley	public	18	70	113	6121	restricted	7 days	$22-28
Jamestown Park	public	18	72	122	6186	restricted	7 days	$25-30
Lexington Golf & Country Club	public	18	70	116	5703	anytime	7 days	$19-21
Lynrock Golf Club	public	18	70	109	5538	anytime	2 days	$22-23
Maple Leaf	public	18	71	n/r	5655	restricted	7 days	$23-26
Meadowlands	public	18	72	n/a	6706	restricted	7 days	$35-42
Mill Creek	semiprivate	18	72	127	7004	no	7 days	$38-45
Monroeton Golf Club	public	18	70	103	5428	anytime	anytime	$11-16
Oak Hollow Golf Course	public	18	72	118	6090	anytime	2 days	$25-28
Oak Valley	public	18	72	n/a	7058	restricted	7 days	$33-45
Pine Knolls	semiprivate	18	72	110	5923	restricted	anytime	$22-28
Pine Tree	semiprivate	18	71	107	6046	restricted	10 days	$25-30
Pudding Ridge	semiprivate	18	70	123	6234	restricted	7 days	$27-30

Reynolds Park	public	18	71	118	5923	restricted	7 day	$22-28
Salem Glen	semiprivate	18	71	131	6603	restricted	7 days	$35-45
Sandy Ridge Golf Course	semiprivate	18	72	n/r	5645	restricted	5 days	$27-30
Southwick Golf Course	public	18	70	111	5431	restricted	anytime	$12-20
Stoney Creek Golf Club	semiprivate	18	72	132	6573	restricted	7 days	$40-45
Tanglewood Park								
Championship Course	public	18	72	135	6638	restricted	7 days	$45-65
Reynolds Course	public	18	72	120	6061.	anytime	7 days	$30

and never has been, a destination for golfers, most of whom would rather visit Pinehurst, just a half-hour south by car.

For 40 years, the members at Asheboro Country Club played on a course built by their forefathers whose rudimentary but sincere efforts produced a layout that lasted until the recent redesign.

In the course of a four-month renovation, Jim Bivins reduced par from 73 to 70, reshaped several fairways and doubled the size of most greens, bringing the course up to modern standards. The most popular addition has been the A1 bentgrass on the greens. One of the most remarkable holes on the course is the 18th, where the second shot must be played close to a dam.

Overall, Asheboro Country Club presents golfers with a fair test through some fine Piedmont scenery.

Amenities include clubhouse, pro shop, range and putting green.

Walking is restricted but the course is walkable. Approximate cost, including cart, is $30 weekdays, $34 weekends.

Bryan Park and Golf Club
6275 Bryan Park Rd., Brown Summit
• (336) 375-2200

The population of the Triad area is fortunate that its municipalities have invested in superior golf complexes. In Greensboro, it's Bryan Park—a complex as fine as any public golf facility in the Carolinas. Well-respected architects designed the two courses. A state-of-the-art practice facility opened in early 1996.

If you're looking for a couple of public courses with real difficulty and serious challenge, visit Bryan Park. Both courses provide excellent value for the golfing dollar and have been recognized for this by *Golf Digest*.

Amenities include a practice green, range, chipping green, snack bar, rental clubs and a pro shop.

Both courses are walkable for the fit; you can walk anytime on the Players and after 4 PM on the Champions. Approximate cost for either course, including cart, is $35 weekdays and $37 on weekends.

Champions Course

Championship Yardage:	7135	
Slope: 130		Par: 72
Men's Yardage:	6622	
Slope: 125		Par: 72
Other Yardage:	5977	
Slope: 118		Par: 72
Ladies' Yardage:	5395	
Slope: 123		Par: 72

Rees Jones designed the Champions Course, which opened in 1990 and is set in open terrain bordered by woods on some holes. Fairways are bermudagrass; greens, bentgrass.

The Champions Course offers some wonderful and difficult holes. Jones made good use of the natural landscape, including several acres bordering Lake Townsend, which comes into play a couple of times. Rees Jones is the son of Robert Trent Jones, and both father and son demonstrate an annoying penchant (from a player's perspective) for mass bunkering. The younger Jones likes them deep and somewhat irregularly placed— some make us wonder whose ball would ever find these traps, they're so out of the way. Perhaps these bunkers exist solely for your viewing pleasure.

There's usually plenty of room off the tee. Wayward drives may end up in woods or bouncing like a pinball around the many large mounds. You might find a bunker. Water comes into play a lot here in the form of the lake, ponds and streams. The greens are large, sloped and flanked by many bunkers and a few embankments. You'll have trouble getting to most of the greens and just as much trouble getting up and down. The Champions Course is so-named for a reason. If you're a high-handicapper, you might be in for a long day, even if you play from the white tees.

The course has lots of muscular and outstanding holes, but the most terrifying might be the shortest par 5, the 481-yard 15th, where water comes into play both off the tee and on the second shot, which is severely uphill. If the first two shots are solid, there's every chance to score. Wayward shots could result in a big, big number.

Players Course

Championship Yardage:	7076	
Slope: 128		Par: 72
Men's Yardage:	6499	
Slope: 120		Par: 72
Other Yardage:	5925	
Slope: 115		Par: 72

INSIDERS' TIP

When the course you're playing is busy, spend a maximum of two or three minutes looking for your errant drive. Or, better still, take a little less club off the tee and concentrate on hitting it straight.

Ladies' Yardage: 5260
Slope: 120   Par: 72

The Players Course at Bryan Park, designed by George Cobb, opened in 1974. The bermudagrass fairways and bentgrass greens are set in open terrain, with woods flanking some holes. Rees Jones made some changes to the Players Course when he built the Champions, but it retained much of its "Cobb feel."

Even from the front tees, the Players Course is difficult; as the scorecard reads, it's "recognized as one of the best public tests of golf."

The Players Course is the more mature of the two, and if you're familiar with the work of George Cobb, you'll recognize this as one of his signature efforts. Rees Jones' modifications likely account for the addition of mounds and some new bunkering. But don't think that the Players Course is an easier version of its sister. From the back, there's still more than 7000 yards of tough golf ahead of you. There isn't nearly as much water on this 18, but you'll still find difficult greens and extensive bunkering. If the Champions Course looks crowded, think about trying the Players. It's still an excellent challenge and one of the best golfing values in North Carolina.

The course begins with the No. 1 handicap hole, a long par 4 of 449 yards. A large fairway bunker awaits the sliced drive. Even a solid swat with the titanium will leave a tough approach to a large green with two enormous bunkers. Even the low handicapper must be slightly happy with a mere five.

The Challenge at Hideaway Farms
Townbranch Rd., Graham
• (336) 578-5070
Championship Yardage: 6935
Slope: 139   Par: 72
Men's Yardage: 6461
Slope: 133   Par: 72
Other Yardage: 5804
Slope: 124   Par: 72
Ladies' Yardage: 4870
Slope: 123   Par: 72

The Challenge at Hideaway Farms opened in 1997. Barry Brantley designed the course on undulating woodland; he used 419 bermudagrass in the fairways and Crenshaw bentgrass on the greens.

In the same county as the smash hit Mill Creek (see subsequent entry), The Challenge at Hideaway Farms has been built and developed to rival the local competition. The Challenge has already been nominated as one of the top new courses in North Carolina.

The most muscular hole surely is the par 5 18th, a 567-yard toughie that only the biggest hitters will reach in two. The tee shot is slightly uphill; the second shot must land between a couple of creeks, leaving a short to mid-iron to a tough green.

The course is already proving popular, most interestingly with a number of golfers driving on I-40/I-85 who want to stop for some challenging golf. The Challenge is yet another fine addition to all the wonderful courses in the Triad.

Amenities include a practice green, range, chipping green, snack bar, rental clubs and a pro shop.

The course is walkable for the fit; you can walk anytime during the week. You can book a tee time one month in advance. Approximate cost, including cart, is $40 weekdays and $48 weekends.

Crescent Golf Club
Laurel Valley Way, Salisbury
• (704) 647-0025
Championship Yardage: 6822
Slope: 129   Par: 72
Men's Yardage: 6331
Slope: 125   Par: 72
Other Yardage: 6767
Slope: 116   Par: 72
Ladies' Yardage: 5163
Slope: 111   Par: 72

Crescent Golf Club opened in 1998. John LaFoy designed the course; he used 419 bermudagrass in the fairways and Crenshaw bentgrass on the greens.

Routed on a former dairy farm, Crescent is fine course that's remarkably mature for its age. Perhaps that's because it's not your typical modern "golf course community" golf course where homesites come first. There was enough good land for a golf course and a housing community, and the result is a fine and fun course that will provide challenges for players of all abilities.

Fine holes abound, but particularly noteworthy is the par 5 14th, 529 from the tips, quite severely downhill with a semi-blind tee shot. With the fairways firm, even the medium-length golfer will find himself with a chance to go for it with a fairway wood, albeit from a downhill lie.

The number one handicap hole is the 3rd, a 453-yard par 4 with the most difficult drive on the course, downhill between two large fairway bunkers. The perfect tee ball finds a slope and gathers some steam, leaving a long iron or fairway wood to the smallish green set at 45 degrees to the fairway. Par here is a fine effort.

Part of the ownership at Crescent is a group of landscaping experts, and their influence is already on display: For a course this young, Crescent's greens are among the best in the Salisbury area.

Crescent is a well-run addition to golf in the Piedmont of North Carolina. It's a what-you-see-is-what-you-get golf course where good play is rewarded with good results.

Amenities include a practice green, range, chipping green, snack bar, rental clubs and a pro shop.

The course is walkable for the fit; you can walk primarily during the week. Approximate cost, including cart, is $30 weekdays and $37 weekends.

Grandover Resort
One Thousand Club Rd., Greensboro
• (336) 294-1800, (800) 472-6301

The East Course opened in 1996, the West Course in 1997. Grandover Resort is the brainchild of Joseph Koury, a Greensboro developer and one of the wealthiest and most influential men in North Carolina.

The two courses are part of a whopping and sumptuous 1,400-acre development that ultimately will include a resort hotel and conference center, custom homes, offices and shopping. Unlike many dual-course facilities, the developer and architects have promised that both East and West courses will be equally magnificent—no "poor uncle" syndrome here.

It's hard to imagine a couple of courses with better access; a portion of the courses at Grandover can be seen from I-85. Described as "world class" by *Triad Golf* magazine, the courses at Grandover are vying to be top dog in the Triad, an area that's already rich in great golf courses. Don't be overly surprised if the Greater Greensboro Chrysler Classic moves to Grandover in the not-too-distant future.

David Graham and Roger Panks designed the courses, with 419 bermudagrass in the fairways and Crenshaw bentgrass on the greens. The developer has gone to great expense with details like granite yardage markers in the fairways; it's truly a first-class facility.

Amenities include a practice green, range, chipping green, snack bar, rental clubs and a pro shop. There's also a spa, world-class restaurant, hotel, and conference amenities. There's also a Ken Venturi Golf Academy. Venturi is the accomplished professional golfer who is now an ornery TV commentator and pitchman for various products, including Orlimar golf clubs.

Both courses are walkable for the fit; you can walk with permission from the pro. Approximate cost for either course, including cart, is $50 weekdays and $60 weekends. It's very important to call ahead for availability, as the resort aims to book as many packages as possible.

East Course

Championship Yardage:	**7100**
Slope: 140	**Par: 72**
Men's Yardage:	**6417**
Slope: 132	**Par: 72**
Ladies' Yardage:	**4991**
Slope: 115	**Par: 72**

The East Course was the first to open and thus it's had a bit more time to mature. It's already gaining rave reviews and *Golf Digest* rated it four stars. It's built on undulating land and features a number of water hazards that could easily lead to some big numbers early in the round.

The 2nd, a 535-yard par 5, offers an early scoring opportunity. You'll have to avoid a small lake on the right hand side of the fairway and the creek to the left of the hole, but solid positioning with the second or third shot could lead to an eagle or birdie. Any sort of wayward shot could lead to a big number.

One of the many muscular holes on the East is the par 4 5th, 460 yards from the back tees. The tee shot to this narrowish fairway must avoid a creek on the left. The approach to the green must clear a bunker front right. Par here is somewhat relative!

There's little in the way of let up on this course. It could very well test the mettle and patience of even the low-handicapper. With its abundance of hazards, undulation and length, Grandover's East Course is not a track for the faint-hearted.

West Course

Championship Yardage:	**6800**
Slope: 136	**Par: 72**
Men's Yardage:	**6499**
Slope: 125	**Par: 72**
Ladies' Yardage:	**5050**
Slope: 116	**Par: 72**

Although it's still long from the tips and still very challenging, the West Course is considered the easier of the two tracks at Grandover. After playing the East Course, "easier" is a relative term.

The best par 5 on the course is the 16th, with a creek inconveniently crossing the fairway about 100 yards from the green. The pic-

The Piedmont of North Carolina features a number of nationally ranked courses. Most of these are set in rolling woodland.

turesque 11th is a 190-yard par 3 over wetlands; it's a beautiful hole if you hit the green. Isn't that always the way?

The first, a 360-yard shortish par 4, is an entertaining opener, with its approach over a stream to a green guarded by bunkers left and back. The 190 yard par 3 11th is an intimidating hole with some bail-out to the left of the slim green. But it's the par 4 13th, at just 330 yards, that's easily the most interesting on the course, offering a variety of options from the tee. The world needs more short two-shotters like this one, with its bunkers in the middle of the fairway getting into the head of the golfer.

With holes like the 11th and 13th, the West course might be the more cerebral of the two excellent courses here at Grandover.

Greensboro National Golf Club
330 Niblick Dr., Summerfield
• (336) 643-4653

Championship Yardage:	**6922**
Slope: No rating	**Par: 72**
Men's Yardage:	**6417**
Slope: No rating	**Par: 72**
Ladies' Yardage:	**4991**
Slope: No rating	**Par: 72**

Greensboro National Golf Club opened in late 1995. The course is set in rolling terrain bordered mostly by woods. In the fairways, you'll find bermudagrass; on the greens, you'll find bentgrass with zoysia collars. Don and Mark Charles designed the course.

Set amid rolling farmland in horse country north of Greensboro, Greensboro National is a wonderful new course that's quickly become one of the more popular tracks in the area. The layout winds through a wonderful piece of land that's as pretty as any in the Piedmont. But more importantly, the designers, staff and developers created the course to be relatively easy to maintain and very golfer-friendly. With its four sets of well-spaced tees, the course is laid out to provide a fun challenge for golfers at all levels.

The layout of most holes is traditional and unassuming—there are few blind shots and no tricks. There are no significant elevation changes. The challenges are in plain view for all to see. Water and wetlands come into play on 10 holes. The strategically placed bunkers need to be avoided if you're going to score well. The greens are large and steadily sloped—there are no significant or awkward undulations. The fairways are wide enough to let you use your driver on many holes—particularly the longer par 4s.

Overall, we think you'll enjoy this track, which is best described as a golfer's golf course; it's a thoroughly well designed and fair test. There are no houses on the course—yet. We also think you'll enjoy the fine amenities and facilities in the unique clubhouse, which looks a lot like a stealth fighter jet... really!

With the game on the line, the final hole, a 562-yard par 5 should provide some climactic and memorable moments. All you need are a solid drive, a well-struck long iron or fairway wood and then a laser-like short iron to the smallish green. Two putts and you've won the match. With nerves on edge and 50 cents on the line, par is easier said than done.

Amenities include a range, practice green, snack bar, rental clubs and a pro shop.

You can walk after 3 PM, but you'll find some significant distances between greens and tees. Approximate cost, including cart, is $35 weekdays and $45 on weekends.

Hickory Hill Country Club
U.S. Hwy. 64 E., Mocksville
• **(910) 998-8746**
Championship Yardage: 6537
Slope: 116   **Par: 70**
Men's Yardage: **5902**
Slope: 110   **Par: 70**
Ladies' Yardage: **4973**
Slope: 109   **Par: 70**

The Golf Course at Hickory Hill Country Club, a Russell McMillan design, opened in 1970. Typical of courses in the Triad, Hickory Hill is primarily open but bordered by woods

on a few holes. In the fairways, you'll find bermudagrass; on the greens, you'll find bentgrass.

Although Hickory Hill is not a terribly old course, it has what might be described as a pre-war design. The layout is an excellent example of minimalist architecture in a pretty, relaxed setting. You'll find good room off the tee and a few lonely grass or sand bunkers. Most of the green complexes are not raised, thus you can play all the run-up shots you want. The greens are mostly flat and have been reseeded with Crenshaw bentgrass to provide patrons with a better putting surface.

A new pro/course manager arrived in 1995, and has been making significant improvements to the course. If you're looking for an ultra-modern moundfest with severely undulating greens, look elsewhere. Hickory Hill harkens back to the early days of golf when every good player knew how to run the ball up to the green from almost anywhere. Where's my mashie?

Back-to-back par 5s on the second and third holes offer entertaining chances to score early in the round, and should provide useful birdies to offset the inevitable bogies that lurk on the back nine, most noticeably at the par 4 12th, 422 from the tips.

All the TLC lavished on this course in the past few years has helped make this one of the better courses in the Triad, particularly for the money.

Amenities include a practice green, range, chipping green, locker room, snack bar, rental clubs and a pro shop.

This course is a good one to walk, and you may walk anytime during the week and after 2 PM on weekends. Approximate cost, including cart, is $24 weekdays and $28 on weekends.

Indian Valley
Indian Valley Dr., Burlington
• **(336) 584-7871**
Championship Yardage: 6610
Slope: 116   **Par: 70**
Men's Yardage: 6121
Slope: 113   **Par: 70**
Ladies' Yardage: 5606
Slope: 115   **Par: 70**

Indian Valley opened in 1975. Ellis Maples designed the course on rolling, wooded terrain with bermudagrass fairways and bentgrass greens. Water comes into play on several holes.

Indian Valley is yet another wonderful municipally owned golf course in the Triad. It's just amazing, isn't it? And to boot, Indian Valley easily holds its own against Tanglewood,

Bryan Park and Oak Hollow, the city-owned courses in Winston-Salem, Greensboro and High Point. Indian Valley actually opened in the mid '60s as a housing development; the development failed and the City of Burlington purchased the property in 1974 and opened the course to the public.

Ellis Maples designed so many fine and wonderful golf courses in North Carolina in the post-war boom that there really should be a statue dedicated to him somewhere. The residents of Burlington should be extremely pleased that they have an Ellis Maples course.

The design features many of those wonderful sweeping doglegs Maples must have loved so much. Fine examples would include the 1st, a par-4 360-yard dogleg left, and the 18th, a more daunting par-4 at 423 yards from the back tees. The consensus favorite hole might be the par 3 8th, 194 yards with a pond to the left of the green and bunkers to the right—little room for a bail out.

As befits such a fine municipal track, the course is busy with men's and women's associations, junior clinics, college matches and other events, so make sure you call ahead for a tee time. Indian Valley is a find, particularly for the price of admission.

Amenities include a practice green, range, and pro shop.

Walking is somewhat restricted, but the course is extremely walkable. Approximate cost, including cart, is $22 weekdays and $28 on weekends.

Jamestown Park Golf Course
200 E. Fork Rd., Jamestown
• (336) 454-4912
Championship Yardage: 6665
Slope: 126   **Par: 72**
Men's Yardage: 6186
Slope: 122   **Par: 72**
Ladies' Yardage: 5298
Slope: 118   **Par: 72**

No one is sure when the golf course at Jamestown Park opened, but we known that John V. Townsend designed it. The course is set in rolling terrain and flanked by woods, with bermudagrass fairways and bentgrass greens.

We're not sure what the "V" in John V. Townsend stands for. In fact, no one is sure who Townsend is; we're told that he may have been a local politician. However, he might have made a decent golf course architect. The course here is pleasant, challenging, sensible and well designed. You won't find a lot of trouble off the tee. The fairways are relatively wide. The greens are large to huge, with the occasional bunker providing a challenge. Three of the par 3s are fronted by gaping bunkers running the entire length of each putting complex. On other greens, you'll be able to run the ball up to the hole. A bit of water comes into play on the back nine, though it's nothing to lose sleep over.

The front nine is pretty enough, but the back nine is more interesting, varied and fun. Dare we say it, but John V. Townsend may have been a fan and imitator of Ellis Maples, for a couple of holes would have made Maples quite happy.

The course here at Jamestown Park is well worth a visit if you're looking for something relaxed yet challenging. Plus it's a good value.

Amenities include a practice green, range, chipping green, locker room, snack bar and pro shop.

You can walk anytime except before 12:30 PM on weekends. Approximate cost, including cart, is $25 weekdays and $30 on weekends.

Lexington Golf and Country Club
200 Country Club Blvd., Lexington
• (336) 248-3950
Championship Yardage: 5582
Slope: 114   **Par: 70**
Regular Yardage: 5254
Slope: 109   **Par: 70**
Ladies Yardage: 4457
Slope: 106   **Par: 70**

Dugan Aycock designed Lexington Golf and Country Club, which opened in 1936. Set on rolling terrain and flanked by houses, Lexington boasts bermudagrass fairways and greens.

You may not have heard of Dugan Aycock, which is a shame. He's quite a character. Aycock played on the U.S. Army golf team during World War II; was friends with the likes of Trevino, Nicklaus and Palmer; encouraged the great Bobby Locke to come to America from South Africa; raised enormous sums of money for charity; and was a golfing partner of Bill "Earthquake" Smith, an officer of the law, former football player at the University of North Carolina at Chapel Hill and an excellent golfer. You can read the full story about Aycock in the men's locker room. Ladies, please knock before you enter.

If times had been different, perhaps Aycock would have been a designer. His product here in Lexington is quirky, erratic, fascinating and short, with enormous character and variety. The course is set on what must be fewer than 100 acres and thus is somewhat tight. Modernists might consider the course to be too ancient and lacking in yards to be of interest, but most would be challenged to hit some of the small targets and score. Lexington is quite a test of shotmaking and accuracy. Big numbers await the even slightly wayward golfer. There aren't many bunkers, but they should be avoided at all costs. The greens are flat and smallish, and you'll be able to run the ball up on a few holes—just like in the 1930s. There are more than a couple of holes that would catch the attention of almost any golf course architect. Play this one if you're in the area and, after your round, devour some Lexington-style barbecue for a real treat.

Big hitters might be tempted to scoff at the 268-yard downhill par 4 2nd, but their laughter will quickly turn to frustration if the tee shot fails to nail the narrow fairway or dribbles into the creek that fronts the small green. More courses need short but dangerous par 4s like the second here at Lexington.

Completely surrounded by homes (but not obnoxiously so), Lexington can't really change that much. Thus, there's an emphasis on making the existing course and its facilities the best they can be. Which is nice.

Amenities include a practice green, locker room, rental clubs and a pro shop.

Walk almost anytime on this eminently walkable golf course. Approximate cost, including cart, is $19 weekdays and $21 on weekends.

Lynrock Golf Club
636 Valley Dr., Eden
• (336) 623-6110

Championship Yardage:	6046	
Slope: 114	**Par: 70**	
Men's Yardage:	5538	
Slope: 109	**Par: 70**	
Ladies' Yardage:	4913	
Slope: 109	**Par: 70**	

Jim Wilson designed Lynrock Golf Club, which opened in 1959 at the beginning of Elvis Presley's reign. The course is set on mostly flat terrain, with bermudagrass fairways and bentgrass greens.

Lynrock offers fun and reasonably demanding country golf on a pretty track that winds around the valley floor immediately adjacent to the confluence of the Dan and Smith rivers. The river is remarkably wide here and comes into play on a couple of holes. This is most noticeable on the par 3 No. 2, which plays 150 yards from the tips. You tee off on one side of the river to a shallow green on the other side. Park it on the dance floor and you get to cross one of the most picturesque and longest bridges

on any golf course in the area—perhaps in the Carolinas. A wonderful way to start the round.

The rest of the course will not disappoint. The fairways are not overly wide, although they are fairly open. The greens are large and sloped; some are crowned and thus will play a little smaller if the greens are firm. Many of the green complexes include a series of medium-size bunkers, and you'll have to fly some of them. On other holes, you'll be able to run the ball up to the pin with a well executed half-shot or some creative use of your Texas wedge.

Amenities include a practice green and rental clubs.

The course is walkable and you can walk almost anytime. Approximate cost, including cart, is $22 weekdays and $23 on weekends.

Maple Leaf Golf Club
4070 Hastings Rd., Kernersville
• (336) 769-9122

Championship Yardage:	6028	
Slope: No rating	**Par: 71**	
Men's Yardage:	5655	
Slope: No rating	**Par: 71**	
Ladies' Yardage:	4643	
Slope: No rating	**Par: 71**	

Maple Leaf Golf Club opened a front nine in 1981, designed by Ellis Maples, and a back nine in 1988, designed by Don Charles. The course is set in rolling wooded terrain, with bermudagrass fairways and bentgrass greens.

You won't find many Canadians here, but you will find a fine secluded course with an outstanding design pedigree. Anyone who has played golf in the Carolinas has heard of the great Ellis Maples. Charles is lesser known, although he assisted with the renowned Legends complex in the Myrtle Beach area.

The result of the combined work of these two architects is a course with great interest and variety. It's not long from the back, but the narrowness of the fairways, in places, makes up for the lack of length. On the front nine, the 5th is a fun hole. Hit a decent drive downhill and you'll have a short iron over water to a small green set on a peninsula. But don't let this hole make you think the course is overly penal. On most holes you can recover from slightly errant shots. Extremely poor shots will leave you dipping into your pocket for an extra ball.

You'll find a variety of options off the tee as well as in the size, shape and structure of the green complexes. With its challenge, picturesque setting, subtleties and sensible pricing, Maple Leaf offers one of the best low-cost golfing venues in the Triad.

The Slope Story

We see those numbers on almost every score card at every golf course. We give it however many grains of salt we care to that day. But what do those slope and course ratings mean, and who assigns them to the course?

The United States Golf Association has committees all over the country that go to member courses to evaluate and assign each course a rating and slope. It is not an arbitrary number the USGA assigns—it's not meted out just because the officials think the course is tough, or the wind was blowing and taking most shots out of bounds on a given day.

The course rating is based on a course's difficulty for a scratch golfer, and the slope rating is the measure of difficulty for a non-scratch golfer. In many cases the rating committee will not even play the course.

The Ocean Course at Kiawah, in South Carolina's Lowcountry, is one of Pete Dye's most controversial designs. Its 149 slope rating from the championship tees is among the highest in the country.

Photo: Kiawah Island Resort

The committee meets with the club pro or general manager to gather information such as total course length, length of the holes into the wind and length of holes downwind. They measure the speed of the greens, the height of the fairways, the height of the rough and the roll on the fairway. They also view and evaluate the tees, the landing areas and greens.

Topography, bunkers, out-of-bounds areas, water hazards and presence or absence of trees, naturally, also come into play when determining the rating and slope. Other factors include target areas, blind shots and holes that force the golfer to lay up. After all variables are accounted for, the numbers are calculated and the course rating and slope are assigned.

What does all of this mean to you and me? If you have a 10 handicap and a USGA index of 12.5 (you have an index if you have a handicap) and you traveled to another course with a higher rating and slope than your home course, your handicap would be adjusted. At the tougher course your 12.5 index factored into a handicap computer results in a higher handicap on that course.

A consistency problem can arise if your home course—where you established your 10 handicap—happens to be very difficult. Your friend might have a handicap of 10 that was established on an easier course. The catch? If you put your respective indexes into the handicap computer at the same course, both of you will have the same adjusted handicap. Although the system is imperfect, it is the best one that we have so far. Many have suggested alternative formulas, but so far none has USGA approval.

So, for good or for ill, those rating and slope numbers on the score card are not just pulled out of the hat and applied to the course. Time, effort and calculations have been put into making the playing field as level as possible for all golfers.

Amenities include a practice green and snack bar.

You can walk anytime during the week and after 4 PM on weekends. You can book a tee time seven days in advance. Approximate cost, including cart, is $23 weekdays and $26 on weekends.

Meadowlands
582 Motsinger Rd., Winston-Salem
• (336) 769-1011

Championship Yardage:	6706
Slope: 123	**Par: 72**
Men's Yardage:	6323
Slope: 119	**Par: 72**
Ladies' Yardage:	4745
Slope: 114	**Par: 72**

Meadowlands opened in late 1995. The course is set in beautiful terrain that's rolling and framed with woods. In the fairways, you'll find bermudagrass; on the greens, you'll putt on bentgrass. Hale Irwin and Stan Gentry designed the course.

No, we're not in New Jersey. We're in bucolic hardwood forests just south of Winston-Salem on the road to Thomasville. Just when you thought there couldn't possibly be any more great golf courses in the Triad, here comes Mead-owlands—a fun and playable course in a magnificent setting that's absolutely free of houses. In terms of setting, Meadowlands rivals Tanglewood.

Hale Irwin is one of the greats of the modern era of professional golf. He holds the course record at Pinehurst #2, and in addition to winning tournaments on that course, he's won at such difficult and treacherous layouts as Winged Foot, Inverness, Medinah, Harbor Town, Butler National and Pebble Beach. There are few players in the game who are more athletic or more consistent. Unlike some of his contemporaries who have ventured into the golf course design game, Irwin (based on the example here at Meadowlands) produces a golf course that mostly follows the lie of the land and is not overly demanding. You won't find excessive carries over water or swamp. You won't find wildly undulating greens. You won't find deep and almost inescapable bunkers lurking near the greens.

Here at Meadowlands, you'll play a relatively straightforward track where most of the problems are easily seen and easily avoided with sound execution. Water comes into play on a few holes, most noticeably the par 4 10th, where you'll need to smack the ball about 200 yards

TRIAD

over a small lake to reach the fairway from the back tees. It's probably the only really intimidating shot on the course. Irwin routed the course to include a number of fine driving holes.

Apart from the sound design work, you'll enjoy Meadowlands for the setting. As we've mentioned, there are no houses on the course, and you really feel like you're miles away from all the clutter and clamor of today's fast-paced lifestyle. Golf should be an escape from the real world, and Meadowlands provides a rare example of a modern course that's designed to follow this belief.

We think you'll find Meadowlands a must-play course in the Triad area. Even though 6703 yards from the tips is relatively short these days, Meadowlands should provide the low-handicapper with a sensible challenge. From the middle and forward tees, Meadowlands will challenge the mid- to high-handicapper. Definitely give this one a try.

You can walk after 3 PM, but sadly, the course is not really designed to be walkable. You can book a tee time a week in advance. Approximate cost, including cart, is $35 weekdays and $42 on weekends.

Mill Creek Golf Club

1700 St. Andrews Dr., Mebane
• (919) 563-4653

Championship Yardage:	7004	
Slope: 141	**Par: 72**	
Men's Yardage:	6387	
Slope: 127	**Par: 72**	
Other Yardage:	5711	
Slope: 122	**Par: 72**	
Ladies' Yardage:	4884	
Slope: 113	**Par: 72**	

The Golf Course at Mill Creek opened in late 1995. The course is set in rolling terrain bordered by woods and homesites. Rick Robbins and Brian Lussier designed the course in association with Gary Koch. You'll find bermudagrass in the fairways and bentgrass on the greens.

In 1995, *North Carolina Magazine* voted Mill Creek the best new public course in North Carolina. It's a well-designed course that presents an excellent challenge for the low-handicap golfer. The course is part of a large and extensive new-home community, creating difficult out-of-bounds situations in plenty of spots.

Overall, the course is full of serious difficulties. For starters, the rough here is rough. It's probably unlike any other rough we've ever seen. You know the thick long grass that grows so well in your back yard? Well, golf fans, that's

the rough you'll find at Mill Creek. Miss the fairway here and your ball might be 4 inches deep in stuff that will not yield to a weed-eater, let alone a five iron. In most cases, your only real option is to chip out and take your medicine. Of course, if you can keep it really straight and really long all the time, then you'll be just fine.

If the suicide rough doesn't cause enough problems, the course offers plenty of other difficulties in the form of water, streams, out of bounds in difficult spots, woods, blind driving holes, large bunkers and some severely sloping greens. If you're having a bad day, things are really going to be awful, and you might end up losing a lot of golf balls and throwing a lot of clubs around. However, once you reach the green, you're going to be really excited. The greens here are magnificently manicured and amazingly fast—especially for a public course that gets a lot of play.

There's ample variety at Mill Creek plus a number of really challenging holes. The 428-yard par 4 finishing hole features a unique touch in the form of a split fairway. It's an interesting aesthetic feature, but it was difficult to discern what it really added to the hole's playability or appeal. There seemed to be no advantage, risk, or reward in choosing fairway A or fairway B. With all the great courses in North Carolina, it's definitely worth a visit to the one voted best new course—in anyone's poll. However, you might find Mill Creek unnecessarily difficult and better suited to the seasoned golfer.

Walking is restricted. As you might expect from a brand-new housing-development course, there are some significant distances between a few of the greens and the subsequent tees. Approximate cost, including cart, is $38 weekdays and $45 on weekends.

Monroeton Golf Club

213 Monroeton Golf Course Rd., Reidsville
• (336) 342-1043

Championship Yardage:	5729	
Slope: 106	**Par: 70**	
Men's Yardage:	5428	
Slope: 103	**Par: 70**	
Other Yardage:	4955	
Slope: No rating	**Par: 70**	
Ladies' Yardage:	4282	
Slope: 105	**Par: 70**	

According to local legend, there was a golf course here when golfers still played on sand greens. Estimates of the date of origin indicate sometime in the 1940s, but the real date play began here might be even earlier. No one is sure who designed this course, which is bordered by woods and houses amid a rolling landscape. In the fairways, you'll find a combination of bermudagrass and native grasses; on the greens, you'll find bentgrass.

You might think that Monroeton Golf Club is a bit of an anachronism, and it is. This classic country track probably has remained untouched since the first golfer teed off here. The fairways are wide and somewhat undefined. Bunkers, there are not. The greens are sloped, crowned and large. If the ground is hard, you'll have to run the ball up to the green because it's unlikely your approach shot will hold. If you want to see what it was like playing golf before earth was moved and sands shifted, you need to play here. Besides, is there a lower cost for 18 holes, including cart, in the Triad?

If you're having some sort of legal dispute either on or off the golf course, you'll be pleased to know that the firm of Griffin and Crapse, with offices adjacent to the 3rd tee, will be more than willing to help you (for a fee). If you call and the secretary says Mr. Crapse is on the golf course and he'll be back in a minute, it's probably true.

Amenities include a practice green, range, locker room and snack bar.

You can walk this course anytime. Approximate cost, including cart, is $11 weekdays and $16 on weekends.

Oak Hollow Golf Course
1400 Oak View, High Point
• (336) 883-3260

Championship Yardage:	6483
Slope: 124	Par: 72
Men's Yardage:	6090
Slope: 118	Par: 72
Ladies' Yardage:	4796
Slope: 114	Par: 72

Oak Hollow Golf Course opened in 1972. Pete Dye designed the course on rolling, primarily open terrain, with a lake bordering many holes on the front nine. Fairways are bermudagrass, and greens are bentgrass. *Golf Digest* ranked the course as one of the best in the United States for less than $50 a round. Bill Coore, who now partners with Ben Crenshaw in the golf course architecture business, learned some of the tricks of the trade while working on this course with Pete Dye.

Yes, *the* Pete Dye designed this course. And what a course, especially for a public track. After the Robert Trent Jones era of golf course architecture came the Pete Dye era, and you'll see many of the features that made Dye one of the most in-demand architects in the universe. Dye began life as a successful life insurance salesman, and there must be many a befuddled golfer who wishes he had stuck to explaining the difference between term and life. During the '60s, Dye and his wife, Alice, herself an accomplished course designer and player, toured Scotland in between designing moderate-cost courses in the Midwest. Oak Hollow was built before Dye's career really took off and Japanese developers began lining up with bunkers-full of cash just to have a Dye course. Oak Hollow is the only Pete Dye course in North Carolina that's open to the public.

Although Dye incorporated a number of Scottish features in his work, this is not a links course. There isn't a great deal of trouble off the tee on most holes. The real work begins around the green complexes, which feature bizarre slopes, bunkers and shapes. It's quite possible to hit a green and still work extremely hard for a par. One of us hit the green on the perilous 6th hole (a 420-yard par 4), found a grassy mound between the ball and the hole and had to get up to the pin with a lob wedge. On many holes, Dye brings Oak Hollow Lake into play in spectacular fashion, particularly on the aforementioned 6th hole, where the tee box sits right in the middle of the lake. Other golf course architects spend time creating subtle shapes and nuances in an effort to create aesthetically pleasing layouts. Dye uses his imagination to create golf holes that are bizarre, penal, wonderful and somewhat mindbending. His goal is to get you thinking; of course, that's when the trouble begins. If you're a student of golf course architecture, make the effort to play this course. It's quite an experience. And at less than $30 per round, it's a Dye course that won't increase your overdraft. It's a must-play in North Carolina.

Amenities include a practice green, range, chipping green, locker room, snack bar, rental clubs and a pro shop.

The course is walkable, and you can walk anytime (also hard to believe). Approximate

INSIDERS' TIP

For a mid- to high-handicapper, bogey is not a bad score, particularly on the more difficult holes. Don't be too disappointed with an occasional bogey. If you're in trouble early off the tee, cut your losses and find the easiest way to make bogey.

TRIAD

cost, including cart, is $25 weekdays and $28 on weekends. Huge value.

Oak Valley Golf Club
261 Oak Valley Blvd., Advance
• **(336) 940-2000**

Championship Yardage:	**7058**
Slope: 134	**Par: 72**
Men's Yardage:	**6684**
Slope: 127	**Par: 72**
Ladies' Yardage:	**5197**
Slope: 115	**Par: 72**

Oak Valley Golf Club opened in late 1995. The course is set in open and gently rolling terrain. In the fairways, you'll find bermudagrass; on the greens, you'll find bentgrass. Arnold Palmer and Ed Seay designed the course, which is part of a housing development.

Just minutes from Tanglewood, Oak Valley is already vying to be one of the top golf course layouts in the quality-rich Triad. It helps that one of the greatest golfers ever attached his name and considerable design reputation to the course. For years, Palmer's designs have been ably implemented by Ed Seay, who oversees an extremely capable group of architects.

Here at Oak Valley, you'll find some of the trademarks of a Palmer/Seay course. The greens undulate gently, and the green complexes feature an artistic combination of bunkers and swales—all designed to make getting up and down a considerable challenge. If you're on the wrong side of a green, a three-putt is a definite possibility. The architects made great use of the land to produce a number of excellent driving holes; these define the course and make it stand out from others in the Triad.

From the tee, you'll find plenty of difficulty lurking in and around the fairways, which are of sensible width. Palmer and Seay like to tempt golfers into "going for it" off the tee. Make the shot and you're in great shape; miss it and you're in a trap, out of bounds or in wetlands. It's a fine example of strategic golf. Making life just a little more difficult at Oak Valley is a stream that meanders through nine holes.

If you like a fine and serious test of golf, try Oak Valley. Once it's had just a bit more time

to mature, it's going to rival some of the other Palmer courses in the state, such as TPC at Piper Glen in Charlotte or Pinehurst Plantation in Southern Pines. Oak Valley looks tough enough to test the professional from the tips, yet fair enough to provide a fun challenge from the forward tees. The course is owned and operated by Carolinas Golf Group, so the quality of your golfing experience should be safely assured. Try this course at least once—you may be tempted to challenge it over and over again.

You can walk on weekdays, but walking is really only for the fit. You can book a tee time a week in advance. Approximate cost, including cart, is $35 weekdays and $45 on weekends.

Pine Knolls Golf Course
1100 Quail Hollow Rd., Kernersville
• **(336) 993-8300**

Championship Yardage:	**6287**
Slope: 121	**Par: 72**
Men's Yardage:	**5923**
Slope: 110	**Par: 72**
Ladies' Yardage:	**4480**
Slope: 92	**Par: 72**

Pine Knolls Golf Course opened in 1969. Most holes are open, and others are bordered by woods or houses. Bermudagrass blankets the fairways, with bentgrass covering the greens.

Yet another Triad golf course with the word "pine" in its name, Pine Knolls offers a fun and mostly straightforward golf outing. The setting is pleasant and relaxed. You won't find a lot of bunkers, but you will find plenty of variety and a decent amount of challenge. The layout is sensible and not overly penal, although really bad shots will yield really bad results. Off the tee, you must think about and choose the correct weapon—use the driver wisely, perhaps sparingly. Around the medium-size greens, you'll find slope and some undulation. A few greens allow you to run the ball up from the fairway. One touch we especially liked was the path cut through the rough from the tee boxes to the fairways. It's a statement from the management that says: "Yes, we like walkers." Pine Knolls is clearly popular; it's also a good value.

Amenities include a practice green, range, chipping green, locker room, snack bar, rental clubs and a pro shop.

INSIDERS' TIP

Take the time to learn something about golf course architects and architecture. Many fine books have been written on the subject (we've referenced several throughout this book), and you'll understand, and probably enjoy, a course more if you're familiar with the architect's style.

TRIAD

Thousands of golf enthusiasts attend the Greater Greensboro Chrysler Classic.

Photo: N.C. Travel & Tourism

spite all the bunkers, you can run the ball up to the pin on a few holes if the ground is hard. Water comes into play here and there but should not cause too much of a problem. Occasional trees near or in the fairways will make you think twice about your next shot. The sweeping dogleg 6th, a wonderful 385-yard par 4 is a particularly fun hole.

The general feeling of being away from it all is what we liked best about Pine Tree. Combine the peaceful setting with a challenging and varied course and you should be in for a good round. It's definitely a good value.

Amenities include a practice green, range, chipping green, locker room, snack bar, restaurant and pro shop.

You can walk Pine Tree only on weekdays. Approximate cost, including cart, is $25 weekdays and $30 on weekends.

Walk Pine Knolls anytime during the week and after 1:30 PM on weekends. Approximate cost, including cart, is $22 weekdays and $28 on weekends.

Pine Tree Golf Club
1680 Pine Tree Ln., Kernersville
• (336) 993-5598

Championship Yardage:	6604
Slope: 113	**Par: 71**
Men's Yardage:	6046
Slope: 107	**Par: 71**
Ladies' Yardage:	4897
Slope: 110	**Par: 71**

Pine Tree Golf Club opened in 1971. Gene Hamm designed the course on rolling, wooded terrain. In the fairways, you'll find bermudagrass; on the greens, bentgrass.

Pine Tree is a course with challenge, scenic beauty and excellent variety. There are virtually no houses lining the course, so you'll be pleasingly far away from the hassles of modern civilization.

For those who play golf for the joys of peace and solitude, Pine Tree is a course you'll find tremendously enjoyable. Gene Hamm is one of the most under-appreciated architects in the Carolinas.

There's ample room off the tee on most holes. Feel free to take out the big stick—you'll need it on many of the longer par 4s. The greens are large and sloped. The green complexes boast an abundance of large and flat bunkers. Quite a few greens are flush with their respective fairways; they're not built up in any way. So, de-

Pudding Ridge Golf Club
224 Cornwallis Dr., Mocksville
• (336) 940-4653

Championship Yardage:	6750
Slope: 128	**Par: 70**
Men's Yardage:	6234
Slope: 123	**Par: 70**
Ladies' Yardage:	4709
Slope: 111	**Par: 70**

Pudding Ridge Golf Club opened in 1994. The course is set in open, rolling terrain, with bermudagrass fairways and bentgrass greens. Mark Charles and Don Bowles teamed up on the design.

Pudding Ridge takes the cake for the most intriguing golf course name. According to local sources, British Gen. Cornwallis' troops coined the name during the American Revolutionary War. The troops thought that the soil looked like pudding, which, as you may know, is the British word for a dessert, e.g. Christmas Pudding.

Pudding Ridge is a new course with an interesting design. The owners of the property took the architectural duties upon themselves, and their work is admirable. Pudding Ridge has gained in maturity, and its openness is unique and in stark contrast to the Triad's many wooded courses. The openness also gives the course a little bit of a linksy feel.

You'll find a lot of room off the tee, some sloping medium to large greens and assorted sizes of bunkers that come into play in varying degrees based on pin placement. One of the great aspects of Pudding Ridge is that, unlike many modern courses, there's an absence of mounds. We like the abandoned grain silo in the 5th fairway—a unique hazard. The question of what happens if the ball falls in the silo is best left to the rules gurus in Far Hills, New Jersey (at USGA headquarters).

Amenities include a practice green, chipping green, locker room, snack bar, restaurant, rental clubs and a pro shop.

The course is walkable for the physically fit, and you can walk anytime during the week and after 3 PM on weekends. Approximate cost, including cart, is $27 weekdays and $30 on weekends.

Reynolds Park Golf Course
2391 Reynolds Park Rd., Winston-Salem
• (336) 650-7660

Championship Yardage:	6320	
Slope: No rating	Par: 71	
Men's Yardage:	5923	
Slope: 118	Par: 71	
Ladies' Yardage:	5538	
Slope: No rating	Par: 75	

Reynolds Park Golf Course opened in 1940. Perry Maxwell designed the original layout, and Ellis Maples revised the track in 1966. The course is primarily open, although woods border a few holes. Fairways are bermudagrass; greens, bentgrass.

Here at Reynolds Park, you'll play a fine old municipal course that's justifiably popular. Maxwell is not a big name in North Carolina, but he's known for another extremely popular municipal course: Hillandale in Durham. He was quite a character, and you can read about him in the Hillandale review in our Triangle chapter. He also designed Winston-Salem's grandest country club course at Old Town.

The course is laid out on a relatively small tract of land, thus some of the fairways are pretty tight. But the course is open, so you won't be out of bounds very often even if your drive strays. It's certainly an entertaining course. There are some holes where it seems like Maples left well enough alone. These holes are somewhat featureless and bunkerless but challeng-

ing. Other holes reveal Maples' influence, featuring large bunkers and sloped greens. The result is a lot of variety and a need for accuracy with approach shots. You'll also notice some fine views of downtown Winston-Salem. The course is evidently quite popular with local golfers—low- and high-handicappers alike.

The par 5 532-yard 4th is a fine hole, downhill to a wide fairway bisected by a stream that may take the driver out of the hands of the big hitters when the ground is baked. The approach shot must avoid a clump of trees on the left-hand side of the fairway. It's one of the many fine driving holes on the golf course.

Amenities include a practice green, range, locker room, snack bar, rental clubs and a pro shop.

You can walk the course anytime during the week and after 1 PM on weekends. Approximate cost, including cart, is $22 weekdays and $28 on weekends.

Salem Glen
100 Glen Day Dr., Clemmons
• (336) 712-1010

Championship Yardage:	7012	
Slope: 136	Par: 71	
Men's Yardage:	6603	
Slope: 131	Par: 71	
Ladies' Yardage:	5054	
Slope: 116	Par: 71	

Salem Glen opened in 1997. Glen Day and Jack Nicklaus designed this course on rolling wooded terrain. In the fairways, you'll find 419 bermudagrass; on the greens, G-2 bentgrass.

Salem Glen is a new housing development golf course near Winston-Salem. Everyone knows Jack Nicklaus, and most who follow the PGA Tour will recognize Glen Day, who won his first PGA Tour event in 1999.

From the tips, Salem Glen is demanding and designed to test the professional or scratch man. Play from the Members' tees and it's a completely different course: a lot friendlier for the mid- to high-handicapper.

The course abuts the Yadkin River, and water comes into play on several holes, providing much of Salem Glen's strategic challenge. In fact, there are 4½ miles of creeks and nine lakes on this tract of land.

The large greens aren't unduly sloped and there's decent room off the tee. The front nine features a number of holes adjacent to the Yadkin River while the back nine features more elevation changes. This might be most noticeable on the par 5 14th, where the approach must clear a ravine to reach a green tucked into an embankment.

Perhaps Salem Glen's calling card is the variety it offers: no two holes are even remotely the same, yet all are set among some of the most majestic scenery in the Triad.

Despite its youth, Salem Glen has already established itself as one of the premier challenges in this exceptional area.

Only members and their guests may walk this course. Approximate cost, including cart, is $35 weekdays and $45 on weekends.

Sandy Ridge Golf Course
2055 Sandy Ridge Rd., Colfax
• (336) 668-0408

Championship Yardage:	6021	
Slope: No rating	Par: 72	
Men's Yardage:	5645	
Slope: No rating	Par: 72	
Ladies' Yardage:	5175	
Slope: No rating	Par: 72	

Sandy Ridge Golf Course opened in 1972. Gene Hamm designed this layout amid rolling wooded terrain. In the fairways, you'll find bermudagrass; on the greens, bentgrass.

Just to the south and west of Greensboro near Piedmont Triad International Airport is the tiny town of Colfax, and this is its one golf course. You're greeted by a docile and somewhat geriatric dog of mixed breed who sniffs at your golf shoes with comforting approval.

A new greenskeeper arrived in 1995, and just after the commencement of his employment, we heard distinct murmurs of approval from golfers with whom we spoke. The design is interesting and varied. Most of the time you'll find plenty of room off the tee, although the back nine seems a little tight in spots. The greens vary in size, are only slightly sloped and, on some holes, are surrounded by small mounds. There are no bunkers, so you'll be able to play some run-up shots if you're a long way from the green and can't land your ball like a well-thrown dart. The terrain is pretty, the golf is relaxed and the dog is well-fed and amiable.

Although it's a short par 5, the 4th still demands the respect of even the long hitter, who must salivate at the 434 yards listed on the scorecard. A lake will devour any ball that skips over the green. The next hole, at 468 yards, also a par 5, might actually offer a better birdie chance.

Amenities include a practice green, locker room, snack bar and dog (again, friendly).

You may walk this course anytime during the week or after noon on weekends. Approximate cost, including cart, is $27 weekdays and $30 on weekends.

Southwick Golf Course
3136 Southwick Dr., Graham
• (336) 227-2582

Championship Yardage:	5778	
Slope: 116	Par: 70	
Men's Yardage:	5431	
Slope: 111	Par: 70	
Ladies' Yardage:	4413	
Slope: 108	Par: 70	

Southwick Golf Course opened in 1960s. Elmo Cobb designed this well-maintained course on predominantly open land, with woods bordering a few holes. It's seeded with bermudagrass fairways and bentgrass greens.

Don't let the abbreviated yardage fool you. Let's just call Southwick a Dudley Moore course: short yet entertaining. It can be plenty tough from the back tees, especially considering the need to play it straight with the driver. The rolling terrain may cause some difficulty with club selection on your approach shots. Call it the *Witches of Southwick* effect (with apologies to John Updike). You won't find Cher here, nor will you find Jack Nicholson, but you will find bewitching greens that vary in size, shape and slope, quite a few devilish bunkers and some water.

Overall, Southwick offers good variety, plenty of doglegs and lots of entertainment. A section of the county amateur tournament is held here, and the staff in the pro shop tells us that scores for that event are always highest here.

Amenities include a practice green, range, snack bar, rental clubs and a pro shop.

You can walk anytime, save weekends before 3 PM in the summer. You can book a tee time anytime. Approximate cost, including cart, is $12 weekdays and $20 on weekends.

Stoney Creek Golf Club
911 Golf House Rd. Stoney Creek
• (336) 449-5688

Championship Yardage:	7063	
Slope: 144	Par: 72	
Men's Regular Yardage:	6573	
Slope: 132	Par: 72	

INSIDERS' TIP

Do you ever go to the practice range *after* your round? Sometimes the most valuable practice time comes right after you've played, when the problems you encountered are fresh in your mind.

Ladies' Yardage: 4737
Slope: 123 **Par: 72**

Stoney Creek Golf Club opened in 1992. Tom Jackson designed the course, which is set in rolling terrain and bordered by woods and houses. Fairways are bermudagrass; greens, bentgrass. In 1993, *Golf Digest* rated Stoney Creek the top new course in North Carolina.

The slope of 144 from the back tees is about as high a rating as you'll find most anywhere in North and South Carolina. Consider that the rating from the back tees for the Ocean Course at Kiawah (South Carolina) is about 149. According to the staff in the pro shop, Stoney Creek from the tips is every bit as difficult as its muscular slope rating; in fact, it's a Monday qualifying site for the Greater Greensboro Chrysler Classic. If you're not a scratch golfer and you're not up for more than 7000 yards of Tom Jackson, consider the other more forgiving tees: There are four sets for your golfing enjoyment. Head for the tips only if you're a five handicap or below.

Ask Tom Jackson about some of his favorite designs and Stoney Creek makes the list—perhaps because Jackson was allowed to lay out the course before the housing development. If you're going to have houses around a golf course, Stoney Creek is a rare example of the proper way to build a housing-development course.

You won't find the abundance of mounds that you might find on other Jackson courses, but you will encounter plenty of bunkering off the tee and around the green complexes. The 1st hole, a tortuous par 5 at a mere 580 from the tips, is probably one of the most difficult starting holes in the area. Many of the bunkers are of the large cloverleaf-shape variety; others are a little smaller but no less penal. Steep embankments flank many of the greens.

Stoney Creek—the creek itself—is not as much a factor as it might seem. The putting surfaces on this course are mostly sloped and large, although some are quite undulating.

Perhaps what separates this Jackson course from others is the excellent variety. Jackson manages to incorporate a number of different looks in most of his courses, but at Stoney Creek he offers increased interest and mental challenge on a playable and not overly penal design. The setting is also remarkably peaceful, given the proximity of houses to many holes.

Just five minutes from I-40/85 between Burlington and Greensboro, Stoney Creek is accessible; it's also an excellent value. Local golfers know how good the course is, but outside the Triad, word has yet to spread, which is why we're spreading it here.

Amenities include a practice green, range, chipping green, snack bar, restaurant and pro shop. A new clubhouse opened in 1999.

The course is walkable for the physically fit, and you may walk anytime during the week and after 3:30 PM on weekends. Approximate cost, including cart, is $40 weekdays and $45 on weekends.

Tanglewood Park

U.S. Hwy. 158 W., Clemmons
• (336) 766-5082

Tanglewood Park boasts two formidable Robert Trent Jones courses: the Championship, which opened in 1959, redesigned in 1973; and the Reynolds, which opened nine holes in 1965, nine more in 1970. Both tracks are set in rolling wooded terrain, although the Championship Course is slightly more open. Both offer bermudagrass fairways and bentgrass greens.

But let's talk about Tanglewood Park. Just west of Winston-Salem, in bucolic and ancient woodlands, you'll find this magnificent amenity. The Reynolds family donated the land. You may have heard of their company: R.J. Reynolds. In a day at Tanglewood, you could play golf, attend a corporate picnic, get married in the wedding chapel, go horseback riding, attend a steeplechase, play tennis, jog, go camping and then be buried in the graveyard adjacent to the 18th green on the Championship Course. There can't be many park complexes like Tanglewood.

But we're here to talk about golf, not parks. There are two wonderful and nationally recognized courses here, both of which have appeared in *Golf Digest's* list of the Top 100 Public Courses. In 1974, the Championship Course hosted the PGA Championship—won by Lee Trevino. Each fall, members of the PGA Senior Tour gather here for one of the richest events of the year, the Vantage Championship. The purse typically brings out the best players on the tour, including Palmer, Trevino, Charles, Rodriguez, Floyd and Irwin.

During the rest of the year, the course attracts people from across North and South Carolina who feel motivated to attack one of the least-vulnerable golf courses anywhere. Estimates vary, but Tanglewood boasts somewhere between 120 and 140 bunkers. It just depends on who you ask. You could ask the maintenance supervisor, but he's probably too busy maintaining the sand to notice your query. We'll get to the bunkers later.

The only problem here, in our minds, is the architecture of the clubhouse, which looks more like an East German chiropractic clinic than a structure befitting two of the prettiest and finest public golf courses in the Carolinas. Anyway, who cares what the clubhouse looks like as long as the burgers and hot dogs are worth their mustard (and they are).

Amenities include a practice green, range, chipping green, locker room, snack bar/grill, rental clubs, a wedding chapel and a pro shop.

The Championship Course is more walkable than the Reynolds; ironically, you can walk the Reynolds Course anytime but may only walk the Championship Course in December, January, July and August. You can book a tee time seven days in advance. Approximate cost, including cart, is $45 weekdays and $48 on weekends for the Championship and $30 every day for the Reynolds. If you live outside North Carolina, the cost for the Championship Course is upwards of $65.

Championship Course
Championship Yardage: 7022
Slope: 140   **Par: 72**
Men's Yardage: 6638
Slope: 135   **Par: 72**
Other Yardage: 6014
Slope: 130   **Par: 72**
Ladies' Yardage: 5119
Slope: 130   **Par: 74**

This might be the prettiest and most challenging public course in the Southeast and about the only course that could qualify as equal to Pinehurst #2. If it's not No. 1, then it's got to be in the top three. The course is long and plays even longer. The fairways are as wide as the rough will allow.

The greens are large and undulating to the point where a two-putt is an accomplishment. But it's the excessive bunkering that makes this course so difficult. It's Bunkers R Us. Just about every shot you play from the tee, and certainly every approach shot, will be influenced by the beach. If you're shooting for a green, it's safest to aim for the middle and hope for the best.

The Seniors

who play the course love it for the lack of housing and other intrusions but have always moaned about the greens. In the past couple of years, management seems to have fixed the situation—finally.

There are so many great holes at Tanglewood that it's virtually impossible to single out one or two. A consensus favorite might be the 424-yard 14th, which requires a solid drive through a chute and over water to a narrow and sloped landing area; the approach is uphill to a large green surrounded on all sides by bunkers. Just one of the many magnificent holes on a course that's more and more underrated each and every year.

Even if your ball is finding the bunkers more than the greens, you can't help appreciating the wonderful setting and ambiance. With its pristine ponds and lakes, its large and mature trees, its chutes and its tranquillity, this outstanding layout feels like an exclusive country club. In fact, probably plenty of country clubs would gladly trade courses with Tanglewood. You'll find magnificent hole after magnificent hole. It's a must-play course in North Carolina, even if the weather preceding your visit has made course maintenance difficult. Play here before you pass on to the great sand trap in the sky.

Reynolds Course
Championship Yardage: 6469
Slope: 125   **Par: 72**
Men's Yardage: 6061
Slope: 120   **Par: 72**

Oak Valley is a fine Arnold Palmer-designed course near Winston-Salem.

Photo: Oak Valley

TRIAD

Ladies' Yardage: 5432
Slope: 120   **Par: 72**

Don't think of the Reynolds Course as the poor sister of the Championship Course. Robert Trent Jones, bless his heart, endowed Reynolds with far less bunkering. The challenge here comes from the dense woods surrounding many of the holes. From the back tees, all the trees make driving the ball a serious challenge. Even if you avoid the trees, you may end up in the deep rough. The greens on this course are predominantly massive, so note the pin position and feel free to fire at it. Even if you miss the green, you'll have a good chance at par if you chip well out of the rough. Water comes into play in the most awkward places, such as right in front of the green on a 214-yard par 3.

Thank you, Mr. Jones. While some of the greens are only slightly sloped, others offer dramatic elevation changes, making putting all the more difficult.

When we visited the course, several greens were in need of serious help, although this may have been caused by the inclement weather preceding our inspection. The course is undergoing a long-term renovation supervised by the head of maintenance. If you can't get on the Championship Course, or if you're in the mood for slightly less bunkering and difficulty, try the Reynolds Course. It would be walkable, except for the fact that the distance between the 9th green and the 10th tee is nearly a mile. Again, it's a wonderfully pretty and peaceful course, just like its sister.

Around the Triad . . .

Fun Things To Do

After you've played the courses, you will find plenty of opportunities for fun in the Triad. On the area's plentiful sunny days, outdoor entertainment abounds. The natural beauty of the Triad lends itself to many green city parks—perfect spots for picnics—and beautiful gardens. The Triad is also home to historical sites and several battlegrounds. If rain is keeping you off the course, visit one of the numerous museums or retail establishments in the area. **Greensboro** and **Winston-Salem** boast several shopping malls; **Burlington** is home to a large number of factory outlet stores; and **High Point** is a renowned furniture destination.

Reynolda Gardens of Wake Forest University, 100 Reynolda Village, Winston-Salem, (336) 759-5325, was made possible by tobacco magnate R.J. Reynolds, who gave this wonderful land to the city. It's now home to some of the most magnificent and extensive gardens in the Triad. Reynolda Gardens is a must-visit for anyone interested in flora.

Old Salem, Old Salem Road, Winston-Salem, (336) 721-7300, offers a slice of history. This Moravian village dates back to the 18th century. More than 80 buildings from the original village have been restored. Re-enactors dressed in period costume act out the daily events of the 18th century in museums and shops along the streets of Old Salem. Don't leave without trying the Moravian sugarcake.

After a hot summer day of golfing, or if you have the kids with you, a trip to **Emerald Point Waterpark,** 3910 Holden Road, Greensboro, (336) 852-9721, may be in order. The 45-acre waterpark features 30 rides and attractions, including a wave pool, several waterslides and bodyslides, and kiddie pools. For the adventurous, the Skycoaster offers an airborne thrill: This huge swing, attached to an arch by steel cables, launches you, secure in your body harness, horizontally 115 feet into the air and swings you back and forth under the arch like Superman.

Greensboro Historical Museum, 130 Summit Avenue, Greensboro, (336) 373-2043, is housed in a former church that dates back to the turn of the century. Exhibits trace the many and varied religious and racial groups that built the city of Greensboro into what it is today. Learn about military history, early transportation and decorative arts.

Those interested in American military history may want to visit the **American Revolution battleground sites** in Greensboro and Bur-lington. The **Guilford Courthouse National Military Battleground Park,** 2332 New Garden Road, Greensboro, (336) 288-1776, was the site of a 1781 battle in the American Revolution. The site features a museum, walking trails, 28 monuments, musket demonstrations and guided tours. The **Alamance Battleground,** 5803 N.C. Highway 62 S., Burlington (Exit 143 off I-85), (336) 227-4785, was the site of a 1771 battle that preceded but was an early part of the Revolutionary War. Re-enactments of the battle, which pitched the Regulators (country farmers) against the troops of Royal Gov. William Tryon, are

TRIAD

held periodically at the battleground. An audiovisual program and tours of the battlefield, monuments and the historic **1780 Allen House** make for an interesting day of learning about the 18th-century battle.

High Point touts itself as "The furniture capital of the world," so if you need furnishings, you might as well check out the bargains. Don't worry about lugging a settee around for the rest of your visit to the Triad; the stores will ship it home for you. More than 50 furniture stores, including **Rose, the Atrium, Furniture Land South** and **Young's,** are scattered around the city. Call the **High Point Convention and Visitors Bureau,** (336) 889-5151, for information. The **Furniture Discovery Center,** 101 W. Green Drive, High Point, (336) 887-3876, is a museum dedicated to the art of furniture making.

Where to Eat

Refer to our Preface for an explanation of the pricing code.

Greensboro

J. Butler's Bar and Grille
$$ • 3709 Battleground Ave., Greensboro
• (336) 282-8080

Across from Brassfield Cinema and Brassfield Shopping Center, J. Butler's offers a feast of sandwiches, gourmet burgers, salads and entrees to enjoy before or after taking in a movie or tackling a shopping expedition. Couple this with a fully stocked bar and you also have a really fun and relaxed place to unwind after a rough day on the links.

Kyoto Fantasy
$$ • 1200 S. Holden Rd., Greensboro
• (336) 299-1003

There's always something fun, funny and bizarre about going to an authentic Japanese steakhouse. The chef comes to your table, and you bear witness to his wizardry as he slices and dices with surgical knives. You'll get the full treatment here at Kyoto Fantasy: Take your shoes off and sit down for your session. Make sure you change your socks before you go. There's also a sushi bar for raw fish fans or the extremely trendy.

Longhorn Steak
Restaurant and Saloon
$$$ • 2925 Battleground Ave., Greensboro
• (336) 545-3200

Longhorn was a pioneer in the introduction of Texas-style steakhouses in the Carolinas. You'll find a large yet friendly environment with a rustic Western-looking decor. There's a bar, and you may have to wait a few minutes here while a table is readied for your appetite. Once you sit down, indulge in a big steak washed down with a couple of beers. Or try the salmon if you're not a steak person. The atmosphere is relaxed, and it's almost essential to wear jeans. You can wear a cowboy hat if you like, but there's no discount for this type of behavior.

Sunset Cafe
$$$ • 4608 W. Market St., Greensboro
• (336) 855-0349

The Sunset Cafe offers a solid alternative to the chain-style restaurants that dominate the local scene. This restaurant specializes in vegetarian, seafood, poultry and lamb dishes served in a warm, cozy atmosphere.

High Point

Barracuda Bistro
$$ • 2801 N. Main St., High Point
• (336) 869-1010

A new and unique concept, especially for High Point, the Barracuda Bistro offers a West Indian feel and menu. At the raw bar, the decor is supposed to make you feel like you're underwater, looking up at the clear blue sky of the Caribbean. And then you hoover a couple of oysters, sink a Red Stripe and listen to the reggae, mon. You're suddenly far from the madding crowds of raging downtown High Point.

The menu is definitely fish-oriented, even though the red-meat eaters among you should try the double-cut pork chops or West Indian ribs. But it's subaquatic fare that will prove most attractive. There's grilled salmon with papaya relish and plantation chips, seared rare tuna with a West Indian vinaigrette,

INSIDERS' TIP

Here's a good exercise to help your short game. Drop a handful of balls all the way around a green, and hit them all with the same club (anything from a 6-iron to a wedge will work). You'll be forced to think and be creative, trying everything from an open stance flop shot to a long bump-and-run.

TRIAD

Caribbean gumbo or blackened grouper. With the Caribbean murals and the abundant banana and mango trees, the ambiance here is tropical—who knows, maybe you'll catch a fish, and maybe it will be a Barracuda. A good value for fresh fish and ambiance.

Noble's
$$$ • 114 S. Main St., High Point
• (336) 889-3354
380 Knollwood St., Winston Salem,
• (336) 777-8477

Noble's is a "dressy casual" restaurant with a fine and varied menu that changes daily. All sauces and desserts are made on the premises, and all the meat and fish are cut that day. The restaurant is known for its oyster salad, which is a popular appetizer. Diners are also fond of the veal tenderloin and free-range chicken, a true rarity in the Carolinas. If you're a fish eater, you should definitely try the salmon, tuna or grouper. When you're finished with your main course, try the apple tart or some of Noble's homemade ice cream. The restaurant sits on two levels: street and basement. There's a jazz trio on Thursday, Friday and Saturday for your further entertainment.

Note that you'll also find a Noble's in Winston-Salem.

Sugar Magnolia
$$$ • 126 E. State Ave., High Point
• (336) 883-1668

No, it's not the song by the Grateful Dead, but one of High Point's most popular restaurants. The menu changes after each High Point furniture show (there's one in the fall and spring), but the establishment boasts enough regular diners that the chef prepares a wide range of specials. Ambiance here is supplied by a wide patio, a bar with a fireplace and a nonsmoking dining room.

Appetizers include baked Brie or a special dish called Three Musketeers, which is marinated beef tips. Once you've disposed with D'Artagnan and shouted "One for all and all for one," it's time to choose a main course. How about angel hair pasta with garlic and wild mushrooms? Or baked sea bass? Or crabcakes? The fish and veal specials change every night, plus there's a solid variety of beef and chicken.

Round everything off with an espresso or glass of port or a stirring rendition of the song named after this eatery. "Takes the wheel when I'm seeing double; pays my ticket when I speed."

Winston-Salem

Par-3 Bistro
$$$ • Bethania Station Rd., Winston-Salem
• (336) 924-9485

One of the most remarkable restaurants in the world, the Par-3 Bistro expertly combines two of America's—and the authors'—favorite pastimes: golf and eating. The nine-hole par 3 course features bermudagrass greens and quite a bit of water. The restaurant is fine dining all the way. Try the roast duck or one of the many veal or beef dishes, all created by chef Michel Claire who has served up fine culinary fare in California, Atlanta and France. It's probably the only place in the world where you can play golf and eat rack of lamb for less than $25.

Szechwan Palace
$$ • 3040 Healy Dr., Winston-Salem
• (336) 768-7123

Tucked away in a somewhat innocuous strip mall in the Hanes Mall area is one of Winston-Salem's best Chinese restaurants. The decor is somewhat clichéd, with a dominant theme of meandering scenes of the Great Wall of China interspersed with red dragons. The menu, however, is less predictable; you'll find some unique creations that go well beyond your typical sweet-and-sour fare—even the name implies some hot and spicy entrees. You can also sip a Chinese beer, although the Chinese are not especially renowned as world leaders in the production of quality adult malt beverages.

Twin City Diner
$$ • 1425A W. First St., Winston-Salem
• (336) 724-4203

Twin City Diner is a relaxed and fun neighborhood restaurant where locals meet and mingle. There's a well-stocked bar where you can swap stories or watch a sports event on the discreetly placed televisions. The menu is extensive. The wings, served in multiples of five, are excellent. Sample some traditional pub fare—hamburgers and sandwiches—or delve into a more substantial entrée, such as Cajun salmon.

Vincenzo's
$$ • 3449 Robin Hood Rd., Winston-Salem
• (336) 765-3176

Vincenzo's is one of those great institutions where you feel right at home the second you walk in the door. The restaurant has been serving up Italian dishes since 1964. There's veal parmigiana, spaghetti, eggplant parmigiana, lasagna, veal marsala, a delightful clam sauce and steamed clams. Plus there's lots of Italian vino to help you wash down all that great pasta.

Where to Stay

Refer to our Preface for an explanation of the pricing code.

Greensboro

Best Western Windsor Suites
$$$ • 2006 Veasley St., Greensboro • (336) 294-9100, (800) 528-1234

Best Westerns are best known for clean and pleasant but basic motel-type rooms and good locations. The Windsor Suites is a step up from the usual—it feels more like a fine hotel. Rooms are elegantly decorated, and there's lots of faux wood paneling. Unlike many hotels, you can actually open the window to the outside world. You'll find plenty of restaurants just around the corner as well as easy access to I-40.

In addition to your larger-than-usual room, amenities here include a separate sitting area, microwaves and refrigerators in the rooms, a complimentary breakfast, a TV with thirty-eight channels, free HBO and ESPN, plus an exercise room with sauna.

Courtyard by Marriott
$$ • 4400 W. Wendover Rd., Greensboro • (336) 294-3800, (800) 321-2211

If you've seen a Courtyard by Marriott before, then you won't be surprised to find this clean, well-kept hotel in a convenient location and run by an efficient staff. Suites boast two TVs and a separate second bedroom with a pull-out couch. Amenities include an outdoor pool, an indoor whirlpool and an exercise room. A restaurant on the premises serves breakfast daily.

Embassy Suites
$$$ • 204 Centreport Dr., Greensboro • (336) 668-4535, (800) 362-2779

Enormous and efficient, the Greensboro Embassy Suites is everything you'd expect from the hotel chain that popularized the free-breakfast concept. As the name implies, at Embassy Suites you get a suite, and there are 221 of them here, 118 of them nonsmoking. This is a great choice if you're taking a family golf vacation—

you'll all have room to spread out. The facility has a restaurant, lounge, cable TV in every suite and a large indoor swimming pool with an adjacent Jacuzzi. If you're the fitness type, we'd recommend a trip to the well-appointed exercise room.

Holiday Inn Four Seasons
$$$$ • 3121 High Point Rd., Greensboro • (336) 292-9161

With 522 rooms, the Holiday Inn Four Seasons is one of the largest and most impressive hotels in Greensboro. As you drive by on I-40, you can't miss the place—it's about 30 stories tall. This hotel offers meeting and convention facilities in addition to a nightclub with live entertainment, a weight room and other amenities, including an indoor/outdoor pool to keep you active. You'll also find four restaurants on site, including Stinger's Bar & Grill and Joseph's, serving Italian cuisine. Shoppers will enjoy the nearby mall as well.

High Point

Holiday Inn – Market Square Convention Center
$$$ • 236 S. Main St., High Point • (336) 886-7011, (800) 647-STAY

Large and extremely busy during the two annual furniture markets, High Point's Holiday Inn is primarily a business hotel, featuring plenty of meeting rooms. There's an outdoor pool, a restaurant offering three meals a day and a lounge where you can hoist a quick one after a hectic day at the market. Rooms feature coffee machines and full cable TV with free Showtime.

Radisson Hotel High Point
$$$$ • 135 S. Main St., High Point • (336) 889-8888, (800) 333-3333

Located right downtown adjacent to the Furniture Market, the large Radisson is targeted at the business traveler who might really enjoy the eighth floor Business Class level. Here, in addition to all the regular amenities, you get free local phone calls, free fax service, free access to the special lounge and free breakfast for two. So, when you're in town for business but also to get in a round or two on the area's great courses, here's your home base. If you're just a regular traveler, the hotel is still pretty spectacular, offering indoor swimming, a Jacuzzi, cable TV (with ESPN) plus a full-service restaurant.

TRIAD

Super 8 Motel
$ • 400 S. Main St., High Point
• (336) 882-4103

You'll find 44 fully renovated rooms here at High Point's outpost of the popular chain. Super 8 offers a host of amenities including satellite TV (with HBO), swimming pool, complimentary breakfast, available waterbeds and a choice of king- or queen-size beds. The convenient location is just a mile from the Furniture Market. You can get AAA rates, commercial rates, family rates, senior rates and special furniture market rates, which are just a hair above regular rates. Right.

Winston-Salem

Adam's Mark
$$$ • 425 N. Cherry St., Winston-Salem
• (336) 725-3500

One of Winston-Salem's largest hotels (315 rooms), the Adam's Mark offers all the amenities you might expect from a top hotel, including an indoor pool, an outdoor sundeck, 24-hour room service, two restaurants, a lounge and a gift shop.

Hampton Inn
$$$ • 1990 Hampton Inn Ct.,
Winston-Salem • (336) 760-1660

This Hampton Inn exemplifies the trade-mark quality that has gained this chain a reputation for clean, well-appointed rooms and friendly service. We recommend the Jacuzzi suites on the third floor as a pleasant and slightly more spacious version of the standard rooms. There's nothing better than a hot bath with swirling jets of water to relax you after a hard day on the links. And once the muscles are loosened up, head for the workout room to tighten them again. Business travelers will appreciate the meeting facilities as well. The hotel is convenient to I-40.

Regency Inn
$$ • 128 N. Cherry St., Winston-Salem
• (336) 723-8861

You probably have seen plenty of Best Westerns around the country on your travels, but this one is a little different from others: It's not the typical motel-style that defines the chain. The Regency Inn is a downtown hotel that's a great place to stay at a sensible price, with cable TV in every room and a full range of amenities. Enjoy the outdoor pool when the weather is right, and don't miss the complimentary continental breakfast.

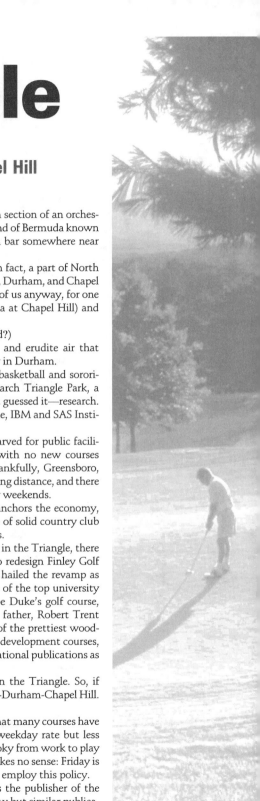

North Carolina's
Triangle

Raleigh/Durham/Chapel Hill

What is the Triangle?

Is it a small instrument found in the percussion section of an orchestra? Is it a block of ocean near the mid-Atlantic island of Bermuda known for swallowing light aircraft? Is it a dark mob-run bar somewhere near Newark?

For the purposes of this book, the Triangle is, in fact, a part of North Carolina's Piedmont. The area is defined by Raleigh, Durham, and Chapel Hill, municipalities best known, in the eyes of one of us anyway, for one major university (the University of North Carolina at Chapel Hill) and two minor ones (North Carolina State and Duke).

(Quick: Which university did one author attend?)

Thus the Triangle boasts a mildly Bohemian and erudite air that sometimes borders on the obnoxious—particularly in Durham.

But there's more to the Triangle than college basketball and sororities. There's industry, tobacco farming, and Research Triangle Park, a massive real estate development dedicated to—you guessed it—research. RTP is inhabited by companies like Glaxo Wellcome, IBM and SAS Institute.

Golf-wise, the Triangle has been somewhat starved for public facilities. Unfortunately, there's little relief in sight, with no new courses planned on increasingly expensive real estate. Thankfully, Greensboro, Winston-Salem, and Pinehurst are within easy driving distance, and there must be quite a pilgrimage to these areas on sunny weekends.

East of the Triangle, where Tobacco farming anchors the economy, life is a little more relaxed and gentrified: A couple of solid country club courses open their doors to the public on weekdays.

Despite the relative scarcity of good public golf in the Triangle, there are some gems. UNC recently hired Tom Fazio to redesign Finley Golf Course; locals, students, alumni, and others have hailed the revamp as extremely successful. It must now be rated as one of the top university facilities in the country. Also on that list must be Duke's golf course, renovated some years back by Rees Jones, whose father, Robert Trent Jones, brilliantly routed the course through some of the prettiest woodland in North Carolina. Some of the more modern development courses, like The Neuse, have garnered solid reviews from national publications as well.

But still, there's a big need for new courses in the Triangle. So, if you're a golf course developer, head over to Raleigh-Durham-Chapel Hill. You'll find that demand far outstrips supply.

One annoying aspect of golf in the Triangle is that many courses have a special Friday greens fee that's more than the weekday rate but less than the weekend rate. Most of us have to play hooky from work to play golf on Friday, so why should we be penalized? Makes no sense: Friday is still a school day. Sadly, most of the better courses employ this policy.

Jay Allred, who lives in Winston-Salem and is the publisher of the excellent publication *Triad Golf Today*, started a new but similar publica-

The Triangle Area

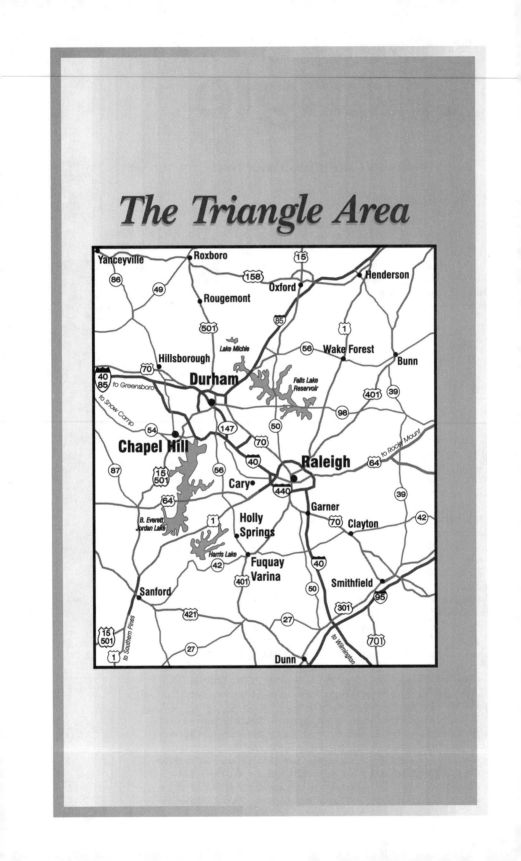

GOLF COURSES IN NORTH CAROLINA'S TRIANGLE

Course	Type	# Holes	Par	Slope	Yards	Walking	Booking	Cost w/Cart
Caswell Pines	public	18	72	114	6270	restricted	5 days	$23-30
Cheviot Hills	semiprivate	18	71	107	5975	restricted	anytime	$26-33
Crooked Creek	public	18	72	116	6028	restricted	7 days	$16-28
Devil's Ridge	semiprivate	18	72	127	6430	restricted	7 days	$40-49
Duke University's Washington Duke Golf & CC	semiprivate	18	72	129	6721	restricted	anytime	$55-65
Eagle Crest	public	18	72	n/r	6038	anytime	anytime	$30-33
Finley Golf Course (UNC)	public	18	72	117	6102	anytime	2 days	$40-55
Hedingham Golf Club	semiprivate	18	72	116	6276	restricted	anytime	$29-38
Hillandale Golf Club	public	18	71	118	6100	restricted	anytime	$28-33
Kerr Lake	semiprivate	18	72	118	6185	anytime	2 days	$27-31
Lake Winds Golf Course	semiprivate	18	72	n/r	6008	anytime	anytime	$24-28
Lochmere Golf Club	semiprivate	18	72	116	6156	restricted	7 days	$33-45
The Neuse Golf Club	semiprivate	18	72	129	6626	restricted	7 days	$40-50
Occoneechee Golf Club	semiprivate	18	71	119	5692	anytime	3-4 days	$26-29
The River	semiprivate	18	72	n/a	6116	anytime	14 days	$25-35
Roxboro Country Club	semiprivate	18	70	113	5364	anytime	2 days	$20-27
Sourwood Golf Club	public	18	72	112	6285	anytime	anytime	$20-25
Wake Forest Country Club	semiprivate	18	72	129	6525	restricted	7 days	$30-40
Wildwood Green C.C.	semiprivate	18	70	117	5100	anytime	7 days	$38-48
Willowhaven	semiprivate	18	72	117	6342	anytime	3-5 days	$31.50-36.50

tion for the Triangle, called, you guessed it, *Triangle Golf Today*. Check out his Website for updates on golf in the Triangle: www.triadgolf.com.

Caswell Pines Golf Club
2380 County Home Rd., Yanceyville
• (910) 694-2255, (800) 694-1888
Championship Yardage: 6651
Slope: 120   **Par: 72**
Men's Yardage: **6270**
Slope: 114   **Par: 72**
Other Yardage: **5720**
Slope: 108   **Par: 72**
Ladies' Yardage: **5145**
Slope: 111   **Par: 72**

Caswell Pines, a Gene Hamm design, opened in 1993. The course is primarily open, but woods and homesites border some holes. In the fairways, you'll find 419 bermudagrass; on the greens, you'll find bentgrass.

Built on what was previously a tobacco farm, Caswell Pines is an exciting and challenging course with a fine design in a pleasant setting. Most of the Gene Hamm courses we've seen tend toward the traditional; this one leans toward the modern: earth-worked and mounded. Hamm is one of the most respected figures in North Carolina golf, having won several tournaments on courses he designed.

Caswell Pines offers excellent variety and some truly outstanding holes, including a number with significant elevation changes. Off the tee, you'll have a decent amount of room: Big hitters will want to play from the back tees and use the driver. The great thing about Caswell Pines is that it makes you think. You'll need to keep your golfing wits about you if you plan to score well. The greens here are typically large, with plenty of subtle and not-so-subtle breaks; two-putting is quite a feat on many holes. Large bunkers around a number of greens make life even more difficult. And did we mention the significant amount of water? Anyway, it's well worth the visit to Yanceyville to play this course.

The most tempting hole might be the par 4 13th. At 337 yards from the tips and water to the left, it requires a heroic decision. With firm course conditions, it might be fun to draw the ball to the hole, but disaster lurks in the tree to the right for the rope hook. Prudence dictates a long iron and wedge, but how often does true sense enter our heads when there's a driveable green right in front of our noses?

Amenities include a practice green, range, snack bar, restaurant, rental clubs and a beverage cart.

The course is walkable for the very fit, but walking is restricted; call for daily details. Approximate cost, including cart, is $23 weekdays and $30 on weekends.

Cheviot Hills Golf Club
7301 Capital Blvd., Raleigh
• (919) 876-9920
Championship Yardage: 6475
Slope: 116   **Par: 71**
Men's Yardage: 5975
Slope: 107   **Par: 71**
Ladies' Yardage: 4965
Slope: 114   **Par: 71**

Cheviot Hills Golf Club opened in 1930. *Architects of Golf* lists Harold Long as the original designer. Gene Hamm came along later to remodel and redesign. The course is set in rolling wooded terrain without a house in sight. In the fairways, you'll find bermudagrass; on the greens, bentgrass.

As you walk up to the 19th-century clubhouse, you'll be greeted by the pro-shop attendant who expertly combines friendliness with brusqueness. You'll feel like you're at a country club, standing among people who have been friends for 50 years.

The course itself is a masterpiece of understatement and traditionalism. There's nothing tricked up, nothing silly. Mounds are uncommon, and the only house you might see belongs to the couple that owns the course. The only thing missing here is a knowledgeable caddie to carry and clean your clubs and help you read putts.

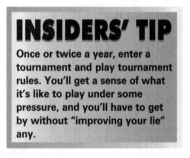

INSIDERS' TIP

Once or twice a year, enter a tournament and play tournament rules. You'll get a sense of what it's like to play under some pressure, and you'll have to get by without "improving your lie" any.

The staff here at Cheviot Hills is justifiably proud of the course—and woe betide you should your cart stray from the path. The aforementioned pro-shop attendant, equipped with binoculars and a sound system that can probably be heard in Virginia, will let you know that "CARTS MUST BE KEPT ON PATHS AT ALL TIMES!"

You'll find some short par 5s and some long par 4s, most with plenty of room off the tee.

The staff informs us that you'll be using all your clubs and hitting all your shots. The course offers particularly good value if you walk.

After the tough 2nd hole, the par 5 3rd arrives as a chance to regain a stroke. At 525 yards, it requires a big drive and solid second to a green that's tucked away behind a small pond. It's safest to lay up to 100 yards and wedge into the shallow green and hopefully putt for birdie, but the big hitter will undoubtedly want to go for it if the fairway is firm.

If you're thinking about skipping Sunday morning services at your chosen house of worship and sneaking onto the course while you should be singing Hymn 315, think again. The course doesn't open until 12:30 PM on Sundays.

Amenities include a practice green, range, chipping green, locker room, snack bar, rental clubs and a pro shop.

The course is walkable and you can walk almost anytime. Approximate cost, including cart, is $26 Monday to Thursday, $29 on Friday and $33 on weekends.

Crooked Creek
4621 Shady Greens Dr., Fuquay-Varina
• (919) 557-7529

Championship Yardage:	6704	
Slope: 120	**Par:** 72	
Men's Yardage:	6028	
Slope: 116	**Par:** 72	
Other Yardage:	5296	
Slope: 112	**Par:** 72	
Ladies' Yardage:	4978	
Slope: 114	**Par:** 72	

Chuck Smith designed Crooked Creek, which opened in late 1995. Fairways are 419 bermudagrass, and greens are bentgrass.

Crooked Creek offers a traditional design that demands accuracy off the tee. The greens are midsize and undulating, with a few bunkers to catch those wayward iron shots you thought you had cured. The course also boasts a number of interesting and well-designed dogleg holes. The greens, on the back nine especially, are rolling. Crooked Creek (have you ever seen a straight one?) is a good addition to the portfolio of courses in the eastern section of the Triangle and is worth a reconnaissance mission if you're in Raleigh and you're interested in surveying a new course.

The par 4 3rd should hold your interest. It's only 378 from the back tees and is everything you'd expect from a hole where precision is more important than power. Water runs down the entire left-hand side. Your drive or three wood needs to play to a narrow landing area. From

there, it's a short iron completely over water to a mid-sized green. For those fearful of the water, there's ample bail-out space to the right of the hole, where a crisp half-wedge and good putt could still yield par. Consider the 3rd good test early in the round and a par gratefully accepted.

Amenities include a practice green, range, chipping green, locker room, snack bar, rental clubs and a pro shop.

Walking is permitted Monday through Friday. Approximate cost, including cart, is $16 Monday through Thursday, $20 on Friday and $28 on weekends.

Devil's Ridge Golf Club
5107 Linksland Dr., Holly Springs
• (919) 557-6100

Championship Yardage:	7002	
Slope: 138	**Par:** 72	
Men's Yardage:	6430	
Slope: 127	**Par:** 72	
Other Yardage:	5852	
Slope: 120	**Par:** 72	
Ladies' Yardage:	5244	
Slope: 121	**Par:** 72	

This John LaFoy design at Devil's Ridge, which opened in 1991, is set on undulating terrain, and houses border many holes. In the fairways, you'll find bermudagrass; on the greens, you'll putt on bentgrass.

John LaFoy is a well-known architect and former associate of George Cobb. LaFoy made frequent trips to Augusta National with Cobb, and when illness slowed Cobb in his later years, LaFoy took over a number of the design responsibilities. In fact, he was most responsible for Linville Ridge Country Club in the mountains of North Carolina. LaFoy began his own design business in 1986.

Here at Devil's Ridge, LaFoy created a tough track with all the trappings of a modern course: mounds, severely undulating greens, tough tee shots, extensive bunkering, elevation changes, more mounds, backbreaking length from the back tees and still more mounds.

It's interesting to see how different this course is from many Cobb designs. You'll certainly want to spend a couple of dollars for the excellent yardage book, especially if you're playing this course for the first time. Keep your cart speed down on the front nine, as a state trooper lives next to one of the greens.

Excessive velocity aside, the course is well designed, greatly varied and interesting. However, if you're not a fan of modern courses, steer toward something more traditional than Devil's

Ridge. A good score requires hitting just about every club in your bag—and hitting it crisply. Particularly interesting are the shapes of the greens: Many look like amoebae on steroids.

Par is a great score on the pre-hot dog 9th, a muscular par 5 at 567 yards from the back tees. The tee shot must avoid two large bunkers to the right, while the second must skirt a large bunker on the left. The huge green is 42 yards deep but quite narrow. A shallow bunker in front of the green provides the final barrier to those who think they can reach in two. Par is a great score here.

We think Devil's Ridge is a must-play course in the Raleigh area, even if you only play it once. Perhaps this description of the 17th hole from the yardage book best summarizes the course:

"This is the hole for which Devil's Ridge got its name. Not too long, not too narrow, not too hard. However, don't miss any shot or you'll post a BIG [their caps] number. Favor the left on your tee shot. If you miss the green to the right and look for your ball, you may never be heard from again." Enough said.

Amenities include a practice green, range, chipping green, snack bar, rental clubs, a beverage cart and a pro shop.

Walking is restricted, although we wouldn't recommend it anyway. Approximate cost, including cart, is $40 Monday to Thursday, $45 on Fridays and $49 on weekends.

Duke University Golf Club
N.C. Hwy. 751 and Science Dr., Durham • (919) 681-2288

Championship Yardage:	7045	
Slope: 137	**Par:** 72	
Men's Yardage:	6721	
Slope: 129	**Par:** 72	
Other Yardage:	6207	
Slope: 119	**Par:** 72	
Ladies' Yardage:	5505	
Slope: 124	**Par:** 72	

The golf course at Washington Duke Golf and Country Club opened in 1957. Robert Trent Jones designed the original course; Rees Jones redesigned and renovated it in 1993. At the time of the renovation, Jones' daughter was a student at Duke, and she persuaded her dad to perform the work for free. This picturesque

track has 419 bermudagrass fairways and bentgrass greens.

This is Duke University's golf course, and it's one of the most magnificent courses in the Triangle. Robert Trent Jones routed the course by cutting it out of Duke Forest; thus, just about every hole is bordered by wonderfully pretty woods replete with towering trees. Rees Jones must have kept the original routing; however, he blew up the tee boxes and green complexes, and the result is nothing short of stunning. The targets are wonderfully defined, and some of the holes are breathtaking. A lot of money was poured into this course, and it shows. However, the lack of air circulation caused by all the trees coupled with the huge number of rounds pumped through here means that conditioning can be an issue, particularly in the summer.

There's subtle mounding in the fairways and quite a few gaping fairway bunkers. You won't always have an even stance in the fairway. And water comes into play on a few holes. But it's the attention to detail around the green complexes that makes the course so spectacular. You'll see large, tiered greens, undulations and obvious slopes. Two-putting any green on this course is an achievement. Embankments flank many greens; but, more importantly, each green complex features a dizzying array of bunkers—some large, some small, but all potentially difficult and score-destroying.

And as if the challenge wasn't great enough, the course finishes with two long and difficult uphill par 4s; you'll have to bust the ball off the tee if you want any chance of reaching the green in regulation. Make sure you play this course before you lose your swing.

We're not sure you'll want to play the course often if you're a high-handicapper. If you get into trouble, particularly around the greens, then you'll be faced with some difficult short-game challenges.

Amenities include a practice green, range, chipping green, locker room, bar, snack bar, restaurant, rental clubs, a beverage cart and a pro shop. You can also spend a night at the well-appointed Washington Duke Inn (see this chapter's subsequent "Where to Stay" section) adjacent to the course.

There are lots of great holes, but the most

INSIDERS' TIP

At least once a year, spend a day at a pro golf tournament. You might want to follow a golfer whose play you enjoy. Or, camp out next to a reachable par 5 and watch the pros demonstrate their short game prowess. Either way, your bound to absorb some tips on what makes these players so good.

picturesque might be the par 3 12th, just 180 from the tips all over water to a peninsula green where a forward pin placement demands accuracy. Bunkers back and left add to the potential problems.

The course is walkable for the physically fit, but walking is restricted; call ahead for daily details. (You'll see lots of students walking out here.) If you're neither a Duke student nor a member of the university's faculty or staff, the approximate cost, including cart, is $55 weekdays and $65 on weekends.

Eagle Crest
4400 Auburn Church Rd., Garner
• (919) 772-6104
Championship Yardage: 6514
Slope: No rating   Par: 72
Men's Yardage: 6038
Slope: No rating   Par: 72
Ladies' Yardage: 4875
Slope: No rating   Par: 72

Eagle Crest opened in 1968. This John Baucom design is set on rolling and primarily open terrain, with bermudagrass fairways and bentgrass greens.

We found a fun, straightforward, relaxing and soundly designed country course at Eagle Crest. You won't encounter any sand traps, so if you hate the beach, you'll love it here all the more. Water comes into play on four holes. Fairways are predominantly wide, although approach shots must hit small greens, some of which are crowned. If the ground is hard, you might be able to run the ball up to the hole with a low running hook. Feel free to use your Texas wedge. You'll find mounds, swales and grass bunkers around some of the greens. If you enjoy a no-frills course with a minimum of fuss and tricks, you'll enjoy the laid-back setting we found here.

With the game almost over, the par 4 350-yard 17th is a hole where par will be welcome. It's a short drive to a landing area then a short iron or wedge over water to the green. The presence of water and nerves makes this one of the most demanding holes on the course.

Amenities include a range, snack bar and rental clubs.

You can walk this course anytime. Approximate cost, including cart, is $30 weekdays and $33 on weekends.

Finley Golf Course
Finley Golf Course Rd., Chapel Hill
• (919) 962-2349
Championship Yardage: 7119
Slope: 141   Par: 72

Men's Yardage: 6579
Slope: 134   Par: 72
Ladies' Yardage: 5543/4954
Slope: 116   Par: 72

The University of North Carolina's Finley Golf Course, designed by George Cobb, opened in 1950. Perhaps the biggest golf course news in the Triangle is the $8 million redesign of Finley, completed in late 1999 by the architect considered by many the best in the world—Tom Fazio. The work is remarkable. The redesign added some undulation to the course, but it's still a relatively flat course. In the fairways, you'll find 419 bermudagrass; on the greens, L93 bentgrass.

Even though the Chapel Hill area is hilly (duh), Finley sits adjacent to Siler's Bog, a swamp/nature reserve that's actually the subject of quite a good book. Since Finley's opening in 1950, parts of it have become Finley's Bog, especially during winter rains and summer downpours. The flatness of the course detracted significantly from what was a pretty decent overall design.

Fazio and his team faced two major challenges. One: drainage. Two: producing an interesting design that would challenge a serious college golfer while still serving the students of PE28: Introduction to Golf. While long carries are fun for the accomplished player, they're disheartening for the beginner.

To meet the needs of the University's golfing community, Fazio completely blew up the old George Cobb design. Much of the work is high-tech, employing lasers to grade fairways and pipes underneath the greens to control the flow of air and water.

Fazio also completely rebuilt the practice area, which is now one of the finest in North Carolina.

Finley provides a thrilling strategic test. Fazio deftly employs bunkers, water hazards and rolling greens to produce a course that boasts interest from the 1st tee to the 18th green.

Two of the tougher holes come late in the round, when pars always seem that much more valuable. The 15th measures 451 yards, a par 4, downhill off the tee with a lake to the left of the green. The 16th is no easier, 423 uphill with a tee shot that must clear a hazard. Perhaps the next, a 540-yard par 5, will provide a respite, but the 18th, at 453, could leave a bad taste in the mouth. It's a stirring finishing stretch.

All the little details are here, from walk mowing the greens every day to the employment of a Border Collie to control the propensity of geese to leave ordure around greensites. With $8 mill to spend, it's no wonder that Finley is now one of the nation's premiere golf facilities.

Golf for Women in the Carolinas

It's different from probably anywhere else in the world.

Those of us who live and play in the Carolinas are accustomed to the absolute fact that women are present, allowed and, yes, welcome... the same as male golfers. Women golfers here possibly take this acceptance for granted until they are asked about it by visitors, usually from northeastern states, who are not accustomed to women being allowed on private courses every day, let alone any time of day. Women are welcome on all of the public or semiprivate golf courses that we researched for *The Insiders' Guide to Golf in the Carolinas*.

More than 5 million women in America play golf, and social acceptance has changed dramatically since the 16th century when Mary Queen of Scots was criticized for taking a liking to the sport of the male nobility.

A recent book by Marcia Chambers, *The Unplayable Lie*, tells of the discrimination that exists in American golf today and of options that help both men and women understand how and why rules can change. The Carolinas, thankfully, are not the setting for any of the cases cited in Chambers' book.

Our differences probably stem from the fact that the vast majority of Carolina courses are public or semiprivate and not country clubs of the type found in many other locations. Also, with a plethora of courses, everyone's business is wanted and needed.

Many clubs do not have women's locker rooms, which might be somewhat annoying, but equal access has been considered for all of the newer clubhouses.

The **Executive Women's Golf League** has chapters in several cities throughout the Carolinas. It's part of a national movement including nearly 10,000 members in more than 100 chapters. The league intends to promote golf by providing a nurturing atmosphere so women will not be intimidated while learning the game. It also emphasizes familiarizing women with the business etiquette of golf as part of professional networking. In fact, the organization pushes etiquette and training to such a point that women might be more

Dana Rader operates one of the most successful golf schools in the country.

Photo: J.J. Bissell

conscious of their proper manners, and even of some rules of golf, than many men.

The camaraderie, including business and social networking, is spoken about among the league's members as an important part of their association. Women new to an area find immediate acceptance among a group with common interests, and those new to golfing find encouragement to learn how to buy clubs and get on a real course.

The leagues in any city welcome visitors from other chapters and invite new members—whether beginning or experienced golfers. For more information, call any of the Executive Women's Golf League Carolina chapters.

In North Carolina:

Charlotte	(704) 892-9274
Pinehurst	(910) 245-3270
Raleigh	(800) 326-3418
	(919) 781-5552
Wilmington	(910) 799-0132

In South Carolina:

Charleston	(843) 881-2014
Hilton Head	(843) 689-1300 Ext. 223
Myrtle Beach	(843) 448-5942 Ext. 18

That was the goal. UNC is a competitive university that wants to be better than its local rivals, Duke and N.C. State, and wants to be recognized around the country for its outstanding physical plants. You have to keep up with the Joneses these days in college golf and with the work at Finley, UNC has done that and then some.

Amenities include a practice green, range, chipping green, snack bar, rental clubs and a pro shop.

You can walk anytime. Approximate cost, including cart, is $40 weekdays (including Fridays) and $55 on weekends.

Hedingham Golf Club
4801 Harbour Town Dr., Raleigh
• (910) 250-3030
Championship Yardage: 6675
Slope: 121   **Par: 72**
Men's Yardage: 6276
Slope: 116   **Par: 72**
Other Yardage: 5565
Slope: 107   **Par: 72**
Ladies' Yardage: 4845
Slope: 107   **Par: 72**

Hedingham Golf Club opened in 1992. David Postlethwait designed a track that's primarily open, although the course is part of a residential community, and houses border some holes. Fairways are bermudagrass, and greens are bentgrass.

We're not familiar with David Postlethwait, but based on the evidence here at this popular Raleigh course, he is in the modern architecture camp. Locals tell us the course is fair—not overly demanding. It's tight off the tee, with out-of-bounds lurking on many holes, so keep the ball in play. Let's say that again. Keep the ball in play.

The greens are medium-size to large, not overly undulating, and boast some potentially difficult subtleties. A few small changes are being made to the course to make it more playable. And as with most modern courses, you'll find plenty of mounds in the fairways and around the green complexes.

The course opens with a bang: a 432-yard par 4 downhill. After a solid drive it's a mid- to long iron over a creek to a green that's only 25 yards deep. It's difficult to be unhappy with a five.

Amenities include a practice green, range, chipping green, locker room, snack bar, rental clubs and a pro shop.

You can walk only at the end of the day. Approximate cost, including cart, is $29 Monday through Thursday, $32 on Friday and $38 on weekends.

Hillandale Golf Course
Hillandale Rd., Durham • (910) 286-4211
Championship Yardage: 6445
Slope: 122   **Par: 71**

Men's Yardage:	6100
Slope: 118	Par: 71
Ladies' Yardage:	5555
Slope: 113	Par: 74

Hillandale opened in the early 1900s. *Architects of Golf* lists Donald Ross as the original designer and Perry Maxwell and George Cobb as redesigners. You'll find information about Ross and Cobb throughout this book. Maxwell was a former banker who took to golf course architecture after World War I. We'll wager you're unaware that he built the first grass greens in the state of Oklahoma. He was known for designing wildly undulating greens and has rebuilt the putting surfaces at such mega-famous courses as Augusta National, Pine Valley and the National Golf Links. Maxwell eventually designed about 70 courses and remodeled 50 others. Thus, Hillandale boasts a fine architectural heritage. The terrain varies between flat and rolling. Bermudagrass covers the fairways, and bentgrass blankets the greens.

The 15th is a wonderful par 3, 190 yards downhill to a large green. It's not an overly difficult hole, but simply demands a straight shot. It's one of the more picturesque on the course.

With more than 50,000 rounds of golf played here every year, Hillandale is probably one of the most popular golf courses in North Carolina. The track is owned and operated by The Durham Foundation, Durham's Community Trust and the Central Carolina Bank and Trust Company. So you might refer to Hillandale as Durham's muni. With so many round being played, you might also refer to it as a golf factory.

The course is fun and relatively straightforward and has the ambiance of an Old World course. Maxwell didn't get too wild with the greens—crowned and midsize to large. On the back nine, three holes have dual greens to accommodate the sheer volume of play. The fairways are relatively wide and open, but water comes into play on a few holes. The course is not overly bunkered, and chipping areas are mowed around the greens, so your ball might roll off if it hits the edge.

The golf shop at Hillandale is one of the best-stocked and largest of any golf course in North Carolina. In 1993, the golf shop was voted the Nation's Most Outstanding by the PGA of America. If you're looking for new or used equipment, stop by Hillandale.

Amenities include a practice green, range, chipping green, locker room, snack bar, rental clubs and a pro shop.

You can—and should—walk this course anytime. Approximate cost, including cart, is $28 Monday through Thursday, $29 on Friday and $33 on weekends.

Kerr Lake Country Club

N.C. Hwy. 3, Henderson • (910) 492-1895

Championship Yardage:	6430
Slope: 122	Par: 72
Men's Yardage:	6185
Slope: 118	Par: 72
Ladies' Yardage:	4799
Slope: 111	Par: 72

The golf course at Kerr Lake Country Club, which opened in the 1960s, is an example of design-by-committee. A group of agricultural types created this open layout, with bermudagrass fairways and bentgrass greens.

Here at Kerr Lake you'll find a fun, entertaining and relaxed course. This well-designed track follows the lay of the land faithfully, and its challenge is due in part to the decent length from the back tees. Locals feel Kerr Lake appears easier than it plays. There isn't a great deal of trouble off the tee, but you'll rarely have an even lie in the fairway. The recent installation of a sprinkler system increased the length of the course. The greens are medium-size and undulating, and their designs mandate good club selection.

Kerr Lake added its first-ever bunker in the spring of 1995! Curiously, the clubhouse at this popular country course resembles a bomb shelter. But, so what? You don't play golf in the snack bar, right?

Amenities include a practice green, range, snack bar, rental clubs and a pro shop.

The course is walkable and you can walk anytime. Approximate cost, including cart, is $27 weekdays and $31 on weekends.

Lake Winds Golf Course

1807 Moores Mill Rd., Rougemont • (910) 471-GOLF

Championship Yardage:	6365
Slope: 120	Par: 72
Men's Yardage:	6088
Slope: No rating	Par: 72
Ladies' Yardage:	5388
Slope: No rating	Par: 72

Lake Winds, a Don Mason design characterized by rolling terrain, with bermudagrass fairways and bentgrass greens, opened in 1982.

A few miles north of Durham, Lake Winds is an example of how good a family-owned, operated and maintained country course can be; it's a tremendously friendly place. The layout meanders around and through tranquil, rolling wooded terrain. The fairways offer decent width, and the greens vary in size and shape. There are some good driving holes. Most of the greens are protected by bunkers whose influence will vary greatly depending on pin placement.

You'll find some surprisingly wonderful golf holes here. Senior PGA Tour professional Jim Thorpe holds his annual charity golf tournament at Lake Winds. Thorpe also holds the course record: 61. The closing three holes are exciting—perfect for those who like to wager while they play, which, of course, is against the law and not condoned by the authors, Insiders' Guides Inc., etc. We're told that the amount of postgame money exchanged will be greatly influenced by these three holes.

This might particularly be the case on the last hole, a short par 4 of just 317 yards. The only obstacle between you and birdie is the water you must shoot over to reach the green on the approach. A fun finishing hole.

Amenities include a practice green, rental clubs and a pro shop.

The course is walkable, and you can walk anytime. Approximate cost, including cart, is $24 weekdays and $28 on weekends.

Lochmere Golf Club
2511 Kildaire Farms Rd., Cary
• **(910) 851-0611**

Championship Yardage:	6867
Slope: 124	**Par: 72**
Men's Yardage:	6156
Slope: 116	**Par: 72**
Ladies' Yardage:	5052
Slope: 113	**Par: 74**

The golf course at Lochmere Golf Club is predominantly flat and laid out in woodlands, with 419 bermudagrass fairways and bentgrass greens. This Gene Hamm-designed track opened in 1985.

Lochmere offers a fun and challenging round in a picturesque setting, even though some holes are bordered by homes. For a modern course, the track is a little short, but don't think that makes it any easier. Many holes are tight off the tee. Once you've banged your ball down the middle of the fairway with your titanium super-mama driver, you'll have to deal with water, bunkers, mounds, embankments and swales. And once you've hit the green, you'll face a sloping putt with all sorts of subtle breaks. Lochmere definitely will test your accuracy and short-game prowess.

The opening hole is a tester, a 506-yard par

5 that will tempt the bold to reach in two and start with birdie or eagle. However, it's a tight hole where a wayward drive could result in a huge number.

Cary is a booming and trendy suburb of Raleigh and is quite busy with traffic and construction. Amid the trendiness and bustle, Lochmere is amazingly peaceful and relaxed—part of what makes it so attractive. It's a commanding but fair track that we recommend you try. It's also host to a couple of minor professional tournaments.

Amenities include a practice green, range, locker room, snack bar, rental clubs, a beverage cart and pro shop.

The course is walkable for the dedicated, and you can walk anytime except before 2 PM on weekends. Approximate cost, including cart, is $33 Monday through Thursday, $40 on Friday and $45 on weekends.

The Neuse Golf Club
918 Birkdale Dr., Clayton
• **(910) 550-0550**

Championship Yardage:	7010
Slope: 136	**Par: 72**
Men's Yardage:	6626
Slope: 129	**Par: 72**
Other Yardage:	6027
Slope: 123	**Par: 72**
Ladies' Yardage:	5478
Slope: 126	**Par: 72**

John LaFoy designed the Neuse Golf Club, which opened in 1994. The course is set in rolling terrain, with houses bordering the fairways. In the fairways, you'll find 419 bermudagrass; on the greens, bentgrass.

The Neuse is a sister club to Devil's Ridge and, like its sister, is owned by Carolinas Golf Group. You can read about LaFoy in the Devil's Ridge write-up above. *Golf Digest* rated the course as one of the best new tracks in the country when it opened, and it's also rated by the same magazine as one of the top 75 public-access courses in the country where you can play for less than $50 a round.

Yes, you might want to think about this course as "The Noose"—and after a round here, you might want to bind, gag and tie Mr. LaFoy to the nearest flagstick. This course appears to be more difficult than Devil's Ridge. The mounds seemed bigger, the elevation changes larger, the undulations on the greens more severe, the bunkers steeper and deeper and the green complexes more menacing. The Neuse River flanks the course and comes into play on the 4th and 17th holes. The difficulties are easily visible from the tee boxes and fairways. The most amazing hole is, in fact, called "The Noose," a tortuous 192-yard par 3, with water and bunkers to the right of the green and a rock the size of a basketball court on the left. It's quite unlike any golf hole in the Triangle or perhaps the entire southeast.

Other holes offer just as much challenge and difficulty. Here's what could happen: Your slightly pushed tee shot ricochets off a mound and ends up out-of-bounds next to the Smiths' Weber grill on their large back deck. Or it might land in one of the deep bunkers. Plop your ball in the middle of the fairway and you might have a lengthy walk from the cart path down a slope only to find that your lie is half a foot above your feet. Your approach shot might hit a mound next to the green and bounce into a grass swale or down an embankment or into a pot bunker. Your first putt might have a three-foot break—or it might end up rolling down a slope to the base of the green. Or you might bang it down the middle of the fairway, hit the middle of the green, one-putt and tell your friends that the course is not as difficult as it looks. Just remember that throwing clubs or smashing them on the cart path won't improve your score.

The Neuse provides an excellent example of an architect strutting his heroic and penal stuff. It's certainly a statement: "I'm going to make this course a challenge. But if you have a good round here and you conquer the challenge, you should feel extremely pleased with yourself."

And that's the point of a modern and challenging golf course. A lot of locals like The Neuse and rate it as the best option in the area. We highly recommend you play this course for the experience—even if you play just once.

Amenities include a practice green, range, chipping green, locker room, snack bar, rental clubs, a beverage cart and pro shop.

The course is not walkable. Approximate cost, including cart, is $40 Monday through Thursday, $45 on Friday and $50 on weekends.

Occoneechee Golf Club
1500 Lawrence Rd., Hillsborough
• (910) 732-3435

Championship Yardage:	**6062**	
Slope: 124		**Par: 71**
Men's Yardage:	**5692**	
Slope: 119		**Par: 71**
Other Yardage:	**4936**	
Slope: 106		**Par: 71**
Ladies' Yardage:	**4681**	
Slope: 113		**Par: 71**

Occoneechee Golf Club opened in 1963. Marvin Ray designed the course, and James Ray renovated it. Set on rolling terrain, you'll find bermudagrass fairways and bentgrass greens.

What a great name for a golf course! Too many tracks have mundane natural or town-oriented names. Nomenclature aside, Occoneechee is a fine and fair track laid out in a pleasant country setting. Frankly, there are more challenging courses out there, but there are less challenging courses as well. This one is set up to provide some interest to the big hitting flat-belly. But it's best suited for the mid-level golfer who wants to play on a good course without losing numerous balls in the woods, without having to hit it 275 yards over water or without carrying it over a morass of bunkers and/or mounds.

The family-run atmosphere is no accident: the Rays have run the course since its inception.

The fairways are medium-width, although out-of-bounds areas make a couple of holes play a bit narrower. The greens are slightly raised and crowned—harder to hit than they appear. There are plenty of pretty trees, some of which might come into play—especially if you're wayward off the tee. Water comes into play on some holes and will affect your strategy if not your shot—ample proof that you don't have to hire a big-name architect to produce a fine and playable golf course. Dare we say the course has an Ellis Maples feel to it? An ongoing course renovation is almost complete. Overall, Occoneechee provides good value for your golfing dollar and boasts a pleasant and relaxed setting that's free of the houses and condos that have turned modern golf courses into the domain of Realtors rather than golfers.

The course opens gently with a birdie hole, a 294-yard par 4 that the big hitter will be tempted to reach in one. All that's required is a big fade. It's a hole that's designed to suit the slicer, which is not a bad thing for an opening hole.

Amenities include a practice green, range, chipping green, locker room, bar, snack bar, beverage cart and pro shop.

The course is walkable, you should walk, and you can walk anytime (hooray!). Approximate cost, including cart, is $26 weekdays and $29 on weekends.

The River Golf and Country Club
Sledge Rd., Bunn • (910) 478-3832

Championship Yardage:	**6407**	
Slope: 122		**Par: 72**

Men's Yardage:	6116
Slope: No rating	Par: 72
Other Yardage:	5870
Slope: No rating	Par: 72
Ladies' Yardage:	4483
Slope: No rating	Par: 72

The golf course at the River Golf and Country Club opened in 1990. We tried to find out who designed the course, but no one knows. Most of the holes are bordered by woods. Fairways are bermudagrass; greens, bentgrass.

The River Golf and Country Club is a serious "find." Bunn is not as remote as you might think, and the course is well worth the drive. For our money, this is one of the best courses in the Triangle. Each hole is well designed and thought out. The setting is both peaceful and magnificent. The fairways vary in width, and there are some fun tee shots from a couple of the elevated tees. The green complexes feature bunkers of various sizes and shapes plus some large undulating greens. There's even a double green on the back nine. Water comes into play on a number of holes in the form of streams and ponds. There's a distinct lack of housing—rare for a newer course.

Perhaps the most tempting hole on this relatively short golf course might be the par 4 seventh, just 260 yards, all downhill to a shallow green that's steeply banked on the far side. Any shot that rolls over the green is instantly a huge number.

Although recently built, the River possesses a traditional feel well beyond its years. Students of golf course architecture might leave the course wondering who is responsible for this outstanding track. The course is also a good value.

Amenities include a practice green, range, snack bar and pro shop.

Walk anytime except weekends before 2 PM. Approximate cost, including cart, is $25 weekdays and $35 on weekends.

Roxboro Country Club
260 Club House Dr., Roxboro
• (910) 599-2332

Championship Yardage:	5663
Slope: 114	Par: 70
Men's Yardage:	5364
Slope: 113	Par: 70

Ladies' Yardage:	4425
Slope: 113	Par: 70

Roxboro Country Club opened in 1945. Ellis Maples rerouted the course and added nine holes in 1969. The course is set amid rolling, slightly wooded terrain, with fairways of bermudagrass and bentgrass greens.

Roxboro Country Club is a fine country club course. It's not the longest course in the world, but it might rate as one of the prettiest in the area. There are plenty of super holes, although those around the turn, which might have been part of the original nine, are not as attractive as some others. As with many Ellis Maples courses, you'll find beautiful sweeping doglegs, excellent use of the land, plenty of room off the tee, deep undulating greens and large bunkers protecting half or two-thirds of the green. You'll find plenty of examples of how Maples matches design elements with the length and pitch of the hole: Long holes have big greens; short holes have smaller greens with more protection. Water comes into play on a few holes, adding a great deal visually to the course.

The first hole is certainly one of Roxboro's most inviting. It's a par 4 of just 292 yards with water along the entire left side. The safest play is to the right side of the fairway, which brings into play two bunkers immediately in front of the green. A duck hook off the tee may hit a duck—and place a big early number on your scorecard.

Amenities include a practice green, range, snack bar and pro shop.

You can walk anytime. You won't need a tee time during the week; call Thursday for a weekend tee time. Approximate cost, including cart, is $20 weekdays and $27 on weekends.

Sourwood Golf Club
8055 Pleasant Hill Church Rd., Snow Camp
• (910) 376-8166

Championship Yardage:	6862
Slope: 117	Par: 72
Men's Yardage:	6285
Slope: 112	Par: 72
Ladies' Yardage:	5017
Slope: 106	Par: 72

Sourwood Golf Course was designed by Elmo Cobb (no relation to George) and opened

> **INSIDERS' TIP**
> If you're playing a course for the first time, or if you're on a particularly difficult course, don't be afraid to play from the mid-front tees. You won't have to use your driver quite as often and you'll probably enjoy your day a lot more.

in 1991 with a mix of open and wooded terrain. In the fairways, you'll find bermudagrass; on the greens, bentgrass.

We found Sourwood to be a fine owner-designed country course; Cobb easily could have made a good golf course architect based on the soundness of this layout. The course is named after the sourwood tree that still shows up in places but, sadly, is disappearing. Most holes are relatively straightforward—neither too easy nor overly difficult, just very playable. There's decent enough room off the tee, so use your driver liberally. The greens are sloped and mid-size.

Even though the course is somewhat remote, it's worth the drive for a break from the city and a fun round of golf in a pleasant country setting on a playable track. Elmo Cobb is reputedly one of the better greenskeepers around, and many area golfers cite Sourwood as a course with good greens.

Amenities include a practice green and snack bar.

You can walk anytime except before 1 PM on weekends. Book a tee time whenever you choose. Approximate cost, including cart, is $20 weekdays and $25 on weekends.

Wake Forest Country Club
13239 Capitol Blvd., Wake Forest
• (919) 556-3416

Championship Yardage:	6956	
Slope: 135	Par: 72	
Men's Yardage:	6525	
Slope: 129	Par: 72	
Other Yardage:	6109	
Slope: 126	Par: 72	
Ladies' Yardage:	5124	
Slope: 122	Par: 72	

Wake Forest Country Club opened in 1968. Gene Hamm designed this course on undulating wooded terrain, with bermudagrass fairways and bentgrass greens.

Wake Forest Country Club is unrelated to Wake Forest University, which is more than an hour's drive to the west. The course is well-known for its opening "world's longest par 5," a 711-yard behemoth on which you'll be happy to reach the ladies' tees on your first shot. If you don't reach the ladies' tees, the normal penalty (whatever yours is) does not apply. Play it from the white tees and it's still an ample 526 yards. And to make matters more difficult, the stream that bisects the hole close to the green easily could destroy your early-round confidence if you're not careful.

The absurd length of the 1st hole aside, Wake

Forest should be better-known for the quality of the layout. You'll find an excellent example here of a fine and playable traditional track that provides plenty of visual attraction and challenge. Attack this course and you'll be rewarded for sound execution, but realize that you'll be penalized proportionally for poor and wayward shots. Occasional trouble off the tee is augmented if the rough has grown up above an inch or two. The greens vary in size, shape, slope and undulation, but we're told that they are true and can get wonderfully fast. Water provides a hazard on a few holes. If you prefer mature, challenging courses, make the trip to Wake Forest Country Club.

Amenities include a practice green, range, chipping green, locker room, bar, snack bar, rental clubs, a beverage cart and pro shop.

Walking is restricted to after 2 PM on weekends; the course is walkable though hilly in places. Approximate cost, including cart, is $30 Monday through Thursday, $32 on Friday and $40 on weekends.

Wildwood Green Country Club
3000 Ballybunion Way., Raleigh
• (910) 846-8376

Championship Yardage:	6500	
Slope: 120	Par: 70	
Men's Yardage:	5100	
Slope: 117	Par: 70	
Ladies' Yardage:	4628	
Slope: 117	Par: 72	

Wildwood Green opened in 1986. Jerry Turner designed the course, which was remodeled entirely in 1996. In the fairways, you'll find bermudagrass; on the greens, G2 bentgrass.

A popular Raleigh course, Wildwood Green benefited from an extensive renovation supervised by the very capable John LaFoy. The course is undulating and, unlike a number of modern courses, the fairways are narrow. The course boasts a number of tricky short par 4s where the driver is best left in the bag, but the most demanding hole has to be the 5th, a 440-yard par 4 with a pond adjacent to the green.

Reaching any green and two-putting is not automatic due to the undulations in the putting surfaces; the new G2 bentgrass means that green speeds can be quick even in the summer. The greenside bunkers are deep and require a deft touch with the sand wedge; a 60-degree wedge might be useful here in certain situations. Overall, this solid course might remind you of an older and more mature track.

Amenities include a practice green, range, snack bar, rental clubs and a pro shop.

Walk anytime except weekends before 2 PM. Approximate cost, including cart, is $38 weekdays and $48 on weekends.

Willowhaven Country Club
253 Country Club Dr., Durham
• **(910) 383-1022**
Championship Yardage: 6655
Slope: 120   **Par: 72**
Men's Yardage: 6342
Slope: 117   **Par: 72**
Other Yardage: 5721
Slope: 111   **Par: 72**
Ladies' Yardage: 5436
Slope: 117   **Par: 75**

The golf course at Willowhaven Country Club opened in 1957. George Cobb designed the course on rolling wooded terrain. In the fairways, you'll find bermudagrass; on the greens, bentgrass.

The course is well over 40 years old, so it's definitely a mature track. It's one of Cobb's earlier efforts, one that clearly demonstrates his skill in taking a pretty piece of land and turning it into a playable and attractive course. At Willowhaven, Cobb has created variety and challenge without anything tricked-up or fancy.

There isn't a lot of trouble off the tee, although it helps to be in the right sector on many of the doglegs. Trouble around the greens comes in the form of large sloped putting surfaces, swales, embankments and basic bunkers. The better golfer won't think that the course offers a huge amount of challenge, but there's easily enough from the back tees. If you're fond of traditional courses, you should make your way to Willowhaven.

Amenities include a practice green, range, snack bar, rental clubs and a pro shop.

Walk anytime. Approximate cost, including cart, is $31.50 weekdays and $36.50 on weekends.

Around the Triangle . . .

Fun Things To Do

Raleigh is North Carolina's capital as well as home to **St. Mary's College, Peace College, Meredith College, St. Augustine's College, Shaw University** and the **North Carolina State University.** Take the time to visit the **Governor's Mansion,** 200 N. Blount Street, home to Gov. James B. Hunt and his family. It's an outstanding example of Queen Anne Cottage Victorian architecture. Call (919) 733-3456 for tour information. You can also tour the **State Capitol building** in downtown Raleigh on Edenton Street; call (919) 733-4994.

For more information about state government sites, contact the **Capital Area Visitor Center,** 301 N. Blount Street, (919) 733-3456, or the **Greater Raleigh Convention and Visitors Bureau,** 225 Hillsborough Street, (800) 849-8499.

North Carolina State University Arboretum, 4301 Berry Road, is worth a visit, especially in the fall and spring; call (919) 515-2011. **The North Carolina Symphony** is based in Raleigh and plays concerts in various locations around Raleigh and the Triangle; call the Symphony office at (919) 733-2750 for information on upcoming concerts.

The North Carolina Museum of Art, 2110 Blue Ridge Avenue, houses permanent displays of the state's art collection, as well as a number of changing exhibitions. There's a gift shop and cafe on site. Call (919) 833-1935 for more information. Admission is free, and daily tours are offered at 1:30 PM.

Durham is perhaps best known for tobacco processing and as the location of the best movie ever about baseball, *Bull Durham.* The movie starred Kevin Costner, Tim Robbins and Susan Sarandon. Sadly, the ballpark where the movie was filmed is no longer used. The **Durham Bulls** now play in a new stadium at 409 Blackwell St. (919) 687-6500.

There's also minor-league play by the **Carolina Mudcats,** who play AA ball in **Zebulon** at Five County Stadium, (919) 269-2287.

If you're not in the mood for baseball or golf, then start with a visit to **Duke University** (for general information on touring campus sites, call (919) 684-8111). You can take in the faux Gothic architecture (the chapel is modeled after

INSIDERS' TIP

If a thunderstorm approaches, get off the course. North Carolina ranks second only to Florida in the number of deaths caused by lightning. Don't just seek shelter under a tree — get indoors.

Princeton University's) in addition to the **Sarah P. Duke Gardens,** located adjacent to the campus, a 55-acre bouquet of daffodils, pansies and students from New Jersey (who seemingly comprise a disproportionate amount of Duke's enrollment). Call the Duke Gardens Office at (919) 684-3698. You might also want to visit the **Duke Homestead and Tobacco Museum,** a state historic site. This attraction is housed in the former home of Washington Duke, father of the tobacco trade, and is located at 2828 Duke Homestead Road; you'll learn a lot about the influence of tobacco on the local economy. Call (919) 477-5498.

West Point on the Eno, on Cole Mill Road, is part of the **Eno River City Park** and is a pleasant and quiet retreat from the city. The park covers 400 acres and is full of wildlife. You can enjoy camping, fishing, rafting, picnicking, hiking and general solitude. Call (919) 471-1623. Another excellent museum is the **North Carolina Museum of Life and Science,** where you'll find hands-on exhibits, live experiments and wildlife. Call (919) 220-5429. The museum is located at 433 Murray Avenue.

Durham is also a major center for medicine; naturally, we hope that you've come to Durham for golf and not for a visit to one of the area's healthcare facilities.

Chapel Hill is where author Scott Martin spent four extremely studious and serious years at the **University of North Carolina.** You should visit **Morehead Planetarium,** one of the finest in the country; call (919) 549-6863. You'll find the building on E. Franklin Street; look for the lovely rose garden out front. While you're in the vicinity, cruise down Franklin Street to take in the general ambiance of one of the prettiest and most eclectic college towns in America. If you want to tour the campus of the University of North Carolina, call (919) 962-2211.

> ## INSIDERS' TIP
> Many professional golfers are very happy to score par on a hole. They shoot for the middle of the fairways and greens to avoid trouble and big numbers, then take the birdie opportunities as they come. Don't try to force a low score—play within your limits.

Those of you who love flowers, trees and shrubberies should visit the **Coker Arboretum** in the **North Carolina Botanical Garden** on the N.C. 15-501 By-pass. Call (919) 962-0522 for more information. Art lovers should visit the **Ackland Art Museum** on S. Columbia Street near the junction of Franklin Street. There's a permanent collection of European and American art in addition to a fine collection of sculpture dating from the Renaissance to the present.

For more information about Chapel Hill and Orange County, contact the **Chapel Hill and Orange County Visitors Bureau,** 105 N. Columbia Street, (919) 968-2060.

Where to Eat

As far as urban areas go in North Carolina, it's probably tough to beat the Triangle for flair and variety. There's plenty of down-home Southern cooking to go around, but the diverse tastes brought here by the universities mean that food lovers are well taken care of here. You'll find plenty of the chain-style eateries you might find at home, but while you're here, why not try something different: There's plenty to sample. The establishments we list here all take major credit cards unless noted otherwise. Refer to our Preface for an explanation of the pricing code.

Raleigh

Angus Barn
$$$$ • U.S. Hwy. 70 at Airport Rd., Raleigh • (919) 781-2444
OK, so we'll start with something a bit traditional, something that will stick to your ribs.

This is one of the busiest and most popular steakhouses in North Carolina and has been— in the same location—for more than 30 years. The restaurant is popular with business people. Bring a big appetite and leave room for a dessert. Don't even think about the word "diet."

In addition to the excellent steaks here at "Beefeaters' Haven," the Angus Barn features seafood, chicken and salads. Top it all off with a fudge sundae and they will be carting you out in a wheelbarrow.

The atmosphere at the Barn, as locals call it, is country elegant—we know that seems contradictory, but you'll see what we mean. While you don't have to really dress up, you'd probably feel somewhat conspicuous if you didn't gussy up at least a little bit.

Est Est Est Tratoria
$$ • 19 W. Hargett St., Raleigh
• (919) 832-8899
Enter on Salisbury Street. The restaurant is popular at lunch and has become even more so

in the evenings. This place is perfect for the romantic in you—and, hopefully, your current or prospective better half too. Pasta is made on the premises. Choose a fine bottle of house wine to wash down your meal. You'll find a variety of entrees that change daily, but the basic menu components include pasta, seafood and lighter meats.

Greenshield's Brewery and Pub
$$ • 214 E. Martin St., Raleigh
• (919) 829-0214

For fine handcrafted beer, you can't go wrong here. The pub is so authentic it's frequented by Anglophiles, real English people (who only drink real beer), rugby players and darts-throwers. When hunger replaces thirst, try the fish and chips or pot pies.

Margaux's
$$$ • 8111 Creedmore Rd., Raleigh
• (919) 846-9846

French cuisine in northern Raleigh? In the land of new houses and shopping centers? Two well-educated chefs turned a sporting goods store into a restaurant that's been acclaimed both in print and by word of mouth. Check it out and be sure to ask about the specials, which might range from Carolina quail to crab casserole.

Durham

Anotherthyme
$$ • 109 N. Gregson St., Durham
• (919) 682-5225

We know locals who call this place home. The menu is varied—French, Italian, Spanish, Chinese—so you never get bored. And besides, all your friends are here, so how could you have anything but a good time. The food is prepared with always-fresh ingredients. Count this one in for lunch, dinner or even a late-night snack. You'll have a great meal at a great price.

Bullock's Bar-B-Cue
$ • 3330 Wortham St., Durham
• (919) 383-3211

There just had to be an establishment with the word "Bull" in it, and this is it. Don't come here for the decor or to be coddled and "waited on." Do come for the variety and quality of the barbecue, the hush puppies and tea so sweet your spoon stands at attention.

Darryl's 1890
$$ • 4603 Chapel Hill Blvd., Durham
• (919) 489-1890

Part of the Darryl's chain, this version offers plenty of food and plenty of ambiance in the form of secluded booths and interesting knickknacks on the walls. The multi-page menu offers everything from seafood to chicken and prime rib to massive desserts and liver-threatening frozen drinks. The restaurant is tremendously popular after football games and other events in Chapel Hill or Durham. Note that there is also a Raleigh location on U.S. Highway 70, just a few miles west of Crabtree Valley Mall.

The Fairview
$$$ • 3001 Cameron Ave., Durham
• (919) 490-0999

You'll find The Fairview inside the Washington Duke Inn, which is adjacent to the majestic Duke Golf Club—a must-play in the Triangle area. Appetizers include mixed baby green salad, crab cakes and stone-baked pizza of the day. Proceed to your entree, which might be pan-seared large sea scallops, grilled breast of chicken, Colorado rack of lamb or a veal chop, all served with fresh vegetables and the latest joke about Dean Smith.

Magnolia Grill
$$$$ • 1002 Ninth St., Durham
• (919) 286-3609

When you just had your best golf day ever and it's time to celebrate, do so at the Magnolia Grill. This is one of the area's best restaurants, and it has the loyal customers to prove it. Your dining pleasure will depend on what's fresh and what's on the chef's ever-changing, always-innovative menu. The menu changes daily, but there's usually a vegetarian dish, steaks, a poultry dish and two or three seafood specialties. You should definitely leave room for dessert. The pastry chef here makes all the ice creams, sorbets and baked goods at the restaurant.

Make reservations here so you won't miss the opportunity to see why the Triangle raves about this fine establishment.

Chapel Hill

Aurora
$$$ • 200 N. Greensboro St., Chapel Hill
• (919) 942-2400

Trendy, and justifiably so, Aurora is not a place to be seen, because you can't be—it's very dimly lit, especially at night. You'll find some of the most acclaimed Italian food in the Triangle. Complement your veal, lamb, poultry or seafood with fresh pasta and dizzying sauces. Match it all with a hearty Italian wine and you're in for a great evening. Make a reservation here.

Carolina Brewery
$$-$$$ • 460 W. Franklin St., Chapel Hill • (919) 942-1800

In the now super-trendy atmosphere that befits the western section of Franklin Street, it's only appropriate that a microbrewery should set up shop. Carolina Brewery's decor is a little upscale for a brewpub, with shiny metalwork to complement the equally shiny copper kettles and other devices designed to produce that most silken and sylvan of beverages: beer. The beer here is pretty good. You might try the Copperline Amber Ale, the Franklin Street Lager, the India Pale Ale or one of the select guest beers from other microbreweries around the country. The great thing about the microbrewery is freshness, so you'll find the beer here especially palatable and varied.

The food matches the ambiance and is symptomatic of the latest in microbrewery fare. You might find the cheesy creole pizza—made with fresh focaccia dough—to your liking. Or, try the marinated citrus chicken sandwich or Louisiana sausage po' boy; either is a perfect complement to your brew. The person with the slightly larger appetite might go for the Duck Trap River smoked red trout pasta or the jambalaya with andouille sausage smothered with spicy creole tomato sauce.

Crook's Corner
$$$ • 610 W. Franklin St., Chapel Hill • (919) 929-7643

Crook's offers one of the most unique and subtly intense dining experiences anywhere. The restaurant itself, which looks like a cross between a hair salon and a former service station, is crowned with a statue of a pig. Wooden animal statuary rounds out the decor. The menu changes so rapidly, you'll never be disappointed. It might be something South American; it might be something like shrimp 'n' grits. It's always praiseworthy—and usually loud and fun. Crook's Corner is a great place for reunions of sorts.

The Fearrington House
$$$$ • 2000 Fearrington Village Center, Pittsboro • (919) 542-2121

One of Chapel Hill's hottest restaurants (and it's been this way for years) isn't in Chapel Hill. It's just down U.S. 15-501 in Pittsboro. The menu changes monthly, but you'll find such mildly exotic fare as boneless leg of rabbit, free range veal loin, baked snapper, roasted guinea hen, or how about the Chilean sea bass? When one author attended Chapel Hill, taking your date here was more impressive than anything,

even if you were left with no money for beer for the next month. It was worth the extravagance.

Pyewacket
$$ • 431 W. Franklin St., Chapel Hill • (919) 929-0291

Pyewacket has been a Chapel Hill fixture with the old-Volvo-and-tweed-jacket academic crowd for years. Or at least that's how it's reputed. Actually, its popularity base has increased to include sorority women on "girls' night out" as well as business people in town to close a deal. The food is the key, and it's mostly within a vegetarian bent. Somehow, it seems light and hearty at the same time. Special entrees vary almost daily, but you can't go wrong with the seafood curry or the vegetarian lasagna. But, what we frequently find ourselves craving the most is their Morning Star salad, a worthy meal in itself. The wine list is also excellent.

The Rathskeller
$ • 157-A Franklin St., Chapel Hill • (919) 942-5158

"The Rat," in its own subterranean fashion, exudes fumes of Chapel Hill past and present. It's a major student hangout, with a large and passionate following among alumni who line up after football games for spaghetti and tea and other such basics. It's not a place for the claustrophobic, but it is a place for those whose blood runs Tar Heel blue. A must.

Where to Stay

Refer to our Preface for an explanation of the pricing code.

Raleigh

Courtyard by Marriott
$$ • 1041 Wakestowne Dr., Raleigh • (919) 821-3400

The Courtyard by Marriott concept is popping up all over the country and is popular with business travelers. This version might look like some of the others you've seen, but there are some important amenities to note, including an on-site gym, whirlpool room and outdoor pool. Guests also have free access to a full-scale gym with extensive facilities across the road. When you're through working out, drop by the restaurant, serving breakfast and light dinners, and the bar. Staff members are quite friendly here. Due to the large volume of business travelers in the area, you should definitely book ahead for a room.

Devil's Ridge near Raleigh is a difficult development course that's popular among locals.

Photo: Devil's Ridge

Hilton Convention Center
$$$-$$$$ • 3415 Wake Forest Rd., Raleigh
• (919) 872-2323

Convenient to Raleigh Community Hospital, and very near the Beltline (I-440), this popular and glitzy hotel boasts 338 rooms and quite a few large-scale political parties.

On the special executive floor, you'll have access to a private cocktail bar; your room will be a little larger than a regular room, plus you'll have an ironing board and a few other bells and whistles at your disposal. The standard rooms are comfortable as well, and all are equipped with coffee makers. Guests receive a free copy of *USA Today* each morning.

Other amenities include a workout room, an indoor pool and a whirlpool. If you're in the mood to boogie, venture forth into Bowties night club, where the price of admission is free if you're staying at the hotel. Enjoy the full-service restaurant; otherwise try one of the 30 restaurants within an hour's drive of the hotel.

Durham

Arrowhead Inn
$$$ • 106 Mason Rd., Durham
• (919) 477-8430

This wonderful bed and breakfast inn features eight guest rooms and is convenient to everywhere in Durham. Relax in the parlor with a game or some light TV. You'll also get a hearty breakfast when you awaken from a peaceful slumber.

Brownstone-Medcenter Inn
$$$ • 2424 Erwin Rd., Durham
• (919) 286-7761

As you enter Durham, the signs tell you that Durham is the City of Medicine; it's also the city of cigarettes. Go figure. Anyway, here's a hotel that has developed to serve those visiting the extensive and well-known medical center. It's also a good place for golfers visiting Durham's golf courses. Here at the Brownstone, you'll find 140 elegant Colonial-design rooms, extensive dining facilities, a banquet room with space for you and 129 of your closest friends, an indoor pool, cable TV (with ESPN), sauna, whirlpool and beauty and barber shop. When you've had enough healthy living for the day, Burley's lounge features beer, wine, vodka, gin, whiskey, rum, tequila and other medicinal potions.

Holiday Inn Durham
$$ • 3460 Hillsborough St., Durham
• (919) 383-1551

Part of the worldwide chain, the Holiday Inn Durham offers 168 comfortable rooms (and two suites) with a full range of amenities. Included in your bill is cable TV (with HBO,

Showtime and ESPN), access to the swimming pool, plus access to Jamie's Restaurant and Lounge. The hotel also offers services for the business traveler, including fax and copy service and a meeting room that can contain (well, maybe) 200 business people.

Washington Duke Inn and Golf Club
$$$ • 3001 Cameron Blvd., Durham
• (919) 490-0999

This 171-room hotel cost roughly $16 million to build, so it had better be nice, right? Well this is one of the finest places in Durham. We've already raved about the golf course, so why not rave about the hotel that dominates the 9th hole, a dangerous par 5.

Service is a key at Washington Duke—room service, turndown service and just the right touches of white-glove style to keep you content. You can relax in their acclaimed restaurant, The Fairview, and enjoy an after-dinner drink in the Bull Durham Lounge. If golf is not your game, you can play tennis, take to the Duke Forest jogging trails or try out the swimming pool. For the business traveler, suites and meeting facilities also are available.

Chapel Hill

The Carolina Inn
$$$ • W. Cameron Ave., Chapel Hill
• (919) 933-2001

Venerable and storied, this is the inn of the University of North Carolina. In 1995, this accommodation underwent a series of changes and improvements to equip it for latter part of the 20th century and prepare it for the 21st. The inn opened in 1924, so it needed some work. You'll love the architecture, designed to resemble Mount Vernon.

Amenities in the completely renovated rooms include coffee machines, cable TV and desks. The inn is within walking distance of downtown Chapel Hill and all of its attractions.

Fearrington House Country Inn
$$$$ • 2000 Fearrington Village Center, Pittsboro • (919) 542-2121

Okay, we know this inn isn't in Chapel Hill proper, but it's less than 10 minutes away, and the experience you'll have at this charming spot is more than worth the drive. The 15 suites at Fearrington House are the definition of luxury but are presented without any of the highbrow attitude that too often accompanies an accommodation of this quality. Each room is unique, with beautiful antiques collected by the owners during trips to Europe. And the surrounding landscaping takes full advantage of the relaxing countryside that once was home to a dairy farm.

You'll also enjoy afternoon teas and a complimentary breakfast served in the on-site restaurant that has been commended by both *Gourmet* and *Food and Wine* magazines. Even if you don't stay the night, dinner here is an experience you'll want to add to your list.

Holiday Inn of Chapel Hill
$$ • U.S. Hwy. 15/501 Bypass, Chapel Hill • (919) 929-2171

Looking for a clean, comfortable hotel that won't take up all your golf money? This is a great choice. It's near a shopping mall and the UNC campus, and offers easy access to I-40, so scooting around the Triangle is convenient. Teddy's restaurant is on-site, and plenty of other good eateries are also nearby. During warmer months, relax in the outdoor pool after your golf round.

North Carolina's
Charlotte
Region

In the past two decades, few cities in the United States have grown with the panache, aggression and swagger as Charlotte, North Carolina. In fact, local big-wigs and civic boosters would prefer that you ditch the "North Carolina" after "Charlotte," seeing as, if the hype is accurate, Charlotte belongs in the same league as cities like Seattle, Atlanta, Kansas City and Dallas—no state name necessary, thank you. That's going a bit far, but there's no denying that Charlotte has exploded and will soon be one of America's largest cities.

In 1980, Charlotte was still pretty much a hard-working, but primarily sleepy, southern *town* best known for... for... well, who knows? There wasn't really much of anything save for a couple of tall buildings downtown, a weird-looking convention center and some large textile factories. Sadly, if you asked people from Philadelphia what they thought about Charlotte, four words routinely emerged: Jim and Tammy Bakker.

How things have changed.

Today, just 20 years later, Charlotte is the nation's second-largest banking center, behind New York City. Now a major USAirways hub, Charlotte-Douglas International Airport is one of the country's busiest and most efficient. Charlotte's downtown is vibrant and busy, even when most of the bankers have retired to the suburbs to count their dough. On average, developers add two new skyscrapers to the Downtown skyline every year. The SouthPark area in south Charlotte is shaping up to be the finest shopping and fashion destination between Atlanta, St. Louis and Washington, D.C. Plus, Charlotte is an arts center, attracting mega-superstar performers from all over the globe.

Major and minor professional sports are huge in Charlotte. The NFL's Carolina Panthers built a brand spanking new 72,000 seat stadium downtown in 1996, and the Charlotte Hornets of the NBA play in the Charlotte Coliseum near the airport. There's serious talk of Major League Baseball arriving in the not-too-distant future, dressed as either the Charlotte Expos or Charlotte Twins.

And even though Daytona (Florida) hosts stock car racing's bureaucratic headquarters, Charlotte is NASCAR's real home: Most of the drivers live in the region, and most of the teams build and maintain their cars near Lowe's Motor Speedway. Many Charlotteans (don't forget that "e") like NASCAR's influence, others find it a bit "below" them. Whatever one's opinion, it's impossible to avoid the influence of NASCAR when the Coca-Cola 600, held every Memorial Day weekend, is the nation's second largest sporting event, after the Indianapolis 500.

The region's "ancient" industries, textile production and trucking, still produce prosperity and jobs, but Charlotte is much more chic and white-collar these days. The thousands of people who relocate to Charlotte each year come to work in new offices and stores, not factories and distribution depots.

The Charlotte Area

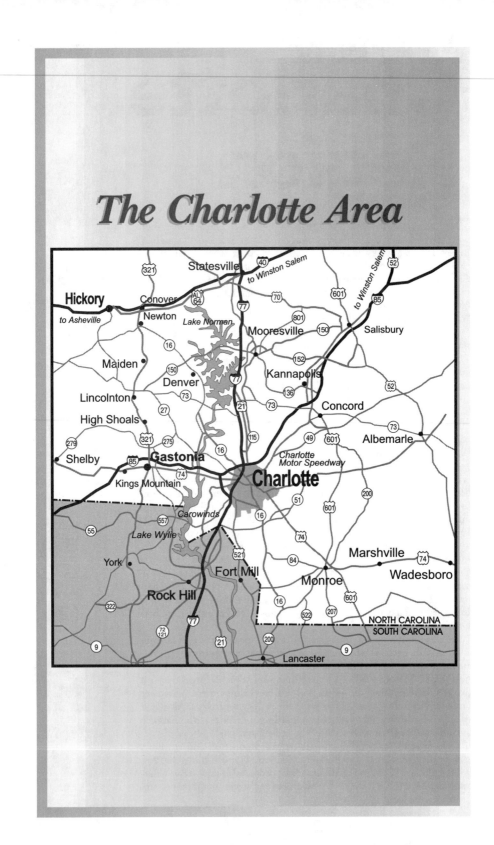

GOLF COURSES IN NORTH CAROLINA'S CHARLOTTE REGION

Course	Type	# Holes	Par	Slope	Yards	Walking	Booking	Approx. Cost w/Cart
Ballantyne Resort	resort	18	71	135	6600	restricted	7 days	$45-59
Birkdale	public	18	72	n/a	n/a	n/a	n/a	$70
Charles T. Myers	public	18	72	122	6002	anytime	anytime	$22-27
Charlotte Golf Links	public	18	71	121	6220	restricted	anytime	$49
Charlotte National	semiprivate	18	72	n/a	7227	restricted	3 days	$30-40
Deer Brook Golf Club	semiprivate	18	72	128	6407	restricted	call	$30-34
The Divide	public	18	72	127	6587	no	3 days	$33-39
Eagle Chase Golf Club	semiprivate	18	72	122	6103	anytime	5 days	$36-45
Emerald Lake	public	18	71	120	6455	restricted	anytime	$36-45
Firethorne Country Club	semiprivate	18	72	133	6406	reatricted	call	$40-60
Fort Mill Golf Club	semiprivate	18	72	118	6373	restricted	3 days	$29-32
Gastonia Municipal	public	18	71	110	5671	anytime	7 days	$25-27
Glen Oaks Country Club	semiprivate	18	70	n/r	6026	restricted	7 days	$28-38
Highland Creek Golf Club	semiprivate	18	72	124	6505	no	3 days	$42-48
King's Mountain	semiprivate	18	72	118	6143	anytime	3-4 days	$27-32
Larkhaven	public	18	72	115	6042	restricted	5 days	$31-35
Lincoln Country Club	semiprivate	18	72	121	6017	anytime	anytime	$25-31
Mallard Head C. C.	semiprivate	18	72	116	6442	restricted	2-3 days	$25-30
Monroe Country Club	semiprivate	18	72	116	6310	restricted	5 days	$26-30
Mooresville Golf Club	public	18	72	121	6102	anytime	3 days	$22.50-26
Olde Sycamore Golf Plantation	semiprivate	18	72	133	6398	no	3 days	$45-50
Piney Point	semiprivate	18	72	115	6385	anytime	anytime	$25-33
Regent Park Golf Club	public	18	72	n/r	6478	no	4-7 days	$45-55
Renaissance Park	public	18	72	121	6880	anytime	7 days	$32-41

River Bend Golf Club	semiprivate	18	72	117	5956	restricted	3 days	$27-34
Rock Barn Club of Golf	semiprivate	18	72	128	6318	anytime	6 days	$32-37
Rocky River Golf Club	public	18	72	119	6028	restricted	6 days	$40-50
Stonebridge Golf Club	public	18	72	127	6374	restricted	4 days	$36-50
The Tradition	public	18	72	n/r	6450	restricted	7 days	$29-39
Verdict Ridge	semiprivate	18	72	131	6347	no	call	$39-54
Westport Golf Course	semiprivate	18	72	118	6291	restricted	3 days	$25-30
The Warrior	public	18	72	121	6193	restricted	call	$35-40
Waterford	public	18	72	125	6513	restricted	call	$36-45
Woodbridge Golf Links	semiprivate	18	72	121	6156	restricted	7 days	$28-38

All this growth led to a massive change in Charlotte's public-access golfing landscape. For many years, Charlotte lagged behind Winston-Salem, Greensboro, Columbia, and even South Carolina's Upstate for its quality and quantity of public-access courses. Most serious Charlotte golfers belonged to one of the many outstanding private clubs like Charlotte Country Club, Myers Park or Quail Hollow. Twenty years ago, the best advice to a daily-fee golfer in search of a solid course was to drive two hours east to Pinehurst or spend the weekend at the beach. Or better still, find someone to invite you to their club.

Around 1990, a national golf organization authored a study that told everyone in Charlotte what everyone already knew: There weren't enough public golf courses close to the city. A lot of developers must have read the survey, and thanks to their efforts and cash, the Charlotte area boasts no fewer than 20 brand-spanking-new public golf courses, all built since "the survey." That's two courses a year for 10 straight years.

Have the devlopers gone barmy? Some local golf professionals argue there's oversupply, but several new courses are under construction or in permitting stages. It's still tough to get a tee time on a sunny weekend in April, but it's particularly easy to play golf quickly on the weekdays in the Charlotte region. While initiation fees at Charlotte's premier country clubs have skyrocketed toward the $50,000 range (please buy more copies of this book), greens fees at public-access courses have remained steady, or even declined at courses that struggle for business. For a top-notch course, you'll pay roughly $35 to play on weekdays, $40 on Fridays and about $48 on weekends and holidays.

Even though the area's sticky clay soil makes it difficult to build and maintain courses in the Charlotte region, the rolling and wooded land is perfect for parkland golf. Charlotte continues to attract many of the country's best golf course architects—the presence of the nation's two largest banks and all their money doesn't hurt.

So while locals might whine about traffic and parking and pollution and "too many Yankees," they can no longer complain about their portfolio of public golf courses, such is the pace and quality of new construction in the past two decades.

(Note: we've also included some South Carolina Midland courses in the Charlotte Region selections, due to their proximity to the Queen City and the volume of Charlotte-area golfers who play there. Even though these courses lie in the Sandlapper State, they're actually in Charlotte's sphere of influence—just don't tell that to people in Rock Hill and Fort Mill.)

Ballantyne Resort
10000 Ballantyne Commons Pkwy.
Charlotte • (704) 341-GOLF(4653)

Championship Yardage:	**6735**
Slope: 137	**Par: 71**
Men's Yardage:	**6600**
Slope: 135	**Par: 71**
Ladies' Yardage:	**4815**
Slope: 118	**Par: 71**

Ballantyne Resort, offically known as the Golf Club at Ballantyne Resort, opened in 1998. Land Design laid out the course in association with a review committee. Fairways are bermudagrass; greens are bentgrass. *North Carolina Magazine* named it the state's Best New Public Course.

First, it's important to get some nomenclature clear. Ballantyne is a massive new 2,000-acre mixed-use development on the southern leg of Charlotte's new outerbelt—I-485, a ring road that's revolutionizing life on the fringes of the metro area. There's a Rees Jones-designed course at Ballantyne Country Club, which is private; that course is most often referred to as simply "Ballantyne." Ballantyne Resort is part of an office and hotel development that's part

of the Ballantyne development. Locals usually refer to this course as "Ballantyne Resort."

Have we completely confused you? One visit to Ballantyne (Resort) will end the confusion. Plus, if you turn up at Ballantyne Country Club hoping to play, the staff will politely tell you to mount your bicycle.

Ballantyne Resort is a fine, and in many ways, amazing golf course. Its owner, real estate developer Smoky Bissell, decided that his Ballantyne office development needed some sizzle, so he took the land he could not use immediately for offices and built an award-winning golf course, without the assistance (and fee) of an architect.

While members of the American Society of Golf Course Architects might not like people like Smoky Bissell, the public does. Ballantyne Resort is one of the busiest courses in the Charlotte area, and it's by no means the least expensive. Several local courses offer serious competition, yet Ballantyne Resort gets the most play.

So why has Ballantyne Resort been so successful? Is it a big marketing and PR budget? Is it the hotdogs at the turn? Is it the cadre of cart girls?

Regulars will tell you that it's the course—built on one of the best natural sites in the area.

The design committee, which included expert and non-expert golfers, produced several interesting strategic holes on a routing that makes excellent use of a relatively tight space.

The green complexes at Ballantyne Resort are the meat of Ballantyne's challenge. Small but shapely mounds and tricky bunkers flank greens that are among the most undulating in the area. Scoring is not easy at Ballantyne Resort.

The par 5 3rd is a solid hole requiring a good smack off the tee to cross a stream. Once over, it's a relatively easy second to set up birdie or eagle. Also memorable is the 10th, a shortish par 3 over water, and the 16th, another par 3, this time about 200 picturesque yards downhill to a large green. The equally scenic 17th, a par 5, requires an accurate tee shot to avoid the water hazard left of the fairway; it can be just a long iron in after that. The 18th, a medium-length par 4, is another superb hole: The tee shot is best shaped right-to-left and must cross a stream. Position 'A' is the left side of the fairway, and from there, it's a mid-iron at most to a receptive green.

Just as receptive is the welcome inside the magnificent 15,000 square-foot clubhouse, easily the finest of all Charlotte's public-access facilities. The clubhouse is geared toward attracting the corporate meeting crowd, and Smoky Bissell has been particularly successful at making this a big part of Ballantyne Resort's success. Outings occur regularly, so plan and call ahead before you venture out.

Most golfers enjoy Ballantyne Resort. From the moment you park you car in the lot, you feel pampered. A headsetted ground crew member removes your bags from your trunk and places them on your cart. Rangers roam the course to help you look for errant balls and rake bunkers—should the need arise. After the round, your clubs are cleaned and placed back in the trunk of your sled.

The course, too, is enjoyable, with mostly wide fairways and generous green complexes that reward laser-like accuracy, but don't punish wayward shots too severely. Only those whose game truly needs serious, serious help will find Ballantyne Resort a bear.

Speaking of help—it's on hand right in the middle of the course, in the form of the Dana Rader Golf School. Rader is a *Golf Magazine* Top 100 teacher and boasts a loyal following throughout the United States. She's even appeared on the Golf Channel. The school's facilities are magnificent and include an indoor classroom that opens up to the range. The school employs seven full-time instructors.

With its outstanding course, service, ambiance and facilities, coupled with owner Smoky Bissell's legendary attention to detail, Ballantyne Resort quickly established itself as one of North Carolina's top-tier public golf facilities.

Amenities include a practice green, driving range, restaurant and pro shop, plus the aforementioned Dana Rader school. Walking is restricted to certain times but the course is walkable. You can book a tee time seven days in advance. Approximate cost, including cart, is $45 Monday to Thursday and $59 Friday to Sunday.

Birkdale

**16500 Birkdale Commons Pkwy.,
Huntersville • (704) 895-8038**

Championship Yardage:	7013	
Slope: 130	**Par: 72**	
Men's Yardage:	6485	
Slope: 126	**Par: 72**	
Ladies' Yardage:	5175	
Slope: 113	**Par: 72**	

Birkdale, designed by Arnold Palmer and Ed Seay, opened in late 1996. The course is routed through woodlands and is bordered by homes and condominiums in a couple of places. Fairways are carpeted with 419 bermudagrass, while greens are seeded with Crenshaw bentgrass.

Birkdale is a development of the Harris Group, a Charlotte commercial real estate company headed by Johnny Harris, one of the most influential and prominent people in the region. Harris is a member of a number of the country's most famous golf clubs, including Augusta National and Pine Valley. He's a close friend of Arnold Palmer and a keen golfer in his own right. If there's one thing you should know about him, it's this: If Johnny Harris is going to do something, then it's going to be done properly, whatever the cost.

In the first half of 1997 and 1998, Birkdale was the talk of the town, mostly because the price of a round outpaced the competition by more than $25. But that's changed. Birkdale advertises itself as an upscale "country club for a day" golf course, from course conditioning to ambiance to quality of design. The smart golfer supposedly adds up the numbers and realizes that it's actually a lot less expensive to plunk down $60 once or twice a week than to join a club and pay the monthly dues and food minimum. That's Birkdale's modus operandi, and time will tell if it's going to be successful.

Arnold Palmer and his team designed a course that's easily one of the best public courses in the Charlotte region. Now that it's had a little time to mature, Birkdale's is one of the best challenges around, especially from the tips. But it's still going to be playable from the forward tees.

The layout begins inauspiciously with a moderate dogleg left par 4 where your approach shot must be played through the main power lines from McGuire Nuclear Station to Charlotte. Should your crisply struck eight-iron plunge most of the largest city in the Carolinas into darkness and chaos, don't worry—it's a free drop. The aforementioned high-tension power line bisects the property and creates a visual nuisance on more than one hole. A pity.

It only takes three holes to realize that Birkdale is a big course. Many greens are huge enough to create a four-club difference, based on pin placement. Fairways are wide enough to land commuter aircraft, and bunkers are deep enough and large enough to accommodate Madonna and her full touring entourage.

But is Birkdale a big hitter's dream course? Perhaps not.

There are spots where discretion is valued more than power. One such spot is the 5th, a 569-yard par 5 and one of two three-shotters that few could reach in two. The hole plays downhill to an enormous fairway. A whack with the big stick is not really a necessity, and the prudent play is to take a three wood out, then play a long iron to lay up at no more than 100 yards. The approach shot to the extremely shallow green fronted by water and backed by a downhill sloping bunker requires a high shot. A punched sand iron from 70 yards might not hold the firm green.

Water is a primary concern on a few holes, most notably the par 4 436-yard 18th, framed by condos to the left, trees to the right and the clubhouse in the background. The hole slopes considerably downhill to a pond, and the big hitter will want to leave the driver in the bag. The approach, depending on pin placement, must traverse the pond to a severely sloping green guarded by some nasty sand. It's a good hole to round off a round, but less exciting than the very reachable downhill 17th, just 511 from the tips to a two-tiered green that slopes away from fairway—quite a rarity these days.

Birkdale's quirks come in the form of a couple of extremely short par 4s of just 330 and 334, holes which play even shorter and are driveable without serious consequence. The muscular par 5 13th, at 595 yards, will irritate the golfer who must avoid a stream placed exactly in the spot where a perfect lay-up might land.

Still, the better courses are unpredictable and shun any degree of cookie-cutter mentality, and thus Birkdale succeeds. Is it worth the price of admission? There are courses that offer better value in the Charlotte region—where just over $20 buys a lot of golf—but we firmly believe plenty of serious golfers will flock to Birkdale and gladly shell out the dough to experience the very best in Charlotte public golf. It's a golf course everyone should play at least once a year, even if it's just a once-in-a-while treat. Is there a better spot north of Charlotte for corporate golf? No. So if you have to entertain a big customer (or vice versa) then head straight for Birkdale.

Amenities include driving range, pro shop, 18-hole putting green, pitching green, Arnie's Tavern (a grill and snack bar) and changing rooms.

You can walk this course anytime, and the course is very walkable. You can book a tee when you wish. Approximate cost, including cart, is $55 during the week and $60 on weekends.

Charles T. Myers

7816 Harrisburg Rd., Charlotte
• (704) 536-1692

Championship Yardage:	**6334**
Slope: 130	**Par: 72**
Men's Yardage:	**6002**
Slope: 122	**Par: 72**
Ladies' Yardage:	**5213**
Slope: 121	**Par: 72**

The front nine of Charles T. Myers opened in 1992; the back nine followed in 1997. Edmund Ault Associates designed the course, which is built on reclaimed land. Fairways are bermudagrass, and greens are bentgrass.

Reclaimed land is the politically correct phrase to describe land formerly used as a landfill. Where there once was garbage, there is now golf. Not a bad swap. The Mecklenburg County Department of Parks and Recreation owns the course and provides local golfers with a decent facility at a sensible price.

The front nine has matured and clearly outshines the back for aesthetic pleasure, even though the phrase "aesthetic pleasure" is not one that should often be used in association with the course. The open layout is the result of the land's former occupation and lends an aura of moonscapishness not found on other Charlotte courses, which tend to be more wooded. On a windy day, gusts might well knock one over—with the smell.

The back nine has not yet had time to mature, and thus a comparison with the front is unfair. Still, it's difficult to say anything pleasing about 10 through 18, except that they makes up the additional nine holes and prevents the tedium of repeating 1 through 9. Time changes all—at least let's hope so.

Several solid holes make the front nine worth the moderate price of admission. The two par 3s are fun: 150 yards downhill over ponds to shallow greens. The 402-yard 6th demands a long and straight drive to set up a mid to short iron to a peninsular green that's quite small for such a long hole. The 301-yard par 4 7th must surely be included as one of the most eclectic holes in the region as the fairway lacks any sort of definition.

Given a choice right now, we might be tempted to play the front nine twice, but in time the back nine should provide added value to a course that will be good enough to warrant its extremely moderate fee structure.

Amenities include a driving range, putting green, chipping green, restaurant and snack bar.

Walking is an option for the fit. You can book a tee time anytime. Approximate cost, including cart, is $22 weekdays and $27 weekends.

Charlotte Golf Links
11500 Providence Rd., Charlotte
• (704) 846-7990

Championship Yardage:	**6700**
Slope: 127	**Par: 71**
Men's Yardage:	**6220**
Slope: 121	**Par: 71**
Ladies' Yardage:	**5279**
Slope: 117	**Par: 72**

Charlotte Golf Links, designed by Tom Doak, opened in 1992. The course is mostly flat and open, with bermudagrass fairways and bentgrass greens.

Doak is a young(ish) architect who, after graduating from Cornell University, spent several months touring Scottish courses, and even spent some time as a caddie at the Old Course at St. Andrews. He's authored two fine books about golf courses, including *Anatomy of a Golf Course*, a must-read for anyone interested in golf course architecture and design. Doak is also an expert golf course photographer. He apprenticed himself to Pete Dye, although you'll find more touches of Donald Ross than Dye.

Doak is quite opinionated about design. In his second book, *The Confidential Guide to Golf Courses*, he's not afraid to pan the work of his competitors and highly praise his own designs. Ironically, Charlotte Golf Links is the only one of Doak's courses of which he is not particularly fond. Credit where credit is due, right?

Charlotte Golf Links is a challenging course and a must-play for the golfing purist. Much of the land here is open. With the wind blowing and a light rain coating the course, you're going to feel like you're in Scotland—or at least that's the idea. The fairways are wide in places, narrow in others, but they boast a number of subtle slopes and undulations just like the genuine article. Many holes were designed to reward the successful risk-taker more than the conservative. However, with risk comes the potential for poor results, and there's always a chance that your ball might find the long native grass that borders many holes. Locals have a name for this "stuff"—it's a scatological word we can't publish in this book.

The green complexes feature a number of small pot bunkers with grass faces and coarse sand. Some of the greens are flat, while others are much more undulating.

Charlotte Golf Links, along with Highland Creek, marked the beginning of a new era in public golf in Charlotte, and it's exciting that one of the newest courses is also one of the most traditional and walkable.

The best time to see and play Charlotte Golf Links is late on a sunny day when the shadows bring out all the subtle shaping in the fairways, and the grass faces of the bunkers are dark and menacing.

The best hole on the course might be the bunkerless 15th, one of the finest short par 4s around. It's a mere 310 from the tips, slightly downhill. On a firm day, with the prevailing wind, the bold golfer will reach for the driver and try to put it on the small and wild green. But disaster lurks in the form of a clump of trees on the left and unkempt mounds on the right. Even a well-struck drive will pinball around on the mounds in front of the putting surface, yielding an unpredictable result. The safety-conscious will take out a mid-iron and lay up safely to the wide expanse of fairway to the left of the direct line; a bit too much to the left and the trees come into play on your approach. Yet the direct lay-up will skirt the long grass to the left and mustn't leak right. Even the most accurate of wedges will have difficulty finding the exact mark due to the severity of the buried elephant green. Par is the just reward for two safe shots, but the bold will more likely find disaster than eagles or birdies.

Arnold Palmer oversees construction of the TPC at Piper Glen in south Charlotte.

Photo: Davie Hinshaw

Those who have played a genuine Scottish links course will find that Charlotte Golf Links is a mediocre imitation of the real thing—mostly because the course (like all others in Charlotte) is on clay while a true links course is on sandly loam. However, after a prolonged dry spell in the spring or fall, the course gets bouncy and can become a true links. This is when the course is at its best.

Still, Charlotte Golf Links stands out from the crowd of newcomers because it's so radically different from the development courses.

Charlotte Golf Links' ownership changed in late 1999—let's hope the new crew pumps some money into a course with a tremendous amount of potential.

Amenities include a practice green, driving range, locker room, snack bar, rental clubs, a beverage cart and pro shop.

You can walk Charlotte Golf Links on weekdays, and weekends after 2 PM. The course is very walkable. You can book a tee time whenever you choose. Approximate cost, including cart, is $35 Monday through Thursday, $39 on Friday and $49 on weekends.

Charlotte National
6920 Howey Bottoms Rd., Charlotte
• (704) 882-8282

Championship Yardage:	7227
Slope: 134	**Par: 72**
Men's Yardage:	6700
Slope: 129	**Par: 72**
Ladies' Yardage:	5423
Slope: 121	**Par: 72**

Charlotte National opened in 1996. Russell Breeden designed the course, which is set on primarily flat land bordered in places by mature woods. Bermudagrass fairways run up to bentgrass greens.

As soon as you step onto the first tee at Charlotte National, it's clear that you're on a Russell Breeden course: The fairways are mostly wide; the bunkers are large and flat; most of the greens are large and subtly sloped. There are no tricks, and the challenges of the course are laid out in front of you—a classic case of what you see is what you get. In today's era of golf course architecture, where good courses are defined by the difficulty of the test, the amount of earth moved and the layers upon layers of severity, Charlotte National is a welcome step back to minimalism. It's a step back we're happy to say has gained favor with several new courses in the Charlotte region in the past five years.

Charlotte National proves that a designer need not move mountains to produce a course that's fun and playable—yet still challenging. There's more than one golfer who firmly believes Charlotte National stands up very well against its more extravagantly built sisters in Union County.

The course is fun so long as you don't play from the tips—a backbreaking 7227 yards. That's longer than any course we've seen, even though Charlotte National drains well and can get quite firm. The course blankets some fine Union County farmland and winds through some attractive woodland; thus, it boasts a pleasant and relaxed air free of houses and other urban encroachments. Water comes into play on some holes but, with the exception of the final four holes, should not prove too hazardous to your score or overall golfing health.

The 18th presents a rousing challenge. More than 450 yards from the tips, it invites the bold driver to cut off the pond at the crux of the dogleg, yet offers ample room for those less courageous who will find themselves faced with 200-plus yards uphill to a green with three distinct levels. The successful risk taker will bomb the green with a mid-iron, which might yield a match-winning birdie.

Like many Breeden courses, this track will not make you say "Wow!" or "Gee whiz, this is amazing!," but you'll probably appreciate its ambiance and playability. It's one of the finest courses in the Charlotte region.

Amenities include a practice green, driving range, snack bar and pro shop.

You can walk this course anytime during the week and on weekend afternoons, and the course is very walkable. You can book a tee time on Wednesday for Saturday, or Thursday for Sunday. Approximate cost, including cart, is $30 during the week and $40 on weekends.

Deer Brook Golf Club
201 Deer Brook Dr., Shelby
• (704) 482-4653

Championship Yardage:	6911	
Slope: 133	Par: 72	
Men's Yardage:	6407	
Slope: 128	Par: 72	
Ladies' Yardage:	5825	
Slope: 123	Par: 72	

Deer Brook opened in 1999. Rick Robbins designed the course, which is set on primarily flat land bordered by mature woods. As at many courses in this region, you'll play from bermudagrass fairways onto bentgrass greens.

Deer Brook is a new and welcome addition to golf in the northwest portion of the Charlotte region. Rick Robbins is a former associate with Jack Nicklaus' design firm. Many golfers lauded Robbins' Mill Creek near Burlington, North Carolina—a new housing development course. Robbins' work here at Deer Brook is just as commendable though less involved.

The site is primarily open—former dairy pasture—with almost perfect undulation. The result is a pretty and playable course where Robbins clearly did not move a lot of earth to achieve a satisfying result.

Playability was obviously a major goal when building Deer Brook. However, the course is by no means a pushover, and good golfers will find that Deer Brook is a decent challenge from the back tees.

Only really poor drivers of the ball will have a hard time at Deer Croft, and the multi-tiered greens are not overly undulating. Getting up and down after a missed green should not be a problem for a golfer with a polished short game. Fairway and greenside bunkers provide ample strategic interest.

While there are many solid one- and two-shot holes on the course, it's the par 5s at Deer Brook that provide the most interest. The 519-yard dogleg 8th is reachable but offers one of the narrower fairways on the course. The fairway on the 533-yard 17th is wider, and a well struck drive leaves a tempting shot over water to a smallish, sloping green that might be better attacked with a wedge or short iron.

Robbins designed the course to provide a fun and easily maintainable layout.

Deer Croft offers several membership options, but daily-fee golfers will find the head pro and his staff extremely welcoming. A new clubhouse opened in the spring.

Amenities include a practice green, driving range, snack bar and pro shop. The course is walkable, though walking is restricted. At press time, there was no set policy for booking in advance. Approximate cost, including cart, is $36 during the week and $46 on weekends.

The Divide
2200 Divide Dr., Matthews
• (704) 882-8088

Championship Yardage:	6973	
Slope: 137	Par: 72	
Men's Yardage:	6587	
Slope: 127	Par: 72	
Other Yardage:	6145	
Slope: 121	Par: 72	
Ladies' Yardage:	5213	
Slope: 121	Par: 72	

The Divide opened in late 1995. John Cassells designed the course, which is set on gently undulating terrain surrounded primarily by woods, although houses will eventually border some holes. Fairways are seeded with 419 bermudagrass, and greens are Pennlinks bentgrass.

The Divide is brought to you by the same group that built Charlotte Golf Links, one of the Queen City's better public courses. So it comes as no surprise that The Divide, despite its youth, is already shaping up as a decent public golf facility.

The par 5s were our favorite holes at the new Deer Brook Golf Club.

Photo:Marc Brady/Deer Brook Golf Club

The Divide marks John Cassells' entry into the noble profession of golf course architecture. Cassells designed the track with the help of Todd Smith and the staff and ownership of the course, thus the emphasis is playability. If you're an average public golfer, then you'll find the course has been built with you in mind. However, if you're a stronger player, this course still should give you a stern test from the back tees (note the 137 slope from the tips).

The fairways are mostly wide, and occasional bunkers lurk, although they tend to be on the small side. On many holes, a wayward drive might find the woods. The green complexes feature mildly undulating putting surfaces, pot bunkers, flat bunkers and embankments. You'll need to bring a strong short game to get up and down successfully. A brook wanders through some of the layout and poses a serious hazard on quite a few holes, including the dramatic 18th, where the big hitter will want to challenge the creek and get to the green in two.

What we liked most about The Divide is that it's straightforward but interesting: It lacks the excesses that make too many public courses too difficult and time consuming. The course clearly has been designed to keep your round less than four hours, and most importantly, it's clearly been designed to put the fun back into public golf. We think that The Divide will ulti-mately become one of Charlotte's most popular public golf courses. You'll also find that it's one of the prettiest once all the housing and construction work is finished—that is, if you don't mind staring into people's back yards while you play.

Amenities include a driving range, putting green, chipping green, bar, restaurant, snack bar, pro shop and beverage cart.

With 8 miles of cart path, you'll need to take a cart. You can book a tee time three days in advance. Approximate cost, including cart, is $33 weekdays and $39 weekends.

Eagle Chase Golf Club
3215 Brantley Rd., Marshville
• **(704) 385-9000**

Championship Yardage: 6723	
Slope: 128	**Par: 72**
Men's Yardage:	6103
Slope: 122	**Par: 72**
Ladies' Yardage:	5139
Slope: 121	**Par: 72**

Eagle Chase Golf Course opened in 1994. Tom Jackson designed this rolling and mostly open course. Bermudagrass covers the fairways, and bentgrass carpets the greens.

To most Charlotteans, Marshville is best known as a town you pass through on your way to the beach. Doze off for a few minutes and you've missed it. It's the boyhood home of country musician Randy Travis and numerous poultry processing plants—two facts that are not necessarily related. Marshville is also home to this outstanding golf course. It's well worth the 45-minute drive from downtown Charlotte.

The most talked-about hole on the course is No. 2, a mid-length par 4 where the elevated tee gives you a great look at the treacherous shot you must negotiate: water to the left and right. The early holes feature significant elevation changes. For the most part, you'll find a decent amount of room off the tee with very few long, forced carries. The bunkers are large and clover-leafed, as you might expect from an architect who spent a couple of years under the tutelage of Robert Trent Jones. The greens also are large but not particularly undulating. The course features a number of interesting and difficult par 3s, where par is a good score.

Even though Eagle Chase is not very close to Charlotte, it can still be counted as one of the best public courses in the Charlotte area. It's quite a challenge from any of the tees and a lot of fun for golfers of all levels.

Amenities include a practice green, driving range, locker room, bar, rental clubs and a pro shop.

We don't recommend walking this course, but you're allowed to anytime. You can book a tee time five days in advance. Approximate cost, including cart, is $30 weekdays and $34 on weekends.

Emerald Lake
1 Tournament Drive, Matthews
• (704) 882-7888

Championship Yardage:	6756
Slope: 124	Par: 71
Men's Yardage:	6455
Slope: 120	Par: 71
Ladies' Yardage:	5120
Slope: 116	Par: 71

Emerald Lake opened in 1997. Gary Wirth designed the course, which is set on undulating land bordered by mature woods, with bermudagrass fairways and bentgrass greens.

Gary Wirth is by no means a well known architect, but his work here at Emerald Lake is extremely commendable: he took a choice site and created, with the possible exception of the 9th, a fine and playable course with significant interest.

Fairways are, for the most part, wide enough to promote use of the driver, while the greens are large yet fair. There is not a lot of fairway bunkering on the course, but most green complexes include at least one trap.

The par 5s at Emerald Lake are particularly good. The 5th requires a long drive over water, but the reward for a well-struck tee shot is a good look at a receptive green. The 14th also requires a good drive over a hazard, but the bold will also try to fly it over a stand of trees, leaving what might be just a seven iron, once again over water—an exciting hole for the gambler. Those trying to reach the par 5 18th in two shots might seriously think about laying up: The green slopes quite severely away from the fairway, and anything coming in hot might bounce through to the water behind the green complex.

The 9th, a long par 4, is the only controversial hole on the course. A good drive might reach a stream that bisects the fairway about 150 yards from the green. It might be a good idea to play this hole like a par 5.

But overall, Emerald Lake is a solid track that compares favorably to the other new courses in the area. It's also a good value.

Amenities include a practice green, driving range, snack bar and pro shop.

Walking is restricted but the course is very walkable. You can book a tee time anytime. Approximate cost, including cart, is $36 during the week and $45 on weekends.

Firethorne Country Club
Marvin Rd., Charlotte
• (704) 843-3111

Championship Yardage:	6904
Slope: 145	Par: 72
Men's Yardage:	6406
Slope: 133	Par: 72
Ladies' Yardage:	5423
Slope: 120	Par: 72

Firethorne opened in 1998. Tom Jackson designed the course, built on hilly land bordered by mature woods. Fairways are bermudagrass; greens are bentgrass. At press time, the course was nearing its membership goal and thus may no longer be open for full-time public play.

Here at Firethorne, Tom Jackson built a spectacular golf course on a difficult site that must have required significant tree clearing and earth moving. The result is admirable: the holes with the least undulation tend to be longer, while the almost mountainous ones are shorter. Still, Firethorne is no pushover, claiming the toughest slope rating in the Charlotte area.

Even though Firethorne is still in its infancy, it boasts the maturity of a much older and grander course. A great example is the long par-5 13th, a muscular 575 yards from the tips, requiring two massive shots to reach the green:

It's a hole that you could slide into any existing country club and nobody would complain.

The one shot holes are particularly notable, especially the 15th, 207 yards from the back tees over a chasm to what looks like one of the tougher greens on the course.

The greens vary in size and undulation.

Even if your golf game isn't going that well, you'll enjoy the ride through one of Charlotte's most picturesque layouts. A special touch: the concrete fords that bridge ponds and streams at three points.

Beginning golfers may find that Firethorne is a bit too much of a test, but the mid- to low-handicapper will relish the challenge.

Amenities include a practice green, driving range, snack bar and pro shop.

You can walk the course at certain times, although it's quite a hike. Approximate cost, including cart, is $50 on Tuesday and Wednesday; $40 on Thursdays and $60 Friday through Sunday.

Fort Mill Golf Club
101 Country Club Dr., Fort Mill, S.C.
• **(803) 547-2044**

Championship Yardage:	**6865**
Slope: 133	**Par: 72**
Men's Yardage:	**6373**
Slope: 118	**Par: 72**
Ladies' Yardage:	**5448**
Slope: 123	**Par: 72**

The front nine at Fort Mill Golf Club opened in the 1947. The back nine opened in the 1970s. Donald Ross designed the front nine just before his death in 1948, and George Cobb designed the back. The front nine is open, and the back is set in rolling terrain. In the fairways, you'll find bermudagrass; on the greens, bentgrass.

Fort Mill has long been a well-known favorite of Charlotte golfers. The club is part of a triumvirate of Springs Industries-owned courses, all of which are popular and well run; the others are in Chester and Lancaster, and each is worth a visit. (You'll find write-ups of each of these South Carolina courses in our Midlands chapter.) Ross also designed the course in Lancaster.

It's difficult to find a golf course that enlisted two better architects than Ross and Cobb. The result is a fine and mature course that's more challenging than it looks. This is a country-club caliber design, and the recent reconstruction of the greens means better conditioning.

The front nine offers plenty of room off the tee. If you're wayward with your driver, the large trees pose the most significant hazards. As you might expect with a Ross course, the trouble begins on and around the greens, where you'll encounter plenty of small bunkers and difficult putts. If you're playing for money, never give your opponent a gimme on the front—make 'em drop it in the hole. Watch as a 2-foot putt is rammed 3 feet past or ends up 2 inches short. ("Hit it, Allis.") It's part of what makes Ross's designs so timeless—and irritating.

Most Donald Ross courses offer a couple of easier par 4s to let the golfer gain his bearings. Not so here at Fort Mill, where the 430-yard 1st yields few fours. The drive must draw around a large oak to avoid another tree on the right, which will block the approach to the small and sloped green, which must be hit on the fly. The 2nd, at 412 yards, also requires a decent thump off the tee. There's water to the right and water directly in front of the large and flattish green. Only the low-handicapper will be dissatisfied with a pair of bogeys.

The back nine is a genuine Cobb championship-caliber test. Many of the holes are truly long and seem to play even longer. The greens are large and not quite as undulating as the Ross greens, but no less difficult. The bunkers are larger and the fairways wider on this nine. Water is sparse, but you'll discover that wayward shots will find the hazard if you're not sensible. Have fun here, and buy textiles made by Springs Industries out of gratitude for their excellent contributions to public golf in South Carolina.

Amenities include a practice green, snack bar and pro shop.

You can walk anytime on weekdays and after 2 PM on weekends. You can book a tee time three days in advance. Approximate cost, including cart, is $29 weekdays and $32 on weekends.

Gastonia Municipal Golf Course
Niblick Dr., Gastonia • **(704) 866-6945**

Championship Yardage:	**6474**
Slope: 115	**Par: 71**
Men's Yardage:	**5671**
Slope: 110	**Par: 71**
Ladies' Yardage:	**4344**
Slope: 110	**Par: 71**

Gastonia Municipal Golf Course opened in the 1930s, although there's no real record of who designed it. The course is set on open and rolling terrain, with bermudagrass fairways and greens.

Gastonia Muni offers a fun and playable

track that's a great value for Gastonia residents. If you live in this lovely town just west of Charlotte, you can walk as many holes as you're able on a weekday for just $10. You can't beat that deal anywhere.

Muni courses have a charm and quality that's sometimes hard to define. Many munis were built on land that was once open countryside. Thus as a metropolis expands, its municipal golf course often becomes an oasis of green in the middle of urban sprawl. That's the case at Gastonia Muni, even though it's difficult to use "Gastonia" and "urban" in the same sentence. A couple of power lines traverse the course in a few places, but for the most part you still feel like you're out in the country.

The front nine is open but the fairways are a little tight in places. The greens are small and sloped, and you can run the ball up to the pin on quite a few holes. You'll find an average of one bunker per green on both the back and front nines. A stream wanders through the track. The course opens with two of its tougher tests: the numbers one and three handicap holes. The 1st is a par 5, 563 from the tips to a small green, and the 2nd is a mere 403 from all the way back. Welcome to Gastonia!

The back nine offers a bit more room off the tee, and many of the holes are more strategic—especially around the green complexes. Still, the setting is pleasant and relaxed, and the course provides a fun and potentially rewarding challenge for all levels of golfer. The more than 40,000 rounds of golf played here per annum prove that Gastonia Muni has something going for it besides sensible greens fees.

Amenities include a practice green, chipping green, locker room, restaurant, beverage cart and pro shop.

The course is walkable anytime. You can book a tee time seven days in advance. Approximate cost, including cart, is $25 weekdays and $27 on weekends. As we mentioned before, the rates are lower if you're a resident of Gastonia, which you should at least think about—if only very briefly.

Glen Oaks Country Club
245 Golf Course Rd., Maiden
• (704) 428-2451

Championship Yardage: 6430	
Slope: 116	**Par:** 70
Men's Yardage: 6026	
Slope: No rating	**Par:** 70
Ladies' Yardage: 4953	
Slope: No rating	**Par:** 70

The golf course at Glen Oaks Country Club opened in 1967. This Bill McRee design is set

on flat terrain with many open holes. Bermudagrass covers the fairways, and bentgrass covers the greens.

Glen Oaks presents a remarkably interesting and challenging course in a country setting. The strength of the course is its variety, although the routing of the holes is a little bizarre. The course is intelligently bunkered. The front nine tends to be a little more wooded than the back and is a little tighter off the tee. The greens are mostly flat and midsize, and many are flush with the fairway, making run-up shots possible and advisable if the fairways, greens and approach aprons are hard. There's quite a bit of water on the back nine, and you'll find your golfing skills tested by a number of approach shots requiring accurate club selection and shot execution. There's even an island green. You might arrive at the 18th with your best score ever only to find the closing hole one of the most difficult on the course. Clearly, Glen Oaks is popular with the local population—for good reason.

Amenities include a practice green, driving range, locker room, bar, snack bar, restaurant, rental clubs and a pro shop.

The course is walkable for the fit and dedicated, and you can walk on weekdays. You can book a tee time seven days in advance. Approximate cost, including cart, is $28 weekdays and $38 on weekends.

Highland Creek Golf Club
7001 Highland Creek Blvd., Charlotte
• (704) 875-9000

Championship Yardage: 7008	
Slope: 133	**Par:** 72
Men's Yardage: 6505	
Slope: 124	**Par:** 72
Other Yardage: 5947	
Slope: 122	**Par:** 72
Ladies' Yardage: 5080	
Slope: 128	**Par:** 72

Highland Creek Golf Club opened in 1993. Lloyd Clifton and Ken Ezell designed the course, which is set in rolling wooded terrain bordered with houses. In the fairways, you'll play on bermudagrass; on the greens, bentgrass.

When it opened, Highland Creek was almost universally acclaimed as the greatest thing for public golf in the Charlotte area since the invention of... public golf. Along with Charlotte Golf Links, Highland Creek marked the end of a drought for Charlotte's public golfer. Here at last was a modern and well-designed course, well kept and within sensible driving distance of Charlotte. Since then, the course has maintained its popularity.

The Clifton-Ezell team hasn't completed a lot of work in North and South Carolina—Highland Creek is only one of two in the Carolinas—but the firm has been active for years in Florida. At Highland Creek, they produced one of the most challenging and demanding public golf courses in the western section of the two states. In places, it's also one of the prettiest and most varied.

On quite a few holes, the course is tight off the tee. Locals will tell you that it's essential to be in just the right place in the fairway; thus, you need to be accurate with whatever you like to use off the tee. Should you spray your shots around somewhat, you'll find your ball in Highland Creek, someone's back yard or the woods. If it seems like Highland Creek comes into play on just about every hole, it's not an illusion. The creek poses quite a hazard, and it's no fun having to fish for your ball.

Easily the most difficult of many, many difficult holes must be the par 5 12th, a solid 550 from the tips. The tee shot is played to a sloping and narrow fairway bordered by woods and the creek. With the ball below the right-handers feet, a long-iron or fairway wood must find the second fairway to the right, again sloping and somewhat narrow. The third is a wedge off a downhill lie to an island green backed by bunkers. A par is cause for massive celebration.

Once you've navigated the hazards off the tee, you must play an accurate approach shot. The greens are predominantly large, as are the bunkers and embankments that flank many of the significantly undulating green complexes. You'll certainly leave here with memories of many holes—and with an opinion about the layout. We think you'll want to come back and challenge this exciting course again. Despite all the new courses opening in the Charlotte region, Highland Creek should keep its place as one of the most difficult and exciting.

The new clubhouse is large and magnificent and offers rooms for corporate meetings and other such events.

Amenities include a practice green, driving range, chipping green, locker room, bar, restaurant, rental clubs, a beverage cart and pro shop.

Walking is not a viable option here. You can book a tee time three days in advance. Approximate cost, including cart, is $42 weekdays and $48 on weekends.

King's Mountain Country Club
Country Club Dr., Kings Mountain
• (704) 739-5871
Championship Yardage: 6483
Slope: 121   **Par:** 72

Men's Yardage:	6143
Slope: 118	**Par:** 72
Ladies' Yardage:	5019
Slope: 119	**Par:** 72

King's Mountain Golf Course opened its first nine holes in the 1940s; the second nine opened in the 1970s. The course is set in rolling wooded terrain, with the typical bermudagrass fairways and bentgrass greens.

King's Mountain offers a couple of varied and thoroughly interesting nines. The front is the original nine and is built much like many courses of its day. The greens are somewhat small and sloped, and there's plenty of room for run-up shots from just about anywhere. Your chipping game will be seriously tested. The few bunkers should not pose too much of a problem. Steep embankments flank many of the greens. What you'll probably notice most about the front nine are the towering pine trees that delineate the fairways. They create quite a frame for many holes.

On the back nine, there's a little more room off the tee. Thick woods border many of the holes, creating quite a hazard. The greens are still relatively flat and somewhat small. It's still possible to run the ball up to many of the holes due to the lack of bunkers fronting the greens. There are also some fun tee placements on a few holes. Overall, it's a relaxed yet challenging course, exhibiting a maturity rarely seen on many modern courses.

Amenities include a practice green and snack bar.

The course is walkable anytime. You can book a tee time whenever you choose for the weekdays, and starting on Wednesday for the weekend. Approximate cost, including cart, is $27 weekdays and $32 on weekends.

Larkhaven Golf Club
4801 Camp Stewart Rd., Charlotte
• (704) 545-GOLF
Championship Yardage: 6464
Slope: 121   **Par:** 72
Men's Yardage: 6042
Slope: 115   **Par:** 72
Ladies' Yardage: 4645
Slope: 110   **Par:** 72

Larkhaven Golf Club opened in 1959. A.B. Connell designed the course, which is set in undulating terrain bordered by woods. You'll find bermudagrass fairways and bentgrass greens here at Larkhaven.

Larkhaven has long been a popular golf course among Charlotte-area public golfers. The course is relatively straightforward; the challenges here come from a couple of water hazards and the tightness of the fairways in places, particularly on the front nine. The key to scoring well here is doing whatever it takes to keep the ball in play.

A couple of holes you'll really enjoy are the par 4 1st, a 262-yard par 4 that tempts you to bang it onto the green with the driver. All you have to do is smack it into a large bank and hope it rolls up to the green. It's a unique opening hole. The 9th, a 207-yard par 3 over water, is an exciting way to finish the front nine.

The greens here at Larkhaven are relatively small and sloped. A few bunkers lurk here and there, but getting up and down from within them should not be too difficult. Overall, we think you'll enjoy your round here. It's a fun course in a relaxed setting where the premium is accuracy, not length. In recent years, management made several improvements to the course, including the addition of practice facilities.

Amenities include a practice green, range, locker room, snack bar and pro shop.

The course is walkable and you can walk during the week. You can book a tee time on Monday for the weekend. Approximate cost, including cart, is $31 weekdays and $35 on weekends.

Lincoln Country Club
2108 Country Club Rd., Lincolnton
• (704) 735-1382

Championship Yardage:	6467	
Slope: 125	Par: 72	
Men's Yardage:	6017	
Slope: 121	Par: 72	
Ladies' Yardage:	5011	
Slope: 118	Par: 72	

The current back nine at Lincoln Country Club opened in 1949, and the front nine opened in 1993. Peter Tufts is credited with Lincoln's recent redesign. The course is set on rolling wooded terrain with bermudagrass fairways and bentgrass greens.

There are two distinct nines here. The front is newer, though not particularly modern or penal in design—it's not a tricked-up course. You'll find some mounds, but they're not of the massive variety. The terrain is pretty and undulating, and trees border many holes. Thankfully, there's decent width off the tee. You'll find a number of tough but short par 4s, each with an interesting and unique feature. The greens are midsize and sloped.

The back nine is older and more traditional in design. If the fairways are dry and hard, you'll be able to play a variety of run-up shots to the greens, which are flush with the fairways. You'll also find a fair amount of sensible bunkering. Overall, it's a fun and playable track that's justifiably popular with the local population.

Amenities include a practice green, driving range, chipping green, locker room, snack bar and pro shop.

Walk this course anytime, and book a tee time whenever you choose during the week and two days before your weekend round. Approximate cost, including cart, is $25 weekdays and $31 on weekends.

Mallard Head Country Club
Brawley School Rd., Mooresville
• (704) 664-7031

Championship Yardage:	6904	
Slope: 121	Par: 72	
Men's Yardage:	6442	
Slope: 116	Par: 72	
Other Yardage:	6233	
Slope: 113	Par: 72	
Ladies' Yardage:	5469	
Slope: 121	Par: 72	

The golf course at Mallard Head Country Club opened in 1979. Porter Gibson designed this course, which is set in rolling terrain. Houses border some of the holes. Fairways are bermudagrass, and greens are bentgrass.

Mallard Head is a popular and reasonably priced golf course that has long attracted golfers from Charlotte and the eastern shores of Lake Norman. The course offers some interesting and diverse golf holes with plenty of challenge, particularly from the back tees. The greens are medium to large in size and flanked by bunkers and the occasional embankment. The front nine is more wooded than the back. Water comes into play on a few holes, and its influence varies in intensity. On most holes, you'll find enough room off the tee to pull out the big stick and take a big whack. Overall, Mallard Head is a fun course that's popular with the locals; it's well worth a visit if you're in the area. Greenskeeper Sam Linker is one of the better manicurists of bentgrass in the Charlotte region, and there must be quite a few country clubs that have tried to lure him from his position. Mallard Head routinely offers some of the best greens around.

Although it's not the number-one handicap hole on the course, the par 4 18th must see its fair share of big numbers. The tee shot must carry a creek: The surrounding ground slopes perilously close and will redirect any poor drive into the murky depths. A solid drive leaves a mid-iron into a smallish green bunkered back

Piedmont courses are often lined with hardwoods.

Photo: Courtesy of The Charlotte Observer

and front. Most are happy to leave with a four and head to the bar in the friendly clubhouse.

Amenities include a practice green, locker room, snack bar, rental clubs and a pro shop.

The course is walkable for the physically fit, and you can walk anytime during the week. You can book a tee time whenever you choose for weekdays and on Thursday for the weekend. Approximate cost, including cart, is $25 weekdays and $30 on weekends.

Monroe Country Club
U.S. Hwy. 601 S., Monroe
• (704) 282-4661

Championship Yardage:	6759	
Slope: 118	**Par: 72**	
Men's Yardage:	6310	
Slope: 116	**Par: 72**	
Ladies' Yardage:	4964	
Slope: 117	**Par: 73**	

The golf course at Monroe Country Club opened in 1936 with nine holes, and a second nine was added in 1984. Tom Jackson designed the newer front nine, and Donald Ross, the original nine, now the back. The course is set on rolling wooded terrain. You'll find bermudagrass on the greens and fairways.

There can't be many better Carolina-based architectural combinations than Donald Ross and Tom Jackson. Both have worked exten-

sively in the area, and their efforts at Monroe Country Club make this course worth playing. It's also an excellent value.

The Jackson nine (no relation to the Jackson Five) is tight and challenging with few mounds. The greens are large and somewhat flat. The bunkers aren't quite as demonic as those on other Jackson layouts. Anyway, the length from the back and the tight fairways will give you all the challenge you want—and then some. Particularly remarkable is the maturity of the new front nine: It looks as though it's been there as long as the original nine.

We're constantly awestruck by the quality and timelessness of a Donald Ross track, and the back nine here is no exception. The simple yet sensible layout might lead you to believe that you'll run away with a low score. But the intelligent placement of bunkers and the small crowned greens make the course more difficult to play than it looks. There's no such thing as a gimme on a Ross course, and with the added element of grainy bermudagrass greens, you'll be praying that your 2- and 3-footers for bogey somehow find the bottom of the cup. The setting is pretty, and many of the holes have an Ellis Maples-like look with a couple of sweeping doglegs. The back nine is wider off the tee. If you're a fan of interesting golf course architecture, take some time to visit this course.

Amenities include a practice green, driving range, snack bar, restaurant and pro shop.

You can walk anytime during the week and after 2 PM on weekends. You can book a tee time five days before you want to play. Approximate cost, including cart, is $26 weekdays and $30 on weekends.

Mooresville Golf Club
W. Wilson Ave., Mooresville
• (704) 663-2539

Championship Yardage:	6528
Slope: 124	Par: 72
Men's Yardage:	6102
Slope: 121	Par: 72
Ladies' Yardage:	4976
Slope: 115	Par: 72

The front nine at Mooresville Golf Club, designed by Donald Ross, opened in the 1940s. The back nine, designed by Porter Gibson, opened in 1978. The front nine is open, and the back is set on rolling terrain. In the fairways, you'll find bermudagrass; on the greens, bentgrass.

There aren't many ultra-low-cost public access Donald Ross courses in the Carolinas, but Mooresville Golf Club is one of them. As with many Ross courses, the layout is excellent. There's plenty of room off the tee. The difficulties include some awkward bunkers and mounding around small greens with numerous minute and irritating undulations. Donald Ross perfected the art of the heart-attack-inducing 2-foot putt, a shot you'll doubtless face many times here. Each hole has a character and challenge all its own. The subtle shaping and innuendoes become magnificently apparent late in the day, when the low sun and long shadows show off the undulations.

To score well on the front nine, you'll need to be precise with club selection and control. You'll also need to drive the ball well and in the correct part of the fairway. Believe it or not, the front nine here at Mooresville is something of a rarity—a relatively untouched and unmolested Donald Ross design. The course management regrew the greens in late 1996, and the resulting success is well worth the whopping $2 increase in greens fees.

The most entertaining hole on the front must be the par 5 7th. Less than 500 yards from the tips and all downhill, it's a hole that even the middle-of-the-road golfer will attempt to hit in two. Yet disaster lurks, and the number of big numbers must reach skyward. Locals call it "The Road Hole" (after the 17th at St. Andrew's, one of the sternest par 4s in all of

golf) due to a heavily-trafficked road that will greet the right-hander's hook. A portion of the Town of Mooresville's water supply beckons on the right but is easily drivable. The solid drive leaves about 200 to 225 yards downhill to a small and tortoise-backed green with bunkers to the left and right. The well-struck long iron will yield a birdie or eagle, but there's little hope for par with any other shot, as two-putts on this green are rare. It's just one of many fine holes on the front nine.

Also daunting from the back tees is the 9th, 200 yards almost entirely over water to a one-club green; hit this one in regulation and walk away with par and you're a player.

The back nine is no less interesting. It's quite tight in places, and some of the holes require a decent thump off the tee if you're going to score well. The greens are larger, as are the bunkers and the embankments that flank some of the greens. Mooresville is a fun and challenging course, a great value and one of our favorites. Despite the sometime boggy nature of the course, many fine golfers in the Charlotte area will tell you that Mooresville National is a superb test from the back tees. Wait for a dry spell before playing here and you'll be similarly impressed.

Amenities include a practice green, driving range, snack bar and pro shop.

Walk anytime you wish. You can book a tee time three days in advance. Approximate cost, including cart, is $22.50 weekdays and $26 on weekends.

Olde Sycamore Golf Plantation
7504 Olde Sycamore Drive., Charlotte
• (704) 573-1000

Championship Yardage:	6965
Slope: 140	Par: 72
Men's Yardage:	6398
Slope: 133	Par: 72
Ladies' Yardage:	4756
Slope: 120	Par: 72

Olde Sycamore Golf Plantation, a Tom Jackson design, opened in 1997. The course is wooded and will ultimately be ringed by large and expensive custom homes. Bermudagrass fairways lead to bentgrass greens.

One of Charlotte's newer courses, Olde Sycamore already rates as one of Charlotte's better public-access facilities. The owners gave the course a chance to mature before it opened, and the result is solid. Tom Jackson is one of the Carolinas' most prominent architects, and this course must rate as one of his better efforts.

Hacked mostly out of woods, Olde Sycamore is a peaceful excursion into a pleasant piece of property where Jackson built a course that's user-friendly in most places. We found no need to pull out the driver until the 9th, a huge par 4, 442 from the tips with an approach shot over water to a large and undulating green. The driver could well stay in the bag on much of the back nine as well, as Jackson emphasizes placement over raw power—at least from the front tees! Once your tee shot splits the fairway, your approach shot needs to find the right portion of the mostly largish greens, but mounds adjacent to many of the putting surfaces will bounce the slightly errant shot back onto the green—the exact opposite of a Donald Ross green complex.

There isn't much water on the golf course, and in true Tom Jackson style, there are no long carries off the tee. The fairways aren't especially wide, and plenty of bunkers lurk in wait of the errant drive. If the fairways are hard, an overhit drive could easily result in a lost ball through the fairway at a dogleg.

The owners built Olde Sycamore as an amenity to their housing development, and the course will surely succeed as such. It should also provide local golfers with an interesting test where even the mid-handicapper might be tempted to head for the tips for the full effect—but only if the fairways are running. Once it's had a couple more years to mature, Olde Sycamore will be yet another solid contribution to Charlotte's public-access golf portfolio.

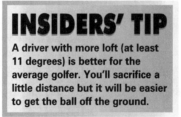

INSIDERS' TIP

A driver with more loft (at least 11 degrees) is better for the average golfer. You'll sacrifice a little distance but it will be easier to get the ball off the ground.

Amenities include a practice green, driving range, chipping green, snack bar, rental clubs and a pro shop.

You will not want to walk this course. You can book a tee time three days in advance of the weekend if you're not a member. Approximate cost, including cart, is $45 Monday through Thursday and $50 on weekends.

Piney Point Golf Club
Piney Point Rd., Norwood
• (704) 474-3985

Championship Yardage:	**6710**
Slope: 118	**Par: 72**
Men's Yardage:	**6385**
Slope: 115	**Par: 72**
Ladies' Yardage:	**4955**
Slope: 111	**Par: 72**

Piney Point Golf Club opened in 1964. Por-

ter Gibson designed the course, which is mostly open, with woods bordering a few holes. The fairways are bermudagrass, and the club redesigned the green complexes with bentgrass in 1998.

This mature golf course, close to Lake Tillery, is justifiably popular among local golfers. The pace and overall ambiance of the course are relaxing and unassuming, offering countrified golf in a pastoral setting. It's only open for public play on weekdays; on weekends, you must play with a member.

There's a lot to like about Piney Point, and there's plenty to make it worth the price of admission, even if you can only play the course during the week. First among its attractions is the solid layout, which features four reachable par 5s, four indifferent but challenging par 3s and some interesting par 4s that vary in length from a mere 376 yards to a muscular 441.

Pride of the par 5s must be the dogleg left 2nd, 490 from the tips downhill to a wide fairway. A good drive on the normally hard surface leaves a tempting 225 or less to a thin green guarded by two bunkers on the left and a large pond on the right. The ball below the feet of the right-hander may push the shot to the right, but a laser-like second could lead to excellent results, while errant approaches will spell early disaster. The 9th, a 390-yard par 4 over water to a fairway set at 45 degrees to the tee, is a justifiably well-known hole that favors the slicer who will find the ball sitting comfortably at the bottom of a swale for the approach to the green.

Perhaps Piney Point is a throwback to a time when architects could take a pleasant piece of property and lay out a golf course without moving too much earth. There are no houses on the course, and wayward drives are more likely to find the next fairway than someone's back yard. The money is clearly spent on the golf course instead of the clubhouse, and the result is a routinely fast track where a downhill shot means two to three fewer clubs. It isn't easy to shoot very low scores on the course, but it's equally difficult to post really huge numbers.

Tipped-out, Piney Point will provide the good golfer with all he could want, particularly on the par 4s, which provide the course with the majority of its interest and challenge.

The club's powers-that-be expertly managed

the recent and much needed redesign of the greens, converted from bermuda to Crenshaw bentgrass. It's always tempting to go overboard with this type of work, but Piney Point members do not want anything too disco and thus the greens are subtle and quirky without being too outrageously difficult to putt or maintain.

You can walk this course anytime. The course is very walkable, and lots of golfers walk here. You can book a tee time anytime, so long as it's not for the weekend. Approximate cost, including cart, is $25 Monday through Friday and $33 on weekends (remember, on weekends you must be with a member).

Regent Park Golf Club
3000 Heritage Pkwy., Fort Mill, S.C.
• (803) 547-1300

Championship Yardage:	**6861**
Slope: No rating	**Par: 72**
Men's Yardage:	**6478**
Slope: No rating	**Par: 72**
Other Yardage:	**6083**
Slope: No rating	**Par: 72**
Ladies' Yardage:	**5258**
Slope: No rating	**Par: 72**

Note: Regent Park is a South Carolina course; however, its proximity to Charlotte (it's less than 10 miles over the state line) and the fact that it is frequented by Charlotte golfers make it a natural addition to this Charlotte Region chapter.

Ron Garl designed Regent Park Golf Club, which opened in 1995. The course is set on rolling wooded terrain. In the fairways, you'll find bermudagrass; on the greens, bentgrass.

The sumptuous Regent Park is the centerpiece of what will eventually be a large housing community. The development also includes a top-quality, state-of-the-art practice facility—the finest in the area.

Playing at Regent Park, you can't help being staggered by and impressed with the money that must have been poured into its construction and design. It's a golfing extravaganza the likes of which you won't find on any public course in the immediate area, even with all the new competition. The result is a number of beautiful golf holes flanked by serious hazards and difficulties. You'll find large bunkers, mounds, water, swamp, tricky lies in the fairway and the type of problems normally reserved for professional and low-handicap golfers. It's as stern a test of golfing skill and patience as you'll find on any top-notch public or private course. Many of the greens are sensible and sloped, while others make you feel like you've

landed on a Putt-Putt course with a few too many under your belt. You'll see what we mean when you visit this course—something you definitely should do.

The pros here are proudest of the dogleg right par 4 8th, 420 from the tips. Your tee shot needs to fade around a large mound on the right side of the fairway, leaving a long iron downhill to an undulating green surrounded by trees. A solid golf hole.

There's a serious emphasis at Regent Park on making this a top-quality public facility. Tee times are spread out at 10-minute intervals, and your tee time is secured by a credit card—so show up for your tee time. As you leave the course, your clubs are cleaned and carried to your car—talk about service. Golfers who show up at the practice range without collars on their shirts are turned away by the style police.

You won't find a larger testament to modern golf anywhere in the Charlotte region than at Regent Park. You must use a cart here.

Amenities include a practice green, driving range, chipping green, snack bar, rental clubs, a beverage cart and pro shop.

You can book a tee time four to seven days in advance for an $8 service charge; otherwise it's three days in advance. Approximate cost, including cart, is $45 weekdays and $55 on weekends.

Renaissance Park Golf Course
1525 Tyvola Rd. W., Charlotte
• (704) 357-3373

Championship Yardage: 7525	
Slope: 126	**Par: 72**
Men's Yardage: 6880	
Slope: 121	**Par: 72**
Other Yardage: 6270	
Slope: 115	**Par: 72**
Ladies' Yardage: 4606	
Slope: No rating	**Par: 72**

Renaissance Park Golf Course opened in 1987. Michael Hurdzan, a well-respected architect and agronomy expert, designed the course with bermudagrass fairways and bentgrass greens on a mix of open and wooded terrain on what used to be a landfill. The course is owned by the City of Charlotte and Mecklenburg County.

Controversial from its very first day in operation, Renaissance Park opened during the "landfill boom" of the 1980s, when municipalities discovered the joys of building golf courses where there used to be garbage. Due to its proximity to downtown Charlotte, the airport and the Charlotte Coliseum, Renaissance packed 'em in during its first few years of life. Those who plunked down the almost $50 (then) to experience the joys of landfill golf found a wide-open links-like design with some interesting and difficult holes, most notably the 1st, a 600-yard par 5 where the only shot was a lay-up with a five iron. And then there was the smell—a sulfurous and nauseating odor oozing out of the earth, borne over the entire layout by the prevailing westerly winds.

Once the competition heated up, Renaissance began to feel the pinch, and the county ordered a $1 million rethink of the project, which coincided with the closure of the clubhouse due to potentially lethal levels of methane. Your tax dollars at work, ladies and gentlemen.

The result of the redesign is a course that's much more user-friendly than the original. Targets have been widened, and many of the blind shots have been eradicated. The price is lower, reducing its impact on the bank account, but most importantly, the smell has subsided. Now, the only obstacles to one's golfing enjoyment are the roaring jets making their final approach to Charlotte-Douglas International Airport, and the distant sound of gunfire from the Police Department's firing range. In his book *The Confidential Guide to Golf Courses*, Tom Doak gave the course a zero out of 10 rating. Things have improved since Tom's visit, making Renaissance a decent course if you're stuck at the airport with more than six hours to kill.

Amenities include a range, practice green, snack bar and rental clubs.

You can walk anytime, but it's not recommended. You can also book a tee time anytime. Approximate cost for Mecklenburg County residents, including cart, is $32 weekdays and $36 on weekends. It's about $5 more for nonresidents.

River Bend Golf Club
Longwood Dr., Shelby • (704) 482-4286

Championship Yardage:	6555
Slope: 130	**Par: 72**
Men's Yardage:	5956
Slope: 117	**Par: 72**
Ladies' Yardage:	4920
Slope: 102	**Par: 72**

River Bend opened in 1965. Russell Breeden designed the course, which is open and set on rolling terrain, with the typical bermudagrass fairways and bentgrass greens.

River Bend has a local reputation as a playable track that's usually in good condition. It's exactly what you'd expect from a Russell

Breeden course. You won't find a ton of trouble off the tee, and your approach shot will be hit to a medium-sized green flanked by a series of bunkers that are not too penal. The owner of the course talks wistfully about Russell Breeden cruising around building the course with the help of his personal earth mover. He also talks proudly about the conditioning. The course is definitely worth a visit, and it's a good value.

Amenities include a practice green, driving range, chipping green, snack bar and pro shop.

The course is walkable, and you can walk on weekdays. You can book a tee time three days in advance. Approximate cost, including cart, is $27 weekdays and $34 on weekends.

Rock Barn Club of Golf
Rock Barn Rd., Conover • (704) 459-9279

Championship Yardage:	6778
Slope: 132	**Par: 72**
Men's Yardage:	6318
Slope: 128	**Par: 72**
Other Yardage:	5921
Slope: 122	**Par: 72**
Ladies' Yardage:	4812
Slope: 117	**Par: 72**

Rock Barn Club of Golf opened in 1968. Russell Breeden designed the course. The club recently added an additional nine holes, designed by Tom Jackson. The course, which is convenient to I-40, is set on rolling terrain, with woods bordering many of the holes. In the fairways, you'll find bermudagrass; on the greens, bentgrass.

Set in the northern reaches of the Charlotte region near Hickory, Rock Barn Club of Golf has long had an excellent reputation for its sound design and great conditioning. We found this to be true. In fact, we think this is perhaps one of Breeden's finest efforts—a course with outstanding variety and playability, laid out in a peaceful setting. Should anyone accuse Breeden of being a cookie-cutter architect, bring them here. There are some wonderful and imaginative holes on this excellent layout. You'll find decent room off the tee, though it helps to be in the right part of the fairway with your drive. The greens are large and sloped. Three-putts are an annoying possibility; there's just enough slope and undulation to make even the shortest putt an adventure. As with many Breeden courses, the large bunkers vary in intensity, depending upon pin placement. You should definitely take time to play here.

The Jackson nine is new and modern in design. The architect unleashed some of his most venomous features. You'll find plenty of major elevation changes, large mounds, nasty bunkers and severely undulating greens. It's certainly a stunning and entertaining track—a strong contrast to Breeden's more mature and less penal 18. After your round on the main course, take a few beers to the new nine and you'll have had all the golf you could possibly want—and more.

The club plans major modifications in 2000, so call first if you'd like to play there.

Amenities include a practice green, driving range, locker room, snack bar, rental clubs and a pro shop.

The original course is walkable for the fit, and you can walk anytime, but we don't recommend you walk the Jackson nine. You can book a tee time six days in advance.

Approximate cost, including cart, is $37 weekdays and $32 on weekends.

Rocky River Golf Club
6900 Speedway Blvd., Concord
• **(704) 455-1200**

Championship Yardage:	6970	
Slope: 132		Par: 72
Men's Yardage:	6028	
Slope: 119		Par: 72
Ladies' Yardage:	4574	
Slope: 119		Par: 72

Dan Maples designed Rocky River, which opened in 1997. The City of Concord owns the course, which is built on rolling woodlands. Greens are bentgrass and fairways are bermudagrass.

This municipally owned course is one of the better tracks northeast of Charlotte. Dan Maples, son of the great Ellis (who built Donald Ross' last golf course at Raleigh Country Club) is a well-known and well-respected architect who makes his home in the Pinehurst area. His work here at Rocky River has been well received and easily outshines all the publicly owned work in the Charlotte region. The course places a strong emphasis on service and conditioning: Charlotte-Mecklenburg Parks and Rec Department take note.

The site is excellent, with wetlands and rock outcroppings providing most of the danger. The rocks provide a quaint, "rugged" look that's unique in this area.

In fact, on the third hole, a solid 555-yard par 5, there's a bus-sized boulder 300 yards out in the middle of the fairway. After that's been negotiated, the approach to the large green is relatively straightforward. Most of the greens at Rocky River are large and somewhat undulating. Many offer the opportunity to bounce

the ball up from the fairway—a design feature that's all too rare these days.

Overall, Rocky River provides an excellent example of what a local government can achieve with a golf course; it's well worth a visit if you're in the Concord area.

The course is walkable—but walking is restricted, which is an absolute crime at a municipal public facility. You can book a tee time six days in advance for weekdays and on Monday for the weekend. Approximate cost, including cart, is $40 weekdays and $50 on weekends. However, the course offers a slew of discounts for students, seniors, residents, etc.

Stonebridge Golf Club
2721 Swilcan Burn Rd., Monroe
• **(704) 283-8998**

Championship Yardage:	6923	
Slope: 132		Par: 72
Men's Yardage:	6374	
Slope: 127		Par: 72
Ladies' Yardage:	5145	
Slope: 120		Par: 72

Stonebridge opened in 1998. Richard Osborne designed the course, which sits on flat land bordered by mature woods. Fairways are bermudagrass; greens are bentgrass. Osborne, who only recently opened his own firm, used to be an associate of Ron Garl, who designed the popular Regent Park.

Drive south and east of Charlotte, past the *house* farms to where you get to the *horse* farms, and you're in some of the prettiest land and scenery in the region. In 20 years or so, most of it will be developed, but for now, it's superb—pristine farmland and woodlands with nary a condo or strip mall in sight.

Stonebridge's developer, a company based in Jacksonville, Florida, found a prime chunk of this fair land upon which to build its course, and the result is outstanding. To the traditionalist or minimalist, Stonebridge is easily the most pleasing of all the new courses built in Charlotte in the past 10 years. In many ways, it's reminiscent of an English countryside parkland course. There are no houses adjacent to the course and civilization, for the most part, has been kept far away.

The imitation of the Swilcan Bridge on the 1st hole, a cracker of a par 5, 574 from the tips, is a bit silly, but overall, the layout is superbly designed. Some holes, particularly on the front are completely hemmed in by woods, while others are quite open and almost linksy. Adding to the Scottish touch is the nomenclature for each hole: the 451 yard par 4 8th is called

"Saddleback." It's a tough hole, with a stand of oaks on the right side of the fairway just 200 yards from the back tee.

Most fairways are wide, and most green complexes offer generous putting surfaces with varying degrees of undulation and bunkering. But while the design is solid, the setting is even better. If you want to get away from it all for a few hours, Stonebridge might be your best bet. Afterwards, relax in the elegant 10,000 square-foot clubhouse.

Amenities include a practice green, driving range, snack bar and pro shop.

The course is very walkable but walking is restricted primarily to weekdays. You can book a tee time four days in advance. Approximate cost, including cart, is $36 during the week and $50 on weekends.

The Tradition
3800 Prosperity Church Rd., Charlotte
• **(704) 549-9779**
Championship Yardage: 6970
Slope: No rating Par: 72
Men's Yardage: 6450
Slope: No rating Par: 72
Ladies' Yardage: 4754
Slope: No rating Par: 72

The Tradition opened in 1996. John Cassells designed the course, which is set on rolling, partially wooded terrain. The fairways are blanketed with bermudagrass; on the greens, you'll putt on bentgrass.

The Tradition is a sister course of The Divide (see write-up above). The taxpayers of Mecklenburg County own the land. A round at The Tradition is bound to be a pleasant ride through the woods over streams and around ponds. The wayward driver will find the course tight and will spend a good deal of time getting to know the woods firsthand.

The greens are midsize and undulating, with shallow bunkers catching off-line shots.

The Tradition offers a sensible value, coming in at a price point that's noticeably lower than other newer public golf courses in the region. Once the course has fully matured and grown in, it'll be a solid addition to public golf in the northeast quadrant of the city.

Amenities include a practice green, driving range, locker room, snack bar, rental clubs and a pro shop.

The course is walkable for the fit, but walking is restricted. You can book a tee time seven days in advance for weekday play and on Monday for the weekend. Approximate cost, including cart, is $29 weekdays and $39 on weekends.

Verdict Ridge
7332 Kidville Rd., Denver
• **(704) 489-1206**
Championship Yardage: 6897
Slope: 142 Par: 72
Men's Yardage: 6347
Slope: 131 Par: 72
Ladies' Yardage: 4932
Slope: 125 Par: 72

Verdict Ridge opened in 1998. Former Charlotte mayor Eddie Knox designed the course in association with the land planning firm Land Design. Bermudagrass fairways lead to bentgrass greens.

Is there a more visually appealing or stunning course in the Charlotte area than Verdict Ridge? Probably not. This site, in rustic east Lincoln County, has to be one of the most scenic in the Charlotte region. You'll feel like you're in the mountains of North Carolina, amid a virgin forest of hardwoods and shrubs, such is the splendor.

In addition to being a prominent citizen and former mayor, founder and designer Knox is also a lawyer, hence the club's name: Verdict Ridge.

Eventually, there will be houses up on the ridge and around the course.

Due to the hilliness of the site, Verdict Ridge is a difficult and challenging golf course. High handicappers might not enjoy themselves on this course and are best advised to leave the clubs at home and enjoy the scenery—particularly magnificent in spring and fall. Even the view from the practice tee is breathtaking!

On most holes, the undulations of the site come into play. Tee shots and approach shots are often quite significantly uphill or downhill, and many shots must be played from tricky sidehill lies, often to greens that are either shallow or narrow. If you don't know how to deal with uneven lies, a day at Verdict Ridge will be quite long.

Adding to the difficulty is the undulating design of the green complexes.

One of the many spectacular holes is the par 4 9th, 351 yards from the back tees. The drive must be played into the side of a hill to the left of the fairway—hopefully, the ball will run down to a relatively flat lie on the right side. From there, it's a short to mid iron to a triple-tiered green flanked by a waterfall. Par here is an achievement that will make your hot dog at the turn taste like caviar.

The 9th is just one of many visually pleasing yet tremendously demanding holes on what might be Charlotte's toughest golf course. We love the scenery. Play it once just for the vistas alone—we'll let you decide whether you're up for the challenge.

Amenities include a practice green, driving range, snack bar and pro shop.

You can't walk this course even though it would make a nice day hike. Approximate cost, including cart, is $39 Monday to Thursday and $54 on weekends (including Fridays.)

The Warrior

890 Lake Wright Rd., China Grove
• (704) 856-0871

Championship Yardage:	**6609**
Slope: 127	**Par: 72**
Men's Yardage:	**6193**
Slope: 121	**Par: 72**
Ladies' Yardage:	**4423**
Slope: 110	**Par: 72**

The Warrior opened in 1999. Stan Gentry designed the course, which is set on undulating acreage bordered by mature woods, with bermudagrass fairways and bentgrass greens.

The Warrior Golf Club in China Grove provides a perfect example of the welcoming new movement towards golf courses designed to bring playability back to public golf in metro Charlotte. The Warrior fills the need for quality public golf in the Salisbury area.

Architect Stan Gentry worked on Meadowlands in Thomasville, a course that's been extremely well received by golfers in the Winston-Salem area. Gentry designed the course golf first and homesites second. The owners of The Warrior originally planned to build a course nearer to Salisbury but happened along this piece of property by accident. And what a piece of land. The centerpiece of the mostly wooded and superbly pitched site is Lake Wright, which supplies a portion of the water for the town of Landis. The small lake borders the first hole and provides a superb backdrop for the 16th, 17th and 18th. It also generates a breeze.

Ponds come into play on Warrior's No. 1 handicap hole, the 407 yard 7th. Players who risk hitting their driver may well end up in one of two water hazards. The big hitter will prudently lay up with a long iron or fairway wood, leaving a mid-iron to one of the few greens on the course with significant undulation.

Off the tee at Warrior, the trouble comes primarily in the form of dense woods, which line many of the fairways. Rope or slice a drive into the forest with the Biggest Big Bertha Ever and it's a lost ball. Thankfully, most of the fairways at Warrior are wide and, at just over 6600 yards from the tips, many players can afford to keep the driver in the bag off the tee.

Once successfully in the fairway, the golfer, should the course be dry, is presented with the option of flying the ball to the pin or running it up to the green. The latter is a rarity on many modern courses, and the bump-and-run will be particularly useful on windy days.

A rarity in this area, Warrior offers a real full-service pro shop, featuring complete club repair and fitting.

Amenities include a practice green, driving range, grill, snack bar and pro shop.

Walking is restricted, but the course is very walkable. Approximate cost, including cart, is $35 during the week and $40 on weekends.

Waterford

1900 Clubhouse Rd., Rock Hill
• (803) 324-0300

Championship Yardage:	**6913**
Slope: 132	**Par: 72**
Men's Yardage:	**6513**
Slope: 125	**Par: 72**
Ladies' Yardage:	**5196**
Slope: 1112	**Par: 72**

Waterford opened in 1997. Hale Irwin designed the course, which is set on undulating land adjacent to the Catawba River. The Senior Tour star had the course seeded with bermudagrass fairways and bentgrass greens.

The Rock Hill area needed a couple more solid public-access courses and Waterford satiates the need extremely well. The site is outstanding, and Irwin produced a fine and scenic course that most golfers will enjoy. Irwin and his crew protected wetlands and streams, and these natural hazards provide most of the strategic challenge. Greens are mostly large and undulating but should not render too much trouble.

The par 4 13th, a decent 423 yards from the back tees, is a magnificent and tricky golf hole. The drive might be best played to the right side

> ## INSIDERS' TIP
> If you drive into trouble, don't try to hit an impossible shot to save par—you'll likely miss the shot and see your score balloon. Instead, do whatever you have to to get your ball safely back in the fairway, and start playing for bogey.

of the sloping, tiered fairway, so that your ball bounces back down to the middle. From there, it's a decent poke uphill to a green that's protected by a stream and long trap in front. Hale Irwin and many other professional golfers would be ecstatic with a par here.

The 9th, another fine hole, measures a whopping 596 yards from the back tees through a relatively narrow opening in the trees. Irwin is famous for his ability to hit consistently straight shots, and his design philosophy somwhat mirrors his playing abilities. This might be especially true on the downhill 15th, a 156-yard par 3 where accuracy is essential—there's water to the left and woods on the right.

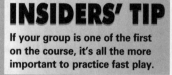

INSIDERS' TIP

If your group is one of the first on the course, it's all the more important to practice fast play.

Even though the soil here is red Piedmont clay, Waterford, with its abundance of tall pines, might remind you of a Pinehurst course, particularly on holes like the aforementioned 9th. It's definitely worth a visit if you're in south Charlotte or York County.

Amenities include a practice green, driving range, snack bar and pro shop.

Walking is restricted, and the course is walkable. Approximate cost, including cart, is $36 during the week and $45 on weekends.

Westport Golf Course
7494 Golf Course Dr., Denver
• (704) 483-5604

Championship Yardage:	6805
Slope: 123	Par: 72
Men's Yardage:	6291
Slope: 118	Par: 72
Ladies' Yardage:	5597
Slope: 118	Par: 72

Westport Golf Course opened in 1968. Porter Gibson designed the course, which is set on rolling wooded terrain. Bermudagrass blankets the fairways, and bentgrass covers the greens.

Westport has been popular for quite some time with the droves of Charlotte golfers who gladly make the 30-minute trek to the western shores of Lake Norman in search of a fun round at a sensible price on a well-designed course.

Even though Lake Norman is close by, it does not come into play, and water is a factor on only a few holes. What makes Westport a popular course is the pretty setting combined with the ample variety and challenge. There's decent room off the tee on most holes, and the greens are medium-size, predominantly sloped and not excessively bunkered. Gibson placed

some light mounding around the green complexes as well. For many years, the course was famous (or infamous) for its 4th hole, a 424-yard par 4 where you had to lay up with a mid-iron off the tee, then hit a long iron or fairway wood off a tight downhill lie over a pond and uphill to a large green. Three-putting was a distinct possibility. The most popular score on the hole was "X." The State of North Carolina recently forced the course to dredge part of the pond—why, we're not sure—and the result was that the hole evened out, making it slightly less difficult.

With all the new courses under construction closer to Charlotte, it will be interesting to see how Westport fares. If courses like Westport are going to prosper, it will be important to groom and maintain the track to consistently high standards year-round.

The ownership of the course has been up in the air for a while, but the new owners set about improving the maintenance, which should help the course compete with all the new tracks that have sprung up. It remains a solid value.

Amenities include a practice green, driving range, locker room, snack bar, rental clubs and a pro shop.

You can walk the course anytime during the week and after 2 PM on weekends. You can book a tee time whenever you choose for the weekdays and on Wednesday for the upcoming weekend. Approximate cost, including cart, is $25 weekdays and $30 on weekends.

Woodbridge Golf Links
1007 New Camp Creek Church Rd.,
Kings Mountain
• (704) 482-0353, (704) 338-9024
(Charlotte Number)

Championship Yardage: 6743	
Slope: 131	Par: 72
Men's Yardage:	6156
Slope: 121	Par: 72
Ladies' Yardage:	5054
Slope: 127	Par: 73

Woodbridge Golf Links opened in 1971. Porter Gibson and Bob Toski designed the course, which is set on rolling, partially wooded terrain. The fairways are blanketed with bermudagrass; on the greens, you'll find bentgrass.

Porter Gibson is a well-known and respected

Charlotte-based golf course architect. He has worked with the likes of Sam Snead and, for a while, Bob Toski, the renowned instructor. Gibson was a leader in the development of wastewater irrigation systems for golf courses. Bet you didn't know that!

Woodbridge is owned by the same people who own the Beck Mercedes auto dealership in Charlotte. The solid ownership has meant that the course has developed a reputation for good maintenance. This reputation has in turn helped the course attract numerous golfers from the Charlotte and Gastonia areas. It's always been a popular and challenging course with a sound design. Woodbridge has also hosted a women's collegiate golf tournament.

The front nine is set in open terrain. The course is at its prettiest on the back nine, where several holes dip into woodland next to a rivulet. A wooden bridge crosses the rivulet after the 600-yard par 5 No. 13 (hence the course's name). The greens are large enough that club selection becomes a significant issue on many holes. There's plenty of room off the tee, so you'll be fine taking the big stick out and giving the ball a good thump. Water comes into play in a number of instances and could really irritate you and lead to some big numbers.

Woodbridge is a fun and playable course that stands a good chance of remaining popular in the face of all the competition from the new courses in the Charlotte area.

Amenities include a practice green, driving range, locker room, snack bar, rental clubs, a beverage cart and pro shop.

The course is walkable for the fit, and you can walk anytime during the week. You can book a tee time seven days in advance for the week and on Monday for the weekend. Approximate cost, including cart, is $28 weekdays and $38 on weekends.

Tournaments

PGA Senior Tour
Home Depot Invitational

Held in mid- to late-spring at The Tournament Players Club at Piper Glen (which isn't written up in this chapter because it's a private course), the Home Depot Invitational is hosted by Arnold Palmer and usually attracts a solid field. Formerly called the World Seniors Invitational and the Paine Webber Invitational, the tournament is one of the oldest on the Senior PGA circuit.

Arnold Palmer and Ed Seay designed the varied course that's bordered by enormous houses. The best place to watch might be the par 5 16th—reachable in two by most players, the hole offers a chance to see the seniors' short games in action, always a marvelous sight.

Others will point you in the direction of the par 3 17th, just a wedge downhill to a multitiered green where birdies are always a possibility.

Home Depot signed on as tournament sponsor for 2000 and should provide a boost for an event that's waned in recent years. Rumor has it that it might move to another course (in the Charlotte area) in the near future.

For tickets and other information, call (704) 442-9797.

Fun Things To Do

Charlotte is a working town, so you're not going to find a large number of really touristy things to do and see: This isn't Orlando. You will, however, discover some major attractions that draw people from all over the city and surrounding counties.

As Charlotte is the retailing epicenter of the Carolinas, **SouthPark Mall,** 4400 Sharon Road, Charlotte, (704) 364-4411, is the retailing epicenter of Charlotte. In addition to anchor department stores Belk, Hecht's and Dillard's, there are more than 100 retail stores, including a Warner Brothers Store, *two* Victoria's Secret shops, Pea in the Pod, the Nature Company and Brooks Brothers. Nordstrom will open a store in 2002. The mall is well run and clean—an excellent place for those who love to shop. Amid the myriad retail stores, you'll find a number of interesting eateries. Besides SouthPark, this area has three other malls offering a fine collection of specialty shops: **Specialty Shops on The Park, Morrocroft Village, Sharon Corners** and **Phillips Place.**

Discovery Place, 301 N. Tryon Street, Charlotte, (704) 845-3882, is a nationally known state-of-the-art science museum. It's a hands-on type of place that will fascinate children of all ages. Wander around the numerous displays and well-designed exhibits. Learn about subjects such as the rain forest, electricity, weather and moon exploration. This is a great place to spend hours discovering the nature of the world around you.

Once you've finished your museum tour, step over to the **Charlotte Observer Omnimax**

Theater. Watch a movie in a special surround-sound environment that truly has to be seen to be believed—it's like watching a movie on all four walls of the theater while sitting in a dentist's chair.

Charlotte is successfully on the map as a big-league sports town. The **Charlotte Hornets** of the National Basketball Association's Eastern Conference play in the Charlotte Coliseum on Tyvola Road West. NBA action Hornets-style is a never-ending barrage of noise and off-court entertainment. If you're a fan of excellent dancing, you'll enjoy the cheerleading squad, affectionately known as the Honeybees. For ticket information, call (704) 357-0252.

The **Carolina Panthers** play in the National Football League, in the NFC West division. One of the newer teams in the NFL, the Panthers reached the NFC Championship game in 1995, just their second season in the league. Their state-of-the-art home is Ericsson Stadium on S. Mint Street Downtown. Call (704) 358-1644 for more information.

If you like ice hockey, the **Charlotte Checkers** play at Independence Arena (known to locals as the "Big I"), 2700 Independence Boulevard, Charlotte, (704) 342-4423. The Checkers play in the East Coast Hockey League, the hockey equivalent of Class AA baseball. The team is affiliated with the New York Rangers of the NHL. The season starts in October and lasts until mid-April. In 1996, the Checkers won the Riley Cup as champions of the league. There's nothing quite like minor league ice hockey. The Checkers were popular in the 1950s, '60s and early '70s until the league folded. The revamped Checkers feature youthful players who hope that their stay in Charlotte lasts but a season. ECHL teams can only have three players with three or more years of professional experience on the roster. Plenty of players are eager to prove themselves worthy of a better league, so the action is always fast, furious and hard-hitting. And, yes, there is the occasional incident where players drop their gloves and engage in fist-to-fist combat. It's part of the game. In the Checkers' first season, the team mascot, a 7-foot-tall bear named Chubby, got into a fight with player Sebastien LaPlante of the Greensboro Monarchs over the use of a water pistol. Yes, there's never a dull moment at a Checkers game. Plenty of home games sell out. As you enter the Big I, turn left and say hello to Betty the ticket-taker.

Opened in 1992 in tandem with the tallest building in the Carolinas—the NationsBank Corporate Center—the **Blumenthal Performing Arts Center,** 130 N. Tryon Street, Charlotte, (704) 372-1000, is a testament to Charlotte's commitment to the arts. The Blumenthal Center is home to the **Charlotte Symphony Orchestra, Opera Carolina** and numerous other performing arts groups. The main performing hall seats about 2,000 patrons.

Events at the Blumenthal might include an opera, a symphony, a rock 'n' roll performance, Carol Channing in *Hello Dolly!,* or a major dance production. The adjacent state-of-the-art **Belk Theater** seats about 400 in a warm and intimate setting. Consult a copy of the *Charlotte Observer* to see what's playing or visit the Observer's Web site: Charlotte.com.

Lowe's Motor Speedway (formerly Charlotte Motor Speedway), N.C. Highway 49 N., Concord, (704) 455-2121, is the place to be for stock car racing, or NASCAR, as it's more commonly known. It's a major industry in the Charlotte region, and many of the top racing teams are headquartered just a smooth 3-wood from the speedway. LMS hosts three major races: the Winston Select and the Coca-Cola 600 in May, and the Mello-Yellow 500 in the fall. Each race event is replete with "extracurricular activities," so come prepared for long days in the sun—the local population provides much of the entertainment. During the year, the venue offers many ancillary events including auto fairs, demonstrations, non-NASCAR races and exhibitions. Call to arrange a tour of the facility. For motorsports fans, a trip to Charlotte is not complete without a stop at LMS.

Paramount's Carowinds, south of Charlotte, just off I-77 on Carowinds Boulevard, Fort Mill, South Carolina, (704) 588-2600, has been one of the Charlotte region's biggest attractions for years. It was called simply "Carowinds" until corporate giant Paramount bought the theme park. It must be one of the most entertaining places in the Carolinas, offering everything from long, screaming roller coasters and water rides to smaller-scale carousels designed for smaller-scale people. The larger, more involved roller coasters are some of the most radical in the Southeast. You'll be turned upside-down at high speeds on The Vortex, a stand-up roller coaster. In addition to the rides, Carowinds' Palladium is a great place to see pop music concerts in the summer months.

The Mint Museum of Art, 3730 Randolph Road, Charlotte, (704) 337-2000, is housed in the city's former 19th-century federal mint, a fact that in part explains why the town is such a

Rock Hill: Charlotte's Bedroom Community

While you're in the Charlotte area for golf, you might want to forget about staying in the usual big hotels downtown and instead stay in Charlotte's bedroom community: Rock Hill, South Carolina. It's not like you will be blazing any trails. Two of Charlotte's professional sports teams, the football Carolina Panthers and the basketball Charlotte Hornets, have training facilities in the area.

Two bed and breakfast inns in Rock Hill are second-to-none when it comes to comfort, accessibility and convenience. The Book & The Spindle, 626 Oakland Avenue, is a lovely, luxurious 1930s home restored by Pam and Warren Bowen. Each of the two suites has its own breakfast nook. Two additional rooms are smaller but still comfortable. All have private baths. Our favorite spot in the whole house is the piazza in the Charleston suite. The Bowens call it a porch dummy. It's a bright little sun room where you can read, work or relax in a wicker chair while communing with the redbirds perched on a branch outside the window. The Camden suite features its own private canopied rooftop patio. With the proper weather, this could be another favorite spot. Each room has a different theme at this charming English-style inn with modern amenities.

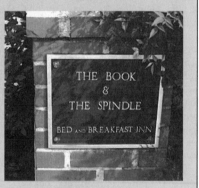

The Book & The Spindle offers grace and charm in Rock Hill, South Carolina.

Photo: Mitch Willard

banking center today. For an art museum nestled in one of Charlotte's oldest neighborhoods, the Mint is a pretty hopping place—for a museum. Various auxiliaries and affiliated organizations spend a lot of time and energy keeping the museum alive and funded, so it's quite a social center as well. There's always at least one exhibit going on in addition to the regular collection, including one of the world's best accumulations of pre-Colombian art.

The museum is closed on Mondays.

Where to Eat

Refer to our Preface for an explanation of the pricing code.

Charlotte

South End Brewery and Smokehouse
$$ • 2100 South Blvd., Charlotte
• (704) 358-4677

Glitzy and big, South End Brewery is the epicenter of Charlotte's bustling and revamped South End district, just a mile or two from Uptown's skyscrapers. Beer is brewed on premises; the India Pale Ale is popular, as is the Carolina Blonde, a wheat lager. In addition to the Blondes, the food is another superb attraction featuring anything from plain burgers to fresh fish. But if you want to be especially cool, head to the Pizza bar where you'll watch the cook work on your pie. After Panther football games, this is where the players head for post-game libations. It's a jumping joint after big wins and is open for lunch and dinner.

Cino Grill
$$-$$$ • 6041 Morrison Blvd., Charlotte
• (704) 365-8226

In the heart of Charlotte's upscale SouthPark area, Cino's clientele is usually an interesting mix of out-of-towners and locals. On weekends, with live jazz, the scene is more local,

Before you go to bed, leave a message with Pam as to what time you want your breakfast served—as long as it's before 10 AM. Promptly at the time you ordered, your breakfast is brought upstairs on a tray. This may be a welcome change from inns where breakfast is served in the dining room, especially if you like to linger in the morning with your significant other. The suites also have full kitchens if you'd prefer to stay in and prepare a meal.

The Book & The Spindle has myriad antiques and fine reproductions displayed about. Rooms overlook the beautiful campus of Winthrop University.

Just a few blocks away at 347 Park Avenue is Park Avenue Inn. Sharon and Donny Neely will make you feel right at home with their Southern hospitality; they open their hearts and home to the fullest. Their tons of knickknacks include antique toys and glass. Also, collections of family memorabilia hang on the walls, creating a homey atmosphere. Breakfast is served between 7 and 9 AM at the dining room table. We think you'll appreciate both the breakfast and the table, a 10-foot-long primitive piece of furniture made from four large boards. The house includes three guest rooms and three baths, and the rooms are quite comfortable.

You will feel right at home at the Park Avenue Inn in Rock Hill, South Carolina.

Photo: Mitch Willard

Rates at both of these inns are no more than you would pay for one of the nationally recognized hotels in the city. For reservations, call The Book & The Spindle, (803) 328-1913, or the Park Avenue Inn, (803) 325-1764.

with trendsetters and heavy-hitters rolling in to be seen with a martini in one hand, a cigar in the other. The bar menu includes an awesome selection of 007's favorite pick-me-up. But Cino is refined enough that by the end of the evening, you'll be stirred, not shaken.

Manzetti's
$$ • 6401 Morrison Blvd., Charlotte
• (704) 364-9334

Set among the SouthPark area's Specialty Shops on the Park, Manzetti's has long been a popular stop on the drinking and dining scene. It's a pretty trendy place, so come expecting to see a number of slightly aging yuppie-types dressed to kill. The atmosphere is definitely "fern bar," with bright brass rails and dark wood predominating. The food is outstanding—menu items include fun appetizers and a number of traditional American entrees. There's plenty to drink at the bar, and it's always crowded with lively people. It's a great place for a relaxed lunch or dinner outing with friends.

Providence Café
$$ • 110 Perrin Pl., Charlotte
• (704) 376-2008

If you're looking for an excellent meal for your dollar, then look no further than Providence Cafe, just off Providence Road near the intersection of Providence and Queens. If you get lost in this area of Charlotte, don't worry—you're not the first and certainly not the last. As you enter Providence Cafe, you might be fooled into thinking that you're going to spend a lot of "cashola," but don't worry—your bill for a big session will be less than you think. In

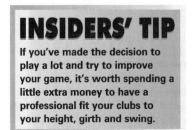

INSIDERS' TIP

If you've made the decision to play a lot and try to improve your game, it's worth spending a little extra money to have a professional fit your clubs to your height, girth and swing.

addition to a fine array of beverages, the mildly eclectic menu features a number of interesting selections that won't increase your overdraft. It's open for lunch and dinner.

Cornelius

Kobe Japanese House of Steak and Seafood
$$$ • 20465 Chartwell Center Dr., Cornelius • (704) 896-7778

If you've never been to a Japanese steakhouse, here's your chance. It's all here, and it's all good. There's the sushi bar, where the expert sushi chef will prepare your California Roll along with that green radioactive horseradish that's guaranteed to clear out your sinuses no matter how bad your head cold is. Then there's the meal itself, the authentic Teppan-Yaki show where the ambidextrous chef dices and slices your dinner right before your eyes, sizzling the rice, making the shrimp dance and the steak do the fandango. Wash it down with some sake and you've received the full Japanese steak house experience. It's best to go in a party of 10 so you can dominate a table and have a chef all to yourself.

Davidson

North Harbor Cafe
$$-$$$ • 181 North Harbor Dr., Davidson Landing • (704) 892-3855

Literally inches from Lake Norman, it's possible to drive your boat right up to the North Harbor Cafe, then drive it back to your lakeside mansion. Because of its accessibility to the lake and its fine views of the water, this ranks as one of the area's hot spots, especially if you dine outside in the middle of a midsummer day. Call ahead for reservations. The menu includes fresh fish, steaks, chicken dishes, fajitas, burgers, sandwiches, soups, salads and a full list of great desserts. It's sounds like pretty standard fare, but the quality of the preparation and the lakeside feel make North Harbor Cafe one of the most popular spots on the eastern shores of Lake Norman.

Denver

Jones Fish Camp
$ • N.C. Hwy. 16, Denver • (704) 483-2480

For more than 43 years, Jones Fish Camp has been serving up the stuff that fish camps are all about—great fish in a down-home, noth-ing-fancy ambiance. In addition to broiled and fried seafood, you'll find ribeye steaks, prime rib and chicken dishes. So there's more to Jones Fish Camp than just fish. But you will also find a staple fish camp specialty here: iced tea that's so sweet and so strong and so iced that a spoon will stand to attention in it.

Gastonia

El Cancun
$ • 516 E. Garrison St., Gastonia • (704) 853-2855

Take a tasty trip to Mexico at one of the Charlotte region's greatest venues. If you like Mexican food but don't want to spend a fortune on it, head for El Cancun. Your waiter or waitress (always Mexican) will bring you chips with excellent salsa. After that, you should skip reading the menu and indulge in the cream burritos. But all the choices on this extensive menu are wonderful. Wash it all down with a Dos Equis or two.

Hillbillys Bar-B-Que and Steaks
$$ • 930 E. Garrison Blvd., Gastonia • (704) 861-8787

Yer invited for supper here at Hillbillys, which describes itself as a "cook-out inside." You'll find some of the best pit-cooked barbecue in town, in addition to hickory-cooked rib eye and New York Strip steaks. Also enjoy ribs, chicken, pork, beef, sizable hot dogs, hamburgers and a pretty extensive kids menu as well. Hillbillys will also cater anything from family reunions to shotgun weddings.

Where to Stay

Refer to our Preface for an explanation of the pricing code.

Charlotte

The Dunhill Hotel
$$$ • 237 N. Tryon St., Charlotte • (704) 332-4141

The Dunhill is in Uptown Charlotte near the new NationsBank tower. It's in a vintage building with the ambiance of an Old World bed and breakfast inn, which makes it a great alternative to the larger chain-style hotels. Yet it's extremely convenient to the central business district, library and Discovery Place (see our "Fun Things To Do" section). You'll find a restaurant on the ground floor, in addition to services tailored to the business traveler.

Hilton at University Place
$$-$$$ • 6929 JM Keynes Dr., Charlotte
• (704) 547-7444

Just off I-85 near the University of North Carolina at Charlotte, the Hilton at University Place is a fully appointed 240-room hotel. The Hilton is convenient to the university area (hence its name), but it's also near Lowe's Motor Speedway, all the new office developments in the area, a couple of fine golf courses (including Highland Creek) and the new hospital. So should you suddenly be hit by a flying golf ball and need some stitches to your head, the Hilton will be a convenient place to recuperate.

The Park Hotel
$$$ • 2200 Rexford Rd., Charlotte
• (704) 364-8220

In the heart of SouthPark, with some of the best shopping in the Southeast just a few steps away, the Park offers great location and excellent service. The Park is well known in Charlotte as one of the best hotels in the city. In fact, it's where the players in the Paine Webber Senior PGA Tournament stay. With nearly 200 rooms, the Park boasts a European feel. Smoky's, on the first floor, is an outstanding place to eat. Amenities at The Park Hotel include several meeting rooms, an outdoor swimming pool with a whirlpool, two ballrooms and a newsstand plus full meeting and banquet facilities. Wayne Shusko is one of the friendliest, most helpful and most experienced hotel managers in Charlotte. The Park enjoys tremendous repeat business, with good reason.

Radisson Plaza Hotel
$$$ • 2 NationsBank Plaza, Charlotte
• (704) 377-0400

The Radisson Plaza in Uptown Charlotte was one of the city's first large hotels with connections to a large chain. It's a magnificent accommodation, with close to 400 rooms and a bunch of meeting rooms and entertainment suites. If you're in Uptown and you're looking for a first-class hotel with every amenity under the sun, you won't go wrong here.

Concord

Holiday Inn Express
$$ • 1601 N.C. Hwy. 29 N., Concord
• (704) 786-5181, (800) 647-STAY

Convenient to I-85 and Concord, this Holiday Inn Express offers a comfortable place to stay at a comfortable rate. You get free local and Charlotte calls, free breakfast bar, free news-

paper and free cable with HBO and ESPN on a 26-inch color TV with remote control. There are in-room refrigerators, nonsmoking rooms and free 18-wheeler parking. In addition, you'll get a discount on your room if you're a member of AARP, and there's fax and copy service.

Cornelius

Holiday Inn Lake Norman
$$ • I-77 and N.C. Hwy. 73, Cornelius
• (704) 892-9120

On the east side of Lake Norman, the Holiday Inn is convenient not only to the lake but to the entire Charlotte region. The hotel has 119 guest rooms, offers a free breakfast buffet, a restaurant and lounge, a pool and a fitness room as well as meeting and banquet facilities. If you're someone who can't survive the day without a cup of coffee, rest easy here: You'll find an in-room coffee maker at your disposal.

Gastonia

Comfort Inn
$$ • I-85 and N.C. Hwy. 161, Gastonia
• (704) 739-7070, (800) 228-5150

Convenient to West Gastonia and I-85, this new and friendly Comfort Inn boasts a number of amenities including in-room microwaves and refrigerators, free deluxe continental breakfast, cable TV with HBO and ESPN, fax and copy service and a laundry room. If you really want to splash out, spend the extra cash for the executive Jacuzzi room.

Econo Lodge
$$ • I-85 and N.C. Hwy. 274, Gastonia
• (704) 867-1821, (800) 555-2666

Just seconds from the always-bustling I-85, Gastonia's Econo Lodge offers a swimming pool, free cable TV with HBO, free local calls, continental breakfast and meeting rooms. Inquire about seniors' and other discounts.

Golf Equipment

One of the leaders in golf retailing in Charlotte is **Pro Golf Discount**. The three stores in Charlotte offer an outstanding variety of equipment for players of all levels. If you want the latest state-of-the-art clubs custom fitted to your swing, you can find them here. If your golfing budget is limited, Pro Golf offers playable clubs perfect for those who are just starting the game. Pro Golf stocks a variety of putters and utility clubs that you won't find anywhere else. You'll also find a good selection of name-brand accessories, including gloves, shoes, shirts, balls and bags. Stop by any of the three locations in Charlotte: Central Avenue, (704) 536-9021; South Boulevard, (704) 523-7262; and Pineville, (704) 541-6950.

An excellent shop for used equipment, expert club fitting, repair, re-shafting and just generally good conversation about golf and unrelated subjects is **John Gamble's Carolina Golf Manufacturing** at 2917-B Central Avenue, (704) 563-0897. Many in Charlotte will tell you that Gamble is the best clubfitter in the Carolinas.

North Carolina's
Mountains

Is there a part of the United States more beautiful and liveable than the mountains of North Carolina? It's hard to argue otherwise. Yes, the mountains out West are spectacular and rugged, and there are spots on the Atlantic and Pacific coasts that are other-worldly. But there's very little to match the visual bounty and peace of North Carolina's mountains—essentially a high and hilly dense deciduous forest that extends from the border with Tennessee to the semi-industrial hinterland and dark red clay of the Piedmont.

The seasons define the beauty of the region.

Winter is dark and grey, the leafless mountainsides bare and exposed. Bright, frigid, windy days give way to prolonged periods of snow and ice, creating a winter playground for visitors and residents.

Spring in this southern portion of the Appalachians means exploding azaleas and dogwoods, the crystal Carolina blue sky cloudless, the trees leafing up, the wildlife returning to full song after months of hibernation or migration to warmer climes. The writer who captured it best wasn't a writer, but a composer—Aaron Copland, whose famous *Appalachian Spring* belongs in the collection of any aficionado of classical music.

Summer is warm, but rarely hot and humid like so much of the mid-Atlantic. If the daytime temperature rises above 80 degrees in the mountains, it's a heatwave. The drenching humidity of cities like Atlanta, Tampa, and Charlotte is non-existent in the mountains. Thus, cities like Hendersonville and Asheville become a Mecca for those seeking refuge from the heat. Most of Florida moves to the mountains of North Carolina in the months of June, July and August; consider yourself warned.

Fall is the queen of the four seasons. Tourists in search of autumnal color venture to Vermont, but many more head for the Mountains of North Carolina, rendering the Blue Ridge Parkway and other visually spectacular thoroughfares clogged processions of tour busses and convertibles crammed with camera-laden passengers going *"Wow!"* It can become crowded, but it's worth battling the hordes—nothing could be more moving to the soul than a warm fall day, the blazing colors of trees readying for their winter rest set against the backdrop of a sky of deepest blue.

Needless to say, people who live in or visit Western North Carolina don't spend all their waking hours gazing at the sky or the sides of mountainsides. There are pastimes a-plenty, including fishing, hunting, climbing, hiking, white-water rafting, eating, drinking, going to plays, discovering waterfalls, dozing and just plain relaxing.

And of course, there's golf.

The terrain and topography of this part of the world limits the number of courses that can be built, thus it's difficult to describe the Mountains of North Carolinas as being "blessed with an abundance of courses," despite what the brochures say. Many of the courses are hyper-private, played and populated by current and former captains and titans of industry retreating from the heat of the cities. These are the types of club where there isn't even a tee sheet and if you have to ask how much it is to join, then you probably can't, etc., etc. You get the picture.

Still, numerous fine and excellent opportunities await the public golfer in the North Carolina Mountains. Architects like Donald Ross, Jack

The Mountains of North Carolina

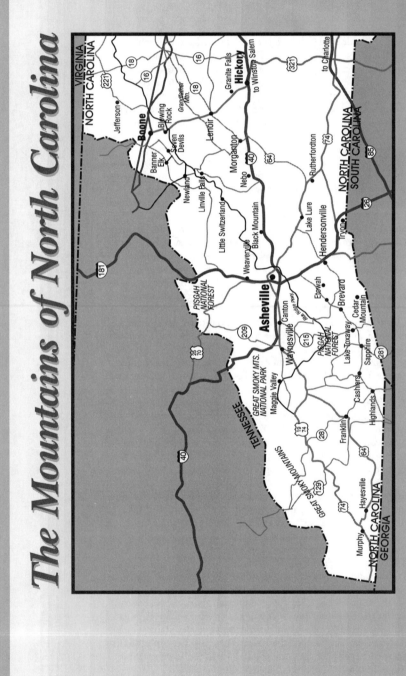

GOLF COURSES IN THE NORTH CAROLINA MOUNTAINS

Course	Type	# Holes	Par	Slope	Yards	Walking	Booking	Cost w/Cart
Apple Valley Golf Club	public	18	72	130	6297	no	30 days	$45
Bald Mountain	public/resort	18	72	121	6125	restricted	30 days	$45
Black Mountain Golf Course	semiprivate	18	71	n/r	5780	restricted	6 dats	$30-35
Blue Ridge C.C.	semiprivate	18	72	123	6362	restricted	anytime	$43-48
Boone Golf Club	semiprivate	18	71	112	5859	restricted	7 days	$45-49
Broadmoor	public	18	72	115	6313	restricted	7 days	$27-32
Buncome County Muni	public	18	72	107	5929	anytime	3 days	$30
Chatuge Shores	public	18	72	118	6269	restricted	3 days	$30
Cleghorn Plantation	public	18	72	126	6313	no	anytime	$38-42
Crooked Creek Golf Club	public	18	72	n/r	6267	restricted	2 days	$30
Cummings Cove Golf and CC	semiprivate	18	70	n/r	5720	restricted	anytime	$30
Etowah Valley Country Club								
South/West Course	resort	18	72	123	6880	restricted	anytime	$50
West/North Course	resort	18	73	122	6700	restricted	anytime	$50
North/South Course	resort	18	73	121	6604	restricted	anytime	$50
Glen Cannon	semiprivate	18	72	121	6272	no	3 days	$50
Granada Farms	semiprivate	18	72	112	5835	restricted	anytime	$23-30
Grassy Creek Golf and CC	public	18	72	116	5774	restricted	7 days	$36-40
Grove Park Inn	semiprivate/resort	18	71	119	6033	restricted	anytime	$80
Hawksnest Ski and Golf	semiprivate	18	72	110	5953	restricted	7 days	$34-39
High Hampton Inn	semiprivate/resort	18	71	120	6012	anytime	1 day	$45-55
Holiday Inn Sunspree	public/resort	18	70	117	5131	restricted	anytime	$30
Hound Ears Club	resort	18	72	120	6036	restricted	anytime	$60
Jefferson Landing	semiprivate/resort	18	72	115	6424	no	anytime	$45-55

Course	Type	Holes	Par	Rating	Yardage	Tee Times	Advance	Price
Lake Junaluska Golf Course	public	18	68	n/r	4579	anytime	anytime	$26
Lake Toxaway	resort	18	71	116	5594	anytime	anytime	$70
Linville Golf Club	resort	18	72	126	6279	restricted	anytime	$50
Maggie Valley Resort and CC	resort	18	72	118	6031	restricted	1 day	$55
Marion Lake Club	semiprivate	18	70	n/r	5710	anytime	anytime	$27
Meadowbrook Golf Club	public	18	72	105	5850	anytime	anytime	$21-28
Mill Creek	semiprivate	18	72	113	5775	restricted	2 days	$40
Mountain Aire	semiprivate	18	71	n/a	5571	anytime	anytime	$28-32
Mountain Glen Golf Club	semiprivate	18	72	119	6195	anytime	7 days	$45
Mount Mitchell Golf Club	public	18	72	116	6110	restricted	14 days	$45-50
Orchard Hills Golf Club	semiprivate	18	72	106	5673	restricted	4 days	$26-30
Quaker Meadows Golf Course	public	18	71	108	6133	restricted	anytime	$20-24
Red Fox Country Club	semiprivate	18	72	124	6393	no	anytime	$30-35
Reems Creek Golf Course	semiprivate	18	72	127	6106	no	anytime	$45-50
Sapphire Mountain Golf Club	public	18	70	118	5690	no	30 days	$35
Springdale Country Club	semiprivate/resort	18	72	121	6437	anytime	anytime	$40
Trillium	public	18	72	129	6118	restricted	restricted	$75
Village of Sugar Mountain GC	public	18	64	91	4198	yes	5 days	$33-35
Waynesville Country Club Inn								
Carolina/Dogwood Course	semiprivate/resort	18	70	100	5395	restricted	anytime	$48
Dogwood/Blue Ridge Course	semiprivate/resort	18	70	100	5258	restricted	anytime	$48
Blue Ridge/Carolina Course	semiprivate/resort	18	70	100	5493	restricted	anytime	$48

Mountain golf is at its best in the fall.

Photo: Courtesy of The Charlotte Observer

Nicklaus, Tom Fazio (who lives in Hendersonville), Fred Hawtree, Martin Hawtree, Tom Jackson, George Cobb and Ellis Maples produced fine work in the mountains, although many of their courses, like Grandfather Mountain, Elk River, and Wade Hampton, are private.

Pick of the public-access courses must be Linville Country Club and The Grove Park Inn. Aficionados of mountain golf might scoff at the choice of the latter, and the course does include a couple of shortish ho-hum holes. But the superb ones more than make up for any perceived deficiencies—plus the grand presence of one of America's great hotels provides a backdrop like no other.

You can play golf without any weather problems from late March to late November. In the winter months, call ahead before planning a golf trip, or better still, bring the skis. Even in the foothills of the mountains, golf is rarely year-round.

Cooler temperatures mean bentgrass on the greens and fairways—a rarity in the Carolinas. Some courses drain poorly and can get quite wet, but greens can be cut to a sixteenth of an inch or less and thus can be amazingly speedy, even in mid-summer. Stay below the hole wherever possible.

Enjoy golf in the mountains. Keep in mind that most people are playing as part of a getaway from the real world, so take the leisurely pace in stride. Enjoy the fine views, the relaxing ambiance and the varied challenges that some of the greatest golf architects in the world have created for your golfing pleasure.

Remember, you are playing in one of the most beautiful areas of the United States. That alone makes golf in the North Carolina Mountains well worth the price of admission.

Note: We've divided this chapter geographically into three sections: the Asheville area and points west, the Boone/Blowing Rock area and the Hickory/Lenoir area. We realize the tourism bureaus probably wouldn't divide things this way, but the mountain region is widespread enough that we thought it helpful to write about the courses that are in your general vicinity, no matter where in the mountains you may be.

Asheville Area

For the most part, the courses we profile in the North Carolina Mountains section are west of Asheville, but we do include a few, such as the Black Mountain Golf Course and Meadowbrook in Rutherford, that lie to the east of the city. We felt these areas were more closely

Tree-lined Fairways on mountain courses give the advantage to the straight hitter.

Photo: The Grove Park Inn Resort

allied with greater Asheville than our other mountain regions.

Apple Valley Golf Club
201 Boulevard of the Mountains, Lake Lure
• (828) 652-2888

Championship Yardage:	**6726**
Slope: 138	**Par: 72**
Men's Yardage:	**6297**
Slope: 130	**Par: 72**
Other Yardage:	**5511**
Slope: 118	**Par: 72**
Ladies' Yardage:	**4661**
Slope: 114	**Par: 72**

Apple Valley opened in 1985. Like its sister course, Bald Mountain (see write-up below), Apple Valley is part of the Fairfield Mountain Golf Resort. Dan Maples, son of Ellis Maples, designed the course. Some holes are flat, while others are set in rolling terrain. Fairways are bermudagrass, and greens are bentgrass.

Apple Valley is a fine mountain course. Interestingly, you'll be hard pressed to understand why the slope rating is so high from the back tees. We must assume that the course is a lot tougher than it looks. Play it from the middle or front tees if you're a mid- to high handicapper.

The course boasts a number of interesting holes. Admirable is the par 4 12th that plays 369 yards from the back tees. A mountain stream bisects the hole. From the tee, you'll have to decide whether to lay up or smack it over the hazard. Go for it successfully, and the approach shot is less fraught with difficulty.

Woods border many of the holes. The greens are fairly large and sloped, with the occasional buried elephant. A couple of holes feature interesting blind shots where local knowledge is a big plus. Water frequently comes into play. Overall, Apple Valley is a fun and interesting course designed by one of the finest and most respected architects in the Carolinas. We'd choose this one over Bald Mountain, although if you're at the resort for two days, by all means play both courses.

Amenities include a practice green, range, locker room, snack bar, rental clubs and pro shop.

You must take a cart here. You can book a tee time up to 30 days in advance. Approximate cost, including cart, is $45 both weekdays and weekends.

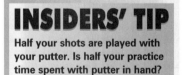

INSIDERS' TIP

Half your shots are played with your putter. Is half your practice time spent with putter in hand?

Bald Mountain
201 Boulevard of the Mountains, Lake Lure
• **(828) 625-3040**

Championship Yardage:	**6575**
Slope: 125	**Par: 72**
Men's Yardage:	**6125**
Slope: 121	**Par: 72**
Other Yardage:	**5208**
Slope: 108	**Par: 72**
Ladies' Yardage:	**4808**
Slope: 112	**Par: 72**

Bald Mountain, a Willie B. Lewis design, opened in 1974. Woods border most of the holes. The rolling fairways are covered with bermudagrass, the greens with bentgrass.

Bald Mountain is part of the Fairfield Mountain Golf Resort. We found it to be a genuine and challenging mountain track that's fun from any of the tees. If you're a movie buff or a fan of Patrick Swayze, you'll enjoy the 16th green, where part of the cinematic masterpiece *Dirty Dancing* was filmed. (How that film failed to make any of those "Top 100 All-Time Best Movies" lists is a complete mystery.) Great movies aside, the course is worth playing, particularly in tandem with Apple Valley, its better-looking sister.

The course layout presents a particular emphasis on hitting it straight off the tee.

The 17th hole might be the most difficult on the course. A solid 423 yards from the tips, the problem with this par 4 is the stream that bisects the fairway at about 100 yards from the green. There's also water short left and right, plus a couple of bunkers in front of the shallow green. A bogey isn't a bad score here.

Amenities include a practice green, range, locker room, bar, snack bar, restaurant, rental clubs, beverage cart and pro shop.

The course is walkable for the physically fit, and you can walk after 2 PM. You can book a tee time 30 days in advance. Approximate cost, including cart, is $45 weekdays and weekends.

Black Mountain Golf Course
17 Ross Dr., Black Mountain
• **(828) 669-2710**

Championship Yardage:	**6181**
Slope: 129	**Par: 71**
Men's Yardage:	**5780**
Slope: No rating	**Par: 71**
Ladies' Yardage:	**4959**
Slope: No rating	**Par: 71**

The front nine at Black Mountain opened in the 1930s, and a second nine opened in the 1960s. Ross Taylor designed the course, which mixes open holes with those bordered and framed with woods. In the fairways, you'll find a combination of bluegrass and bentgrass; on the greens, strictly bentgrass.

Here at Black Mountain, we found a playable and justifiably popular course, with good variety and interest. Locals say that the back nine is more difficult than the front. The front provides significant difficulties in the form of streams, small greens, small mounds, bunkers and narrow fairways. Difficulties on the back come from some longer par 4s, plenty of creeks, undulating greens plus one of the world's longest holes—the 747-yard 17th, an arduous par 6.

The fairways are generous in most spots; the small greens provide the bulk of the challenge here at Black Mountain.

Amenities include a practice green, snack bar, rental clubs and pro shop.

The course is walkable for the fit and you can walk anytime except weekend mornings. You can book a tee time six days in advance. Approximate cost, including cart, is $30 weekdays and $35 weekends.

Broadmoor
5 French Broad Ave., Asheville
• **(828) 687-8545**

Championship Yardage:	**6857**
Slope: 120	**Par: 72**
Men's Yardage:	**6313**
Slope: 115	**Par: 72**
Other Yardage:	**5881**
Slope: 111	**Par: 72**
Ladies' Yardage:	**5082**
Slope: 113	**Par: 72**

Broadmoor opened in 1993; the name changed from French Broad Golf Center. Karl Litten designed the course. The layout is remarkably flat and wide open, with woods bordering the course. In the fairways, you'll find rye grass, while you'll putt on bentgrass greens. The course sits directly in the path of Asheville's airport, so if a 737 cruises by less than 100 feet over your head while you're in the middle of a testy 3-footer that your opponent should have conceded, you still have to drain it—you've been warned.

Okay, so who is this Karl Litten guy? Aside from the fact that he's a graduate of Steubenville College, he's an accomplished architect who apprenticed under the flamboyant Robert von Hagge, surely the greatest and most prolific architect never to have designed a course in North Carolina. Litten formed his own firm in 1979 and, like his teacher, was very busy in Florida in the 1980s. Litten formed a design partnership with Gary Player in 1987 that continued through 1989. Litten's design here, just south of Asheville, is remarkable in that the ground is almost totally flat—just like in Florida. Trees have been planted, but they shouldn't come into play for years. The result is an interesting and subtly varied design with a links flavor. It's really not a mountain course at all. Play the course in a fresh wind and you might feel like you're in Scotland.

Off the tee, the fairways are relatively wide, with mounds presenting most of the trouble. Upon initial glance, you might be tempted to think that the green complexes have a certain similarity. But on closer inspection, you'll find that Litten has used the flatness to develop approach shots that require a great deal of thought and strategy. On some holes, for instance, a low, running bounce-up shot is possible—even advisable—if the course is dry and there's a hearty wind. The greens are typically medium-size and mostly flat or slightly sloped. Bunkers provide most of the problems around the green. Water comes into play on the majority of holes on the front nine and is a factor on the back nine on a few holes. Interestingly, the final three holes provide excellent scoring opportunities for the better player, particularly the 18th, a 500-yard par 5 where the big hitter will have to avoid a pond on the left hand side of the green to reach the putting surface in two shots. Overall, French Broad is a fine course that you should make an effort to play.

Amenities include a practice green, range, chipping green, snack bar, bar and restaurant, rental clubs, beverage cart and pro shop.

Walking is not allowed, even though it's one of the most walkable courses in Western North Carolina—amazing isn't it? You can book a tee time seven days in advance. Approximate cost, including cart, is $27 weekdays and $32 on weekends.

Buncombe County Municipal Golf Course
226 Fairway Dr., Asheville
• (828) 298-1867

Championship Yardage:	6356
Slope: 115	Par: 72
Men's Yardage:	5929
Slope: 107	Par: 72
Ladies' Yardage:	4897
Slope: 109	Par: 72

Buncombe County Municipal Golf Course opened in 1927. Donald Ross designed the course. Fairways are bermudagrass, and greens are bentgrass. The front nine is flat and open,

while the wooded, tighter back nine boasts much more undulation.

Quick, how many counties in the Carolinas are home to a municipal course designed by the famed Donald Ross? Answer: Not many. Here at Buncombe Municipal, you'll play one of them, a fine and straightforward Ross layout that doesn't look like it's been touched since it opened. We found a sensible layout, with small and flat bunkers fronting large crowned greens. The significant difference in layout between the back and the front nines makes the course all the more interesting.

We were told that the course is host to close to 50,000 rounds a year. If you've got a 20-spot burning a hole in your pocket, and if you've never played a Donald Ross course, you should stop by for a round. Just be careful on the 9th hole. If you air mail your approach shot, you'll hit a car in the parking lot—and no free drop from the front seat of a Jaguar, even if you've just smashed the windshield.

Amenities include a practice green, snack bar, rental clubs and pro shop.

The course is walkable, you can walk anytime, and you should walk. You'll only need a tee time on weekends and holidays, and you can book three days in advance. Approximate cost, including cart, is $30 on both weekends and weekdays.

Chatuge Shores Golf Course
Myers Chapel Rd., Hayesville
• (828) 389-8940

Championship Yardage:	6687
Slope: 123	Par: 72
Men's Yardage:	6269
Slope: 118	Par: 72
Ladies' Yardage:	4950
Slope: 120	Par: 72

Chatuge Shores Golf Course, designed by J. Townsend, opened in 1969. Some holes are flat, but most feature some undulation. You'll drive onto bermudagrass fairways and putt on bentgrass greens. Water comes into play on some of the holes.

Chatuge Shores offers a fun, friendly and mature course, presenting challenges for golfers of all levels. The layout is fairly straightforward. Some of the fairways are wide, some are narrow. Trees delineate the fairways. The greens are slightly rolling, but not overly bunkered—the varying size and shape of the greens provides the main interest. There aren't many public courses in the immediate area, and the cost is sensible, so Chatuge Shores is definitely worth

The Cashiers area boasts some excellent opportunities for the accomplished golfer.

Photo: Cashiers Chamber of Commerce

MOUNTAINS

a visit if you're vacationing nearby. It's clearly a popular track—you won't be alone.

Amenities include a practice green, range, chipping green, snack bar, rental clubs and pro shop.

The course is walkable. You can book a tee time three days in advance. Approximate cost, including cart, is $30.

Cleghorn Plantation Golf and Country Club
200 Golf Cir., Rutherfordton
• (828) 286-9117

Championship Yardage:	6903	
Slope: 134	**Par: 72**	
Men's Yardage:	6313	
Slope: 126	**Par: 72**	
Other Yardage:	5679	
Slope: 115	**Par: 72**	
Ladies' Yardage:	4751	
Slope: 111	**Par: 73**	

The golf course at Cleghorn Plantation, a George Cobb design, opened in 1969. The course is set amid rolling terrain, and homes and woods border many holes. In the fairways, you'll find bermudagrass, with bentgrass on the greens.

Cleghorn Plantation is a real find. Original plans called for a private track, but financial hard times in the 1980s probably facilitated the change. Management made a number of recent improvements, and it looks like the course is shaping up to be one of the finest in the North Carolina foothills. Many of Cobb's resort/vacation courses are less demanding than his more serious efforts. Cleghorn is not a vacation course.

Play the tips and you're in for a long day, unless you can hit the ball a country mile off the tee. Play it from the men's or forward tees for a more sensible outing. The course features a number of epic sweeping holes, including elevated tee shots followed by uphill approach shots to large and heavily bunkered greens, which pitch and roll significantly.

The attractions of the course are the excellent layout, great variety, playability and sensible combination of natural and manmade hazards. It's great news for area golfers that this outstanding golf course is on the way up in the world. If you're visiting the area, this is the course to play. If you live in Western North Carolina and you're up for a serious challenge, Cleghorn is a must-play for you too. It's an excellent value.

With water bordering both sides of the fairway, the 418-yard 2nd hole is probably the most picturesque yet difficult driving hole on the golf course. Once you've negotiated the drive, which might be most prudently played with a fairway wood, the approach must avoid the tough bunkering around the green.

Amenities include a practice green, range, snack bar and pro shop.

A cart is required to play Cleghorn; you may book a tee time whenever you choose. Approximate cost, including cart, is $38 weekdays and $42 on weekends.

Crooked Creek Golf Club
764 Crooked Creek Rd., Hendersonville
• (828) 692-2011

Championship Yardage:	**6652**
Slope: No rating	**Par: 72**
Men's Yardage:	**6267**
Slope: No rating	**Par: 72**
Ladies' Yardage:	**5546**
Slope: No rating	**Par: 72**

Alex Guin and Stewart Goodin designed Crooked Creek Golf Club, which opened in 1968. The course has a wide-open feel—many of the holes are flat and others are set in rolling terrain. Fairways are bermudagrass, and greens are bentgrass.

First, an interesting note about the clubhouse. Warner Brothers executives built it during World War II, fearful that the Japanese might invade California, necessitating a move to the East Coast. So if Bugs Bunny shows up unexpectedly and says "What's up, Doc?" right in the middle of your back swing, you'll know why. You've been warned: No mulligan.

This is one of the earliest examples of a course set in a housing development. Homes and out-of-bounds provide potential threats on many holes. You'll find good variety on this course. Some of your tee shots must negotiate narrow fairways. Some of the greens are small,

others are midsize to large. Many greens are crowned and sloped, others offer significant undulations. There isn't a lot of water on the course. The most omnipresent hazards are the bunkers around the green complexes, which come in an interesting variety of shapes and sizes. Overall, it's a fun and straightforward track that will provide a decent challenge from the back tees.

While it's difficult to describe Crooked Creek as a muscular golf course, the final hole makes up for the lack of length. At 555 yards from the tips, it's a true three-shot hole for all but biggest hitters. Still, three well-struck shots could produce a birdie for the rest of us.

Amenities include a practice green, range, snack bar and pro shop.

The course is walkable, although walking is restricted. You can book a tee time two days in advance. Approximate cost, including cart, is $30.

INSIDERS' TIP

For more information on courses in the North Carolina Mountains, contact the Great Smoky Mountains Golf Associatrion, P.O. Box 18556, Asheville, NC 28801.

Cummings Cove Golf and Country Club
3000 Cummings Rd., Hendersonville
• (828) 891-9412

Championship Yardage:	**6008**
Slope: No rating	**Par: 70**
Men's Yardage:	**5720**
Slope: No rating	**Par: 70**

Cummings Cove Golf and Country Club, originally called Horseshoe Country Club, opened in 1986. Robert Cupp, a man with an interesting background, designed the course. Cupp is certainly a prolific architect, having designed courses in almost every state in the Union. In the North Carolina Mountains, he assisted Jack Nicklaus in the design of Elk River, one of the state's most revered private courses. Cupp's resumé includes a Master of Fine Arts degree from the University of Alaska, advertising experience, pro shop management, an associate's degree in agronomy and a significant stint as an associate in the Jack Nicklaus design firm. Cupp has worked with a variety of touring pros-turned-designers, including Tom Kite and Fuzzy Zoeller.

Cupp created a challenging course here at Cummings Cove. Your tee shots need to be precise though not always very long. Your approach shots must hit small and undulating greens with little or no bailout potential. Embankments flank many of the greens. Woods and homes border the course.

Two holes will stick in your golf hole memory bank. The 10th, a 370-yard par 4 bordered by a lake, allows one of the smallest tee-shot landing areas of any course anywhere. And the green on the par 5 No. 5 is horseshoe-shaped—hit the ball to the wrong level of this green and your putter won't get the job done—you may have to bring out the lob wedge to get it close to the hole. Please replace your divot.

Take the challenge of this course if you get the chance. There's an awful lot of target golf here, so keep it straight and you'll have a good round.

Amenities include a practice green and snack bar.

The course is not easy to walk, but you may skip the cart anytime during the week and after 2 PM on weekends. You can book a tee time whenever you choose. Approximate cost, including cart, is $30.

Etowah Valley Country Club
Brickyard Rd., Etowah Resort
• (828) 891-7022, (828) 891-9412

South/West Course

Championship Yardage:	7108	
Slope: 125	Par: 72	
Men's Yardage:	6880	
Slope: 123	Par: 72	
Other Yardage:	6287	
Slope: 118	Par: 72	
Ladies' Yardage:	5480	
Slope: 119	Par: 72	

West/North Course

Championship Yardage:	7003	
Slope: 124	Par: 73	
Men's Yardage:	6700	
Slope: 122	Par: 73	
Other Yardage:	6215	
Slope: 121	Par: 73	
Ladies' Yardage:	5319	
Slope: 117	Par: 73	

North/South Course

Championship Yardage:	6909	
Slope: 124	Par: 73	
Men's Yardage:	6604	
Slope: 121	Par: 73	
Other Yardage:	6156	
Slope: 118	Par: 73	
Ladies' Yardage:	5391	
Slope: 115	Par: 73	

The South and West courses at Etowah Valley opened in 1967. The North course opened in 1988. Edmund B. Ault designed all three. Ault's credits include only two courses in North Carolina and one 18-hole course in Myrtle Beach, South Carolina. However, he was a prolific designer who built and redesigned more than 100 courses, primarily in Maryland, Arkansas, Pennsylvania and Virginia. He was a scratch golfer at one stage and played in the national amateur championship. (Bet you didn't know that!)

These well-maintained courses have bentgrass fairways and greens. Overall, all three courses are playable, fun and laid out in a picturesque and mostly flat setting. Bunkers of varying shapes and sizes will influence all of your approach shots. On the longer par 4s, you'll often have a chance to run the ball up to the green if the approaches are firm. All of the green complexes offer bailout areas; if you're a good chipper, head for these areas and avoid the bunkers.

The South Course is somewhat narrow. Water comes into play on quite a few holes in the form of large ponds and mountain streams. The greens are mostly midsized and quite undulating. Play from the back tees and you'll have a long course to negotiate. If you want a more sensible outing and you're not a long hitter, play from the other (white) tees.

The West Course is also primarily flat, although three holes offer elevation changes. From the tips, the course is even longer than the South Course. The greens might be a little larger, but so are the bunkers.

The newest nine is the North Course. The terrain is more rolling, giving the course a more open feel. A stream comes into play on most holes. The greens are large and undulating. Once again, bunkers will make you think about the most sensible approach to the green.

There's a lodge where you should stay if you definitely want to play Etowah Valley. If you don't stay here, you may be able to get on this course if you call in advance, although resort guest play and member play take priority. So there will be times when you'll be told "Sorry, members and guests only." Your chances of playing here if you're not a guest at Etowah Resort are best out of season.

The ninth hole on the North course might be the most entertaining of all 27. It's a short par 5, just 490 from the tips. A solid drive will avoid the stream to the right of the fairway, leaving the bold with an approach shot of not much more than 200 yards over water and bunkers. Two good shots mean birdie; one bad shot means double bogey or worse. Are you bold enough to take the risk?

Amenities include three practice greens, a

MOUNTAINS

range, bar, snack bar, restaurant, beverage gazebo, rental clubs and pro shop.

Walking is restricted, although the first two nines are walkable, and you should walk. You can book a tee time with your lodging reservation or two days in advance. Approximate cost for 18 holes, including cart, is $50.

Glen Cannon Country Club
Wilson Rd., Pisgah Forest
• (828) 884-9160

Championship Yardage:	6548	
Slope: 124		Par: 72
Men's Yardage:	6272	
Slope: 121		Par: 72
Ladies' Yardage:	5172	
Slope: 117		Par: 72

Glen Cannon Country Club opened in 1966. According to *Architects of Golf*, Willie B. Lewis of Greenville, South Carolina, designed the course. Lewis used to be an associate of George Cobb. For a mountain track, this course has a remarkably wide-open feel; also remarkable is its flatness. Fairways are bermudagrass; greens are bentgrass.

Locals tell us that Glen Cannon is one of the more private semiprivate courses in the area, so make sure you call for a tee time.

Glen Cannon offers a fine, playable and relatively straightforward mountain course that winds around a lush and wide valley floor. Trees and shrubs delineate the spacious fairways. The greens are medium-size to large. The grass around the greens is mostly bentgrass: If it's more than a couple of inches deep, try to avoid it at all costs. Most of the greens are sloped and not overly rolling. Water hazards come in the form of several branches of a mountain stream—watch out for it. Bunkers provide frequent hazards, and many are grass-faced; some are in the fairway, others are around the greens. The back nine is a little hillier and offers fine views from some tee boxes. Particularly appealing is a small but beautiful waterfall that complements the 2nd hole.

If you're looking for a good course in the Brevard area with a sound design and plenty of variety, try Glen Cannon. You'll likely have an enjoyable round. Just make sure you ring the bell before venturing toward the 17th hole. The bell alerts those on the driving range that you're about to cross their line of fire.

Amenities include a practice green, range, chipping green, locker room, bar, snack bar, restaurant, rental clubs, beverage cart and pro shop.

The course is walkable, but you must use a cart if you're not a member. You can book a tee time three days in advance. Approximate cost, including cart, is $50.

Holiday Inn Sunspree
1 Hilton Inn Dr., Asheville
• (828) 254-3211

Championship Yardage:	5600	
Slope: 118		Par: 70
Men's Yardage:		5131
Slope: 117		Par: 70
Ladies' Yardage:		4502
Slope: 112		Par: 70

The golf course at Great Smokies Resort opened in 1975; it used to be part of the Hilton organization, but now it's part of the Holiday Inn empire. According to *Architects of Golf*, Willie B. Lewis designed the course. The course is somewhat tight, particularly on the front nine, with woods bordering many of the holes. You'll find bluegrass and fescue in the fairways and bentgrass on the greens.

Corporate takeovers and changes have affected, if not the course, then at least the name of the hotel attached to this interesting mountain track. The course opened as Great Smokies Hilton, but the Holiday Inn chain took over and renamed the complex a Sunspree Resort, for what that's worth.

The golf course is a truly challenging mountain layout with a solid design. While cruising around the course, we sensed that someone had redesigned the layout and perhaps some of the holes, though we couldn't verify this. You'll find plenty of elevation changes. Hazards come in the form of well-placed bunkers and potentially pesky mountain streams. You'll need to keep it straight off the tee and think about your approach shots. The course is not long, but don't think that this makes it easy: Errant tee shots mean lost balls. The greens are predominantly large and sloped. The first four or five holes seem particularly tight. When you arrive on the 5th tee, you're confronted with your mortality as you tee off next to a small graveyard. Hello! The 5th hole is a solid one, a short 140-yard par 3 downhill over a stream. Bunkers guard the back left and right portions of the green.

Octagonal holiday chalets dot the course, and certain holes are dominated by the 279-room hotel whose aspects lie firmly in the East German school of architecture.

Amenities include a practice green, bar, snack bar, restaurant, rental clubs and pro shop.

The course is walkable for the fit and dedicated, and you can walk after 1 PM Monday through Thursday. You can book a tee time with your hotel or octagonal holiday chalet res-

The Grove Park Inn is an old and storied hotel in Asheville.

Photo: The Grove Park Inn

ervation, although you don't need to stay here to play here. Approximate cost, including cart, is $30 weekdays and weekends.

The Grove Park Inn Resort
230 Macon Ave., Asheville
• (828) 252-2711, (800) 438-5800

Championship Yardage:	**6520**
Slope: 125	**Par: 71**
Blue Yardage:	**6033**
Slope: 119	**Par: 71**
Ladies' Yardage:	**4987**
Slope: 111	**Par: 71**

The golf course at The Grove Park Inn opened in February 1899. Architects Willie Park Jr., Herbert Barker, Donald Ross and Russell Breeden all worked on or influenced the course. Ask the excellent staff here who had the biggest influence and they'll tell you it was Donald Ross. The course lies on the hillside beneath the magnificent and storied Grove Park Inn. You'll find Vamont bermudagrass in the fairways leading to Penncross bentgrass greens.

Over a century old now, the golf course at The Grove Park Inn is steeped in history. But first, let's investigate the Grove Park Inn itself. There's a book about this venerable lodge, and it's worth the small investment. Few resorts can rival the Grove Park Inn's legacy and physical appearance. From F. Scott Fitzgerald to George Bush, Beau Bridges and Tammy Wynette, the Grove Park Inn's list of guest luminaries is unsurpassed in its depth and variety. There's something extremely special about staying in a room just a corridor away from where Fitzgerald spent time with a pen in his hand.

Today, guests come to The Grove Park Inn from all over the world to relax in the well-appointed rooms, eat in the fine restaurants, dance in the nightclub or relax with a drink on the balcony overlooking Asheville. And if you're up for an amazing Sunday brunch, visit the Grove Park Inn, but make reservations for this feast.

But this is a book about golf, not hotels, right? So let's talk about this wonderful course—a top-3 favorite of ours. If you're an architecture fan, the first thing you'll notice is that this track was built in a remarkably tight area—covering just 80 acres. Just as remarkable is the fact that despite the limited acreage, very few of the holes are noticeably narrow. The front nine is flat(ish), while the back nine, which is closer to the hotel, makes greater use of the slope beneath the inn. The greens vary in shape, size and slope. Errant tee and approach shots risk landing in bunkers, but the course is not overly penal. Water comes into play mostly on the front nine. The yardage book is a useful guide if you're playing the course for the first time.

People complain that the course is too short to be interesting for the big hitter.

Balderdash.

While it may be true that the par 5s are mostly on the short side and there are three or four short par 4s, we'd still challenge the long hitter to score par or better on the short holes. Each of the short holes features a unique challenge that could lead to a bogey or worse. For example, the par 4 11th runs only about 350 yards, but it's an uphill hole with a small green that slopes away from the fairway. Thus a decently struck short iron can easily end up in the thick rough behind the green, leaving you with a tricky up and down. For those who don't feel that the course is long enough, it boasts a couple of long par 3s and some par 4s that are longer than 400 yards. Combine this with the fact that the fairways usually offer very little roll and a number of difficult stances and you'll be pleased to score well on this course. If there's a layout that proves you don't need a lot of length to be challenging, this is it.

Another hole you'll enjoy is the par 4 18th, where you tee off literally right next to the walls of the inn. You drive downhill to an extremely narrow V-shaped fairway, where you're more than likely to have a difficult stance for your second shot, which you'll have to hit uphill to a large green flanked by trees and deep bunkers.

Perhaps the Donald Ross influence can be most easily seen in the par 3s. The best of this outstanding bunch might be the two No. 7s. The first is shorter at 167 yards from the tips, but must traverse a pond. Hole 7a is longer but without the water. These two are two of the best short holes in North Carolina.

As you might expect from a course touched by the hands of Donald Ross, there's plenty of variety and interest. Every hole has its own character and charm, including the 9th, supposedly one of Bobby Jones's favorites and another great par 3. It's a lengthy and tight par 3 (more than 200 yards from the tips) with a long green fronted by three large and flat bunkers—a great way to finish the front nine.

But the layout is only a part of the story. Golfers who have played here include such greats as the aforementioned Bobby Jones, Ben Hogan, Jack Nicklaus, Arnold Palmer, Fuzzy Zoeller and Walter Hagen. There's a wonderful story about Ben Hogan scoring 11 on the par 3 7th and 4 on the par 5 8th; fable has it that his expression never changed.

From about the mid-'20s to the mid-'50s, the course hosted a stop on the PGA Tour. During that period, many of the pros would come to the inn for the summer and play for big bucks with the wealthy guests who were here to escape the heat of the cities. So when you play at The Grove Park Inn, you're walking in the footsteps of giants.

Finally, let's not forget that the course is 100 years old—few courses have such grand views and maturity. One of the magnificent sights will be you as you putt on the 17th green in full view of the guests in the Sammons Wing of the inn. You can play at the Grove Park Inn without staying at the hotel; but that's a lot like visiting the Metropolitan Museum of Art without taking a look at the paintings. Still, even if you're in the Asheville area staying elsewhere, you must play this golf course.

Amenities include a practice green, rental clubs, locker room, bar, snack bar, restaurant, beverage cart and pro shop. The hotel is building a spa that will open in late 2000—perfect for your pre-round massage with the Swedish Prime Minister.

You can walk after 3 PM—if you're fit. You can book a tee time whenever you choose. Approximate cost, including cart, is $80 weekdays and weekends. It's essential to book early because the course hosts numerous corporate outings and can get clogged up. If you're not staying at the hotel, or if you're on your own, try playing in the morning.

High Hampton Inn and Country Club
N.C. Hwy. 107 S., Cashiers Inn, Cashiers
• (828) 743-2450, (800) 334-2551
Men's Yardage: 6012
Slope: 120 **Par: 71**

The golf course at High Hampton Inn and Country Club opened in 1923 and was designed by J. Victor East. George Cobb redesigned the course in 1958 and again in 1980 with the help of John LaFoy. Some of the holes are flat, but most include undulations. Bentgrass carpets both the fairways and greens.

General public play at this fine old course is limited to after noon. Guests at the inn can play anytime.

High Hampton offers a mature track with plenty of variety. Its most remarkable feature is the varying length of the holes. For example, the par 5 No. 3 measures a significant 572 yards; next up is the par 4 No. 4, just 229 yards. This pattern is often repeated. But don't be fooled into thinking the short holes are easy. You'll be shooting to small crowned greens that become extremely fast in the spring and fall. On the longer holes, including two monster par 3s, you'll still find that the greens are not overly large. So, you'll need to be accurate to score well. The course presents a variety of fairway widths. You'll also find some imaginative tee sites. Interestingly, the course is devoid of bunkers, and water only comes into play on a few holes, most noticeably on the par 3 No. 8, where you might be tempted to take more club than you actually need.

Even if your golf isn't going too well, enjoy the setting—it has to be one of the finest of any public-access course in the mountains. Woods border a number of the holes, mountain streams crisscross the track and wonderful views of the surrounding peaks await from the elevated tees. You might think that 6012 yards isn't the longest course, but there are some significantly long holes where your drive through a chute has to be long and accurate. Don't be fooled by the distance; the course is tough enough for all levels of golfer.

One throwback to the 1920s is the lack of yardage markers. You'll be on your own when it comes to choosing clubs—no cart-mounted laser-guided yardage aids here. Most holes offer a 150-yard marker, but that's it. The course is apt to be wet.

Amenities include a practice green, range, chipping green, snack bar, bar, restaurant, locker room, rental clubs and pro shop.

The course is walkable, you can walk anytime and you should walk. If you're not staying at the inn, you can only book a tee time one day in advance. Approximate cost, including cart, is $55; it's $45 for guests at the inn.

Lake Junaluska Golf Course
19 Golf Course Rd., Waynesville
• **(828) 456-5777**

Championship Yardage:	4962
Slope: No rating	Par: 68
Men's Yardage:	4579
Slope: No rating	Par: 68
Ladies' Yardage:	3792
Slope: No rating	Par: 68

There's evidence of the first nine holes of a golf course as far back as 1919, and the course added a new nine in 1993. The architect of the front nine is unknown, but Jim Moulin shaped the back. The course is well maintained, and efforts are ongoing to improve it. It's primarily wide open and set in rolling terrain. You'll find bluegrass in the fairways and bentgrass on the greens.

Lake Junaluska Golf Course is owned and

operated by a conglomeration of Lake Junaluska Assembly, SEJ Administrative Council and the United Methodist Church. So if you want a beer with your mid-round hot dog, forget it. In fact, the brochure clearly states that the course has a "No alcohol—no profanity" policy. Two retired ministers serve as part-time rangers and golf course maintenance experts. We played with one of them who, at age 72, could still drive the ball more than 270 yards. And that's after having had surgery on three of the vertebrae in his neck!

This friendly course is an interesting old track with small greens. If the ground is hard, you'll have to take one less club than normal and let the ball run onto the putting surface. If you miss a green, you'll have to negotiate a tough chip or pitch up an embankment. A small pond and the occasional mountain stream come into play. You'll especially enjoy the 135-yard par 3 9th, where the winds can sweep off the lake and influence a short shot to one of the smallest greens in Christendom. You might be tempted to think that the course is too short to be fun, but think otherwise.

There's plenty of entertainment here, and if you're not satiated after your round, you can pick up a copy of *Tee-Ology*, a book by John Freeman about golf's lessons for Christians and other seekers—a must at about $10. If you like unmolested old courses without any gimmicks or trickery, take a look at this track.

Amenities include a practice green, snack bar, rental clubs and pro shop.

The course is walkable anytime. You can book a tee time whenever you choose. Approximate cost, including cart, is $26.

Lake Toxaway Country Club
353 W. Club Blvd., Lake Toxaway
• **(828) 966-4661**

Championship Yardage:	6234
Slope: 122	Par: 71
Men's Yardage:	5594
Slope: 116	Par: 71
Ladies' Yardage:	4627
Slope: 109	Par: 71

If you want to play this course, you have to stay at the inn.

The golf course at Lake Toxaway opened in 1960. According to *Architects of Golf*, R.D. Heinitsh designed the original layout. However, John LaFoy redesigned the course. LaFoy is a well-known architect who designed several fine tracks throughout the Southeast. LaFoy apprenticed under George Cobb, making frequent visits to Augusta National to study the design.

When Cobb was slowed by illness, LaFoy took over many well-known Cobb projects, including Linville Ridge near Grandfather Mountain.

Most of the holes on the course are bordered by woods. The layout is undulating, with a number of significant elevation changes. You'll find bluegrass in the fairways and bentgrass and poa annua on the greens.

Lake Toxaway's course is well designed and boasts a beautiful environment. The course starts with a bang: a 445-yard par 5 uphill to a raised green fronted by a mean bunker. You'll find plenty of traps—some in the fairways, some around the greens. Most of the holes on the front boast just one bunker, but it's placed in a difficult spot and will force you to think about how heroic you plan to be on your approach shot. Lake Toxaway proves that you don't need a multitude of bunkers to make a hole interesting and challenging—remember what Donald Ross said about there being no misplaced bunkers on a golf course. Some bunkers have steep faces. The greens are midsize to large, crowned and sloped, with subtle undulations. The fairways are of a sensible width. Steep embankments flank some of the greens, usually on the side opposite the bunker. Note the Astroturf cart path next to the green on No. 10: Is this still a free drop, or must you hit from the fake stuff?

Things get more difficult on the back nine. First, there are more bunkers and some steeper embankments. The 11th hole (where the Wards and their canine, Mulligan, live) is a relatively gentle par 4. Then begins a long and treacherous series of holes, including a 429-yard par 4, a 659-yard par 5 and a 230-yard par 3. So don't be lulled into a state of semi-catatonic complacency when, upon first glance at the scorecard, you see a mere 6234 yards from the tips. There are some big holes here.

The course will be fun and entertaining for golfers of all levels. Go ahead and splurge on a night at the inn and enjoy yourself on this wonderful track. You'll love the golf as well as the opportunity to relax on the veranda overlooking the 10th tee as you recount the gory details of your round, tell a few lies, collect on the bet and sip a cold beer.

Amenities include a practice green, range, chipping green, locker room, bar, snack bar, restaurant, rental clubs, beverage cart and pro shop.

The course is walkable for the fit, and you can walk anytime. Book your tee with your room. Approximate cost, including cart, is $70.

Maggie Valley Resort and Country Club
340 Country Club Rd., Maggie Valley
• (828) 926-1616

Championship Yardage:	6336		
Slope: 121		**Par:** 72	
Men's Yardage:	6031		
Slope: 118		**Par:** 72	
Other Yardage:	5344		
Slope: 111		**Par:** 72	
Ladies' Yardage:	4645		
Slope: 105		**Par:** 72	

The golf course at Maggie Valley opened in 1963. William Prevost Sr. designed the course, although Emmett Mitchell also receives a credit. The course is relatively open, with trees defining the fairways on which you'll find bluegrass; on the greens, you'll putt on bentgrass. You'll also find it easiest to get a tee time at Maggie Valley if you're staying at the resort.

The advertisements exclaim: "You gotta meet Maggie!" And indeed you should(n't). The 2-mile stretch of tourist traps that defines the town of Maggie Valley may lead you to think that the course is similar in its attitude towards aesthetics. Don't worry; the layout at Maggie Valley is one of the better and prettier courses in the area. Maggie has hosted four N.C. Open Championships, the women's state senior championship, the Western North Carolina PGA Assistant Pro Championship and a number of other competitions. Tom Doak, a golf course architect and a noted golf course architecture writer, didn't see much here of interest, but we'd disagree.

The front and back nines are quite different. The front winds along the valley floor, while the back is much hillier and presents some fine views from some of the tee boxes. Perhaps the front nine is a little tighter off the tee, although you shouldn't notice a big difference. Problems come in the form of the streams that crisscross the course; take a good look at the layout on the scorecard and make a note of where the creeks are. The large, flat bunkers will influence your approach shots. The greens are rolling, and a few are two- or even three-tiered; on some of the putting surfaces, just the

INSIDERS' TIP

If you're a mid- or high handicapper, time spent practicing your short game will help you avoid big blowups and big numbers. Once your short game has improved, you can plan your approach shots to maximize the effectiveness of your short game.

slope and pitch will give you fits. The scorecard gives you green depths, which is useful considering the vastness of some of the greens. Despite all the hazards and undulations, Maggie is not overly penal, and you'll be able to score well here if you keep your game under control. In any case, you'll find excellent variety and interest at Maggie Valley. It's well worth a visit if you're in the area.

The best hole is probably the 556-yard 18th, a suitable finishing hole to a fun course. The downhill drive needs to find the landing area between to streams. From there, it's a lay up to a long and undulating green or better still, a strong fairway wood to provide a birdie opportunity.

Amenities include a practice green, range, chipping green, locker room, bar, snack bar, restaurant, rental clubs, beverage cart and pro shop.

The course is walkable for the fit, and you can walk after 2:30 PM. Book your tee time with your stay at the resort or one day ahead for the public. Approximate cost, including cart, is $55 (the highest midseason rate).

Meadowbrook Golf Club
Meadowbrook Rd., Rutherfordton
• (828) 863-2690

Championship Yardage:	6378	
Slope: 110	**Par: 72**	
Men's Yardage:	5850	
Slope: 105	**Par: 72**	
Ladies' Yardage:	5208	
Slope: 108	**Par: 75**	

Meadowbrook opened in 1964. The course is set on rolling terrain, with bermudagrass fairways and bentgrass greens. Some of the holes are open, others are bordered by woods.

This fun and relatively straightforward course has a mountain feel to it despite the fact that it's a bit west of where the real mountains begin their ascent. If you hate bunkers, you'll love this course—there are none.

Except for a few narrow fairways, you won't find a great deal of trouble off the tee. This is especially true on the front nine, which is more open than the back. Don't be fooled by the clubhouse: It looks like a hay storage facility. But the course is set in pretty surroundings and has a pleasant and peaceful ambiance not usually found on purely public courses. Credit the ever-underrated architect, Willie B. Lewis. The greens are predominantly midsize to large, with subtle undulations. There's plenty of water to contend with in the form of a mountain stream as well as a pond on two holes. This track is certainly worth a look if you're fond of courses with a traditional feel.

The most intriguing hole on the course might be the par 5 12th. It's just 478 from the tips and it doglegs left, which should help the better right-handed player who can hit a draw. The main hazard is a significant stream that crosses the hole in two places and almost forces a second shot straight to the green.

Amenities at Meadowbrook include a practice green, locker room, snack bar, restaurant, rental clubs and pro shop.

You can and should walk anytime. You can book a tee time whenever you choose. Approximate cost, including cart, is $21 weekdays and $28 on weekends.

Mill Creek Country Club
100 Mill Creek Rd., Franklin
• (828) 524-6458

Championship Yardage:	6167	
Slope: 115	**Par: 72**	
Men's Yardage:	5775	
Slope: 113	**Par: 72**	
Ladies' Yardage:	4483	
Slope: 113	**Par: 72**	

Mill Creek Country Club opened in 1968. After numerous queries and additional research, we've discovered that no one knows who designed this course. The layout is primarily wide open with some elevation changes. You'll be playing on bentgrass in the fairways and on the greens.

This Mecca of golf in Franklin is a fun and straightforward course with plenty of challenge for golfers of all levels and abilities. The greens are small to midsize and protected by flat bunkers that could prove disastrous if your sand technique isn't up to snuff. The greens are sloped. The most notable landscaping feature is the preponderance of mature willow trees, some of which come into play. You'll have some fine mountain views, particularly from the elevated tees. If you're in the area, stop by the course for a fun round.

The hole that offers the most joy might be the picturesque 3rd, a short par 3 with water right and center.

Amenities include a practice green, chipping green, snack bar, rental clubs and pro shop.

You can walk the course after 2 PM. Book a tee time two days in advance, if you wish. Approximate cost, including cart, is $40.

Red Fox Country Club
2 Club Rd., Tryon • (828) 894-8251

Championship Yardage:	7104	
Slope: 136	**Par: 72**	
Men's Yardage:	6393	
Slope: 124	**Par: 72**	

MOUNTAINS

Other Yardage:	5705
Slope: 111	Par: 72
Ladies' Yardage:	5286
Slope: 118	Par: 73

Red Fox Country Club opened in 1966. Ellis Maples designed the course, a primarily open track, with woods and houses bordering some holes. In the fairways, you'll find bermudagrass; on the greens, bentgrass.

Red Fox is an excellent example of Ellis Maples' architectural talent. Maples took a pretty piece of land and turned it into a fine and tough country golf course. The fairways are wide, and the greens are large and sloped. Plenty of bunkers surround the green complexes. (These are basic details that match many of Maples' courses.) The beauty of the course comes from the layout: the sweeping doglegs, the variety of shots you have to play and the subtle shaping of the large flat bunkers. Ellis Maples courses often feature a number of uphill approach shots that tend to be semi-blind. Some people don't like this. Still, we've heard a number of better golfers rave about this course as one of the best undiscovered secrets in the foothills of the mountains. At least it's been a secret until now, right?

It's difficult to describe the essence of this fine old course, so we recommend you play it and take in its attractions and challenges. Play it from the Red Fox tees (the tips), and you'll be in for a long day. If you're up for less of a challenge, play it from one of the forward sets. We have a feeling you'll go out of your way to play this course over and over again.

Amenities include a practice green, range, locker room, snack bar, rental clubs and pro shop.

You must take a cart here, but you can book a tee time whenever you choose. Approximate cost, including cart, is $30 weekdays and $35 on weekends.

Reems Creek Golf Course
Pink Fox Cove Rd., Weaverville
• (828) 645-4393

Championship Yardage:	6477
Slope: 130	Par: 72
Men's Yardage:	6106
Slope: 127	Par: 72
Other Yardage:	5357
Slope: 119	Par: 72
Ladies' Yardage:	4605
Slope: 114	Par: 72

Reems Creek Golf Course, a Martin Hawtree design just north of Asheville, opened in 1989. This is a mountain track, and you'll encounter plenty of significant elevation changes. Most of the holes are open, and woods border a few. Bentgrass blankets the fairways and covers the greens.

Englishman Martin Hawtree represents the third generation of the Hawtree family, famous for its fine and prolific golf course designs, most of which are in the British Isles. Martin Hawtree has a doctorate in land planning from Liverpool University. His father, Fred, designed nearby Mount Mitchell Course. European PGA Tour player Simon Gidman assisted in the design of Reems Creek.

Reems Creek is Martin Hawtree's only golf course in America. After playing it, you might be thankful there isn't a second effort anywhere. It's an ambitious track that's a sort of hybrid mountain/links course. The result is an extremely challenging layout that will test every aspect of your game and make you use every club in your bag.

The serious elevation changes mean you'll often have to negotiate a severe uphill or downhill shot. The lack of length means you'll be playing some target golf as well. If the weather has been hot and the greenskeeper has saturated the fairways, the course will play a little wider than it looks. Hit a straight drive and you're still not out of trouble. Your approach shots to the mostly large greens need to be placed just right if you're going to score par. Some of the greens, particularly on the back nine, must slope up to 6 or 7 feet from back to front: Take our advice and do everything you can to stay below the hole. In fact, in our opinion some greens verge on being unfair. So make sure you check the pin placement and hit your approach shots to the sensible portion of the green. Oh, you'll also find plenty of mounding to help define the fairways and green complexes. Bunkers are everywhere as well, and Hawtree has taken a page out of Robert Trent Jones's book and made them cloverleaf-shaped. There are also some grass bunkers around some of the greens.

One of many picturesque holes is the par 4 5th hole, at 348 yards from the tips, a short dogleg to the left. The drive is downhill to a landing area, then a precise short iron will yield at least a par. Danger lurks on the left in the form of a lake and a bunker awaits on the right. Trees defend the direct route to the green, and there must be quite a few big hitters who have been tempted to try a high hook to cut out the dogleg.

Reems Creek seems to be a much-admired and talked about course among the local golf-

The North Carolina mountains are home to some stunning golf courses—Hound Ears is one of them.

Photo: Clay Nolen

ing population. If you're looking for a challenging modern course in the Asheville area, you'll get all you can handle at this impressive track.

Amenities include a practice green, range, snack bar, grill, rental clubs and pro shop.

You must use a cart at Reems Creek. You can book a tee time whenever you like. Approximate cost, including cart, is $45 weekdays and $50 on weekends.

Sapphire Mountain Golf Club
30 Slicers Ave., Sapphire
• (828) 743-1174

Championship Yardage:	6147
Slope: 119	Par: 70
Men's Yardage:	5690
Slope: 118	Par: 70
Ladies' Yardage:	4515
Slope: 112	Par: 70

The course used to be called Holly Forest. The management attributes the current design to Ron Garl, although *Architects of Golf* says Tom Jackson designed the course. Woods border most of the holes. The course, owned and operated by LinksCorp, features bentgrass on the greens and in the fairways. There are two other courses in the Cashiers area with the name Sapphire. Sapphire Mountain is the only course bearing the Sapphire nomenclature that's open to the public.

The first thing you'll notice about the course is its somewhat bizarre routing, which must have been changed from the original. As your round progresses, you'll see that perhaps the rerouting was completed to produce the remarkable par 3s that define this course. Each one has its own character, and each is quite dramatic. For example, on the 203-yard 4th hole, you'll smack your tee shot to a green with a large rock on the left and a steep embankment to the right and front—and it's only the No. 14 handicap. Go figure. The 15th hole, measuring just 138 yards, features an undulating island green.

Although the par 3s alone are worth the price of admission, the 401-yard par 4 No. 14 is surely one of the most dramatic and difficult golf holes in North Carolina. You have to drive from an elevated tee to a narrow landing area with a stream on the lefthand side. Your approach shot will travel to a significantly elevated two-tiered green. Miss the green to the right and your ball will be swallowed by a waterfall. A dramatic and difficult hole, No. 14 can be counted a good effort with par. Overall, good variety, bizarre routing, tricky greens and some large bunkers will make your golfing life difficult and interesting. And if the greenskeeper lets the rough grow, finesse shots become more

difficult. In an area where most of the courses are private, Sapphire Mountain provides a modern public course in a pleasant setting.

Amenities include a snack bar, rental clubs, a locker room, bar, restaurant, beverage cart and pro shop.

Walking is not permitted here. You can book a tee time 30 days in advance. Approximate cost, including cart, is $35 weekdays and weekends.

Springdale Country Club
200 Golf Watch Rd., Canton
• (828) 235-8451

Championship Yardage:	6812
Slope: 126	Par: 72
Men's Yardage:	6437
Slope: 121	Par: 72
Other Yardage:	5734
Slope: 113	Par: 72
Ladies' Yardage:	5421
Slope: 121	Par: 74

All 18 holes at Springdale Country Club opened in 1970. Joseph Holmes laid out the original course, and according to the staff at Springdale, Fred Tingle revised the track. Most of the course is set in rolling terrain and includes some decent elevation changes. You'll play on rye grass fairways and bentgrass greens.

The fairways vary in width. The greens vary in shape, but most are fairly large and undulating. A number of changes were completed recently, including the construction of a new practice putting green, the renovation of the practice range and the redesign of all bunkers. Springdale also recently hired a full-time PGA professional as director of golf.

You don't have to stay at one of the guest cottages or at the inn to play here, but we recommend it. The resort is family-owned and operated and, according to the staff, enjoys strong repeat visits. The focus here is golf. As the brochure firmly states: "Here, the game of golf reigns supreme; no pools, spas or tennis courts." That's what we like to hear!

The golf course is a challenging mountain track with plenty of variety. Play it all the way from the back and you're in for a long day. Play it from the front and the course is kinder and gentler. Some fairways are narrow and bordered by woods; others are wide and more forgiving. The back nine is more open than the front. You'll enjoy driving the ball from some of the elevated tees. The greens are midsize and sloped. Streams come into play on some of the holes. Overall, Springdale is a beautiful and fun course that will provide a challenge for any golfer.

And just in case you're worried about playing too slowly, each golf cart is equipped with

MOUNTAINS

an egg timer. If it dings, then you've spent too much time on that hole and need to go the next.

The course opens with a strong par 5, 547 yards from the tips. With your swing not yet in gear, it's best to pull out a fairway wood for two shots, then approach with a wedge or short iron.

Amenities include a practice green, range, chipping green, locker room, snack bar, restaurant, rental clubs, beverage cart and pro shop.

You can walk anytime, if you are fit! And you can book a tee time whenever you choose. Approximate cost, including cart, is $40.

Trillium
Hwy. 107 North., Cashiers
• (888) 909-7171

Championship Yardage:	**6505**
Slope: 134	**Par: 72**
Men's Yardage:	**6118**
Slope: 129	**Par: 72**
Other Yardage:	**5451**
Slope: 122	**Par: 72**
Ladies' Yardage:	**4340**
Slope: 120	**Par: 74**

Trillium opened in 1998. PGA Tour veteran Morris Hatalsky designed the course on superb mountainous terrain. Greens, tees and fairways are bentgrass.

Trillium is Morris Hatalsky's first golf course. Hatalksy, who now makes his home in Asheville, is a familiar name to anyone who follows the PGA Tour. Now in the semi-limbo between the main tour and the Senior circuit, Hatalsky occasionally uses a veteran exemption to play in a tournament. Nobody would say that he possesses the ball striking ability of a Tom Watson, but nobody would argue that there was anyone better with a blade in his hand than Morris Hatalsky, who, based on statistics, was the best putter on the PGA Tour in the 1980s. That alone helped him to four wins and helped him keep his tour card for twenty years. Hatalsky is living proof of the importance of the short game.

Most recently, Hatalsky has been busy in the mountains just to the north of Cashiers, building a much-needed daily fee course on a beautiful but tricky site. The result is visually stunning, yet very playable. Views throughout the course are nothing short of sensational. Designers built most of the courses in this chapter along valley floors and on primarily flat sites. Here at Trillium, Hatalsky takes the golfer up the sides of mountains, over ridges, down through deep forests of rhododendron, past burbling brooks and streams.

Sites like this pose a significant challenge to the golf course architect: How do you make all the holes on the course playable while maintaining the integrity of the site? And in these days of mega-permitting, it's even more difficult.

Remarkably, Hatalsky and his associates succeeded where other bigger names might have failed. Whereas it would have been easier to produce a penal, target-style course, Hatalsky offer a number of strategic options to help the mid- to high-handicapper keep the ball in play.

Still, Trillium is no pushover from tee to green and thus the green complexes are not particularly severe. In designing the greens, Hatalsky eschewed multi-tiered sorcery so common on so many courses in favor of a subtler, more Ross-like approach. It's a welcome throwback.

Trillium's signature hole must surely be the 8th, a 280-yard uphill par 4. From the tee, the challenge is daunting, a fairway wood or long iron quite severely uphill to a landing area cut between tall hardwoods. The successful tee shot leaves just a short iron or wedge to a small pear-shaped green seemingly perched in mid air. On a cloudless day in mid-fall, the bold and perfectly executed par or birdie on this hole will remain etched in the golfer's memory for years to come.

It's unlikely that a golfer's first visit to Trillium will be the last. Off the tee, the course requires local knowledge and prudence in club selection. A three wood or long iron will often be the wisest choice—as befits a par 71 course with the tips at 6,500 yards and only four uphill tee shots. A tee shot to the short grass sets up scoring opportunities and thus the wise golfer will use the driver sparingly at Trillium, particularly from the forward tees.

But that's on the par 4s and 5s. On the picture postcard par 3s, the course stresses accuracy over strength, mind over muscle.

Amenities include a practice green, range, locker room, snack bar, restaurant, rental clubs, beverage cart and pro shop.

Trillium would be a nice day hike, but not with golf clubs attached to your back—you are not allowed to walk. Call ahead to book a tee time, particularly during the summer. Approximate cost, including cart, is $75.

Waynesville Country Club Inn
Country Club Dr., Waynesville
• (828) 452-4617
Carolina/Dogwood Course
Championship Yardage:	**5798**
Slope: 103	**Par: 70**

Men's Yardage: 5395
Slope: 100   Par: 70
Ladies' Yardage: 4927
Slope: 103   Par: 70
Dogwood/Blue Ridge Course
Championship Yardage: 5803
Slope: 105   Par: 70
Men's Yardage: 5258
Slope: 100   Par: 70
Ladies' Yardage: 4565
Slope: 100   Par: 70
Blue Ridge/Carolina Course
Championship Yardage: 5943
Slope: 104   Par: 70
Men's Yardage: 5493
Slope: 100   Par: 70
Ladies' Yardage: 5002
Slope: 104   Par: 70

Golfers started swinging at Waynesville Country Club Inn in 1926, and the course has an interesting design history. Little known is the fact that Donald Ross designed the initial routing. John Drake finished the construction of the course. Ross Taylor revised the layout. Then Tom Jackson arrived to add the third nine and revise the course again in 1989. If you ask in the pro shop who built the course, they'll tell you it was Tom Jackson. In the fairways, you'll find bluegrass; on the greens, you'll find bentgrass.

The inn here is magnificent. You can get on the course even if you're not staying here, but you'll probably find it easier to get a tee time if you're a guest. You can also rent a condo or vacation cottage, or whatever it's called these days. All sorts of packages are available.

You won't find tremendous "let it rip with the titanium driver" length on any of the three nine-hole courses, but you'll enjoy a bit more room off the tee on the Carolina nine, which is flatter and a little more straightforward than the Dogwood and Blue Ridge courses. The latter two courses are placement tracks where judgment is more important than brute strength. We think you'll find that all three courses are much more user-friendly than some of today's modern earth-moving impossibilities. There's very little that's unfair about any of these three, at least from the tee to the green. A few mountain streams provide the water hazards, and the courses are only moderately bunkered.

But it's on and around the greens where the courses become trickier. We're in a valley here, thus reading putts is extremely difficult and likely to add to your score. Such are the joys of mountain golf. The setting is super, and you'll enjoy a round on any of the courses, particularly if your strengths are putting and hitting it straight but not especially far.

A beautiful hole is the par 3 2nd on the Blue Ridge course, a testy 184 yards from the tips over water.

Amenities include a practice green, locker room, bar, snack bar, restaurant, rental clubs and pro shop.

Walking is restricted. You can book a tee time with your reservation or one day in advance. Approximate cost for 18 holes, including cart, is $48.

Boone/Blowing Rock Area

Blue Ridge Country Club
N.C. Hwy. 181, Linville Falls
• (828) 756-7001
Championship Yardage: 6862
Slope: 128   Par: 72
Men's Yardage: 6362
Slope: 123   Par: 72
Ladies' Yardage: 5203
Slope: 116   Par: 72

Blue Ridge Country Club opened nine holes in 1995 and opened all 18 in spring 1996. Ken Ezell and Lloyd Clifton designed the course, which is set on the side of a mountain near Linville Caverns on the way to Linville and Boone. Greens are bentgrass, and the fairways are a mixture of bluegrass, rye and fine fescue. Many of the holes feature significant elevation changes.

If you've already read the Charlotte chapter of this book, you're familiar with the design team of Lloyd Clifton and Ken Ezell. They produced one of Charlotte's most popular and challenging public courses, Highland Creek. They also designed a significant number of courses in Florida.

Their course here at Blue Ridge Country Club is both challenging and picturesque. On most holes, you don't have to drive the ball a long way, but you mustn't spray it—if you do, you've probably lost your ball for good. If the rough is up, the course becomes particularly difficult.

The greens here are mostly large and quite undulating, flanked by a series of bunkers and embankments that could make getting up and down quite difficult. An aspect you'll really like about the course is that it's been designed so that almost all of the problems and challenges are easily seen. A lot of tee boxes are elevated, so you're provided with an abundance of down-

MOUNTAINS

Whatever It Takes

In the course of my travels as I investigated and researched golf courses, I played golf with a lot of interesting characters, some of whom I enjoyed, some of whom I'll be happy not to see again. One person who is part of the former category is an assistant pro at one of the larger resorts in Pinehurst. He used to be a caddie on the pro tour. Apart from his ability to play golf very well and his ability to recite most of the words from one of the best movies ever made, *Caddyshack*, this golfer told me about the players on the PGA tour, where the big boys play.

"The pros do whatever it takes to be in the middle of the fairway. After that, every iron is going right where it needs to go and every chip and putt looks like it's going in."

Personally, this advice or method of playing golf strikes me as excellent, if you can practice enough to get there. If you can follow this general game plan, then you'll probably enjoy the game a lot more, even if your scoring average isn't 69.23. Doing whatever it takes to be in the fairway means taking a fairway wood or even a mid-iron off the tee. You may hit the ball only 150 to 200 yards, but that's a lot better than being in the woods or in a stream or in the back yard of somebody's house—someone who, despite spending all the money to own a house next to a golf course, is amazed when golf balls and golfers appear in their back yard.

A second shot where it needs to be may be short of the green and thus short of all the trouble that often surrounds the green complex. After these two good shots, a well-executed pitch or chip and two (or even one) good putts means no more than bogey on even a long par 4. One less than 18 bogeys and you've shot in the 80s.

So take the advice of a caddie who's seen the best in the world play golf. Let the course come to you instead of stretching to do something you can't do, and you'll enjoy golf a lot more . . . and save money on golf balls to boot. —Scott Martin

Bring a good short game with you when you visit the Carolinas; getting up and down isn't impossible.

Photo: Courtesy of The Charlotte Observer

hill tee shots. This effect is created by the excellent routing of the course. We think you'll really enjoy the ambiance here, the pretty setting and the variety of challenges presented for your golfing enjoyment. Just check your driver at the door unless you're able to hit it consistently straight.

There's quite an emphasis here on making the course a destination with a resort-type atmosphere. You'll find a number of well-appointed rooms at the small inn, which also features a pleasant restaurant. The facility is proving popular as a corporate retreat. Retirees are already purchasing lots adjacent to the golf course, so you're going to find a lot of houses being built quite soon.

The 7th is one of a number of menacing par 5s—a solid 542 from the tips. The problem here is the narrowness of the fairway, which will take the driver out of the hands of all but the most proficient.

Amenities include a practice green, range, restaurant, snack bar, meeting room, rental clubs and pro shop.

You can walk here at anytime, but you'll find it quite a hike. You can book a tee time whenever you please. Approximate cost, including cart, is $43 weekdays and $48 on weekends.

Boone Golf Club
Fairway Dr., Boone • (828) 264-8760

Championship Yardage:	**6401**
Slope: 120	**Par: 71**
Men's Yardage:	**5859**
Slope: 112	**Par: 71**
Ladies' Yardage:	**5172**
Slope: 103	**Par: 75**

Boone Golf Club, an Ellis Maples course, opened in 1959. The course is flat in places, rolling in others, with bentgrass fairways and greens.

At Boone Golf Club we found a formidable and mature Ellis Maples design that's close to Boone and well worth a visit. It's one of Maples' first courses, as well as one of his first in the mountains. One of Maples' sons, Joe, was formerly the head pro here. Ellis Maples had been an architect for just six years when the Boone club was built, and you'll see here many of the features that later came to be standards on his other fine courses.

You probably won't encounter a great deal of trouble off the tee, but it will help to be long from the tips. Trees border many of the fairways. The greens are midsize and undulating—in fact, we noticed some buried elephants on a couple—so make sure your approach shots are well placed. You'll also find some intelligent and sneaky bunker placements around the greens. A couple of small tributaries of the New River come into play on some holes.

The 1st hole is a fun 390-yard par 4 downhill to a large green. It's a wonderful driving hole.

If you're in Boone and looking for a fine Ellis Maples' design, drop by for 18 holes. You

won't be disappointed. The club boasts about 500 members.

Amenities include a practice green, restaurant, rental clubs and pro shop.

Nonmembers can walk after 2 PM. You can book a tee time seven days in advance. Approximate cost, including cart, is $45 weekdays and $49 on weekends.

Hawksnest Ski and Golf
2058 Skyland Dr., Seven Devils
• (828) 898-5135, (800) 822-4295

Championship Yardage:	**6244**
Slope: 117	**Par: 72**
Men's Yardage:	**5953**
Slope: 110	**Par: 72**
Other Yardage:	**5181**
Slope: 102	**Par: 72**
Ladies' Yardage:	**4799**
Slope: 120	**Par: 72**

Hawksnest opened in 1965. You need to stay at the accompanying lodge to play the course. A committee of local residents designed the course. Woods border most of the holes. In the fairways, you'll find bluegrass; on the greens, you'll find bentgrass. If you arrive at the course and it's dumping snow, leave your sticks in the car, strap on your skis and head for the slopes above the first tee.

Standing on the area just outside the pro shop, with the course spreading out below, you might think this layout is wide open. It isn't. Leave your driver in the trunk of your Porsche or Rolls unless you can keep the ball extremely straight: If you miss the fairway, you're in the thick woods and reaching into your bag for a fresh ball.

INSIDERS' TIP

A lesson from a PGA professional demonstrating the proper technique for playing out of a sand trap is well worth the small investment. One lesson is all it takes to get some valuable sand pointers, and you'll see instant improvement in shots that most amateurs struggle with.

Narrow fairways aside, Hawksnest proves that designing a golf course by committee can sometimes work. With the mountainside above you and magnificent views from some of the tees, this course is surely one of the most striking in the mountains. You'll find a pleasant mix of flat holes and those with elevation changes, which include terraced fairways. The greens are medium-size and sloped just enough to make for some tricky putts. Miss the green and you may find your ball in a bunker, but it's more likely that you'll be playing from the well-groomed chipping areas. It's always nice to find a course that rewards and encourages skillful chipping. To score well here, choose less club than you think you'll need off the tee, keep your ball in play and shoot for the middle of the greens.

The most spectacular hole must be the par 3 2nd, which drops about 150 feet and is just 158 yards long from the tips. So take out that short iron and fire one into the deep blue sky. There's not much room for error around the green!

Amenities include a practice green, range, chipping green, locker room, snack bar, rental clubs and pro shop.

You can walk after 6 PM if you've got the stamina. You can book a tee time seven days in advance. Approximate cost, including cart, is $34 weekdays and $39 on weekends. Remember, you can't walk off the street to play this course.

Hound Ears Club
N.C. Hwy. 105 S., Blowing Rock
• (828) 963-5831

Championship Yardage:	**6165**
Slope: 122	**Par: 72**
Men's Yardage:	**6036**
Slope: 120	**Par: 72**
Other Yardage:	**5639**
Slope: 115	**Par: 72**
Ladies' Yardage:	**4959**
Slope: 110	**Par: 73**

The golf course at Hound Ears Club, designed by George Cobb, opened in 1963. We found a pleasant mix of open and wooded holes, carpeted with bluegrass on the fairways and bentgrass on the greens.

You must stay at the well-appointed lodge to play Hound Ears. It may be worth the cashola if you're looking for a first-rate mountain resort, away from it all in a peaceful and pampered setting. The course and the lodge seem to be extremely popular with the well-to-do seasoned-citizen set. And with good reason: The golf course is a fine example of an excellent mountain track. Some of the holes are flat, while others offer dramatic elevation changes. The fairways are predominantly wide, and the greens are large and undulating. The three-tiered 12th green, a par 5 hole, must surely be one of the most difficult in western North Carolina; you can be proud of a three-putt here. An interesting story accompanies this hole: In 1995, Peter Rucker, the head pro, scored consecutive double eagles here. Peter Rucker is the brother of David Rucker, the head pro at Myers Park Country Club in Charlotte and the man who attempts to teach one of us how to strike a golf

ball so that it lands somewhere near the intended target. A tough task indeed.

Most of the greens at Hound Ears are built-up and protected by bunkers that should only be a hazard if the pin is placed nearby and you play for it. Hit your approach shot to the middle of the green and you'll be fine. As for water, you've got the Watauga River and a tributary stream, both of which come into play on a number of holes. There's also a pond on the back nine that could prove irritating. Make sure you study the card if you've never played the course before.

We would be remiss if we failed to describe, or at least tried to describe, the general ambiance of the course. The mountains rise above you, streams burble as you pull your club back, you drive your cart under ancient and cool rhododendron bushes and you feel relaxed and at ease with the world. Until, sadly, you pull your tee shot into the woods. It's a wonderful resort course, and it's a great place to be pampered.

Amenities include a practice green, range, snack bar, rental clubs and pro shop.

The course is walkable for the fit, and you can walk before 8 AM and after 6 PM. Book your tee time in conjunction with your lodge reservations. Approximate cost, including cart, is $60 every day.

Jefferson Landing
N.C. Hwy. 16-88, Jefferson
• (336) 246-5555

Championship Yardage:	**7111**
Slope: 121	**Par: 72**
Men's Yardage:	**6424**
Slope: 115	**Par: 72**
Other Yardage:	**5720**
Slope: 109	**Par: 72**
Ladies' Yardage:	**4960**
Slope: 103	**Par: 72**

The golf course at Jefferson Landing opened in 1991. Dennis Lehmann and Larry Nelson designed the course. You may know Dennis Lehmann as the associate of Jack Nicklaus responsible for Elk River in Banner Elk—a private course rated as one of the finest in North Carolina. This course, for a mountain track, has a remarkably wide-open feel; also remarkable is its occasional flatness. In the fairways, you'll find an interesting combination of bluegrass and fescue, while the greens are seeded with bentgrass.

First, a note about the resort and the development. At Jefferson Landing, you can purchase a pre-existing home or homesite, stay at the well-appointed lodge or rent a townhouse for a week. It's up to you. And you can enjoy an adult beverage or two. We mention that because the course is situated in Ashe County, a Gobi Desert when it comes to adult beverages.

And you can, of course, play golf. The layout, while relatively fresh, is straightforward and well designed. There are no trick holes; there are no frivolously designed holes. There's plenty of water in the form of streams and ponds, but it doesn't always come into play. Quite a few tee boxes render dramatic downhill tee shots. From the back tees, at a whopping 7111 yards, the course provides all the challenge you want and then some: Water comes into play more often from the tips than from the forward tees.

The strength of the course lies in its tremendous variety—again, not in tricks or gimmicks. What you see is what you get from the tee, as well as with respect to your approach shots. The well-kept Penncross bentgrass greens provide an excellent example of why this type of green should be the grass of choice on putting surfaces in the new millennium: It's true, resilient, fair and easier to maintain than pure bentgrass. The greens are medium-size, as are the bunkers protecting them, and are flattish and tricky. The management planted a large number of trees to define the fairways. Overall, Jefferson Landing is worth a visit if you're looking for a fine mountain golf course with good amenities and pleasant surroundings.

Additional features include a practice green, range, chipping green, snack bar, rental clubs, beverage cart and pro shop.

The course is not walkable. You can book a tee time whenever you choose. Approximate cost, including cart, is $45 weekdays and $55 on weekends (including Fridays).

Linville Golf Club
N.C. Hwy. 221, Linville
• (828) 733-4363

Championship Yardage:	6780	
Slope: 132		**Par:** 72
Men's Yardage:	6279	
Slope: 126		**Par:** 72
Other Yardage:	5437	
Slope: 113		**Par:** 72
Ladies' Yardage:	5086	
Slope: 117		**Par:** 72

A golf course called Tanglewood opened adjacent to the current course in 1892. The old course no longer exists (a victim of the Great Depression) although a portion is used as the driving range. Donald Ross designed the new course in 1924. Linville Golf Club is set among majestic and wonderful wooded scenery in the well-heeled retirement and second-home town of Linville. In the fairways, you'll play off bentgrass; on the greens, you'll find poa annua. Linville Golf Club is private—you must play as the guest of a member or be a guest at the excellent Eseeola Lodge. The course is open from May through October.

Among golfers in North Carolina, Linville Golf Club is known as one of the best mountain golf courses, and maybe as one of the top courses in the Carolinas. It's the finest public-access course in the mountains. Most golfers would happily choose this course over one of the more modern, earth-moving extravaganzas with houses bordering (and interfering with) almost every hole. A lot of factors make the course particularly interesting and particularly good.

For starters, Linville is something of a rarity: a true Donald Ross course that looks like it's relatively untouched. Richard S. Tufts, who died in 1980 and who used to own Pinehurst Resort, revised the course a little, but for the most part, it's pure Ross. This means that the layout is excellent: There are no silly or poorly conceived holes on the course. You'll also find plenty of those Ross greens that play smaller than they look. Getting up and down from a greenside bunker is no easy task, and we'll give you a short-game proficiency certificate if you can get up and down from behind the green. Like many great Ross courses, you need to let the course come to you, and you need to stay below the hole on your approach shots, chips and pitches.

From the tee, many of the holes are relatively wide, while others are somewhat narrow; spray the ball off the tee and you're probably going to be in the woods or on an adjacent fairway. From the middle tees, a well struck 3 wood may be your wisest choice.

Ross courses (in North Carolina, at least) don't usually feature a lot of water, and Linville is a bit of an exception in that a couple of streams regularly come into play, although they shouldn't really bother a good shot. If your other favorite pastime is fly fishing, you'll wish you could bring your rod—giant trout wander around in the streams, just waiting to be hooked, safe in the knowledge that they are protected by a "No Fishing" sign.

The course boasts a number of magnificent holes, most notably the par 4 3rd that measures 449 yards from the tips. The aforementioned stream bisects the hole at about 150 yards from the front of the turtlebacked green, which is perched on a small knoll. Most of the fairway slopes significantly downhill from right to left, making the approach short even more difficult. Par here is a great score. Golf course architect and golf writer Tom Doak believes this hole is one of the greatest par 4s in the world. He's seen a lot of excellent par 4s, so it's difficult to disagree with his assessment.

But don't think that the third hole is the only great one on the course. You'll find the 2nd, 8th, 11th, 12th and 18th to be fine and testing challenges. Linville is mostly a placement golf course. You don't have to hit the ball a mile to score well here. You just need to be in the right place at the right time and let the course come to you. Even if things are going badly here for you, remember that you're in a special place.

One other notable feature are the poa annua greens. Most course superintendents hate the stuff, due to the theory that it can take over and ruin the consistency of a good bentgrass green. We think you may find the greens here are some of the best you'll ever play, and some of the trickiest to putt in the early and late season. It's simply crucial to stay beneath the hole on most greens, lest you find yourself with an almost impossible downhill putt. One of the great things about the greens is that they are so true—a well-struck putt is most often rewarded with a great result.

With its fine architectural pedigree and its majestic setting, Linville proves that a basic layout can be a great layout. If you're a fan of really good, old golf courses, you should bribe a member to let you on or stay at the Eseeola Lodge and invest in a golf package. It's well worth the cashola.

Amenities include a practice green, range, chipping green, snack bar after the 11th hole, rental clubs and pro shop.

The course is walkable, but, sadly, you're not allowed to walk before 4 PM. It's a tragedy that such a great old course won't let you strap your bag to your own shoulder or to that of a caddie. You can book a tee time when you reserve at the Eseeola Lodge, which offers golf packages. Approximate cost, including cart, is $50 weekdays and weekends.

Mountain Aire Golf Course
1104 Golf Course Rd., West Jefferson
• (336) 877-4716

Championship Yardage:	6107
Slope: No rating	**Par: 71**
Men's Yardage:	5571
Slope: No rating	**Par: 71**
Other Yardage:	4935
Slope: No rating	**Par: 71**
Ladies' Yardage:	4143
Slope: No rating	**Par: 71**

No one seems to know when Mountain Aire opened or who designed the course. The course is primarily open and features some dramatic topography. It features bluegrass fairways along with the bentgrass greens typical of the region.

Deep in the heart of Jefferson County, Mountain Aire is perched on the side of a significant and pretty mountain. The result is a course with

Mountain golf courses often feature dramatic par 3s.

Photo: Courtesy of The Charlotte Observer

stunning elevation changes, most noticeably on the 452-yard par 4, where you tee off from what seems like the top of a cliff. The left side of the fairway features an embankment dotted with grassy pot bunkers—a unique hole. Also interesting is the 2nd hole, a par 3 listed as 89 yards, although it may be even less.

We looked hard to find a hole here that's flat, and we couldn't find one. Expect to hit either uphill or downhill on just about every shot. The greens are predominantly small and slightly sloped. Overall, Mountain Aire is a pleasant course, affording fine views and some challenging holes.

Amenities include a practice green, range, snack bar and rental clubs.

The course is walkable for the physically fit, and you can walk anytime. You can book a tee time whenever you choose. Approximate cost, including cart, is $28 weekdays and $32 weekends.

Mount Mitchell Golf Club
7590 N.C. Hwy. 80 S., Burnsville
• (828) 675-5454

Championship Yardage:	6475	
Slope: 121	Par: 72	
Men's Yardage:	6110	
Slope: 116	Par: 72	
Ladies' Yardage:	5455	
Slope: 117	Par: 72	

Mount Mitchell Golf Course opened in 1975. Fred Hawtree designed the course on a valley floor, thus it's predominantly flat. You'll find bentgrass in the fairways and on the greens.

Fred Hawtree is the son of Frederic George Hawtree, well known in the United Kingdom as one of the great designers in the first half of the 20th century. Fred Hawtree continued his father's design excellence. After a distinguished record in World War II, including a stint as a POW in a Japanese camp, Hawtree designed and built numerous courses in England and France in addition to a few in Germany, Iran, the Netherlands, South Africa, Spain, Switzerland and Wales. Mount Mitchell is his only course in the United States. Fred Hawtree's son, Martin, continued the architectural firm and is, himself, a prolific designer. You can see an example of Martin's work at Reems Creek Golf Course just north of Asheville in Weaverville (see the write-up in this chapter).

Comparing Reems Creek to Mount Mitchell is like comparing the artist formerly known as Prince to Mozart. Whereas Reems Creek is a masterpiece of modern earth-moving prowess, Mount Mitchell is a kinder, gentler course. Rumor has it that Ben Wright and Charlie "Choo-choo" Justice had houses on the course at one stage. Justice would sit on his porch and let golfers know how the putts were breaking.

The routing is magnificent. There are no bad holes, and each shot requires thought and a degree of precision. The holes have a gentle shape and appearance yet are quite challenging, due mostly to the tightness off the tee and the potential for big score disasters posed by mountain streams and several bunkers. It's probably one of the prettiest public courses in the mountains. As you drive up to the course through the winding mountain road and come upon the crosscut fairways, you can't help drooling a little at the sight.

The key to scoring well here is keeping the ball in play. If you're wild with your driver, lock it in the trunk and rely on your short game to keep you out of the big-number doghouse. The greens offer a great deal of variety. Some are sloped, others are tiered, others still are undulating.

Even though the course is a little remote, make the time to get here, particularly in the fall, when the greens are fast and the trees blaze magnificently with color. Mt. Mitchell is the highest peak east of the Mississippi River, and the scenery is stupendous.

The hole you'll remember is the par 4 18th, 400 yards straight downhill, then over a creek to a large green. It's just one of many holes with superb views.

Perhaps because it doesn't spend a lot on PR and promotion, Mount Mitchell rarely cracks those annoying "Top 100" and "Best Course in the Universe" lists. That's unfortunate—Mount Mitchell is one of North Carolina's jewels and is much better than most of the state's "ranked" and highly publicized courses.

Amenities include a practice green, locker room, snack bar, restaurant, rental clubs and pro shop.

The course is walkable for the fit, and you can walk after 1 PM Monday through Thursday. You can book a tee time two weeks in advance. Approximate cost, including cart, is $45 weekdays and $50 on weekends.

Mountain Glen Golf Club
N.C. Hwy. 194, Newland
• (828) 733-5804

Championship Yardage:	6723	
Slope: 129	Par: 72	
Men's Yardage:	6195	
Slope: 119	Par: 72	
Ladies' Yardage:	5506	
Slope: 110	Par: 72	

Mountain Glen Golf Course opened in 1964.

This George Cobb design features rolling, relatively open terrain, with trees delineating the bluegrass fairways. The greens are bentgrass.

Mountain Glen is an example of a George Cobb resort/vacation course with excellent routing. Cobb believed this type of course should be more straightforward and less fraught with difficulty than a country club course that a member might play many times a year. After all, you're on vacation! If you still want a challenge, play it from the back tees. (Actually, the course is quite long even from the ladies' tees.)

The fairways are medium-width, and the greens are medium-size and sloped, with subtle breaks. Mountain streams comprise most of the water hazards. There's plenty of bunkering around the greens, so plan your approach to avoid them. Most of the bunkers are built to catch shots that are wide and short. If you don't like the look of a bunker, take an extra club or two.

The fourth is one of many solid par 3s on the course. It's 205 from the tips to a difficult green flanked by two bunkers.

This is a fun and relatively challenging course that's worth the price of admission. An interesting local rule is that no beginning golfers are allowed on the course on weekends and holidays before 4 PM. A good move for those of us trying to get around in under five hours.

Amenities include a practice green, chipping green, locker room, snack bar, rental clubs and pro shop.

The course is pleasantly walkable, and you can walk anytime (hooray!). You can book a tee time seven days in advance. Approximate cost, including cart, is $45 weekdays and weekends.

The Village of Sugar Mountain Golf Course

Village of Sugar Mountain, Banner Elk
• (828) 898-6464
Championship Yardage: 4488
Slope: 94   Par: 64
Men's Yardage: 4198
Slope: 91   Par: 64
Ladies' Yardage: 3470
Slope: 90   Par: 64

The golf course at Sugar Mountain opened in the early 1970s, according to local legend. The staff here did not know who designed the course, and we couldn't glean any information from our typically reliable sources, but if we could hazard a guess, it might be Russell Breeden. Some holes are set in open terrain, while others are wooded. The course is primarily flat, with some minor elevation changes. Fairways are bluegrass; greens, bentgrass.

Sugar Mountain is best known as one of the largest ski areas in the Southeast. It's still small by Western standards, but it's very popular and often crowded in the middle of the season. A large, multistory concrete-sided building, which looks like an East German government building, is annoyingly perched on top of the mountain and must surely win the prize for the structure most deserving of the wrecking ball.

Architectural snafus aside, the Village of Sugar Mountain offers a fine and somewhat unique golf course. This par 64 course is defined by its nine varied, interesting and thoroughly hazardous par 3s, most notably the 187-yard 7th. The other holes offer decent length and width off the tee, although a few are tighter. It looks like little earth was moved during construction. A couple of streams provide hazards, as do some large bunkers. The greens are built-up and medium-sized; they are primarily sloped and slightly undulating. This friendly course is a good place for the beginner and interesting enough for the better and more experienced player who will be happy to keep the score close to par. Overall, Sugar Mountain is a course where residents and visitors alike will have a lot of fun.

Amenities include a practice green and rental clubs.

The course is walkable, and you should walk here—we were told that several octogenarians keep themselves atrophy-free by walking the course on a regular basis. Hey, maybe it'll work for you. You can book a tee time five days in advance. Approximate cost, including cart, is $33 weekdays and $35 on weekends.

Hickory/Lenoir Area

Granada Farms

10 River Dr., Granite Falls
• (828) 396-2313
Championship Yardage: 6661
Slope: 121   Par: 72
Men's Yardage: 5835
Slope: 112   Par: 72
Ladies' Yardage: 4821
Slope: 103   Par: 72

According to *Architects of Golf*, Granada Farms opened in 1978, although the pro shop staff cite a somewhat earlier date. Tom Jackson designed the course on rolling terrain. Some of the holes have an open feel, while woods and houses line others. Bermudagrass blankets the fairways; bentgrass covers the greens.

A well-struck 4-wood from the textile mills of Granite Falls sits Granada Farms Country

MOUNTAINS

Club, a housing development with one of Tom Jackson's first solo designs. Since this effort, Jackson's stock has risen: The houses around his golf courses are bigger, the mounds around the greens are more ominous, the greens are more demonic and the distance from the back tee has increased.

Granite Farms is a good example of why Jackson became such a hot and well-respected designer in the Carolinas. You'll also see the links elements that have continued to define Jackson's work since the construction of Granada Farms. The fairways here are mostly wide, with bunkers and the occasional mound coming into play. The greens are midsize to large, and the green complexes include a multitude of bunkers, mounds and hollows. Water comes into play on a few holes and is ingeniously employed. The course is certainly worth a look if you're in the area, especially if you're a fan of Tom Jackson.

The par 4 5th is only a medium-length par 4 at 400 yards, but the water hazard right in front of the green must cause its fair share of problems.

Amenities include a practice green, range, locker room, snack bar and pro shop.

The course is walkable (amazing for a Tom Jackson course), and you can walk after noon on weekends and anytime during the week. You can book a tee time whenever you choose. Approximate cost, including cart, is $23 weekdays and $30 on weekends.

Grassy Creek Golf and Country Club
101 Golf Course Rd., Spruce Pine
• (828) 765-7436

Championship Yardage:	**6277**
Slope: 120	**Par: 72**
Men's Yardage:	**5744**
Slope: 116	**Par: 72**
Ladies' Yardage:	**4797**
Slope: 109	**Par: 72**

Grassy Creek opened its first nine holes in 1956 and the next nine in 1966. The course is laid out on rolling terrain. Fairways combine bluegrass and bentgrass; greens are strictly bentgrass.

At Grassy Creek we found a fine, mature course that's more challenging than it looks. Hit a long or wild hook off the first tee and

your ball will land smack in the middle of a McDonald's drive-through. After this, the course becomes a lot prettier. It's predominately tight off the tee, although you can escape by hitting onto the adjacent fairway. The greens are sloped, sometimes crowned, small to midsize on the front nine and slightly larger on the back. Many of the greens are protected by bunkers of various sizes and shapes. Steep embankments flank some. A mountain stream comes into play on some holes. Have a go here if you're looking for a relaxed outing.

Amenities include a practice green, range, chipping green, locker room, snack bar, restaurant, rental clubs and pro shop.

You can walk this course anytime except Saturday before noon. You can book a tee time seven days in advance. Approximate cost, including cart, is $36 weekdays and $40 on weekends.

Marion Lake Club
N.C. Hwy. 126, Nebo • (828) 652-6232

Championship Yardage:	**6110**
Slope: No rating	**Par: 70**
Men's Yardage:	**5710**
Slope: No rating	**Par: 70**
Ladies' Yardage:	**4826**
Slope: No rating	**Par: 74**

The first nine at Lake Marion opened in 1923, and the second nine opened in the early 1970s. The track is set in rolling terrain. In the fairways and on the greens, you'll find bermudagrass. No one is certain about who designed this course, although a staff member said many knowledgeable golfers believe the layout of the original nine smacks of Donald Ross, and the second nine is the work of Russell Breeden.

Here at Lake Marion, you'll find a country course in a pleasant setting. The older holes, on the back nine, feature small greens, and you can run the ball up to the hole if the ground gets hard. The greens are generally medium-size on the front and often flanked by steep embankments that you'll want to avoid. The back nine are highlighted by views of the lake. The 14th hole features a tee shot near a very attractive house just 30 yards from the tee. This popular and pretty course is worth a visit the next time you're in Marion.

Amenities include a practice green, range, locker room, snack bar and pro shop.

INSIDERS' TIP

If you've only got a few minutes before your round, spend them on the practice green. Getting a feel for the speed of the putting surface will help you save the most strokes once you begin play.

You can walk this course and book a tee time whenever you choose. Approximate cost, including cart, is $27.

Orchard Hills Golf Club
Colony Springs Rd., Granite Falls
• **(828) 728-3560**

Championship Yardage:	6134
Slope: 111	Par: 72
Men's Yardage:	5673
Slope: 106	Par: 72
Ladies' Yardage:	4803
Slope: 105	Par: 74

W. Pitts designed Orchard Hills, which opened in the 1950s. The course is set on undulating terrain, with bermudagrass fairways and bentgrass greens.

At Orchard Hills, we found a mature, sloped and predominately open course, with a number of uphill shots. You won't run into a lot of trouble off the tee. There is a small stream that comes into play on a few holes, and a pond could affect one hole. The greens are midsize and sloped, with some bunkers protecting them.

The course closes with a difficult hole, a 427-yard par 4 that's bordered by an apple orchard. The green is one of the more heavily bunkered on the course. It's unlikely that you'll leave Orchard Hills with a birdie, but you'll be more than happy with a well-earned par.

Amenities include a practice green, range, chipping green, locker room, snack bar and pro shop.

You can walk anytime during the week and after 2 PM on weekends. You can book a tee time as early as Tuesday for the following weekend. Approximate cost, including cart, is $26 weekdays and $30 on weekends.

Quaker Meadows Golf Club
N.C. Hwy. 181, Morganton
• **(828) 437-2677**

Championship Yardage:	6704
Slope: 111	Par: 71
Men's Yardage:	6133
Slope: 108	Par: 71
Ladies' Yardage:	5625
Slope: No rating	Par: 71

The golf course at Quaker Meadows opened in 1969. This Russell Breeden design is open and primarily flat, with bermudagrass fairways and bentgrass greens.

We failed to find any Quakers, but we did find a fine, well-designed Breeden course. Typical of a Breeden track, we found little trouble off the tee, save the occasional stream or out-of-bounds area. The greens are classic Breeden: large, undulating, sloped and flanked by well-shaped and strategically placed bunkers that vary in intensity depending on pin placement. The course is clearly popular with the local golfing citizenry and with good reason—it's playable, fun and challenging without being tricked up. At par 71, the course offers significant distance from the tips. Only one hole presents a water hazard to be feared—the 422-yard 9th.

Amenities include a practice green, range, locker room, snack bar, restaurant, rental clubs and pro shop.

You can walk this course anytime except weekends before 2 PM. Book a tee time whenever you choose. Approximate cost, including cart, is $20 weekdays and $24 on weekends.

INSIDERS' TIP
Afternoon showers are fairly common in the Carolinas, especially in the summer. Keep an umbrella and a light rainsuit in your bag so you'll be prepared when the rains come.

MOUNTAINS

Around the Mountains . . .

Fun Things To Do

North Carolina's mountains make for a playground unlike any other. It's perfectly possible to do anything but play golf here and still find plenty to do.

Hang on. Did we really say that?

Let's try again. You'll find plenty to do here once you've finished playing golf.

That's better.

Once you've finished playing, try mountain biking, antique hunting, roller-coastering and horseback riding. In fact, there's enough going on to fill a rather large book, and may we be so bold as to suggest *The Insiders' Guide to North Carolina's Mountains* as an excellent resource? Look for it at fine bookstores or call (800) 582-2665 to order a copy.

Here are just a few major attractions that you shouldn't miss if you're in the mountains:

In Boone, check out **Horn in the West**, (828) 264-2120, off N.C. Highway 105 and U.S. highways 321 and 421, an outdoor drama depicting the trials and travails of those who settled the North Carolina mountains, including Daniel Boone. It's two hours of history and entertainment rolled into one. The season lasts from mid-June to mid-August.

Tweetsie Railroad, between Boone and Blowing Rock on U.S 321/221, is a great place to take the family. In addition to the 100-year-old locomotive, there's much to see, do and sample, including a petting farm, Mouse Mine #9, caramel apples and a Ferris wheel and other rides. Call (800) 526-5740 for more information. The season runs from May to Labor Day.

If you're not particularly claustrophobic, **Linville Caverns** is an entertaining option. Initially discovered by Native Americans in the 1820s, the limestone caverns also served as hideouts for Civil War deserters. It's a great place to see some serious caves and experience total darkness when the guides cut the lights. The caves are between Linville and Marion, 4 miles south of the Blue Ridge Parkway on U.S. 221. Call (828) 756-4171 for more information.

For those of you who prefer life in the fast lane to life underground, the **New Asheville Speedway** in Asheville (surprise!) at 219 Amboy Road will satisfy your need for speed. This short track used to be a regular NASCAR stop; despite the present-day absence of the big boys, there's still plenty of competition. Enjoy racing action every Friday night from April to September. The speedway's clever tag line, "Each year, 80,000 fans buy seats, but they only use the edge," sums it up. Call (828) 254-4627 for more information.

There are quite a few "touristy" spots in the North Carolina Mountains, and **Maggie Valley** might be the most touristy of them all. One of the major attraction here is the well-known **Ghost Town in the Sky**, Soco Road (U.S. 19), (828) 926-1140 or (800) GHOST TOWN. You must take the incline railroad or a chair lift to get here. The Wild West theme is accentuated by gunfights, jail breaks, bank robberies, country music and Indian dances. You'll also find more than 20 rides, including the Red Devil roller coaster. There is also tons of food to eat, most of it deliciously loaded with calories. Ghost Town in the Sky is open 9 AM to 6 PM from May to October.

No trip to Asheville is complete without a visit to what many must consider North Carolina's premier attraction, the **Biltmore Estate**. The aforementioned *Insiders' Guide to North Carolina's Mountains* devotes an entire chapter to the Biltmore Estate, and justifiably so. George Vanderbilt completed this magnificent chateau in 1895, and the home is still in the possession of his descendants who graciously open it to the public. In addition to the house, check out the estate's winery. Some currently produced wines are gaining significant praise from wine connoisseurs. The Biltmore House itself boasts more than 225 rooms, 50 of which are open to the public.

Biltmore plans plenty of annual events, but perhaps the best time to see the estate is during the Christmas holidays, when the house is decorated in a fashion that will drop your jaw and make you happy that you chose the Biltmore House over the golf course. You'll also find four places to eat on the Estate: Deer Park Restaurant, the Stable Cafe, the Winery Cafe and The Bistro. For more information about Biltmore Estate, call (800) 543-2961. It's off N.C. 25 at the junction of Hendersonville Road and McDowell Street.

Waterfalls

No trip to the mountains is complete without a trip down a waterfall. Or if you're not the type to envelop yourself in a barrel and take the plunge, at least you should go see one. It's probably safer. A number of golf courses in the mountains feature waterfalls of various shapes and sizes—often where you least expect them. Following is a selection of non-golf course waterfalls.

Avery County: **Elk Falls'** 65 feet of power cascade into one of the largest post-waterfall pools in the mountains. Travel north on U.S. 19 E. to Elk Park (just inside the North Carolina–Tennessee border). Turn right on Elk River Road and proceed 4 miles to a parking area next to the Elk River. Hike the short trail to the falls.

Burke County: One of the best known of all mountain waterfalls, **Linville Falls** tumults down the deep Linville Gorge. The upper and lower falls are equally dramatic. Access Linville Falls at milepost 316.3 on the Blue Ridge Parkway, where there's a visitors center for your convenience.

Transylvania County: One of the most accessible of all mountain waterfalls, **Looking Glass**

Falls is also one of the prettiest. It's on U.S. 276, 5.5 miles into Pisgah Forest and the junction with U.S. 64 near Brevard. Your total hike from car to view and back may be less than 30 feet.

Jackson County: You're an eight-hour drive from the beach, so take what you can get and lounge and sunbathe on the sand next to the pool at the foot of **Silver Run Falls**. Why not bring your 60-degree wedge and practice getting out of bunkers? Drive south from Cashiers on N.C. 107 for 4 miles. Park at the gravel-covered pull-off on the left. Follow the short path to the falls.

Blue Ridge Parkway

One of the most remarkable attractions, if we could call it such, is the **Blue Ridge Parkway**. Construction began in 1935, part of a government project designed to employ then-unemployed people during the Great Depression. The roadway links Great Smoky Mountains National Park in North Carolina and Shenandoah National Park in Virginia. Thus a large portion of the Parkway winds through the North Carolina Mountains. In some cases, it's a useful if somewhat circuitous route to some of the golf courses, one we recommend if you're not in a hurry and enjoy a scenic drive. Mount Mitchell Golf Course, for example, is just a few miles from the Parkway.

Cruising this picturesque roadway provides some of the greatest motoring pleasure anywhere. As you enter, a sign reads "No Commercial Vehicles;" thus, your journey will not be cluttered by the inevitable delivery trucks and 18-wheelers. Likewise, the protected Parkway provides a respite from the fast food joints and tourist traps that are sadly all too common on other mountain roads. It's the sort of road that makes you wish for an Italian sports convertible with a close-ratio stick shift, a rocket under the hood and a suspension so tight you go around curves like you're on rails. This is real motoring.

Regularly during your trip, you'll be tempted to stop at one of the wonderful overlooks to take in the view. Do it. There are also numerous trails and picnic tables for your convenience. Like the mountains themselves, the Parkway changes dramatically by season. Enjoy the colorful fall. Get up early in the morning and rise above the clouds. Dip into morning fog so thick you can't see 5 feet in front of you. But drive safely—if you're in the driver's seat, keep your eyes on the road and your hands upon the wheel. Catch the views at the overlooks, not from behind the wheel.

The Parkway emergency number is (800) 727-5928. For general Parkway information, call (828) 298-0398.

Skiing

It's actually quite a good idea to plan a trip with both golf and skiing in mind—if you're that ambitious. If it's cold, then it's quite likely that the course you came to play will be closed. If it's warm, then you won't be able to ski, but you'll be able to play golf.

Skiing in the North Carolina Mountains is not like skiing in the West. Most of the time, 90 percent of the snow is manmade and the slopes get icy. If there's real snow, it may be wet, which will turn icy in the late-afternoon shadows. About once every five years a winter of big storms will create optimal snow conditions, even if the runs tend to be a little short. We're sure you've heard that a bad day on the golf course is better than a good day in the office. Well, if you take the same attitude about skiing to the North Carolina Mountains, you'll have lots of fun.

Here are some of the area's major ski areas.

Hawksnest Golf and Ski Resort, 1800 Skyland Drive, Banner Elk, (828) 963-6561, offers 11 slopes: two beginner, five intermediate and four advanced, with a 619-foot vertical drop. The golf course here is interesting too (see our review in this chapter).

Beech Mountain Ski Resort, Beech Mountain, (828) 387-2011, is the highest ski resort in eastern North America, at approximately 5,500 feet. It's got quite a complex attached to it, including shops, ski rental, restaurants, an ice rink and a nursery. There are 14 trails in all with a vertical drop of 830 feet. Ample accommodations are available at the resort.

Sugar Mountain, Banner Elk, (828) 898-5421, lies 5,300 feet above sea level and features 18 slopes. Tackle the whopping (for North Carolina) 1,200-foot drop over and over again until the lactic acid buildup makes your quadriceps scream "No more!" Plenty of chair lifts assure you won't have to wait too long between runs. Ski rentals, lessons, lockers, a nursery and a cafeteria are available.

Appalachian Ski Mountain, Blowing Rock, (828) 295-7828, is a family-owned resort that's been in business since 1962. There are eight slopes with a vertical drop of 365 feet. Check out the giant fireplace in the Bavarian-style lodge overlooking the slopes.

Where to Eat

You'll discover hundreds of excellent restaurants in the mountains. While we're confident the head pro at the golf course you're visiting can provide a sound dining recommendation, here are a few places you might want to go to celebrate that 76 you just posted (even if it was for nine holes). Be aware that America's bout with temperance lives on in full force in a number of counties in the North Carolina Mountains. If you're in the mood for a bottle of claret to wash down your steak, you might be out of luck. *In vino non veritas.* Refer to our Preface for an explanation of the pricing code.

Asheville Area

Boston Pizza
$ • 501 Merrimon Ave., Asheville
• (828) 252-9474

Boston Pizza is about a Tiger Woods drive away from the University of North Carolina at Asheville. There's a sort of college-campus beer-and-pizza ambiance to the place, which is also well-suited for families. When school's in session and the weather is a little chilly, you'll probably run into a few students who look like they're right out of the Seattle "grunge" scene, complete with oversize faded sweaters, Kurt Cobain look-alike three-day beard growth and pierced body parts, some of which you'll be able to see.

Alternative music aside, the pizza at Boston Pizza is wonderful. You can also devour subs and other Italian staples. Since this is a student hangout, adult beverage is never in short supply.

The Grove Park Inn
$$$ • 290 Macon Ave., Asheville
• (828) 252-2711

Even if your taste in accommodations is on the lower end of the scale, we recommend you splurge on the culinary delights at the Grove Park Inn, in part because there's a strong chance (particularly if you ask) that your table may overlook the golf course. You'll be dining next to a Donald Ross masterpiece. And you'll be dining in the hotel with the greatest golf history outside of Pinehurst. There are other places for blowouts in Asheville, but this one has golf attached to it. You can eat just a stone's throw away from where golfing giants once smacked the ball around.

You'll find three restaurants: Blue Ridge Dining Room, Sunset Terrace and Horizons. Book a tee time on Sunday afternoon and precede your best-ever round with the awe-inspiring brunch in the Blue Ridge. Or have lunch at the Sunset Terrace, with its wonderful views, after an early morning round. Perhaps you're entertaining guests for golf and dinner at Horizons . . . it's hard to miss here.

Louie Michaud's Mountain Brook Center
$$-$$$ • Mallard Sq., Highlands
• (828) 526-3573

We'll risk the cliché, but there's something for everyone here at Louie Michaud's: pasta, steak, ribs, lamb, chicken and big salads. Try the prime rib buffet on Wednesday and the seafood buffet on Friday. There's also a belly-bulging brunch buffet on Sundays.

Relia's Garden Restaurant
$-$$ • U.S. Hwy. 19-74, Bryson City
• (828) 488-9186

Relia's is just 20 minutes from Bryson City at the Nantahala Outdoor Center. You must cross a steel bridge over the Nantahala River to get to the restaurant. If the weather's right, you should sit on the open-air porch overlooking the herb and vegetable gardens that supply the restaurant. Talk about seeing what you're eating! Thus, you'll find a fresh touch here that few other restaurants can match. Go for the trout or one of the many vegetarian dishes.

Boone/Blowing Rock Area

Famous Louise's Rock House Restaurant
$-$$, no credit cards • U.S. Hwy. 221, Linville Falls • (828) 765-2702

Louise's Rock House sits right on the border of three counties: Burke, McDowell and Avery. While this might lead to an intra-county identity crisis, it also leads to good food in a storied atmosphere. The building used to be a Prohibition-era roadhouse before becoming a restaurant.

The food here is primarily down-home. Menu items include pork loin, country-style steak, roast beef, turkey with all the fixin's, fried chicken and a full complement of side dishes. There's also fresh seafood delivered three times weekly from the coast.

Pepper's Restaurant
$-$$ • 2066 Blowing Rock Rd., Boone
• (828) 262-1250

Pepper's has been well known in Boone for

more than 20 years. It's particularly popular due mainly to the light, airy interior with its wooden floors and comfortable booths. The specialties here include seafood, pasta and sandwiches. Or try the mountain trout served à la Pepper.

Tumbleweed Grill & Microbrewery
$-$$ • 122 Blowing Rock Rd., Boone
• (828) 264-7111

Tumbleweed serves up a great combination of fine Mexican food and excellent hand-crafted beer in an intimate atmosphere. The restaurant is popular and small, so you might want to make a reservation if you're on some sort of official schedule (but who is in the mountains?). Otherwise, enjoy an ale while you wait for your table.

At your table, how about enjoying another beer with your chipotle shrimp Caesar salad or Anasazi chicken sauteed with ancho chiles and goat cheese and rounded off with a Madeira wine sauce and tobacco onions. Yum! Have another beer, and the excess nature of your caloric intake will soon match the excess nature of the lies you'll be telling about how you got up and down for birdie from the stream on the back nine at Boone Golf Course. Yeah, right.

Hickory/Lenoir Area

1859 Café
$$$ • 443 Second Ave. S.W., Hickory
• (828) 322-1859

In the heart of bustling downtown Hickory sits the 1859 Café. We wouldn't wear shorts, but you won't have to walk in wearing black tie. Dinner is served nightly except Sunday and features an outstanding selection of beef, seafood, duck, lamb and a variety of pasta dishes. One of our favorite items on the menu is the Sesame Salmon with Ginger Soy Sauce. If the temperature is pleasant, you might enjoy the outdoor patio. The restaurant also features periodic live entertainment.

Ham's Restaurant
$$ • 204 U.S. Hwy. 321, Hickory
• (828) 326-4267

Ham's is part of a small and good chain of well-run restaurants in North Carolina. There's one in Chapel Hill as well. The restaurant offers breakfast, lunch and dinner and boasts all ABC (alcohol) permits. Ham's provides good basic food in a relaxed atmosphere where you are welcome to show up in whatever clothes you feel like wearing; the restaurant is particu-larly good at deli-style sandwiches. Ham's is an excellent place to go when there's a sporting event going on that you'd like to watch on their big-screen TV with a couple of friends over a couple of pitchers of beer and a few meaty hamburgers with stacks of French fries and onion rings.

Where to Stay

The variety of accommodations in western North Carolina is as massive as the mountains themselves. All the major chains have built a significant presence here. In addition, there are some wonderful old inns and hotels that date back to the 19th century. Numerous small and intimate bed and breakfasts dot the pastoral landscape. Many of the places to stay are affiliated with a golf course and can help you secure a tee time. Refer to our Preface for an explanation of the pricing code.

Asheville Area

Best Western Mountainbrook Inn
$$-$$$ • U.S. Hwy. 19, Maggie Valley
• (828) 926-3962, (800) 752-6230

In this busy tourist town, the Best Western offers a range of amenities including a pool, hot tub and your own personal rocking chair where you can sit, relax and watch the mountains. You're within walking distance of many of Maggie Valley's attractions.

Cedar Crest
$$$$ • 674 Biltmore Ave., Asheville
• (828) 252-1389

Just north of the Biltmore Estate entrance lies this wonderful Victorian bed and breakfast. Asheville businessman William Breese built the home in 1891, but after his death, the house fell into disrepair. Jack and Barbara McEwan came all the way from Wisconsin to renovate the house and open the inn. Their renovation efforts are nothing short of astounding. If you stay in one of the guest rooms, you'll find yourself back in the 1890s. All rooms feature personal telephones (a plus, in our opinion, since many bed and breakfasts have only central phones), and there's even a croquet court out back. Cedar Crest is open all year.

Inn on Main Street
$ • 88 S. Main St., Weaverville
• (828) 645-3442

You can't miss the Inn on Main Street. It's the big, blue house on—you guessed it!—Main

MOUNTAINS

Street. The house dates back to 1900, when it was built as a combination office and home for Dr. Zebulon Richardson, a physician who just may have left his practice every Wednesday afternoon for his customary and sacred 1:34 tee time. Who knows? The inn has been renovated recently, and the rooms are elegantly furnished with fine antiques.

Monte Vista Hotel
$$ • 308 W. State St., Black Mountain • (828) 669-2119, (800) 441-5400

The Monte Vista is one of those fine, old boardinghouse inns that used to dot the landscape of the South. The minute you enter the spacious lobby with its roaring fireplace, lofty ceiling, ornately carved Victorian settees and overstuffed armchairs, with an army of family photographs and vintage prints decorating every available space, you know you've passed the threshold of time.

This is America in the early '20s and '30s, when gasoline cost pennies a gallon and motoring was an adventure. You can just imagine an excited vacation party arriving at the Monte Vista, children bounding up the grand old staircase to a pleasantly appointed room, then back downstairs for a buffet meal in the cheery dining room. The 55 guest rooms are furnished in a comfy collection of 19th-century antiques and Depression-era pieces. Rooms have quaint private baths, no telephones and no televisions— they've pulled the plug on the hectic pace of the 1990s.

The Monte Vista offers golf packages at area courses including Reems Creek, Black Mountain and the Blue Ridge Golf and Country Club. The packages include lodging, breakfast and golf with cart. One- to three-night packages are available.

The Phelps House Bed & Breakfast Inn
$ • W. Main St., Highlands • (828) 526-2590

You'll find lots of charm in this modestly priced bed and breakfast that's close to all the fine golf courses in the area. The house dates back to 1885. Each room has a private bath. You'll get a massive and hearty breakfast to push you along while you walk your 18 holes of choice.

The Lion and the Rose
$$$$ • 276 Montford Ave., Asheville • (828) 255-7673

Located right in the middle of Asheville's historic district, the Lion and the Rose also features a witch and a wardrobe—just kidding. In fact, this friendly bed and breakfast features six Victorian guest rooms, each with private bathrooms, and a Southern-style breakfast with all sorts of bacon and ham and jam and other such delights.

The Plaza Motel
$$ • 111 Hendersonville Rd., Asheville • (828) 274-2050

Built in the 1940s but completely refurbished, the Plaza Motel is a comfortable, clean, reasonably priced place to stay that's convenient to the Biltmore Village and Biltmore Estate. Many of the other motels in the area are more expensive.

Richmond Hill Inn
$$$$ • 87 Richmond Hill Dr., Asheville • (828) 252-7313

This superb 12-room bed and breakfast inn was built in 1889 and used to be the home of diplomat Richmond Pearson. Facing the bulldozer in the 1970s, the inn survived extinction and flourished under the ownership of a Greensboro businessman, Albert Michel, who spent three years renovating it. The rooms are beautifully furnished in the Victorian style and feature cable TV, with ESPN. If a room at the inn isn't available, then it's best to try the Croquet Cottages, which, even though they were built in 1991, complement the main house. The Richmond Hill Inn is open all year, and your visit will not be complete without a visit to the wonderful restaurant, one of Asheville's best.

Sycamores
$$$ • 150 Royal Pines Drive, Asheville • (828) 681-5227, (888) 353-5227

Sycamores features contemporary Southern Cuisine served in a restored 1847 Mansion. Duck, lamb, seafood, steaks, pastas and vegetarian dishes are featured. Fresh-made breads, butters and desserts compliment the extensive beer and wine selection. Two dining rooms, covered porch, and patio for dining. Live dinner music on Friday and Saturday evenings on our patio.

Boone/Blowing Rock Area

The Burgiss Farm Bed and Breakfast
$$ • N.C. Hwy. 18, Laurel Springs • (336) 359-2995

Innkeepers Tom and Nancy Burgiss created a fun atmosphere and offer great hospitality. Additions to this 1897 farmhouse mingle Old World charm with modern conveniences like private baths, a massive great room, a wet bar and a large Jacuzzi room. All this means great privacy, which makes the inn quite popular with honeymooners.

Enjoy select items from Nancy's breakfast menu, which must be one of the most creative around. It features such delicacies as Hawaiian pancakes and baked fruit.

Days Inn—Blowing Rock
$$-$$$ • U.S. Hwy. 321 Bypass,
Blowing Rock • (828) 295-4422

This Days Inn offers a good value in an area replete with golf courses. Choose from a variety of configurations among the 118 guest rooms. Also enjoy the enclosed atrium with hot tub.

Eseeola Lodge
$$$$ • U.S. Hwy. 221, Linville
• (828) 733-4311

The original Eseeola Lodge, destroyed by fire in 1936, opened somewhere near the turn of the century, and thus there's a great deal of history and tradition associated with this well-known establishment. The railroad made this remote section of the mountains somewhat accessible, and well-heeled vacationers made Eseeola a fine establishment frequented by the well-to-do of the Southeast. The rates, which in the middle of summer are upwards of $250 per night (including dinner and breakfast), are still geared toward the monied, so be prepared to shell out some serious plastic if you're going to stay here.

Still, it's well worth it if you enjoy excellent service, fine food and wonderfully appointed rooms. There are 29 rooms in all, most with private porches, surrounding a large main room with an inviting fireplace. Next to this main gathering room is the Lodge dining room. Gentlemen must wear a jacket and tie for dinner.

One of the biggest benefits of being a guest at the Lodge is access to one of the best golf courses in the Carolinas—Linville Golf Club (see the description earlier in this chapter). Golf packages are available only in May, June, September and October and are quite popular due to the quality of the course and accommodations.

If golf is not your game, Eseeola offers tennis on clay courts, swimming and croquet. There are 2,000 acres for hiking and fishing and special recreation programs for children as well.

Maple Lodge
$$-$$$ • Sunset Dr., Blowing Rock
• (828) 295-3331

If you're looking for a wonderful and homey place to stay in the mountains, look no further than the Maple Lodge. You'll find a place that's graceful, simple, elegant and convenient to Main Street in Blowing Rock and to the Blowing Rock Stage Company, which performs in the summer months.

There are 12 guest rooms at the Maple Lodge, and each room is named after a flower. Each room offers a private bath, and some even come complete with crocheted canopies—how about that for elegance! Your room fee includes a large breakfast that will set you up perfectly for the rest of the day. The spread includes muffins (homemade) and other breads, egg dishes and

MOUNTAINS

fresh fruit. The meal is served in the sun room, overlooking the flower garden. Innkeeper Marilyn Bateman will make sure your stay here is memorable and relaxing.

The Ragged Garden Inn
$$-$$$ • Sunset Dr., Blowing Rock
• (828) 295-9703

The first thing you'll notice at the Ragged Garden Inn is the stunning stone staircase in the grand hall. You'll also notice the English-style flower gardens and the chestnut bark siding found on older homes in this region. Innkeepers Joyce and Joe Villani tap into their extensive experience as restaurateurs in Connecticut and Florida to produce a sumptuous breakfast. Each of the inn's five guest rooms has a private bath. The inn is open from April to January; a good time to be here is in the spring when the garden is at its best.

The Switzerland Inn
$$$ • Blue Ridge Pkwy., M.P. 334,
Little Switzerland
• (828) 762-2153, (800) 654-4026

Just a well-struck 5-iron from the Blue Ridge Parkway, this fine old inn offers 55 rooms and an outstanding view of the mountains. Enjoy fine dining here as well. It's a friendly place, and you'll end up meeting and mingling with other guests, perhaps even sharing a tee time at a local course. Fall is the peak season.

Hickory/Lenoir Area

Holiday Inn Express
$$ • 142 Wilkesboro Blvd., Lenoir
• (828) 758-4403

The Holiday Inn Express of Lenoir offers clean, comfortable and sensibly priced lodgings in an area where there aren't many hotels. Your room price includes continental breakfast, access to the outdoor swimming pool, cable TV (with HBO and ESPN) plus free access to a local gymnasium where you can further develop your golfing muscles.

The Hickory Bed and Breakfast
$$$ • 464 Seventh St. SW, Hickory
• (828) 324-0548

A half-mile from downtown Hickory, you'll find The Hickory Bed and Breakfast, run by Bob and Pat Lynch. Bob spent 30 years serving his country in the Coast Guard and has augmented the charm of his already-charming 1908 Georgian house with a unique collection of collectibles from around the world. The Lynch's offer four rooms, all with queen-size beds and adjoining bathrooms. Being near all the furniture factories, the inn also features fine antiques. Before you leave for your daily business or pleasure, the Lynch's will cook you up a large breakfast.

Howard Johnson Hotel
$$ • 483 U.S. Hwy. 70 SW, Hickory
• (828) 322-1600

Convenient to I-40 and all Hickory's major thoroughfares, the Hickory Howard Johnson offers a full range of amenities and goodies including a restaurant and lounge, banquet facilities, family rates, senior rates, cable TV (with ESPN and free HBO), swimming pool, fitness center, sauna, Laundromat and fax service.

MOUNTAINS

Index of Advertisers

Index

INDEX